Julie C. Meloni

Sams **Teach Yourself**

PHP, MySQL & JavaScript

All

in **One**

SIXTH EDITION

Pearson

Sams Teach Yourself PHP, MySQL & JavaScript All in One, Sixth Edition

ISBN-13: 978-0-672-33770-3

ISBN-10: 0-672-33770-3

Library of Congress Control Number: 2017911865

Printed in the United States of America

1   17

Trademarks

All terms mentioned in this book that are known to be trademarks or service marks have been appropriately capitalized. Pearson cannot attest to the accuracy of this information. Use of a term in this book should not be regarded as affecting the validity of any trademark or service mark.

Warning and Disclaimer

Every effort has been made to make this book as complete and as accurate as possible, but no warranty or fitness is implied. The information provided is on an "as is" basis. The author and the publisher shall have neither liability nor responsibility to any person or entity with respect to any loss or damages arising from the information contained in this book or from the use of the CD or programs accompanying it.

Special Sales

For information about buying this title in bulk quantities, or for special sales opportunities (which may include electronic versions; custom cover designs; and content particular to your business, training goals, marketing focus, or branding interests), please contact our corporate sales department at corpsales@pearsoned.com or (800) 382-3419.

For government sales inquiries, please contact governmentsales@pearsoned.com.

For questions about sales outside the U.S., please contact intlcs@pearson.com.

Editor
Mark Taber

Managing Editor
Sandra Schroeder

Project Editor
Mandie Frank

Copy Editor
Bart Reed

Indexer
Erika Millen

Proofreader
Abby Manheim

Technical Editor
Timothy Boronczyk

Editorial Assistant
Vanessa Evans

Designer
Chuti Prasertsith

Compositor
codeMantra

Contents at a Glance

Table of Contents

Part IV: Integrating a Database into Your Applications

About the Author

Julie C. Meloni is a technical consultant who has been developing web-based applications since the Web first saw the light of day. She has authored numerous books and articles on web-based programming and scripting languages and database topics, and you can find translations of her work in 18 different languages. She barely maintains a blog at thickbook.com, and can typically be found camping in national parks or cozying up to craft cocktail bars in and around Washington, D.C.

Acknowledgments

The Apache Software Foundation, the PHP Group, and MySQL AB deserve much more recognition than they ever get for creating these super products that drive the vast majority of the Web.

Accessing the Free Web Edition

Your purchase of this book in any format, print or electronic, includes access to the corresponding Web Edition, which provides several special online-only features to help you learn:

- ▶ The complete text of the book

- ▶ Updates and corrections as they become available

The Web Edition can be viewed on all types of computers and mobile devices with any modern web browser that supports HTML5.

To get access to the Web Edition of *Sams Teach Yourself PHP, MySQL & JavaScript All in One, Sixth Edition*, all you need to do is register this book:

1. Go to www.informit.com/register.

2. Sign in or create a new account.

3. Enter ISBN: 9780672337703.

4. Answer the questions as proof of purchase.

The Web Edition will appear under the Digital Purchases tab on your Account page. Click the Launch link to access the product.

Introduction

Welcome to *Sams Teach Yourself PHP, MySQL & JavaScript All in One.* This book takes the most useful parts of *Sams Teach Yourself HTML, CSS & JavaScript All in One (Second Edition)* and *Sams Teach Yourself PHP, MySQL & Apache All in One (Fifth Edition)*, refreshes the content for the inevitable changes in technology that happen every day, and provides you with a foundation for "full stack" web application development.

This foundation is provided by example; this book scaffolds your understanding of HTML, CSS, JavaScript, and PHP (plus database interactivity with MySQL) by showing you code that builds upon other code, explaining the details of the code, and providing you with sample output—what it might look like on your screen.

The goal of this book is not to make you an expert in any one of these technologies but instead to give you a solid foundation in the skills you need to create modern, standards-compliant web applications. The following are of particular note:

▶ Every example in this book is validated HTML5 and CSS3.

▶ All the examples in the book have been tested for compatibility with the latest version of every major web browser. That includes Apple Safari, Google Chrome, Microsoft Internet Explorer, Mozilla Firefox, and Opera. You'll learn from the start to be compatible with the past, yet ready for the future.

▶ All of the PHP code runs beautifully with PHP 7, but is backward compatible to PHP 5.6.x, which is still in use by thousands of web hosting providers.

Attention to many of these essentials are what made the many editions of the previous books bestsellers, and this updated edition is no different. A solid foundation is key to your future development no matter if you choose to specialize in HTML and CSS, JavaScript, PHP, or all of the above.

As always, it is important to remember that this book should be a first step—and by no means your only step—toward a more advanced understanding of technical development. It takes 10,000 hours of practice to become an expert in something, which is so much longer than you'll spend reading this book.

Who Should Read This Book?

This book is geared toward individuals who possess a general understanding of the concepts of the World Wide Web, meaning that there is a thing called the World Wide Web and people connect to sites on it using web browsers. That's it—no other knowledge is assumed.

The chapters that delve into programming with PHP assume no previous knowledge of the language. However, if you have experience with other programming languages, you will find the going much easier because of your familiarity with such programming elements as variables, control structures, functions, objects, and the like. Similarly, if you have worked with databases other than MySQL, you already possess a solid foundation for working through the MySQL-related lessons.

How This Book Is Organized

This book is divided into five parts, corresponding to particular topic groups. You should read the chapters within each part one right after another, with each chapter building on the information found in those before it:

▶ Part I, "Web Application Basics," takes you from understanding communication on the Web to writing basic PHP scripts, with stops along the way to provide a foundation in HTML, CSS, and JavaScript. Even if you are familiar with one or more of these technologies at a basic level, you should still skim these chapters as a refresher. Much of the rest of the book builds on the lessons in these initial chapters.

▶ Part II, "Getting Started with Dynamic Websites," is almost fully devoted to the use and syntax of JavaScript, which provides the dynamism in dynamic websites; where HTML and CSS often just sit there looking pretty, JavaScript makes the thing *go*…at least until you throw PHP and databases in the mix.

▶ Part III, "Taking Your Web Applications to the Next Level," moves beyond the front end and into the back end of your applications. You'll learn the basics of the PHP language, including structural elements such as arrays and objects, and you'll learn how to wield cookies and user sessions to your advantage. This is also the part of the book where you learn more than you (probably) ever wanted to know about forms.

▶ Part IV, "Integrating a Database into Your Applications," contains chapters devoted to working with databases in general, such as database normalization, as well as using PHP to connect to and work with MySQL. Included is a basic SQL primer, which also includes MySQL-specific functions and other information.

▶ Part V, "Getting Started with Application Development," consists of chapters devoted to performing a particular task using PHP and MySQL, integrating all the knowledge you gained throughout the book. Projects include creating a discussion forum, a basic online storefront, and a simple calendar.

At the end of each chapter, a few quiz questions test how well you've learned the material. Additional exercises provide another way to apply the information learned in the chapter and guide you toward using this newfound knowledge in the next chapter.

About the Book's Source Code

All the code that appears in listings throughout the chapters is also available on GitHub at https://github.com/jcmeloni/PMJAiO. You may also download the source code bundle from the author's website at http://www.thickbook.com/.

Typing the code on your own provides useful experience in making typos, causing errors, and performing the sometimes mind-numbing task of tracking down errant semicolons. However, if you want to skip that lesson and just upload the working code to your website, feel free!

Conventions Used in This Book

This book uses different typefaces to differentiate between code and plain English and to help you identify important concepts. Throughout the chapters, code, commands, and text you type or see onscreen appear in a `computer typeface`. New terms appear in *italics* at the point in the text where they are defined. In addition, icons accompany special blocks of information:

NOTE
_____
A Note presents an interesting piece of information related to the current topic.
_____

TIP
_____
A Tip offers advice or teaches an easier method for performing a task.
_____

CAUTION
_____
A Caution warns you about potential pitfalls and explains how to avoid them.
_____

Q&A, Quiz, and Exercises

Every chapter ends with a short question-and-answer session that addresses the kind of "dumb questions" everyone wishes they dared to ask. A brief but complete quiz lets you test yourself to be sure you understand everything presented in the chapter. Finally, one or two optional exercises give you a chance to practice your new skills before you move on.

CHAPTER 1
Understanding How the Web Works

What You'll Learn in This Chapter:

- ▶ A very brief history of the World Wide Web
- ▶ What is meant by the term *web page*, and why that term doesn't always reflect all the content involved
- ▶ How content gets from your personal computer to someone else's web browser
- ▶ How to select a web hosting provider
- ▶ How different web browsers and device types can affect your content
- ▶ How to transfer files to your web server using FTP
- ▶ Where files should be placed on a web server
- ▶ How to distribute web content without a web server

Before you learn the intricacies of HTML (Hypertext Markup Language), CSS (Cascading Style Sheets), and JavaScript—not to mention the back-end programming language PHP—it is important to gain a solid understanding of the technologies that help transform these plain-text files to the rich multimedia displays you see on your computer, tablet, or smartphone when browsing the World Wide Web.

For example, a file containing markup and client-side code (HTML, CSS, and JavaScript) is useless without a web browser to view it, and no one besides yourself will see your content unless a web server is involved—this is especially true when server-side technologies such as PHP are put into the mix. Web servers make your content available to others who, in turn, use their web browsers to navigate to an address and wait for the server to send information to them. You will be intimately involved in this publishing process because you must create files and then put them on a web server to make the content available in the first place, and you must ensure that your content will appear to the end user as you intended.

A Brief History of HTML and the World Wide Web

Once upon a time, back when there weren't any footprints on the moon, some farsighted folks decided to see whether they could connect several major computer networks. I'll spare you the names and stories (there are plenty of both), but the eventual result was the "mother of all networks," which we call the Internet.

Until 1990, accessing information through the Internet was a rather technical affair. It was so hard, in fact, that even Ph.D.-holding physicists were often frustrated when trying to exchange data and documents. One such physicist, the now-famous (and knighted) Sir Tim Berners-Lee, cooked up a way to easily cross-reference text on the Internet through hypertext links.

This wasn't a new idea, but his simple Hypertext Markup Language (HTML) managed to thrive while more ambitious hypertext projects floundered. *Hypertext* originally meant text stored in electronic form with cross-reference links between pages. It is now a broader term that refers to just about any object (text, images, files, and so on) that can be linked to other objects. *Hypertext Markup Language* is a language for describing how text, graphics, and files containing other information are organized and linked.

By 1993, only 100 or so computers throughout the world were equipped to serve up HTML pages. Those interlinked pages were dubbed the *World Wide Web (WWW)*, and several web browser programs had been written to enable people to view web content. Because of the growing popularity of the Web, a few programmers soon wrote web browsers that could view graphical images along with text. From that point forward, the continued development of web browser software and the standardization of web technologies including HTML, CSS, and JavaScript have led us to the world we live in today, one in which more than a billion websites serve trillions (or more) of text and multimedia files.

NOTE

For more information on the history of the World Wide Web, see the Wikipedia article on this topic: http://en.wikipedia.org/wiki/History_of_the_Web.

These few paragraphs really are a brief history of what has been a remarkable period. Today's college students have never known a time in which the World Wide Web didn't exist, and the idea of always-on information and ubiquitous computing will shape all aspects of our lives moving forward. Instead of seeing dynamic web content creation and management as a set of skills possessed by only a few technically oriented folks (okay, call them geeks, if you will), by the end of this book, you will see that these are skills that anyone can master, regardless of inherent geekiness.

Creating Web Content

You might have noticed the use of the term *web content* rather than *web pages*—that was intentional. Although we talk of "visiting a web page," what we really mean is something like "looking at all the text and the images at one address on our computer." The text that we read and the images that we see are rendered by our web browsers, which are given certain instructions found in individual files.

Those files contain text that is *marked up* with, or surrounded by, HTML codes that tell the browser how to display the text—as a heading, as a paragraph, in a bulleted list, and so on. Some HTML markup tells the browser to display an image or video file rather than plain text, which brings me back to this point: Different types of content are sent to your web browser, so simply saying *web page* doesn't begin to cover it. Here we use the term *web content* instead, to cover the full range of text, image, audio, video, and other media found online.

In later chapters, you'll learn the basics of linking to or creating the various types of multimedia web content found in websites, and for creating dynamic content from server-side scripts using PHP. All you need to remember at this point is that *you* are in control of the content a user sees when visiting your website. Beginning with the file that contains text to display or code that tells the server to send a graphic along to the user's web browser, you have to plan, design, and implement all the pieces that will eventually make up your web presence. As you will learn throughout this book, it is not a difficult process as long as you understand all the little steps along the way.

In its most fundamental form, web content begins with a simple text file containing HTML markup. In this book, you'll learn about and compose standards-compliant HTML5 markup. One of the many benefits of writing standards-compliant code is that, in the future, you will not have to worry about having to go back to your code to fundamentally alter it so that it works on multiple types of browsers and devices. Instead, your code will (likely) always work as intended for as long as web browsers adhere to standards and the backwards compatibility to previous standards (which is hopefully a long time).

Understanding Web Content Delivery

Several processes occur, in many different locations, to eventually produce web content that you can see. These processes occur very quickly—on the order of milliseconds—and happen behind the scenes. In other words, although we might think all we are doing is opening a web browser, typing in a web address, and instantaneously seeing the content we requested, technology in the background is working hard on our behalf. Figure 1.1 shows the basic interaction between a browser and a server.

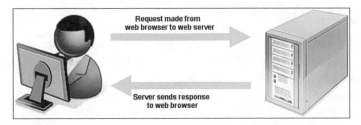

FIGURE 1.1
A browser request and a server response.

However, the process involves several steps—and potentially several trips between the browser and the server—before you see the entire content of the site you requested.

Suppose you want to do a Google search, so you dutifully type **www.google.com** in the address bar or select the Google bookmark from your bookmarks list. Almost immediately, your browser shows you something like what's shown in Figure 1.2.

FIGURE 1.2
Visiting www.google.com.

Figure 1.2 shows a website that contains text plus one image (the Google logo). A simple version of the processes that occurred to retrieve that text and image from a web server and display it on your screen follows:

1. Your web browser sends a request for the `index.html` file located at the http://www.google. com address. The `index.html` file does not have to be part of the address that you type in the address bar; you'll learn more about the `index.html` file farther along in this chapter.

2. After receiving the request for a specific file, the web server process looks in its directory contents for the specific file, opens it, and sends the content of that file back to your web browser.

3. The web browser receives the content of the index.html file, which is text marked up with HTML codes, and renders the content based on these HTML codes. While rendering the content, the browser happens upon the HTML code for the Google logo, which you can see in Figure 1.2. The HTML code looks something like this:

```
<img alt="Google" height="92" width="272" id="hplogo" src="/images/branding/
googlelogo/2x/googlelogo_color_272x92dp.png">
```

The HTML code for the image is an `<img>` tag, and it also provides attributes that tell the browser the file source location (`src`), width (`width`), and height (`height`) necessary to display the logo. You'll learn more about attributes throughout later lessons.

4. The browser looks at the `src` attribute in the `<img>` tag to find the source location. In this case, the image `googlelogo_color_272x92dp.png` can be found in a subdirectory of the `images` directory at the same web address (www.google.com) from which the browser retrieved the HTML file.

5. The browser requests the file at the web address http://www.google.com/images/branding/googlelogo/2x/googlelogo_color_272x92dp.png.

6. The web server interprets that request, finds the file, and sends the contents of that file to the web browser that requested it.

7. The web browser displays the image on your monitor.

As you can see in the description of the web content delivery process, web browsers do more than simply act as picture frames through which you can view content. Browsers assemble the web content components and arrange those parts according to the HTML commands in the file.

You can also view web content locally, or on your own hard drive, without the need for a web server. The process of content retrieval and display is the same as the process listed in the previous steps, in that a browser looks for and interprets the codes and content of an HTML file, but the trip is shorter: The browser looks for files on your own computer's hard drive rather than on a remote machine. A web server would be needed to interpret any server-based programming language embedded in the files, but that is outside the scope of this book. In fact, you could work through all the HTML, CSS, and JavaScript lessons in this book without having a web server to call your own, but then nobody but you could view your masterpieces.

Selecting a Web Hosting Provider

Despite my just telling you that you can work through all the HTML, CSS, and JavaScript lessons in this book without having a web server, having a web server is the recommended method for continuing. Although the appendixes describe how to install a full-blown web server and database on your local machine for personal development, invariably you will want your static or dynamic websites to be visible to the public. Don't worry—obtaining a hosting provider is usually a quick, painless, and relatively inexpensive process. In fact, you can get your own domain name and a year of web hosting for just slightly more than the cost of the book you are reading now.

If you type **web hosting provider** in your search engine of choice, you will get millions of hits and an endless list of sponsored search results (also known as *ads*). Not this many web hosting providers exist in the world, although it might seem otherwise. Even if you are looking at a managed list of hosting providers, it can be overwhelming—especially if all you are looking for is a place to host a simple website for yourself or your company or organization.

You'll want to narrow your search when looking for a provider and choose one that best meets your needs. Some selection criteria for a web hosting provider follow:

- ▶ **Reliability/server "uptime"**—If you have an online presence, you want to make sure people can actually get there consistently.

- ▶ **Customer service**—Look for multiple methods for contacting customer service (phone, email, chat), as well as online documentation for common issues.

- ▶ **Server space**—Does the hosting package include enough server space to hold all the multimedia files (images, audio, video) you plan to include in your website (if any)?

- ▶ **Bandwidth**—Does the hosting package include enough bandwidth that all the people visiting your site and downloading files can do so without your having to pay extra?

- ▶ **Domain name purchase and management**—Does the package include a custom domain name, or must you purchase and maintain your domain name separately from your hosting account?

- ▶ **Price**—Do not overpay for hosting. If you see a wide range of prices offered, you should immediately wonder, "What's the difference?" Often the difference has little to do with the quality of the service and everything to do with company overhead and what the company thinks it can get away with charging people. A good rule of thumb is that if you are paying more than $75 per year for a basic hosting package and domain name, you are probably paying too much.

Here are three reliable web hosting providers whose basic packages contain plenty of server space and bandwidth (as well as domain names and extra benefits) at a relatively low cost. If you don't go with any of these web hosting providers, you can at least use their basic package descriptions as a guideline as you shop around.

NOTE

The author has used all these providers (and then some) over the years and has no problem recom-
mending any of them; predominantly, she uses DailyRazor as a web hosting provider, especially for
advanced development environments.

▶ **A Small Orange (http://www.asmallorange.com)**—The Tiny and Small hosting packages
  are perfect starting places for any new web content publisher.

▶ **DailyRazor (http://www.dailyrazor.com)**—Even its personal-sized hosting package is
  full-featured and reliable.

▶ **Lunarpages (http://www.lunarpages.com)**—The Starter hosting package is suitable for
  many personal and small business websites.

One feature of a good hosting provider is that it offers a "control panel" for you to manage
aspects of your account. Figure 1.3 shows the control panel for my own hosting account at
DailyRazor. Many web hosting providers offer this particular control panel software, or some
control panel that is similar in design—clearly labeled icons leading to tasks you can perform to
configure and manage your account.

FIGURE 1.3
A sample control panel.

You might never need to use your control panel, but having it available to you simplifies the installation of databases and other software, the viewing of web statistics, and the addition of email addresses (among many other features). If you can follow instructions, you can manage your own web server—no special training required.

Testing with Multiple Web Browsers

Now that we've just discussed the process of web content delivery and the acquisition of a web server, it might seem a little strange to step back and talk about testing your websites with multiple web browsers. However, before you go off and learn all about creating websites with HTML and CSS, do so with this very important statement in mind: Every visitor to your website will potentially use hardware and software configurations that are different from your own. From their device types (desktop, laptop, tablet, smartphone) to their screen resolutions, browser types, browser window sizes, and speed of connections—you cannot control any aspect of what your visitors use when they view your site. So just as you're setting up your web hosting environment and getting ready to work, think about downloading several web browsers so that you have a local test suite of tools available to you. Let me explain why this is important.

Although all web browsers process and handle information in the same general way, some specific differences among them result in things not always looking the same in different browsers. Even users of the same version of the same web browser can alter how a page appears by choosing different display options and/or changing the size of their viewing windows. All the major web browsers allow users to override the background and fonts the web page author specifies with those of their own choosing. Screen resolution, window size, and optional toolbars can also change how much of a page someone sees when it first appears on the screen. You can ensure only that you write standards-compliant HTML and CSS.

NOTE

In Chapter 3, "Understanding the CSS Box Model and Positioning," you'll learn a little bit about the concept of responsive web design, in which the design of a site shifts and changes automatically depending on the user's behavior and viewing environment (screen size, device, and so on).

Do not, under any circumstances, spend hours on end-designing something that looks perfect only on your own computer—unless you are willing to be disappointed when you look at it on your friend's computer, on a computer in the local library, or on your iPhone.

You should always test your websites with as many of these web browsers as possible, on standard, portable, and mobile devices:

▶ Apple Safari (http://www.apple.com/safari/) for Mac

▶ Google Chrome (http://www.google.com/chrome) for Mac, Windows, and Linux/UNIX

▶ Microsoft Internet Explorer (http://www.microsoft.com/ie) and Microsoft Edge (https://www.microsoft.com/microsoft-edge) for Windows

▶ Mozilla Firefox (http://www.mozilla.com/firefox/) for Mac, Windows, and Linux/UNIX

Now that you have a development environment set up, or at least some idea of the type you'd like to set up in the future, let's move on to creating a test file.

Creating a Sample File

Before we begin, take a look at Listing 1.1. This listing represents a simple piece of web content—a few lines of HTML that print "Hello World! Welcome to My Web Server." in large, bold letters on two lines centered within the browser window. You'll learn more about the HTML and CSS used within this file as you move forward in this book.

LISTING 1.1 Our Sample HTML File

```
<!DOCTYPE html>
<html>
  <head>
    <title>Hello World!</title>
  </head>
  <body>
    <h1 style="text-align: center">Hello World!<br>
    Welcome to My Web Server.</h1>
  </body>
</html>
```

To make use of this content, open a text editor of your choice, such as Notepad (on Windows) or TextEdit (on a Mac). Do not use WordPad, Microsoft Word, or other full-featured word processing software because those programs create different sorts of files from the plain-text files we use for web content.

Type the content that you see in Listing 1.1 and then save the file using `sample.html` as the filename. Be sure your editor does not change the extension you give it; the `.html` extension tells the web server that your file is, indeed, full of HTML. When the file contents are sent to the web browser that requests it, the browser will also know from it is HTML and will render it appropriately.

Now that you have a sample HTML file to use—and hopefully somewhere to put it, such as a web hosting account—let's get to publishing your web content.

Using FTP to Transfer Files

As you've learned so far, you have to put your web content on a web server to make it accessible to others. This process typically occurs by using the *File Transfer Protocol (FTP)*. To use FTP, you need an FTP client—a program used to transfer files from your computer to a web server.

FTP clients require three pieces of information to connect to your web server; this information will have been sent to you by your hosting provider after you set up your account:

- ▶ The hostname, or address, to which you will connect

- ▶ Your account username

- ▶ Your account password

When you have this information, you are ready to use an FTP client to transfer content to your web server.

Selecting an FTP Client

Regardless of the FTP client you use, FTP clients generally use the same type of interface. Figure 1.4 shows an example of FireFTP, which is an FTP client used with the Firefox web browser. The directory listing of the local machine (your computer) appears on the left of your screen, and the directory listing of the remote machine (the web server) appears on the right. Typically, you will see right-arrow and left-arrow buttons, as shown in Figure 1.4. The right arrow sends selected files from your computer to your web server; the left arrow sends files from the web server to your computer. Many FTP clients also enable you to simply select files and then drag and drop those files to the target machines.

Many FTP clients are freely available to you, but you can also transfer files via the web-based file management tool that is likely part of your web server's control panel. However, that method of file transfer typically introduces more steps into the process and isn't nearly as streamlined (or simple) as the process of installing an FTP client on your own machine.

Here are some popular free FTP clients:

- ▶ Classic FTP (http://www.nchsoftware.com/classic/) for Mac and Windows

- ▶ Cyberduck (http://cyberduck.ch) for Mac

- ▶ Fetch (http://fetchsoftworks.com) for Mac

- ▶ FileZilla (http://filezilla-project.org) for all platforms

- ▶ FireFTP (http://fireftp.mozdev.org) Firefox extension for all platforms

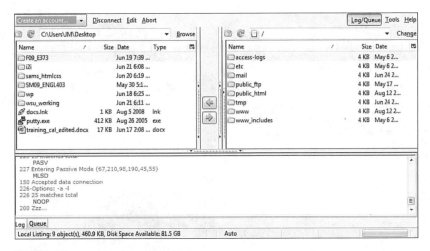

FIGURE 1.4
The FireFTP interface.

When you have selected an FTP client and installed it on your computer, you are ready to upload and download files from your web server. In the next section, you'll see how this process works using the sample file in Listing 1.1.

Using an FTP Client

The following steps show how to use Classic FTP to connect to your web server and transfer a file. However, all FTP clients use similar, if not identical, interfaces. If you understand the following steps, you should be able to use any FTP client. (Remember, you first need the hostname, the account username, and the account password.)

1. Start the Classic FTP program and click the Connect button. You are prompted to fill out information for the site to which you want to connect, as shown in Figure 1.5.

2. Fill in each of the items shown in Figure 1.5 as described here:

   ▶ The FTP Server is the FTP address of the web server to which you need to send your content. Your hosting provider will have given you this address. It probably is *yourdomain*.com, but check the information you received when you signed up for service.

   ▶ Complete the User Name field and the Password field using the information your hosting provider gave you.

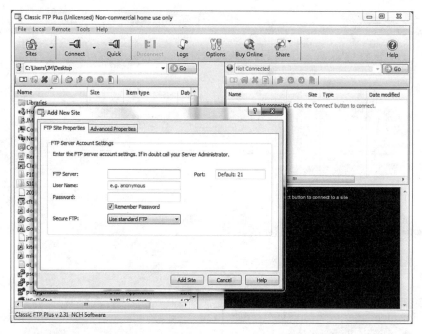

FIGURE 1.5
Connecting to a new site in Classic FTP.

3. You can switch to the Advanced tab and modify the following optional items, shown in Figure 1.6:

   ▶ The Site Label is the name you'll use to refer to your own site. Nobody else will see this name, so enter whatever you want.

   ▶ You can change the values for Initial Remote Directory on First Connection and Initial Local Directory on First Connection, but you might want to wait until you have become accustomed to using the client and have established a workflow.

4. When you're finished with the settings, click Add Site to save them. You can then click Connect to establish a connection with the web server.

You will see a dialog box indicating that Classic FTP is attempting to connect to the web server. Upon a successful connection, you will see an interface like the one in Figure 1.7, showing the contents of the local directory on the left and the contents of your web server on the right.

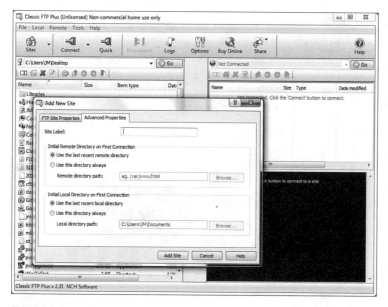

FIGURE 1.6
The advanced connection options in Classic FTP.

5. You are now *almost* ready to transfer files to your web server. All that remains is to change directories to what is called the *document root* of your web server. The document root of your web server is the directory that is designated as the top-level directory for your web content—the starting point of the directory structure, which you'll learn more about later in this chapter. Often, this directory is named `public_html`, www (because www has been created as an alias for `public_html`), or `htdocs`. You do not have to create this directory; your hosting provider will have created it for you.

   Double-click the document root directory name to open it. The display shown on the right of the FTP client interface changes to show the contents of this directory (it will probably be empty at this point, unless your web hosting provider has put placeholder files in that directory on your behalf).

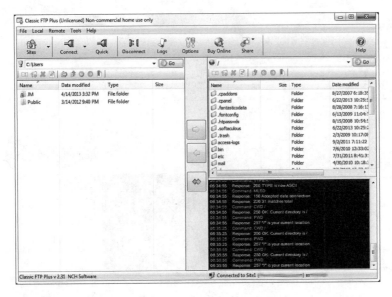

FIGURE 1.7
A successful connection to a remote web server via Classic FTP.

6. The goal is to transfer the `sample.html` file you created earlier from your computer to the web server. Find the file in the directory listing on the left of the FTP client interface (navigate if you have to) and click it once to highlight the filename.

7. Click the right-arrow button in the middle of the client interface to send the file to the web server. When the file transfer completes, the right side of the client interface refreshes to show you that the file has made it to its destination.

8. Click the Disconnect button to close the connection, and then exit the Classic FTP program.

These steps are conceptually similar to the steps you take anytime you want to send files to your web server via FTP. You can also use your FTP client to create subdirectories on the remote web server. To create a subdirectory using Classic FTP, click the Remote menu and then click New Folder. Different FTP clients have different interface options to achieve the same goal.

Understanding Where to Place Files on the Web Server

An important aspect of maintaining web content is determining how you will organize that content—not only for the user to find, but also for you to maintain on your server. Putting files in directories helps you manage those files.

Naming and organizing directories on your web server, and developing rules for file maintenance, is completely up to you. However, maintaining a well-organized server makes your management of its content more efficient in the long run.

Basic File Management

As you browse the Web, you might have noticed that URLs change as you navigate through websites. For instance, if you're looking at a company's website and you click on graphical navigation leading to the company's products or services, the URL probably changes from

http://www.*companyname*.com/

to

http://www.*companyname*.com/products/

or

http://www.*companyname*.com/services/

In the preceding section, I used the term *document root* without really explaining what that is all about. The document root of a web server is essentially the trailing slash in the full URL. For instance, if your domain is *yourdomain*.com and your URL is http://www.*yourdomain*.com/, the document root is the directory represented by the trailing slash (/). The document root is the starting point of the directory structure you create on your web server; it is the place where the web server begins looking for files requested by the web browser.

If you put the `sample.html` file in your document root as previously directed, you will be able to access it via a web browser at the following URL:

http://www.*yourdomain*.com/sample.html

If you entered this URL into your web browser, you would see the rendered `sample.html` file, as shown in Figure 1.8.

However, if you created a new directory within the document root and put the `sample.html` file in that directory, the file would be accessed at this URL:

http://www.*yourdomain*.com/newdirectory/sample.html

FIGURE 1.8
The `sample.html` file accessed via a web browser.

If you put the `sample.html` file in the directory you originally saw upon connecting to your server—that is, you did *not* change directories and place the file in the document root—the `sample.html` file would not be accessible from your web server at any URL. The file will still be on the machine that you know as your web server, but because the file is not in the document root—where the server software knows to start looking for files—it will never be accessible to anyone via a web browser.

The bottom line? Always navigate to the document root of your web server before you start transferring files.

This is especially true with graphics and other multimedia files. A common directory on web servers is called `images`, where, as you can imagine, all the image assets are placed for retrieval. Other popular directories include `css` for style sheet files (if you are using more than one) and `js` for JavaScript files. Alternatively, if you know that you will have an area on your website where visitors can download many types of files, you might simply call that directory `downloads`.

Whether it's a ZIP file containing your art portfolio or an Excel spreadsheet with sales numbers, it's often useful to publish a file on the Internet that isn't simply a web page. To make available on the Web a file that isn't an HTML file, just upload the file to your website as if it *were* an HTML file, following the instructions earlier in this chapter for uploading. After the file is uploaded to the web server, you can create a link to it (as you'll learn in Chapter 2, "Structuring HTML and Using Cascading Style Sheets"). In other words, your web server can serve much more than HTML.

Here's a sample of the HTML code you will learn more about later in this book. The following code would be used for a file named `artfolio.zip`, located in the `downloads` directory of your website, and with link text that reads `Download my art portfolio!`:

```
<a href="/downloads/artfolio.zip">Download my art portfolio!</a>
```

Using an Index Page

When you think of an index, you probably think of the section in the back of a book that tells you where to look for various keywords and topics. The index file in a web server directory can serve that purpose—if you design it that way. In fact, that's where the name originates.

The `index.html` file (or just *index file*, as it's usually referred to) is the name you give to the page you want people to see as the default file when they navigate to a specific directory in your website.

Another function of the index page is that users who visit a directory on your site that has an index page but who do not specify that page will still land on the main page for that section of your site—or for the site itself.

For instance, you can type either of the following URLs and land on Apple's iPhone informational page:

http://www.apple.com/iphone/

http://www.apple.com/iphone/index.html

Had there been no `index.html` page in the `iphone` directory, the results would depend on the configuration of the web server. If the server is configured to disallow directory browsing, the user would have seen a "Directory Listing Denied" message when attempting to access the URL without a specified page name. However, if the server is configured to allow directory browsing, the user would have seen a list of the files in that directory.

Your hosting provider will already have determined these server configuration options. If your hosting provider enables you to modify server settings via a control panel, you can change these settings so that your server responds to requests based on your own requirements.

Not only is the index file used in subdirectories, but it's used in the top-level directory (or document root) of your website as well. The first page of your website—or *home page* or *main page*, or however you like to refer to the web content you want users to see when they first visit your domain—should be named `index.html` and placed in the document root of your web server. This ensures that when users type **http://www.*yourdomain*.com/** into their web browsers, the server responds with the content you intended them to see (instead of "Directory Listing Denied" or some other unintended consequence).

Summary

This chapter introduced you to the concept of using HTML to mark up text files to produce web content. You also learned that there is more to web content than just the "page"—web content also includes image, audio, and video files. All this content lives on a web server—a remote machine often far from your own computer. On your computer or other device, you use a web browser to request, retrieve, and eventually display web content on your screen.

You learned the criteria to consider when determining whether a web hosting provider fits your needs. After you have selected a web hosting provider, you can begin to transfer files to your web server, which you also learned how to do, using an FTP client. You also learned a bit about web server directory structures and file management, as well as the very important purpose of the `index.html` file in a given web server directory. In addition, you learned that you can distribute web content on removable media, and you learned how to go about structuring the files and directories to achieve the goal of viewing content without using a remote web server.

Finally, you learned the importance of testing your work in multiple browsers after you've placed it on a web server. Writing valid, standards-compliant HTML and CSS helps ensure that your site looks reasonably similar for all visitors, but you still shouldn't design without receiving input from potential users outside your development team—it is even *more* important to get input from others when you are a design team of one!

Q&A

Q. I've looked at the HTML source of some web sites on the Internet, and it looks frighteningly difficult to learn. Do I have to think like a computer programmer to learn this stuff?

A. Although complex HTML pages can indeed look daunting, learning HTML is much easier than learning actual programming languages—we're saving that for later on in this book, and you'll do just fine with it as well. HTML is a markup language rather than a programming language; you mark up text so that the browser can render the text a certain way. That's a completely different set of thought processes than developing a computer program. You really don't need any experience or skill as a computer programmer to be a successful web content author.

One of the reasons the HTML behind many commercial websites looks complicated is that it was likely created by a visual web design tool—a "what you see is what you get" (WYSIWYG) editor that uses whatever markup its software developer told it to use in certain circumstances—as opposed to being hand-coded (where you are completely in control of the resulting markup). In this book, you are taught fundamental coding from the ground up, which typically results in clean, easy-to-read source code. Visual web design tools have a knack for making code difficult to read and for producing code that is convoluted and not standards compliant.

Q. Running all the tests you recommend would take longer than creating my pages! Can't I get away with less testing?

A. If your pages aren't intended to make money or provide an important service, it's probably not a big deal if they look funny to some users or produce errors once in a while. In that case, just test each page with a couple different browsers and call it a day. However, if you need to project a professional image, there is no substitute for rigorous testing.

Q. Seriously, who cares how I organize my web content?

A. Believe it or not, the organization of your web content does matter to search engines and potential visitors to your site. But overall, having an organized web server directory structure helps you keep track of content that you are likely to update frequently. For instance, if you have a dedicated directory for images or multimedia, you know exactly where to look for a file you want to update—no need to hunt through directories containing other content.

Workshop

The Workshop contains quiz questions and exercises to help you solidify your understanding of the material covered. Try to answer all questions before looking at the "Answers" section that follows.

Quiz

1. How many files would you need to store on a web server to produce a single web page with some text and two images on it?

2. What are some of the features to look for in a web hosting provider?

3. What three pieces of information do you need in order to connect to your web server via FTP?

4. What is the purpose of the `index.html` file?

5. Does your website have to include a directory structure?

Answers

1. You would need three: one for the web page itself, which includes the text and the HTML markup, and one for each of the two images.

2. Look for reliability, customer service, web space and bandwidth, domain name service, site-management extras, and price.

3. You need the hostname, your account username, and your account password.

4. The `index.html` file is typically the default file for a directory within a web server. It enables users to access http://www.*yourdomain*.com/*somedirectory*/ without using a trailing filename and still end up in the appropriate place.

5. No. Using a directory structure for file organization is completely up to you, although using one is highly recommended because it simplifies content maintenance.

Exercises

▶ Get your web hosting in order—are you going to move through the lessons in this book by viewing files locally on your own computer, or are you going to use a web hosting provider? Note that most web hosting providers will have you up and running the same day you purchase your hosting plan.

▶ If you are using an external hosting provider, then using your FTP client, create a subdirectory within the document root of your website. Paste the contents of the `sample.html` file into another file named `index.html`, change the text between the `<title>` and `</title>` tags to something new, and change the text between the `<h1>` and `</h1>` tags to something new. Save the file and upload it to the new subdirectory. Use your web browser to navigate to the new directory on your web server and see that the content in the `index.html` file appears. Then, using your FTP client, delete the `index.html` file from the remote subdirectory. Return to that URL with your web browser, reload the page, and see how the server responds without the `index.html` file in place.

▶ Using the same set of files created in the preceding exercise, place these files on a removable media device such as a USB drive. Use your browser to navigate this local version of your sample website, and think about the instructions you would have to distribute with this removable media so that others could use it.

CHAPTER 2

Structuring HTML and Using Cascading Style Sheets

What You'll Learn in This Chapter:

▶ How to create a simple web page in HTML

▶ How to include the HTML tags that every web page must have

▶ How to use links within your web pages

▶ How to organize a page with paragraphs and line breaks

▶ How to organize your content with headings

▶ How to use the semantic elements of HTML5

▶ How to begin using basic CSS

In the first chapter, you got a basic idea of the process behind creating web content and viewing it online (or locally, if you do not yet have a web hosting provider). In this chapter, we get down to the business of explaining the various elements that must appear in an HTML file so that it is displayed appropriately in your web browser.

In general, this chapter provides an overview of HTML basics and gives some practical tips to help you make the most of your time as a web developer. You'll begin to dive a bit deeper into the theory behind it all as you learn about the HTML5 elements that enable you to enhance the semantics—the meaning—of the information that you provide in your marked-up text. You'll take a closer look at six elements that are fundamental to solid semantic structuring of your documents: `<header>`, `<section>`, `<article>`, `<nav>`, `<aside>`, and `<footer>`. Finally, you'll learn the basics of fine-tuning the display of your web content using *Cascading Style Sheets (CSS)*, which enable you to set a number of formatting characteristics, including exact typeface controls, letter and line spacing, and margins and page borders, just to name a few.

Throughout the remainder of this book, you will see HTML tags and CSS styles used appropriately in the code samples, so this chapter makes sure that you have a good grasp of their meaning before we continue.

Getting Started with a Simple Web Page

In the first chapter, you learned that a web page is just a text file that is marked up by (or surrounded by) HTML code that provides guidelines to a browser for displaying the content. To create these text files, use a plain-text editor such as Notepad on Windows or TextEdit on a Mac—do not use WordPad, Microsoft Word, or other full-featured word-processing software because those create different sorts of files than the plain-text files used for web content.

CAUTION

I'll reiterate this point because it is very important to both the outcome and the learning process itself: Do not create your first HTML file with Microsoft Word or any other word processor, even if you can save your file as HTML, because most of these programs will write your HTML for you in strange ways, potentially leaving you totally confused.

Additionally, I recommend that you *not* use a graphical, what-you-see-is-what-you-get (WYSIWYG) editor such as Adobe Dreamweaver. You'll likely find it easier and more educational to start with a simple text editor that forces you to type the code yourself as you're learning HTML and CSS.

Before you begin working, you should start with some text that you want to put on a web page:

1. Find (or write) a few paragraphs of text about yourself, your family, your company, your pets, or some other subject that holds your interest.

2. Save this text as plain, standard ASCII text. Notepad (on Windows) and most simple text editors always save files as plain text, but if you're using another program, you might need to choose this file type as an option (after selecting File, Save As).

As you go through this chapter, you will add HTML markup (called *tags*) to the text file, thus turning it into content that is best viewed in a web browser.

When you save files containing HTML tags, always give them a name ending in .html. This is important—if you forget to type the .html at the end of the filename when you save the file, most text editors will give it some other extension (such as .txt). If that happens, you might not be able to find the file when you try to look at it with a web browser; if you find it, it certainly won't display properly. In other words, web browsers expect a web page file to have a file extension of .html and to be in plain-text format.

When visiting websites, you might also encounter pages with a file extension of .htm, which is another acceptable file extension to use. You might find other file extensions used on the Web, such as .jsp (Java Server Pages), .aspx (Microsoft Active Server Pages), and .php (PHP: Hypertext Preprocessor). These files also contain HTML in addition to the programming language—although the programming code in those files is executed on the server side and all you would see on the client side is the HTML output. If you looked at the source files, you would likely see some intricate weaving of programming and markup codes. You'll learn more about this process in later chapters as you learn to integrate PHP into your websites.

Listing 2.1 shows an example of text you can type and save to create a simple HTML page. If you opened this file with your web browser, you would see the page shown in Figure 2.1. Every web page you create must include a `<!DOCTYPE>` declaration, as well as `<html></html>`, `<head></head>`, `<title></title>`, and `<body></body>` tag pairs.

LISTING 2.1   The `<html>`, `<head>`, `<title>`, and `<body>` Tags

```
<!DOCTYPE html>
<html lang="en">
  <head>
    <title>The First Web Page</title>
  </head>

  <body>
    <p>
      In the beginning, Tim created the HyperText Markup Language. The
      Internet was without form and void, and text was upon the face of
      the monitor and the Hands of Tim were moving over the face of the
      keyboard. And Tim said, Let there be links; and there were links.
      And Tim saw that the links were good; and Tim separated the links
      from the text. Tim called the links Anchors, and the text He
      called Other Stuff. And the whole thing together was the first
      Web Page.
    </p>
  </body>
</html>
```

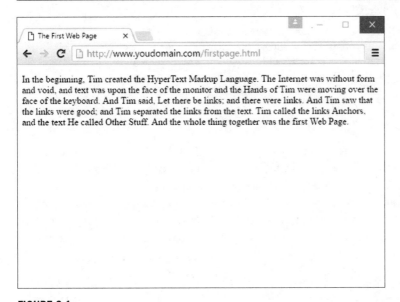

FIGURE 2.1
When you save the text in Listing 2.1 as an HTML file and view it with a web browser, only the actual title and body text are displayed.

In Listing 2.1, as in every HTML page, the words starting with < and ending with > are actually coded commands. These coded commands are called *HTML tags* because they "tag" pieces of text and tell the web browser what kind of text it is. This allows the web browser to display the text appropriately.

The first line in the document is the document type declaration; you are *declaring* that it is HTML (specifically, HTML5) because `html` is the value used to declare a document as HTML5 in the `<!DOCTYPE>` tag.

▼ TRY IT YOURSELF

Creating and Viewing a Basic Web Page

Before you learn the meaning of the HTML tags used in Listing 2.1, you might want to see exactly how I went about creating and viewing the document itself. Follow these steps:

1. Type all the text in Listing 2.1, including the HTML tags, in Windows Notepad (or use Macintosh TextEdit or another text editor of your choice).

2. Select File, Save As. Be sure to select plain text (or ASCII text) as the file type.

3. Name the file `firstpage.html`.

4. Choose the folder on your hard drive where you want to keep your web pages—and remember which folder you choose! Click the Save or OK button to save the file.

5. Now start your favorite web browser. (Leave Notepad running, too, so you can easily switch between viewing and editing your page.)

In Internet Explorer, select File, Open and click Browse. If you're using Firefox, select File, Open File. Navigate to the appropriate folder and select the `firstpage.html` file. Some browsers and operating systems also enable you to drag and drop the `firstpage.html` file onto the browser window to view it.

Voila! You should see the page shown in Figure 2.1.

If you have obtained a web hosting account, you could use FTP at this point to transfer the `firstpage.html` file to the web server. In fact, from this chapter forward, the instructions assume that you have a hosting provider and are comfortable sending files back and forth via FTP; if that is not the case, you should review the first chapter before moving on. Alternatively, if you are consciously choosing to work with files locally (without a web host), be prepared to adjust the instructions to suit your particular needs (such as ignoring the commands "transfer the files" and "type in the URL").

NOTE

You don't need to be connected to the Internet to view a web page stored on your own computer. By default, your web browser probably tries to connect to the Internet every time you start it, which makes sense most of the time. However, this can be a hassle if you're developing pages locally on your hard drive (offline) and you keep getting errors about a page not being found. If you have a full-time web connection via a cable modem, DSL, or Wi-Fi, this is a moot point because the browser will never complain about being offline. Otherwise, the appropriate action depends on your breed of browser; check the options under your browser's Tools menu.

HTML Tags Every Web Page Must Have

The time has come for the secret language of HTML tags to be revealed to you. When you understand this language, you will have creative powers far beyond those of other humans. Don't tell the other humans, but it's really pretty easy.

The first line of code is the document type declaration; in HTML5, this is simply `<!DOCTYPE html>`.

This declaration identifies the document as being HTML5, which then ensures that web browsers know what to expect and can prepare to render content in HTML5.

Many HTML tags have two parts: an *opening tag*, which indicates where a piece of text begins, and a *closing tag*, which indicates where the piece of text ends. Closing tags start with a forward slash (/) just after the < symbol.

Another type of tag, or element, is the *empty element*, which is different in that it doesn't include a pair of matching opening and closing tags. Instead, an empty element consists of a single tag that starts with the < symbol and ends with the > symbol. You may see some empty elements end with />, which is no longer required in HTML5 but did exist in previous versions of HTML.

Following is a quick summary of these three types of tags, just to make sure you understand the role each plays:

▶ An *opening tag* is an HTML tag that indicates the start of an HTML command; the text affected by the command appears after the opening tag. Opening tags always begin with < and end with >, as in `<html>`.

▶ A *closing tag* is an HTML tag that indicates the end of an HTML command; the text affected by the command appears before the closing tag. Closing tags always begin with `</` and end with >, as in `</html>`.

▶ An *empty tag* or *empty element* is an HTML tag that issues an HTML command without enclosing any text in the page. Examples include `<br>` for line breaks and `<img>` for images.

NOTE

You no doubt noticed in Listing 2.1 that there is some extra code associated with the `<html>` tag. This code consists of the language attribute (`lang`), which is used to specify additional information related to the tag. In this case, it specifies that the language of the text within the HTML is English. If you are writing in a different language, replace the `en` (for English) with the language identifier relevant to you.

For example, the `<body>` tag in Listing 2.1 tells the web browser where the actual body text of the page begins, and `</body>` indicates where it ends. Everything between the `<body>` and `</body>` tags appears in the main display area of the web browser window, as shown in Figure 2.1.

The very top of the browser window (refer to Figure 2.1) shows title text, which is any text that is located between `<title>` and `</title>`. The title text also identifies the page on the browser's Bookmarks or Favorites menu, depending on which browser you use. It's important to provide titles for your pages so that visitors to the page can properly bookmark them for future reference; search engines also use titles to provide a link to search results.

You will use the `<body>` and `<title>` tag pairs in every HTML page you create because every web page needs a title and body text. You will also use the `<html>` and `<head>` tag pairs, which are the other two tags shown in Listing 2.1. Putting `<html>` at the very beginning of a document simply indicates that the document is a web page. The `</html>` at the end indicates that the web page is over.

Within a page, there is a head section and a body section. Each section is identified by `<head>` and `<body>` tags. The idea is that information in the head of the page somehow describes the page but isn't actually displayed by a web browser. Information placed in the body, however, is displayed by a web browser. The `<head>` tag always appears near the beginning of the HTML code for a page, just after the opening `<html>` tag.

TIP

You might find it convenient to create and save a bare-bones page (also known as a *skeleton* page, or *template*) with just the DOCTYPE and opening and closing `<html>`, `<head>`, `<title>`, and `<body>` tags, similar to the document in Listing 2.1. You can then open that document as a starting point whenever you want to make a new web page and save yourself the trouble of typing all those obligatory tags every time.

The `<title>` tag pair used to identify the title of a page appears within the head of the page, which means it is placed after the opening `<head>` tag and before the closing `</head>` tag. In upcoming lessons, you'll learn about some other advanced header information that can go between `<head>` and `</head>`, such as style sheet rules for formatting the page.

The `<p></p>` tag pair in Listing 2.1 encloses a paragraph of text. You should enclose your chunks of text in the appropriate container elements whenever possible; you'll learn more about container elements as you move forward in your lessons.

Using Hyperlinks in Web Pages

There is no rule that says you have to include links in your web content, but you would be hard-pressed to find a website that doesn't include at least one link either to another page on the same domain (for example, yourdomain.com), another domain, or even the same page. Links are all over the web, but it is important to understand a little bit of the "under the hood" details of links.

When files are part of the same domain, you can link to them by simply providing the name of the file in the `href` attribute of the `<a>` tag. An *attribute* is an extra piece of information associated with a tag that provides further details about the tag. For example, the `href` attribute of the `<a>` tag identifies the address of the page to which you are linking.

When you have more than a few pages, or when you start to have an organizational structure to the content in your site, you should put your files into directories (or *folders*, if you will) whose names reflect the content within them. For example, all your images could be in an `images` directory, company information could be in an `about` directory, and so on. Regardless of how you organize your documents within your own web server, you can use relative addresses, which include only enough information to find one page from another. A *relative address* describes the path from one web page to another, instead of a full (or *absolute*) Internet address which includes the full protocol (`http` or `https`) and the domain name (like www.yourdomain.com).

As you recall from Chapter 1, "Understanding How the Web Works," the document root of your web server is the directory designated as the top-level directory for your web content. In web addresses, that document root is represented by the forward slash (/). All subsequent levels of directories are separated by the same type of forward slash. Here's an example:

```
/directory/subdirectory/subsubdirectory/
```

CAUTION

The forward slash (/) is always used to separate directories in HTML. Don't use the backslash (\, which is normally used in Windows) to separate your directories. Remember, everything on the Web moves forward, so use forward slashes.

Suppose you are creating a page named `zoo.html` in your document root, and you want to include a link to pages named `african.html` and `asian.html` in the `elephants` subdirectory. The links would look like the following:

```
<a href="/elephants/african.html">Learn about African elephants.</a>
<a href="/elephants/asian.html">Learn about Asian elephants.</a>
```

Linking Within a Page Using Anchors

The <a> tag—the tag responsible for hyperlinks on the Web—got its name from the word *anchor*, because a link serves as a designation for a spot in a web page. The <a> tag can be used to mark a spot on a page as an anchor, enabling you to create a link that points to that exact spot. For example, the top of a page could be marked as:

```
<a name="top"></a>
```

The <a> tag normally uses the href attribute to specify a hyperlinked target. The <a href> is what you click, and <a id> is where you go when you click there. In this example, the <a> tag is still specifying a target, but no actual link is created that you can see. Instead, the <a> tag gives a name to the specific point on the page where the tag occurs. The </a> tag must be included and a unique name must be assigned to the id attribute, but no text between <a> and </a> is necessary.

To link to this location, you would use the following:

```
<a href="#top">Go to Top of Page</a>
```

Linking to External Web Content

The only difference between linking to pages within your own site and linking to external web content is that when linking outside your site, you need to include the full address to that content. The full address includes the http:// before the domain name and then the full pathname to the file (for example, an HTML file, an image file, or a multimedia file).

For example, to include a link to Google from within one of your own web pages, you would use this type of absolute addressing in your <a> link:

```
<a href="http://www.google.com/">Go to Google</a>
```

CAUTION

As you might know, you can leave out the http:// at the front of any address when typing it into most web browsers. However, you *cannot* leave that part out when you type an Internet address into an <a href> link on a web page.

You can apply what you learned in previous sections to creating links to named anchors on other pages. Linked anchors are not limited to the same page. You can link to a named anchor on another page by including the address or filename followed by # and the anchor name. For example, the following link would take you to an anchor named photos within the african.html page inside the `elephants` directory on the (fictional) domain www.takeme2thezoo.com:

```
<a href="http://www.takeme2thezoo.com/elephants/african.html#photos">
Check out the African Elephant Photos!</a>
```

If you are linking from another page already on the www.takeme2thezoo.com domain (because you are, in fact, the site maintainer), your link might simply be as follows:

```
<a href="/elephants/african.html#photos">Check out the
African Elephant Photos!</a>
```

The `http://` and the domain name would not be necessary in that instance, as you have already learned.

CAUTION
Be sure to include the # symbol only in `<a href>` link tags. Don't put the # symbol in the `<a id>` tag; links to that name won't work in that case.

Linking to an Email Address

In addition to linking between pages and between parts of a single page, the `<a>` tag enables you to link to email addresses. This is the simplest way to enable your web page visitors to talk back to you. Of course, you could just provide visitors with your email address and trust them to type it into whatever email programs they use, but that increases the likelihood for errors. By providing a clickable link to your email address, you make it almost completely effortless for them to send you messages and eliminate the chance for typos.

An HTML link to an email address looks like the following:

```
<a href="mailto:yourusername@yourdomain.com">Send me an
email message.</a>
```

The words `Send me an email message` will appear just like any other `<a>` link.

Having taken this brief foray into the world of hyperlinks, let's get back to content organization and display.

Organizing a Page with Paragraphs and Line Breaks

When a web browser displays HTML pages, it pays no attention to line endings or the number of spaces between words in the underlying text file itself. For example, the top version of the poem in Figure 2.2 appears with a single space between all words, even though that's not how it's shown in Listing 2.2. This is because extra whitespace in HTML code is automatically reduced to a single space when rendered by the web browser. Additionally, when the text reaches the edge of the browser window, it automatically wraps to the next line, no matter where the line breaks were in the original HTML file.

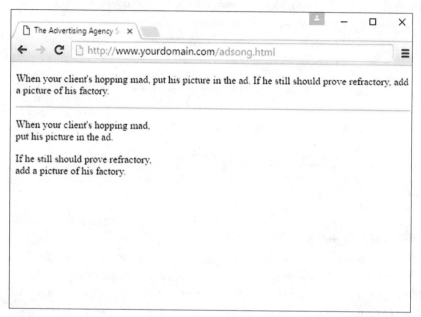

FIGURE 2.2
When the HTML in Listing 2.2 is viewed as a web page, line and paragraph breaks appear only where there are <br> and <p> tags.

LISTING 2.2   HTML Containing Paragraph and Line Breaks

```
<!DOCTYPE html>

<html lang="en">
  <head>
    <title>The Advertising Agency Song</title>
  </head>

  <body>
    <p>
      When your client's     hopping mad,
      put his picture in the ad.

      If he still should     prove refractory,
      add a picture of his factory.
    </p>
```

```
    <hr>
    <p>
      When your client's hopping mad,<br>
      put his picture in the ad.
    </p>
    <p>
      If he still should prove refractory,<br>
      add a picture of his factory.
    </p>
  </body>
</html>
```

You must use HTML tags if you want to control where line and paragraph breaks actually appear. When text is enclosed within the `<p></p>` container tags, a line break is assumed after the closing tag. In later chapters, you'll learn to control the height of the line break using CSS. The `<br>` tag forces a line break within a paragraph. Unlike the other tags you've seen so far, `<br>` doesn't require a closing `</br>` tag—this is one of those empty elements discussed earlier.

The poem in Listing 2.2 and Figure 2.2 shows the `<br>` and `<p>` tags used to separate the lines and verses of an advertising agency song. You might have also noticed the `<hr>` tag in the listing, which causes a horizontal rule line to appear on the page (see Figure 2.2). Inserting a horizontal rule with the `<hr>` tag also causes a line break, even if you don't include a `<br>` tag along with it. Like `<br>`, the `<hr>` horizontal rule tag is an empty element and, therefore, never gets a closing `</hr>` tag.

TRY IT YOURSELF ▼

Formatting Text in HTML

Try your hand at formatting a passage of text as proper HTML:

1. Add `<html><head><title>`*My Title*`</title></head><body>` to the beginning of the text (using your own title for your page instead of *My Title*). Also include the boilerplate code at the top of the page that takes care of meeting the requirements of standard HTML.

2. Add `</body></html>` to the very end of the text.

3. Add a `<p>` tag at the beginning of each paragraph and a `</p>` tag at the end of each paragraph.

4. Use `<br>` tags anywhere you want single-spaced line breaks.

5. Use `<hr>` to draw horizontal rules separating major sections of text, or wherever you'd like to see a line across the page.

6. Save the file as *mypage*`.html` (using your own filename instead of *mypage*).

CAUTION

If you are using a word processor to create the web page, be sure to save the HTML file in plain-text or ASCII format.

7. Open the file in a web browser to see your web content. (Send the file via FTP to your web hosting account, if you have one.)

8. If something doesn't look right, go back to the text editor to make corrections and save the file again (and send it to your web hosting account, if applicable). You then need to click Reload/Refresh in the browser to see the changes you made.

Organizing Your Content with Headings

When you browse web pages on the Internet, you'll notice that many of them have a heading at the top that appears larger and bolder than the rest of the text. Listing 2.3 is sample code and text for a simple web page containing an example of a heading as compared to normal paragraph text. Any text between the <h1> and </h1> tags will appear as a large heading. Additionally, <h2> and <h3> make progressively smaller headings, all the way down to <h6>.

LISTING 2.3   Using Heading Tags

```
<!DOCTYPE html>

<html lang="en">
  <head>
    <title>My Widgets</title>
  </head>

  <body>
    <h1>My Widgets</h1>
    <p>My widgets are the best in the land. Continue reading to
    learn more about my widgets.</p>

    <h2>Widget Features</h2>
    <p>If I had any features to discuss, you can bet I'd do
    it here.</p>

    <h3>Pricing</h3>
    <p>Here, I would talk about my widget pricing.</p>
```

```
      <h3>Comparisons</h3>
      <p>Here, I would talk about how my widgets compare to my
      competitor's widgets.</p>
  </body>
</html>
```

NOTE

By now, you've probably caught on to the fact that HTML code is often indented by its author to reveal the relationship between different parts of the HTML document, as well as for simple ease of reading. This indentation is entirely voluntary—you could just as easily run all the tags together with no spaces or line breaks, and they would still look fine when viewed in a browser. The indentations are for you so that you can quickly look at a page full of code and understand how it fits together. Indenting your code is another good web design habit and ultimately makes your pages easier to maintain, both for yourself and for anyone else who might pick up where you leave off.

As you can see in Figure 2.3, the HTML that creates headings couldn't be simpler. In this example, the phrase "My Widgets" is given the highest level of heading, and is prominently displayed, by surrounding it with the `<h1></h1>` tag pair. For a slightly smaller (level 2) heading—for information that is of lesser importance than the title—use the `<h2>` and `</h2>` tags around your text. For content that should appear even less prominently than a level 2 heading, use the `<h3>` and `</h3>` tags around your text.

However, bear in mind that your headings should follow a content hierarchy; use only one level 1 heading, have one (or more) level 2 headings after the level 1 heading, use level 3 headings only after level 2 headings, and so on. Do not fall into the trap of assigning headings to content just to make that content display a certain way, such as by skipping headings. Instead, ensure that you are categorizing your content appropriately (as a main heading, a secondary heading, and so on) while using display styles to make that text render a particular way in a web browser.

You can also use `<h4>`, `<h5>`, and `<h6>` tags to make progressively less important headings. By default, web browsers seldom show a noticeable difference between these headings and the `<h3>` headings—although you can control that with your own CSS. Also, content usually isn't displayed in such a manner that you'd need six levels of headings to show the content hierarchy.

It's important to remember the difference between a *title* and a *heading*. These two words are often interchangeable in day-to-day English, but when you're talking HTML, `<title>` gives the entire page an identifying name that isn't displayed on the page itself; it's displayed only on the browser window's title bar. The heading tags, on the other hand, cause some text on the page to be displayed with visual emphasis. There can be only one `<title>` per page, and it must appear within the `<head>` and `</head>` tags; on the other hand, you can have as many `<h1>`, `<h2>`, and `<h3>` headings as you want, in any order that suits your fancy. However, as

I mentioned before, you should use the heading tags to keep tight control over content hierarchy (logic dictates only one `<h1>` heading); do not use headings as a way to achieve a particular look, because that's what CSS is for.

FIGURE 2.3
Using three levels of headings shows the hierarchy of content on this sample product page.

CAUTION

Don't forget that anything placed in the head of a web page is not intended to be viewed on the page, whereas everything in the body of the page *is* intended for viewing.

Peeking at Other Designers' Pages

Given the visual and sometimes audio pizzazz present in many popular web pages, you probably realize that the simple pages described in this lesson are only the tip of the HTML iceberg. Now that you know the basics, you might surprise yourself with how much of the rest you can pick up just by looking at other people's pages on the Internet. You can see the HTML for any page by right-clicking and selecting View Source in any web browser.

Don't worry if you aren't yet able to decipher what some HTML tags do or exactly how to use them yourself. You'll find out about all those things as you move forward in the book. However, sneaking a preview now will show you the tags that you do know in action and give you a taste of what you'll soon be able to do with your web pages.

Understanding Semantic Elements

HTML5 includes tags that enable you to enhance the semantics—the meaning—of the information you provide in your marked-up text. Instead of simply using HTML as a presentation language, as was the practice in the very early days when <b> for bold and <i> for italics was the norm, modern HTML has as one of its goals the separation of presentation and meaning. While using CSS to provide guidelines for presentation, composers of HTML can provide meaningful names within their markup for individual elements, not only through the use of IDs and class names (which you'll learn about later in this chapter), but also through the use of semantic elements.

Some of the semantic elements available in HTML5 follow:

▶ **<header></header>**—This might seem counterintuitive, but you can use multiple <header> tags within a single page. The <header> tag should be used as a container for introductory information, so it might be used only once in your page (likely at the top), but you also might use it several times if your page content is broken into sections. Any container element can have a <header> element; just make sure that you're using it to include introductory information about the element it is contained within.

▶ **<footer></footer>**—The <footer> tag is used to contain additional information about its containing element (page or section), such as copyright and author information or links to related resources.

▶ **<nav></nav>**—If your site has navigational elements, such as links to other sections within a site or even within the page itself, these links go in a <nav> tag. A <nav> tag typically is found in the first instance of a <header> tag, just because people tend to put navigation at the top and consider it introductory information—but that is not a requirement. You can put your <nav> element anywhere (as long as it includes navigation), and you can have as many on a page as you need (often no more than two, but you might feel otherwise).

▶ **<section></section>**—The <section> tag contains anything that relates thematically; it can also contain a <header> tag for introductory information and possibly a <footer> tag for other related information. You can think of a <section> as carrying more meaning than a standard <p> (paragraph) or <div> (division) tag, which typically conveys no meaning at all; the use of <section> conveys a relationship between the content elements it contains.

▶ **<article></article>**—An <article> tag is like a <section> tag, in that it can contain a <header>, a <footer>, and other container elements such as paragraphs and divisions. But the additional meaning carried with the <article> tag is that it is, well, like an article in a newspaper or some other publication. Use this tag around blog posts, news articles, reviews, and other items that fit this description. One key difference between an <article> and a <section> is that an <article> is a standalone body of work, whereas a <section> is a thematic grouping of information.

▶ `<aside></aside>`—Use the `<aside>` tag to indicate secondary information; if the
`<aside>` tag is within a `<section>` or an `<article>`, the relationship will be to those
containers; otherwise, the secondary relationship will be to the overall page or site itself. It
might make sense to think of the `<aside>` as a sidebar—either for all the content on the
page or for an article or other thematic container of information.

These semantic elements will become clearer as you practice using them. In general, using
semantic elements is a good idea because they provide additional meaning not only for you
and other designers and programmers reading and working with your markup, but also for
machines. Web browsers and screen readers will respond to your semantic elements by using
them to determine the structure of your document; screen readers will report a deeper meaning
to users, thus increasing the accessibility of your material.

One of the best ways to understand the HTML5 semantic elements is to see them in action, but
that can be a little difficult when the primary purpose of these elements is to provide *meaning* rather than design. That's not to say that you can't add design to these elements—you most certainly
can. But the "action" of the semantic elements is to hold content and provide meaning through
doing so, as in Figure 2.4, which shows a common use of semantic elements for a basic web page.

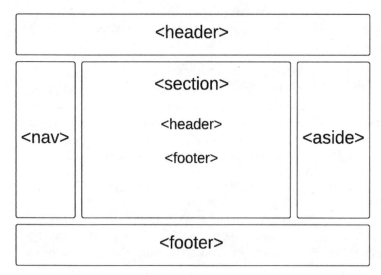

FIGURE 2.4
Showing basic semantic elements in a web page.

Initially, you might think, "Of *course*, that makes total sense, with the header at the top and the
footer at the bottom," and feel quite good about yourself for understanding semantic elements
at first glance—and you should! A second glance should then raise some questions: What if

you want your navigation to be horizontal under your header? Does an aside have to be (literally) on the side? What if you don't want any asides? What's with the use of `<header>` and `<footer>` again within the main body section? And that's just to name a few! Something else you might wonder about is where the `<article>` element fits in; it isn't shown in this example but will be used later in this chapter.

This is the time when conceptualizing the page—and specifically the page *you* want to create—comes into play. If you understand the content you want to mark up and you understand that you can use any, all, or none of the semantic elements and still create a valid HTML document, then you can begin to organize the content of your page in the way that makes the most sense for it and for you (and, hopefully, for your readers).

NOTE

Although you do not need to use semantic elements to create a valid HTML document, even a minimal set is recommended so that web browsers and screen readers can determine the structure of your document. Screen readers are capable of reporting a deeper meaning to users, thus increasing the accessibility of your material.

(If this note were marked up in an HTML document, it would use the `<aside>` element.)

Let's take a look at the elements used in Figure 2.4 before moving on to a second example and then a deeper exploration of the individual elements themselves. In Figure 2.4, you see a `<header>` at the top of the page and a `<footer>` at the bottom—straightforward, as already mentioned. The use of a `<nav>` element on the left side of the page matches a common display area for navigation, and the `<aside>` element on the right side of the page matches a common display area for secondary notes, pull quotes, helper text, and "for more information" links about the content. In Figure 2.5, you'll see some of these elements shifted around, so don't worry—Figure 2.4 is not some immutable example of semantic markup.

Something you might be surprised to see in Figure 2.5 is the `<header>` and `<footer>` inside the `<section>` element. As you'll learn shortly, the role of the `<header>` element is to introduce a second example and then a deeper exploration of the individual elements themselves. In Figure 2.4, you see a `<header>` at the top of the page and a `<footer>` at the bottom—straightforward, as already mentioned. The use of a `<nav>` element on the left side of the page matches the content that comes after it, and the `<header>` element itself does not convey any level in a document outline. Therefore, you can use as many as you need to mark up your content appropriately; a `<header>` at the beginning of the page might contain introductory information about the page as a whole, and the `<header>` element within the `<section>` element might just as easily and appropriately contain introductory information about the content within it. The same is true for the multiple appearances of the `<footer>` element in this example.

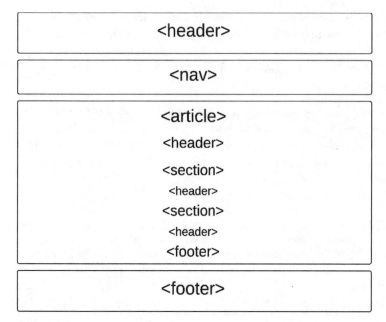

FIGURE 2.5
Using nested semantic elements to add more meaning to the content.

Let's move on to Figure 2.5, which shifts around the `<nav>` element and also introduces the use of the `<article>` element.

In Figure 2.5, the `<header>` and `<nav>` elements at the beginning of the page, and the `<footer>` element at the bottom of the page, should make perfect sense to you. And, although we haven't talked about the `<article>` element yet, if you think about it as a container element that has sections (`<section>`s, even!), with each of those sections having its own heading, then the chunk of semantic elements in the middle of the figure should make sense, too. As you can see, there's no single way to conceptualize a page; you should conceptualize content, and that content will be different on each page in a web site.

If you marked up some content in the structure shown in Figure 2.5, it might look like Listing 2.4.

LISTING 2.4   Semantic Markup of Basic Content

```
<!DOCTYPE html>

<html lang="en">
  <head>
    <title>Semantic Example</title>
```

```
    </head>
    <body>
      <header>
          <h1>SITE OR PAGE LOGO GOES HERE</h1>
      </header>
      <nav>
          SITE OR PAGE NAV GOES HERE.
      </nav>
      <article>
          <header>
              <h2>Article Heading</h2>
          </header>
          <section>
              <header>
                  <h3>Section 1 Heading</h3>
              </header>
              <p>Section 1 content here.</p>
          </section>
          <section>
              <header>
                  <h3>Section 2 Heading</h3>
              </header>
              <p>Section 2 content here.</p>
          </section>
          <footer>
              <p>Article footer goes here.</p>
          </footer>
      </article>
      <footer>
          SITE OR PAGE FOOTER HERE
      </footer>
    </body>
</html>
```

If you opened this HTML document in your web browser, you would see something like what's shown in Figure 2.6—a completely unstyled document, but one that has semantic meaning (even if no one can "see" it).

FIGURE 2.6
The output of Listing 2.4.

Just because there is no visible styling doesn't mean the meaning is lost; as noted earlier in this section, machines can interpret the structure of the document as provided for through the semantic elements. You can see the outline of this basic document in Figure 2.7, which shows the output of this file after examination by the HTML5 Outline tool at http://gsnedders.html5.org/outliner/.

TIP

Using the HTML5 Outline tool is a good way to check that you've created your headers, footers, and sections; if you examine your document and see "untitled section" anywhere, and those untitled sections do not match up with a `<nav>` or `<aside>` element (which has more relaxed guidelines about containing headers), then you have some additional work to do.

Now that you've seen some examples of conceptualizing the information represented in your documents, you're better prepared to start marking up those documents. The sections that follow take a look at the semantic elements individually.

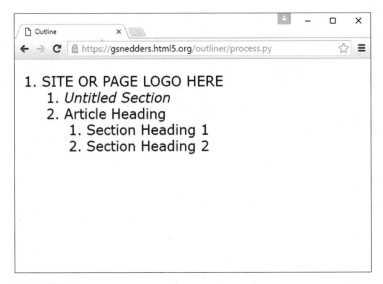

FIGURE 2.7
The outline of this document follows the semantic markup.

Using `<header>` in Multiple Ways

At the most basic level, the `<header>` element contains introductory information. That information might take the form of an actual `<h1>` (or other level) element, or it might simply be a logo image or text contained within a `<p>` or `<div>` element. The *meaning* of the content should be introductory in nature, to warrant its inclusion within a `<header></header>` tag pair.

As you've seen in the examples so far in this lesson, a common placement of a `<header>` element is at the beginning of a page. When it's used in this way, containing a logo or an `<h1>`-level title makes sense, such as here:

```
<header>
     <img src="acmewidgets.jpg" alt="ACME Widgets LLC">
</header>
```

Or even here:

```
<header>
     <img src="acmewidgets.jpg" alt="ACME Widgets LLC">
     <h1>The finest widgets are made here!</h1>
</header>
```

Both snippets are valid uses of `<header>` because the information contained within them is introductory to the page overall.

As you've also seen in this chapter, you are not limited to only one <header>. You can go crazy with your <header> elements, as long as they are acting as containers for introductory information—Listing 2.4 showed the use of <header> elements for several <section> elements within an <article>, and this is a perfectly valid use of the element:

```
<section>
   <header>
       <h3>Section 1 Heading</h3>
   </header>
   <p>Section 1 content here.</p>
</section>
<section>
   <header>
       <h3>Section 2 Heading</h3>
   </header>
   <p>Section 2 content here.</p>
</section>
```

The <header> element can contain any other element in the flow content category, of which it is also a member. This means that a <header> *could* contain a <section> element, if you wanted, and be perfectly valid markup. However, when you are conceptualizing your content, think about whether that sort of nesting makes sense before you go off and do it.

NOTE

In general, *flow content* elements are elements that contain text, images, or other multimedia embedded content; HTML elements fall into multiple categories.

If you want to learn more about the categorization of elements into content models, see http://www.w3.org/TR/2011/WD-html5-20110525/content-models.html.

The only exceptions to the permitted content within <header> are that the <header> element cannot contain *other* <header> elements and it cannot contain a <footer> element. Similarly, the <header> element cannot be contained within a <footer> element.

Understanding the <section> Element

The <section> element has a simple definition: It is a "generic section of a document" that is also a "thematic grouping of content, typically with a heading." That sounds pretty simple to me, and probably does to you as well. So you might be surprised to find that if you type "difference between section and article in HTML5" in your search engine of choice, you'll find tens of thousands of entries talking about the differences because the definitions trip people up all the time. We first discuss the <section> element and then cover the <article> element—and hopefully avoid any of the misunderstandings that seem to plague new web developers.

In Listing 2.4, you saw a straightforward example of using `<section>` within an `<article>` (repeated here). In this example, you can easily imagine that the `<section>`s contain a "thematic grouping of content," which is supported by the fact that they each have a heading:

```
<article>
    <header>
        <h2>Article Heading</h2>
    </header>
    <section>
        <header>
            <h3>Section 1 Heading</h3>
        </header>
        <p>Section 1 content here.</p>
    </section>
    <section>
        <header>
            <h3>Section 2 Heading</h3>
        </header>
        <p>Section 2 content here.</p>
    </section>
    <footer>
        <p>Article footer goes here.</p>
    </footer>
</article>
```

But here's an example of a perfectly valid use of `<section>` with no `<article>` element in sight:

```
<section>
    <header>
        <h1>Super Heading</h1>
    </header>
    <p>Super content!</p>
</section>
```

So what's a developer to do? Let's say you have some generic content that you know you want to divide into sections with their own headings. In that case, use `<section>`. If you need to only *visually* delineate chunks of content (such as with paragraph breaks) that do not require additional headings, then `<section>` isn't for you—use `<p>` or `<div>` instead.

Because the `<section>` element can contain any other flow content element, and can be contained within any other flow content element (except the `<address>` element, discussed later in this chapter), it's easy to see why, without other limitations and with generic guidelines for use, the `<section>` element is sometimes misunderstood.

Using `<article>` Appropriately

Personally, I believe that a lot of the misunderstanding regarding the use of `<section>` versus `<article>` has to do with the name of the `<article>` element. When I think of an article, I think specifically about an article in a newspaper or a magazine. I don't naturally think "any standalone body of work," which is how the `<article>` element is commonly defined. The HTML5 recommended specification defines it as "a complete, or self-contained, composition in a document, page, application, or site and that is, in principle, independently distributable or reusable," such as "a forum post, a magazine or newspaper article, a blog entry, a user-submitted comment, an interactive widget or gadget, or any other independent item of content."

In other words, an `<article>` element could be used to contain the entire page of a website (whether or not it is an article in a publication), an actual article in a publication, a blog post anywhere and everywhere, part of a threaded discussion in a forum, a comment on a blog post, and as a container that displays the current weather in your city. It's no wonder there are tens of thousands of results for a search on "difference between section and article in HTML5."

A good rule of thumb when you're trying to figure out when to use `<article>` and when to use `<section>` is simply to answer the following question: Does this content make sense on its own? If so, then no matter what the content seems to be to you (for example, a static web page, not an article in the *New York Times*), start by using the `<article>` element. If you find yourself breaking it up, do so in `<section>`s. And if you find yourself thinking that your "article" is, in fact, part of a greater whole, then change the `<article>` tags to `<section>` tags, find the beginning of the document, and surround it from there with the more appropriately placed `<article>` tag at a higher level.

Implementing the `<nav>` Element

The `<nav>` element seems so simple (`<nav>` implies *navigation*), and it ultimately is—but it can also be used incorrectly. In this section, you'll learn some basic uses, and also some incorrect uses to avoid. If your site has any navigational elements at all, either sitewide or within a long page of content, you have a valid use for the `<nav>` element.

For that sitewide navigation, you typically find a `<nav>` element within the primary `<header>` element; you are not required to put it there, but if you want your navigational content to be introductory (and omnipresent in your template), you can easily make a case for your primary `<nav>` element to appear within the primary `<header>`. More important, that is valid HTML (as is `<nav>` outside a `<header>`) because a `<nav>` element can appear within any flow content, as well as contain any flow content.

The following code snippet shows the main navigational links of a website, placed within a `<header>` element:

```
<header>
    <img src="acmewidgets.jpg" alt="ACME Widgets LLC"/>
    <h1>The finest widgets are made here!</h1>
    <nav>
        <ul>
            <li><a href="#">About Us</a></li>
            <li><a href="#">Products</a></li>
            <li><a href="#">Support</a></li>
            <li><a href="#">Press</a></li>
        </ul>
    </nav>
</header>
```

You are not limited to a single <nav> element in your documents, which is good for site developers who create templates that include both primary *and* secondary navigation. For example, you might see horizontal primary navigation at the top of a page (often contained within a <header> element), and then vertical navigation in the left column of a page, representing the secondary pages within the main section. In that case, you simply use a second <nav> element, not contained within the <header>, placed and styled differently to delineate the two types visually in addition to semantically.

Remember, the <nav> element is used for *major* navigational content—primary and secondary navigation both count, as does the inclusion of tables of contents within a page. For good and useful semantic use of the <nav> element, do not simply apply it to every link that allows a user to navigate anywhere. Note that I said "good and useful" semantic use, not necessarily "valid" use—it's true that you could apply <nav> to any list of links, and it would be valid according to the HTML specification because links are flow content. But it wouldn't be particularly *useful*—it wouldn't add meaning—to surround a list of links to social media sharing tools with the <nav> element.

When to Use <aside>

As you'll see by the number of tips and notes from me throughout this book, I'm a big fan of the type of content that is most appropriately marked up within the <aside> element. The <aside> element is meant to contain any content that is tangentially related to the content around it—additional explanation, links to related resources, pull quotes, helper text, and so on. You might think of the <aside> element as a sidebar, but be careful not to think of it only as a *visual* sidebar, or a column on the side of a page where you can stick anything and everything you want, whether or not it's related to the content or site at hand.

In Figure 2.8, you can see how content in an <aside> is used to create a *pull quote*, or a content excerpt that is specifically set aside to call attention to it. The <aside>, in this case, is used to highlight an important section of the text, but it could also have been used to define a term or link to related documents.

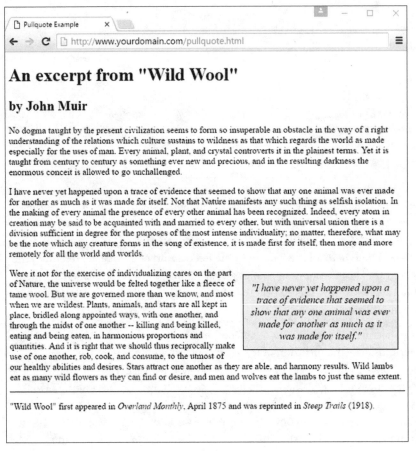

FIGURE 2.8
Using `<aside>` to create meaningful pull quotes.

When determining whether to use the `<aside>` element, think about the content you want to add. Is it related directly to the content in which the `<aside>` would be contained, such as a definition of terms used in an article or a list of related links for the article? If your answer is an easy yes, that's great! Use `<aside>` to your heart's content. If you're thinking of including an `<aside>` outside a containing element that is itself full of content, just make sure that the content of the `<aside>` is reasonably related to your site overall and that you're not just using the `<aside>` element for visual effect.

Using `<footer>` Effectively

The counterpart to the `<header>` element, the `<footer>` element, contains additional information about its containing element. The most common use of the `<footer>` element is to contain copyright information at the bottom of a page, such as here:

```
<footer>
    <p>&copy; 2017 Acme Widgets, LLC. All Rights Reserved.</p>
</footer>
```

Similar to the `<header>` element, the `<footer>` element can contain any other element in the flow content category, of which it is also a member, with the exception of *other* `<footer>` or `<header>` elements. Additionally, a `<footer>` element cannot be contained within an `<address>` element, but a `<footer>` element can contain an `<address>` element—in fact, a `<footer>` element is a common location for an `<address>` element to reside in.

Placing useful `<address>` content within a `<footer>` element is one of the most effective uses of the `<footer>` element (not to mention the `<address>` element) because it provides specific contextual information about the page or section of the page to which it refers. The following snippet shows a use of `<address>` within `<footer>`:

```
<footer>
    <p>&copy; 2017 Acme Widgets, LLC. All Rights Reserved.</p>
    <p>Copyright Issues? Contact:</p>
        <address>
        Our Lawyer<br>
        123 Main Street<br>
        Somewhere, CA 95128<br>
        <a href="mailto:lawyer@example.com">lawyer@example.com</a>
        </address>
</footer>
```

As with the `<header>` element, you are not limited to only one `<footer>`. You can use as many `<footer>` elements as you need, as long as they are containers for additional information about the containing element—Listing 2.4 showed the use of `<footer>` elements for both a page and an `<article>`, both of which are valid.

How CSS Works

In the preceding sections, you learned the basics of HTML, including how to set up a skeletal HTML template for all your web content, use hyperlinks, and generally organize your content. In this section, you'll learn the basics of fine-tuning the visual display of your web content using *Cascading Style Sheets (CSS)*.

The concept behind style sheets is simple: You create a style sheet document that specifies the fonts, colors, spacing, and other characteristics that establish a unique look for a website. You then link every page that should have that look to the style sheet instead of specifying all those styles repeatedly in each separate document. Therefore, when you decide to change your official corporate typeface or color scheme, you can modify all your web pages at once just by changing one or two entries in your style sheet—you don't have to change them in all your static web files. So a *style sheet* is a grouping of formatting instructions that control the appearance of several HTML pages at once.

Style sheets enable you to set a great number of formatting characteristics, including exact type-face controls, letter and line spacing, and margins and page borders, just to name a few. Style sheets also enable you to specify sizes and other measurements in familiar units, such as inches, millimeters, points, and picas. In addition, you can use style sheets to precisely position graphics and text anywhere on a web page, either at specific coordinates or relative to other items on the page.

In short, style sheets bring a sophisticated level of display to the Web—and they do so, if you'll pardon the expression, with style.

NOTE
___

If you have three or more web pages that share (or should share) similar formatting and fonts, you might want to create a style sheet for them as you read this chapter. Even if you choose not to create a complete style sheet, you'll find it helpful to apply styles to individual HTML elements directly within a web page.

___

A *style rule* is a formatting instruction that can be applied to an element on a web page, such as a paragraph of text or a link. Style rules consist of one or more style properties and their associated values. An *internal style sheet* is placed directly within a web page, whereas an *external style sheet* exists in a separate document and is simply linked to a web page via a special tag—more on this tag in a moment.

The *cascading* part of the name Cascading Style Sheets refers to the manner in which style sheet rules are applied to elements in an HTML document. More specifically, styles in a CSS style sheet form a hierarchy in which more specific styles override more general styles. It is the responsibility of CSS to determine the precedence of style rules according to this hierarchy, which establishes a cascading effect. If that sounds a bit confusing, just think of the cascading mechanism in CSS as being similar to genetic inheritance, in which general traits are passed from parents to a child, but more specific traits are entirely unique to the child. Base-style rules are applied throughout a style sheet but can be overridden by more specific style rules.

NOTE
___

You might notice that I use the term *element* a fair amount in this chapter (and I do in the rest of the book, for that matter). An *element* is simply a piece of information (content) in a web page, such as an image, a paragraph, or a link. Tags are used to mark up elements, and you can think of an element as a tag, complete with descriptive information (attributes, text, images, and so on) within the tag.

___

A quick example should clear things up. Take a look at the following code to see whether you can tell what's going on with the color of the text:

```
<div style="color:green">
  This text is green.
  <p style="color:blue">This text is blue.</p>
  <p>This text is still green.</p>
</div>
```

In the preceding example, the color green is applied to the `<div>` tag via the `color` style property. Therefore, the text in the `<div>` tag is colored green. Because both `<p>` tags are children of the `<div>` tag, the green text style cascades down to them. However, the first `<p>` tag overrides the color style and changes it to blue. The end result is that the first line (not surrounded by a paragraph tag) is green, the first official paragraph is blue, and the second official paragraph retains the cascaded green color.

If you made it through that description on your own and came out on the other end unscathed, congratulations—that's half the battle. Understanding CSS isn't like understanding rocket science—the more you practice, the more it will become clear. The real trick is developing the aesthetic design sense that you can then apply to your online presence through CSS.

Like many web technologies, CSS has evolved over the years. The original version of CSS, known as *Cascading Style Sheets Level 1* (*CSS1*), was created in 1996. The later CSS2 standard was created in 1998, and CSS2 is still in use today; all modern web browsers support CSS2. The latest version of CSS is CSS3, which builds on the strong foundation laid by its predecessors but adds advanced functionality to enhance the online experience. In the following sections you'll learn core CSS, and throughout the rest of the book when CSS is discussed or used, I'll refer to CSS3.

The rest of this chapter explains the basics of putting CSS to good use, but it's not a reference for all things CSS. Nor is the rest of this book, which will show plenty of examples of basic CSS in use as you learn to build dynamic web applications. However, you can find a developer-oriented guide to CSS at https://developer.mozilla.org/en-US/docs/Web/CSS that gets into excruciating detail regarding everything you can do with CSS. This guide can be an invaluable reference to you as you continue on your web development journey.

A Basic Style Sheet

Despite their power, style sheets are simple to create. Consider the web pages shown in Figures 2.9 and 2.10. These pages share several visual properties that can be put into a common style sheet:

▶ They use a large, bold Verdana font for the headings and a normal-size and normal-weight Verdana font for the body text.

▶ They use an image named `logo.gif` floating within the content and on the right side of the page.

▶ All text is black except for subheadings, which are purple.

▶ They have margins on the left side and at the top.

▶ They include vertical space between lines of text.

▶ They include a footer that is centered and in small print.

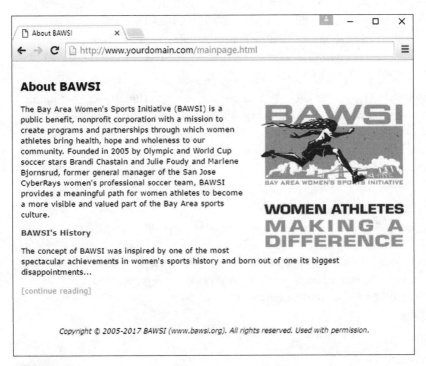

FIGURE 2.9
This page uses a style sheet to fine-tune the appearance and spacing of the text and images.

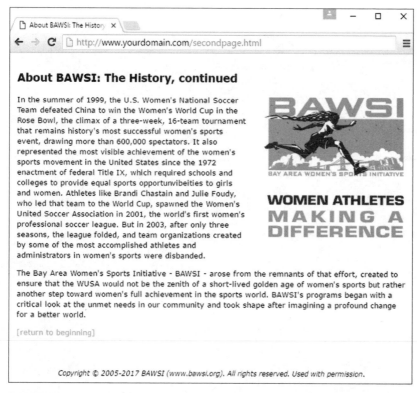

FIGURE 2.10
This page uses the same style sheet as the one in Figure 2.9, thus maintaining a consistent look and feel.

Listing 2.5 shows the CSS used in a style sheet to specify these properties.

LISTING 2.5   A Single External Style Sheet

```
body {
    font-size: 10pt;
    font-family: Verdana, Geneva, Arial, Helvetica, sans-serif;
    color: black;
    line-height: 14pt;
    padding-left: 5pt;
    padding-right: 5pt;
    padding-top: 5pt;
}


h1 {
    font: 14pt Verdana, Geneva, Arial, Helvetica, sans-serif;
    font-weight: bold;
    line-height: 20pt;
}
```

```
p.subheader {
  font-weight: bold;
  color: #593d87;
}

img {
  padding: 3pt;
  float: right;
}

a {
  text-decoration: none;
}

a:link, a:visited {
  color: #8094d6;
}

a:hover, a:active {
  color: #FF9933;
}

footer {
  font-size: 9pt;
  font-style: italic;
  line-height: 12pt;
  text-align: center;
  padding-top: 30pt;
}
```

This might initially appear to be a lot of code, but if you look closely, you'll see that there isn't a lot of information on each line of code. It's fairly standard to place individual style rules on their own line, to help make style sheets more readable, but that is a personal preference; you could put all the rules on one line as long as you kept using the semicolon to separate each rule (more on that in a bit). Speaking of code readability, perhaps the first thing you noticed about this style sheet code is that it doesn't look anything like normal HTML code. CSS uses a syntax all its own to specify style sheets.

Of course, the listing includes some familiar HTML tags (although not all tags require an entry in the style sheet). As you might guess, body, h1, p, img, a, and footer in the style sheet refer to the corresponding tags in the HTML documents to which the style sheet will be applied. The curly braces after each tag name describe how all content within that tag should appear.

In this case, the style sheet says that all body text should be rendered at a size of 10 points, in the Verdana font (if possible), and with the color black, with 14 points between lines. If the user does not have the Verdana font installed, the list of fonts in the style sheet represents the order in which the browser should search for fonts to use: Geneva, then Arial, and then Helvetica. If the user has none of those fonts, the browser uses whatever default sans-serif font is available. Additionally, the page should have left, right, and top padding of 5 points each.

Any text within an `<h1>` tag should be rendered in boldface Verdana at a size of 14 points. Moving on, any paragraph that uses only the `<p>` tag inherits all the styles indicated by the body element. However, if the `<p>` tag uses a special class named `subheader`, the text appears bold and in the color #593d87 (a purple color).

The `pt` after each measurement in Listing 2.5 means *points* (there are 72 points in an inch). If you prefer, you can specify any style sheet measurement in inches (`in`), centimeters (`cm`), pixels (`px`), or "widths of a letter *m*," which are called ems (`em`).

You might have noticed that each style rule in the listing ends with a semicolon (`;`). Semicolons are used to separate style rules from each other. It is therefore customary to end each style rule with a semicolon so that you can easily add another style rule after it. Review the remainder of the style sheet in Listing 2.5 to see the presentation formatting applied to additional tags.

NOTE

You can specify font sizes as large as you like with style sheets, although some display devices and printers do not correctly handle fonts larger than 200 points.

To link this style sheet to HTML documents, include a `<link>` tag in the `<head>` section of each document. Listing 2.6 shows the HTML code for the page shown in Figure 2.9. It contains the following `<link>` tag:

```
<link rel="stylesheet" type="text/css" href="styles.css">
```

This assumes that the style sheet is stored under the name `styles.css` in the same folder as the HTML document. As long as the web browser supports style sheets—and all modern browsers do—the properties specified in the style sheet will apply to the content in the page without the need for any special HTML formatting code. This meets one of the goals of HTML, which is to provide a separation between the content in a web page and the specific formatting required to display that content.

LISTING 2.6   HTML Code for the Page Shown in Figure 2.9

```
<!DOCTYPE html>

<html lang="en">
  <head>
    <title>About BAWSI</title>
    <link rel="stylesheet" type="text/css" href="styles.css">
  </head>
```

```
<body>
    <section>

    <header>
    <h1>About BAWSI</h1>
    </header>

    <p><img src="logo.gif" alt="BAWSI logo">The Bay Area Women's
    Sports Initiative (BAWSI) is a public benefit, nonprofit
    corporation with a mission to create programs and partnerships
    through which women athletes bring health, hope and wholeness to
    our community. Founded in 2005 by Olympic and World Cup soccer
    stars Brandi Chastain and Julie Foudy and Marlene Bjornsrud,
    former general manager of the San Jose CyberRays women's
    professional soccer team, BAWSI provides a meaningful path for
    women athletes to become a more visible and valued part of the
    Bay Area sports culture.</p>

    <p class="subheader">BAWSI's History</p>

    <p>The concept of BAWSI was inspired by one of the most
    spectacular achievements in women's sports history and born out
    of one its biggest disappointments... </p>

    <p><a href="secondpage.html">[continue reading]</a></p>
    </section>


    <footer>
    Copyright &copy; 2005-2017 BAWSI (www.bawsi.org).
    All rights reserved.  Used with permission.
    </footer>
  </body>
</html>
```

TIP

In most web browsers, you can view the style rules in a style sheet by opening the .css file and choosing Notepad or another text editor as the helper application to view the file. (To determine the name of the .css file, look at the HTML source of any web page that links to it.) To edit your own style sheets, just use a text editor.

The code in Listing 2.6 is interesting because it contains no formatting of any kind. In other words, nothing in the HTML code dictates how the text and images are to be displayed—no colors, no fonts, nothing. Yet the page is carefully formatted and rendered to the screen, thanks to the link to the external style sheet, styles.css. The real benefit to this approach is that you can easily create a site with multiple pages that maintains a consistent look and feel. And you have the benefit of isolating the visual style of the page to a single document (the style sheet) so that one change impacts all pages.

NOTE

Not every browser's support of CSS is flawless. To find out how major browsers compare to each other in terms of CSS support, take a look at these websites: http://www.quirksmode.org/css/contents.html and http://caniuse.com.

TRY IT YOURSELF ▼

Create a Style Sheet of Your Own

Starting from scratch, create a new text document called `mystyles.css` and add some style rules for the following basic HTML tags: `<body>`, `<p>`, `<h1>`, and `<h2>`. After creating your style sheet, make a new HTML file that contains these basic tags. Play around with different style rules and see for yourself how simple it is to change entire blocks of text in paragraphs with one simple change in a style sheet file.

A CSS Style Primer

You now have a basic knowledge of CSS style sheets and how they are based on style rules that describe the appearance of information in web pages. The next few sections of this chapter provide a quick overview of some of the most important style properties and enable you to get started using CSS in your own style sheets.

CSS includes various style properties that are used to control fonts, colors, alignment, and margins, to name just a few. The style properties in CSS can be generally grouped into two major categories:

▶ Layout properties, which consist of properties that affect the positioning of elements on a web page, such as margins, padding, and alignment

▶ Formatting properties, which consist of properties that affect the visual display of elements within a website, such as the font type, size, and color

Basic Layout Properties

CSS layout properties determine how content is placed on a web page. One of the most important layout properties is the `display` property, which describes how an element is displayed with respect to other elements. The `display` property has four basic values:

- ▶ `block`—The element is displayed on a new line, as in a new paragraph.

- ▶ `list-item`—The element is displayed on a new line with a list-item mark (bullet) next to it.

- ▶ `inline`—The element is displayed inline with the current paragraph.

- ▶ `none`—The element is not displayed; it is hidden.

NOTE
___

The `display` property relies on a concept known as *relative positioning*, which means that elements are positioned relative to the location of other elements on a page. CSS also supports *absolute positioning*, which enables you to place an element at an exact location on a page, independent of other elements. You'll learn more about both of these types of positioning in Chapter 3, "Understanding the CSS Box Model and Positioning."

___

Understanding the `display` property is easier if you visualize each element on a web page occupying a rectangular area when displayed—the `display` property controls the manner in which this rectangular area is displayed. For example, the `block` value results in the element being placed on a new line by itself, whereas the `inline` value places the element next to the content just before it. The `display` property is one of the few style properties that can be applied in most style rules. Following is an example of how to set the `display` property:

```
display: block;
```

You control the size of the rectangular area for an element with the `width` and `height` properties. As with many size-related CSS properties, `width` and `height` property values can be specified in several different units of measurement:

- ▶ `in`—Inches

- ▶ `cm`—Centimeters

- ▶ `mm`—Millimeters

- ▶ `%`—Percentage

- ▶ `px`—Pixels

- ▶ `pt`—Points

You can mix and match units however you choose within a style sheet, but it's generally a good idea to be consistent across a set of similar style properties. For example, you might want to stick with points for font properties and pixels for dimensions. Following is an example of setting the width of an element using pixel units:

```
width: 200px;
```

Basic Formatting Properties

CSS formatting properties are used to control the appearance of content on a web page, as opposed to controlling the physical positioning of the content. One of the most popular formatting properties is the `border` property, which establishes a visible boundary around an element with a box or partial box. Note that a border is always present in that space is always left for it, but the border does not appear in a way that you can see unless you give it properties that make it visible (like a color). The following border properties provide a means of describing the borders of an element:

- **`border-width`**—The width of the border edge
- **`border-color`**—The color of the border edge
- **`border-style`**—The style of the border edge
- **`border-left`**—The left side of the border
- **`border-right`**—The right side of the border
- **`border-top`**—The top of the border
- **`border-bottom`**—The bottom of the border
- **`border`**—All the border sides

The `border-width` property establishes the width of the border edge. It is often expressed in pixels, as the following code demonstrates:

```
border-width: 5px;
```

Not surprisingly, the `border-color` and `border-style` properties set the border color and style. Following is an example of how these two properties are set:

```
border-color: blue;
border-style: dotted;
```

The `border-style` property can be set to any of the following basic values:

- **`solid`**—A single-line border
- **`double`**—A double-line border
- **`dashed`**—A dashed border
- **`dotted`**—A dotted border
- **`groove`**—A border with a groove appearance
- **`ridge`**—A border with a ridge appearance

- ▶ **inset**—A border with an inset appearance

- ▶ **outset**—A border with an outset appearance

- ▶ **none**—No border

- ▶ **hidden**—Effectively the same as none in that no border is displayed, but if two elements are next to each other with collapsed space between them, hidden ensures that a collapsed visible border does not show within the area of the element with a hidden border.

The default value of the border-style property is none, which is why elements don't have a border *unless* you set the border property to a different style. Although solid is the most common border style, you will also see the other styles in use.

The border-left, border-right, border-top, and border-bottom properties enable you to set the border for each side of an element individually. If you want a border to appear the same on all four sides, you can use the single border property by itself, which expects the following styles separated by a space: border-width, border-style, and border-color. Following is an example of using the border property to set a border that consists of two (double) red lines that are a total of 10 pixels in width:

```
border: 10px double red;
```

Whereas the color of an element's border is set with the border-color property, the color of the inner region of an element is set using the color and background-color properties. The color property sets the color of text in an element (foreground), and the background-color property sets the color of the background behind the text. Following is an example of setting both color properties to predefined colors:

```
color: black;
background-color: orange;
```

You can also assign custom colors to these properties by specifying the colors in hexadecimal or as RGB (Red, Green, Blue) decimal values:

```
background-color: #999999;
color: rgb(0,0,255);
```

You can also control the alignment and indentation of web page content without too much trouble. This is accomplished with the text-align and text-indent properties, as the following code demonstrates:

```
text-align: center;
text-indent: 12px;
```

When you have an element properly aligned and indented, you might be interested in setting its font. The following basic font properties set the various parameters associated with fonts:

▶ **font-family**—The family of the font

▶ **font-size**—The size of the font

▶ **font-style**—The style of the font (normal or italic)

▶ **font-weight**—The weight of the font (normal, lighter, bold, bolder, and so on)

The font-family property specifies a prioritized list of font family names. A prioritized list is used instead of a single value to provide alternatives in case a font isn't available on a given system. The font-size property specifies the size of the font using a unit of measurement, often in points. Finally, the font-style property sets the style of the font, and the font-weight property sets the weight of the font. Following is an example of setting these font properties:

```
font-family: Arial, sans-serif;
font-size: 36pt;
font-style: italic;
font-weight: normal;
```

Now that you know a whole lot more about style properties and how they work, refer to Listing 2.5 and see whether it makes a bit more sense. Here's a recap of the style properties used in that style sheet, which you can use as a guide for understanding how it works:

▶ **font**—Lets you set many font properties at once. You can specify a list of font names separated by commas; if the first is not available, the next is tried, and so on. You can also include the words bold and/or italic and a font size. Alternatively, you can set each of these font properties separately with font-family, font-size, font-weight, and font-style.

▶ **line-height**—Also known in the publishing world as *leading*. This sets the height of each line of text, usually in points.

▶ **color**—Sets the text color using the standard color names or hexadecimal color codes.

▶ **text-decoration**—Is useful for turning off link underlining; simply set it to none. The values of underline, italic, and line-through are also supported.

▶ **text-align**—Aligns text to the left, right, or center, along with justifying the text with a value of justify.

▶ **padding**—Adds padding to the left, right, top, and bottom of an element; this padding can be in measurement units or a percentage of the page width. Use padding-left and padding-right if you want to add padding to the left and right of the element independently. Use padding-top or padding-bottom to add padding to the top or bottom of the element, as appropriate. You'll learn a bit more about these style properties in Chapter 3.

Using Style Classes

Whenever you want some of the text on your pages to look different from the other text, you can create what amounts to a custom-built HTML tag. Each type of specially formatted text you define is called a *style class*, which is a custom set of formatting specifications that can be applied to any element in a web page.

Before showing you a style class, I need to take a quick step back and clarify some CSS terminology. First off, a CSS *style property* is a specific style that you can assign a value, such as `color` or `font-size`. You associate a style property and its respective value with elements on a web page by using a selector. A *selector* is used to identify tags on a page to which you apply styles. Following is an example of a selector, a property, and a value all included in a basic style rule:

```
h1 { font: 36pt Courier; }
```

In this code, `h1` is the selector, `font` is the style property, and `36pt Courier` is the value. The selector is important because it means that the font setting will be applied to all `h1` elements in the web page. But maybe you want to differentiate between some of the `h1` elements—what then? The answer lies in style classes.

Suppose you want two different kinds of `<h1>` headings for use in your documents. You create a style class for each one by putting the following CSS code in a style sheet:

```
h1.silly { font: 36pt 'Comic Sans'; }
h1.serious { font: 36pt Arial; }
```

Notice that these selectors include a period (`.`) after `h1`, followed by a descriptive class name. To choose between the two style classes, use the `class` attribute, like this:

```
<h1 class="silly">Marvin's Munchies Inc. </h1>
<p>Text about Marvin's Munchies goes here. </p>
```

Or you could use this:

```
<h1 class="serious">MMI Investor Information</h1>
<p>Text for business investors goes here.</p>
```

When referencing a style class in HTML code, simply specify the class name in the `class` attribute of an element. In the preceding example, the words `Marvin's Munchies Inc.` would appear in a 36-point Comic Sans font, assuming that you included a `<link>` to the style sheet at the top of the web page and that the user has the Comic Sans font installed. The words `MMI Investor Information` would appear in the 36-point Arial font instead. You can see another example of classes in action in Listing 2.5; look for the `specialtext` `<p>` class.

What if you want to create a style class that can be applied to any element instead of just headings or some other particular tag? In your CSS, simply use a period (`.`) followed by any style class name you make up and any style specifications you choose. That class can specify any number of font, spacing, and margin settings all at once. Wherever you want to apply your custom tag in a page, just use an HTML tag plus the `class` attribute, followed by the class name you created.

For example, the style sheet in Listing 2.5 includes the following style class specification:

```
p.specialtext {
  font-weight: bold;
  color: #593d87;
}
```

This style class is applied in Listing 2.6 with the following tag:

```
<p class="specialtext">
```

TIP

You might have noticed a change in the coding style when a style rule includes multiple properties. For style rules with a single style, you'll commonly see the property placed on the same line as the rule, like this:

```
p.specialtext { font-weight: bold; }
```

However, when a style rule contains multiple style properties, it's much easier to read and understand the code if you list the properties one per line, like this:

```
p.specialtext {
  font-weight: bold;
  color: #593d87;
}
```

Everything between that tag and the closing `</p>` tag in Listing 2.6 appears in bold purple text.

If no element selector were present in your style sheet, meaning that the rule looked like this:

```
.specialtext {
  font-weight: bold;
  color: #593d87;
}
```

Then any element could refer to `specialtext` and have the text rendered as bold purple, not just a `<p>` element.

What makes style classes so valuable is how they isolate style code from web pages, effectively enabling you to focus your HTML code on the actual content in a page, not on how it is going to appear on the screen. Then you can focus on how the content is rendered to the screen by fine-tuning the style sheet. You might be surprised by how a relatively small amount of code in a style sheet can have significant effects across an entire website. This makes your pages much easier to maintain and manipulate.

Using Style IDs

When you create custom style classes, you can use those classes as many times as you like—they are not unique. However, in some instances, you want precise control over unique elements for layout or formatting purposes (or both). In such instances, look to IDs instead of classes.

A *style ID* is a custom set of formatting specifications that can be applied to only one element in a web page. You can use IDs across a set of pages, but only once per time within each page.

For example, suppose you have a title within the body of all your pages. Each page has only one title, but all the pages themselves include one instance of that title. Following is an example of a selector with an ID indicated, plus a property and a value:

```
p#title {font: 24pt Verdana, Geneva, Arial, sans-serif}
```

Notice that this selector includes a hash mark, or pound sign (#), after p, followed by a descriptive ID name. When referencing a style ID in HTML code, simply specify the ID name in the id attribute of an element, like so:

```
<p id="title">Some Title Goes Here</p>
```

Everything between the opening and closing `<p>` tags will appear in 24-point Verdana text—but only once on any given page. You often see style IDs used to define specific parts of a page for layout purposes, such as a header area, footer area, main body area, and so on. These types of areas in a page appear only once per page, so using an ID rather than a class is the appropriate choice.

Internal Style Sheets and Inline Styles

In some situations, you want to specify styles that will be used in only one web page. You can enclose a style sheet between `<style>` and `</style>` tags and include it directly in an HTML document. Style sheets used in this manner must appear in the `<head>` of an HTML document. No `<link>` tag is needed, and you cannot refer to that style sheet from any other page (unless you copy it into the beginning of that document too). This kind of style sheet is known as an internal style sheet, as you learned earlier in the chapter.

Listing 2.7 shows an example of how you might specify an internal style sheet.

LISTING 2.7   A Web Page with an Internal Style Sheet

```
<!DOCTYPE html>

<html lang="en">
  <head>
    <title>Some Page</title>
```

```
    <style type="text/css">
      footer {
        font-size: 9pt;
        line-height: 12pt;
        text-align: center;
      }
    </style>
  </head>
  <body>
  ...
    <footer>
    Copyright 2017 Acme Products, Inc.
    </footer>
  </body>
</html>
```

In the listing code, the footer style class is specified in an internal style sheet that appears in the head of the page. The style class is now available for use within the body of this page, and only within this page. In fact, it is used in the body of the page to style the copyright notice.

Internal style sheets are handy if you want to create a style rule that is used multiple times within a single page. However, in some instances, you might need to apply a unique style to one particular element. This calls for an inline style rule, which enables you to specify a style for only a small part of a page, such as an individual element. For example, you can create and apply a style rule within a <p>, <div>, or <span> tag via the style attribute. This type of style is known as an *inline style* because it is specified right there in the middle of the HTML code.

NOTE

The <span> and </span> tags are dummy tags that do nothing in and of themselves except specify a range of content to apply any style attributes that you add. The only difference between <div> and <span> is that <div> is a block element and, therefore, forces a line break, whereas <span> is an inline element and doesn't force a break. Therefore, you should use <span> to modify the style of any portion of text that is to appear in the middle of a sentence or paragraph without any line break.

Here's how a sample style attribute might look:

```
<p style="color:green">
  This text is green, but <span style="color:red">this text is
  red.</span>
  Back to green again, but...
</p>
<p>
  ...now the green is over, and we're back to the default color
  for this page.
</p>
```

This code makes use of the <span> tag to show how to apply the color style property in an inline style rule. In fact, both the <p> tag and the <span> tag in this example use the color property as an inline style. What's important to understand is that the color:red style property overrides the color:green style property for the text between the <span> and </span> tags. Then, in the second paragraph, neither of the color styles applies because it is a completely new paragraph that adheres to the default color of the entire page.

CAUTION

Using inline styles isn't considered a best practice when used beyond page-level debugging or beyond trying out new things in a controlled setting. The best practice of all is having your pages link to a centrally maintained style sheet so that changes are immediately reflected in all pages that use it.

Validate Your Style Sheets

Just as it is important to validate your HTML markup, it is important to validate your style sheet. You can find a specific validation tool for CSS at http://jigsaw.w3.org/css-validator/. You can point the tool to a web address, upload a file, or paste content into the form field provided. The ultimate goal is a result like the one in Figure 2.11: valid!

FIGURE 2.11
The W3C CSS Validator shows there are no errors in the style sheet contents of Listing 2.5.

Summary

This chapter introduced the basics of what web pages are and how they work. You learned that coded HTML commands are included in a text file, and you saw that typing HTML text yourself is better than using a graphical editor to create HTML commands for you—especially when you're learning HTML.

You were introduced to the most basic and important HTML tags. By adding these coded commands to any plain-text document, you can quickly transform it into a bona fide web page. You learned that the first step in creating a web page is to put a few obligatory HTML tags at the beginning and end, including adding a title for the page. You can then mark where paragraphs and lines end and add horizontal rules and headings, if you want them. You also got a taste of some of the semantic tags in HTML5, which are used to provide additional meaning by delineating the types of content your pages contain (not just the content itself). Table 2.1 summarizes the basic HTML tags introduced in this chapter.

Beyond HTML, you learned that a style sheet can control the appearance of many HTML pages at once. It can also give you extremely precise control over the typography, spacing, and positioning of HTML elements. You also learned that, by adding a `style` attribute to almost any HTML tag, you can control the style of any part of an HTML page without referring to a separate style sheet document.

You learned about three main approaches to including style sheets in your website: a separate style sheet file with the extension `.css` that is linked to in the `<head>` of your documents, a collection of style rules placed in the head of the document within the `<style>` tag, and rules placed directly in an HTML tag via the `style` attribute (although the latter is not a best practice for long-term use). Table 2.2 summarizes tags with attributes discussed in this chapter.

TABLE 2.1 HTML Tags Covered in this Chapter

Tag	Function
`<html>...</html>`	Encloses the entire HTML document.
`<head>...</head>`	Encloses the head of the HTML document. Used within the `<html>` tag pair.
`<title>...</title>`	Indicates the title of the document. Used within the `<head>` tag pair.
`<body>...</body>`	Encloses the body of the HTML document. Used within the `<html>` tag pair.
`<p>...</p>`	Encloses a paragraph; skips a line between paragraphs.
` `	Indicates a line break.
`<hr>`	Displays a horizontal rule line.

Tag	Function
`<h1>`...`</h1>`	Encloses a first-level heading.
`<h2>`...`</h2>`	Encloses a second-level heading.
`<h3>`...`</h3>`	Encloses a third-level heading.
`<h4>`...`</h4>`	Encloses a fourth-level heading.
`<h5>`...`</h5>`	Encloses a fifth-level heading.
`<h6>`...`</h6>`	Encloses a sixth-level heading.
`<header>`...`</header>`	Contains introductory information.
`<footer>`...`</footer>`	Contains supplementary material for its containing element (commonly a copyright notice or author information).
`<nav>`...`</nav>`	Contains navigational elements.
`<section>`...`</section>`	Contains thematically similar content, such as a chapter of a book or a section of a page.
`<article>`...`</article>`	Contains content that is a standalone body of work, such as a news article.
`<aside>`...`</aside>`	Contains secondary information for its containing element.
`<address>`...`</address>`	Contains address information related to its nearest `<article>` or `<body>` element, often contained within a `<footer>` element.

TABLE 2.2 **HTML Tags with Attributes Covered in This Chapter**

Tag/Attributes	Function
Tag	
`<a>`	Indicates a hyperlink to a position in the current document or to another document.
Attributes	
`href="url"`	The address of the linked content.
Tag	
`<style>`...`</style>`	Allows an internal style sheet to be included within a document. Used between `<head>` and `</head>`.
Attribute	
`type="contenttype"`	The Internet content type. (Always `"text/css"` for a CSS style sheet.)

Tag/Attributes	Function
Tag	
`<link>`	Links to an external style sheet (or other document type). Used in the `<head>` section of the document.
Attributes	
`href="url"`	The address of the style sheet.
`type="contenttype"`	The Internet content type. (Always `"text/css"` for a CSS style sheet.)
`rel="stylesheet"`	The relationship to a referenced document. (Always `"stylesheet"` for style sheets.)
Tag	
`<span>...</span>`	Does nothing but provide a place to put style or other attributes. (Similar to `<div>...</div>`, but does not cause a line break.)
Attribute	
`style="style"`	Includes inline style specifications. (Can be used in `<span>`, `<div>`, `<body>`, and most other HTML tags.)

Q&A

Q. I've created a web page, but when I open the file in my web browser, I see all the text, including the HTML tags. Sometimes I even see weird gobbledygook characters at the top of the page. What did I do wrong?

A. You didn't save the file as plain text. Try saving the file again, being careful to save it as Text Only or ASCII Text. If you can't quite figure out how to get your word processor to do that, don't stress. Just type your HTML files in Notepad or TextEdit instead, and everything should work just fine. (Also, always make sure that the filename of your web page ends in `.html` or `.htm`.)

Q. I've seen web pages on the Internet that don't have `<!DOCTYPE>` or `<html>` tags at the beginning. You said pages always have to start with these tags. What's the deal?

A. Many web browsers will forgive you if you forget to include the `<!DOCTYPE>` or `<html>` tag and will display the page correctly anyway. However, it's a very good idea to include it because some software does need it to identify the page as valid HTML. Besides, you want your pages to be bona fide HTML pages so that they conform to the latest web standards.

Q. **Do I have to use semantic markup at all? Didn't you say throughout this lesson that pages are valid with or without it?**

A. True, none of these elements is required for a valid HTML document. You don't have to use any of them, but I urge you to think beyond the use of markup for visual display only and think about it for semantic meaning as well. Visual display is meaningless to screen readers, but semantic elements convey a ton of information through these machines.

Q. **Say I link a style sheet to my page that says all text should be blue, but there's a** `<span style="font-color:red">` **tag in the page somewhere. Will that text display as blue or red?**

A. Red. Local inline styles always take precedence over external style sheets. Any style specifications you put between `<style>` and `</style>` tags at the top of a page also take precedence over external style sheets (but not over inline styles later in the same page). This is the cascading effect of style sheets that I mentioned earlier in the chapter. You can think of cascading style effects as starting with an external style sheet, which is overridden by an internal style sheet, which is overridden by inline styles.

Q. **Can I link more than one style sheet to a single page?**

A. Sure. For example, you might have a sheet for formatting (text, fonts, colors, and so on) and another one for layout (margins, padding, alignment, and so on). Just be sure to include a `<link>` for both. Technically, the CSS standard requires web browsers to give the user the option to choose between style sheets when multiple sheets are presented via multiple `<link>` tags. However, in practice, all major web browsers simply include every style sheet unless it has a `rel="alternate"` attribute. The preferred technique for linking in multiple style sheets involves using the special `@import` command. The following is an example of importing multiple style sheets with `@import`:

```
@import url(styles1.css);
@import url(styles2.css);
```

Similar to the `<link>` tag, the `@import` command must be placed in the head of a web page.

Workshop

The Workshop contains quiz questions and exercises to help you solidify your understanding of the material covered. Try to answer all questions before looking at the "Answers" section that follows.

Quiz

1. Which five tags does every HTML5 page require?

2. Which of the semantic elements discussed in this chapter is appropriate for containing the definition of a word used in an article?

3. Do you have to use an `<h1>`, `<h2>`, `<h3>`, `<h4>`, `<h5>`, or `<h6>` element within a `<header>` element?

4. How many different `<nav>` elements can you have in a single page?

5. How many different ways are there to ensure that style rules can be applied to your content?

Answers

1. Every HTML page requires `<html>`, `<head>`, `<title>`, and `<body>` (along with their closing tags, `</html>`, `</head>`, `</title>`, and `</body>`, respectively), plus `<!DOCTYPE html>` on the very first line.

2. The `<aside>` element is appropriate for this situation.

3. No. The `<header>` element can contain any other flow content besides another `<header>` element or a `<footer>` element. However, a heading element (`<h1>` through `<h6>`) is not required in a `<header>` element.

4. You can have as many `<nav>` elements as you need. The trick is to "need" only a few (perhaps for primary and secondary navigation only); otherwise, the meaning is lost.

5. Three: externally, internally, and inline.

Exercises

▶ Even if your main goal in reading this book is to create web content for your business, you might want to make a personal web page just for practice. Type a few paragraphs to introduce yourself to the world, and use the HTML tags you learned in this chapter to make them into a web page.

▶ Throughout the book, you'll be following along with the code examples and making pages of your own. Take a moment now to set up a basic document template containing the document type declaration and tags for the core HTML document structure. That way, you can be ready to copy and paste that information whenever you need it.

▶ Develop a standard style sheet for your website, and link it into all your pages. (Use internal style sheets and/or inline styles for pages that need to deviate from it.) If you work for a corporation, chances are it has already developed font and style specifications for printed materials. Get a copy of those specifications and follow them for company web pages too.

CHAPTER 3

Understanding the CSS Box Model and Positioning

What You'll Learn in This Chapter:

▶ How to conceptualize the CSS box model

▶ How to position your elements

▶ How to control the way elements stack up

▶ How to manage the flow of text

▶ How fixed layouts work

▶ How fluid layouts work

▶ How to create a fixed/fluid hybrid layout

▶ How to think about and begin to implement a responsive design

In the preceding chapter, you learned a lot about the basic structure and syntax of HTML and CSS. In this chapter, you'll take that knowledge one step further and learn about the CSS box model, which is the guiding force behind the layout of elements on your screen—be it a desktop or mobile display.

It's important to spend some time focusing on and practicing working with the box model, because if you have a good handle on how the box model works, you won't tear your hair out when you create a design and then realize that the elements don't line up or that they seem a little "off." You'll know that, in almost all cases, something—the margin, the padding, the border—just needs a little tweaking.

You'll also learn more about CSS positioning, including stacking elements on top of each other in a three-dimensional way (instead of a vertical way), as well as controlling the flow of text around elements using the `float` property. You'll then build on this information and learn about the types of overall page layouts: fixed and fluid (also referred to as liquid). But it's also possible to use a combination of the two, with some elements fixed and others fluid. We end the chapter with a brief mention of responsive web design, which is an important topic upon which entire books have been written.

The CSS Box Model

Every element in HTML is considered a "box," whether it is a paragraph, a <div>, an image, or anything else. Boxes have consistent properties, whether we see them or not, and whether the style sheet specifies them or not. They're always present, and as designers, we have to keep their presence in mind when creating a layout.

Figure 3.1 is a diagram of the box model. The box model describes the way in which every HTML block-level element has the potential for a border, padding, and margin and, specifically, how the border, padding, and margin are applied. In other words, all elements have some padding between the content and the border of the element. Additionally, the border might or might not be visible, but there is space for it, just as there is a margin between the border of the element and any other content outside the element.

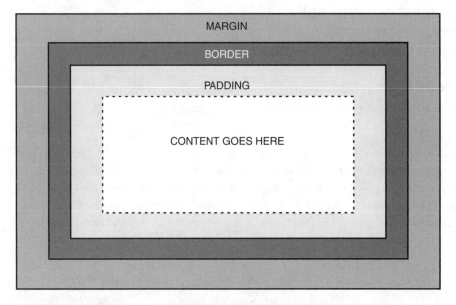

FIGURE 3.1
Every element in HTML is represented by the CSS box model.

Here's yet another explanation of the box model, going from the outside inward:

> ▶ The *margin* is the area outside the element. It never has color; it is always transparent.

> ▶ The *border* extends around the element, on the outer edge of any padding. The border can be of several types, widths, and colors.

> ▶ The *padding* exists around the content and inherits the background color of the content area.

> ▶ The *content* is surrounded by padding.

Here's where the tricky part comes in: To know the true height and width of an element, you have to take all the elements of the box model into account. Think back to the example from the preceding chapter: Despite the specific indication that a <div> should be 250 pixels wide and 100 pixels high, that <div> had to grow larger to accommodate the padding in use.

You already know how to set the width and height of an element using the width and height properties. The following example shows how to define a <div> that is 250 pixels wide and 100 pixels high, with a red background and a black single-pixel border:

```
div {
    width: 250px;
    height: 100px;
    background-color: #ff0000;
    border: 1px solid #000000;
}
```

Figure 3.2 shows this simple <div>.

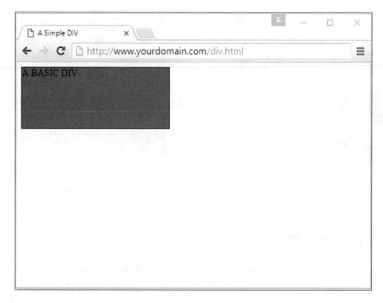

FIGURE 3.2
This is a simple styled <div>.

If we define a second element with these same properties, but also add margin and padding properties of a certain size, we begin to see how the size of the element changes. This is because of the box model.

The second `<div>` is defined as follows, just adding 10 pixels of margin and 10 pixels of padding to the element:

```
div#d2 {
  width: 250px;
  height: 100px;
  background-color: #ff0000;
  border: 5px solid #000000;
  margin: 10px;
  padding: 10px;
}
```

The second `<div>`, shown in Figure 3.3, is defined as the same height and width as the first one, but the overall height and width of the entire box surrounding the element itself is much larger when margins and padding are put in play.

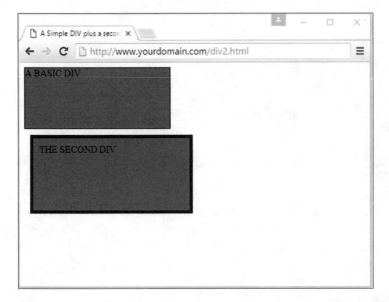

FIGURE 3.3
This is supposed to be another simple `<div>`, but the box model affects the size of the second `<div>`.

The total *width* of an element is the sum of the following:

```
width + padding-left + padding-right + border-left + border-right +
margin-left + margin-right
```

The total *height* of an element is the sum of the following:

```
height + padding-top + padding-bottom + border-top + border-bottom +
margin-top + margin-bottom
```

Therefore, the second <div> has an actual width of 300 (250 + 10 + 10 + 5 + 5 + 10 + 10) and an actual height of 150 (100 + 10 + 10 + 5 + 5 + 10 + 10).

By now, you can begin to see how the box model affects your design. Let's say that you have only 250 pixels of horizontal space, but you would like 10 pixels of margin, 10 pixels of padding, and 5 pixels of border on all sides. To accommodate what you would like with what you have room to display, you must specify the width of your <div> as only 200 pixels so that 200 + 10 + 10 + 5 + 5 + 10 + 10 adds up to that 250 pixels of available horizontal space.

The mathematics of the model are important as well. In dynamically driven sites or sites in which user interactions drive the client-side display (such as through JavaScript events), your server-side or client-side code could draw and redraw container elements on the fly. In other words, your code will produce the numbers, but you have to provide the boundaries.

Now that you've been introduced to the way of the box model, keep it in mind throughout the rest of the work you do in this book and in your web design. Among other things, it will affect element positioning and content flow, which are the two topics we tackle next.

The Whole Scoop on Positioning

Relative positioning is the default type of positioning HTML uses. You can think of relative positioning as being akin to laying out checkers on a checkerboard: The checkers are arranged from left to right, and when you get to the edge of the board, you move on to the next row. Elements that are styled with the block value for the display style property are automatically placed on a new row, whereas inline elements are placed on the same row immediately next to the element preceding them. As an example, <p> and <div> tags are considered block elements, whereas the <span> tag is considered an inline element.

The other type of positioning CSS supports is known as *absolute positioning* because it enables you to set the exact position of HTML content on a page. Although absolute positioning gives you the freedom to spell out exactly where an element is to appear, the position is still relative to any parent elements that appear on the page. In other words, absolute positioning enables you to specify the exact location of an element's rectangular area with respect to its parent's area, which is very different from relative positioning.

With the freedom of placing elements anywhere you want on a page, you can run into the problem of overlap, when an element takes up space another element is using. Nothing is stopping you from specifying the absolute locations of elements so that they overlap. In this case, CSS relies on the z-index of each element to determine which element is on the top and which is on the bottom. You'll learn more about the z-index of elements later in this lesson. For now, let's look at exactly how you control whether a style rule uses relative or absolute positioning.

The type of positioning (relative or absolute) a particular style rule uses is determined by the position property, which is capable of having one of the following four values:

▶ **static**—The default positioning according to the normal flow of the content

▶ **relative**—The element is positioned relative to its normal position, using offset properties discussed below

▶ **absolute**—The element is positioned relative to its nearest ancestor element, or according to the normal flow of the page if no ancestor is present

▶ **fixed**—The element is fixed relative to the viewport—this type of positioning is used for images that scroll along with the page (as an example)

After specifying the type of positioning, you provide the specific position using the following properties:

▶ **left**—The left position offset

▶ **right**—The right position offset

▶ **top**—The top position offset

▶ **bottom**—The bottom position offset

You might think that these position properties make sense only for absolute positioning, but they actually apply to relative and fixed positioning as well. For example, under relative positioning, the position of an element is specified as an offset relative to the original position of the element. So if you set the left property of an element to 25px, the left side of the element shifts over 25 pixels from its original (relative) position. An absolute position, on the other hand, is specified relative to the ancestor element to which the style is applied. So if you set the left property of an element to 25px under absolute positioning, the left side of the element appears 25 pixels to the right of the ancestor element's left edge. On the other hand, using the right property with the same value positions the element so that its *right* side is 25 pixels to the right of the ancestor's *right* edge.

Let's return to the color-blocks example to see how positioning works. In Listing 3.1, the four color blocks have relative positioning specified. As you can see in Figure 3.4, the blocks are positioned vertically.

LISTING 3.1 Showing Relative Positioning with Four Color Blocks

```
<!DOCTYPE html>

<html lang="en">
 <head>
  <title>Positioning the Color Blocks</title>
   <style type="text/css">
   div {
      position: relative;
      width: 250px;
      height: 100px;
      border: 5px solid #000;
      color: black;
      font-weight: bold;
      text-align: center;
    }
    div#d1 {
     background-color: #ff0000;
    }
    div#d2 {
     background-color: #00ff00;
    }
    div#d3 {
     background-color: #0000ff;
    }
    div#d4 {
     background-color: #ffff00;
    }
   </style>
 </head>
 <body>
  <div id="d1">DIV #1</div>
  <div id="d2">DIV #2</div>
  <div id="d3">DIV #3</div>
  <div id="d4">DIV #4</div>
 </body>
</html>
```

The style sheet entry for the `<div>` element itself sets the `position` style property for the `<div>` element to `relative`. Because the remaining style rules are inherited from the `<div>` style rule, they inherit its relative positioning. In fact, the only difference between the other style rules is that they have different background colors.

Notice in Figure 3.4 that the `<div>` elements are displayed one after the next, which is what you would expect with relative positioning. But to make things more interesting, which is what we're here to do, you can change the positioning to absolute and explicitly specify the placement of the colors. In Listing 3.2, the style sheet entries are changed to use absolute positioning to arrange the color blocks.

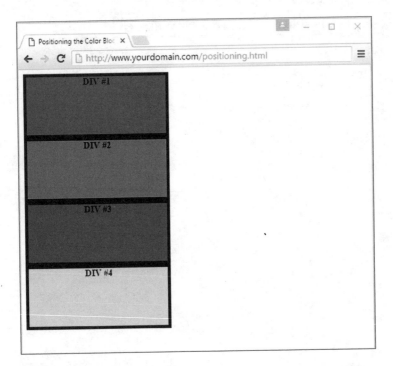

FIGURE 3.4
The color blocks are positioned vertically, with one on top of the other.

LISTING 3.2   Using Absolute Positioning of the Color Blocks

```
<!DOCTYPE html>

<html lang="en">
 <head>
  <title>Positioning the Color Blocks</title>
    <style type="text/css">
    div {
     position: absolute;
     width: 250px;
     height: 100px;
     border: 5px solid #000;
     color: black;
     font-weight: bold;
     text-align: center;
    }
    div#d1 {
     background-color: #ff0000;
     left: 0px;
     top: 0px;
    }
```

```
      div#d2 {
       background-color: #00ff00;
       left: 75px;
       top: 25px;
       }
      div#d3 {
       background-color: #0000ff;
       left: 150px;
       top: 50px;
       }
      div#d4 {
       background-color: #ffff00;
       left: 225px;
       top: 75px;
       }
      </style>
   </head>
   <body>
      <div id="d1">DIV #1</div>
      <div id="d2">DIV #2</div>
      <div id="d3">DIV #3</div>
      <div id="d4">DIV #4</div>
   </body>
</html>
```

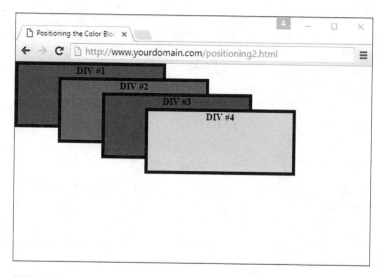

FIGURE 3.5
The color blocks are displayed using absolute positioning.

This style sheet sets the position property to absolute, which is necessary for the style sheet to use absolute positioning. Additionally, the left and top properties are set for each of the inherited <div> style rules. However, the position of each of these rules is set so that the elements are displayed overlapping each other, as Figure 3.5 shows.

Now we're talking layout! Figure 3.5 shows how absolute positioning enables you to place elements exactly where you want them. It also reveals how easy it is to arrange elements so that they overlap. You might be curious about how a web browser knows which elements to draw on top when they overlap. The next section covers how you can control stacking order.

Controlling the Way Things Stack Up

In certain situations, you want to carefully control the manner in which elements overlap each other on a web page. The z-index style property enables you to set the order of elements with respect to how they stack on top of each other. The name z-index might sound a little strange, but it refers to the notion of a third dimension (Z) that points into the computer screen, in addition to the two dimensions that go across (X) and down (Y) the screen. Another way to think of the z-index is to consider the relative position of a single magazine within a stack of magazines. A magazine nearer the top of the stack has a higher z-index than a magazine lower in the stack. Similarly, an overlapped element with a higher value for its z-index is displayed on top of an element with a lower value for its z-index.

The z-index property is used to set a numeric value that indicates the relative z-index of a style rule. The number assigned to z-index has meaning only with respect to other style rules in a style sheet, which means that setting the z-index property for a single rule doesn't mean much. On the other hand, if you set z-index for several style rules that apply to overlapped elements, the elements with higher z-index values appear on top of elements with lower z-index values.

NOTE

Regardless of the z-index value you set for a style rule, an element displayed with the rule will always appear on top of its parent.

Listing 3.3 contains another version of the color-blocks style sheet and HTML that uses z-index settings to alter the natural overlap of elements.

LISTING 3.3   Using `z-index` to Alter the Display of Elements in the Color-Blocks Example

```
<!DOCTYPE html>

<html lang="en">
 <head>
   <title>Positioning the Color Blocks</title>
    <style type="text/css">
    div {
       position: absolute;
       width: 250px;
       height: 100px;
       border: 5px solid #000;
       color: black;
       font-weight: bold;
       text-align: center;
     }
    div#d1 {
      background-color: #ff0000;
      left: 0px;
      top: 0px;
      z-index: 0;
     }
    div#d2 {
      background-color: #00ff00;
      left: 75px;
      top: 25px;
      z-index: 3;
     }
    div#d3 {
      background-color: #0000ff;
      left: 150px;
      top: 50px;
      z-index: 2;
     }
    div#d4 {
      background-color: #ffff00;
      left: 225px;
      top: 75px;
      z-index: 1;
     }
   </style>
 </head>
 <body>
  <div id="d1">DIV #1</div>
  <div id="d2">DIV #2</div>
  <div id="d3">DIV #3</div>
  <div id="d4">DIV #4</div>
 </body>
</html>
```

The only change in this code from what you saw in Listing 3.2 is the addition of the z-index property in each of the numbered div style classes. Notice that the first numbered div has a z-index setting of 0, which should make it the lowest element in terms of the z-index, whereas the second div has the highest z-index. Figure 3.6 shows the color-blocks page as displayed with this style sheet, which clearly shows how the z-index affects the displayed content and makes it possible to carefully control the overlap of elements.

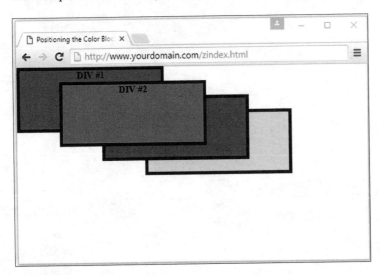

FIGURE 3.6
Using z-index to alter the display of the color blocks.

Although the examples show color blocks that are simple <div> elements, the z-index style property can affect any HTML content, including images.

Managing the Flow of Text

Now that you've seen some examples of placing elements relative to other elements or placing them absolutely, it's time to revisit the flow of content around elements. The conceptual *current line* is an invisible line used to place elements on a page. This line has to do with the flow of elements on a page; it comes into play as elements are arranged next to each other across and down the page. Part of the flow of elements is the flow of text on a page. When you mix text with other elements (such as images), it's important to control how the text flows around those other elements.

Following are some style properties that give you control over text flow:

▶ **float**—Determines how text flows around an element

▶ **clear**—Stops the flow of text around an element

▶ **overflow**—Controls the overflow of text when an element is too small to contain all the text

The `float` property controls how text flows around an element. It can be set to either `left` or `right`. These values determine where to position an element with respect to flowing text. So setting an image's `float` property to `left` positions the image to the left of flowing text.

As you learned in the preceding chapter, you can prevent text from flowing next to an element by using the `clear` property, which you can set to `none`, `left`, `right`, or `both`. The default value for the `clear` property is `none`, indicating that text is to flow with no special considerations for the element. The `left` value causes text to stop flowing around an element until the left side of the page is free of the element. Likewise, the `right` value means that text is not to flow around the right side of the element. The `both` value indicates that text isn't to flow around either side of the element.

The `overflow` property handles overflow text, which is text that doesn't fit within its rectangular area; this can happen if you set the `width` and `height` of an element too small. The `overflow` property can be set to `visible`, `hidden`, or `scroll`. The `visible` setting automatically enlarges the element so that the overflow text fits within it; this is the default setting for the property. The `hidden` value leaves the element the same size, allowing the overflow text to remain hidden from view. Perhaps the most interesting value is `scroll`, which adds scrollbars to the element so that you can move around and see the text.

Understanding Fixed Layouts

A fixed layout, or fixed-width layout, is just that: a layout in which the body of the page is set to a specific width. That width is typically controlled by a master "wrapper" element that contains all the content. The `width` property of a wrapper element, such as a `<div>`, is set in the style sheet entry if the `<div>` was given an ID value such as `main` or `wrapper` (although the name is up to you).

When you're creating a fixed-width layout, the most important decision is determining the minimum screen resolution you want to accommodate. For many years, 800×600 was the "lowest common denominator" for web designers, resulting in a typical fixed width of approximately 760 pixels. However, the number of people using 800×600 screen resolution for non-mobile browsers is now less than 4%. Given that, many web designers consider 1,024×768 the current minimum screen resolution, so if they create fixed-width layouts, the fixed width typically is somewhere between 800 and 1,000 pixels wide.

CAUTION

Remember, the web browser window contains nonviewable areas, including the scrollbar. So if you are targeting a 1,024-pixel-wide screen resolution, you really can't use all 1,024 of those pixels.

A main reason for creating a fixed-width layout is so that you can have precise control over the appearance of the content area. However, if users visit your fixed-width site with smaller or much larger screen sizes or resolutions than the size or resolution you had in mind while you designed it, they will encounter scrollbars (if their size or resolution is smaller) or a large amount of empty space (if their size or resolution is greater). Finding fixed-width layouts is difficult among the most popular websites these days because site designers know they need to cater to the largest possible audience (and therefore make no assumptions about browser size). However, fixed-width layouts still have wide adoption, especially by site administrators using a content management system with a strict template.

The following figures show one such site, for San Jose State University (university websites commonly use a strict template and content management system, so this was an easy example to find); it has a wrapper element fixed at 960 pixels wide. In Figure 3.7, the browser window is a shade under 900 pixels wide. On the right side of the image, important content is cut off (and at the bottom of the figure, a horizontal scrollbar displays in the browser).

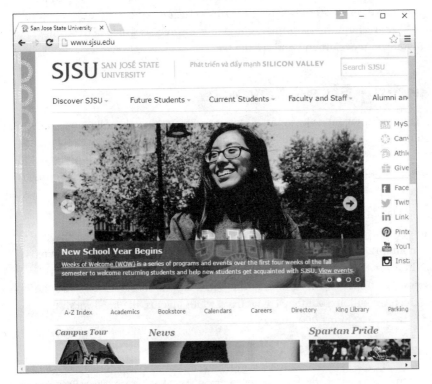

FIGURE 3.7
A fixed-width example with a smaller screen size.

However, Figure 3.8 shows how this site looks when the browser window is more than 1,300 pixels wide: You see a lot of empty space (or "real estate") on both sides of the main body content, which some consider aesthetically displeasing.

FIGURE 3.8
A fixed-width example with a larger screen size.

Besides the decision to create a fixed-width layout in the first place is the task of determining whether to place the fixed-width content flush left or center it. Placing the content flush left produces extra space on the right side only; centering the content area creates extra space on both sides. However, centering at least provides balance, whereas a flush-left design could end up looking like a small rectangle shoved in the corner of the browser, depending on the size and resolution of a user's monitor.

Understanding Fluid Layouts

A fluid layout—also called a *liquid* layout—is one in which the body of the page does not use a specified width in pixels, although it might be enclosed in a master "wrapper" element that uses a percentage width. The idea behind the fluid layout is that it can be perfectly usable and still retain the overall design aesthetic even if the user has a very small or very wide screen.

Figures 3.9, 3.10, and 3.11 show three examples of a fluid layout in action.

In Figure 3.9, the browser window is approximately 745 pixels wide. This example shows a reasonable minimum screen width before a horizontal scrollbar appears. In fact, the scrollbar does not appear until the browser is 735 pixels wide. On the other hand, Figure 3.10 shows a very small browser window (less than 600 pixels wide).

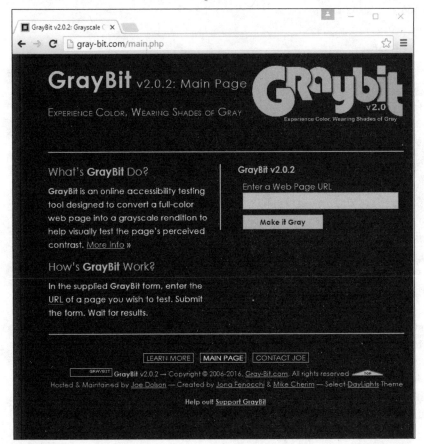

FIGURE 3.9
A fluid layout as viewed in a relatively small screen.

In Figure 3.10, you can see a horizontal scrollbar; in the header area of the page content, the logo graphic is beginning to take over the text and appear on top of it. But the bulk of the page is still quite usable. The informational content on the left side of the page is still legible and is sharing the available space with the input form on the right side.

Figure 3.11 shows how this same page looks in a very wide screen. In Figure 3.11, the browser window is approximately 1,200 pixels wide. There is plenty of room for all the content on the page to spread out. This fluid layout is achieved because all the design elements have a percentage width specified (instead of a fixed width). Thus, the layout makes use of all the available browser real estate.

The fluid layout approach might seem like the best approach at first glance—after all, who wouldn't want to take advantage of all the screen real estate available? But there's a fine line between taking advantage of space and not allowing the content to breathe. Too much content is overwhelming; not enough content in an open space is underwhelming.

FIGURE 3.10
A fluid layout as viewed in a very small screen.

FIGURE 3.11
A fluid layout as viewed in a wide screen.

The pure fluid layout can be impressive, but it requires a significant amount of testing to ensure that it is usable in a wide range of browsers at varying screen resolutions. You might not have the time and effort to produce such a design; in that case, a reasonable compromise is the fixed/fluid hybrid layout, or a fully responsive design, as you'll learn about later in this chapter.

Creating a Fixed/Fluid Hybrid Layout

A fixed/fluid hybrid layout is one that contains elements of both types of layouts. For example, you could have a fluid layout that includes fixed-width content areas either within the body area or as anchor elements (such as a left-side column or as a top navigation strip). You can even create a fixed content area that acts like a frame, in which a content area remains fixed even as users scroll through the content.

Starting with a Basic Layout Structure

In this example, you'll learn to create a template that is fluid but with two fixed-width columns on either side of the main body area (which is a third column, if you think about it, only much wider than the others). The template also has a delineated header and footer area. Listing 3.4 shows the basic HTML structure for this layout.

LISTING 3.4   Basic Fixed/Fluid Hybrid Layout Structure

```
<!DOCTYPE html>

<html lang="en">
  <head>
    <title>Sample Layout</title>
    <link href="layout.css" rel="stylesheet" type="text/css">
  </head>

  <body>
    <header>HEADER</header>
    <div id="wrapper">
        <div id="content_area">CONTENT</div>
        <div id="left_side">LEFT SIDE</div>
        <div id="right_side">RIGHT SIDE</div>
    </div>
    <footer>FOOTER</footer>
  </body>
</html>
```

First, note that the style sheet for this layout is linked to with the `<link>` tag instead of included in the template. Because a template is used for more than one page, you want to be able to control the display elements of the template in the most organized way possible. This means you need to change the definitions of those elements in only one place—the style sheet.

Next, notice that the basic HTML is just that: extremely basic. Truth be told, this basic HTML structure can be used for a fixed layout, a fluid layout, or the fixed/fluid hybrid you see here because all the actual styling that makes a layout fixed, fluid, or hybrid happens in the style sheet.

With the HTML structure in Listing 3.4, you actually have an identification of the content areas you want to include in your site. This planning is crucial to any development; you have to know what you want to include before you even think about the type of layout you are going to use, let alone the specific styles that will be applied to that layout.

NOTE

I am using elements with named identifiers in this example instead of the semantic elements such as `<section>` or `<nav>` because I'm illustrating the point in the simplest way possible without being prescriptive to the content itself. However, if you know that the `<div>` on the left side is going to hold navigation, you should use the `<nav>` tag instead of a `<div>` element with an id something like left_side—but this type of naming can become problematic as depending on repositioning that content might not end up displaying on the left side of anything, so best to name based on purpose rather than appearance.

At this stage, the layout.css file includes only this entry:

```
body {
    margin: 0;
    padding: 0;
}
```

Using a 0 value for margin and padding allows the entire page to be usable for element placement.

If you look at the HTML in Listing 3.4 and say to yourself, "But those <div> elements will just stack on top of each other without any styles," you are correct. As shown in Figure 3.12, there is no layout to speak of.

FIGURE 3.12
A basic HTML template with no styles applied to the container elements.

Defining Two Columns in a Fixed/Fluid Hybrid Layout

We can start with the easy things to get some styles and actual layout in there. Because this layout is supposed to be fluid, we know that whatever we put in the header and footer areas will extend the width of the browser window, regardless of how narrow or wide the window might be.

Adding the following code to the style sheet gives the header and footer area each a width of 100% as well as the same background color and text color:

```
header, footer {
    float: left;
    width: 100%;
    background-color: #7152f4;
    color: #ffffff;
}
```

Now things get a little trickier. We have to define the two fixed columns on either side of the page, plus the column in the middle. In the HTML we're using here, note that a `<div>` element, called `wrapper`, surrounds both. This element is defined in the style sheet as follows:

```
#wrapper {
  float: left;
  padding-left: 200px;
  padding-right: 125px;
}
```

The two padding definitions essentially reserve space for the two fixed-width columns on the left and right of the page. The column on the left will be 200 pixels wide, the column on the right will be 125 pixels wide, and each will have a different background color. But we also have to position the items relative to where they would be placed if the HTML remained unstyled (see Figure 3.12). This means adding `position: relative` to the style sheet entries for each of these columns. Additionally, we indicate that the `<div>` elements should float to the left.

But in the case of the `<div>` element `left_side`, we also indicate that we want the rightmost margin edge to be 200 pixels in from the edge (this is in addition to the column being defined as 200 pixels wide). We also want the margin on the left side to be a full negative margin; this will pull it into place (as you will soon see). The `<div>` element `right_side` does not include a value for `right`, but it does include a negative margin on the right side:

```
#left_side {
  position: relative;
  float: left;
  width: 200px;
  background-color: #52f471;
  right: 200px;
  margin-left: -100%;
}
```

```
#right_side {
  position: relative;
  float: left;
  width: 125px;
  background-color: #f452d5;
  margin-right: -125px;
}
```

At this point, let's also define the content area so that it has a white background, takes up 100% of the available area, and floats to the left relative to its position:

```
#content_area {
  position: relative;
  float: left;
  background-color: #ffffff;
  width: 100%;
}
```

At this point, the basic layout should look something like Figure 3.13, with the areas clearly delineated.

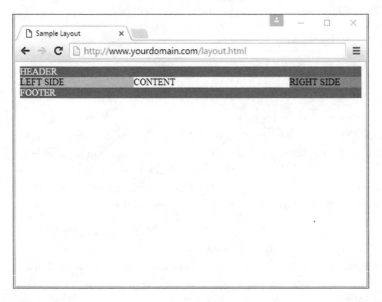

FIGURE 3.13
A basic HTML template after some styles have been put in place.

However, there's a problem with this template if the window is resized below a certain width. Because the left column is 200 pixels wide and the right column is 125 pixels wide, and we want at least *some* text in the content area, you can imagine that this page will break if the window is only 350 to 400 pixels wide. We address this issue in the next section.

Setting the Minimum Width of a Layout

Although users won't likely visit your site with a desktop browser that displays less than 400 pixels wide, the example serves its purpose within the confines of this lesson. You can extrapolate and apply this information broadly: Even in fixed/fluid hybrid sites, at some point, your layout will break down unless you do something about it.

One of those "somethings" is to use the min-width CSS property. The min-width property sets the minimum width of an element, not including padding, borders, and margins. Figure 3.14 shows what happens when min-width is applied to the <body> element.

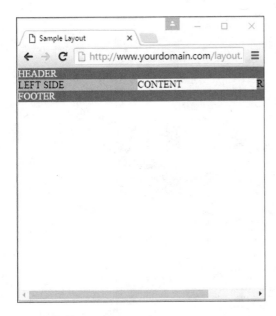

FIGURE 3.14
A basic HTML template resized to around 400 pixels, with a minimum width applied.

Figure 3.14 shows a small portion of the right column after the screen has been scrolled to the right, but the point is that the layout does not break apart when resized below a minimum width. In this case, the minimum width is 525 pixels:

```
body {
  margin: 0;
  padding: 0;
  min-width: 525px;
}
```

The horizontal scrollbar appears in this example because the browser window itself is less than 500 pixels wide. The scrollbar disappears when the window is slightly larger than 525 pixels wide.

Handling Column Height in a Fixed/Fluid Hybrid Layout

This example is all well and good except for one problem: It has no content. When content is added to the various elements, more problems arise. As Figure 3.15 shows, the columns become as tall as necessary for the content they contain.

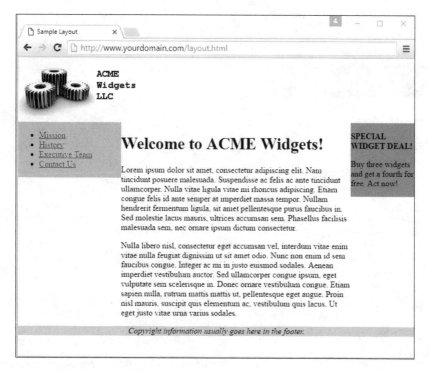

FIGURE 3.15
Columns are only as tall as their content.

NOTE

Because we have moved beyond the basic layout example, I also took the liberty to remove the background and text color properties for the header and footer, which is why the example no longer shows white text on a very dark background. Additionally, I've centered the text in the `<footer>` element, which now has a light gray background.

Because you cannot count on a user's browser being a specific height, or the content always being the same length, you might think this poses a problem with the fixed/fluid hybrid layout. Not so. If you think a little outside the box, you can apply a few more styles to bring all the pieces together.

First, add the following declarations in the style sheet entries for the `left_side`, `right_side`, and `content_area` IDs:

```
margin-bottom: -2000px;
padding-bottom: 2000px;
```

These declarations add a ridiculous amount of padding and assign a too-large margin to the bottom of all three elements. You must also add `position:relative` to the footer element definitions in the style sheet so that the footer is visible despite this padding.

At this point, the page looks as shown in Figure 3.16—still not what we want, but closer.

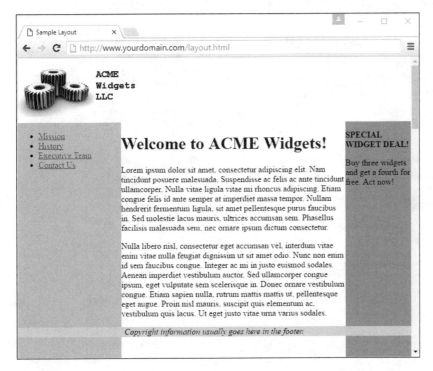

FIGURE 3.16
Color fields are now visible, despite the amount of content in the columns.

To clip off all that extra color, add the following to the style sheet for the `wrapper` ID:

```
overflow: hidden;
```

Figure 3.17 shows the final result: a fixed-width/fluid hybrid layout with the necessary column spacing. I also took the liberty of styling the navigational links and adjusting the margin around the welcome message; you can see the complete style sheet in Listing 3.6.

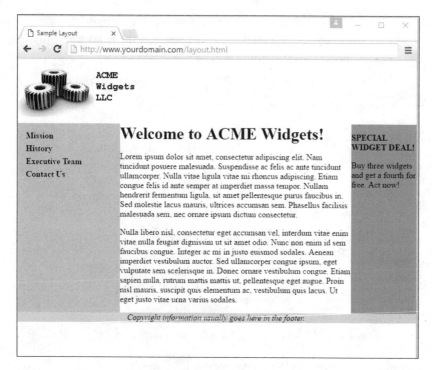

FIGURE 3.17
Congratulations! It's a fixed-width/fluid hybrid layout (although you'll want to do something about those colors!).

The full HTML code appears in Listing 3.5, and Listing 3.6 shows the final style sheet.

LISTING 3.5   **Basic Fixed/Fluid Hybrid Layout Structure (with Content)**

```
<!DOCTYPE html>

<html lang="en">
  <head>
    <title>Sample Layout</title>
    <link href="layout.css" rel="stylesheet" type="text/css">
  </head>

  <body>
    <header><img src="acmewidgets.jpg" alt="ACME Widgets
      LLC"/></header>
    <div id="wrapper">
      <div id="content_area">
        <h1>Welcome to ACME Widgets!</h1>
        <p>Lorem ipsum dolor sit amet, consectetur adipiscing elit.
```

Nam tincidunt posuere malesuada. Suspendisse ac felis ac ante tincidunt ullamcorper. Nulla vitae ligula vitae mi rhoncus adipiscing. Etiam congue felis id ante semper at imperdiet massa tempor. Nullam hendrerit fermentum ligula, sit amet pellentesque purus faucibus in. Sed molestie lacus mauris, ultrices accumsan sem. Phasellus facilisis malesuada sem, nec ornare ipsum dictum consectetur.</p>

```
<p>Nulla libero nisl, consectetur eget accumsan vel, interdum
vitae enim vitae nulla feugiat dignissim ut sit amet odio.
Nunc non enim id sem faucibus congue. Integer ac mi in justo
euismod sodales. Aenean imperdiet vestibulum auctor. Sed
ullamcorper congue ipsum, eget vulputate sem scelerisque in.
Donec ornare vestibulum congue. Etiam sapien nulla, rutrum
mattis mattis ut, pellentesque eget augue. Proin nisl mauris,
suscipit quis elementum ac, vestibulum quis lacus. Ut eget
justo vitae urna varius sodales. </p>
</div>
<div id="left_side">
  <ul>
  <li><a href="#">Mission</a></li>
  <li><a href="#">History</a></li>
  <li><a href="#">Executive Team</a></li>
  <li><a href="#">Contact Us</a></li>
</ul>
</div>
<div id="right_side">
  <p><strong>SPECIAL WIDGET DEAL!</strong></p>
  <p>Buy three widgets and get a fourth for free. Act now!</p>
</div>
</div>
<footer>Copyright information usually goes here in the
footer.</footer>
</body>
</html>
```

LISTING 3.6   Full Style Sheet for Fixed/Fluid Hybrid Layout

```css
body {
  margin: 0;
  padding: 0;
  min-width: 525px;
}

header {
  float: left;
  width: 100%;
}
```

```css
footer {
  position: relative;
  float: left;
  width: 100%;
  background-color: #cccccc;
  text-align: center;
  font-style: italic;
}

#wrapper {
  float: left;
  padding-left: 200px;
  padding-right: 125px;
  overflow: hidden;
}

#left_side {
  position: relative;
  float: left;
  width: 200px;
  background-color: #52f471;
  right: 200px;
  margin-left: -100%;
  margin-bottom: -2000px;
  padding-bottom: 2000px;
}

#right_side {
  position: relative;
  float: left;
  width: 125px;
  background-color: #f452d5;
  margin-right: -125px;
  margin-bottom: -2000px;
  padding-bottom: 2000px;
}

#content_area {
  position: relative;
  float: left;
  background-color: #ffffff;
  width: 100%;
  margin-bottom: -2000px;
  padding-bottom: 2000px;
}

h1 {
  margin: 0;
}
```

```
#left_side ul {
  list-style: none;
  margin: 12px 0px 0px 12px;
  padding: 0px;
}

#left_side li a:link, #nav li a:visited {
  font-size: 12pt;
  font-weight: bold;
  padding: 3px 0px 3px 3px;
  color: #000000;
  text-decoration: none;
  display: block;
}

#left_side li a:hover, #nav li a:active {
  font-size: 12pt;
  font-weight: bold;
  padding: 3px 0px 3px 3px;
  color: #ffffff;
  text-decoration: none;
  display: block;
}
```

Considering a Responsive Web Design

In 2010, web designer Ethan Marcotte coined the term *responsive web design* to refer to a web design approach that builds on the basics of fluid design you just learned a bit about. The goal of a responsive web design is that content is easy to view, read, and navigate, regardless of the device type and size on which you are viewing it. In other words, a designer who sets out to create a responsive website is doing to so to ensure that the site is similarly enjoyable to and usable by audience members viewing on a large desktop display, a small smartphone, or a medium-size tablet.

The underlying structure of a responsive design is based on fluid (liquid) grid layouts, much as you learned about earlier in this chapter, but with a few modifications and additions. First, those grid layouts should always be in relative units rather than absolute ones. In other words, designers should use percentages rather than pixels to define container elements.

Second—and this is something we have not discussed previously—all images should be flexible. By this, I mean that instead of using a specific height and width for each image, we use relative percentages so that the images always display within the (relatively sized) element that contains them.

Finally, until you get a handle on intricate creations of style sheets for multiple uses, spend some time developing specific style sheets for each media type, and use media queries to employ these different rules based on the type. As you advance in your work and understanding of responsive design—well beyond the scope of this book—you will learn to progressively enhance your layouts in more meaningful ways.

Remember, you can specify a link to a style sheet like the following:

```
<link rel="stylesheet" type="text/css"
   media="screen and (max-device-width: 480px)"
   href="wee.css">
```

In this example, the `media` attribute contains a type and a query: The type is screen and the query portion is (`max-device-width: 480px`). This means that if the device attempting to render the display is one with a screen and the horizontal resolution (device width) is less than 480 pixels wide—as with a smartphone—then load the style sheet called `wee.css` and render the display using the rules found within it.

Of course, a few short paragraphs in this book cannot do justice to the entirety of responsive web design. I highly recommend reading Marcotte's book *Responsive Web Design* (http://www.abookapart.com/products/responsive-web-design) after you have firmly grounded yourself in the basics of HTML5 and CSS3 that are discussed and used throughout this book. Additionally, several of the HTML and CSS frameworks discussed in Chapter 22, "Managing Web Applications," take advantage of principles of responsive design, and that makes a great starting point for building up a responsive site and tinkering with the fluid grid, image resizing, and media queries that make it so.

Summary

This chapter began with an important discussion about the CSS box model and how to calculate the width and height of elements when taking margins, padding, and borders into consideration. The lesson continued by tackling absolute positioning of elements, and you learned about positioning using `z-index`. You then learned about a few nifty style properties that enable you to control the flow of text on a page.

Next, you saw some practical examples of the three main types of layouts: fixed, fluid, and a fixed/fluid hybrid. In the third section of the lesson, you saw an extended example that walked you through the process of creating a fixed/fluid hybrid layout in which the HTML and CSS all validate properly. Remember, the most important part of creating a layout is figuring out the sections of content you think you might need to account for in the design.

Finally, you were introduced to the concept of responsive web design, which itself is a book-length topic. Given the brief information you learned here, such as using a fluid grid layout, responsive images, and media queries, you have some basic concepts to begin testing on your own.

Q&A

Q. How would I determine when to use relative positioning and when to use absolute positioning?

A. Although there are no set guidelines regarding the usage of relative versus absolute positioning, the general idea is that absolute positioning is required only when you want to exert a finer degree of control over how content is positioned. This has to do with the fact that absolute positioning enables you to position content down to the exact pixel, whereas relative positioning is much less predictable in terms of how it positions content. This isn't to say that relative positioning can't do a good job of positioning elements on a page; it just means that absolute positioning is more exact. Of course, this also makes absolute positioning potentially more susceptible to changes in screen size, which you can't really control.

Q. If I don't specify the z-index of two elements that overlap each other, how do I know which element will appear on top?

A. If the `z-index` property isn't set for overlapping elements, the element that appears later in the web page will appear on top. The easy way to remember this is to think of a web browser drawing each element on a page as it reads it from the HTML document; elements read later in the document are drawn on top of those that were read earlier.

Q. I've heard about something called an elastic layout. How does that differ from the fluid layout?

A. An *elastic layout* is a layout whose content areas resize when the user resizes the text. Elastic layouts use ems, which are inherently proportional to text and font size. An em is a typographical unit of measurement equal to the point size of the current font. When ems are used in an elastic layout, if a user forces the text size to increase or decrease in size using Ctrl and the mouse scroll wheel, the areas containing the text increase or decrease proportionally.

Q. You've spent a lot of time talking about fluid layouts and hybrid layouts—are they better than a purely fixed layout?

A. *Better* is a subjective term; in this book, the concern is with standards-compliant code. Most designers will tell you that fluid layouts take longer to create (and perfect), but the usability enhancements are worth it, especially when it leads to a responsive design. When might the time not be worth it? If your client does not have an opinion and is paying you a flat rate instead of an hourly rate. In that case, you are working only to showcase your own skills (that might be worth it to you, however).

Workshop

The Workshop contains quiz questions and exercises to help you solidify your understanding of the material covered. Try to answer all questions before looking at the "Answers" section that follows.

Quiz

1. What's the difference between relative positioning and absolute positioning?

2. Which CSS style property controls the manner in which elements overlap each other?

3. What does `min-width` do?

Answers

1. In relative positioning, content is displayed according to the flow of a page, with each element physically appearing after the element preceding it in the HTML code. Absolute positioning, on the other hand, enables you to set the exact position of content on a page.

2. The `z-index` style property controls the manner in which elements overlap each other.

3. The `min-width` property sets the minimum width of an element, not including padding, borders, and margins.

Exercises

▶ Practice working with the intricacies of the CSS box model by creating a series of elements with different margins, padding, and borders, and see how these properties affect their height and width.

▶ Figure 3.17 shows the finished fixed/fluid hybrid layout, but notice a few areas for improvement: There isn't any space around the text in the right-side column, there aren't any margins between the body text and either column, the footer strip is a little sparse, and so on. Take some time to fix these design elements.

▶ Using the code you fixed in the preceding exercise, try to make it responsive, using only the brief information you learned in this chapter. Just converting container elements to relative sizes should go a long way toward making the template viewable on your smartphone or other small device, but a media query and alternative style sheet certainly wouldn't hurt, either.

CHAPTER 4
Introducing JavaScript

What You'll Learn in This Chapter:

▶ What web scripting is and what it's good for

▶ How scripting and programming are different (and similar)

▶ What JavaScript is and where it came from

▶ How to include JavaScript statements in a web page

▶ What JavaScript can do for your web pages

▶ Beginning and ending scripts

▶ Formatting JavaScript statements

▶ How a script can display a result

▶ Including a script within a web document

▶ Testing a script in your browser

▶ Moving scripts into separate files

▶ Basic syntax rules for avoiding JavaScript errors

▶ What JSON is and how it can be used

▶ Dealing with errors in scripts

The World Wide Web (WWW) began as a text-only medium—the first browsers didn't even support images within web pages. The Web has come a long way since those early days. Today's websites include a wealth of visual and interactive features in addition to useful content: graphics, sounds, animation, and video. Using a web scripting language such as JavaScript is one of the easiest ways to spice up a web page and to interact with users in new ways. In fact, using JavaScript is the next step in taking the static HTML you've learned about in the chapters so far and turning it into something dynamic.

The first part of this chapter introduces the concept of web scripting and the JavaScript language. As the chapter moves ahead, you'll learn how to include JavaScript commands directly in your HTML documents, and how your scripts will be executed when the page is viewed in a browser. You will work with a simple script, edit it, and test it in your browser, all the while learning the basic tasks involved in creating and using JavaScript scripts.

Learning Web Scripting Basics

You already know how to use one type of computer language: HTML. You use HTML tags to describe how you want your document formatted, and the browser obeys your commands and shows the formatted document to the user. But because HTML is a simple text markup language, it can't respond to the user, make decisions, or automate repetitive tasks. Interactive tasks such as these require a more sophisticated language: a programming language or a *scripting* language.

Whereas many programming languages are complex, scripting languages are generally simple. They have a simple syntax, can perform tasks with a minimum of commands, and are easy to learn. JavaScript is a web scripting language that enables you to combine scripting with HTML to create interactive web pages.

Here are a few of the things you can do with JavaScript:

▶ Display messages to the user as part of a web page, in the browser's status line, or in alert boxes.

▶ Validate the contents of a form and make calculations (for example, an order form can automatically display a running total as you enter item quantities).

▶ Animate images or create images that change when you move the mouse over them.

▶ Create ad banners that interact with the user, rather than simply displaying a graphic.

▶ Detect features supported by browsers and perform advanced functions only on browsers that support those features.

▶ Detect installed plug-ins and notify the user if a plug-in is required

▶ Modify all or part of a web page without requiring the user to reload it

▶ Display or interact with data retrieved from a remote server

Scripts and Programs

A movie or a play follows a script—a list of actions (or lines) for the actors to perform. A web script provides the same type of instructions for the web browser. A script in JavaScript can range from a single line to a full-scale application. (In either case, JavaScript scripts usually run within a browser.)

Some programming languages must be *compiled*, or translated, into machine code before they can be executed. JavaScript, on the other hand, is an *interpreted* language: The browser executes each line of script as it comes to it.

There is one main advantage to interpreted languages: Writing or changing a script is very simple. Changing a JavaScript script is as easy as changing a typical HTML document, and the change is enacted as soon as you reload the document in the browser.

How JavaScript Fits into a Web Page

Using the `<script>` tag, you can add a short script (in this case, just one line) to a web document, as shown in Listing 4.1. The `<script>` tag tells the browser to start treating the text as a script, and the closing `</script>` tag tells the browser to return to HTML mode. In most cases, you can't use JavaScript statements in an HTML document except within `<script>` tags. The exception is event handlers, which are described later in this chapter.

LISTING 4.1 A Simple HTML Document with a Simple Script

```
<!DOCTYPE html>

<html lang="en">
  <head>
    <title>A Spectacular Time!</title>
  </head>

  <body>
    <h1>It is a Spectacular Time!</h1>
    <p>What time is it, you ask?</p>
    <p>Well, indeed it is: <br>
    <script type="text/javascript">
    var currentTime = new Date();
    document.write(currentTime);
    </script>
    </p>
  </body>
</html>
```

JavaScript's `document.write` method, which you'll learn more about later, sends output as part of the web document. In this case, it displays the current date and time, as shown in Figure 4.1.

In this example, we placed the script within the body of the HTML document. There are actually four places where you might place scripts:

- **In the body of the page**—In this case, the script's output is displayed as part of the HTML document when the browser loads the page.

- **In the header of the page between the `<head>` tags**—Scripts in the header should not be used to create output within the `<head>` section of an HTML document because that would likely result in poorly formed and invalid HTML documents, but these scripts can be referred to by other scripts here and elsewhere. The `<head>` section is often used for functions—groups of JavaScript statements that can be used as a single unit. You will learn more about functions in Chapter 9, "Understanding JavaScript Event Handling."

▶ **Within an HTML tag, such as `<body>` or `<form>`**—This is called an *event handler*, and it enables the script to work with HTML elements. When using JavaScript in event handlers, you don't need to use the `<script>` tag. You'll learn more about event handlers in Chapter 9.

▶ **In a separate file entirely**—JavaScript supports the use of files that can be included by specifying a file in the `<script>` tag. Although the `.js` extension is a convention, scripts can actually have any file extension, or none.

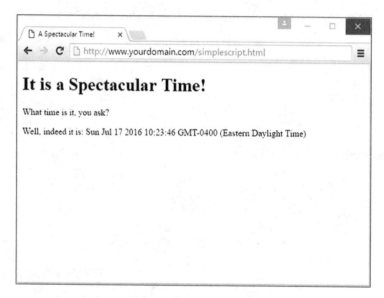

FIGURE 4.1
Using `document.write` to display the current date.

Using Separate JavaScript Files

When you create more complicated scripts, you'll quickly find that your HTML documents become large and confusing. To avoid this problem, you can use one or more external JavaScript files. These are files with the `.js` extension that contain JavaScript statements.

External scripts are supported by all modern browsers. To use an external script, you specify its filename in the `<script>` tag, like so—and don't forget to close the `<script>` tag using `</script>`:

```
<script type="text/javascript" src="filename.js"></script>
```

Because you'll be placing the JavaScript statements in a separate file, you don't need anything between the opening and closing `<script>` tags—in fact, anything between them will be ignored by the browser.

You can create the .js file using a text editor. It should contain one or more JavaScript state-ments, and only JavaScript—don't include <script> tags, other HTML tags, or HTML com-ments. Save the .js file in the same directory as the HTML documents that refer to it.

TIP

External JavaScript files have a distinct advantage: You can link to the same .js file from two or more HTML documents. Because the browser stores this file in its cache, the time it takes your web pages to display is reduced.

Using Basic JavaScript Events

Many of the useful things you can do with JavaScript involve interacting with the user, and that means responding to *events*—for example, a link or a button being clicked. You can define event handlers within HTML tags to tell the browser how to respond to an event. For example, Listing 4.2 defines a button that displays a message when clicked.

LISTING 4.2 A Simple Event Handler

```
<!DOCTYPE html>

<html lang="en">
  <head>
    <title>Event Test</title>
  </head>

  <body>
    <h1>Event Test</h1>
    <button type="button"
            onclick="alert('You clicked the button.');">
            Click Me!</button>
  </body>
</html>
```

In various places throughout this book, you'll learn more about JavaScript's event model and how to create simple and complex event handlers—in some cases, invoking PHP scripts for even greater dynamic experiences as you'll learn in Chapter 11, "AJAX: Getting Started with Remote Scripting".

Exploring JavaScript's Capabilities

If you've spent any time browsing the Web, you've undoubtedly seen lots of examples of JavaScript, even if you were not aware that JavaScript was powering your interactions. Here are some brief descriptions of typical applications for JavaScript.

Validating Forms

Form validation is a common use of JavaScript, although the form validation features of HTML5 have stolen a lot of JavaScript's thunder here. A simple script can read values the user types into a form and make sure they're in the right format, such as with ZIP Codes, phone numbers, and email addresses. This type of client-side validation enables users to fix common errors without waiting for a response from the web server telling them that their form submission was invalid.

Special Effects

One of the earliest, and admittedly most annoying, uses of JavaScript was to create attention-getting special effects—for example, scrolling a message in the browser's status line or flashing the background color of a page.

These techniques have fortunately fallen out of style, but thanks to the W3C DOM and the latest browsers, some more impressive effects are possible with JavaScript—for example, creating objects that can be dragged and dropped on a page, or creating fading transitions between images in a slideshow. Additionally, some developers use HTML5, CSS3, and JavaScript in tandem to create fully functioning interactive games.

Remote Scripting (AJAX)

For a long time, one of the greatest limitations of JavaScript was that there was no way for it to communicate with a web server. For example, you could use JavaScript to verify that a phone number had the right number of digits, but you could not use JavaScript to look up the user's location in a database based on the number.

However, now your scripts can get data from a server without loading a page or sending data back to be saved. These features are collectively known as AJAX (Asynchronous JavaScript and XML), or *remote scripting*. You'll learn how to develop AJAX scripts in Chapter 11.

You've seen AJAX in action if you've used Google's Gmail mail application, Facebook, or any online news site that allows you to comment on stories, vote for favorites, or participate in a poll (among many other things). All of these use remote scripting to present you with a dynamic user interface that interacts with a server in the background.

Basic JavaScript Language Concepts

As you build on your knowledge, there are a few foundational concepts you should know that form the basic building blocks of JavaScript.

Statements

Statements are the basic units of programs, be it a JavaScript or PHP program (or any other language). A statement is a section of code that performs a single action. For example, the following four statements create a new `Date` object and then assign the values for the current hour, minutes, and seconds into variables called `hours`, `mins`, and `secs`, respectively. You can then use these variables elsewhere in your JavaScript code.

```
now = new Date();
hours = now.getHours();
mins = now.getMinutes();
secs = now.getSeconds();
```

Although a statement is typically a single line of JavaScript, this is not a rule—it's possible (and fairly common) to break a statement across multiple lines, or to include more than one statement in a single line.

A semicolon marks the end of a statement, but you can also omit the semicolon if you start a new line after the statement—if that is your coding style. In other words, these are three valid JavaScript statements:

```
hours = now.getHours()
mins = now.getMinutes()
secs = now.getSeconds()
```

However, if you combine statements into a single line, you must use semicolons to separate them. For example, the following line is valid:

```
hours = now.getHours(); mins = now.getMinutes(); secs = now.getSeconds();
```

But this line is invalid:

```
hours = now.getHours() mins = now.getMinutes() secs = now.getSeconds();
```

Again, your style is always up to you but I personally recommend always using semicolons to end statements.

Combining Tasks with Functions

Functions are groups of JavaScript statements that are treated as a single unit—this is a term you'll use in PHP as well. A statement that uses a function is referred to as a *function call*. For example, you might create a function called `alertMe`, which produces an alert when called, like so:

```
function alertMe() {
    alert("I am alerting you!");
}
```

When this function is called, a JavaScript alert pops up and the text I am alerting you! is displayed.

Functions can take arguments—the expression inside the parentheses—to tell them what to do. Additionally, a function can return a value to a waiting variable. For example, the following function call prompts the user for a response and stores it in the text variable:

```
text = prompt("Enter some text.")
```

Creating your own functions is useful for two main reasons: First, you can separate logical portions of your script to make it easier to understand. Second, and more important, you can use the function several times or with different data to avoid repeating script statements.

NOTE

Entire chapters of this book are devoted to learning how to create and use functions both in JavaScript and in PHP.

Variables

Variables are containers that can store a number, a string of text, or another value. For example, the following statement creates a variable called food and assigns it the value cheese:

```
var food = "cheese";
```

JavaScript variables can contain numbers, text strings, and other values. You'll learn more about variables in much greater detail in Chapter 7, "JavaScript Fundamentals: Variables, Strings, and Arrays," and in the context of PHP in Chapter 12, "PHP Fundamentals: Variables, Strings, and Arrays."

Objects

JavaScript also supports *objects*. Like variables, objects can store data—but they can store two or more pieces of data at once. As you'll learn throughout the JavaScript-specific chapters of this book, using built-in objects and their methods is fundamental to JavaScript—it's one of the ways the language works, by providing a predetermined set of actions you can perform. For example, the document.write functionality you saw earlier in this chapter is actually a situation in which you use the write method of the document object to output text to the browser for eventual rendering.

The data stored in an object is called a *property* of the object. For example, you could use objects to store information about people in an address book. The properties of each person object might include a name, an address, and a telephone number.

You'll want to become intimately familiar with object-related syntax, because you will see objects quite a lot, even if you don't build your own. You'll definitely find yourself using built-in objects, and objects will very likely form a large part of any JavaScript libraries you import for use. JavaScript uses periods to separate object names and property names. For example, for a person object called Bob, the properties might include `Bob.address` and `Bob.phone`.

Objects can also include *methods*. These are functions that work with the object's data. For example, our person object for the address book might include a `display()` method to display the person's information. In JavaScript terminology, the statement `Bob.display()` would display Bob's details.

Don't worry if this sounds confusing—you'll be exploring objects in much more detail later in this book both in the context of learning JavaScript fundamentals and PHP fundamentals. For now, you just need to know the basics, which are that JavaScript supports three kinds of objects:

▶ *Built-in objects* are built in to the JavaScript language. You've already encountered one of these: `Date`. Other built-in objects include `Array`, `String`, `Math`, `Boolean`, `Number`, and `RegExp`.

▶ *DOM (Document Object Model) objects* represent various components of the browser and the current HTML document. For example, the `alert()` function you used earlier in this chapter is actually a method of the `window` object.

▶ *Custom objects* are objects you create yourself. For example, you could create a `Person` object, as mentioned earlier in this section.

Conditionals

Although you can use event handlers to notify your script (and potentially the user) when something happens, you might need to check certain conditions yourself as your script runs. For example, you might want to validate on your own that a user entered a valid email address in a web form.

JavaScript supports *conditional statements*, which enable you to answer questions like this. A typical conditional uses the `if` keyword, as in this example:

```
if (count == 1) {
    alert("The countdown has reached 1.");
}
```

This compares the variable count with the constant 1 and displays an alert message to the user if they are the same. It is quite likely you will use one or more conditional statements like this in most of your scripts, and more space is devoted to this concept in Chapter 8, "JavaScript Fundamentals: Functions, Objects, and Flow Control."

Loops

Another useful feature of JavaScript—and most other programming languages—is the capability to create *loops*, or groups of statements that repeat a certain number of times. For example, these statements display the same alert 10 times, greatly annoying the user but showing how loops work:

```
for (i=1; i<=10; i++) {
    alert("Yes, it's yet another alert!");
}
```

The `for` statement is one of several statements JavaScript uses for loops. This is the sort of thing computers are supposed to be good at—performing repetitive tasks. You will use loops in many of your scripts, in much more useful ways than this example, as you'll see in Chapter 8.

Event Handlers

As mentioned previously, not all scripts are located within `<script>` tags. You can also use scripts as *event handlers*. Although this might sound like a complex programming term, it actually means exactly what it says: Event handlers are scripts that handle events. You learned a little bit about events already, but not to the extent you'll read about now or learn in Chapter 9, "Understanding JavaScript Event Handling."

In real life, an event is something that happens to you. For example, the things you write on your calendar are scheduled events, such as "Dentist appointment" and "Fred's birthday." You also encounter unscheduled events in your life, such as a traffic ticket and an unexpected visit from relatives.

Whether events are scheduled or unscheduled, you probably have normal ways of handling them. Your event handlers might include things such as *When Fred's birthday arrives, send him a present* and *When relatives visit unexpectedly, turn off the lights and pretend nobody is home.*

Event handlers in JavaScript are similar: They tell the browser what to do when a certain event occurs. The events JavaScript deals with aren't as exciting as the ones you deal with—they include such events as *When the mouse button is pressed* and *When this page is finished loading.* Nevertheless, they're a very useful part of JavaScript's environment.

Many events (such as mouse clicks, which you've seen previously) are caused by the user. Rather than doing things in a set order, your script can respond to the user's actions. Other events don't involve the user directly—for example, an event can be triggered when an HTML document finishes loading.

Each event handler is associated with a particular browser object, and you can specify the event handler in the tag that defines the object. For example, images and text links have an event, onmouseover, that happens when the mouse pointer moves over the object. Here is a typical HTML image tag with an event handler:

```
<img src="button.gif" onmouseover="highlight();">
```

You specify the event handler as an attribute within the HTML tag and include the JavaScript statement to handle the event within the quotation marks. This is an ideal use for functions because function names are short and to the point and can refer to a whole series of statements.

TRY IT YOURSELF ▼

Using an Event Handler

Here's a simple example of an event handler that will give you some practice setting up an event and working with JavaScript without using `<script>` tags. Listing 4.3 shows an HTML document that includes a simple event handler.

LISTING 4.3   An HTML Document with a Simple Event Handler

```
<!DOCTYPE html>

<html lang="en">
  <head>
    <title>Simple Event Handler Example</title>
  </head>

  <body>
    <h1>Simple Event Handler Example</h1>
    <p><a href="http://www.google.com/"
          onclick="alert('A-ha! An Event!');">Go to Google</a>
    </p>
  </body>
</html>
```

The event handler is defined with the following `onclick` attribute within the `<a>` tag that defines a link:

```
onclick="alert('A-ha! An Event!');"
```

This event handler uses the DOM's built-in `alert` method of the `window` object to display a message when you click the link; after you click OK to dismiss the alert, your browser will continue on to the URL. In more complex scripts, you will usually define your own functions to act as event handlers.

You'll use other event handlers throughout this book, leading up to a more comprehensive lesson in Chapter 9.

After you click the OK button to dismiss the alert, the browser follows the link defined in the `<a>` tag. Your event handler could also stop the browser from following the link, as you will learn in Chapter 9.

Which Script Runs First?

You are not limited to a single script within a web document: one or more sets of `<script>` tags, external JavaScript files, and any number of event handlers can be used within a single document. With all of these scripts, you might wonder how the browser knows which to execute first. Fortunately, this is done in a logical fashion:

▶ Sets of `<script>` tags within the `<head>` element of an HTML document are handled first, whether they include embedded code or refer to a JavaScript file. Because scripts in the `<head>` element will not create output in the web page, it's a good place to define functions for use later.

▶ Sets of `<script>` tags within the `<body>` section of the HTML document are executed after those in the `<head>` section, while the web page loads and displays. If there are two or more scripts in the body, they are executed in order.

▶ Event handlers are executed when their events happen. For example, the `onload` event handler is executed when the body of a web page loads. Because the `<head>` section is loaded before any events, you can define functions there and use them in event handlers.

JavaScript Syntax Rules

JavaScript is a simple language, but you do need to be careful to use its *syntax*—the rules that define how you use the language—correctly. The rest of this book covers many aspects of JavaScript syntax, but there are a few basic rules you can begin to keep in mind now, throughout the chapters in this book, and then when you are working on your own.

Case Sensitivity

Almost everything in JavaScript is *case sensitive*: You cannot use lowercase and capital letters interchangeably. Here are a few general rules:

▶ JavaScript keywords, such as `for` and `if`, are always lowercase.

▶ Built-in objects such as `Math` and `Date` are capitalized.

▶ DOM object names are usually lowercase, but their methods are often a combination of capitals and lowercase. Usually capitals are used for all but the first word, as in `setAttribute` and `getElementById`.

When in doubt, follow the exact case used in this book or another JavaScript reference. If you use the wrong case, the browser will usually display an error message.

Variable, Object, and Function Names

When you define your own variables, objects, or functions, you can choose their names. Names can include uppercase letters, lowercase letters, numbers, and the underscore (_) character. Names must begin with a letter or an underscore.

You can choose whether to use capitals or lowercase in your variable names, but remember that JavaScript is case sensitive: `score`, `Score`, and `SCORE` would be considered three different variables. Be sure to use the same name each time you refer to a variable.

Reserved Words

One more rule for variable names: They must not be *reserved words*. These include the words that make up the JavaScript language, such as `if` and `for`, DOM object names such as `window` and `document`, and built-in object names such as `Math` and `Date`.

A list of JavaScript reserved words can be found at https://developer.mozilla.org/en-US/docs/Web/JavaScript/Reference/Reserved_Words.

Spacing

Blank space (known as *whitespace* by programmers) is mostly ignored by JavaScript. You can usually include spaces and tabs within a line, or blank lines, without causing an error, although if your statements are not clearly terminated or bracketed you may get into a sticky situation. Overall, whitespace often makes the script more readable, so do not hesitate to use it.

Using Comments

JavaScript *comments* enable you to include documentation within your script. Brief documentation is useful if someone else needs to understand the script, or even if you try to understand it after returning to your code after a long break. To include comments in a JavaScript program, begin a line with two slashes, as in this example:

```
// this is a comment.
```

You can also begin a comment with two slashes in the middle of a line, which is useful for documenting a script. In this case, everything on the line after the slashes is treated as a comment and ignored by the JavaScript. For example, the following line is a valid JavaScript statement followed by a comment explaining what is going on in the code:

```
a = a + 1; // add 1 to the value of the variable a
```

JavaScript also supports C-style comments, which begin with /* and end with */. These comments can extend across more than one line, as the following example demonstrates:

```
/* This script includes a variety
of features, including this comment. */
```

Because JavaScript statements within a comment are ignored, this type of comment is often used for *commenting out* sections of code. If you have some lines of JavaScript that you want to temporarily take out of the picture while you debug a script, you can add /* at the beginning of the section and */ at the end.

Best Practices for JavaScript

Now that you've learned some of the very basic rules for writing valid JavaScript, it's also a good idea to follow a few *best practices*. The following practices are not required, but you'll save yourself and others some headaches if you begin to integrate them into your development process:

▶ *Use comments liberally.* These make your code easier for others to understand, and also easier for you to understand when you edit it later. Comments are also useful for marking the major divisions of a script.

▶ *Use a semicolon at the end of each statement, and use only one statement per line.* Although you learned in this chapter that semicolons are not necessary to end a statement (if you use a new line), using semicolons and only one statement per line will make your scripts easier to read and also easier to debug.

▶ *Use separate JavaScript files whenever possible.* Separating large chunks of JavaScript makes debugging easier, and also encourages you to write modular scripts that can be reused.

▶ *Avoid being browser-specific.* As you learn more about JavaScript, you'll learn some features that work in only one browser. Avoid them unless absolutely necessary, and always test your code in more than one browser.

▶ *Keep JavaScript optional.* Don't use JavaScript to perform an essential function on your site—for example, the primary navigation links. Whenever possible, users without JavaScript should be able to use your site, although it might not be quite as attractive or convenient. This strategy is known as *progressive enhancement*.

There are many more best practices involving more advanced aspects of JavaScript. You'll learn about them not only as you progress through the chapters, but also over time and as you collaborate with others on web development projects.

Understanding JSON

Although JSON, or *JavaScript Object Notation*, is not a part of the core JavaScript language, it is in fact a common way to structure and store information either used by or created by JavaScript-based functionality on the client side. Now is a good time to familiarize yourself with JSON (pronounced "Jason") and some of its uses.

JSON-encoded data is expressed as a sequence of parameter and value pairs, with each pair using a colon to separate parameter from value. These "parameter":"value" pairs are themselves separated by commas, as shown here:

```
"param1":"value1", "param2":"value2", "param3":"value3"
```

Finally, the whole sequence is enclosed between curly braces to form a JSON object; the following example creates a variable called yourJSONObject:

```
var yourJSONObject = {
    "param1":"value1",
    "param2":"value2",
    "param3":"value3"
}
```

Note that there is no comma after the final parameter—doing so would be a syntax error since no additional parameter follows.

JSON objects can have properties accessed directly using the usual dot notation, such as this:

```
alert(yourJSONObject.param1); // alerts 'value1'
```

More generally, though, JSON is a general-purpose syntax for exchanging data in a string format. It is then easy to convert the JSON object into a string by a process known as serialization; serialized data is convenient for storage or transmission around networks. You'll see some uses of serialized JSON objects as this book progresses.

One of the most common uses of JSON these days is as a data interchange format used by application programming interfaces (APIs) and other data feeds consumed by a front-end application that uses JavaScript to parse this data. This increased use of JSON in place of other data formats such as XML has come about because JSON is

► Easy to read for both people and computers

► Simple in concept, with a JSON object being nothing more than a series of "parameter":"value" pairs enclosed by curly braces

► Largely self-describing

► Fast to create and parse

► No special interpreters or other additional packages are necessary

Using the JavaScript Console to Debug JavaScript

As you develop more complex JavaScript applications, you're going to run into errors from time to time. JavaScript errors are usually caused by mistyped JavaScript statements.

To see an example of a JavaScript error message, modify the statement you added in the preceding section. We'll use a common error: omitting one of the parentheses. Change the last `document.write` statement in Listing 4.1 to read as follows:

```
document.write(currentTime;
```

Save your HTML document again and load the document into the browser. Depending on the browser version you're using, one of two things will happen: Either an error message will be displayed or the script will simply fail to execute.

If an error message is displayed, you're halfway to fixing the problem by adding the missing parenthesis. If no error was displayed, you should configure your browser to display error messages so that you can diagnose future problems:

▶ In Firefox, you can select the Developer option, then Browser Console from the main menu.

▶ In Chrome, select More Tools, Developer Tools from the main menu. A console displays in the bottom of the browser window. The console is shown in Figure 4.2, displaying the error message you created in this example.

▶ In Microsoft Edge, select F12 Developer Tools from the main menu.

The error we get in this case is `Uncaught SyntaxError` and it points to line 15. In this case, clicking the name of the script takes you directly to the highlighted line containing the error, as shown in Figure 4.3.

Most modern browsers contain JavaScript debugging tools such as the one you just witnessed. These tools will be incredibly useful to you as you begin your journey in web application development.

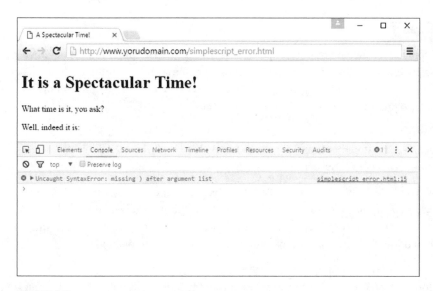

FIGURE 4.2
Showing an error in the JavaScript console in Chrome.

FIGURE 4.3
Chrome helpfully points out the offending line.

Summary

In this chapter, you learned what web scripting is and what JavaScript is. You also learned how to insert a script into an HTML document or refer to an external JavaScript file, what sorts of things JavaScript can do, and how JavaScript differs from other web languages. You also wrote a simple JavaScript program and tested it using a web browser.

In the process of writing this script, you have used some of JavaScript's basic features: variables, the `document.write` statement, and functions for working with dates and times. You were also introduced to the concept of JavaScript functions, objects, event handlers, conditions, and loops.

Additionally, you learned how to use JavaScript comments to make your script easier to read, and we looked at a simple example of an event handler. Finally, you were introduced to JSON, a data interchange format that is commonly used by JavaScript-based applications, and what happens when a JavaScript program runs into an error (and how to debug it).

Now that you've learned a bit of JavaScript syntax, you're ready to build on that in future chapters. But before that, take a moment in the next chapter to learn a similar set of basic information about a server-side scripting language: PHP.

Q&A

Q. **Do I need to test my JavaScript on more than one browser?**

A. In an ideal world, any script you write that follows the standards for JavaScript will work in all browsers, and 98% of the time (give or take) that's true in the real world. But browsers do have their quirks, and you should test your scripts in Chrome, Internet Explorer, and Firefox at a minimum.

Q. **When I try to run my script, the browser displays the actual script in the browser window instead of executing it. What did I do wrong?**

A. This is most likely caused by one of three errors. First, you might be missing the beginning or ending `<script>` tags. Check them, and then also verify that the first reads `<script type="text/javascript">`. Finally, your file might have been saved with a `.txt` extension, causing the browser to treat it as a text file. Rename it to `.htm` or `.html` to fix the problem.

Q. **I've heard the term object-oriented applied to languages such as C++ and Java. If JavaScript supports objects, is it an object-oriented language?**

A. Yes, although it might not fit some people's strict definitions. JavaScript objects do not support all the features that languages such as C++ and Java support, although the latest versions of JavaScript have added more object-oriented features.

Workshop

The Workshop contains quiz questions and exercises to help you solidify your understanding of the material covered. Try to answer all questions before looking at the "Answers" section that follows.

Quiz

1. When a user views a page containing a JavaScript program, which machine actually executes the script?

    A. The user's machine running a web browser

    B. The web server

    C. A central machine deep within Netscape's corporate offices

2. What software do you use to create and edit JavaScript programs?

    A. A browser

    B. A text editor

    C. A pencil and a piece of paper

3. What are variables used for in JavaScript programs?

    A. Storing numbers, dates, or other values

    B. Varying randomly

    C. Causing high-school algebra flashbacks

4. What should appear at the very end of a JavaScript script embedded in an HTML file?

    A. The `<script type="text/javascript">` tag

    B. The `</script>` tag

    C. The `END` statement

5. Which of the following is executed first by a browser?

    A. A script in the `<head>` section

    B. A script in the `<body>` section

    C. An event handler for a button

Answers

1. **A.** JavaScript programs execute on the web browser. (There is actually a server-side version of JavaScript, but that's another story.)

2. **B.** Any text editor can be used to create scripts. You can also use a word processor if you're careful to save the document as a text file with the `.html` or `.htm` extension.

3. **A.** Variables are used to store numbers, dates, or other values.

4. **B.** Your script should end with the `</script>` tag.

5. **A.** Scripts defined in the `<head>` section of an HTML document are executed first by the browser.

Exercises

▶ Examine the simple time display script you created and comment the code to explain everything that is happening all along the way. Verify that the script still runs properly.

▶ Use the techniques you learned in this chapter to create a script that displays the current date and time in an alert box when the user clicks a link.

CHAPTER 5
Introducing PHP

What You'll Learn in This Chapter:

▶ How PHP works with the web server as a "server-side" language
▶ How to include PHP code in a web page
▶ Beginning and ending PHP scripts
▶ How to use HTML, JavaScript, and PHP in the same file

In the first four chapters of this book, you worked with client-side or front-end languages: HTML and JavaScript. In this chapter, you'll learn a bit about PHP, which is a server-side scripting language that operates on a web server. You'll learn how to include PHP code into your HTML documents and how these scripts are executed when you refer to a page in your web browser that accesses a remote web server. This is a short chapter that is meant to be a bridge between the front end functionality you just learned about, and the backend functionality that you'll pick up again in Part III of this book.

How PHP Works with a Web Server

Often, when a user submits a request to a web server for a web page, the server reads a simple HTML file (that may or may not include JavaScript) and sends its contents back to the browser in response. If the request is for a PHP file, or for an HTML document that includes PHP code, and the server supports PHP, then the server looks for PHP code in the document, executes it, and includes the output of that code in the page in place of the PHP code. Here's a simple example:

```
<!DOCTYPE html>
<html>
    <head>
      <title>There's PHP in Here</title>
    </head>
    <body>
        <?php echo "Howdy!"; ?>
    </body>
</html>
```

If this page is requested from a web server that supports PHP, the HTML sent to the browser will look like this:

```
<!DOCTYPE html>
<html>
   <head>
     <title>There's PHP in Here</title>
   </head>
   <body>
      Howdy!
   </body>
</html>
```

When the user requests the page, the web server determines that it is a PHP page rather than a regular HTML page. If a web server supports PHP, it usually treats any files with the extension .php as PHP pages. Assuming this page is called something like howdy.php, when the web server receives the request, it scans the page looking for PHP code and then runs any code it finds. PHP code is distinguished from the rest of a page by PHP tags, which you'll learn more about in the next section.

Whenever the server finds those tags, it treats whatever is within them as PHP code. That's not so different from the way things work with JavaScript, where anything inside <script> tags is treated as JavaScript code.

The Basics of PHP Scripts

Let's jump straight into the fray with the simplest PHP script possible that also produces some meaningful output. To begin, open your favorite text editor. Like HTML documents, PHP files are made up of plain text. You can create them with any text editor, and most popular HTML editors and programming IDEs (integrated development environments) provide support for PHP.

TIP

If you have an IDE or simple text editor that you enjoy using for HTML and JavaScript, it's likely to work just fine with PHP as well.

Type in the example shown in Listing 5.1 and save the file to the document root of your web server, using a name something like test.php.

LISTING 5.1   A Simple PHP Script

```
<?php
    phpinfo();
?>
```

This script simply tells PHP to use the built-in function called `phpinfo()`. This function automatically generates a significant amount of detail about the configuration of PHP on your system. You can also begin to see the power of a scripting language, in which a little bit of text can go a long way toward producing something useful.

If you are not working directly on the machine that will be serving your PHP script, you need to use a File Transfer Protocol (FTP) or Secure Copy Protocol (SCP) client to upload your saved document to the server. When the document is in place on the server, you should be able to access it using your browser. If all has gone well, you should see the script's output. Figure 5.1 shows the output from the `test.php` script.

FIGURE 5.1
Success: the output from `test.php`.

Beginning and Ending a Block of PHP Statements

When writing PHP, you need to inform the PHP engine that you want it to execute your commands. If you don't do this, the code you write will be mistaken for HTML and will be output to the browser. You can designate your code as PHP with special tags that mark the beginning and end of PHP code blocks. Table 5.1 shows the two possible PHP delimiter tags.

TABLE 5.1 PHP Start and End Tags

Tag Style	Start Tag	End Tag
Standard tags	`<?php`	`?>`
Short tags	`<?`	`?>`

Standard tags are highly recommended and are the default expectation by the PHP engine. If you want to use short tags, you must explicitly enable short tags in your PHP configuration by making sure that the `short_open_tag` switch is set to On in `php.ini`:

```
short_open_tag = On;
```

Such a configuration change will require a restart of your web server. This is largely a matter of preference, although if you intend to include XML in your script, you should not enable the short tags (`<?` and `?>`) and should work with the standard tags (`<?php` and `?>`). Standard tags will be used throughout this book, but you should be aware you may run into this other type of tag if you are reading other people's code; if you use that code, you must adjust the PHP tags before you use it.

CAUTION

The character sequence `<?` tells an XML parser to expect a processing instruction and is therefore often included in XML documents. If you include XML in your script and have short tags enabled, the PHP engine is likely to confuse XML processing instructions and PHP start tags. Definitely do not enable short tags if you intend to incorporate XML in your document. Again, the standard tags will really serve you best in the long run.

Let's run through the two ways in which you can legally write the code in Listing 5.1, including using short tags if that configuration option is enabled:

```
<?php
    phpinfo();
?>

<?
    phpinfo();
?>
```

You can also put single lines of code in PHP on the same line as the PHP start and end tags:

```
<?php phpinfo(); ?>
```

Now that you know how to define a block of PHP code with PHP tag delimiters, let's move forward.

The `echo` and `print()` Statements

The following bit of PHP code does exactly one thing—it displays "Hello!" on the screen:

```php
<?php
    echo "Hello!";
?>
```

The `echo` statement, which is what we used here, outputs data. In most cases, anything output by `echo` ends up viewable in the browser. Alternatively, you could have used the `print()` statement in place of the `echo` statement. Using `echo` or `print()` is a matter of taste; when you look at other people's scripts, you might see either used, which is why I mention both here.

Referring back to the code you have seen so far, note the only line of code in Listing 5.1 ended with a semicolon. The semicolon informs the PHP engine that you have completed a statement, and it's probably the most important bit of coding syntax you could learn at this stage.

A *statement* represents an instruction to the PHP engine. Broadly, it is to PHP what a sentence is to written or spoken English. A sentence should usually end with a period; a statement should usually end with a semicolon. Exceptions to this rule include statements that enclose other statements and statements that end a block of code. In most cases, however, failure to end a statement with a semicolon will confuse the PHP engine and result in an error.

Combining HTML and PHP

The script in Listing 5.1 is pure PHP, but that does not mean you can only use PHP in PHP scripts. You can use PHP and HTML (and JavaScript too!) in the same document by simply ensuring that all of the PHP is enclosed by PHP start and end tags, as shown in Listing 5.2.

LISTING 5.2 Some PHP Embedded Inside HTML

```html
<!DOCTYPE html>
<html lang="en">
  <head>
    <title>Some PHP Embedded Inside HTML</title>
  </head>
  <body>
    <h1><?php echo "Hello World!"; ?></h1>
  </body>
</html>
```

As you can see, incorporating PHP code into a predominantly HTML document is simply a matter of typing in the code because the PHP engine ignores everything outside the PHP start and end tags.

Save the contents of Listing 5.2 as `helloworld.php`, place it in your document root, and then view it with a browser. You should see the string `Hello World!` in a large, bold heading, as shown in Figure 5.2. If you were to view the document source, as shown in Figure 5.3, the listing would look exactly like a normal HTML document, because all of the processing by the PHP engine will have already taken place before the output gets to the browser for rendering.

FIGURE 5.2
The output of `helloworld.php` as viewed in a browser.

You can include as many blocks of PHP code as you need in a single document, interspersing them with HTML however it makes sense. Although you can have multiple blocks of code in a single document, they combine to form a single continuous script as far as the PHP engine is concerned.

FIGURE 5.3
The output of `helloworld.php` as HTML source code.

Adding Comments to PHP Code

Code that seems clear at the time you write it can seem like a hopeless tangle when you try to amend it 6 months later. Adding comments to your code as you write can save you time later on and make it easier for other programmers to work with your code.

A *comment* is text in a script that is ignored by the PHP engine. Comments can make code more readable or can be use to annotate a script.

Single-line comments begin with two forward slashes (//), which is the preferred style, or a single hash or pound sign (#), which you may see in other people's code if those folks are more used to working in Perl or other languages where that comment type is more the norm. Regardless of which valid comment type you use, the PHP engine ignores all text between these marks and either the end of the line or the PHP close tag:

```
// this is a comment
#  this is another comment
```

Multiline comments begin with a forward slash followed by an asterisk (/*) and end with an asterisk followed by a forward slash (*/):

```
/*
this is a comment
none of this will
be parsed by the
PHP engine
*/
```

Code comments, just like HTML and JavaScript (and anything else that isn't PHP), are ignored by the PHP engine and will not cause errors that halt the execution of your scripts.

Code Blocks and Browser Output

In the previous section, you learned that you can slip in and out of HTML mode at will using the PHP start and end tags. In later chapters, you'll learn more about how you can present distinct output to the user according to a decision-making process you can control by using what are called *flow control statements*, which exist in both JavaScript and PHP. Although flow control in both languages will be discussed at length as the book moves forward, I use a basic example here to continue the lesson about mingling PHP and HTML with ease.

Imagine a script that outputs a table of values only when some condition is true, and doesn't output anything when a condition is false. Listing 5.3 shows a simplified HTML table constructed with the code block of an `if` statement.

LISTING 5.3   PHP Displays Text if a Condition Is True

```
<!DOCTYPE html>
<html lang="en">
<head>
    <title>More PHP Embedded Inside HTML</title>
    <style type="text/css">
    table, tr, th, td {
        border: 1px solid #000;
        border-collapse: collapse;
        padding: 3px;
    }
    th {
        font-weight: bold;
    }
    </style>
    </head>
    <body>
    <?php
    $some_condition = true;
```

```
        if ($some_condition) {
            echo "<table>
            <tr><th colspan=\"3\">
            Today's Prices
            </th></tr>
            <tr><td>14.00</td><td>32.00</td><td>71.00</td></tr>
            </table>";
        }
        ?>
        </body>
</html>
```

If the value of $some_condition is true, the table is printed. For the sake of readability, we split the output into multiple lines surrounded by one echo statement, and we use the backslash to escape any quotation marks used in the HTML output.

Put these lines into a text file called embedcondition.php and place this file in your web server document root. When you access this script through your web browser, it should look like Figure 5.4.

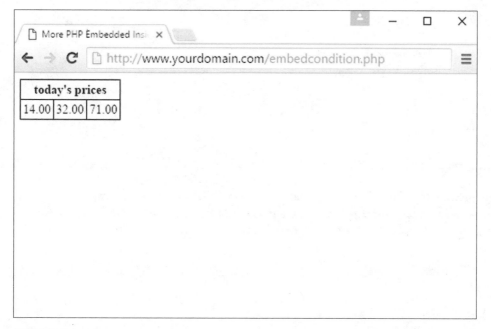

FIGURE 5.4
Output of embedcondition.php.

There's nothing wrong with the way this is coded, but you may find your code more readable to slip back into HTML mode within the code block itself. Listing 5.4 does just that.

LISTING 5.4   Returning to HTML Mode Within a Code Block

```
<!DOCTYPE html>
<html lang="en">
<head>
    <title>More PHP Embedded Inside HTML</title>
    <style type="text/css">
    table, tr, th, td {
        border: 1px solid #000;
        border-collapse: collapse;
        padding: 3px;
    }
    th {
        font-weight: bold;
    }
    </style>
</head>
<body>
    <?php
    $some_condition = true;
    if ($some_condition) {
    ?>
    <table>
    <tr><th colspan="3">Today's Prices</th></tr>
    <tr><td>14.00</td><td>32.00</td><td>71.00</td></tr>
    </table>
    <?php
    }
    ?>
</body>
</html>
```

The important thing to note here is that the shift to HTML mode occurs only if the condition of the `if` statement is fulfilled. Slipping in and out of PHP or HTML mode like this can save you from the time and effort of escaping quotation marks and wrapping output in `echo` statements. This approach might, however, affect the readability of the code in the long run, especially if the script grows larger.

Summary

In this chapter, you learned the concept of using PHP as a server-side scripting language, and using the `phpinfo()` function, you produced a list of the PHP configuration values for the server you are using. You created a simple PHP script using a text editor, and you learned about the tags you can use to begin and end blocks of PHP code.

You learned how to use the `echo` and `print` statements to send data to the browser, and you brought HTML and PHP together into the same script. You also looked at a technique for using PHP start and end tags in conjunction with conditional code blocks, as another way to embed PHP within HTML.

The first five chapters in this book lay the groundwork for creating web applications by introducing you to the idea of interactive websites and basic concepts used when developing web content with HTML, JavaScript, and PHP. The PHP language and its use on the back end of applications (the server side), as opposed to the front end (your web browser), makes it the more complex of the three. However, there are many similarities in the fundamentals and syntax of both PHP and JavaScript, such that directly after this chapter we will refocus on JavaScript for a bit before returning to PHP to build interactive and dynamic applications.

Q&A

Q. Which are the best start and end tags to use?

A. It is largely a matter of preference. For the sake of portability, the standard tags (`<?php` and `?>`) are preferred.

Q. What editors should I avoid when creating PHP code?

A. Do not use word processors that format text for printing (Microsoft Word, for example). Even if you save files created using this type of editor in plain-text format, hidden characters are likely to creep into your code.

Q. When should I comment my code?

A. Again, this is a matter of preference. Some short scripts will be self-explanatory, even when you return to them after a long interval. For scripts of any length or complexity, you should comment your code. Comments in your code often save you time and frustration in the long run.

Workshop

The Workshop is designed to help you review what you've learned and begin putting your knowledge into practice.

Quiz

1. Can a person browsing your website read the source code of a PHP script you have successfully installed?

2. Is the following a valid PHP script that will run without errors? If so, what will display in the browser?

```
<?php echo "Hello World!" ?>
```

3. Is the following a valid PHP script that will run without errors? If so, what will display in the browser?

```
<?php
// I learned some PHP!
?>
```

Answers

1. No, the user will see only the output of your script.

2. No, this code will produce an error because the `echo` statement is not terminated by a semicolon.

3. Yes, this code will run without errors. However, it will produce nothing in the browser because the only code within the PHP start and end tags is a PHP comment, which will be ignored by the PHP engine. Therefore, no output will be rendered.

Exercises

1. Familiarize yourself with the process of creating, uploading, and running PHP scripts. In particular, create your own "Hello World" script. Add HTML code to it as well as additional blocks of PHP.

## CHAPTER 6

Understanding Dynamic Websites and HTML5 Applications

What You'll Learn in This Chapter:

▶ How to conceptualize different types of dynamic content

▶ How to display randomized text with JavaScript

▶ How the W3C DOM standard makes dynamic pages easier to control

▶ The basics of the standard DOM objects: `window`, `document`, `history`, and `location`

▶ How to work with DOM nodes, parents, children, and siblings

▶ How to access and use the properties of DOM nodes

▶ How to access and use DOM node methods

▶ How to control element positioning with JavaScript

▶ How to hide and show elements with JavaScript

▶ How to add and modify text within a page with JavaScript

▶ How to change images using JavaScript and user events

▶ How to debug HTML, CSS, and JavaScript using developer tools

▶ How to begin thinking ahead to putting all the pieces together to create HTML5 applications

The term *dynamic* means something active or something that motivates another person to become active. A dynamic website is one that incorporates interactivity into its functionality and design, but also motivates a user to take an action—read more, purchase a product, and so on. In this chapter, you'll learn about the types of interactivity that can make a site dynamic, including information about both server-side and client-side scripting (as well as some practical examples of the latter).

This chapter will also help you better understand the Document Object Model (or DOM), which is the structured framework of a document within a web browser. Using JavaScript objects, methods, and other functionality (in addition to basic HTML), you can control the DOM to develop rich user experiences. After learning about the different technologies, you'll use JavaScript and your knowledge of the DOM to display a random quote upon a load loading as well as swap images based on user interaction. Finally, having learned at least the keywords and the basic concept of putting the HTML, CSS, and JavaScript pieces together, you'll be introduced to the possibilities that exist when you're creating HTML5 applications.

Refresher on the Different Types of Scripting

In web development in general, two types of scripting exist: server side and client side. *Server-side* scripting refers to scripts that run on the web server, which then sends results to your web browser. If you have ever submitted a form at a website (which includes using a search engine), you have experienced the results of a server-side script. You were introduced to PHP in the previous chapter, and PHP is a server-side scripting language.

On the other hand, *client-side scripting* refers to scripts that run within your web browser—no interaction with a web server is required for the scripts to run. By far the most popular client-side scripting language is *JavaScript*, which you learned about in Chapter 4, "Introducing JavaScript." For several years, research has shown that more than 99% of all web browsers have JavaScript enabled.

As you work through the book, we'll focus on using JavaScript for client-side scripting and PHP for server-side scripting.

Displaying Random Content on the Client Side

In Chapter 4, you learned the basics of JavaScript, such as how it fits into a web page. As an example of doing something dynamic on the client side, this section walks you through adding random content to a web page through JavaScript. You can use JavaScript to display something different each time a page loads. Maybe you have a collection of text or images you find interesting enough to include in your pages.

I'm a sucker for a good quote. If you're like me, or plenty of other people creating personal websites, you might find it fun to incorporate an ever-changing quote into your web pages. To create a page with a quote that changes each time the page loads, you must first gather all your quotes, along with their respective sources. You then place these quotes into a JavaScript *array*, which is a special type of variable in programming languages that is handy for holding lists of items.

After the quotes are loaded into an array, the JavaScript that's used to pluck out a quote at random is relatively small. Listing 6.1 contains the complete HTML and JavaScript code for a web page that displays a random quote each time it loads.

LISTING 6.1 A Random-Quote Web Page

```
<!DOCTYPE html>

<html lang="en">
  <head>
    <title>Quotable Quotes</title>
```

```
    <script type="text/javascript">
      <!-- Hide the script from old browsers
      function getQuote() {
        // Create the arrays
        var quotes = new Array(4);
        var sources = new Array(4);

        // Initialize the arrays with quotes
        quotes[0] = "Optimism is the faith that leads to achievement.";
        sources[0] = "Helen Keller";

        quotes[1] = "If you don't like the road you're walking, " +
        "start paving another one.";
        sources[1] = "Dolly Parton";

        quotes[2] = "The most difficult thing is the decision to act, " +
        "the rest is merely tenacity.";
        sources[2] = "Amelia Earhart";

        quotes[3] = "What's another word for thesaurus?";
        sources[3] = "Steven Wright";

        // Get a random index into the arrays
        i = Math.floor(Math.random() * quotes.length);

        // Write out the quote as HTML
        document.write("<p style='background-color: #ffb6c1;
                        text-align:center'>\"");
        document.write(quotes[i] + "\"");
        document.write("<em>- " + sources[i] + "</em>");
        document.write("</p>");
      }
      // Stop hiding the script -->
  </script>
  </head>

  <body>
    <h1>Quotable Quotes</h1>
    <p>Following is a random quotable quote. To see a new quote just
    reload this page.</p>
    <script type="text/javascript">
      <!-- Hide the script from old browsers
      getQuote();
      // Stop hiding the script -->
    </script>
  </body>
</html>
```

Although this code looks kind of long, a lot of it consists of just the four quotes available for display on the page.

The large number of lines between the first set of `<script></script>` tags creates a JavaScript function called `getQuote()`. After a function is defined, it can be called in other places in the same page, which you see later in the code. Note that if the function existed in an external file, the function could be called from all your pages.

If you look closely at the code, you will see some lines like this:

```
// Create the arrays
```

and

```
// Initialize the arrays with quotes
```

These are code comments. A developer uses these types of comments to leave notes in the code so that anyone reading it has an idea of what the code is doing in that particular place. After the first comment about creating the arrays, you can see that two arrays—initialized using the keyword *var*—are created—one called `quotes` and one called `sources`, each containing four elements:

```
var quotes = new Array(4);
var sources = new Array(4);
```

After the second comment (about initializing the arrays with quotes), four items are added to the arrays. Let's look closely at one of them, the first quote by Helen Keller:

```
quotes[0] = "Optimism is the faith that leads to achievement.";
sources[0] = "Helen Keller";
```

You already know that the arrays are named `quotes` and `sources`. But the variables to which values are assigned (in this instance) are called `quotes[0]` and `sources[0]`. Because `quotes` and `sources` are arrays, each item in the array has its own position. When you're using arrays, the first item in the array is not in slot #1—it is in slot #0. In other words, you begin counting at 0 instead of 1, which is typical in programming and is true in JavaScript as well as PHP—just file that away as an interesting and useful note for the future (or as a good trivia answer). Therefore, the text of the first quote (a value) is assigned to `quotes[0]` (a variable). Similarly, the text of the first source is assigned to `source[0]`.

Text strings are enclosed in quotation marks. However, in JavaScript, a line break indicates an end of a statement, so the third quote would cause problems in the code if it were written like this:

```
quotes[2] = "The most difficult thing is the decision to act,
the rest is merely tenacity.";
```

Therefore, you see that the string is built as a series of strings enclosed in quotation marks, with a plus sign (+) connecting the strings (this plus sign is called a *concatenation operator*):

```
quotes[2] = "The most difficult thing is the decision to act, " +
"the rest is merely tenacity.";
```

The next chunk of code definitely looks the most like programming; this line generates a random number and assigns that value to a variable called i:

```
i = Math.floor(Math.random() * quotes.length);
```

But you can't just pick any random number—the purpose of the random number is to determine which of the quotes and sources should be printed, and there are only four quotes. So this line of JavaScript does the following:

▶ Uses Math.random() to get a random number between 0 and 1. For example, 0.5482749 might be a result of Math.random().

▶ Multiplies the random number by the length of the quotes array, which is currently 4; the length of the array is the number of elements in the array. If the random number is 0.5482749 (as shown previously), multiplying that by 4 results in 2.1930996.

▶ Uses Math.floor() to round the result down to the nearest whole number. In other words, 2.1930996 turns into 2; remember that we start counting elements in an array at 0, so rounding up would always mean a chance that we would refer to an element that does not exist.

▶ Assigns the variable i a value of 2 (for example).

The rest of the function should look familiar, with a few exceptions. First, as you learned in Chapter 4, document.write() is used to write HTML that the browser then renders. Next, the strings are separated to clearly indicate when something needs to be handled differently, such as escaping the quotation marks with a backslash when they should be printed literally (\) or when the value of a variable is substituted. The actual quote and source that are printed are the ones that match quotes[i] and sources[i], where i is the number determined by the mathematical functions noted previously.

But the act of simply writing the function doesn't mean that any output will be created. Further on in the HTML, you can see getQuote(); between the two <script></script> tags—that is how the function is called. Wherever that function call is made, that is where the output of the function will be placed. In this example, the output displays below a paragraph that introduces the quotation.

Figure 6.1 shows the Quotable Quotes page as it appears when loaded in a web browser. When the page reloads, there is a one-in-four chance that a different quote displays—it is random, after all!

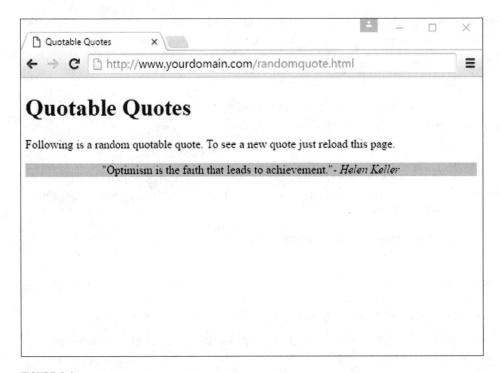

FIGURE 6.1
The Quotable Quotes page displays a random quote each time it is loaded.

Keep in mind that you can easily modify this page to include your own quotes or other text that you want to display randomly. You can also increase the number of quotes available for display by adding more entries in the `quotes` and `sources` arrays in the code. And of course, you can modify the HTML output and style it however you'd like.

If you use the Quotable Quotes page as a starting point, you can easily alter the script and create your own interesting variation on the idea. If you make mistakes along the way, so be it. The trick to getting past mistakes in script code is to be patient and carefully analyze the code you've entered. You can always remove code to simplify a script until you get it working, and then add new code one piece at a time to make sure each piece works.

Understanding the Document Object Model

One advantage that JavaScript has over plain HTML is that these client-side scripts can manipulate the web browser and documents (including their contents) right there in the browser after the content has been loaded. Your script can load a new page into the browser, work with parts of the browser window and the loaded document, open new windows, and even modify text within the page—all dynamically, without requiring additional page loads from a server.

To work with the browser and documents, JavaScript uses the hierarchy of parent and child objects found within the DOM. These objects are organized into a tree-like structure, and they represent all the content and components of a web document and the browser that renders it.

NOTE

The DOM is not part of JavaScript or any other programming language—rather, it's an API (application programming interface) built into the browser.

The objects in the DOM have *properties* that describe the web browser or document, and *methods*, or built-in code that enables you to work with parts of the web browser or document. You'll learn more about these properties and methods, and will practice referencing or using them, as this chapter moves forward.

You've seen DOM object notation already in this book, even if it wasn't called out as such. When you refer to a DOM object, you use the parent object name followed by the child object name or names, separated by periods. For example, if you need to refer to a specific image loaded in your web browser, this is a child object of the document object. But that document object, in turn, is a child of the DOM's window object. So to reference an image called logo_image, the DOM object notation would look like this:

```
window.document.logo_image
```

Using window **Objects**

At the top of the browser object hierarchy is the window object, which represents a browser window. You've already used at least one method of the window object: alert(), which displays a message in an alert box.

A user might have several windows open at a time, each with its own distinct window object, since different documents will presumably be loaded in each window. Even if the same document is loaded into two or more windows, they are considered distinct window objects because they are in fact distinct instances of the browser. However, when you reference window.document (or just document, as the window object is the default parent object so we don't need to explicitly refer to it) in your JavaScript, the reference is interpreted to be the window currently in focus—the one actively being used.

The window object is the parent object for all the objects we will be looking at in this chapter. Figure 6.2 shows the window section of the DOM object hierarchy and a variety of its objects.

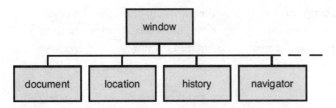

FIGURE 6.2
The window section of the DOM object hierarchy, and some of its children.

Working with the document Object

Just like it sounds, the document object represents a web document. Web documents are displayed within browser windows, so it shouldn't surprise you to learn that the document object is a child of the window object. Because the window object always represents the current window, as you learned in the preceding section, you can use window.document to refer to the current document. You can also simply refer to document, which automatically refers to the current window.

In the following sections, you will look at some of the properties and methods of the document object that will be useful in your scripting.

Getting Information About the Document

Several properties of the document object include information about the current document in general:

- ▶ document.URL specifies the document's URL, and you (or your code) cannot change the value of this property.

- ▶ document.title refers to the title of the current page, defined by the HTML <title> tag. You can change the value of this property.

- ▶ document.referrer returns the URL of the page the user was viewing before the current page—usually, the page with a link to the current page. As with document.URL, you cannot change the value of document.referrer. Note that document.referrer will be blank if a user has accessed a given URL directly.

- ▶ document.lastModified is the date the document was last modified. This date is sent from the server along with the page.

- ▶ document.cookie enables you to read or set a cookie used within the document.

- ▶ document.images returns a collection of images used in the document.

As an example of a document property, Listing 6.2 shows a short HTML document that displays its last modified date using JavaScript.

LISTING 6.2   Displaying the Last Modified Date

```html
<!DOCTYPE html>

<html lang="en">
  <head>
    <title>Displaying the Last Modified Date</title>
  </head>
  <body>
    <h1>Displaying the Last Modified Date</h1>
    <p>This page was last modified on:
    <script type="text/javascript">
       document.write(document.lastModified);
    </script>
    </p>
  </body>
</html>
```

Figure 6.3 shows the output of Listing 6.2.

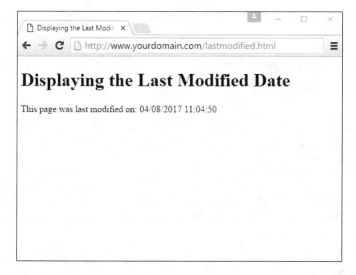

FIGURE 6.3
Viewing the last modified date of a document.

If you use JavaScript to display the value of this document property, you don't have to remember to update the date each time you modify the page, should you choose to expose this information to the user. (You could also use the script to always print the current date instead of the last modified date, but that would be cheating.)

NOTE

You might find that the `document.lastModified` property doesn't work on your web pages or returns the wrong value. The date is received from the web server, and some servers do not maintain modification dates correctly.

Writing Text in a Document

The simplest `document` object methods are also the ones you will use most often. In fact, you've used one of them already, even in the most basic examples in this book so far. The `document.write` method prints text as part of the HTML in a document window. An alternative statement, `document.writeln`, also prints text, but it includes a newline (\n) character at the end. This is handy when you want your text to be the last thing on the line in your source code.

CAUTION

Bear in mind that the newline character is displayed as a single space by the browser, except inside a `<pre></pre>` container. You will need to use the `<br>` tag if you want an actual line break to be shown in the browser.

You can use these methods only within the body of the web page; you can't use these methods to add to a page that has already loaded without reloading it. You *can* write new content for a document, however, as the next section explains.

NOTE

You can also directly modify the text of a web page by using more advanced features of the DOM, which you'll learn about later in this chapter.

The `document.write` method can be used within a `<script>` tag in the body of an HTML document. You can also use it in a function, provided you include a call to the function within the body of the document, as shown in Listing 6.2.

Using Links and Anchors

Another child of the `document` object is the `link` object. There can be, and very likely are, multiple `link` objects in a document. Each `link` object includes information about a link to another location or to an anchor.

You can access `link` objects through the `links` array. Each member of the array is one of the `link` objects in the current page. A property of the `links` array, `document.links.length`, indicates the number of links in the page. You might use the `document.links.length` property in a script to first determine how many links there are, before performing additional tasks such as dynamically changing the display of a certain number of links, and so on.

Each `link` object (or member of the `links` array) has a list of properties defining the URL that is ultimately stored in the object. The `href` property contains the entire URL, and other properties define other, smaller portions of it. The link object uses the same property names as the `location` object, defined later in this chapter, so after you commit one set to memory, you will also know the other set.

You can refer to a property by indicating the link number, or position within the array, and the property name. For example, the following statement assigns the entire URL of the first link stored in the array to the variable `link1`:

```
var link1 = links[0].href;
```

The `anchor` objects are also children of the `document` object. Each `anchor` object represents an anchor in the current document—a particular location that can be jumped to directly.

As with links, you can access anchors using an array; this one is called `anchors`. Each element of this array is an `anchor` object. The `document.anchors.length` property gives you the number of elements in the `anchors` array. An example of using the `anchors` array to your advantage would be to use JavaScript to loop through all the anchors on a given page, to dynamically generate a table of contents at the top of the page.

Accessing Browser History

The `history` object is another child (property) of the `window` object. This object holds information about the locations (URLs) that have been visited before and after the current one, and it includes methods to go to previous or next locations.

The `history` object has one property you can access:

▶ `history.length` keeps track of the length of the history list—in other words, the number of different locations that the user has visited.

The `history` object has three methods you can use to move through the history list:

▶ `history.go()` opens a URL from the history list. To use this method, specify a positive or negative number in parentheses. For example, `history.go(-2)` is equivalent to clicking the Back button twice.

▶ `history.back()` loads the preceding URL in the history list—equivalent to `history.go(-1)` or to clicking the Back button.

▶ `history.forward()` loads the next URL in the history list, if available. This is equivalent to `history.go(1)` or to clicking the Forward button.

You can use the `back` and `forward` methods of the `history` object to add your own Back and Forward buttons to a web document. The browser already has Back and Forward buttons, of course, but sometimes it is useful (or provides a better user experience) to include your own links that serve the same purpose.

Suppose you wanted to create a script that displays Back and Forward buttons and uses these methods to navigate the browser. Here's the code that will create the Back button:

```
<button type="button" onclick="history.back();">Go Back</button>
```

In the preceding snippet, the `<button>` element defines a button labeled Go Back. The `onclick` event handler uses the `history.back()` method to go to the preceding page in the browser's history. The code for a Go Forward button is similar:

```
<button type="button" onclick="history.forward();">Go Forward</button>
```

Let's take a look at these in the context of a complete web page. Listing 6.3 shows a complete HTML document, and Figure 6.4 shows a browser's display of the document. After you load this document into a browser, visit other URLs and make sure the Go Back and Go Forward buttons work as expected.

LISTING 6.3   A Web Page That Uses JavaScript to Include Back and Forward Buttons

```
<!DOCTYPE html>

<html lang="en">
  <head>
    <title>Using Custom Go Back and Go Forward Buttons</title>
  </head>
  <body>
    <h1>Using Custom Go Back and Go Forward Buttons</h1>
    <p>Buttons on this page allow you to go back or forward in
    your history list.</p>
    <p>These buttons should be the equivalent of the back
    and forward arrow buttons in your browser's toolbar.</p>
    <div>
    <button type="button"
            onclick="history.back();">Go Back</button>
    <button type="button"
            onclick="history.forward();">Go Forward</button>
    </div>
  </body>
</html>
```

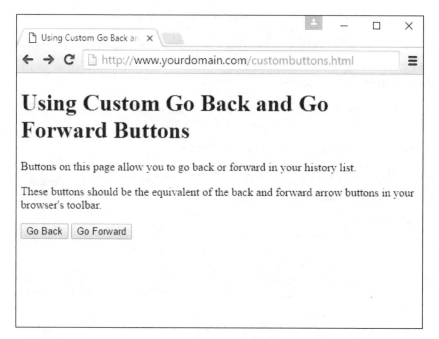

FIGURE 6.4
Showing custom Go Back and Go Forward buttons.

Working with the `location` Object

Another child of the `window` object is the `location` object. This object stores information about the current URL loaded in the browser window. For example, the following JavaScript statement loads a URL into the current window by assigning a value to the `href` property of this object:

```
window.location.href="http://www.google.com";
```

The `href` property contains the entire URL of the window's current location. Using JavaScript, you can access portions of the URL through various properties of the `location` object. To understand these properties a bit better, consider the following URL:

```
http://www.google.com:80/search?q=javascript
```

The following properties represent parts of the URL:

- ▶ `location.protocol` is the protocol part of the URL (`http` in the example).
- ▶ `location.hostname` is the hostname of the URL (`www.google.com` in the example).
- ▶ `location.port` is the port number of the URL (`80` in the example).

▶ `location.pathname` is the filename part of the URL (`search` in the example).

▶ `location.search` is the query portion of the URL, if any (`q=javascript` in the example).

Unused in this example but also accessible are the following:

▶ `location.host` is the hostname of the URL plus the port number (`www.google.com:80` in the example).

▶ `location.hash` is the anchor name used in the URL, if any.

The `link` object, introduced earlier in this chapter, also uses this list of properties for accessing portions of the URL found in the `link` object.

CAUTION

Although the `location.href` property usually contains the same URL as the `document.URL` property described earlier in this chapter, you can't change the `document.URL` property. Always use `location.href` to load a new page in a given window.

The `location` object has three methods:

▶ `location.assign()` loads a new document when used as follows:

```
location.assign("http://www.google.com")
```

▶ `location.reload()` reloads the current document. This is the same as using the Reload button on the browser's toolbar. If you optionally include the `true` parameter when calling this method, it will ignore the browser's cache and force a reload whether the document has changed or not.

▶ `location.replace()` replaces the current location with a new one. This is similar to setting the `location` object's properties yourself. The difference is that the `replace` method does not affect the browser's history. In other words, the Back button can't be used to go to the preceding location. This is useful for splash screens or temporary pages that it would be useless to return to.

More About the DOM Structure

Previously in this chapter, you learned how some of the most important DOM objects are organized: The `window` object is a parent to the `document` object, and so on. Whereas these objects were the only ones available in the original conception of the DOM years ago, the modern DOM adds objects under the `document` object for every element of a page.

To better understand the concept of a `document` object for every element, let's look at the simple HTML document in Listing 6.4. This document has the usual `<head>` and `<body>` sections, plus a heading and a single paragraph of text.

LISTING 6.4   A Simple HTML Document

```
<!DOCTYPE html>

<html lang="en">
  <head>
    <title>A Simple HTML Document</title>
  </head>
  <body>
    <h1>This is a Level-1 Heading.</h1>
    <p>This is a simple paragraph.</p>
  </body>
</html>
```

Like all HTML documents, this one is composed of various *containers* and their contents. The <html> tags form a container that includes the entire document, the <body> tags contain the body of the page, and so on.

In the DOM, each container within the page and its contents are represented by an object. The objects are organized into a treelike structure, with the document object itself at the root of the tree, and with individual elements such as the heading and paragraph of text at the leaves of the tree. Figure 6.5 shows a diagram of these relationships.

In the following sections, you will examine the structure of the DOM more closely.

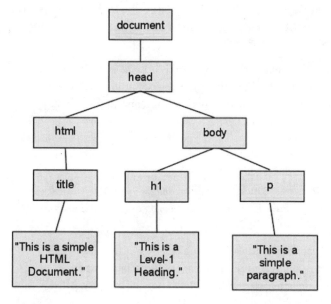

FIGURE 6.5
How the DOM represents an HTML document.

NOTE

Don't worry if this tree structure confuses you right now; just understand you can assign IDs to elements and refer to them in your JavaScript. Further on, you will look at more complicated examples that use this newfound information about how objects are organized in the DOM.

Nodes

Each container or element in a document is called a *node* in the DOM. In the example in Figure 6.5, each of the objects in boxes is a node, and the lines represent the relationships between the nodes.

You will often need to refer to individual nodes in scripts. You can do this by assigning an ID, or by navigating the tree using the relationships between the nodes. You will get plenty of practice with nodes as you move forward in this book; it's a good word to know.

Parents and Children

As you have already learned, an object can have a *parent* (an object that contains it) and can also have *children* (objects that it contains). The DOM uses the same terminology as JavaScript in this regard.

In Figure 6.5, the document object is the parent object for the other objects shown and does not have a parent itself explicitly listed, although as you learned previously, the document object is a child of the window object. The html object is the parent of the head and body objects, and the h1 and p objects are children of the body object.

Text nodes work a bit differently. The actual text in the paragraph is a node in itself and is a child of the p object, rather than being a grandchild of the body object. Similarly, the text within the <h1> tags is a child of the h1 object. Don't worry, we'll refer to this concept further on in the book to reinforce understanding.

Siblings

The DOM also uses another term for the organization of objects: *siblings*. As you might expect, this refers to objects that have the same parent—in other words, objects at the same level in the DOM object tree.

In Figure 6.5, the h1 and p objects are siblings because both are children of the body object. Similarly, the head and body objects are siblings under the html object. There's not a lot of practical use in knowing which objects are siblings, but it is offered here as some knowledge that completes the family tree.

Working with DOM Nodes

As you've seen, the DOM organizes objects within a web page into a tree-like structure. Each node (object) in this tree can be accessed in JavaScript. In the next sections, you will learn how you can use the properties and methods of nodes to manage them.

NOTE

The following sections describe only the most important properties and methods of nodes, and those that are supported by current browsers. For a complete list of available properties, see the W3C's DOM specification at http://www.w3.org/TR/DOM-Level-3-Core/.

Basic Node Properties

Previously in this book, you used the `style` property of nodes to change their presentation. Each node also has a number of basic properties that you can examine or set. These include the following:

▶ `nodeName` is the name of the node (not the ID). For a node based on an HTML tag, such as `<p>` or `<body>`, the name is the tag name: p or body. For the document node, the name is a special code: #document. Similarly, text nodes have the name #text. This is a read-only value.

▶ `nodeType` is an integer describing the node's type, such as 1 for normal HTML tags, 3 for text nodes, and 9 for the document node. This is a read-only value.

▶ `nodeValue` is the actual text contained within a text node. This property returns `null` for other types of nodes.

▶ `innerHTML` is the HTML content of any node. You can assign a value, including the HTML tags that provide a rich display, to this property and change the DOM child objects for a node dynamically.

▶ `innerText` is the text-only content of any node. You can assign a value to this property and change the DOM child objects for a node dynamically.

Node Relationship Properties

In addition to the basic properties described previously, each node has various properties that describe its relation to other nodes. These include the following read-only properties:

▶ `parentNode` is the primary node of an element; for example, in a list the `parentNode` would be `<ul>` or `<ol>` while the `childNodes` would include an array of `<li>` elements.

▶ `firstChild` is the first child object for a node. For nodes that contain text, such as h1 and p, the text node containing the actual text is the first child.

- ▶ `lastChild` is the node's last child object.

- ▶ `childNodes` is an array that includes all of a node's child nodes. You can use a loop with this array to work with all the nodes under a given node.

- ▶ `previousSibling` is the sibling (node at the same level) previous to the current node.

- ▶ `nextSibling` is the sibling after the current node.

CAUTION

Remember that, like all JavaScript objects and properties, the node properties and functions described here are case sensitive. Be sure you type them exactly as shown.

Document Methods

The `document` node itself has several methods you might find useful. The `document` node's methods include the following:

- ▶ `getElementById`(*id*) returns the element with the specified `id` attribute.

- ▶ `getElementsByTagName`(*tag*) returns an array of all the elements with a specified tag name. You can use the wildcard * to return an array containing all the nodes in the document.

- ▶ `createTextNode`(*text*) creates a new text node containing the specified text, which you can then add to the document.

- ▶ `createElement`(*tag*) creates a new HTML element for the specified tag. As with `createTextNode`, you need to add the element to the document after creating it. You can assign content within the element by changing its child objects or the `innerHTML` property.

Node Methods

Each node within a page has a number of methods available. Which of these are valid depends on the node's position in the page, and whether it has parent or child nodes. These include the following:

- ▶ `appendChild`(*new*) appends the specified new node after all the object's existing nodes.

- ▶ `insertBefore`(*new, old*) inserts the specified new child node before the specified old child node, which must already exist.

▶ replaceChild(*new, old*) replaces the specified old child node with a new node.

▶ removeChild(*node*) removes a child node from the object's set of children.

▶ hasChildNodes() returns a Boolean value of true if the object has one or more child nodes, or false if it has none.

▶ cloneNode() creates a copy of an existing node. If a parameter of true is supplied, the copy will also include any child nodes of the original node.

Creating Positionable Elements (Layers)

Now that you understand a little more about how the DOM is structured, you should be able to start thinking about how you can control any element in a web page, such as a paragraph or an image. For example, you can use the DOM to change the position, visibility, and other attributes of an element.

Before the W3C DOM and CSS2 standards (remember, we're now on CSS3), you could only reposition *layers*, or special groups of elements defined with a proprietary tag. Although you can now position any element individually, it's still useful to work with groups of elements in many cases.

You can effectively create a layer, or a group of HTML objects that can be controlled together, using the <div> container element.

To create a layer with <div>, enclose the content of the layer between the two division tags and specify the layer's properties in the style attribute of the <div> tag. Here's a simple example:

```
<div id="layer1" style="position:absolute; left:100px; top:100px;">
This is the content of the layer.
</div>
```

This code defines a container with the name layer1. This is a movable container positioned 100 pixels down and 100 pixels to the right of the upper-left corner of the browser window.

NOTE

As you've learned previously, you can specify CSS properties such as the position property in a <style> block, in an external style sheet, or in the style attribute of an HTML tag, and then control these properties using JavaScript. The code snippet shown here uses properties in the style attribute rather than in a <style> block, just because it is a snippet of an example and not a full code listing.

You've already learned about the positioning properties and seen them in action in Chapter 3, "Understanding the CSS Box Model and Positioning." The remaining examples in this chapter use HTML and CSS like what you've already seen in this book, but they describe JavaScript-based interactions with the DOM.

Controlling Positioning with JavaScript

Using the code snippet from the preceding section, you'll see an example in this section of how you can control the positioning attributes of an object, using JavaScript.

Here is our sample layer (a `<div>`):

```
<div id="layer1" style="position:absolute; left:100px; top:100px;">
This is the content of the layer.
</div>
```

To move this layer up or down within the page using JavaScript, you can change its `style.top` attribute. For example, the following statements move the layer 100 pixels down from its original position:

```
var obj = document.getElementById("layer1");
obj.style.top = 200;
```

The `document.getElementById()` method returns the object corresponding to the layer's `<div>` tag, and the second statement sets the object's `top` positioning property to 200px. You can also combine these two statements, like so:

```
document.getElementById("layer1").style.top = 200;
```

This simply sets the `style.top` property for the layer without assigning a variable to the layer's object.

NOTE

Some CSS properties, such as `text-indent` and `border-color`, have hyphens in their names. When you use these properties in JavaScript, you combine the hyphenated sections and use a capital letter: `textIndent` and `borderColor`.

Now let's create an HTML document that defines a container and then combine it with a script to allow the container to be moved, hidden, or shown using buttons. Listing 6.5 shows the HTML document that defines the buttons and the container. The script itself (`position.js`) follows in Listing 6.6.

LISTING 6.5   The HTML Document for the Movable Container Example

```
<!DOCTYPE html>

<html lang="en">
  <head>
    <title>Positioning Elements with JavaScript</title>
    <script type="text/javascript" src="position.js"></script>
    <style type="text/css">
    #buttons {
        text-align: center;
    }
    #square {
        position: absolute;
        top: 150px;
        left: 100px;
        width: 200px;
        height: 200px;
        border: 2px solid black;
        padding: 10px;
        background-color: #e0e0e0;
    }
    div {
        padding: 10px;
    }
    </style>
  </head>
  <body>
    <h1>Positioning Elements</h1>
    <div id="buttons">
    <button type="button" name="left"
      onclick="pos(-1,0);">Left</button>
    <button type="button" name="right"
      onclick="pos(1,0);">Right</button>
    <button type="button" name="up"
      onclick="pos(0,-1);">Up</button>
    <button type="button" name="down"
      onclick="pos(0,1);">Down</button>
    <button type="button" name="hide"
      onclick="hideSquare();">Hide</button>
    <button type="button" name="show"
      onclick="showSquare();">Show</button>
    </div>
    <hr>
    <div id="square">
    This square is an absolutely positioned container
    that you can move using the buttons above.
    </div>
  </body>
</html>
```

In addition to some basic HTML, Listing 6.5 contains the following:

▶ The `<script>` tag in the header reads a script called `position.js`, which is shown in Listing 6.6.

▶ The `<style>` section is a brief style sheet that defines the properties for the movable layer. It sets the `position` property to `absolute` to indicate that it can be positioned at an exact location, sets the initial position in the `top` and `left` properties, and sets `border` and `background-color` properties to make the layer clearly visible.

▶ The `<button>` tags define six buttons: four to move the layer left, right, up, or down, and two to control whether it is visible or hidden.

▶ The `<div>` section defines the layer itself. The `id` attribute is set to the value `"square"`. This `id` is used in the style sheet to refer to the layer and will also be used in your script.

If you load the HTML into a browser, you should see the buttons and the `"square"` layer, but the buttons won't do anything yet. The script in Listing 6.6 adds the capability to use the actions. When you load the code in Listing 6.5 into your browser, it should look as shown in Figure 6.6.

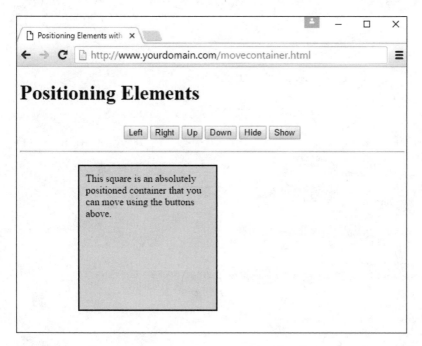

FIGURE 6.6
The movable container, ready to be moved.

Listing 6.6 shows the JavaScript variables and functions that are called in the HTML in Listing 6.5. This code is expected (by the `<script>` tag) to be in a file called `position.js`.

LISTING 6.6   The Script for the Movable Layer Example

```
var x=100;
var y=150;

function pos(dx,dy) {
    if (!document.getElementById) return;
    x += 30*dx;
    y += 30*dy;
    var obj = document.getElementById("square");
    obj.style.top=y + "px";
    obj.style.left=x + "px";
}
function hideSquare() {
    if (!document.getElementById) return;
    var obj = document.getElementById("square");
    obj.style.display="none";
}
function showSquare() {
    if (!document.getElementById) return;
    var obj = document.getElementById("square");
    obj.style.display="block";
}
```

The `var` statement at the beginning of the script defines two variables, x and y, that will store the current position of the container. The pos function is called by the event handlers for all four of the movement buttons.

The parameters of the pos() function, dx and dy, tell the script how the container should move: If dx is negative, a number is subtracted from x, moving the container to the left. If dx is positive, a number is added to x, moving the container to the right. Similarly, dy indicates whether to move up or down.

The pos() function begins by making sure the getElementById() function is supported, so it won't attempt to run in older browsers. It then multiplies dx and dy by 30 (to make the movement more obvious) and applies them to x and y. Finally, it sets the top and left properties to the new position (including the "px" to indicate the unit of measurement), thus moving the container layer.

Two more functions, hideSquare() and showsquare(), hide or show the container by setting its display property to "none" (hidden) or "block" (shown).

To use this script, save it as `position.js` and then load the HTML document in Listing 6.6 into your browser. Figure 6.7 shows this script in action—well, after an action, that is. Figure 6.7 shows the script after the Right button has been clicked four times and the Down button five times.

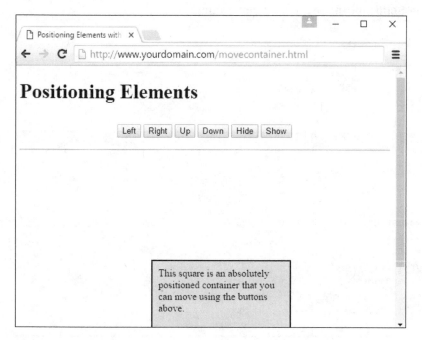

FIGURE 6.7
The movable container has been moved.

Hiding and Showing Objects

In the preceding example, you saw some functions that could be used to hide or show the "square." In this section, we'll take a closer look at hiding and showing objects within a page.

As a refresher, objects have a `visibility` style property that specifies whether they are currently visible within the page:

```
object.style.visibility="hidden"; // hides an object
object.style.visibility="visible"; // shows an object
```

Using this property, you can create a script that hides or shows objects in either browser. Listing 6.7 shows the HTML document for a script that allows two headings to be shown or hidden.

LISTING 6.7   Hiding and Showing Objects

```
<!DOCTYPE html>

<html lang="en">
  <head>
    <title>Hiding or Showing Objects</title>
    <script type="text/javascript">
    function showHide() {
        if (!document.getElementById) return;
        var heading1 = document.getElementById("heading1");
        var heading2 = document.getElementById("heading2");
        var showheading1 = document.checkboxform.checkbox1.checked;
        var showheading2 = document.checkboxform.checkbox2.checked;
        heading1.style.visibility=(showheading1) ? "visible" : "hidden";
        heading2.style.visibility=(showheading2) ? "visible" : "hidden";
    }
    </script>
  </head>
  <body>
    <h1 id="heading1">This is the first heading</h1>
    <h1 id="heading2">This is the second heading</h1>
    <p>Using the W3C DOM, you can choose whether to show or hide
    the headings on this page using the checkboxes below.</p>
    <form name="checkboxform">
    <input type="checkbox" name="checkbox1"
        onclick="showHide();" checked="checked" />
    <span style="font-weight:bold">Show first heading</span><br>
    <input type="checkbox" name="checkbox2"
        onclick="showHide();" checked="checked" />
    <span style="font-weight:bold">Show second heading</span><br>
    </form>
  </body>
</html>
```

The `<h1>` tags in this document define headings with IDs of `head1` and `head2`. Inside the `<form>` element are two check boxes, one for each of these headings. When a check box is modified (checked or unchecked), the `onclick` method calls the JavaScript `showHide()` function to perform an action.

The `showHide()` function is defined within the `<script>` tag in the header. This function assigns the objects for the two headings to two variables named `heading1` and `heading2`, using the `getElementById()` method. Next, it assigns the value of the check boxes within the form to the `showheading1` and `showheading2` variables. Finally, the function uses the `style.visibility` attributes to set the visibility of the headings.

TIP

The lines that set the `visibility` property might look a bit strange. The `?` and `:` characters create *conditional expressions*, a shorthand way of handling `if` statements. You'll learn more about these conditional expressions in Chapter 8, "JavaScript Fundamentals: Functions, Objects, and Flow Control."

Figure 6.8 shows this example in action. In the figure, the first heading's check box has been unchecked, so only the second heading is visible.

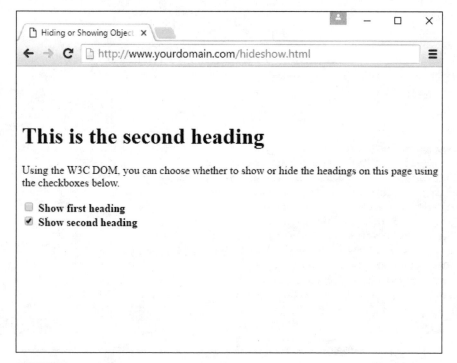

FIGURE 6.8
The text-hiding/showing example in action.

Modifying Text Within a Page

You can also create a simple script to modify the contents of a heading within a web page (or any element, for that matter). As you learned earlier in this chapter, the `nodeValue` property of a text node contains its actual text, and the text node for a heading is a child of that heading. Thus, the syntax to change the text of a heading with the identifier `head1` would be

```
var heading1 = document.getElementById("heading1");
heading1.firstChild.nodeValue = "New Text Here";
```

This assigns the heading's object to the variable called `heading1`. The `firstChild` property returns the text node that is the only child of the heading, and its `nodeValue` property contains the heading text.

Using this technique, it's easy to create a page that allows the heading to be changed dynamically. Listing 6.8 shows the complete HTML document for a script that does just that.

LISTING 6.8   The Complete Text-Modifying Example

```
<!DOCTYPE html>

<html lang="en">
  <head>
    <title>Dynamic Text in JavaScript</title>
    <script type="text/javascript">
    function changeTitle() {
        if (!document.getElementById) return;
        var newtitle = document.changeform.newtitle.value;
        var heading1 = document.getElementById("heading1");
        heading1.firstChild.nodeValue=newtitle;
    }
    </script>
  </head>
  <body>
    <h1 id="heading1">Dynamic Text in JavaScript</h1>
    <p>Using the W3C DOM, you can dynamically change the
    heading at the top of this page.</p>
    <p>Enter a new title and click the Change! button. </p>

    <form name="changeform">
    <input type="text" name="newtitle" size="40" />
    <button type="button" onclick="changeTitle();">Change!</button>
    </form>
  </body>
</html>
```

This example defines a form that enables the user to enter a new heading for the page. Clicking the button calls the `changeTitle()` function, defined in the `<script>` tag in the `<head>` element. This JavaScript function gets the value the user entered in the form, and it changes the heading's value to the new text by assigning the value of the input to the `heading1.firstChild.nodeValue` property.

Figure 6.9 shows this page in action after a new title has been entered and the Change! button has been clicked.

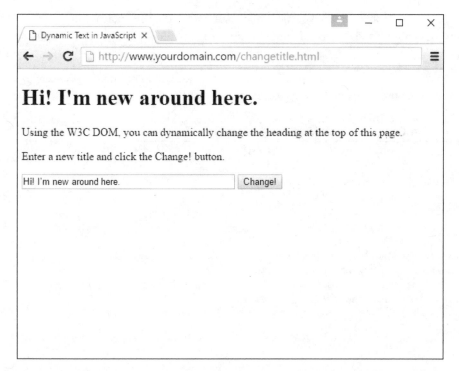

FIGURE 6.9
The heading-modification example in action.

Adding Text to a Page

You can create a script that actually adds text to a page rather than just changing existing text. To do this, you must first create a new text node. This statement creates a new text node with the text "this is a test":

```
var node=document.createTextNode("this is a test");
```

Next, you can add this node into the document. To do this, you use the `appendChild` method. The text can be added to any element that can contain text, but in this example we will just use a paragraph. The following statement adds the text node defined previously to the paragraph with the identifier `paragraph1`:

```
document.getElementById("paragraph1").appendChild(node);
```

Listing 6.9 shows the HTML document for a complete example that uses this technique, using a form to allow the user to specify text to add to the page.

LISTING 6.9   Adding Text to a Page

```
<!DOCTYPE html>

<html lang="en">
  <head>
    <title>Adding Text to a Page</title>
    <script type="text/javascript">
    function addText() {
        if (!document.getElementById) return;
        var sentence=document.changeform.sentence.value;
        var node=document.createTextNode(" " + sentence);
        document.getElementById("paragraph1").appendChild(node);
        document.changeform.sentence.value="";
    }
    </script>
  </head>
  <body>
    <h1 id="heading1">Create Your Own Content</h1>
    <p id="paragraph1"> Using the W3C DOM, you can dynamically add
    sentences to this paragraph.</p>
    <p>Type a sentence and click the Add! button.</p>
    <form name="changeform">
    <input type="text" name="sentence" size="65" />
    <button type="button" onclick="addText();">Add!</button>
    </form>
  </body>
</html>
```

In this example, the `<p>` element with the ID of `paragraph1` is the paragraph that will hold the added text. The `<form>` element is a form with a text field called `sentence` and an Add! button that calls the `addText()` function when clicked. This JavaScript function is defined in the `<script>` tag in the `<head>` element. The `addText()` function first assigns text typed in the text field to the `sentence` variable. Next, the script creates a new text node containing the value of the `sentence` variable and then appends the new text node to the paragraph.

Load this document into a browser to test it, and try adding several sentences by typing them and clicking the Add! button. Figure 6.10 shows this document after several sentences have been added to the paragraph.

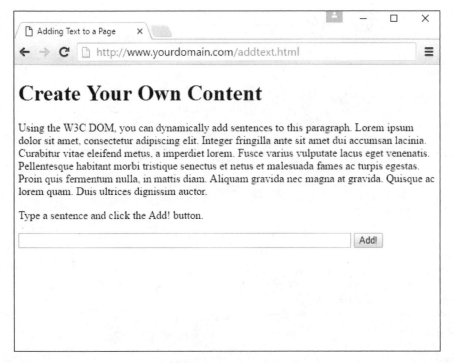

FIGURE 6.10
The text-addition example in action.

Changing Images Based on User Interaction

Chapter 4 introduced you to the concept of user interaction events and their event handlers, such as the `onclick` event handler when a click action is made by the user. In that chapter, you invoked changes in a window display based on user interaction; in this section, you'll see an example of a visible type of interaction that is both practical and dynamic.

Figure 6.11 shows a page that contains one large image with some text next to it, and three small images farther down the page. If you look closely at the list of small images, you might notice that the first small image is, in fact, a smaller version of the large image that is displayed. This is a common display type for a small gallery, such as one you might see in an online catalog where an item has a description and a few alternate views of the product. Although close-up images of the details of products are important to the potential buyer, using several large images on a page becomes unwieldy from both a display and bandwidth point of view, so this type of gallery view is a popular way to display alternative images. I don't personally have products to sell, but I do have pictures of big trees that I can use as an example, as you can see in the figure.

FIGURE 6.11
An informational page with a main image and alternative images ready to click and view.

The large image on the page is called using the following `<img>` tag:

```
<img
    id="large_photo"
    style="border: 1px solid black; margin-right: 13px;"
    src="mariposa_large_1.jpg"
    alt="large photo">
```

The `style`, `src`, and `alt` attributes should all make sense to you at this stage of the game. Additionally, as you can see, this image is given an ID of `large_photo`. Therefore, this image exists in the DOM as `document.images['large_photo']`—images are referred to by their ID. This is important because a bit of JavaScript functionality enables us to dynamically change the value of `document.images['large_image'].src`, which is the source (`src`) of the image.

The following code snippet creates the third small image in the group of three images shown at the bottom of Figure 6.11. The `onclick` event indicates that when the user clicks on this small image, the value of `document.images['large_image'].src`—the large image slot—is filled with the path to a matching large image.

```
<a href="#"
  onclick="document.images['large_photo'].src =
  'mariposa_large_1.jpg'">
<img
  style="border: 1px solid black; margin-right: 3px;"
  src="mariposa_small_1.jpg"
  alt="photo #1"></a>
```

Figure 6.12 shows the same page, but not reloaded by the user. The slot for the large image is filled by a different image when the user clicks one of the other smaller images at the bottom of the page.

FIGURE 6.12
The large image is replaced when the user clicks a smaller image.

Thinking Ahead to Developing HTML5 Applications

I'm not going to lie—there's a pretty big difference between a basic website built with HTML, CSS, and a little JavaScript, and comprehensive applications that use some of the advanced features of HTML5 and the latest JavaScript frameworks. But it's important to your understanding of

HTML, the language of the Web, to have some idea of just how far you can extend it (it's pretty far, as it turns out). Beyond basic markup, HTML5 extends to include APIs (application programming interfaces) for complex applications, beginning with the native integration of audio and video elements, as you learned in previous chapters, and going all the way to built-in offline storage mechanisms that allow full-blown applications to be accessed and run (and data stored on the client side) even without a network connection.

Although HTML5 is incredibly rich, the creation of highly interactive HTML5 websites and applications—including mobile applications—doesn't happen in isolation. Interactivity comes when HTML5 is paired with a client-side language such as JavaScript, which then reaches back into the server and talks to a server-side language such as PHP (and others) through a persistent connection called a *web socket*. With this connection open and talking to some server-side code that is, for example, talking to a database or performing some calculation, the browser can relay a bundle of information that is additionally processed by JavaScript and finally rendered in HTML5. Be it a video game, a word processing program, or an email or Twitter client, just to name a few types of applications, the combination of the advanced features of HTML5 plus JavaScript really makes the opportunities limitless when it comes to application creation.

In this book, you'll learn key features of technologies involved in HTML5 application creation, and the foundation you will have in standards-compliant HTML5, CSS3, JavaScript, and PHP development will serve you well once you think outside the box containing the lessons in this book.

Summary

In this chapter, you learned about the differences between server-side scripting and client-side scripting, but mostly you learned a lot about the Document Object Model (DOM), which creates a hierarchy of web browser and document objects that you can access via JavaScript. You learned how you can use the `document` object to work with documents, and you used the `history` and `location` objects to control the current URL displayed in the browser.

Additionally, you learned the methods and properties you can use to manage DOM objects, and you created sample scripts to hide and show elements within a page, modify existing text, and add to existing text. You also learned how to use HTML and CSS to define a positionable container, and how you can use positioning properties dynamically with JavaScript.

By applying the knowledge you've gained here, you can use client-side scripting to make elements on a web page respond to user interactions. Although they are simple in their construction, these types of interactions are some of the basic JavaScript-based interactions that form the foundation of web applications.

Q&A

Q. If I want to use the random-quote script from this lesson, but I want to have a library of a lot of quotes, do I have to put all the quotes in each page?

A. If you're working entirely on the client side, you can also put these quotes in a separate document and reference it in your code. This method will work as long as each item in the array is present in the browser in some way. However, you can begin to see a bit of a tipping point between something that can be on the client side and something that is better dealt with on the server side. If you have a true library of random quotations and only one is presented at any given time, it's probably best to store those items in a database table and use a little piece of server-side scripting to connect to that database, retrieve the text, and print it on the page.

Q. Can I avoid assigning an id attribute to every DOM object I want to handle with a script?

A. Yes. Although the scripts in this chapter typically use the `id` attribute for convenience, you can actually locate any object in the page by using combinations of node properties such as `firstChild` and `nextSibling`. However, keep in mind that any change you make to the HTML can change an element's place in the DOM hierarchy, so the `id` attribute is a reliable recommended way to handle this.

Q. Can I change history entries or prevent the user from using the Back and Forward buttons?

A. You can't change the history entries. Additionally, you can't prevent the use of the Back and Forward buttons, but you can use the `location.replace()` method to load a series of pages that don't appear in the history. There are a few tricks for preventing the Back button from working properly, but I don't recommend them—that's the sort of thing that gives JavaScript a bad reputation.

Workshop

The Workshop contains quiz questions and activities to help you solidify your understanding of the material covered. Try to answer all questions before looking at the "Answers" section that follows.

Quiz

1. What does the plus sign mean in the following context?

```
document.write('This is a text string ' + 'that I have created.');
```

2. Which of the following DOM objects never has a parent node?

A. `body`

B. `div`

C. `document`

3. Which of the following is the correct syntax to get the DOM object for a heading with the identifier `heading1`?

   A. `document.getElementById("heading1")`

   B. `document.GetElementByID("heading1")`

   C. `document.getElementsById("heading1")`

Answers

1. The plus sign (+) joins two strings together.

2. **C.** The `document` object is the root of the DOM object tree, and has no parent object.

3. **A.** `getElementById` has a lowercase **g** at the beginning and a lowercase **d** at the end, contrary to what you might know about normal English grammar. Additionally, the name includes Element (singular) rather than Elements (plural).

Exercises

▶ Modify the Back and Forward example in Listing 6.3 to include a Reload button along with the Back and Forward buttons. (This button would trigger the `location.reload()` method.)

▶ Modify the positioning example in Listings 6.5 and 6.6 to move the square 1 pixel at a time rather than 30 at a time.

▶ Add a third check box to Listing 6.7 to allow the paragraph of text to be shown or hidden. You will need to add an `id` attribute to the `<p>` tag, add a check box to the form, and add the appropriate lines to the script.

## CHAPTER 7

JavaScript Fundamentals: Variables, Strings, and Arrays

What You'll Learn in This Chapter:

▶ How to name and declare variables

▶ How to choose whether to use local or global variables

▶ How to assign values to variables

▶ How to convert between different data types

▶ How to use variables and literals in expressions

▶ How strings are stored in `String` objects

▶ How to create and use `String` objects

▶ How to create and use arrays of numbers and strings

Now that you have learned some of the fundamentals of JavaScript and the DOM (not to mention a bit of PHP), it's time to dig into more details of the JavaScript language before moving forward to create interactive applications.

In this chapter, you'll learn three basic tools for storing data in JavaScript: *variables*, which are often used to store numbers or text but can also store complex data structures as well; *arrays*, which are data structures that hold multiple variables. Variables, strings, and arrays are not the most exciting elements of any programming language when described individually, but as you will see throughout this book, variables, strings, and arrays are fundamental to just about every bit of complex JavaScript that you'll develop—and for that matter, PHP as well.

Using Variables

You've already used a few variables as you progressed through the initial chapters of this book. You probably can also figure out how to use a few more without any help from me. Nevertheless, there are some aspects of working with variables you haven't learned yet, and these are covered in the next few sections.

Choosing Variable Names

As a reminder, *variables* are named containers that can store data (for example, a number, a text string, or an object). As you learned earlier in this book, every variable has a unique name of your choosing. However, there are rules you must follow when choosing a variable name:

▶ Variable names can include letters of the alphabet, both upper- and lowercase. They can also include the digits 0–9 and the underscore (_) character.

▶ Variable names cannot include spaces or any other punctuation characters.

▶ The first character of the variable name must be either a letter or an underscore.

▶ Variable names are case sensitive—`totalnum`, `Totalnum`, and `TotalNum` are interpreted as separate variable names.

▶ There is no official limit on the length of variable names, but they must fit on one line. Frankly, if your variable names are longer than that—or even longer than 25 or so characters—you might consider a different naming convention.

Using these rules, the following are examples of valid variable names:

```
total_number_of_fish
LastInvoiceNumber
temp1
a
_var39
```

NOTE

You can choose to use either friendly, easy-to-read names or completely cryptic ones. Do yourself a favor: Use longer (but not too long), friendly names whenever possible. Although you might remember the difference between `a`, `b`, `x`, and `x1` right now, you might not after a few days away from the code, and someone who isn't you most certainly won't understand your cryptic naming convention without some documentation.

Using Local and Global Variables

Some computer languages require you to declare a variable before you use it. JavaScript includes the `var` keyword, which can be used to declare a variable. You can omit `var` in many cases; the variable is still declared the first time you assign a value to it.

To understand where to declare a variable, you will need to understand the concept of *scope*. A variable's scope is the area of the script in which that variable can be used. There are two types of variables:

▶ *Global variables* have the entire script (and other scripts in the same HTML document) as their scope. They can be used anywhere, even within functions.

▶ *Local variables* have a single use as their scope. They can be used only within the function where they are created.

To create a global variable, you declare (and define) it in the main script, outside any functions. You can use the `var` keyword to declare (and define) the variable, as in this example:

```
var students = 25;
```

This statement declares (and defines) a variable called `students` and assigns it a value of 25. If this statement is used outside functions, it creates a global variable. The `var` keyword is optional in this case, so this statement is equivalent to the preceding one:

```
students = 25;
```

Before you get in the habit of omitting the `var` keyword, be sure you understand exactly when it's required. It's actually a good idea to always use the `var` keyword—you'll avoid errors and make your script easier to read, and it won't usually cause any trouble.

A local variable belongs to a particular function. Any variable you declare with the `var` keyword in a function is a local variable. Additionally, the variables in the function's parameter list are always local variables.

To create a local variable within a function, you *must* use the `var` keyword. This forces JavaScript to create a local variable, even if there is a global variable with the same name. However, try to keep your variable names distinct, even if you are using them in different scopes.

You should now understand the difference between local and global variables. If you're still a bit confused, don't worry—if you use the `var` keyword every time, you'll usually end up with the right type of variable.

Assigning Values to Variables

As you learned in Chapter 4, "Introducing JavaScript," you use the equal sign to assign a value to a variable. For example, this statement assigns the value 40 to the variable `lines`:

```
var lines = 40;
```

You can use any expression to the right of the equal sign, including other variables. You have used this syntax earlier to add 1 to a variable:

```
lines = lines + 1;
```

Because incrementing or decrementing variables is quite common, JavaScript includes two types of shorthand for this syntax. The first is the += operator, which enables you to create the following shorter version of the preceding example:

```
lines += 1;
```

Similarly, you can subtract a number from a variable using the -= operator:

```
lines -= 1;
```

If you still think that's too much to type, JavaScript also includes the increment and decrement operators, ++ and --. This statement adds 1 to the value of lines:

```
lines++;
```

Similarly, this statement subtracts 1 from the value of lines:

```
lines--;
```

You can alternatively use the ++ or -- operator before a variable name, as in ++lines. However, these are not identical. The difference is in when the increment or decrement happens:

▶ If the operator is after the variable name, the increment or decrement happens *after* the current expression is evaluated.

▶ If the operator is before the variable name, the increment or decrement happens *before* the current expression is evaluated.

This difference is an issue only when you use the variable in an expression and increment or decrement it in the same statement. As an example, suppose you have assigned the lines variable the value 40. The following two statements have different effects:

```
alert(lines++);
alert(++lines);
```

The first statement displays an alert with the value 40, and then increments lines to 41. The second statement first increments lines to 41, then displays an alert with the value 41.

NOTE

The increment and decrement operators are strictly for your convenience. If it makes more sense to you to stick to lines = lines + 1, do it—your script won't suffer.

Understanding Expressions and Operators

An *expression* is a combination of variables and values that the JavaScript interpreter can evaluate to a single value, like 2 + 2 = 4. The characters that are used to combine these values, such as + and /, are called *operators*.

TIP

Along with variables and constant values, expressions can also include function calls that return results.

Using JavaScript Operators

In the basic JavaScript examples so far in this book, you've already used some operators, such as the + sign (addition) and the `increment` and `decrement` operators. Table 7.1 lists some of the most important (and common) operators used in JavaScript expressions.

TABLE 7.1 Common JavaScript Operators

Operator	Description	Example
+	Concatenate (combine) strings	`message="this is" + " a test";`
+	Add	`result = 5 + 7;`
-	Subtract	`score = score - 1;`
*	Multiply	`total = quantity * price;`
/	Divide	`average = sum / 4;`
%	Modulo (remainder)	`remainder = sum % 4;`
++	Increment	`tries++;`
--	Decrement	`total--;`

Along with these, there are also many other operators used in conditional statements—you'll learn about these in Chapter 8, "JavaScript Fundamentals: Functions, Objects, and Flow Control."

Operator Precedence

When you use more than one operator in an expression, JavaScript uses rules of *operator precedence* to decide how to calculate the value. Table 7.1 lists the operators from lowest to highest precedence, and operators with highest precedence are evaluated first. For example, consider this statement:

```
result = 4 + 5 * 3;
```

If you try to calculate this result, there are two ways to do it. You could multiply 5 * 3 first and then add 4 (result: 19) or add 4 + 5 first and then multiply by 3 (result: 27). JavaScript solves this dilemma by following the precedence rules: Because multiplication has a higher precedence than addition, it first multiplies 5 * 3 and then adds 4, producing a result of 19.

NOTE

If you're familiar with any other programming languages, you'll find that the operators and precedence in JavaScript work, for the most part, the same way as those in C, C++, and Java, as well as web scripting languages such as PHP.

Sometimes operator precedence doesn't produce the result you want. For example, consider this statement:

```
result = a + b + c + d / 4;
```

This is an attempt to average four numbers by adding them all together and then dividing by 4. However, because JavaScript gives division a higher precedence than addition, it will divide the d variable by 4 before adding the other numbers, producing an incorrect result.

You can control precedence by using parentheses. Here's the working statement to calculate an average:

```
result = (a + b + c + d) / 4;
```

The parentheses ensure that the four variables are added first and then the sum is divided by 4.

TIP

If you're unsure about operator precedence, you can use parentheses to make sure things work the way you expect and to make your script more readable.

Data Types in JavaScript

In some computer languages, you have to specify the type of data a variable will store (for example, a number or a string). In JavaScript, you don't need to specify a data type in most cases. However, you should know the types of data JavaScript can deal with.

These are the basic JavaScript data types:

▶ *Numbers*, such as 3, 25, and 1.4142138. JavaScript supports both integers and floating-point numbers.

▶ *Boolean*, or logical values. These can have one of two values: true or false. These are useful for indicating whether a certain condition is true.

▶ *Strings*, such as `"I like cheese"`. These consist of one or more characters of text. (Strictly speaking, these are `String` objects, which you'll learn about later in this chapter.)

▶ *Objects*, which are collections of properties. For example, a book object contains properties such as `title`, `author`, `subject`, and `page_count`. Those properties have values, such as "The Awesomeness of Cheese", "John Doe", "cheese", and 231.

▶ *The null value*, represented by the keyword `null`. This is the value of an undefined variable. For example, the statement `document.write(fig)` will result in this value (and an error message) if the variable `fig` has not been previously used or defined.

Although JavaScript keeps track of the data type currently stored in each variable, it doesn't restrict you from changing types midstream. For example, suppose you declared a variable by assigning it a value:

```
var total = 31;
```

This statement declares a variable called `total` and assigns it the value of `31`. This is a numeric variable. Now suppose you changed the value of `total`:

```
total = "albatross";
```

This assigns a string value to `total`, replacing the numeric value. JavaScript will not display an error when this statement executes; it's perfectly valid, although it's probably not a very useful "total."

NOTE

Although this feature of JavaScript is convenient and powerful, it can also make it easy to make a mistake. For example, if the `total` variable was later used in a mathematical calculation, the result would be invalid—but JavaScript does not warn you that you've made this mistake.

Converting Between Data Types

JavaScript handles conversions between data types for you whenever it can. For example, you've already used statements like this:

```
document.write("The total is " + total);
```

This statement prints out the message such as `"The total is 40"`. Because the `document.write` function works with strings, the JavaScript interpreter automatically converts any nonstrings in the expression (in this case, the value of `total`) to strings before performing the function.

This works equally well with floating-point and Boolean values. However, there are some situations in which it won't work. For example, the following statement will work fine if the value of `total` is `40`:

```
average = total / 3;
```

However, the `total` variable could also contain a string; in this case, the preceding statement would result in an error.

In some situations, you might end up with a string containing a number and need to convert it to a regular numeric variable. JavaScript includes two functions for this purpose:

- ▶ **parseInt()**—Converts a string to an integer number
- ▶ **parseFloat()**—Converts a string to a floating-point number

Both of these functions will read a number from the beginning of the string and return a numeric version. For example, these statements convert the string `"30 angry polar bears"` to a number:

```
var stringvar = "30 angry polar bears";
var numvar = parseInt(stringvar);
```

After these statements execute, the `numvar` variable contains the number `30`; the nonnumeric portion of the string is ignored.

NOTE

These functions look for a number of the appropriate type at the beginning of the string. If a valid number is not found, the function returns the special value `NaN`, meaning **_not a number_**.

Using `String` Objects

You've already used several strings in the brief JavaScript examples found in previous chapters. Strings store a group of text characters, and their defining variables follow typical naming conventions mentioned earlier. As a simple example, this statement assigns the string `This is a test` to a string variable called `stringtest`:

```
var stringtest = "This is a test";
```

In the following sections, you'll learn a little more about the `String` object and see it in action in a full script.

Creating a `String` Object

JavaScript stores strings as `String` objects. You usually don't need to worry about this piece of information—that your strings are in fact objects—but it will explain some of the common techniques you'll see for working with strings, which use methods (built-in functions) of the `String` object.

There are two ways to create a new `String` object. The first is the one you've already used, whereas the second uses object-oriented syntax. The following two statements create the same string:

```
var stringtest = "This is a test";
stringtest = new String("This is a test");
```

The second statement uses the `new` keyword, which you use to create objects. This tells the browser to create a new `String` object containing the text `This is a test` and then assigns it to the variable `stringtest`.

Assigning a Value

You can assign a value to a string in the same way as any other variable. Both of the examples in the preceding section assigned an initial value to the string. You can also assign a value after the string has already been created. For example, the following statement replaces the contents of the `stringtest` variable with a new string:

```
var stringtest = "This is only a test.";
```

You can also use the concatenation operator (+) to combine the values of two strings. Listing 7.1 shows a simple example of assigning and combining the values of strings.

LISTING 7.1 Assigning Values to Strings and Combining Them

```
<!DOCTYPE html>

<html lang="en">
  <head>
    <title>String Text</title>
  </head>

  <body>
      <h1>String Test</h1>
      <script type="text/javascript">
       var stringtest1 = "This is a test. ";
       var stringtest2 = "This is only a test.";
       var bothstrings = stringtest1 + stringtest2;
       alert(bothstrings);
      </script>
  </body>
</html>
```

This script assigns values to two string variables, `stringtest1` and `stringtest2`, and then displays an alert with their combined value (the variable `bothstrings`). If you load this HTML document in a browser, your output should resemble what's shown in Figure 7.1.

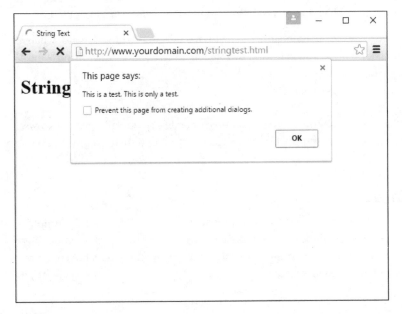

FIGURE 7.1
The output of the string sample script.

In addition to using the + operator to concatenate two strings, you can use the += operator to add text to a string. For example, this statement adds a period to the current contents of a string variable named `sentence`:

```
sentence += ".";
```

NOTE

The plus sign (+) is also used to add numbers in JavaScript. The browser knows whether to use addition or concatenation based on the types of data you use with the plus sign. If you use it between a number and a string, the number is converted to a string and concatenated.

Calculating the String's Length

From time to time, you might find it useful to know how many characters a string variable contains. You can do this with the `length` property of `String` objects, which you can use with any string. To use this property, type the string's name followed by `.length`.

For example, `stringtest.length` refers to the length of the `stringtest` string. Here is an example of this property:

```
var stringtest = "This is a test.";
document.write(stringtest.length);
```

The first statement assigns the string `This is a test.` to the `stringtest` variable. The second statement displays the length of the string—in this case, 15 characters. The `length` property is a read-only property, so you cannot assign a value to it to change a string's length.

NOTE

Remember that although `stringtest` refers to a string variable, the value of `stringtest.length` is a number and can be used in any numeric expression.

Converting the String's Case

Two methods of the `String` object enable you to convert the contents of a string to all uppercase or all lowercase:

▶ **`toUpperCase()`**—Converts all characters in the string to uppercase

▶ **`toLowerCase()`**—Converts all characters in the string to lowercase

For example, the following statement displays the value of the `stringtest` string variable in lowercase:

```
document.write(stringtest.toLowerCase());
```

Assuming that this variable contained the text is `This Is A Test`, the result would be the following string:

```
this is a test
```

Note that the statement doesn't change the value of the `stringtest` variable. These methods return the upper- or lowercase version of the string, but they don't change the string itself. If you want to change the string's value, you can use a statement like this:

```
stringtest = stringtest.toLowerCase();
```

Working with Substrings

In the short examples so far, you've worked only with entire strings. Like most programming languages, JavaScript also enables you to work with *substrings*, or portions of a string. You can use the `substring` method to retrieve a portion of a string, or the `charAt` method to get a single character. These are explained in the following sections.

Using Part of a String

The `substring` method returns a string consisting of a portion of the original string between two index values, which you must specify in parentheses. For example, the following statement displays the fourth through sixth characters of the `stringtest` string:

```
document.write(stringtest.substring(3,6));
```

At this point, you're probably wondering where the 3 and the 6 come from. There are three things you need to understand about using index parameters, regardless of when you're using them:

▶ Indexing starts with 0 for the first character of the string, so the fourth character is actually index 3.

▶ The second index is noninclusive. A second index of 6 includes up to index 5 (the sixth character).

▶ You can specify the two indexes in either order. The smaller one will be assumed to be the first index. In the previous example, (6,3) would have produced the same result. Of course, there is rarely a reason to use the reverse order.

As another example, suppose you defined a string called `alpha` to hold an uppercase version of the alphabet:

```
var alpha = "ABCDEFGHIJKLMNOPQRSTUVWXYZ";
```

The following are examples of the `substring()` method using the `alpha` string:

▶ `alpha.substring(0,4)` returns ABCD.

▶ `alpha.substring(10,12)` returns KL.

▶ `alpha.substring(12,10)` also returns KL. Because 10 is the smaller of the two values, it's is used as the first index.

▶ `alpha.substring(6,7)` returns G.

▶ `alpha.substring(24,26)` returns YZ.

▶ `alpha.substring(0,26)` returns the entire alphabet.

▶ `alpha.substring(6,6)` returns the `null` value, an empty string. This is true whenever the two index values are the same.

Getting a Single Character

The `charAt` method is a simple way to grab a single character from a specified position within a string. To use this method, specify the character's index, or position, in parentheses. As you've learned, the index begins at 0 for the first character. Here are a few examples of using the `charAt` method on the `alpha` string:

- ▶ `alpha.charAt(0)` returns A.

- ▶ `alpha.charAt(12)` returns M.

- ▶ `alpha.charAt(25)` returns Z.

- ▶ `alpha.charAt(27)` returns an empty string because there is no character at that position.

Finding a Substring

Another use for substrings is to find a string within another string. One way to do this is with the `indexOf` method. To use this method, add `indexOf` to the string you want to search and then specify the string to search for in the parentheses. This example searches for "this" in the `stringtest` string and assigns the result to a variable called `location`:

```
var location = stringtest.indexOf("this");
```

CAUTION

As with most JavaScript methods and property names, `indexOf` is case sensitive. Make sure you type it exactly as shown here when you use it in scripts.

The value returned in the `location` variable is an index into the string, similar to the first index in the `substring` method. The first character of the string is index 0.

You can specify an optional second parameter in this method, to indicate the index value to begin the search. For example, this statement searches for the word `fish` in the `moretext` string, starting with the 20th character:

```
var newlocation = moretext.indexOf("fish",19);
```

NOTE

One use for the second parameter of this method is to search for multiple occurrences of a string. After finding the first occurrence, you search starting with that location for the second one, and so on.

A second method, `lastIndexOf()`, works the same way but finds the *last* occurrence of the string. It searches the string backward, starting with the last character. For example, this statement finds the last occurrence of `Fred` in the `names` string:

```
var namelocation = names.lastIndexOf("Fred");
```

As with `indexOf()`, you can specify a location to search from as the second parameter. In this case, the string will be searched backward starting at that location.

Using Numeric Arrays

An *array* is a numbered group of data items that you can treat as a single unit. For example, you might use an array called `scores` to store several scores for a game. Arrays can contain strings, numbers, objects, or other types of data. Each item in an array is called an *element* of the array.

Creating a Numeric Array

Unlike most other types of JavaScript variables, you typically need to declare an array before you use it. The following example creates an array with four elements:

```
scores = new Array(4);
```

To assign a value to the array, you use an index in brackets. As you've seen earlier in this chapter, indexes begin with 0, so the elements of the array in this example would be numbered 0 to 3. These statements assign values to the four elements of the array:

```
scores[0] = 39;
scores[1] = 40;
scores[2] = 100;
scores[3] = 49;
```

You can also declare an array and specify values for elements at the same time. This statement creates the same `scores` array in a single line:

```
scores = new Array(39,40,100,49);
```

You can also use a shorthand syntax to declare an array and specify its contents. The following statement is an alternative way to create the `scores` array:

```
scores = [39,40,100,49];
```

TIP

Remember to use parentheses when declaring an array with the `new` keyword, as in a `= new Array(3,4,5)`, and use brackets when declaring an array without `new`, as in `a = [3,4,5]`. Otherwise, you'll run into JavaScript errors.

Understanding Array Length

Like strings, arrays have a `length` property. This tells you the number of elements in the array. If you specified the length when creating the array, this value becomes the `length` property's value. For example, these statements would print the number 30:

```
scores = new Array(30);
document.write(scores.length);
```

You can declare an array without a specific length as well as change the length later by assigning values to elements or changing the `length` property. For example, these statements create a new array and assign values to two of its elements:

```
test = new Array();
test[0]=21;
test[5]=22;
```

In this example, because the largest index number assigned so far is 5, the array has a `length` property of 6—remember, elements are numbered starting at 0.

Accessing Array Elements

You can read the contents of an array using the same notation you used when assigning values. For example, the following statements would display the values of the first three elements of the `scores` array:

```
scoredisplay = "Scores: " + scores[0] + ", " + scores[1] +
   ", " + scores[2];
document.write(scoredisplay);
```

TIP

Looking at this example, you might imagine it would be inconvenient to display all the elements of a large array. This is an ideal job for loops, which enable you to perform the same statements several times with different values. You'll learn all about loops in Chapter 8.

Using String Arrays

So far, you've used arrays of numbers. JavaScript also enables you to use *string arrays*, or arrays of strings. This is a powerful feature that enables you to work with a large number of strings at the same time.

Creating a String Array

You declare a string array in the same way as a numeric array—in fact, JavaScript does not make a distinction between them:

```
names = new Array(30);
```

You can then assign string values to the array elements:

```
names[0] = "John H. Watson";
names[1] = "Sherlock Holmes";
```

As with numeric arrays, you can also specify a string array's contents when you create it. Either of the following statements would create the same string array as the preceding example:

```
names = new Array("John H. Watson", "Sherlock Holmes");
names = ["John H. Watson", "Sherlock Holmes"];
```

You can use string array elements anywhere you would use a string. You can even use the string methods introduced earlier. For example, the following statement prints the first four characters of the first element of the `names` array, resulting in `John`:

```
document.write(names[0].substring(0,4));
```

Splitting a String

JavaScript includes a string method called `split`, which splits a string into its component parts. To use this method, specify the string to split and a character to divide the parts:

```
name = "John Q. Public";
parts = name.split(" ");
```

In this example, the `name` string contains the name `John Q. Public`. The `split` method in the second statement splits the `name` string at each space, resulting in three strings. These are stored in a string array called `parts`. After the sample statements execute, the elements of `parts` contain the following:

- ▶ `parts[0] = "John"`
- ▶ `parts[1] = "Q."`
- ▶ `parts[2] = "Public"`

JavaScript also includes an array method, `join`, that performs the opposite function. This statement reassembles the `parts` array into a string:

```
fullname = parts.join(" ");
```

The value in the parentheses specifies a character to separate the parts of the array. In this case, a space is used, resulting in the final string John Q. Public. If you do not specify a character, commas are used.

Sorting a String Array

JavaScript also includes a sort method for arrays that returns an alphabetically sorted version of the array. For example, the following statements initialize an array of four names and sort it:

```
names[0] = "Public, John Q.";
names[1] = "Doe, Jane";
names[2] = "Duck, Daisy";
names[3] = "Mouse, Mickey";
sortednames = names.sort();
```

The last statement sorts the names array and stores the result in a new array, sortednames.

Sorting a Numeric Array

Because the sort method sorts alphabetically, it won't work with a numeric array—at least not the way you'd expect. If an array contains the numbers 4, 10, 30, and 200, for example, it would sort them as 10, 200, 30, 4—not even close. Fortunately, there's a solution: You can specify a function in the sort method's parameters, and that function is used to compare the numbers. The following code sorts a numeric array correctly:

```
function numbercompare(a,b) {
    return a-b;
}
numbers = new Array(30, 10, 200, 4);
sortednumbers = numbers.sort(numbercompare);
```

This example defines a simple function, numbercompare, that subtracts the two numbers. After you specify this function in the sort method, the array is sorted in the correct numeric order: 4, 10, 30, 200.

NOTE

JavaScript expects the comparison function to return a negative number if a belongs before b, 0 if they are the same, or a positive number if a belongs after b. This is why a-b is all you need for the function to sort numerically.

▼ TRY IT YOURSELF

Sorting and Displaying Names

To gain more experience working with JavaScript's string and array features, you can create a script that enables the user to enter a list of names and then displays the list in sorted form.

Because this will be a larger script, you will create separate HTML and JavaScript files. First, the `sort.html` file will contain the HTML structure and form fields for the script to work with. Listing 7.2 shows the HTML document.

LISTING 7.2 The HTML Document for the Sorting Example

```
<!DOCTYPE html>

<html lang="en">
  <head>
    <title>Array Sorting Example</title>
    <script type="text/javascript" src="sort.js"></script>
  </head>

  <body>
    <h1>Sorting String Arrays</h1>
    <p>Enter two or more names in the field below,
    and the sorted list of names will appear in the
    textarea.</p>
    <form name="theform">
    Name:
    <input type="text" name="newname" size="20">
    <input type="button" name="addname" value="Add"
    onclick="SortNames();">
    <br/>
    <h2>Sorted Names</h2>
    <textarea cols="60" rows="10" name="sorted">
    The sorted names will appear here.
    </textarea>
    </form>
  </body>
</html>
```

Because the script will be in a separate document, the `<script>` tag in the header of this document uses the `src` attribute to include a JavaScript file called `sort.js`. You will create this file next.

This document defines a form named `theform`, a text field named `newname`, an `addname` button, and a text area named `sorted`. Your script will use these form fields as its user interface.

Listing 7.3 provides the JavaScript necessary for the sorting process.

LISTING 7.3   The JavaScript File for the Sorting Example

```
// initialize the counter and the array
var numbernames=0;
var names = new Array();
function SortNames() {
    // Get the name from the text field
    thename=document.theform.newname.value;
    // Add the name to the array
    names[numbernames]=thename;
    // Increment the counter
    numbernames++;
    // Sort the array
    names.sort();
    document.theform.sorted.value=names.join("\n");
}
```

The script begins by defining two variables with the `var` keyword: `numbernames` is a counter that increments as each name is added, and the `names` array stores the names.

When you type a name into the text field and click the button, the `onclick` event handler calls the `SortNames` function. This function stores the text field value in a variable, `thename`, and then adds the name to the `names` array using `numbernames` as the index. It then increments `numbernames` to prepare for the next name.

The final section of the script sorts the names and displays them. First, the `sort()` method is used to sort the `names` array. Next, the `join()` method is used to combine the names, separating them with line breaks, and display them in the text area.

To test the script, save it as `sort.js` and then load the `sort.html` file you created previously into a browser. You can then add some names and test the script. Figure 7.2 shows the result after several names have been sorted.

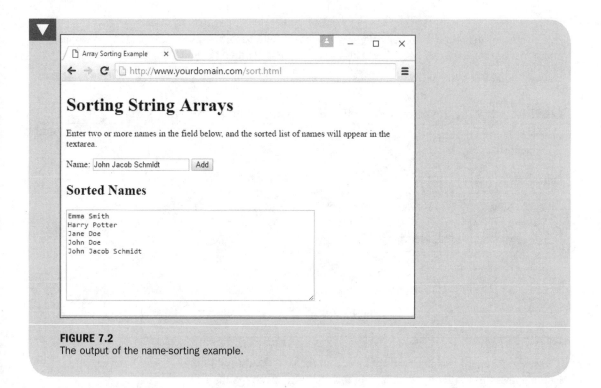

FIGURE 7.2
The output of the name-sorting example.

Summary

In this chapter, the lessons focused on variables and how JavaScript handles them. You learned how to name variables, how to declare them, and the differences between local and global variables. You also explored the data types supported by JavaScript and how to convert between them.

You also learned about JavaScript's more complex variable types—strings and arrays—and looked at the features that enable you to perform operations on them, such as converting strings to uppercase and sorting arrays. Not only is all of the information in this chapter useful as foundational JavaScript knowledge, but the topics covered are conceptually similar to those you'll learn and practice in the foundational PHP chapters later in this book.

In the next chapter, you'll continue your foundational JavaScript education by learning more about three additional key features: functions, objects, and flow control.

Q&A

Q. What is the importance of the `var` keyword? Should I always use it to declare variables?

A. You only need to use `var` to define a local variable in a function. However, if you're unsure at all, it's always safe to use `var`. Using it consistently will help you keep your scripts organized and error free.

Q. Is there any reason I would want to use the `var` keyword to create a local variable with the same name as a global one?

A. Not on purpose. The main reason to use `var` is to avoid conflicts with global variables you might not know about. For example, you might add a global variable in the future, or you might add another script to the page that uses a similar variable name. This is more of an issue with large, complex scripts.

Q. What good are Boolean variables?

A. Often in scripts you'll need a variable to indicate whether something has happened—for example, whether a phone number the user has entered is in the right format. Boolean variables are ideal for this; they're also useful in working with conditions, as you'll see in Chapter 8.

Q. Can I store other types of data in an array? For example, can I have an array of dates?

A. Absolutely. JavaScript enables you to store any data type in an array.

Q. What about two-dimensional arrays?

A. These are arrays with two indexes (such as columns and rows). JavaScript does not directly support this type of array, but you can use objects to store more complex data.

Workshop

The Workshop contains quiz questions and exercises to help you solidify your understanding of the material covered. Try to answer all questions before looking at the "Answers" section that follows.

Quiz

1. Which of the following is *not* a valid JavaScript variable name?

   A. `2names`

   B. `first_and_last_names`

   C. `FirstAndLast`

2. If the statement `var fig=2` appears in a function, which type of variable does it declare?

    A. A global variable

    B. A local variable

    C. A constant variable

3. If the string `test` contains the value `The eagle has landed.`, what would be the value of `test.length`?

    A. `4`

    B. `21`

    C. `The`

4. Using the same sample string, which of these statements would return the word `eagle`?

    A. `test.substring(4,9)`

    B. `test.substring(5,9)`

    C. `test.substring("eagle")`

5. What will be the result of the JavaScript expression `31 + " angry polar bears"`?

    A. An error message

    B. 32

    C. "31 angry polar bears"

Answers

1. A. `2names` is an invalid JavaScript variable name because it begins with a number. The others are valid, although they're probably not ideal choices for names.

2. B. Because the variable is declared in a function, it is a local variable. The `var` keyword ensures that a local variable is created.

3. B. The length of the string is 21 characters.

4. A. The correct statement is `test.substring(4,9)`. Remember that the indexes start with `0` and that the second index is noninclusive.

5. C. JavaScript converts the whole expression to the string `"31 angry polar bears"`. (No offense to polar bears, who are seldom angry and rarely seen in groups this large.)

Exercises

▶ Modify the sorting example in Listing 7.3 to convert the names to all uppercase before sorting and displaying them.

▶ Modify Listing 7.3 to display a numbered list of names in the textarea.

CHAPTER 8

JavaScript Fundamentals: Functions, Objects, and Flow Control

---

What You'll Learn in This Chapter:

- ▶ How to define, call, and return values from functions
- ▶ How to define custom objects
- ▶ How to use object properties and values
- ▶ How to define and use object methods
- ▶ How to use objects to store data and related functions
- ▶ How to use the `Math` object's methods
- ▶ How to use `with` to work with objects
- ▶ How to use the `Date` object to work with dates
- ▶ How to test conditions with the `if` statement
- ▶ How to use comparison operators to compare values
- ▶ How to use logical operators to combine conditions
- ▶ How to use alternative conditions with `else`
- ▶ How to create expressions with conditional operators
- ▶ How to test for multiple conditions
- ▶ How to perform repeated statements with the `for` loop
- ▶ How to use `while` and `do...while` loops
- ▶ How to create infinite loops (and why you shouldn't)
- ▶ How to escape from loops and continue loops
- ▶ How to loop through object properties

In this chapter, you'll learn about several key JavaScript concepts that you'll use in your future JavaScript endeavors. First, you'll learn the details of creating and using functions, which enable you to group any number of statements into a single block. Functions are useful for creating reusable sections of code, and you can create functions that accept parameters and return values for later use.

Whereas functions enable you to group sections of code, objects enable you to group data—you can use objects to combine related data items and functions for working with the data. You'll learn how to define and use objects and their methods, and you'll work specifically with two more useful objects built in to JavaScript: `Math` and `Date`.

Finally, you'll learn about flow control. Statements in a JavaScript program generally execute in the order in which they appear, one after the other. Because this order isn't always practical, most programming languages provide *flow control* statements that let you control the order in which code is executed. Functions are one type of flow control—although a function might be defined first in your code, its statements can be executed anywhere in the script. You'll look at two other types of flow control in JavaScript: conditions, which allow a choice of different options depending on values that are tested, and loops, which allow statements to repeat based on certain conditions.

Using Functions

The JavaScript scripts you've seen so far in this book have generally been simple lists of instructions. The browser begins with the first statement after the `<script>` tag and follows each instruction in order until it reaches the closing `</script>` tag (or encounters an error).

Although this is a straightforward approach for short scripts, it can be confusing to read a longer script written in this fashion. To make it easier for you to organize your scripts, JavaScript supports functions. In this section, you will learn how to define and use functions.

Defining a Function

Functions are groups of JavaScript statements that can be treated as a single unit. To use a function, you must first define it. Here is a simple example of a function definition:

```
function greet() {
    alert("Greetings!");
}
```

This snippet defines a function that displays an alert message to the user. This begins with the `function` keyword followed by the name you're giving to the function—in this case, the function's name is `greet`. Notice the parentheses after the function's name. As you'll learn in short order, the space between them is not always empty as it is here.

The first and last lines of the function include curly braces (that is, { and }). You use these curly braces to enclose all the statements within the function. The browser uses the curly braces to determine where the function begins and ends.

Between the braces is the core JavaScript code of the function. This particular function contains a single line that invokes the JavaScript `alert` method, which displays an alert message to the user. The message contains the text "Greetings!"

CAUTION

Function names are case sensitive. If you define a function such as greet with a lowercase letter, be sure you use the identical name when you call the function. That is to say, if you define the function with the name greet but you attempt to call the function using Greet, it will not work.

Now, about those parentheses. The greet function shown earlier always does the same thing: Each time you use it, it displays the same message in the alert pop-up window.

To make this (or any) function more flexible, you can add *parameters*. These are variables that are received by the function each time it is called. For example, you can add a parameter called who that tells the function the name of the person to greet, based on the value of that parameter, called the *argument*, when the function is called. Here is the modified greet function:

```
function greet(who) {
    alert("Greetings, " + who + "!");
}
```

To call this function and see its behavior in action, you need to include it in an HTML document. Traditionally, the best place for a function definition is within the <head> section of the document. Because the statements in the <head> section are executed first, this ensures that the function is defined before it is used.

Listing 8.1 shows the greet function embedded in the header section of an HTML document, but not yet called into action.

LISTING 8.1   The greet Function in an HTML Document

```
<!DOCTYPE html>

<html lang="en">
  <head>
    <title>Functions</title>
    <script type="text/javascript">
    function greet(who) {
        alert("Greetings, " + who + "!");
    }
    </script>
  </head>
  <body>
    <p>This is the body of the page.</p>
  </body>
</html>
```

Calling the Function

You have now defined a function and placed it in an HTML document. However, if you load Listing 8.1 into a browser, you'll notice that it does absolutely nothing besides display the text "This is the body of the page." This lack of action is because the function is defined—ready to be used—but we haven't used it yet.

Making use of a function is referred to as *calling* the function. To call a function, use the function's name as a statement in a script or as an action associated with an event. To call a function, you need to include the parentheses and the values for the function's parameters, if any. For example, here's a statement that calls the `greet` function:

```
greet("Fred");
```

This tells the JavaScript interpreter to go ahead and start processing the first statement in the `greet` function. Calling the function in this manner, with an argument within the parentheses, passes the value of `"Fred"` to the function. This value of `"Fred"` is then assigned to the `who` variable inside the function.

TIP

Functions can have more than one parameter. To define a function with multiple parameters, list a variable name for each parameter, separated by commas. To call the function, specify values for each parameter separated by commas.

Listing 8.2 shows a complete HTML document that includes the function definition and a few buttons within the page that call the function as an action associated with an event. To demonstrate the usefulness of functions, we'll call it twice to greet two different people—using two different parameters.

LISTING 8.2   The Complete Function Example

```
<!DOCTYPE html>

<html lang="en">
  <head>
    <title>Functions</title>
    <script type="text/javascript">
    function greet(who) {
        alert("Greetings, " + who + "!");
    }
    </script>
  </head>
  <body>
    <h1>Function Example</h1>
    <p>Who are you?</p>
```

```
    <button type="button" onclick="greet('Fred');">I am Fred</button>
    <button type="button" onclick="greet('Ethel');">I am Ethel</button>
  </body>
</html>
```

This listing includes two buttons, each of which calls the greet function a bit differently—with a different parameter associated with the call from each button.

Now that you have a script that actually does something, try loading it into a browser. If you click one of the buttons, you should see something like the screen in Figure 8.1, which shows the alert that appears when one of the buttons is clicked (I am Ethel, in this case).

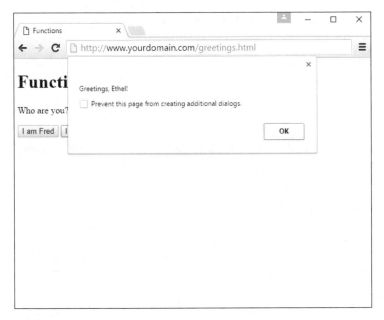

FIGURE 8.1
The output of the greet function example, with one button clicked.

Returning a Value

The function you created in the preceding example displays a message to the user in an alert pop-up, but functions can also return a value to the script that called them. This enables you to use functions to calculate values. As an example, let's create a function that averages four numbers.

As usual, your function should begin with the function keyword, the function's name, and the parameters it accepts. We will use the variable names a, b, c, and d for the four numbers to average. Here is the first line of the function:

```
function average(a,b,c,d) {
```

NOTE

I've also included the opening brace ({) on the first line of the function. This is a common style, but you can also place the brace on the next line or on a line by itself.

Next, the function needs to calculate the average of the four parameters. You can calculate this by adding them and then dividing by the number of parameters (in this case, 4). Thus, here is the next line of the function:

```
var result = (a + b + c + d) / 4;
```

This statement creates a variable called `result` and calculates the value assigned to `result` by adding the four numbers and then dividing by 4. (The parentheses are necessary to tell JavaScript to be absolutely sure to perform the addition before the division.)

To send this result back to the script that called the function, you use the `return` keyword. Here is the last part of the function:

```
return result;
}
```

Listing 8.3 shows the complete `average` function in an HTML document. This HTML document also includes a small script in the `<body>` section that calls the `average` function and displays the result.

LISTING 8.3   The `average` Function in an HTML Document

```
<!DOCTYPE html>

<html lang="en">
  <head>
    <title>Function Example: Average</title>
    <script type="text/javascript">
    function average(a,b,c,d)  {
        var result = (a + b + c + d) / 4;
        return result;
    }
    </script>
  </head>
  <body>
    <h1>Function Example: Average</h1>
    <p>The following is the result of the function call.</p>
    <script type="text/javascript">
    var score = average(3,4,5,6);
    document.write("The average is: " + score);
    </script>
  </body>
</html>
```

If you open the script in Listing 8.3 in your web browser, you will see something like the result displayed in Figure 8.2, which shows the average printed on the screen, courtesy of the `document.write` method.

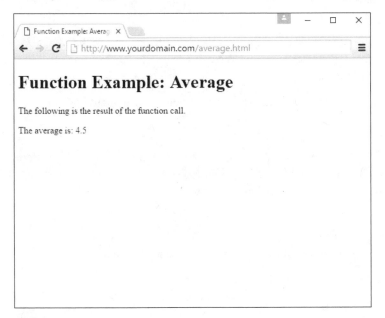

FIGURE 8.2
The output of the `average` function example.

You can use a variable with the function call, as shown in this listing. This statement averages the numbers 3, 4, 5, and 6 and stores the result in a variable called `score`:

```
var score = average(3,4,5,6);
```

TIP

You can also use the function call directly in an expression. For example, you could use the `alert` statement to display the result of the function `alert(average(1,2,3,4))`.

Introducing Objects

In the preceding chapter, you learned how to use variables to represent different kinds of data in JavaScript. JavaScript also supports *objects*, or data structures that can store multiple data items and functions; objects were mentioned briefly in that chapter as well. Whereas a variable can have only one value at a time, an object can contain multiple values, which enables you to group related data items into a single object.

In this chapter, you'll learn how to define and use your own objects. You've already worked with some of them, including the following:

- ▶ **DOM objects**—These objects enable your scripts to interact with elements of the web browser and web documents. You learned about these in Chapter 6, "Understanding Dynamic Websites and HTML5 Applications."

- ▶ **Built-in objects**—These include strings and arrays, which you learned about in Chapter 7, "JavaScript Fundamentals: Variables, Strings, and Arrays."

The syntax for working with all three types of objects—DOM objects, built-in objects, and custom objects—is the same, so even if you don't end up creating your own objects, you should have a good understanding of JavaScript's object terminology and syntax.

Creating Objects

When you created an array in the preceding chapter, you used the following JavaScript statement:

```
var scores = new Array(4);
```

The new keyword tells the JavaScript interpreter to use built-in functionality to create an object of the Array type. Objects have one or more *properties*—essentially, properties are variables, with values, that are stored within the object. For example, in Chapter 6, you learned you can use the location.href property to give you the URL of the current document because the value (the URL) is assigned to that property, just as a value is assigned to a variable. The href property is one of the properties of the location object in the DOM.

You've also used the length property of String objects, as in the following example from the preceding chapter:

```
var stringtest = "This is a test.";
document.write(stringtest.length);
```

To reiterate, as with variables, each object property has a *value*. To read a property's value, you simply reference the object name and property name, separated by a period, in any expression—the example you just saw uses stringtest.length. You can change a property's value using the = operator, just as you can change the assignment of a value to a variable. The following example sends the browser to a new URL by assigning a new variable to the location.href property:

```
location.href = "http://www.google.com";
```

Understanding Methods

Along with properties, each object can have one or more *methods*. These are functions that work with the object's data. For example, the following JavaScript statement reloads the current document, as you learned in Chapter 6:

```
location.reload();
```

When you use the `reload()` method, you're using a method of the `location` object. Like other functions, methods can accept arguments in parentheses and can return values. Each object type in JavaScript has its own list of built-in methods. For example, a list of built-in methods for the `Array` object can be found at https://developer.mozilla.org/en-US/docs/Web/JavaScript/ Reference/Global_Objects/Array/prototype#Methods.

Using Objects to Simplify Scripting

Although JavaScript's variables and arrays are versatile ways to store data, sometimes you need a more complicated structure, which is when objects are useful. For example, suppose you are creating a script to work with a business card database that contains names, addresses, and phone numbers for various people.

If you were using regular variables, you would need several separate variables for each person in the database: a name variable, an address variable, and so on. This would be very confusing, not to mention quite lengthy to define.

Arrays would improve things, but only slightly. You could have a names array, an addresses array, and a phone number array. Each person in the database would have an entry in each array. This would be more convenient than many, many individually named variables, but still not perfect.

With objects, you can make the variables that store the database as logical as the physical business cards they are supposed to represent. Each person could be represented by a new `Card` object, which would contain properties for name, address, and phone number. You can even add methods to the object to display or work with the information, which is where the real power of using objects comes into play.

In the following sections, you'll use JavaScript to create a `Card` object and some properties and methods. Later in this chapter, you'll use the `Card` object in a script that will be used to display information for several members of this data store you've created through the use of objects.

Defining an Object

The first step in creating an object is to name it and its properties. We've already decided to call the object a `Card` object. Each object will have the following properties:

- name

- email

- address

- phone

The first step in using this object in a JavaScript program is to create a function to make new `Card` objects. This function is called the *constructor* for an object. Here is the constructor function for the `Card` object:

```
function Card(name,email,address,phone) {
    this.name = name;
    this.email = email;
    this.address = address;
    this.phone = phone;
}
```

The constructor is a simple function that accepts parameters to initialize a new object and assigns them to the corresponding properties. You can think of it like setting up a template for the object. The `Card` function in particular accepts several parameters from any statement that calls the function, and then it assigns these parameters as properties of an object. Because the function is called `Card`, the object created is a `Card` object.

Notice the `this` keyword. You'll use it any time you create an object definition. Use `this` to refer to the current object—the one that is being created by the function.

Defining an Object Method

Next, you will create a method to work with the `Card` object. Because all `Card` objects will have the same properties, it might be handy to have a function that prints the properties in a neat format. Let's call this function `printCard`.

Your `printCard` function will be used as a method for `Card` objects, so you don't need to ask for parameters. Instead, you can use the `this` keyword again to refer to the current object's properties. Here is a function definition for the `printCard()` function:

```
function printCard() {
    var name_line = "Name: " + this.name + "<br/>\n";
    var email_line = "Email: " + this.email + "<br/>\n";
    var address_line = "Address: " + this.address + "<br/>\n";
    var phone_line = "Phone: " + this.phone + "<hr/>\n";
    document.write(name_line, email_line, address_line, phone_line);
}
```

This function simply reads the properties from the current object (`this`), prints each one with a label string before it, and then creates a new line.

You now have a function that prints a card, but it isn't officially a method of the `Card` object. The last thing you need to do is make `printCard` part of the function definition for `Card` objects. Here is the modified function definition:

```
function Card(name,email,address,phone) {
    this.name = name;
    this.email = email;
    this.address = address;
    this.phone = phone;
    this.printCard = printCard;
}
```

The added statement looks just like another property definition, but it refers to the `printCard` function. This new method will now work so long as `printCard` has its own function definition elsewhere in your script. Methods are essentially properties that define a function rather than a simple value.

TIP

The previous example uses lowercase names such as `address` for properties and a mixed-case name (`printCard`) for the method. You can use any case for property and method names, but this is one way to make it clear that `printCard` is a method rather than an ordinary property.

Creating an Object Instance

Now let's use the object definition and method you just created. To use an object definition, you create a new object using the `new` keyword. This is the same keyword you've already used to create `Date` and `Array` objects.

The following statement creates a new `Card` object called `tom`:

```
var tom = new Card("Tom Jones", "tom@jones.com",
            "123 Elm Street, Sometown ST 77777",
            "555-555-9876");
```

As you can see, creating an object is easy. All you do is call the `Card()` function (the object definition) and enter the required attributes in the same order as you defined originally (in this case, the parameters: name, email, address, phone).

After this statement executes, you will have a new object to hold Tom's information. This new object, now named `tom`, is called an *instance* of the `Card` object. Just as there can be several string variables in a program, there can be several instances of an object you define.

Rather than specifying all the information for a card with the new keyword, you can assign the data after the fact. For example, the following script creates an empty Card object called holmes and then assigns its properties:

```
var holmes = new Card();
holmes.name = "Sherlock Holmes";
holmes.email = "sherlock@holmes.com";
holmes.address = "221B Baker Street";
holmes.phone = "555-555-3456";
```

After you've created an instance of the Card object using either of these methods, you can use the printCard() method to display its information. For example, this statement displays the properties of the tom card:

```
tom.printCard();
```

▼ TRY IT YOURSELF

Storing Data in Objects

Now you've created a new object to store business cards and a method to print them. As a final demonstration of objects, properties, functions, and methods, you will now use this object in a web page to display data for several cards.

Your script will need to include the function definition for printCard, along with the function definition for the Card object. You will then create three cards and print them in the body of the document. We will use separate HTML and JavaScript files for this example. Listing 8.4 shows the complete script.

LISTING 8.4   A Sample Script that Uses the Card Object

```
// define the functions
function printCard() {
    var nameLine = "<strong>Name: </strong>" + this.name + "<br>";
    var emailLine = "<strong>Email: </strong>" + this.email + "<br>";
    var addressLine = "<strong>Address: </strong>" + this.address + "<br>";
    var phoneLine = "<strong>Phone: </strong>" + this.phone + "<hr>";
    document.write(nameLine, emailLine, addressLine, phoneLine);
}

function Card(name,email,address,phone) {
    this.name = name;
    this.email = email;
    this.address = address;
    this.phone = phone;
    this.printCard = printCard;
}
```

```
// Create the objects
var sue = new Card("Sue Suthers", "sue@suthers.com", "123 Elm Street,
        Yourtown ST 99999", "555-555-9876");
var fred = new Card("Fred Fanboy", "fred@fanboy.com", "233 Oak Lane,
        Sometown ST 99399", "555-555-4444");
var jimbo = new Card("Jimbo Jones", "jimbo@jones.com", "233 Walnut Circle,
        Anotherville ST 88999", "555-555-1344");

// Now print them
sue.printCard();
fred.printCard();
jimbo.printCard();
```

Notice that the `printCard()` function has been modified slightly to make things look good with the labels in boldface. To prepare to use this script, save it as `cards.js`. Next, you'll need to include the `cards.js` script in a simple HTML document. Listing 8.5 shows the HTML document for this example.

LISTING 8.5 The HTML File for the `Card` Object Example

```
<!DOCTYPE html>

<html lang="en">
  <head>
    <title>JavaScript Business Cards</title>
  </head>
  <body>
    <h1>JavaScript Business Cards</h1>
    <p>External script output coming up...</p>
    <script type="text/javascript" src="cards.js"></script>
    <p>External script output has ended.</p>
  </body>
</html>
```

To test the complete script, save this HTML document in the same directory as the `cards.js` file you created earlier and then load the HTML document into a browser. The browser's display of this example is shown in Figure 8.3.

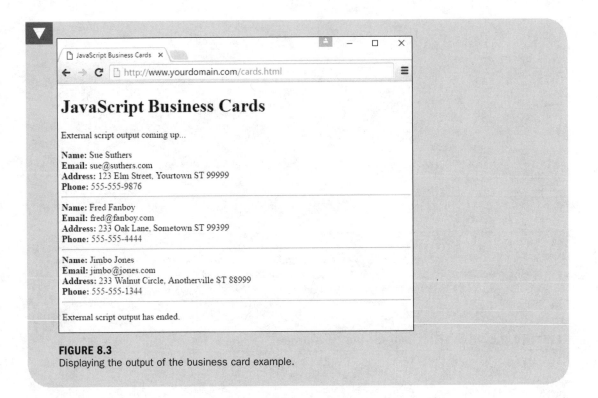

FIGURE 8.3
Displaying the output of the business card example.

Extending Built-in Objects

JavaScript includes a feature that enables you to extend the definitions of built-in objects. For example, if you think the String object doesn't quite fit your needs, you can extend it by adding a new property or method. This might be very useful if you are creating a large script that uses many strings and manipulates those strings in unique ways, but you should use this sparingly and only if you have a really good reason.

You can add both properties and methods to an existing object by using the prototype keyword. (A *prototype* is another name for an object's definition, or constructor function.) The prototype keyword enables you to change the definition of an object outside its constructor function.

As an example, let's add a method to the String object definition. You will create a method called heading, which converts a string into an HTML heading. The following statement defines a string called myTitle:

```
var myTitle = "Fred's Home Page";
```

This statement would output the contents of the `myTitle` string as an HTML level 1 heading:

```
document.write(myTitle.heading(1));
```

Listing 8.6 adds a `heading` method to the `String` object definition that will display the string as a heading, and then it displays three headings using the new method.

LISTING 8.6   Adding a Method to the `String` Object

```
<!DOCTYPE html>

<html lang="en">
  <head>
    <title>Test of Heading Method</title>
  </head>
  <body>
    <script type="text/javascript">
    function addHeading(level) {
       var html = "h" + level;
       var text = this.toString();
       var opentag = "<" + html + ">";
       var closetag = "</" + html + ">";
       return opentag + text + closetag;
    }
    String.prototype.heading = addHeading;
    document.write("This is a heading 1".heading(1));
    document.write("This is a heading 2".heading(2));
    document.write("This is a heading 3".heading(3));
    </script>
  </body>
</html>
```

First, you define the `addHeading()` function, which will serve as the new string method. It accepts a number to specify the heading level. The `opentag` and `closetag` variables are used to store the HTML "begin heading tag" and "end heading tag" tags, such as `<h1>` and `</h1>`.

After the function is defined, use the `prototype` keyword to add it as a method of the `String` object. You can then use this method on any `String` object or, in fact, any JavaScript string. This is demonstrated by the last three statements, which display quoted text strings as level 1, 2, and 3 headings.

If you load this document into a browser, it should look something like what's shown in Figure 8.4.

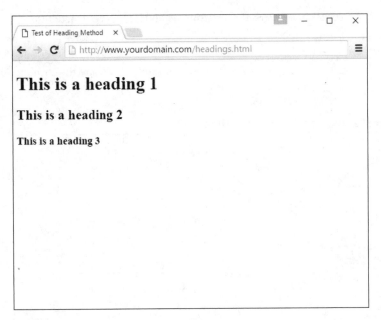

FIGURE 8.4
Displaying the dynamic heading example.

Using the Math Object

The Math object is a built-in JavaScript object that includes math constants and functions. You'll never need to create a Math object because it exists automatically in any JavaScript program. The Math object's properties represent mathematical constants, and its methods are mathematical functions. If you're working with numbers in any way in your JavaScript, the Math object will be your new best friend.

Rounding and Truncating

Three of the most useful methods of the Math object enable you to round decimal values up and down:

- ▶ Math.ceil() rounds a number up to the next integer.

- ▶ Math.floor() rounds a number down to the next integer.

- ▶ Math.round() rounds a number to the nearest integer.

All of these methods take the number to be rounded as their only parameter. You might notice one thing missing: the capability to round to a decimal place, such as for dollar amounts.

Fortunately, you can easily simulate this, as is shown in this simple function that rounds numbers to two decimal places:

```
function round(num) {
    return Math.round(num * 100) / 100;
}
```

The function shown here multiplies the value by 100 to move the decimal and then rounds the number to the nearest integer. Finally, the value is divided by 100 to restore the decimal to its original position.

Generating Random Numbers

One of the most commonly used methods of the Math object is the Math.random() method, which generates a random number. This method doesn't require any parameters. The number it returns is a random decimal number between 0 and 1.

You'll usually want a random number between 1 and some predetermined value. You can do this with a general-purpose random number function. The following function generates random numbers between 1 and the parameter you send it:

```
function rand(num) {
    return Math.floor(Math.random() * num) + 1;
}
```

This function multiplies a random number by the value specified in the num parameter and then converts it to an integer between 1 and the number by using the Math.floor() method.

Other Math Methods

The Math object includes many methods beyond those you've looked at here. For example, Math.sin() and Math.cos() calculate sines and cosines. The Math object also includes properties for various mathematical constants, such as Math.PI. You can see a list of all the built-in methods you can use with the Math object at https://developer.mozilla.org/en-US/docs/Web/JavaScript/Reference/Global_Objects/Math#Methods.

Working with Math Methods

The Math.random method generates a random number between 0 and 1. However, it's very difficult for a computer to generate a truly random number. (It's also hard for a human being to do so—that's why dice were invented.) Today's computers do reasonably well at generating random numbers, but just how good is JavaScript's Math.random function? One way to test it is to generate many random numbers and calculate the average of all of them.

In theory, the average of all generated numbers should be somewhere near 0.5, or halfway between 0 and 1. The more random values you generate, the closer the average should get to this middle ground. To really do this test, let's create a script that tests JavaScript's random number function by generating 5,000 random numbers and calculating their average.

This example will use a `for` loop, which you'll learn more about in the next chapter, but this is a simple enough example that you should be able to follow along. In this case, the `for` loop will generate the random numbers. You may be surprised how fast JavaScript can do this.

To begin your script, initialize a variable called `total`. This variable will store a running total of all the random values, so it's important that it starts at 0:

```
var total = 0;
```

Next, begin a loop that will execute 5,000 times. Use a `for` loop because you want it to execute for a fixed number of times (in this case, 5,000):

```
for (i=0; i<=5000; i++) {
```

Within the `for` loop, you will need to create a random number and add its value to the `total` variable. Here are the statements that do this and continue with the next iteration of the loop:

```
    var num = Math.random();
    total += num;
}
```

Depending on the speed of your computer, it might take a few seconds to generate those 5,000 random numbers. Just to be sure something is happening, let's have the script display a status message after each 1,000 numbers:

```
if (i % 1000 == 0) {
    document.write("Generated " + i + " numbers...<br>");
}
```

NOTE

The % symbol in the previous code is the *modulo operator*, which gives you the remainder after dividing one number by another. Here it is used to find even multiples of 1,000.

The final part of your script will calculate the average by dividing the value of the `total` variable by 5,000. Let's also round the average to three decimal places, for fun:

```
var average = total / 5000;
average = Math.round(average * 1000) / 1000;
document.write("<p>Average of 5000 numbers is: " + average + "</p>");
```

To test this script and see just how random those numbers are, combine the complete script with an HTML document and `<script>` tags. Listing 8.7 shows the complete random number testing script.

LISTING 8.7   A Script to Test JavaScript's Random Number Function

```
<!DOCTYPE html>

<html lang="en">
  <head>
    <title>Math Example</title>
  </head>
  <body>
    <h1>Math Example</h1>
    <p>How random are JavaScript's random numbers?<br>
    Let's generate 5000 of them and find out.</p>

    <script type="text/javascript">
    var total = 0;
    for (i=0; i<=5000; i++) {
      var num = Math.random();
      total += num;
      if (i % 1000 == 0) {
         document.write("Generated " + i + " numbers...<br>");
       }
    }
    var average = total / 5000;
    average = Math.round(average * 1000) / 1000;
    document.write("<p>Average of 5000 numbers is: " + average + "</p>");
    </script>

  </body>
</html>
```

To test the script, load the HTML document into a browser. After a short delay, you should see a result. If it's close to 0.5, the numbers are reasonably random. My result was 0.501, as shown in Figure 8.5. If you reload the page, you'll likely get different results, but they should all be around 0.5.

NOTE

The average you've used here is called an *arithmetic mean*. This type of average isn't a perfect way to test randomness. Actually, all it tests is the distribution of the numbers above and below 0.5. For example, if the numbers turned out to be 2,500 0.4's and 2,500 0.6's, the average would be a perfect 0.5—but they wouldn't be very random numbers. (Thankfully, JavaScript's random numbers don't have this problem.)

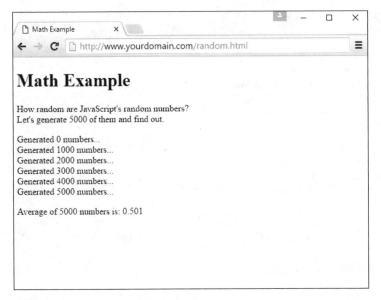

FIGURE 8.5
The random number testing script in action.

Working with Dates

The `Date` object is a built-in JavaScript object that enables you to work more easily with dates and times. You can create a `Date` object any time you need to store a date, and you can use the `Date` object's methods to work with the date. The `Date` object has no properties of its own. To set or obtain values from a `Date` object, use the methods described in the next section.

NOTE

JavaScript dates are stored as the number of milliseconds since midnight, January 1, 1970. This date is called the *epoch*. Dates before 1970 weren't allowed in early versions but are now represented by negative numbers.

Creating a `Date` Object

You can create a `Date` object using the `new` keyword. You can also optionally specify the date to store in the object when you create it. You can use any of the following formats:

```
birthday = new Date();
birthday = new Date("April 8, 2017 08:00:00");
birthday = new Date(4,8, 2017);
birthday = new Date(4,8,2017, 8, 0, 0);
```

You can choose any of these formats, depending on which values you want to set. If you use no parameters, as in the first example, the current date is stored in the object. You can then set the values using the set methods, described in the next section.

Setting Date Values

Various set methods enable you to set components of a Date object to values:

- ▶ setDate() sets the day of the month.

- ▶ setMonth() sets the month. JavaScript numbers the months from 0 to 11, starting with January (0).

- ▶ setFullYear() sets the year.

- ▶ setTime() sets the time (and the date) by specifying the number of milliseconds since January 1, 1970.

- ▶ setHours(), setMinutes(), and setSeconds() set the time.

As an example, the following statement sets the year of a Date object called holiday to 2017:

```
holiday.setFullYear(2017);
```

Reading Date Values

You can use the get methods to get values from a Date object. This is the only way to obtain these values because they are not available as properties. Here are the available get methods for dates:

- ▶ getDate() gets the day of the month.

- ▶ getMonth() gets the month.

- ▶ getFullYear() gets the year.

- ▶ getTime() gets the time (and the date) as the number of milliseconds since January 1, 1970.

- ▶ getHours(), getMinutes(), getSeconds(), and getMilliseconds() get the components of the time.

NOTE

Along with setFullYear and getFullYear, which require four-digit years, JavaScript includes setYear and getYear methods, which use two-digit year values.

Working with Time Zones

Finally, a few functions are available to help your `Date` objects work with local time values and time zones:

- ▶ The `getTimeZoneOffset()` function gives you the local time zone's offset from UTC (Coordinated Universal Time, based on the old Greenwich Mean Time standard). In this case, *local* refers to the location of the browser. (Of course, this works only if the user has set his or her system clock accurately.)

- ▶ The `toUTCString()` function converts the `date` object's time value to text, using UTC.

- ▶ The `toLocalString()` function converts the `date` object's time value to text, using local time.

Along with these basic functions, JavaScript includes UTC versions of several of the functions described previously. These are identical to the regular commands, but they work with UTC instead of local time:

- ▶ The `getUTCDate()` function gets the day of the month in UTC time.

- ▶ The `getUTCDay()` function gets the day of the week in UTC time.

- ▶ The `getUTCFullYear()` function gets the four-digit year in UTC time.

- ▶ The `getUTCMonth()` function returns the month of the year in UTC time.

- ▶ The `getUTCHours()`, `getUTCMinutes()`, `getUTCSeconds()`, and `getUTCMilliseconds()` functions return the components of the time in UTC.

- ▶ The `setUTCDate()`, `setUTCFullYear()`, `setUTCMonth()`, `setUTCHours()`, `setUTCMinutes()`, `setUTCSeconds()`, and `setUTCMilliseconds()` functions set the time in UTC.

Converting Between Date Formats

Two special methods of the `Date` object enable you to convert between date formats. Instead of using these methods with a `Date` object you created, you use them with the built-in object `Date` itself. These include the following:

- ▶ The `Date.parse()` method converts a date string, such as `April 8, 2017`, to a `Date` object (number of milliseconds since 1/1/1970).

- ▶ The `Date.UTC()` method does the opposite. It converts a `Date` object value (number of milliseconds) to a UTC (GMT) time.

The `if` **Statement**

No matter if you're using functions, built-in objects, or objects of your own creation, one of the most important features of any computer language is the capability to flow through a series of statements that might change based on the values of variables or input from the user. An example of flow control is the use of the `if` statement.

The `if` statement is the main conditional statement in JavaScript. This statement means much the same in JavaScript as it does in English—for example, here is a typical conditional statement in English:

If the phone rings, answer it.

This statement consists of two parts: a condition (*If the phone rings*) and an action (*answer it*). The `if` statement in JavaScript works much the same way. Here is an example of a basic `if` statement:

```
if (a == 1) alert("I found a 1!");
```

This statement includes a condition (if a equals 1) and an action (display a message). This statement checks the variable a and, if it has a value of 1, displays an alert message. Otherwise, it does nothing.

If you use an `if` statement like the preceding example (that is, all on one line), you can use only a single statement as the action. However, you can also use multiple statements for the action by enclosing the entire `if` statement in curly braces ({ }), as shown here:

```
if (a == 1) {
    alert("I found a 1!");
    a = 0;
}
```

This block of statements checks the variable a once again. If the value of the variable matches 1, it displays a message and sets a back to 0.

It's up to you, as a matter of personal style, whether you use the curly braces for single statements within flow control structures. Some people (such as me) find it easier to read if all the flow control structures are clearly delineated through the use of curly braces no matter their length, and other developers are perfectly happy using a mix of single-line conditional statements and statements within braces. It doesn't really matter which you use; just try to use them consistently for easier ongoing maintenance, and follow any practices dictated by your team or project.

Conditional Operators

The action part of an `if` statement can include any JavaScript statement, but the condition part of the statement uses its own syntax. This is called a *conditional expression*.

A conditional expression usually includes two values to be compared (in the preceding example, the values were a and 1). These values can be variables, constants, or even expressions in themselves.

NOTE

Either side of the conditional expression can be a variable, a constant, or an expression. You can compare a variable and a value, or two variables. (You can also compare two constants, but there's usually no reason to.)

Between the two values to be compared is a *conditional operator*. This operator tells JavaScript how to compare the two values. For instance, the == operator that you saw in the preceding section is used to test whether the two values are equal.

Various conditional operators are available:

- ==—Is equal to
- !=—Is not equal to
- <—Is less than
- >—Is greater than
- >=—Is greater than or equal to
- <=—Is less than or equal to
- ===—Is equal to, both in value and type

CAUTION

Be sure not to confuse the equality operator (==) with the assignment operator (=), even though they both might be read or referred to as "equals." Remember to use = when *assigning* a value to a variable, and use == when *comparing* values. Confusing these two is one of the most common mistakes in programming (JavaScript or otherwise).

Combining Conditions with Logical Operators

Often, you'll want to check a variable for more than one possible value, or check more than one variable at once. JavaScript includes *logical operators*, also known as Boolean operators, for this purpose. For example, the following two statements check different conditions and use the same action:

```
if (phone == "") alert("error!");
if (email == "") alert("error!");
```

Using a logical operator, you can combine them into a single statement:

```
if ((phone == "") || (email == "")) alert("Something Is Missing!");
```

This statement uses the logical Or operator (||) to combine the conditions. Translated into English, this would be, "If the phone number is blank or the email address is blank, display an error message."

An additional logical operator is the And operator, &&. Consider this statement:

```
if ((phone == "") && (email == "")) alert("Both Values Are Missing!");
```

In this case, the error message will be displayed only if *both* the email address and phone number variables are blank.

TIP

If the JavaScript interpreter discovers the answer to a conditional expression before reaching the end, it does not evaluate the rest of the condition. For example, if the first of two conditions separated by the || operator is true, the second is not evaluated because the condition (one or the other) has already been met. You can take advantage of operators to improve the speed of your scripts.

A third logical operator is the exclamation mark (!), which means Not. It can be used to invert an expression—in other words, a true expression would become false, and a false one would become true. For example, here's a statement that uses the Not operator:

```
if (!phone == "") alert("phone is OK");
```

In this statement, the ! (Not) operator inverts the condition, so the action of the if statement is executed only if the phone number variable is *not* blank. You could also use the != (Not equal) operator to simplify this statement:

```
if (phone != "") alert("phone is OK");
```

Both of the preceding statements will alert you if the phone variable has a value assigned to it (if is not blank, or null).

TIP

Logical operators are powerful, but it's easy to accidentally create an impossible condition with them. For example, the condition ((a < 10) && (a > 20)) might look correct at first glance. However, if you read it out loud, you get "If a is less than 10 and a is greater than 20"—an impossibility in our universe. In this case, Or (||) should have been used to make a meaningful condition.

The `else` Keyword

An additional feature of the `if` statement is the `else` keyword. Much like its English-language counterpart, `else` tells the JavaScript interpreter what to do if the condition in the `if` statement isn't met. The following is a simple example of the `else` keyword in action:

```
if (a == 1) {
   alert("Found a 1!");
   a = 0;
} else {
   alert("Incorrect value: " + a);
}
```

This snippet displays a message and resets the variable a if the condition is met. If the condition is *not* met (if a is not 1), a different message is displayed courtesy of the `else` statement.

NOTE

Like the `if` statement, `else` can be followed either by a single action statement or by a number of statements enclosed in braces.

Using Shorthand Conditional Expressions

In addition to the `if` statement, JavaScript provides a shorthand type of conditional expression that you can use to make quick decisions. This uses a peculiar syntax that is also found in other languages, such as C. A conditional expression can look like this:

```
variable = (condition) ? (value if true) : (value if false);
```

This construction ends up assigning one of two values to the variable: one value if the condition is true, and another value if it is false. Here is an example of a conditional expression:

```
value = (a == 1) ? 1 : 0;
```

This statement might look confusing, but it is equivalent to the following `if` statement:

```
if (a == 1) {
   value = 1;
} else {
   value = 0;
}
```

In other words, the value directly after the question mark (?) will be used if the condition is true, and the value directly after the colon (:) will be used if the condition is false. The colon and what follows represent the `else` portion of the statement, were it written as an if...else statement, and, like the `else` portion of the `if` statement, it is optional.

These shorthand expressions can be used anywhere JavaScript expects a value. They provide a quick way to make simple decisions about values. As an example, here's a quick way to display a grammatically correct message about a variable:

```
document.write("Found " + counter +
    ((counter == 1) ? " word." : " words."));
```

This prints the message Found 1 word. if the `counter` variable has a value of 1, and Found 2 words. if its value is 2 or greater. You might, in fact, find that conditional expressions are not quicker or easier for you to use, and that is perfectly fine. You should, however, know what they look like and how to read them, should you encounter them in someone else's code in the future.

Testing Multiple Conditions with `if` and `else`

You now have all the pieces necessary to create a script using `if` and `else` statements to control flow. We'll use that knowledge here as you create a script that uses conditions to display a greeting that depends on the time: "Good morning," "Good afternoon," "Good evening," or "Good day." To accomplish this task, you can use a combination of several `if` statements; this is rather verbose to emphasize the logic:

```
if (hour_of_day < 10)  {
    document.write("Good morning.");
}  else if ((hour_of_day >= 14) && (hour_of_day <= 17))  {
    document.write("Good afternoon.");
}  else if (hour_of_day >= 17)  {
    document.write("Good evening.");
}  else {
    document.write("Good day.");
}
```

The first statement checks the hour_of_day variable for a value less than 10—in other words, it checks whether the current time is before 10:00 a.m. If so, it displays the greeting "Good morning."

The second statement checks whether the time is between 2:00 p.m. and 5:00 p.m. and, if so, displays "Good afternoon." This statement uses else if to indicate that this condition will be tested only if the preceding one failed—if it's morning, there's no need to check whether it's afternoon. Similarly, the third statement checks for times after 5:00 p.m. and displays "Good evening."

The final statement uses a simple else, meaning it will be executed if none of the previous conditions matched. This covers the times between 10:00 a.m. and 2:00 p.m. (neglected by the other statements) and displays "Good day."

The HTML File

To try this example in a browser, you'll need an HTML file. We will keep the JavaScript code separate, so Listing 8.8 is the complete HTML file. Save it as `timegreet.html` but don't load it into the browser until you've prepared the JavaScript file in the next section.

LISTING 8.8   The HTML File for the Time and Greeting Example

```html
<!DOCTYPE html>

<html lang="en">
  <head>
    <title>Time Greet Example</title>
  </head>
  <body>
    <h1>Current Date and Time</h1>
    <script type="text/javascript" src="timegreet.js" > </script>
  </body>
</html>
```

The JavaScript File

Listing 8.9 shows the complete JavaScript file for the time-greeting example. This uses the built-in `Date` object functions to find the current date and store it in `hour_of_day`, `minute_of_hour`, and `seconds_of_minute` variables. Next, `document.write` statements display the current time, and the `if` and `else` statements introduced earlier display an appropriate greeting.

LISTING 8.9   A Script to Display the Current Time and a Greeting

```javascript
// Get the current date
now = new Date();

// Delineate hours, minutes, seconds
hour_of_day = now.getHours();
minute_of_hour = now.getMinutes();
seconds_of_minute = now.getSeconds();


// Display the time
document.write("<h2>");
document.write(hour_of_day + ":" + minute_of_hour +
               ":" + seconds_of_minute);
document.write("</h2>");

// Display a greeting
document.write("<p>");
if (hour_of_day < 10) {
```

```
        document.write("Good morning.");
} else if ((hour_of_day >= 14) && (hour_of_day <= 17)) {
        document.write("Good afternoon.");
} else if (hour_of_day >= 17)  {
        document.write("Good evening.");
} else  {
        document.write("Good day.");
}
document.write("</p>");
```

To try this example, save this file as `timegreet.js` and then load the `timegreet.html` file into your browser. Figure 8.6 shows the results of this script.

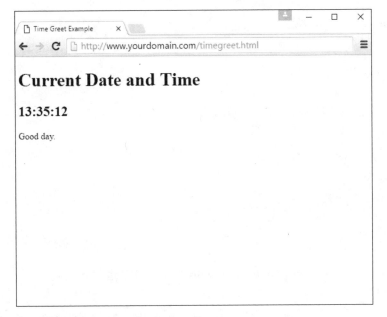

FIGURE 8.6
The output of the time-greeting example.

Using Multiple Conditions with `switch`

In Listing 8.9, you used several `if...else` statements in a row to test for different conditions. Here is another example of this technique:

```
if (button == "next") {
        window.location = "next.html";
} else if (button == "previous") {
        window.location = "previous.html";
```

```
} else if (button == "home") {
    window.location = "home.html";
} else if (button == "back") {
    window.location = "menu.html";
}
```

Although this construction is a logical way of doing things, this method can get messy if each `if` statement has its own block of code with several statements in it. As one alternative, JavaScript includes the `switch` statement, which enables you to combine several tests of the same variable or expression into a single block of statements. The following shows the same example converted to use `switch`:

```
switch (button) {
    case "next":
        window.location = "next.html";
        break;
    case "previous":
        window.location = "previous.html";
        break;
    case "home":
        window.location = "home.html";
        break;
    case "back":
        window.location = "menu.html";
        break;
    default:
        window.alert("Wrong button.");
}
```

The `switch` statement has several components:

▸ The initial `switch` statement. This statement includes the value to test (in this case, `button`) in parentheses.

▸ Braces ({ and }) enclose the contents of the `switch` statement, similar to a function or an `if` statement.

▸ One or more `case` statements. Each of these statements specifies a value to compare with the value specified in the `switch` statement. If the values match, the statements after the `case` statement are executed. Otherwise, the next `case` is tried.

▸ The `break` statement is used to end each case. This skips to the end of the `switch`. If `break` is not included, statements in multiple cases might be executed whether or not they match; always include a `break` to avoid what's known as *fall through*.

▸ Optionally, the `default` case can be included and followed by one or more statements that are executed if none of the other cases was matched.

NOTE

You can use multiple statements after each `case` statement within the `switch` structure, and not just the single-line statements shown here. You don't need to enclose them in braces. If the case matches, the JavaScript interpreter executes statements until it encounters a `break` or the next `case`.

One of the main benefits of using a `switch` statement instead of an `if...else` statement is readability—in one glance you know that all the conditional tests are for the same expression, and therefore you can focus on understanding the desired outcome of the conditional tests. But using a `switch` statement is purely optional—you might find you prefer `if...else` statements, and there's nothing wrong with that. Any efficiency gains in using a `switch` statement instead of an `if...else` statement will not be noticeable to human eyes, if any is even present at all. The bottom line is this: Use what you like.

Using for Loops

The `for` keyword is the first tool to consider for creating loops, much as you saw in the preceding chapter during the random-number example. A `for` loop typically uses a variable (called a *counter* or an *index*) to keep track of how many times the loop has executed, and it stops when the counter reaches a certain number. A basic `for` statement looks like this:

```
for (somevar = 1; somevar < 10; somevar++) {
    // more code
}
```

There are three parameters to the `for` loop, each separated by semicolons:

▶ The first parameter (`somevar = 1` in the example) specifies a variable and assigns an initial value to it. This is called the *initial expression* because it sets up the initial state for the loop.

▶ The second parameter (`somevar < 10` in the example) is a condition that must remain true to keep the loop running. This is called the *condition* of the loop.

▶ The third parameter (`somevar++` in the example) is a statement that executes with each iteration of the loop. This is called the *increment expression* because it is typically used to increment the counter. The increment expression executes at the end of each loop iteration. Increment is just an example here—any operation can be performed.

After the three parameters are specified, a left brace ({) is used to signal the beginning of a block. A right brace (}) is used at the end of the block. All the statements between the braces will be executed with each iteration of the loop.

The parameters for a `for` loop might sound a bit confusing, but after you're used to them, you'll use `for` loops frequently. Here is a simple example of this type of loop:

```
for (i=0; i<10; i++) {
    document.write("This is line " + i + "<br>");
}
```

These statements define a loop that uses the variable i, initializes it with a value of 0, and loops as long as the value of i is less than 10. The increment expression, i++, adds 1 to the value of i with each iteration of the loop. Because this happens at the end of the loop, the output will be nine lines of text.

When a loop includes only a single statement between the braces, as in this example, you can omit the braces if you want. The following statement defines the same loop without braces:

```
for (i=0; i<10; i++)
    document.write("This is line " + i + "<br>");
```

TIP

It's a good style convention to use braces with all loops, regardless of whether they contain one statement or many statements. This makes it easy to add statements to the loop later without causing syntax errors.

The loop in this example contains a `document.write` statement that will be repeatedly executed. To see just what this loop does, you can add it to a `<script>` section of an HTML document, as shown in Listing 8.10.

LISTING 8.10 A Loop Using the `for` Keyword

```
<!DOCTYPE html>

<html lang="en">
  <head>
    <title>Using a for Loop</title>
  </head>
  <body>
    <h1>Using a for loop</h1>
    <p>The following is the output of the <strong>for</strong> loop:</p>
    <script type="text/javascript">
    for (i=1;i<10;i++) {
        document.write("This is line " + i + "<br>");
    }
    </script>
  </body>
</html>
```

This example displays a message containing the current value of the loop's counter during each iteration. The output of Listing 8.10 is shown in Figure 8.7.

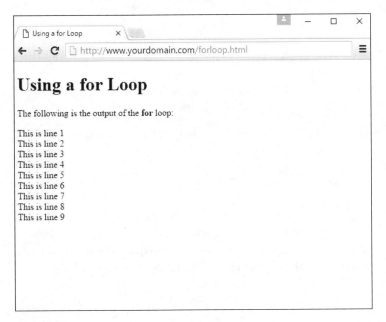

FIGURE 8.7
The results of the `for` loop example.

Notice that the loop was executed only nine times. This is because the conditional is `i<10`, and i is less than `10`. When the counter (`i`) is incremented to `10`, the expression is no longer true. If you want the loop to count to `10`, you will have to change the conditional; either `i<=10` or `i<11` will work fine.

The `for` loop is traditionally used to count from one number to another, but you can use just about any statement for the initialization, condition, and increment. However, there's usually a better way to do other types of loops with the `while` keyword, described in the next section.

Using while Loops

Another keyword for loops in JavaScript is `while`. Unlike `for` loops, `while` loops don't necessarily use a variable to count. Instead, they continue to execute as long as a condition is true. In fact, if the condition starts out as false, the statements won't execute at all.

The `while` statement includes the condition in parentheses, and it is followed by a block of statements within braces, just like a `for` loop. Here is a simple `while` loop:

```
while (total < 10) {
    n++;
    total += values[n];
}
```

This loop uses a counter, n, to iterate through the `values` array. Rather than stopping at a certain count, however, it stops when the total of the values reaches 10.

You might have thought that you could have done the same thing with a `for` loop, and you'd be correct:

```
for (n = 0; total < 10; n++) {
    total += values[n];
}
```

As a matter of fact, the `for` loop is nothing more than a special kind of `while` loop that handles an initialization and an increment for you all in one line. You can generally use `while` for any loop. However, it's best to choose whichever type of loop makes the most sense for the job, or takes the least amount of typing.

Using `do...while` **Loops**

JavaScript, like many other programming languages, includes a third type of loop: the do... while loop. This type of loop is similar to an ordinary `while` loop, with one difference: The condition is tested at the *end* of the loop rather than the beginning. Here is a typical do...while loop:

```
do {
    n++;
    total += values[n];
}
while (total < 10);
```

As you've probably noticed, this is basically an upside-down version of the previous `while` example. There is one difference: With the do loop, the condition is tested at the *end* of the loop. This means that the statements in the loop will always be executed at least once, even if the condition is never true.

NOTE

As with the `for` and `while` loops, the do loop can include a single statement without braces, or a number of statements enclosed in braces.

Working with Loops

Although you can use simple `for` and `while` loops for straightforward tasks, there are some considerations you should make when using more complicated loops. In the next sections, we'll look at infinite loops (to be avoided!) and the `break` and `continue` statements, which give you more control over the execution of your loops.

Creating an Infinite Loop

The `for` and `while` loops give you quite a bit of control over the loop. In some cases, this can cause problems if you're not careful. For example, look at the following loop code:

```
while (i < 10) {
    n++;
    values[n] = 0;
}
```

There's a mistake in this example. The condition of the `while` loop refers to the i variable, but that variable doesn't actually change during the loop—the n variable does. This creates an *infinite loop*. The loop will continue executing until the user stops it, or until it generates an error of some kind.

Infinite loops can't always be stopped by the user, except by quitting the browser—and some loops can even prevent the browser from quitting, or cause a crash.

Obviously, infinite loops are something to avoid; another common reason for infinite loops is using the wrong comparison overall or performing the wrong operation on a counter. Infinite loops can be difficult to spot because JavaScript won't give you an error that actually tells you there is an infinite loop. Thus, each time you create a loop in a script, you should be careful to make sure there's a way out.

NOTE

Depending on the browser version in use, an infinite loop might even make the browser stop responding to the user because all the memory is used up. Be sure you provide an escape route from infinite loops, and be sure to always test your work.

Occasionally, you might want to create a long-running and seemingly infinite loop deliberately. For example, you might want your program to execute until the user explicitly stops it, or until you provide an escape route with the `break` statement, as mentioned previously. Here's an easy way to create an infinite loop:

```
while (true) {
   //more code
}
```

Because the value `true` is the conditional, this loop will always find its condition to be true.

Escaping from a Loop

There is a way out of a long-running and seemingly infinite loop. You can use the break statement at some point during the loop to exit immediately and continue with the first statement after the loop. Here is a simple example of the use of break:

```
while (true) {
    n++;
    if (values[n] == 1) break;
}
```

Although the while statement is set up as an infinite loop, the if statement checks the corresponding value of an array, and if it finds a value of 1, it exits the loop.

When the JavaScript interpreter encounters a break statement, it skips the rest of the loop and continues the script with the first statement after the right brace at the loop's end. You can use the break statement in any type of loop, whether infinite or not. This provides an easy way to exit if an error occurs, or if another condition is met.

Continuing a Loop

One more JavaScript statement is available to help you control the execution of a loop. The continue statement skips the rest of the loop but, unlike break, it continues with the next iteration of the loop. Here is a simple example:

```
for (i=1; i<21; i++) {
    if (score[i]==0) continue;
    document.write("Student number "+ i + ", Score: "
    + score[i] + "<br>");
}
```

This script uses a for loop to print scores for 20 students, stored in the score array (not shown here). The if statement is used to check for scores with a value of 0. The script assumes that a score of 0 means that the student didn't take the test, so it continues the loop without printing that score.

Looping Through Object Properties

Yet another type of loop is available in JavaScript. The for...in loop is not as flexible as an ordinary for or while loop, but it is specifically designed to perform an operation on each property of an object.

For example, the built-in `navigator` object contains properties that describe the user's browser. You can use `for...in` to display this object's properties:

```
for (i in navigator) {
    document.write("<p>Property: " + i + "<br>");
    document.write("Value: " + navigator[i] + "</p>");
}
```

Like an ordinary `for` loop, this type of loop uses an index variable (`i` in the example). For each iteration of the loop, the variable is set to the next property of the object. This makes it easy when you need to check or modify each of an object's properties.

 TRY IT YOURSELF ▼

Working with Arrays and Loops

To apply your knowledge of loops, you will now create a script that works with arrays using loops. As you progress through this script, try to imagine how difficult it would be without JavaScript's looping features.

This simple script will prompt the user for a series of names. After all the names have been entered, it will display the list of names in a numbered list. To begin the script, initialize some variables:

```
var names = new Array();
var i = 0;
```

The `names` array will store the names the user enters. You don't know how many names will be entered, so you don't need to specify a dimension for the array. The `i` variable will be used as a counter in the loops.

Next, use the `prompt` statement to prompt the user for a series of names. Use a loop to repeat the prompt for each name. You want the user to enter at least one name, so a `do` loop is ideal:

```
do {
    next = prompt("Enter the Next Name", " ");
    if (next > " ") {
      names[i] = next;
    }
    i = i + 1;
} while (next > " ");
```

This loop prompts for a string called `next`. If a name was entered and isn't blank, it's stored as the next entry in the `names` array. The `i` counter is then incremented. The loop repeats until the user doesn't enter a name or clicks Cancel in the prompt dialog box.

Next, your script can display the number of names that was entered:

```
document.write("<h2>" + (names.length) + " names entered</h2>");
```

This statement displays the `length` property of the `names` array, surrounded by level 2 header tags for emphasis.

Next, the script should display all the names in the order in which they were entered. Because the names are in an array, the `for...in` loop is a good choice:

```
document.write("<ol>");
for (i in names) {
    document.write("<li>" + names[i] + "</li>");
}
document.write("</ol>");
```

Here you have a `for...in` loop that loops through the `names` array, assigning the counter `i` to each index in turn. The script then prints the name between opening and closing `<li>` tags as an item in an ordered list. Before and after the loop, the script prints beginning and ending `<ol>` tags.

You now have everything you need for a working script. Listing 8.11 shows the HTML file for this example, and Listing 8.12 shows the JavaScript file.

LISTING 8.11　**A Script to Prompt for Names and Display Them (HTML)**

```
<!DOCTYPE html>

<html lang="en">
  <head>
    <title>Loops Example</title>
  </head>
  <body>
    <h1>Loops Example</h1>
    <p>Enter a series of names and JavaScript will display them
    in a numbered list.</p>
    <script type="text/javascript" src="loops.js"></script>
  </body>
</html>
```

LISTING 8.12　**A Script to Prompt for Names and Display Them (JavaScript)**

```
// create the array
names = new Array();
var i = 0;

// loop and prompt for names
do {
    next = prompt("Enter the Next Name", "");
    if (next > " ") {
      names[i] = next;
```

```
    }
    i = i + 1;
} while (next > " ");

document.write("<h2>" + (names.length) + " names entered</h2>");

// display all of the names
document.write("<ol>");
for (i in names) {
    document.write("<li>" + names[i] + "</li>");
}
document.write("</ol>");
```

To try this example, save the JavaScript file as `loops.js` and then load the HTML document into a browser. You'll be prompted for one name at a time. Enter several names and then click Cancel to indicate that you're finished. Figure 8.8 shows what the final results should look like in a browser.

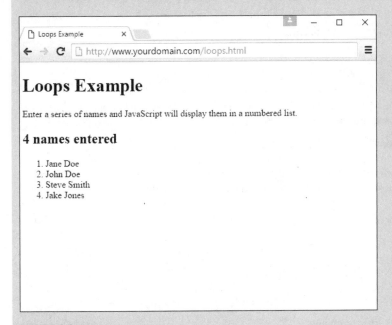

FIGURE 8.8
The output of the names example.

Summary

In this chapter, you learned several important features of JavaScript. First, you learned how to use functions to group JavaScript statements, and how to call functions and use the values they return. Next, you learned about JavaScript's object-oriented features—defining objects with constructors, creating object instances, and working with properties, property values, and methods.

As an example of these object-oriented features, we looked closer at the Math and Date objects built in to JavaScript, and you learned more than you ever wanted to know about random numbers.

You also learned two ways to control the flow of your scripts. You learned how to use the if statement to evaluate conditional expressions and react to them. You also learned a shorthand form of conditional expression using the ?: operator, as well as the switch statement for working with multiple conditions. You also learned about JavaScript's looping capabilities using for, while, and the do...while loops, and how to control loops further using the break and continue statements.

Not only are these structures important in JavaScript, they are very similar (if not exact, in some cases) to structures found in other programming languages, including PHP. These similarities will become apparent quickly in the next few chapters.

Q&A

Q. Many objects in JavaScript, such as DOM objects, include parent and child objects. Can I include child objects in my custom object definitions?

A. Yes. Just create a constructor function for the child object, and then add a property to the parent object that corresponds to it. For example, if you created a Nicknames object to store several nicknames for a person in the card file example, you could add it as a child object in the Card object's constructor: this.nick = new Nicknames();.

Q. Can I create an array of custom objects?

A. Yes. First, create the object definition as usual and define an array with the required number of elements. Then assign a new object to each array element (for example, cardarray[1] = new Card();). You can use a loop to assign objects to an entire array at once.

Q. Can I modify all properties of objects?

A. With custom objects, yes—but this varies with built-in objects and DOM objects. For example, you can use the length property to find the length of a string, but it is a *read-only property* and cannot be modified.

Q. Why don't I get a friendly error message if I accidentally use = instead of ==?

A. In some cases, this does result in an error. However, the incorrect version often appears to be a correct statement. For example, in the statement `if (a=1)`, the variable `a` is assigned the value `1`.

Workshop

The Workshop contains quiz questions and activities to help you solidify your understanding of the material covered. Try to answer all questions before looking at the "Answers" section that follows.

Quiz

1. What JavaScript keyword is used to create an instance of an object?

    A. `object`

    B. `new`

    C. `instance`

2. What is the meaning of the `this` keyword in JavaScript?

    A. The current object.

    B. The current script.

    C. It has no meaning.

3. What is the range of random numbers generated by the `Math.random` function?

    A. Between 1 and 100

    B. Between 1 and the number of milliseconds since January 1, 1970

    C. Between 0 and 1

4. What does the `switch` statement do?

    A. Tests a variable or expression for a number of different values

    B. Turns a variable on or off

    C. Makes ordinary `if` statements longer and more confusing

5. Within a loop, what does the `break` statement do?

    A. Crashes the browser

    B. Starts the loop over

    C. Escapes the loop entirely

Answers

1. A. The `new` keyword creates an object instance.

2. A. The `this` keyword refers to the current object.

3. C. The `Math` object returns a random number between 0 and 1.

4. A. The `switch` statement can test the same variable or expression for a number of different values.

5. C. The `break` statement escapes the loop.

Exercises

▶ Modify the definition of the `Card` object to include a property called `personal_notes` to store your own notes about the person. Modify the object definition and `printCard` function in Listings 8.4 and 8.5 to include this property.

▶ Modify Listings 8.11 and 8.12 to prompt for exactly 10 names. What happens if you click the Cancel button instead of entering a name?

## CHAPTER 9

Understanding JavaScript Event Handling

What You'll Learn in This Chapter:

▶ How event handlers work

▶ How event handlers relate to objects

▶ How to create an event handler

▶ How to detect mouse and keyboard actions

▶ How to use `onclick` to change the appearance of `<div>`

In your experience with JavaScript so far, most of the scripts you've written have executed in a calm, orderly fashion, quietly and methodically moving from the first statement to the last. You've seen a few event handlers in use in sample scripts used to focus your attention on other aspects of programming, and it is likely that you used your common sense to follow along with the actions—`onclick` really does mean "when a click happens." That alone speaks to the relative ease and simplicity of using JavaScript event handlers within your HTML.

In this chapter, you'll learn to use various event handlers supported by JavaScript. Rather than executing statements in a methodical order, the user can interact directly with different parts of your scripts when he or she invokes an event handler. You'll use event handlers in just about every bit of JavaScript you write throughout the rest of this book, and in fact they're likely to feature prominently in most JavaScript you will write, period.

Understanding Event Handlers

As you learned in Chapter 4, "Introducing JavaScript," JavaScript programs don't have to execute in order. You also learned they can detect *events* and react to them. Events are things that happen within the scope of the browser—the user clicks a button, the mouse pointer moves, or a web page finishes loading from the server (just to name a few). Various events enable your scripts to respond to the mouse, the keyboard, and other circumstances. Events are the key methods JavaScript uses to make web documents interactive.

The script that you create and use to detect and respond to an event is generally referred to as an *event handler*. Event handlers are among the most powerful features of JavaScript. Luckily, they're also among the easiest features to learn and use—often, a useful event handler requires only a single statement.

Objects and Events

As you learned in Chapter 6, "Understanding Dynamic Websites and HTML5 Applications," JavaScript uses a set of objects to store information about the various parts of a web page—the buttons, links, images, windows, and so on that you interact with. An event can often happen in more than one place (for example, the user could click any one of the links on the page), so each event is associated with an object.

Each event has a name. For example, the `mouseover` event occurs when the mouse pointer moves over an object on the page. When the pointer moves over a particular link, the `mouseover` event is sent to that link's event handler, if it has one. In the next few sections, you'll learn more about creating and using event handlers in your own code.

Creating an Event Handler

You don't need the `<script>` tag to invoke an event handler. Instead, you use the event name and code to invoke the event handler as an attribute of an individual HTML tag. For example, here is the HTML markup for a link that invokes an event handler script when a `mouseover` occurs on that linked bit of text:

```
<a href="http://www.google.com/"
    onmouseover="alert('You moved over the link.');">
    This is a link.</a>
```

Note that this snippet is all one `<a>` element, although it's split into multiple lines for readability here. In this example, the `onmouseover` attribute specifies a JavaScript statement to invoke—namely, an alert message is displayed when the user's mouse moves over the link.

NOTE

The previous example uses single quotation marks to surround the text. This is necessary in an event handler because double quotation marks are used to surround the event handler itself. You can also use single quotation marks to surround the event handler and double quotes within the script statements—just don't use the same type of quotation marks because that is a JavaScript syntax error.

You can invoke JavaScript statements like the preceding one in response to an event, but if you need to invoke more than one statement, it's a good idea to use a function instead. Just define the function elsewhere in the document or in a referenced document and then call the function as the event handler, like this:

```
<a href="#bottom" onmouseover="doIt();">Move the mouse over this
    link.</a>
```

This example calls a function called doIt when the user moves the mouse over the link. Using a function in this type of situation is convenient because you can use longer, more readable JavaScript routines as event handlers—not to mention you can reuse the function elsewhere without duplicating all of its code.

TIP

For simple event handlers, you can use two statements if you separate them with a semicolon. However, in most cases, it's just easier and more maintainable to use a function to perform these multiple statements.

Defining Event Handlers with JavaScript

Rather than specifying an event-handling script each time you want to invoke it, best practices call for assigning a specific function as the default event handler for an event. This enables you to set event handlers conditionally, turn them on and off, and dynamically change the function that handles an event.

TIP

Setting up event handlers this way enables you to use an external JavaScript file to define the function and set up the event, keeping the JavaScript code completely separate from the HTML file.

To define an event handler in this way, first define a function and then assign the function as an event handler. Event handlers are stored as properties of the document object or another object that can receive an event. For example, these statements define a function called mousealert and then assign it as the event handler for all instances of mousedown in the current document:

```
function mousealert() {
    alert("You clicked the mouse!");
}
document.onmousedown = mousealert;
```

You can use this technique to set up an event handler for only a specific HTML element, but an additional step is required to achieve that goal: You must first find the object corresponding to the element. To do this, use the document.getElementById function.

First, define an element in the HTML document and specify an id attribute:

```
<a href="http://www.google.com/" id="link1">
```

Next, in the JavaScript code, find the object and apply the event handler:

```
var link1_obj = document.getElementById("link1");
link1_obj.onclick = myCustomFunction;
```

You can do this for any object as long as you've defined it and therefore can reference it by a unique id attribute in the HTML file. Using this technique, you can easily assign the same function to handle events for multiple objects without adding clutter to your HTML code.

Supporting Multiple Event Handlers

What if you want more than one thing to happen when you click an element? For example, suppose you want two functions called update and display both to execute when a button is clicked? It's very easy to run into syntax errors or logic errors such that two functions assigned to the same event won't work as expected. One solution for clean separation and execution is to define a single function that calls both functions:

```
function updateThenDisplay() {
    update();
    display();
}
```

This isn't always the ideal way to do things. For example, if you're using two third-party scripts and both of them want to add a load event to the page, there should be a way to add both events. The W3C DOM standard defines a function, addEventListener, for this purpose. This function defines a *listener* for a particular event and object, and you can add as many listener functions as you need.

Using the Event Object

When an event occurs, you might want or need to know more about the event in order for your script to perform different actions—for example, for a keyboard event, you might want to know which key was pressed, especially if your script performs different actions depending on whether the J key or the L key was pressed. The DOM includes an Event object that provides this type of granular information.

To use the Event object, you can pass it on to your event handler function. For example, this statement defines a keypress event that passes the Event object to a function:

```
<body onkeypress="getKey(event);">
```

You can then define your function to accept the event as a parameter:

```
function getKey(e) {
    // more code
}
```

In Firefox, Safari, and Chrome, an `Event` object is automatically passed to the event handler function, so this will work even if you use JavaScript rather than HTML to define an event handler. In Internet Explorer, the most recent event is stored in the `window.event` object. In the preceding HTML snippet, this object is passed to the event handler function; therefore, depending on your browser, the wrong object (or no object) might be passed along in this scenario and your JavaScript code will need to do a little work to determine the correct object:

```
function getkey(e) {
    if (!e) e=window.event;
    // more code
}
```

In this case, the `if` statement checks whether the e variable is already defined. If it is not (because the user's browser is Internet Explorer), it gets the `window.event` object and stores it in e. This ensures that you have a valid `event` object in any browser.

Unfortunately, although both Internet Explorer and non–Internet Explorer browsers support `Event` objects, these objects have different properties. One property that is the same in both browsers is `Event.type`, which is the type of event. This is simply the name of the event, such as `mouseover` and `keypress`. The following sections list some additional useful properties for each browser.

Internet Explorer `Event` Properties

The following are some of the commonly used properties of the `Event` object for Internet Explorer:

▶ `Event.button`—The mouse button that was pressed. This value is 1 for the left button and usually 2 for the right button.

▶ `Event.clientX`—The x coordinate (column, in pixels) where the event occurred.

▶ `Event.clientY`—The y coordinate (row, in pixels) where the event occurred.

▶ `Event.altKey`—A flag that indicates whether the Alt key was pressed during the event.

▶ `Event.ctrlKey`—A flag that indicates whether the Ctrl key was pressed.

▶ `Event.shiftKey`—A flag that indicates whether the Shift key was pressed.

▶ `Event.keyCode`—The key code (in Unicode) for the key that was pressed.

▶ `Event.srcElement`—The object where the event occurred.

Non–Internet Explorer `Event` Properties

The following are some of the commonly used properties of the `Event` object for modern browsers that are not Internet Explorer:

▶ `Event.modifiers`—A flag that indicates which modifier keys (Shift, Ctrl, Alt, and so on) were held down during the event. This value is an integer that combines binary values representing the different keys.

▶ `Event.pageX`—The x coordinate of the event within the web page.

▶ `Event.pageY`—The y coordinate of the event within the web page.

▶ `Event.which`—The key code for keyboard events (in Unicode), or the button that was pressed for mouse events. (It's best to use the cross-browser `button` property instead.)

▶ `Event.button`—The mouse button that was pressed. This works just like Internet Explorer except that the left button's value is 0 and the right button's value is 2.

▶ `Event.target`—The object where the element occurred.

NOTE

The `Event.pageX` and `Event.pageY` properties are based on the top-left corner of the element where the event occurred, not always the exact position of the mouse pointer.

Using Mouse Events

The DOM includes a number of event handlers for detecting mouse actions. Your script can detect the movement of the mouse pointer and when a button is clicked, released, or both. Some of these will be familiar to you already because you have seen them in action in previous chapters.

Over and Out

You've already seen the first and most common event, `mouseover`, which is called when a user's mouse pointer moves over a link or another object. Note that `mouseout` is the opposite—it is called when the user's mouse pointer moves out of the object's border. Unless something strange happens and the user's mouse never moves again while the viewer is viewing the particular document, you can count on `mouseout` happening sometime after `mouseover`.

`mouseout` is particularly useful if your script has made a visual change within the document when the user's mouse pointer moved over the object—for example, displaying a message in the status line or changing an image. You can use a `mouseout` event to undo the action when the pointer moves away.

However, when considering using `mouseover` and `mouseout` events, be mindful that not all devices actually include a mouse pointing event. An example is mobile devices—if you keep important information behind a mouse-based barrier, your mobile users will never see it.

TIP
_____

One of the most common uses for `mouseover` and `mouseout` event handlers is to create _rollovers_—images that change when the mouse moves over them. You'll learn how to create these later in the chapter.

Ups and Downs (and Clicks)

You can also use events to detect when the mouse button is clicked. The basic event for this is `click`. An event handler can be called when the mouse button is clicked while positioned over the appropriate object.

For example, you can use the following to display an alert when a link is clicked:

```
<a href="http://www.google.com/"
    onclick="alert('You are about to leave this site.');">
    Go Away</a>
```

In this case, the `click` event invokes the JavaScript `alert` before the linked page is loaded into the browser. This is useful for making links conditional or displaying a disclaimer before sending the user away to the linked page.

If your `click` event handler returns the `false` value, the link will not be followed. For example, the following is a link that displays a confirmation dialog box. If you click Cancel, the link is not followed; if you click OK, the new page is loaded:

```
<a href="http://www.google.com/"
    onclick="return(window.confirm('Are you sure?'));">
    Go Away</a>
```

This example uses the `return` statement to enclose the event handler. This ensures that the `false` value that is returned when the user clicks Cancel is returned from the event handler, which prevents the link from being followed.

The `dblclick` event is similar, but is used only if the user double-clicks an object. Because links usually require only a single click, you could use this to make a link do two different things depending on the number of clicks. (Needless to say, this could be confusing to the user, but it _is_ technically possible.) You can also detect double-clicks on images and other objects.

To give you even more control of what happens when the mouse button is pressed, two more events are included:

▶ mousedown is used when the user presses the mouse button.

▶ mouseup is used when the user releases the mouse button.

These two events are the two halves of a mouse click. If you want to detect an entire click, use click, but you can use mouseup and mousedown to detect just one or the other.

To detect which mouse button is pressed, you can use the button property of the Event object. This property is assigned the value 0 or 1 for the left button, and 2 for the right button. This property is assigned for click, dblclick, mouseup, and mousedown events.

CAUTION

Browsers don't normally detect click or dblclick events for the right mouse button. If you want to detect the right button, mousedown is the most reliable way.

As an example of these event handlers, you can create a script that displays information about mouse button events and determines which button is pressed. Listing 9.1 shows a script that handles some mouse events.

LISTING 9.1 The JavaScript File for the Mouse-Click Example

```
function mouseStatus(e) {
    if (!e) e = window.event;
    btn = e.button;
    whichone = (btn < 2) ? "Left" : "Right";
    message=e.type + " : " + whichone + "<br>";
    document.getElementById('testarea').innerHTML += message;
}
obj=document.getElementById('testlink');

obj.onmousedown = mouseStatus;
obj.onmouseup = mouseStatus;
obj.onclick = mouseStatus;
obj.ondblclick = mouseStatus;
```

This script includes a function, mouseStatus, that detects mouse events. This function uses the button property of the Event object to determine which button was pressed. It also uses the type property to display the type of event, since the function will be used to handle multiple event types.

After the function, the script finds the object for a link with the id attribute testlink and assigns its mousedown, mouseup, click, and dblclick events to the mousestatus function.

Save this script as `click.js`. Next, you will need an HTML document to work with the script; this is shown in Listing 9.2.

LISTING 9.2   The HTML File for the Mouse-Click Example

```html
<!DOCTYPE html>

<html lang="en">
  <head>
    <title>Mouse Click Text</title>
  </head>
  <body>
    <h1>Mouse Click Test</h1>
    <p>Click the mouse on the test link below. A message
    will indicate which button was clicked.</p>
    <p><a href="#" id="testlink">Test Link</a></p>
    <div id="testarea"></div>
    <script type="text/javascript" src="click.js"></script>
  </body>
</html>
```

This file defines a test link with the `id` property `testlink`, which is used in the script to assign event handlers. It also defines a `<div>` with an `id` of `testarea`, which is used by the script to display the message regarding the events. To test this document, save it in the same folder as the JavaScript file you created previously and load the HTML document into a browser. Some sample results are shown in Figure 9.1.

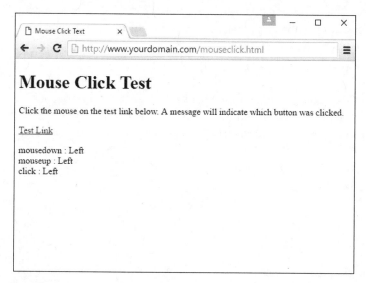

FIGURE 9.1
The mouse-click example in action.

NOTE

Notice that a single click of the left mouse button triggers three events: `mousedown`, `mouseup`, and then `click`, whereas clicking the right mouse button triggers only two events.

Using Keyboard Events

JavaScript can also detect keyboard actions. The main event for this purpose is `keypress`, which occurs when a key is pressed and released, or held down. As with mouse buttons, you can detect the down and up parts of the key press with `keydown` and `keyup` event handlers.

Of course, you might find it useful to know which key the user pressed. You can find this out with the `Event` object, which is sent to your event handler when the event occurs. In Internet Explorer, `Event.keyCode` stores the ASCII character code for the key that was pressed. In non–Internet Explorer browsers, the `Event.which` property stores the ASCII character code for the key that was pressed.

NOTE

ASCII (American Standard Code for Information Interchange) is the standard numeric code used by most computers to represent characters. It assigns the numbers 0 to 128 to various characters—for example, the capital letters *A* through *Z* are ASCII values 65 to 90.

If you'd rather deal with actual characters than key codes, you can use the `String` method called `fromCharCode` to convert them. This method converts a numeric ASCII code to its corresponding string character. For example, the following statement converts the `Event.which` property to a character and stores it in the `key` variable:

```
var key = String.fromCharCode(event.which);
```

Because different browsers have different ways of returning the key code, displaying keys independently of the browser is a bit harder. However, you can create a script that displays keys for both Internet Explorer and non–Internet Explorer browsers. The following function displays each key as it is typed:

```
function displayKey(e) {
    // which key was pressed?
    if (e.keyCode) {
        var keycode=e.keyCode;
    } else {
        var keycode=e.which;
    }
    character=String.fromCharCode(keycode);
```

```
    // find the object for the destination paragraph
    var keysParagraph = document.getElementById('keys');

    // add the character to the paragraph
    keysParagraph.innerHTML += character;
}
```

The `displayKey` function receives the `Event` object from the event handler and stores it in the variable e. It checks whether the `e.keyCode` property exists and then stores it in the `keycode` variable if present. Otherwise, it assumes that the browser is not Internet Explorer and assigns `keycode` to the `e.which` property.

The remaining lines of the function convert the key code to a character and add it to the paragraph in the document with the `id` attribute `keys`. Listing 9.3 shows a complete example using this function.

NOTE

The final lines in the `displayKey` function use the `getElementById` function and the `innerHTML` attribute to display the keys you type within a paragraph on the page—in this case, a paragraph with an `id` of `keys`.

LISTING 9.3   Displaying Typed Characters

```
<!DOCTYPE html>

<html lang="en">
  <head>
    <title>Displaying Keypresses</title>
    <script type="text/javascript">
    function displayKey(e) {
       // which key was pressed?
       if (e.keyCode) {
          var keycode=e.keyCode;
       } else {
          var keycode=e.which;
       }
       character=String.fromCharCode(keycode);

       // find the object for the destination paragraph
       var keysParagraph = document.getElementById('keys');

       // add the character to the paragraph
       keysParagraph.innerHTML += character;
    }
    </script>
```

```
  </head>
  <body onkeypress="displayKey(event)">
    <h1>Displaying Typed Characters</h1>
    <p>This document includes a simple script that displays
    the keys you type as a new paragraph below. Type a few keys
    to try it. </p>
    <div id="keys"></div>
  </body>
</html>
```

When you load this example, type and then watch the characters you've typed appear in a paragraph of the document. Figure 9.2 shows the result of some typing, but you should really try it yourself to see the full effect!

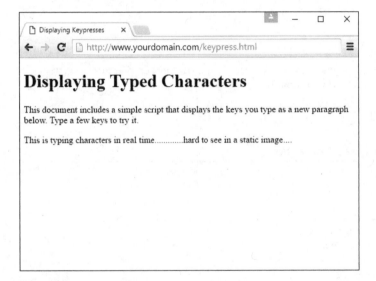

FIGURE 9.2
Displaying the output of the keys that were pressed.

Using the `load` and `unload` Events

Another event you might use often is `load`. This event occurs when the current page (including all of its images) finishes loading from the server.

The `load` event is related to the `window` object, and to define it you use an event handler in the `<body>` tag. For example, the following is a `<body>` element that uses a simple event handler to display an alert when the page finishes loading:

```
<body onload="alert('Loading complete.');">
```

CAUTION

Because the `load` event occurs after the HTML document has finished loading and displaying, you should not use the `document.write` or `document.open` statement within a `load` event handler, because it would overwrite the current document.

Images can also have a `load` event handler. When you define a `load` event handler for an `<img>` element, it is triggered as soon as the specified image has completely loaded.

To set a `load` event using JavaScript, you assign a function to the `onload` property of the window object:

```
window.onload = MyFunction;
```

You can also specify an `unload` event for the `<body>` element. This event will be triggered whenever the browser unloads the current document—this occurs when another page is loaded or when the browser window is closed.

Using `click` to Change a `<div>`'s Appearance

As you've learned already in this chapter, the `click` event can be used to invoke all sorts of actions. You might think of a mouse click as a way to submit a form by clicking a button, but you can capture this event and use it to provide interactivity within your pages as well. In the example that follows, you will see how you can use the `click` event to show or hide information contained in a `<div>` element.

In this case, you will be adding interactivity to a web page by allowing the user to show previously hidden information when he or she clicks a piece of text. I refer to it as a *piece of text* because, strictly speaking, the text is not a link. That is to say, to the user it will look like a link and act like a link, but it will not be marked up within an `<a>` tag.

Listing 9.4 provides the complete code for this example, which we'll walk through momentarily.

LISTING 9.4 Using `onclick` to Show or Hide Content

```
<!DOCTYPE html>

<html lang="en">
  <head>
    <title>Steptoe Butte</title>
    <style type="text/css">
    a {
       text-decoration: none;
       font-weight: bold;
    }
```

```
  img {
     margin-right: 12px;
     margin-bottom: 6px;
     border: 1px solid #000;
  }
  .mainimg {
     float: left;
  }
  #hide_e {
     display: none;
  }
  #elevation {
     display: none;
  }
  #hide_p {
     display: none;
  }
  #photos {
     display: none;
  }
  #show_e {
     display: block;
  }
  #show_p {
     display: block;
  }
  .fakelink {
     cursor: pointer;
     text-decoration: none;
     font-weight: bold;
     color: #E03A3E;
  }
  section {
     margin-bottom: 6px;
  }
   </style>
 </head>
<body>
  <header>
     <h1>Steptoe Butte</h1>
  </header>

  <section>
     <h2>General Information</h2>
     <p><img src="steptoebutte.jpg" alt="View from Steptoe Butte"
      class="mainimg">Steptoe Butte is a quartzite island jutting out of
      the silty loess of the <a
      href="http://en.wikipedia.org/wiki/Palouse">Palouse </a> hills in
      Whitman County, Washington. The rock that forms the butte is over
```

400 million years old, in contrast with the 15-7 million year old
`<a href="http://en.wikipedia.org/wiki/Columbia_River">Columbia`
`River</a>` basalts that underlie the rest of the Palouse (such
"islands" of ancient rock have come to be called buttes, a butte
being defined as a small hill with a flat top, whose width at
top does not exceed its height).`</p>`
`<p>`A hotel built by Cashup Davis stood atop Steptoe Butte from
1888 to 1908, burning down several years after it closed. In 1946,
Virgil McCroskey donated 120 acres (0.49 km2) of land to form
Steptoe Butte State Park, which was later increased to over 150
acres (0.61 km2). Steptoe Butte is currently recognized as a
National Natural Landmark because of its unique geological value.
It is named in honor of
`<a href="http://en.wikipedia.org/wiki/Colonel_Edward_`
`Steptoe">Colonel`
`Edward Steptoe</a>.</p>`
`</section>`

```
<section>
   <h2>Elevation</h2>
   <div class="fakelink"
     id="show_e"
     onclick="this.style.display='none';
     document.getElementById('hide_e').style.display='block';
     document.getElementById('elevation').style.display='inline';
   ">&raquo; Show Elevation</div>
   <div class="fakelink"
     id="hide_e"
     onclick="this.style.display='none';
     document.getElementById('show_e').style.display='block';
     document.getElementById('elevation').style.display='none';
   ">&raquo; Hide Elevation</div>

   <div id="elevation">3,612 feet (1,101 m), approximately
   1,000 feet (300 m) above the surrounding countryside.</div>
</section>

<section>
   <h2>Photos</h2>
   <div class="fakelink"
     id="show_p"
     onclick="this.style.display='none';
     document.getElementById('hide_p').style.display='block';
     document.getElementById('photos').style.display='inline';
   ">&raquo; Show Photos from the Top of Steptoe Butte</div>

   <div class="fakelink"
     id="hide_p"
     onclick="this.style.display='none';
```

```
      document.getElementById('show_p').style.display='block';
      document.getElementById('photos').style.display='none';
   ">&raquo; Hide Photos from the Top of Steptoe Butte</div>

   <div id="photos"><img src="steptoe_sm1.jpg" alt="View from Steptoe
   Butte"><img  src="steptoe_sm2.jpg" alt="View from Steptoe
   Butte"><img  src="steptoe_sm3.jpg" alt="View from Steptoe
   Butte"></div>
</section>

<footer>
  <em>Text from
  <a href="http://en.wikipedia.org/wiki/Steptoe_Butte">
  Wikipedia</a>, photos by the author.</em>
</footer>
</body>
</html>
```

If you take a look at this code as rendered in your browser, you will see something like Figure 9.3.

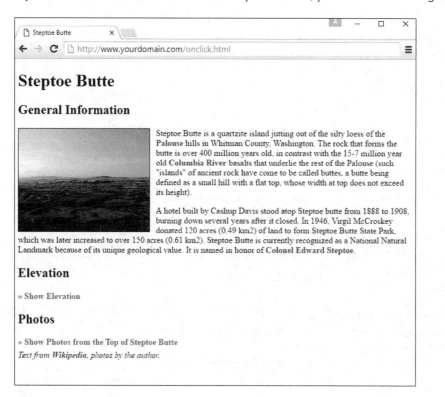

FIGURE 9.3
The initial display of Listing 9.4.

When your mouse pointer hovers over the red text link, it should change to a hand despite the fact it is not an `<a>` link.

To begin, look at the 11 entries in the style sheet. The first entry simply styles links that are surrounded by the `<a></a>` tag pair; these links display as non-underlined, bold, blue links. You can see these regular links in the two paragraphs of text in Figure 9.3 (and in the line at the bottom of the page). The next two entries make sure that the images used in the page have appropriate margins; the entry for the `<img>` element sets some margins and a border, and the `.mainimg` class enables you to apply a style to the main image on the page, but not the set of three images at the bottom of the page.

The next four entries are for specific IDs, and those IDs are all set to be invisible (`display: none`) when the page initially loads. In contrast, the two IDs that follow are set to display as block elements when the page initially loads. Again, strictly speaking, these two IDs do not have to be defined as block elements because that is the default display. However, this style sheet includes these entries to illustrate the differences between the two sets of elements. If you count the number of `<div>` elements in Listing 9.4, you will find six in the code: four invisible and two that are visible upon page load.

The goal in this example is to change the display value of two IDs when another ID is clicked. But first you have to make sure users realize that a piece of text is clickable, and that typically happens when users see their mouse pointers change to reflect a present link. Although you can't see it in Figure 9.3, if you load the sample code on your machine and view it in your browser, the mouse pointer changes to a hand with a finger pointing at a particular link.

This functionality is achieved by defining a class for this particular text; the class is called fakelink, as you can see in this snippet of code:

```
<div class="fakelink"
     id="show_e"
     onclick="this.style.display='none';
     document.getElementById('hide_e').style.display='block';
     document.getElementById('elevation').style.display='inline';
">&raquo; Show Elevation</div>
```

The `fakelink` class ensures that the text is rendered as non-underlined, bold, and red; `cursor: pointer` causes the mouse pointer to change in such a way that users think the text is a link of the type that would normally be enclosed in an `<a>` element. But the really interesting stuff happens when we associate an `onclick` attribute with a `<div>`. In the sample snippet just shown, the value of the `onclick` attribute is a series of commands that change the current value of CSS elements.

Let's look at them separately:

```
this.style.display='none';
document.getElementById('hide_e').style.display='block';
document.getElementById('elevation').style.display='inline';
```

In the first line of the snippet, the `this` keyword refers to the element itself. In other words, `this` refers to the `<div>` ID called `show_e`. The keyword `style` refers to the `style` object; the style object contains all the CSS styles that you assign to the element. In this case, we are most interested in the `display` style. Therefore, `this.style.display` means "the display style of the `show_e` ID," and we are setting the value of the `display` style to `none` when the text itself is clicked.

But three actions also occur within the `onclick` attribute. The other two actions begin with `document.getElementById()` and include a specific ID name within the parentheses. We use `document.getElementById()` instead of `this` because the second and third actions set CSS style properties for elements that are not the parent element. As you can see in the snippet, in the second and third actions, we are setting the display property values for the element IDs `hide_e` and `elevation`. When users click the currently visible `<div>` called `show_e`, the following happens:

▸ The `<div>` element called `show_e` becomes invisible.

▸ The `<div>` element called `hide_e` becomes visible and is displayed as a block.

▸ The `<div>` element called `elevation` becomes visible and is displayed inline.

Figure 9.4 shows the result of these actions.

FIGURE 9.4
When Show Elevation is clicked, the visibility of it and other `<div>` elements changes based on the commands in the `onclick` attribute.

Another set of `<div>` elements exists in the code in Listing 9.4: the ones that control the visibility of the additional photos. These elements are not affected by the `onclick` actions in the elevation-related elements. That is, when you click either Show Elevation or Hide Elevation, the photos-related `<div>` elements do not change. You can show the elevation and not the photos (as shown in Figure 9.4), the photos and not the elevation, or both the elevation and the photos at the same time (see Figure 9.5).

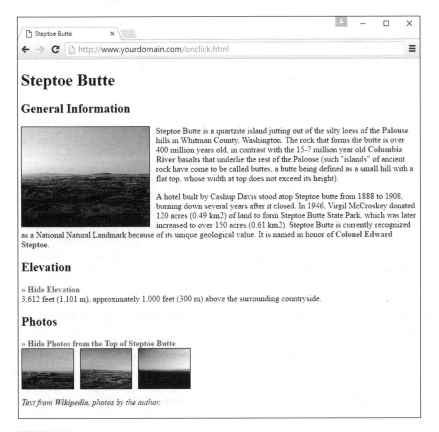

FIGURE 9.5
The page after both Show Elevation and Show Photos from the Top of Steptoe Butte have been clicked.

This brief example has shown you the very beginning of the layout and interaction possibilities that await you when you master CSS in conjunction with events. For example, you can code your pages so that your users can change elements of the style sheet, change to an entirely different style sheet, move blocks of text to other places in the layout, take quizzes, submit forms, and do much, much more.

Summary

In this chapter, you learned to use events to detect mouse actions, keyboard actions, and other events, such as the loading of the page. You can use event handlers to perform a simple JavaScript statement when an event occurs, or to call a more complicated function.

JavaScript includes various other events. Many of these are related to forms, which you'll learn more about in Chapter 15, "Working with Web-Based Forms." In a longer example at the end of this chapter, you saw how to use `onclick` to show or hide text in a page with some design elements in it. Some new CSS was introduced: the use of the `cursor` property. Assigning a `cursor` property of `pointer` enabled you to indicate to users that particular text was acting as a link even though it was not enclosed within `<a>` and `</a>` tags, as you are used to seeing.

Q&A

Q. Can I capture mouse or keyboard events on elements other than text, such as images?

A. Yes, these types of events can be applied to actions related to clicking on or rolling over images as well as text. However, other multimedia objects, such as embedded YouTube videos and Flash files, are not interacted with in the same way, because those objects are played via additional software for which other mouse or keyboard actions are applicable. For instance, if you click a YouTube video that is embedded in your web page, you are interacting with the YouTube player and no longer your actual web page—that action cannot be captured in the same way.

Q. What happens if I define both `keydown` and `keypress` event handlers? Will they both be called when a key is pressed?

A. The `keydown` event handler is called first. If it returns `true`, the `keypress` event is called. Otherwise, no key press event is generated.

Q. When I use the `load` event, my event handler sometimes executes before the page is done loading, or before some of the graphics. Is there a better way?

A. This is a bug in some older browsers. One solution is to add a slight delay to your script using the `setTimeout` method.

Workshop

The Workshop contains quiz questions and exercises to help you solidify your understanding of the material covered. Try to answer all questions before looking at the "Answers" section that follows.

Quiz

Test your knowledge of JavaScript events by answering the following questions.

1. Which of the following is the correct event for detecting a mouse click on a link?

    A. `mouseup`

    B. `link`

    C. `click`

2. When does a `load` event handler for the `<body>` element execute?

    A. When an image is finished loading

    B. When the entire page is finished loading

    C. When the user attempts to load another page

3. Which of the following `Event` object properties indicates which key was pressed for a `keypress` event in Internet Explorer?

    A. `Event.which`

    B. `Event.keyCode`

    C. `Event.onKeyPress`

Answers

1. **A.** The event for a mouse click is `click`.

2. **B.** The `<body>` element's `load` event handler executes when the page and all its images are finished loading.

3. **C.** In Internet Explorer, the `Event.keyCode` property stores the character code for each key press.

Exercises

To gain more experience using event handlers in JavaScript, try the following exercise:

▶ Extend any (or all!) of the sample scripts in this chapter to check for specific values of key press actions before continuing on to execute the underlying JavaScript statements within their associated functions.

▶ Add commands to the `onclick` attributes in Listing 9.4 such that only one of the `<div>` elements (the elevation or photos) is visible at a time.

CHAPTER 10
The Basics of Using jQuery

What You'll Learn in This Chapter:

▶ Why you might use a third-party JavaScript library
▶ How to use jQuery's `$().ready` handler
▶ How to use jQuery to select page elements and manipulate HTML content
▶ How to chain commands together and handle events with jQuery

Third-party JavaScript libraries, or code libraries written and maintained by another party for easy implementation in your own code, offer many advantages to always writing your own code. First and foremost, using these libraries enables you to avoid reinventing the wheel for common tasks. Additionally, these libraries enable you to implement cross-browser scripting and sophisticated user interface elements without first having to become an expert in JavaScript.

There are many third-party JavaScript libraries out there, and in this chapter you'll gain a brief introduction to the most popular one: jQuery.

By the end of this chapter, you will likely see why jQuery is so popular, and why developers continue to contribute plug-ins to this open-source project for the rest of the development community to use. With just a few keystrokes here and there, you'll see how useful this library can be for adding interactivity to your website or web-based application.

Using Third-Party JavaScript Libraries

When you use JavaScript's built-in and often-used `Math` and `Date` functions, JavaScript does most of the work—you don't have to figure out how to convert dates between formats or calculate a cosine; you just use the function JavaScript provides. Third-party libraries are those libraries not directly included with JavaScript, but they serve a similar purpose: they enable you to do complicated things with only a small amount of code, because that small amount of code refers to something bigger under the hood that someone else has already created.

Although in general most people are big fans of third-party libraries, you should be aware of some of the common objections:

▶ You won't ever really know how the code works because you're simply employing someone else's algorithms and functions.

▶ JavaScript libraries contain a lot of code you'll never use but the browser has to download anyway.

Blindly implementing code is never a good thing; you should endeavor to understand what is happening behind the scenes when you use any library. But that understanding could be limited to knowing that someone else wrote a complicated algorithm that you could not—and it's fine if that's all you know, as long as you implement it appropriately and understand possible weaknesses.

To the point about libraries containing a lot of extraneous code, that should be a consideration especially if you know that your target users have bandwidth limitations or if the size of the library is disproportionate to the feature you're using from it. For example, if your code requires the browser to load a 1MB library just to use one function, look into ways to fork the library (if it is open source) and use just the sections you need, find other features of the library you can use to make it worthwhile, look for another library that does what you want but with less overhead, or use a minified version of the library.

However, regardless of the objections, there are numerous good reasons for using third-party JavaScript libraries, which in my opinion outweigh the negative objections:

▶ Using a well-written library can really take away some of the headaches of writing cross-browser JavaScript. You won't have every browser always at your disposal, but the library writers—and their communities of users—will have tested using several versions of all major browsers.

▶ Why invent code that somebody else has already written? Popular JavaScript libraries tend to contain the sorts of abstractions that programmers often need to use—which means you'll likely need those functions too from time to time. The thousands of downloads and pages of online documentation and commentary generated by the most-used libraries pretty much guarantee that the code these libraries contain will be more thoroughly tested and debugged than the ordinary user's home-cooked code would be.

▶ Advanced functionality such as drag and drop and JavaScript-based animation is, well, really advanced and rather complex in its implementation. Truly cross-browser solutions for this type of functionality have always been one of the trickiest effects to code for all browsers, and well-developed and well-tested libraries can help you achieve these types of features and are incredibly valuable in terms of the time and effort they will save you.

Using a third-party JavaScript library is usually as simple as copying one or more files to your server (or linking to an external but stable location) and including a `<script>` tag in your document to load the library, thus making its code available to your own scripts.

jQuery Arrives on the Scene

The first implementation of jQuery was introduced in 2006 and has grown from an easy, cross-browser means of DOM manipulation to a stable, powerful library. This library contains not just DOM manipulation tools, but many additional features that make cross-browser JavaScript coding much more straightforward and productive. In fact, many JavaScript frameworks, which you'll learn about later in this chapter, rely on the jQuery library for their own functionality.

The current version (at the time of writing) is 3.2.1, and jQuery also has an additional advanced user interface extensions library that can be used alongside the existing library to rapidly build and deploy rich user interfaces or to add various attractive effects to existing components.

NOTE

jQuery's home page is at http://jquery.com/, where you not only can download the latest version, but also gain access to extensive documentation and sample code. The companion UI library can be found at http://jqueryui.com/.

TIP

If you don't want to download and store the jQuery library on your own local development machine or production server, you can use a remotely hosted version from a content delivery network, such as the one hosted by Google. Instead of referring to a locally hosted `.js` file in your HTML files, use the following code to link to a stable and minified version of the code:

```
<script
src="http://ajax.googleapis.com/ajax/libs/jquery/3.2.1/jquery.min.js"
type="text/javascript"></script>
```

In many cases, this provides better performance than hosting your own version, due to Google's servers being optimized for low-latency, massively parallel content delivery. Additionally, anyone visiting your page who has also visited another page that references this same file will have the file cached in their browser and will not need to download it again.

jQuery has at its heart a sophisticated, cross-browser method for selection of page elements. The selectors used to obtain elements are based on a combination of simple CSS-like selector styles, so with the CSS techniques you learned in earlier chapters of this book, you should have no problem getting up to speed with jQuery. Following are a few brief examples of jQuery code, to illustrate my point.

For example, if you want to get an element that has an ID of *someElement*, all you do is use this:

```
$("#someElement")
```

Or to return a collection of elements that have the *someClass* class name, you can simply use this:

```
$(".someClass")
```

We can very simply get or set values associated with our selected elements. Let's suppose, for example, that we want to hide all elements having the class name hideMe. We can do that, in a fully cross-browser manner, in just one line of code:

```
$(".hideMe").hide();
```

Manipulating HTML and CSS properties is just as straightforward. To append the phrase "powered by jQuery" to all paragraph elements, for example, we would simply write the following:

```
$("p").append(" powered by jQuery");
```

To then change the background color of those same elements, we can manipulate their CSS properties directly:

```
$("p").css("background-color","yellow");
```

Additionally, jQuery includes simple cross-browser methods for determining whether an element has a class, adding and removing classes, getting and setting the text or HTML content of an element, navigating the DOM, getting and setting CSS properties, and handling cross-browser events easily. The associated jQuery UI library adds a huge range of UI widgets (such as date pickers, sliders, dialog boxes, and progress bars), animation tools, drag-and-drop capabilities, and much more.

Preparing to Use jQuery

As you learned in previous chapters, including any JavaScript library in your code is as simple as linking to it via a <script> element.

You have two options for storing the library: You can download and store it on your own server, or you can use a remotely hosted version from a content delivery network, such as the one hosted by Google or even the jQuery folks themselves.

If you download jQuery and keep it on your own server, I would suggest keeping it in a directory called js (for "javascript") or another directory specifically for assets (in fact, you could even call it assets) so that it doesn't get lost among all the other files you maintain. Then, you reference it like so:

```
<script src="/js/jquery-3.2.1.min.js" type="text/javascript"></script>
```

NOTE

The "min" in the filename is for the *minified* version of the library, or a version that is fully functioning but has all the whitespace, line breaks, and other unnecessary characters removed from the source code. Minified versions also rename internal variable and function names to shorter versions (since humans aren't reading the minified version). This minified version is thus smaller in size, which requires less time and bandwidth for the end user to download, while retaining all original functionality. Minified code is not easy for human eyes to read, but computers have no issues with it, because the unnecessary spacing doesn't matter to them.

I typically use the Google content delivery network, which means a `<script>` tag that looks like the following:

```
<script
    src="http://ajax.googleapis.com/ajax/libs/jquery/3.2.1/jquery.min.js"
    type="text/javascript">
</script>
```

However, you should use whatever is more comfortable for you, as long as you know the difference.

Becoming Familiar with the `$().ready` Handler

Previously in this book, you used a `window.onload` event handler to open a new window when a page was loaded. jQuery has its own handler that serves the same purpose, but is perhaps more explicitly named; this handler ensures that nothing within the page can be manipulated until a state of DOM readiness has been detected.

TIP

Readiness means that the full DOM is ready for manipulation, but does not necessarily mean all assets (such as images and other multimedia) have been fully downloaded and are available.

The syntax of the `$().ready` handler is simply this:

```
$().ready(function() {
    // jQuery code goes here
});
```

Pretty much all the jQuery code you write will be executed from within a statement like this. Like the JavaScript `onload` event handler you saw previously, the `$().ready` handler accomplishes two things:

▶ It ensures that the code does not run until the DOM is available; that is, it ensures that any elements your code might be trying to access already exist, so your code doesn't return any errors.

▶ It helps make your code unobtrusive by separating it from the semantic (HTML) and presentation (CSS) layers.

Listing 10.1 enables you to watch the state of readiness occur by loading a document and watching jQuery write a message to the console when the DOM is available and thus a state of readiness has been achieved.

LISTING 10.1   Ensuring a State of Readiness

```
<!DOCTYPE html>
<html lang="en">
    <head>
    <title>Hello World!</title>
    <script
        src="http://ajax.googleapis.com/ajax/libs/jquery/3.2.1/jquery.min.js"
        type="text/javascript">
    </script>

    <script type="text/javascript">
        $().ready(function() {
            console.log("Yes, I am ready!");
        });
    </script>

    </head>
    <body>
        <h1 style="text-align: center">Hello World!<br>Are you ready?</h1>
    </body>
</html>
```

If you open your web browser, open Developer Tools, and then switch to the console, you should see the "Yes, I am ready!" message printed to the console when you load this specific web page, as shown in Figure 10.1. This message is printed by jQuery when the document reaches a ready state.

FIGURE 10.1
jQuery has written a message to the console, declaring a state of readiness.

After your document has reached a ready state—which should take milliseconds and is really imperceptible to human eyes unless you're looking for a console log statement—your page can continue on to be as interactive as you've planned.

Selecting DOM and CSS Content

With your documents in a ready state, *you* should be ready to do more with code. Before diving deeper into specific acts of manipulating content with jQuery, let's take a look at some of the jQuery statements that enable you to select HTML elements. The first step in manipulating content is figuring out the content that you want to manipulate, and the following statements help you out with that.

These jQuery statements each return an object containing an array of the DOM elements specified by the expression that you see. Each of these statements builds off the jQuery wrapper syntax: `$("")`.

```
$("span"); // all HTML span elements
$("#theElement"); // the HTML element having an ID of "theElement"
$(".theClassname"); // HTML elements having a class of "theClassname"
$("div#theElement"); // the <div> element with an ID of "theElement"
$("ul li a.theClassname"); // anchors with class "theClassname"
                           // that are within list items
$("p > span"); // spans that are direct children of paragraphs
$("input[type=password]"); // inputs that have the specified type
$("p:first"); // the first paragraph on the page
$("p:even"); // all even numbered paragraphs
```

These examples are all DOM and CSS selectors, but jQuery also has its own custom selectors, such as the following:

```
$(":header"); // all header elements (h1 to h6)
$(":button"); // any button elements (inputs or buttons)
$(":radio"); // all radio buttons
$(":checkbox"); // all check boxes
$(":checked"); // all selected check boxes or radio buttons
```

If you notice, none of the preceding lines of jQuery has any actions associated with it. These selectors just get the required elements from the DOM. In the next few sections, you'll learn how to work with the content you've selected.

Manipulating HTML Content

jQuery's `html()` and `text()` methods enable you to get and set the content of any elements you've selected (using the statements in the preceding section), and the `attr()` method helps you get and set the values of individual element attributes. Let's see some examples in the code snippets that follow.

The `html()` method gets the HTML of any element or collection of elements, and as such is very similar to JavaScript's `innerHTML` that you've seen in earlier chapters. In the snippet that follows, the variable `htmlContent` will contain all the HTML and text inside an element with an ID of `theElement`:

```
var htmlContent = $("#theElement").html();
```

Using a similar syntax, you can *set*, and not just retrieve, the HTML content of a specified element or collection of elements:

```
$("#theElement").html("<p>Here is some new content for within
    theElement ID.</p>");
```

However, if you want only the text content of an element or collection of elements, without the HTML that surrounds it, you can use the `text()` method:

```
var textContent = $("#theElement").text();
```

If the previous snippets were used in order in your script, the value of `textContent` would be `"Here is some new content for within theElement ID."` (note the lack of surrounding `<p>` and `</p>` tags).

You could again change the content—but now only the text content—of the specified elements using the following snippet:

```
$("#theElement").text("Here is some new content for that element.");
```

In the snippets given previously, you can see how the use of jQuery selectors makes the process of selecting or referencing specific DOM elements pretty easy. In all of those snippets, you could swap out `$("#theElement")` with any of the selectors in the preceding section (and then some), as appropriate to your needs. Want to change the text of all anchor elements within a list to `"Click Me!"`? You can do that:

```
$("ul li a").text("Click Me!");
```

You can also append content rather than replacing it outright:

```
$("#theElement").append("<p>Here is even more new content.</p>");
```

In this snippet, the element with the ID `theElement` would now contain two paragraphs: the modified original from two previous snippets, and the new paragraph of content here.

Another useful trick is the capability to select specific attributes of particular elements. Using the `attr()` method, if you pass an argument containing the name of an attribute, jQuery will return the value of that attribute for the specified element.

For example, if you have an element such as

```
<a id="theElement" title="The Title Goes Here">The Title Goes Here</a>
```

then the following jQuery will return the value of the title attribute, or "The Title Goes Here":

```
var title = $("#theElement").attr("title");
```

You can also pass a second argument to the attr() method to set an attribute value:

```
$("#theElement").attr("title", "This is the new title.");
```

Showing and Hiding Elements

With plain-old JavaScript, showing and hiding page elements usually means manipulating the value of the display or visibility property of the element's style object. Although that works just fine, it can lead to pretty long lines of code, such as this:

```
document.getElementById("theElement").style.visibility = 'visible';
```

You can use jQuery's show() and hide() methods to carry out these tasks with less code. The jQuery methods also offer some additional functionality that's quite useful, as you will see in the following code snippets. First, here is a simple way to make an element or a set of elements visible by calling the show() method:

```
$("#theElement").show(); // makes an element show if it has an ID of "theElement"
```

However, you can also add some additional parameters to spice up the transition. In the following example, the first parameter (fast) determines the speed of the transition. As an alternative to fast or slow, jQuery will happily accept a number of milliseconds for this argument as the required duration of the transition. If no value is set, the transition will occur instantly, with no animation.

TIP

The value "slow" corresponds to 600ms, and "fast" is equivalent to 200ms.

The second argument to the show() method can be a function that operates as a callback; that is, the specified function executes after the transition is complete:

```
$("#theElement").show("fast", function() {
    // do something once the specified element is shown
});
```

The hide() method is, as expected, the exact reverse of show(), enabling you to make page elements invisible with the same optional arguments as you saw for hide():

```
$("#theElement").hide("slow", function() {
    // do something once the specified element is hidden
});
```

Additionally, the `toggle()` method changes the current state of an element or a collection of elements; it makes visible any element in the collection that is currently hidden and hides any that are currently being shown. The same optional duration and callback function parameters are also available to the `toggle()` method:

```
$("#theElement").toggle(1000, function() {
    // do something once the specified element is shown or hidden
});
```

TIP
***
Remember that the `show()`, `hide()`, and `toggle()` methods can be applied to collections of elements, so the elements in that collection will appear or disappear all at once.
***

Animating Elements

As part of its rich feature set, jQuery also has methods for fading elements in and out, as well as optionally setting the transition duration in milliseconds and adding a callback function to the process.

To fade out to invisibility, use the `fadeout()` method:

```
$("#theElement").fadeOut("slow", function() {
    // do something after fadeout() has finished executing
});
```

To fade in, use the `fadeIn()` method, here using the duration in milliseconds:

```
$("#theElement").fadeIn(500, function() {
    // do something after fadeIn() has finished executing
});
```

You can also fade an element only partially, either in or out, using the `fadeTo()` method, also using a duration in milliseconds:

```
$("#theElement").fadeTo(3000, 0.5, function() {
    // do something after fadeTo() has finished executing
});
```

The second parameter in the `fadeIn()` method (here set to `0.5`) represents the target opacity. Its value works similarly to the way opacity values are set in CSS, in that whatever the value of opacity is before the method is called, the element will be animated until it reaches the value specified in the argument.

In addition to fading elements in or out, you can also slide elements upward or downward without a change in opacity. The jQuery methods for sliding an element are direct corollaries to the fading methods you've just seen, and their arguments follow exactly the same rules.

For example, use the `slideDown()` method to slide an element down:

```
$("#theElement").slideDown(150, function() {
    // do something when slideDown() is finished executing
});
```

To slide an element up, use the `slideUp()` method:

```
$("#theElement").slideUp("slow", function() {
    // do something when slideUp() is finished executing
});
```

To provide a visual change to the element in an animated way, you do so by using jQuery to specify the new CSS styles that you want to have applied to the element. jQuery will then impose the new styles but in a gradual manner (instead of applying them instantly as in plain CSS/JavaScript), thus creating an animation effect.

You can use the `animate()` method on a wide range of numerical CSS properties. In this example, the width and height of an element are animated to a size of 400×500 pixels; after the animation is complete, the callback function is used to fade the element to invisibility:

```
$("#theElement").animate(
    {
    width: "400px",
    height: "500px"
    }, 1500, function() {
        $(this).fadeOut("slow");
    }
);
```

NOTE

Most jQuery methods return a jQuery object that can then be used in your call to another method. You could combine two of the methods in the previous examples, through what is called *command chaining*, like this:

```
$("#theElement").fadeOut().fadeIn();
```

In this example, the selected element will fade out and then fade back in. The number of items you can chain is arbitrarily large, allowing for several commands to successively work on the same collection of elements:

```
$("#theElement").text("Hello from jQuery").fadeOut().fadeIn();
```

Putting the Pieces Together to Create a jQuery Animation

Given what you've learned in this chapter so far, you can begin to put the pieces together into a more cohesive whole. Listing 10.2 shows a complete listing of the code used in a basic jQuery animation example; following the listing is an explanation of all the code used.

LISTING 10.2   A jQuery Animation Example

```
<!DOCTYPE html>
<html lang="en">
<head>
    <style>
        #animateMe {
            position: absolute;
            top: 100px;
            left: 100px;
            width: 100px;
            height: 400px;
            border: 2px solid black;
            background-color: red;
            padding: 20px;
        }
    </style>
    <title>Animation Example</title>
    <script
        src="http://ajax.googleapis.com/ajax/libs/jquery/3.2.1/jquery.min.js"
        type="text/javascript">
    </script>

    <script type="text/javascript">
        $().ready(function() {
            $("#animateMe").text("Changing shape...").animate(
                {
                width: "400px",
                height: "200px"
                }, 5000, function() {
                    $(this).text("Fading away...").fadeOut(4000);
                }
            );
        });
    </script>
</head>
<body>
    <div id="animateMe"></div>
</body>
</html>
```

If you put the code from Listing 10.1 into a file and open it with your web browser, you will see something like what's shown in Figures 10.2 and 10.3—bear in mind that it's difficult to capture animation examples in screenshots!

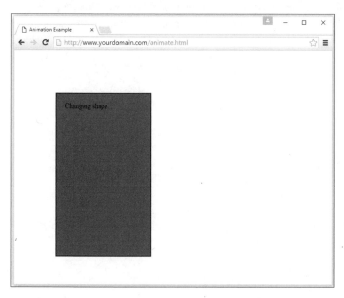

FIGURE 10.2
The animation example shows the element changing shape.

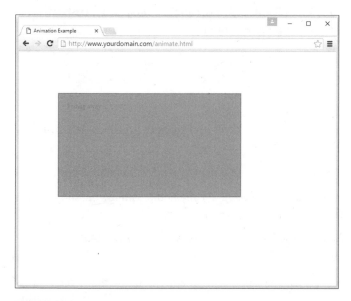

FIGURE 10.3
The animation example shows the element fading away after having changed shape.

Let's take a closer look at the code that produced these examples. First, in the `<style>` section of the script, an element with an ID of `animateMe` is defined as an absolutely positioned rectangle that is 100 pixels wide and 400 pixels high, with the upper-left corner of that rectangle positioned 100 pixels from the top and 100 pixels from the left edge of the browser. This rectangle has a red background and a 2-pixel solid black border, with an inside padding of 20 pixels on all sides.

```
#animateMe {
    position: absolute;
    top: 100px;
    left: 100px;
    width: 100px;
    height: 400px;
    border: 2px solid black;
    background-color: red;
    padding: 20px;
}
```

The first `<script>` element contains a link to the Google Code CDN, which stores the particular version of the jQuery library we are using in this script, jQuery 3.2.1:

```
<script
    src="http://ajax.googleapis.com/ajax/libs/jquery/3.2.1/jquery.min.js"
    type="text/javascript">
</script>
```

The magic happens in the next `<script>` element, which contains actual jQuery. First, ensure that the document is in a ready state by wrapping the primary commands in the `$().ready()` handler:

```
$().ready(function() {
    // more code goes here
});
```

Within the `$().ready()` handler is a chain of commands and callback functions that ensure these actions happen to any element with an ID of `animateMe`:

1. Use the `text()` method to place text within the element labeled "Changing shape...."

2. Over a period of 5000 milliseconds, use the `animate()` method to change the shape of the element to one that is 400 pixels wide and 200 pixels high.

3. When the shape change is complete, use the `text()` method to place text within the element labeled "Fading away...."

4. Over a period of 4000 milliseconds, use the `fadeOut()` method to cause the element to disappear from view.

All the preceding steps are found in this chunk of the code:

```
$("#animateMe").text("Changing shape...").animate(
    {
    width: "400px",
    height: "200px"
    }, 5000, function() {
        $(this).text("Fading away...").fadeOut(4000);
    }
);
```

Finally, within the body of the HTML document, you see a `<div>` with an ID of `animateMe`. This `<div>`, which contains no text in the HTML, is the DOM element that all the jQuery code is manipulating:

```
<div id="animateMe"></div>
```

Although there's no text inside the `<div>` element originally, the jQuery `text()` method adds it in for display as the script executes. That's really all there is to it—you have some basic DOM elements that this powerful jQuery library can manipulate in many ways to produce an interactive experience for your users. Modifications to the display can happen automatically, as in the preceding example, or by capturing events that the user enacts, such as mouse clicks and key presses.

Handling Events with jQuery

All the examples in this chapter so far show jQuery that simply runs when the script is loaded in the browser. But as you've seen already in this book—specifically in Chapter 9, "Understanding JavaScript Event Handling" —and in your experience online in general, interactivity occurs when a user invokes actions through mouse clicks or key presses. For example, you may click a button to start a process, hover over an image to see a larger version, and so on.

jQuery has its own syntax for handling events, which is as straightforward as the basic HTML and JavaScript you've seen in Chapter 9. For example, you can attach event handlers to elements or collections of elements—such as all `<a>` elements, an `<a>` element with given ID, all `<a>` elements with a given class name, and so on.

Capturing click events happens directly with the jQuery `.click()` event handler:

```
$("a").click(function() {
    // execute this code when any anchor element is clicked
});
```

You can also handle a click event, `.click()`, using a named function:

```
function hello() {
    alert("Hello from jQuery");
}
$("a").click(hello);
```

In both instances, the code within the curly braces or the named function (depending on which you have used) will be executed when any anchor is clicked. Note that the `.click()` event handler is not the only one available to you; other event handlers include the following, which correspond to events you've seen in more detail in Chapter 9 of this book:

- ▶ `.keydown()`—Handles a `keydown` JavaScript event

- ▶ `.keypress()`—Handles a `keypress` JavaScript event

- ▶ `.keyup()`—Handles a `keyup` JavaScript event

- ▶ `.dblclick()`—Handles a `dblclick` (double-click) JavaScript event

- ▶ `.focusout()`—Handles a `focusout` JavaScript event

- ▶ `.mousedown()`—Handles a `mousedown` JavaScript event

- ▶ `.mouseenter()`—Handles a `mouseenter` JavaScript event

- ▶ `.mouseleave()`—Handles a `mouseleave` JavaScript event

- ▶ `.mousemove()`—Handles a `mousemove` JavaScript event

- ▶ `.mouseout()`—Handles a `mouseout` JavaScript event

- ▶ `.mouseover()`—Handles a `mouseover` JavaScript event

- ▶ `.mouseup()`—Handles a `mouseup` JavaScript event

For more information and documentation on other methods available in jQuery to handle JavaScript events, visit http://api.jquery.com/category/events/.

Summary

In this chapter, you took a closer look at the basics of using jQuery in your interactive sites, which begins by including the library and verifying the ready state of your document. From that point forward, you learned how to select page elements by referencing their element name, ID, class, or other position within the DOM, and how to manipulate the text within or the appearance of those elements.

Additionally, you learned about chaining jQuery commands together, and how to handle JavaScript events with jQuery so that users can initiate visual display or other changes through actions they take with their keyboard or mouse.

Q&A

Q. **Can I use more than one third-party library in the same script?**

A. Yes, in theory: If the libraries are well written and designed not to interfere with each other, there should be no problem with combining them. In practice, this will depend on the libraries you need and how they were written, but many JavaScript libraries can be used together or will include a warning about incompatibilities. For example, $ is an alias for jQuery, so if you are using other libraries that use $ as an alias, you should call `jQuery.noConflict()` in your scripts and replace all uses of `$()` with `jQuery()`. You can learn more at http://learn.jquery.com/using-jquery-core/avoid-conflicts-other-libraries/.

Q. **This chapter was short, but isn't jQuery huge?**

A. Remarkably, even though jQuery is very powerful, it is not in fact a huge codebase, nor is it particularly unwieldy. Clocking in at 10,000 lines of code or so, and around 275KB (when not minimized), it's definitely bigger than a web page, that's for sure! But it is true that packed into those 10,000 lines of code are many features we have not discussed here. We will talk a little more about the jQuery UI library in the next chapter, but even that is not sufficient to cover everything you might find in the technical documentation at http://api.jquery.com/ or in the more user-friendly documentation and tutorials site at http://learn.jquery.com/.

Workshop

The Workshop contains quiz questions and exercises to help you solidify your understanding of the material covered. Test your knowledge of JavaScript libraries by answering the following questions. Try to answer all questions before looking at the "Answers" section that follows.

Quiz

1. How could you select all page elements having a class of `sidebar`?

   A. `$(".sidebar")`

   B. `$("class: sidebar")`

   C. `$("#sidebar")`

2. The expression `$("p:first").show()` does what, exactly?

   A. Displays `<p>` elements before displaying any other elements

   B. Makes the first `<p>` element on the page visible

   C. Makes the first line of all `<p>` elements visible

3. When used with methods for fading, sliding, and animating elements, which of the following is not a valid value?

   A. `fast`

   B. `1000`

   C. `quick`

Answers

1. **A.** `$(".sidebar")`

2. **B.** Makes the first paragraph element on the page visible

3. **C.** `quick`

Exercises

To further explore the JavaScript features you learned about in this chapter, you can perform the following exercises:

▶ Modify the example in Listing 10.2 to react to mouse events, using jQuery.

▶ Go back to scripts used in earlier chapters that use JavaScript events for interactivity. Rewrite those examples using basic jQuery you learned here.

## CHAPTER 11

AJAX: Remote Scripting

What You'll Learn in This Chapter:

▶ How AJAX enables JavaScript to communicate with server-side programs and files

▶ Using the `XMLHttpRequest` object's properties and methods

▶ Creating your own AJAX library

▶ Using AJAX to read data from an XML file

▶ Debugging AJAX applications

▶ Using AJAX to communicate with a PHP program

Remote scripting, also known as AJAX—which stands for Asynchronous JavaScript and XML—is a browser feature that enables JavaScript to escape its client-side boundaries and work with files on a web server or with server-side programs. In this chapter, you'll learn how AJAX works and create two working examples of client-side to server-side interactivity using AJAX requests. This chapter builds on the JavaScript you have learned in the previous chapters, and reintroduces you to PHP, which you will learn much more about as the book moves forward.

Introducing AJAX

Traditionally, one of the major limitations of JavaScript was that it couldn't communicate with a web server because it is a client-side technology—JavaScript runs within the browser. For example, although you can create a game purely in JavaScript, keeping a list of high scores stored on a server requires some form of submitting data to a server-side script, which JavaScript alone could not do (because it originally wasn't meant to do that).

Speaking purely about user interactions, one of the early limitations of web pages in general was that getting data from the user to the server, or from the server to the user, generally required a new page to be loaded and displayed. But in 2017, you would be hard-pressed to find some website in your daily browsing that *doesn't* allow you to interact with content without loading a new page every time you click a button or submit a form. For example, if you use web-based email such as Google or Yahoo! Mail, or if you use Facebook or Twitter, then you're interacting with some AJAX-based functionality.

AJAX was the answer to both of the problems indicated previously. AJAX, which you may also see written as just "Ajax," refers to JavaScript's capability to use a built-in object, XMLHttpRequest, to communicate with a web server without submitting a form or loading a page. This object is supported by Internet Explorer, Firefox, Chrome, and all other modern browsers.

Although the term AJAX was coined in 2005, the XMLHttpRequest object has been supported by browsers for years—it was developed by Microsoft and first appeared in Internet Explorer 5 (if you're keeping track at home, that's *really* old). In the past decade, it has become one of the cornerstones of advanced web application development. Another name for this technique is *remote scripting*.

NOTE

The term AJAX first appeared in an online article by Jesse James Garrett of Adaptive Path on February 18, 2005. It still appears here, which is well worth a read: http://adaptivepath.org/ideas/ajax-new-approach-web-applications/.

In the next few sections, we'll look at the individual components of AJAX in a little more detail.

The JavaScript Client (Front End)

Traditionally, JavaScript had one way of communicating with a server: through an HTML form submission. Remote scripting allows for much more versatile communication with the server. The A in *AJAX* stands for *asynchronous*, which means that the browser (and the user) isn't left hanging while waiting for the server to respond. Here's how a typical AJAX request works:

1. The script creates an XMLHttpRequest object and sends it to the web server. After sending the request, the script can continue performing other tasks.

2. The server responds by sending the contents of a file, or the output of a server-side program.

3. When the response arrives from the server, a JavaScript function is triggered to act on the data.

4. Because the goal is a more responsive user interface, the script usually displays the data from the server using the DOM, eliminating the need for a page refresh.

In practice, this happens very quickly—almost imperceptible to the user—but even with a slow server, it will still work. Also, because the requests are asynchronous, more than one request can be in progress at a time.

The Server-Side Script (Back End)

The part of an application that resides on the web server is commonly referred to as the *back end*. You've learned about this concept in this book already, in your brief introduction to PHP in Chapter 5, "Introducing PHP." The simplest back-end script is a static file on the server—JavaScript can request the file with XMLHttpRequest and then read and act on its contents.

Most back-end scripts are typically server-side programs running in a language such as PHP, but they can also be static files full of data that is simply being returned to the user.

JavaScript can send data to a server-side program using the GET and POST methods; these are the same two methods an HTML form uses. In a GET request, the data is encoded in the URL that loads the program. In a POST request, the data is sent separately and the packet can contain more data than a GET request. If it helps, think of the AJAX request as mimicking the action of an HTML-based form, only without the <form> and other related tags.

XML

The *X* in *AJAX* stands for *XML* (Extensible Markup Language), the universal markup language designed to store and transport data. A server-side file or program can send data in XML format, and JavaScript can act on the data using its methods for working with XML. These methods are similar to the DOM methods you've already used—for example, you can use the getElements-ByTagName() method to find elements with a particular tag in the data.

Keep in mind that XML is just one way to send data, and not always the easiest. The server could just as easily send plain text, which the script could display, or HTML, which the script could insert into the page using the innerHTML property. In fact, over the past decade that AJAX has been in use, a shift has occurred such that it is more typical to see data transferred in JSON format than in XML format. However, "AJAJ" doesn't have the same ring to it.

NOTE
JSON (JavaScript Object Notation) takes the idea of encoding data in JavaScript and formalizes it. See http://www.json.org/ for details and code examples in many languages.

Popular Examples of AJAX

Although typical HTML and JavaScript are used to build web pages and sites, AJAX techniques often result in *web applications*—web-based services that perform work for the user. Here are a few well-known examples of AJAX:

▶ Google's Gail mail client (http://mail.google.com/) uses AJAX to make a fast-responding email application. You can delete messages and perform other tasks without waiting for a new page to load.

▶ Amazon.com uses AJAX for many functions. For example, if you click one of the Yes/No voting buttons for a product comment, it sends your vote to the server and a message appears next to the button thanking you, all without loading a page.

▶ Facebook uses AJAX all over the place, such as every time you "like" something, or as used to produce the "infinite scroll" that allows you to peruse your timeline unless the server no longer has anything to send back to you to fulfill your request for more.

These are just a few examples. Subtle bits of remote scripting appear all over the Web, and you might not even notice them—you'll just be annoyed a little bit less often at waiting for a page to load. Because remote scripting can be complicated, several frameworks and libraries have been developed to simplify AJAX programming. For starters, the JavaScript libraries and frameworks described in the previous chapter include functions that simplify remote scripting.

Using `XMLHttpRequest`

We will now look at how to use `XMLHttpRequest` to communicate with a server. This might seem a bit complex, but the process is the same for any request. In fact, it's so similar that later in this chapter you will create a reusable code library to simplify this process.

Creating a Request

The first step in creating a request is to create an `XMLHttpRequest` object. To do this, you use the `new` keyword, just like when you create other JavaScript objects, as you learned in Chapter 8, "JavaScript Fundamentals: Functions, Objects, and Flow Control." The following statement creates an `XMLHttpRequest` request object:

```
var ajaxreq = new XMLHttpRequest();
```

The variable you use (`ajaxreq` in the example) stores the `XMLHttpRequest` object, and you'll use the methods of this object to open and send a request, as explained in the following sections.

Opening a URL

The `open()` method of the `XMLHttpRequest` object specifies the filename as well as the method in which data will be sent to the server: `GET` or `POST`. These are the same methods supported by web forms; we'll spend more time on these methods in later chapters of the book, as appropriate to the work you'll be doing.

```
ajaxreq.open("GET","filename");
```

For the `GET` method, the data you send is included in the URL. For example, this command opens the `search.php` script stored on your server and sends the value `John` to the script as the `query` parameter:

```
ajaxreq.open("GET","search.php?query=John");
```

Sending the Request

You use the `send()` method of the `XMLHttpRequest` object to send the request to the server. If you are using the `POST` method, the data to send is the argument for `send()`. For a `GET` request, you can use the `null` value instead:

```
ajaxreq.send(null);
```

Awaiting a Response

After the request is sent, your script will continue without waiting for a result. Because the result could come at any time, you can detect it with an event handler. The XMLHttpRequest object has an onreadystatechange event handler for this purpose. You can create a function to deal with the response and set it as the handler for this event:

```
ajaxreq.onreadystatechange = MyFunc;
```

The request object has a property, readyState, that indicates its status, and this event is triggered whenever the readyState property changes. The values of readyState range from 0 for a new request to 4 for a complete request, so your event-handling function usually needs to watch for a value of 4.

Although the request is complete, it might not have been successful. The status property is set to 200 if the request succeeded or an error code if it failed. The statusText property stores a text explanation of the error or OK for success.

CAUTION

As usual with event handlers, be sure to specify the function name without parentheses. With parentheses, you're referring to the *result* of the function; without them, you're referring to the function itself.

Interpreting the Response Data

When the readyState property reaches 4 and the request is complete, the data returned from the server is available to your script in two properties: responseText is the response in raw text form, and responseXML is the response as an XML object. If the data was not in XML format, only the text property will be available.

JavaScript's DOM methods are meant to work on XML, so you can use them with the responseXML property. Later in this chapter, you'll use the getElementsByTagName() method to extract data from XML.

Creating a Simple AJAX Library

You should be aware by now that AJAX requests can be a bit complex, and to repeat that complex code in every page that calls it definitely makes for unwieldy pages that are no fun to maintain. To make things easier, you can create an AJAX library and simply reference it in your pages, as you do any external script. This library can then provide functions that handle making a request and receiving the result, which you can reuse any time you need AJAX functions.

The library in Listing 11.1 will be used in the two examples later in this chapter. This listing shows the complete AJAX library, in a bit of a verbose fashion so that you can see all the inner-workings as you go.

LISTING 11.1 The AJAX Library

```
// global variables to keep track of the request
// and the function to call when done
var ajaxreq=false, ajaxCallback;

// ajaxRequest: Sets up a request
function ajaxRequest(filename) {
    try {
        //make a new request object
        ajaxreq= new XMLHttpRequest();
    } catch (error) {
        return false;
    }
    ajaxreq.open("GET", filename);
    ajaxreq.onreadystatechange = ajaxResponse;
    ajaxreq.send(null);
}

// ajaxResponse: Waits for response and calls a function
function ajaxResponse() {
    if (ajaxreq.readyState !=4) return;
    if (ajaxreq.status==200) {
        // if the request succeeded...
        if (ajaxCallback) ajaxCallback();
    } else alert("Request failed: " + ajaxreq.statusText);
    return true;
}
```

The following sections explain the library's code in a bit more detail.

The `ajaxRequest` Function

The `ajaxRequest` function handles all the steps necessary to create and send an `XMLHttpRequest`. First, it creates the `XMLHttpRequest` object. We use `try` and `catch` when creating the request just to ensure that we do not continue moving forward if an error occurs.

The `ajaxResponse` Function

The `ajaxResponse` function is used as the `onreadystatechange` event handler. This function first checks the `readyState` property for a value of 4. If it has a different value, the function returns without doing anything. The full range of values are:

- ▶ 0—not initialized

- ▶ 1—connection established with server

- ▶ 2—request received

- ▶ 3—processing

- ▶ 4—request complete

Next, it checks the `status` property for a value of `200`, which indicates that the request was successful. If so, it runs the function stored in the `ajaxCallback` variable. If not, it displays the error message in an alert box. For a useful list of HTTP status codes and what they mean, please see https://developer.mozilla.org/en-US/docs/Web/HTTP/Status.

Using the Library

To use this library, follow these steps:

1. Save the library file as `ajax.js` in the same folder as your HTML documents and scripts.

2. Include the script in the `<head>` of your document, using a `<script>` tag. It should be included before any other scripts that use its features.

3. In your script, create a function to be called when the request is complete, and set the `ajaxCallback` variable to the function.

4. Call the `ajaxRequest()` function. Its parameter is the filename of the server-side program or file. (This version of the library supports `GET` requests only, so you don't need to specify the method.)

5. Your function specified in `ajaxCallback` will be called when the request completes successfully, and the global variable `ajaxreq` will store the data in its `responseXML` and `responseText` properties.

The two remaining examples in this chapter make use of this library to create AJAX applications.

Creating an AJAX Quiz Using the Library

Now that you have a reusable AJAX library, you can use it to create simple JavaScript applications that take advantage of remote scripting. This first example displays quiz questions on a page and prompts you for the answers.

Rather than including the questions in the script, this example reads the quiz questions and answers from an XML file on the server as a demonstration of AJAX.

CAUTION

Unlike most of the scripts in this book, this example requires a web server. It does not work on a local machine due to browsers' security restrictions on remote scripting.

The HTML File

The HTML for this example is straightforward. It defines a simple form with an Answer field and a Submit button, along with some hooks for the script. The HTML for this example is shown in Listing 11.2.

LISTING 11.2   The HTML File for the Quiz Example

```
<!DOCTYPE html>
<html lang="en">
  <head>
    <title>AJAX Quiz Test</title>
    <script type="text/javascript" src="ajax.js"></script>
  </head>
  <body>
    <h1>AJAX Quiz Example</h1>
    <button id="start_quiz">Start Quiz</button>

    <p><strong>Question:</strong><br>
    <span id="question">[Press Button to Start Quiz]</span></p>

    <p><strong>Answer:</strong><br>
    <input type="text" name="answer" id="answer"></p>

    <button id="submit">Submit Answer</button>

    <script type="text/javascript" src="quiz.js"></script>
  </body>
</html>
```

This HTML file includes the following elements:

▶ The <script> tag in the <head> section includes the AJAX library you created in the preceding section from the ajax.js file.

▶ The <script> tag in the <body> section includes the quiz.js file, which will contain the quiz script.

▶ The <span id="question"> tag sets up a place for the question to be inserted by the script.

▶ The text field with the id value "answer" is where the user will answer the question.

▶ The button with the id value "submit" will submit an answer.

▶ The button with the id value "start_quiz" will start the quiz.

You can test the HTML document at this time by placing the file on your web server and accessing it via the URL, but the buttons won't work until you add the XML and JavaScript files, as you'll learn in the next two sections.

The XML File

The XML file for the quiz is shown in Listing 11.3. I've filled it with a few JavaScript questions, but it could easily be adapted for another purpose.

LISTING 11.3 The XML File Containing the Quiz Questions and Answers

```
<?xml version="1.0" ?>
<quiz>
    <question>What DOM object contains URL information for the window?</question>
    <answer>location</answer>
    <question>Which method of the document object finds the
        object for an element?</question>
    <answer>getElementById</answer>
    <question>If you declare a variable outside a function,
        is it global or local?</question>
    <answer>global</answer>
    <question>What is the formal standard for the JavaScript language
    called?</question>
    <answer>ECMAScript</answer>
</quiz>
```

The `<quiz>` tag encloses the entire file, and each question and each answer is enclosed in `<question>` and `<answer>` tags. Remember, this is XML, not HTML—these are not standard HTML tags, but tags that were created for this example. Because this file will be used only by your script, it does not need to follow a standard format.

To use this file, save it as `questions.xml` in the same folder as the HTML document. It will be loaded by the script you create in the next section.

Of course, with a quiz this small, you could have made things easier by storing the questions and answers in a JavaScript array. But imagine a much larger quiz, with thousands of questions, or a server-side program that pulls questions from a database, or even a hundred different files with different quizzes to choose from, and you can see the benefit of using a separate XML file.

The JavaScript File

Because you have a separate library to handle the complexities of making an AJAX request and receiving the response, the script for this example needs to deal only with the action for the quiz itself. Listing 11.4 shows the JavaScript file for this example.

LISTING 11.4 The JavaScript File for the Quiz Example

```
// global variable questionNumber is the current question number
var questionNumber=0;

// load the questions from the XML file
function getQuestions() {
   obj=document.getElementById("question");
   obj.firstChild.nodeValue="(please wait)";
   ajaxCallback = nextQuestion;
   ajaxRequest("questions.xml");
}

// display the next question
function nextQuestion() {
   questions = ajaxreq.responseXML.getElementsByTagName("question");
   obj=document.getElementById("question");
   if (questionNumber < questions.length) {
      question = questions[questionNumber].firstChild.nodeValue;
      obj.firstChild.nodeValue=question;
   } else {
      obj.firstChild.nodeValue="(no more questions)";
   }
}

// check the user's answer
function checkAnswer() {
   answers = ajaxreq.responseXML.getElementsByTagName("answer");
   answer = answers[questionNumber].firstChild.nodeValue;
   answerfield = document.getElementById("answer");
   if (answer == answerfield.value) {
      alert("Correct!");
   }
   else {
      alert("Incorrect. The correct answer is: " + answer);
   }
   questionNumber = questionNumber + 1;
   answerfield.value="";
   nextQuestion();
}

// Set up the event handlers for the buttons
obj=document.getElementById("start_quiz");
obj.onclick=getQuestions;
ans=document.getElementById("submit");
ans.onclick=checkAnswer;
```

This script consists of the following:

▶ The first `var` statement defines a global variable, `questionNumber`, which keeps track of which question is currently displayed. It is initially set to zero for the first question.

▶ The `getQuestions()` function is called when the user clicks the Start Quiz button. This function uses the AJAX library to request the contents of the `questions.xml` file. It sets the `ajaxCallback` variable to the `nextQuestion()` function.

▶ The `nextQuestion()` function is called when the AJAX request is complete. This function uses the `getElementsByTagName()` method on the `responseXML` property to find all the questions (`<question>` tags) and store them in the `questions` array.

▶ The `checkAnswer()` function is called when the user submits an answer. It uses `getElementsByTagName()` to store the answers (`<answer>` tags) in the `answers` array, and then compares the answer for the current question with the user's answer and displays an alert indicating whether the user was right or wrong.

▶ The script commands after this function set up two event handlers. One attaches the `getQuestions()` function to the Start Quiz button to set up the quiz; the other attaches the `checkAnswer()` function to the Submit button.

Testing the Quiz

To try this example, you'll need all four files in the same folder: `ajax.js` (the AJAX library), `quiz.js` (the quiz functions), `questions.xml` (the questions), and the HTML document. All but the HTML document need to have the correct filenames so that they will work correctly. Also remember that because it uses AJAX, this example requires a web server.

Figure 11.1 shows the quiz in action. The second question has just been answered.

FIGURE 11.1
The quiz example loaded in a web browser.

Debugging AJAX-Based Applications

Dealing with remote scripting means working with several languages at once—JavaScript, server-side languages such as PHP, data markup such as XML or JSON, and of course HTML and CSS. Thus, when you find an error, it can be difficult to track down. Here are some tips for debugging AJAX-based applications:

- ▶ Be sure that all filenames are correct and that the paths for all of these files are indicated correctly in your code.

- ▶ If you are using a server-side language, test the script without using the AJAX request: Load the script in the browser and make sure it works, and try passing variables to the script via the URL and checking the resulting output.

- ▶ Check the `statusText` property for the results of your request—an `alert` message or a message logged to the console is helpful here. It is often a clear message such as `"File not found"` that ends up explaining the problem.

- ▶ If you're using a third-party library, check its documentation—many libraries have built-in debugging features you can enable to examine what's going on.

▼ TRY IT YOURSELF

1. One of the most impressive demonstrations of AJAX is *live search*: Whereas a normal search form requires that you click a button and wait for a page to load to see the results, a live search displays results within the page immediately as you type in the search field. As you type letters or press the Backspace key, the results are updated instantly to make it easy to find the result you need.

2. Using the AJAX library you created earlier, live search is not too hard to implement. This example uses a PHP script on the server to provide the search results.

CAUTION

Once again, because it uses AJAX, this example requires a web server. You'll also need PHP to be installed, which it is by default for the vast majority of hosting services.

The HTML Form

The HTML for this example simply defines a search field and leaves some room for the dynamic results. The HTML document is shown in Listing 11.5.

LISTING 11.5   The HTML File for the Live Search Example

```
<!DOCTYPE html>
<html lang="en">
  <head>
```

```
  <title>AJAX Live Search Example</title>
  <script type="text/javascript" src="ajax.js"></script>
</head>
<body>
  <h1>AJAX Live Search Example</h1>

  <p><strong>Search for:</strong>
  <input type="text" size="40" id="searchlive"></p>

  <div id="results">
     <ul id="list">
     <li>[Search results will display here.]</li>
     </ul>
   </div>
  <script type="text/javascript" src="search.js"></script>
  </body>
</html>
```

This HTML document includes the following:

▶ The <script> tag in the <head> section includes the AJAX library, ajax.js.

▶ The <script> tag in the <body> section includes the search.js script, which you'll create next.

▶ The <input> element with the id value "searchlive" is where you'll type your search query.

▶ The <div> element with the id value "results" acts as a container for the dynamically fetched results. A bulleted list is created with a <ul> tag; this will be replaced with a list of results when you start typing.

The PHP Back End

Next, you'll need a server-side program to produce the search results. This PHP program includes a list of names stored in an array. It will respond to a JavaScript query with the names that match what the user has typed so far. The names will be returned in XML format. For example, here is the output of the PHP program when searching for "smith":

```
<names>
<name>John Smith</name>
<name>Jane Smith</name>
</names>
```

Although the list of names is stored within the PHP program here for simplicity, in a real application it would more likely be stored in a database—and this script could easily be adapted to work with a database containing thousands of names. The PHP program is shown in Listing 11.6.

LISTING 11.6   The PHP Code for the Live Search Example

```php
<?php
  header("Content-type: text/xml");
  $names = array (
   "John Smith", "John Jones", "Jane Smith", "Jane Tillman",
   "Abraham Lincoln", "Sally Johnson", "Kilgore Trout",
   "Bob Atkinson", "Joe Cool", "Dorothy Barnes",
   "Elizabeth Carlson", "Frank Dixon", "Gertrude East",
   "Harvey Frank", "Inigo Montoya", "Jeff Austin",
   "Lynn Arlington", "Michael Washington", "Nancy West" );
echo "<?xml version=\"1.0\" ?>\n";
echo "<names>\n";
while (list($k,$v)=each($names)) {
    if (stristr($v,$_GET['query'])) {
       echo "<name>$v</name>\n";
    }
}
echo "</names>\n";
?>
```

You've seen PHP scripts before but haven't gone full steam ahead with PHP (that's up next!), so here's a summary of how this program works:

▶ The `header` statement sends a header indicating that the output is in XML format. This is required for `XMLHttpRequest` to correctly use the `responseXML` property.

▶ The `$names` array stores the list of names. You can use a much longer list of names without changing the rest of the code.

▶ The program looks for a GET variable called `query` and uses a loop to output all the names that match the query.

▶ Save the PHP script as `search.php` in the same folder as the HTML file. You can test it by typing a query such as **search.php?query=John** in the browser's URL field. Use the View Source command to view the XML result.

The JavaScript Front End

Finally, the JavaScript for this example is shown in Listing 11.7.

LISTING 11.7   The JavaScript File for the Live Search Example

```javascript
// global variable to manage the timeout
var t;

// Start a timeout with each keypress
```

```
function startSearch() {
   if (t) window.clearTimeout(t);
   t = window.setTimeout("liveSearch()",200);
}


// Perform the search
function liveSearch() {
   // assemble the PHP filename
   query = document.getElementById("searchlive").value;
   filename = "search.php?query=" + query;
   // DisplayResults will handle the Ajax response
   ajaxCallback = displayResults;
   // Send the Ajax request
   ajaxRequest(filename);
}


// Display search results
function displayResults() {
   // remove old list
   ul = document.getElementById("list");
   div = document.getElementById("results");
   div.removeChild(ul);

   // make a new list
   ul = document.createElement("ul");
   ul.id="list";
   names = ajaxreq.responseXML.getElementsByTagName("name");
   for (i = 0; i < names.length; i++) {
      li = document.createElement("li");
      name = names[i].firstChild.nodeValue;
      text = document.createTextNode(name);
      li.appendChild(text);
      ul.appendChild(li);
   }
   if (names.length==0) {
      li = document.createElement("li");
      li.appendChild(document.createTextNode("No results"));
      ul.appendChild(li);
   }

   // display the new list
   div.appendChild(ul);
}


// set up event handler
obj=document.getElementById("searchlive");
obj.onkeydown = startSearch;
```

This script includes the following components:

▶ A global variable, t, is defined. This stores a pointer to the timeout used later in the script.

▶ The startSearch() function is called when the user presses a key. This function uses setTimeout() to call the liveSearch() function after a 200-millisecond delay. The delay is necessary so that the key the user types has time to appear in the search field.

▶ The liveSearch() function assembles a filename that combines search.php with the query in the search field and then launches an AJAX request using the library's ajaxRequest() function.

▶ The displayResults() function is called when the AJAX request is complete. It deletes the bulleted list from the <div id="results"> section and then assembles a new list using the W3C DOM and the AJAX results. If there are no results, it displays a "No results" message in the list.

▶ The final lines of the script set up the startSearch() function as an event handler for the keydown event of the search field.

Making It All Work

To try this example, you'll need three files on a web server: ajax.js (the library), search.js (the search script), and the HTML file. Figure 11.2 shows this example in action.

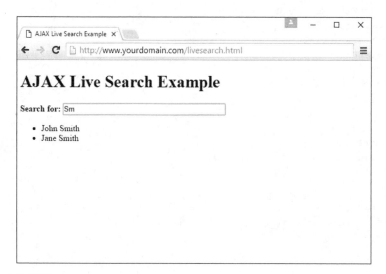

FIGURE 11.2
The live search example as displayed in the browser.

Using jQuery's Built-in Functions for AJAX

Having learned (and practiced) the "long" way of implementing AJAX requests in your website, you should know that jQuery has its own built-in functions for performing the same tasks. If you are already using jQuery, the following code snippets should make your programming life a lot easier.

NOTE

Of course, you can also include the jQuery library just to use its AJAX-related functionality, but if you do so, recognize you're requiring the user's browser to download a lot of code that you otherwise will not be using.

There are numerous AJAX-related jQuery functions and methods, which you can read about in great detail at http://api.jquery.com/category/ajax/. For the purposes of a quick introduction, the following three jQuery shorthand methods enable you to do most of what you need in a basic AJAX implementation. To try these examples, you need to load the jQuery library via a `<script>` tag, as you learned in Chapter 10, "The Basics of Using jQuery."

The first of these shorthand methods is `load()`, which enables you to get a document from the server and display it "as is." This method is useful if you have a set of static HTML pages that you want to piece together to form a cohesive view. For example, in the code that follows, the jQuery `load()` method gets the content from the file on the server called `newContent.html` and replaces the text of the element with an ID value of `newContentHere` with the content that is in the `newContent.html` document:

```
$(function() {
    $("#newContentHere").load("newContent.html");
});
```

If all of that seems a little too magical—if it hides the functionality from view and gives you less control than you would like—there are two other jQuery shorthand methods that provide more opportunities for AJAX scripting, both of which provide you with more control over what is going on. The `get()` and `post()` methods in jQuery enable you to specify a target script to either `GET` or `POST` as well as to send parameters and values along with your request.

In the example that follows, the `get()` jQuery method is used to send two parameters to the script called `serverScript.php`, via the `GET` HTTP method. These parameters are called `param1` and `param2`, with values of `value1` and `value2`, respectively. When the request has been made and has returned a result, an alert is displayed.

```
$.get("serverScript.php",
    {param1: "value1", param2: "value2"},
    function (data) {
        alert("Server responded: " + data);
    }
);
```

When the `post()` jQuery method is used, the syntax is essentially the same:

```
$.post("serverScript.php",
    {param1: "value1", param2: "value2"},
    function (data) {
        alert("Server responded: " + data);
    }
);
```

Summary

In this chapter, you learned how AJAX, or remote scripting, enables JavaScript to communicate with a web server and retrieve results in a seemingly uninterrupted way for the user. You created a reusable AJAX library that can be used to create any number of AJAX applications, and you created a sample quiz using questions and answers stored in an XML file. Finally, you created a live search form using AJAX and PHP and then learned you could perform similar functions using jQuery's built-in AJAX functionality.

Q&A

Q. **What happens if the server is slow, or never responds to the request?**

A. When your server is slow, the callback function is called late or not at all. This can cause trouble with overlapping requests: For example, in the live search example, an erratic server might cause the responses for the first few characters typed to come in a few seconds apart, thus confusing the user. You can remedy this problem by checking the `readyState` property to make sure that a request is not already in progress before you start another one.

Q. **In the live search example, why is the `onkeydown` event handler necessary? Wouldn't the `onchange` event be easier to use?**

A. Although `onchange` tells you when a form field has changed, it is not triggered until the user moves on to a different field—it doesn't work for "live" search, so you have to watch for key presses instead. The `onkeypress` handler would work; however, in some browsers it doesn't detect the Backspace key, and it's nice to have the search update when you backspace to shorten the query.

Workshop

The Workshop contains quiz questions and exercises to help you solidify your understanding of the material covered. Test your knowledge of AJAX by answering the following questions. Try to answer all questions before looking at the "Answers" section that follows.

Quiz

1. Which of the following is the *A* in *AJAX*?

    A. Advanced

    B. Asynchronous

    C. Application

2. Which property of an `XMLHttpRequest` object indicates whether the request was successful?

    A. `status`

    B. `readyState`

    C. `success`

3. True or false? jQuery has numerous AJAX-related functions that you could use instead of creating your own.

Answers

1. B. AJAX stands for Asynchronous JavaScript and XML.

2. A. The `status` property indicates whether the request was successful; `readyState` indicates whether the request is complete, but it does not indicate success.

3. True, but it comes at the cost of loading additional information in the user's browser.

Exercises

If you want to gain more experience with AJAX, try the following exercises:

▶ Build your own XML file of questions and answers on your favorite topic and try it with the quiz example.

▶ Use the AJAX library to add an AJAX feature to your site or create a simple example of your own.

▶ Rewrite the quiz example using one or more of jQuery's built-in AJAX functions.

CHAPTER 12
PHP Fundamentals: Variables, Strings, and Arrays

What You'll Learn in This Chapter:

▸ All about variables—what they are, why you need to use them, and how to use them

▸ Understanding and using data types

▸ How to use some of the more commonly used operators

▸ How to use operators to create expressions

▸ How to define and use constants

▸ How to create associative and multidimensional arrays

▸ How to use the numerous array-related functions built in to PHP

In this chapter, you get your hands dirty with some of the nuts and bolts of the PHP scripting language, including variables, strings, operators, and arrays. It might sound like a lot, but even if this is your first foray into PHP, don't worry—the earlier chapters on JavaScript fundamentals have prepared you for this one. No matter that JavaScript is on the client side and PHP is on the server side, these languages contain similar concepts and structures.

Even if you're fully familiar with these concepts as used in JavaScript, this chapter covers a few PHP-specific features with regard to global variables, data types, and changing types. Similarly, the functions discussed that enable you to create, modify, and manipulate arrays are specific to PHP.

Variables

Just as in JavaScript, a *variable* in PHP is a special container that you can define, which then "holds" a value, such as a number, string, object, array, or a Boolean. Variables are fundamental to all kinds of programming languages. Without variables, you would be forced to hard-code each specific value used in your scripts. With variables, you can create templates for operations, such as adding two numbers, without worrying about the specific values the variables represent. Values are given to the variables when the script is run, possibly through user input, through a database query, or from the result of another action earlier in the script. In other words, variables should be used whenever the data in your script is liable to change—either during the lifetime of the script or when it is passed to another script for later use.

In PHP, a variable consists of a name of your choosing, preceded by a dollar sign ($). Variable names can include letters, numbers, and the underscore character (_), but they cannot include spaces. Names must begin with a letter or an underscore. The following list shows some legal variables:

```
$a
$a_longish_variable_name
$_24563
$sleepyZZZZ
```

NOTE

Your variable names should be meaningful as well as consistent in style. For example, if your script deals with name and password values, do not create a variable called $n for the name and $p for the password—those are not meaningful names for anyone other than you, at that particular moment. If you pick up that script weeks later, you might think that $n is the variable for *number* rather than *name* and that $p stands for *page* rather than *password*. And what if a co-worker has to modify your script? How will that person know what $n and $p stand for? You can use whatever naming convention you want for variables in your scripts, as long as the names are descriptive and follow some sort of pattern that others can understand.

A semicolon (;), also known as the *instruction terminator*, is used to end a PHP statement. The semicolons in the next fragments of code are not part of the variable names but are used to end the statement that declares the variable as "alive and kicking," if you will. To declare a variable, you need only include it in your script. When you declare a variable, you usually assign a value to it in the same statement, as shown here:

```
$num1 = 8;
$num2 = 23;
```

The preceding lines declare two variables and use the assignment operator (=) to assign values to them. You will learn about assignment in more detail in the "Using Expressions and Operators" section later in this chapter. After you assign values to your variables, you can treat them exactly as if they were the values themselves. In other words,

```
echo $num1;
```

is equivalent to

```
echo 8;
```

as long as $num1 is assigned a value of 8.

Global Variables

In addition to the rules for naming variables in PHP, there are rules regarding the availability of variables. In general, the assigned value of a variable is present only within the function or script where it resides. For example, if you have `scriptA.php` that holds a variable called `$name` with a value of `joe`, and you want to create `scriptB.php` that also uses a `$name` variable, you can assign to that second `$name` variable a value of `jane` without affecting the variable in `scriptA.php`. The value of the `$name` variable is *local* to each script, and the assigned values are independent of each other.

However, you can also define the `$name` variable as *global* within a script or function. If the `$name` variable is defined as a global variable in both `scriptA.php` and `scriptB.php`, and these scripts are connected to each other (that is, one script calls the other or includes the other), there will be just one value for the now-shared `$name` variable. Examples of global variable scope are explained in more detail in Chapter 13, "PHP Fundamentals: Functions, Objects, and Flow Control."

Superglobal Variables

In addition to global variables of your own creation, PHP has several predefined variables called *superglobals*. These variables are always present, and their values are available to all your scripts. Each of the following superglobals is actually an array of other variables:

- ▶ `$_GET` contains any variables provided to a script through the GET method.
- ▶ `$_POST` contains any variables provided to a script through the POST method.
- ▶ `$_COOKIE` contains any variables provided to a script through a cookie.
- ▶ `$_FILES` contains any variables provided to a script through file uploads.
- ▶ `$_SERVER` contains information such as headers, file paths, and script locations.
- ▶ `$_ENV` contains any variables provided to a script as part of the server environment.
- ▶ `$_REQUEST` contains any variables provided to a script via GET, POST, or COOKIE input mechanisms.
- ▶ `$_SESSION` contains any variables that are currently registered in a session.

The examples in this book use superglobals in all applicable situations. Using superglobals is crucial in creating secure applications because, in part, they reduce the likelihood of user-injected input to your scripts. By coding your scripts to accept only what you want, in a manner defined by you (from a form using the POST method or from a session, for example), you can eliminate some of the problems created by loosely written scripts.

Data Types

Different types of data take up different amounts of memory and may be treated differently when they are manipulated by a script. Some programming languages therefore demand that the programmer declare in advance which type of data a variable will contain. By contrast, PHP is *loosely typed*, meaning that it automatically determines the data type at the time data is assigned to each variable.

This automatic typing is a mixed blessing. On the one hand, it means that variables can be used flexibly—in one instance, a variable can hold a string and then later in the script it can hold an integer or some other data type. On the other hand, this flexibility can lead to problems in larger scripts if you are specifically expecting a variable to hold one data type when in fact it holds something completely different. For example, suppose you have created code to manipulate an array variable. If the variable in question instead contains a number value and no array structure is in place, errors will occur when the code attempts to perform array-specific operations on the variable.

Table 12.1 shows the eight standard data types available in PHP.

TABLE 12.1 Standard Data Types

Type	Example	Description
Boolean	`true`	One of the special values `true` or `false`
Integer	5	A whole number
Float or double	`3.234`	A floating-point number
String	`"hello"`	A collection of characters
Object		An instance of a class
Array		An ordered set of keys and values
Resource		Reference to a third-party resource (a database, for example)
NULL		An uninitialized variable

Resource types are often returned by functions that deal with external applications or files. For example, you will see references to "the MySQL resource ID" in Chapter 18, "Interacting with MySQL Using PHP." The NULL type is reserved for variables that have been declared but no value has been assigned to them.

PHP has several functions available to test the validity of a particular type of variable—one for each type, in fact. The `is_*` family of functions tests whether a given value is a certain data type; for example, `is_bool()`, tests whether a given value is a Boolean. Listing 12.1 assigns different data types to a single variable and then tests the variable with the appropriate `is_*` function. The comments in the code show you where the script is in the process.

NOTE

You will learn more about calling functions in Chapter 13.

LISTING 12.1 Testing the Type of a Variable

```
1:  <?php
2:  $testing; // declare a NULL value
3:  echo "is null? ".is_null($testing); // checks if null
4:  echo "<br>";
5:  $testing = 5;
6:  echo "is an integer? ".is_int($testing); // checks if integer
7:  echo "<br>";
8:  $testing = "five";
9:  echo "is a string? ".is_string($testing); // checks if string
10: echo "<br>";
11: $testing = 5.024;
12: echo "is a double? ".is_double($testing); // checks if double
13: echo "<br>";
14: $testing = true;
15: echo "is boolean? ".is_bool($testing); // checks if boolean
16: echo "<br>";
17: $testing = array('apple', 'orange', 'pear');
18: echo "is an array? ".is_array($testing); // checks if array
19: echo "<br>";
20: echo "is numeric? ".is_numeric($testing); // checks if numeric
21: echo "<br>";
22: echo "is a resource? ".is_resource($testing); // checks if a resource
23: echo "<br>";
24: echo "is an array? ".is_array($testing); // checks if an array
25: echo "<br>";
26: ?>
```

Put these lines into a text file called testtype.php and place this file in your web server document root. When you access this script through your web browser, it produces the following output:

```
is null? 1
is an integer? 1
is a string? 1
is a double? 1
is boolean? 1
is an array? 1
is numeric?
is a resource?
is an array? 1
```

When the $testing variable is declared in line 2, it is it given a NULL value, so when the variable is tested in line 3 to see whether it is NULL (using is_null()), the result is 1 (true).

After the check to see whether $testing is NULL, values are assigned to $testing by using the = sign and then the variable is tested using the appropriate is_* function. An integer, assigned to the $testing variable in line 5, is a whole or real number. In simple terms, you can think of a *whole number* as a number without a decimal point. A *string*, assigned to the $testing variable in line 8, is a collection of characters. When you work with strings in your scripts, they should always be surrounded by double or single quotation marks (" or '). A *double*, assigned to the $testing variable in line 11, is a floating-point number (that is, a number that includes a decimal point). A *Boolean*, assigned to the $testing variable in line 14, can have one of two special values: true or false. In line 17, an array is created using the array() function, which you learn more about later in this chapter. This particular array contains three items, and the script dutifully reports $testing to have a type of array.

From line 20 through the end of the script, no value is reassigned to $testing—only the type is tested. Lines 20 and 22 test whether $testing is a numeric or resource type, respectively, and because it is not, no value is displayed to the user. In line 24, the script tests again to see whether $testing is an array, and because it is, the value of 1 is displayed.

Changing Type with settype()

PHP also provides the function settype(), which is used to change the type of a variable. To use settype(), you place the variable to change and the type to change it to between the parentheses and separate the elements with a comma, like this:

```
settype($variabletochange, 'new type');
```

Listing 12.2 converts the value 3.14 (a float) to each of the four standard types examined in this chapter.

LISTING 12.2   Changing the Type of a Variable with settype()

```
1:   <?php
2:   $undecided = 3.14;
3:   echo "is ".$undecided." a double? ".is_double($undecided)."<br>"; // double
4:   settype($undecided, 'string');
5:   echo "is ".$undecided." a string? ".is_string($undecided)."<br>"; // string
6:   settype($undecided, 'integer');
7:   echo "is ".$undecided." an integer? ".is_integer($undecided)."<br>"; // integer
8:   settype($undecided, 'double');
9:   echo "is ".$undecided." a double? ".is_double($undecided)."<br>"; // double
10: settype($undecided, 'bool');
11: echo "is ".$undecided." a boolean? ".is_bool($undecided)."<br>"; // boolean
12: ?>
```

In each case, we use the appropriate is_* function to confirm the new data type and to print the value of the variable $undecided to the browser using echo. When we convert the string "3.14" to an integer in line 6, any information beyond the decimal point is lost forever. That's why $undecided contains 3 after we change it back to a double in line 8. Finally, in line 10, we convert $undecided to a Boolean. Any number other than 0 becomes true when converted to a Boolean. When you print a Boolean in PHP, true is represented as 1, and false is represented as an empty string; so in line 11, $undecided is printed as 1.

Put these lines into a text file called settype.php and place this file in your web server document root. When you access this script through your web browser, it produces the following output:

```
is 3.14 a double? 1
is 3.14 a string? 1
is 3 an integer? 1
is 3 a double? 1
is 1 a boolean? 1
```

Changing Type by Casting

The principal difference between using settype() to change the type of an existing variable and changing the type by *casting* is the fact that casting produces a copy, leaving the original variable untouched. To change type through casting, you indicate the name of a data type, in parentheses, in front of the variable you are copying. For example, the following line creates a copy of the $originalvar variable, with a specific type (integer) and a new name ($newvar). The $originalvar variable is still available and is its original type; $newvar is a completely new variable.

```
$newvar = (integer) $originalvar
```

Listing 12.3 illustrates changing data types through casting.

LISTING 12.3   Casting a Variable

```
1:   <?php
2:   $undecided = 3.14;
3:   $holder = (double) $undecided;
4:   echo "is ".$holder." a double? ".is_double($holder)."<br>"; // double
5:   $holder = (string) $undecided;
6:   echo "is ".$holder." a string? ".is_string($holder)."<br>"; // string
7:   $holder = (integer) $undecided;
8:   echo "is ".$holder." an integer? ".is_integer($holder)."<br>"; // integer
9:   $holder = (double) $undecided;
10:  echo "is ".$holder." a double? ".is_double($holder)."<br>"; // double
11:  $holder = (boolean) $undecided;
12:  echo "is ".$holder." a boolean? ".is_bool($holder)."<br>"; // boolean
```

```
13: echo "<hr>";
14: echo "original variable type of $undecided: ";
15: echo gettype($undecided); // double
16: ?>
```

Listing 12.3 never actually changes the type of the $undecided variable, which remains a double throughout this script, as illustrated on line 15, where the gettype() function is used to determine the type of $undecided.

In fact, casting $undecided creates a copy that is then converted to the type specified at the time of the cast and stored in the variable $holder. This casting occurs first in line 3 and again in lines 5, 7, 9, and 11. Because the code is working with only a copy of $undecided and not the original variable, it never lost its original value, as the $undecided variable did in line 6 of Listing 12.2 when its type changed from a string to an integer.

Put the contents of Listing 12.3 into a text file called casttype.php and place this file in your web server document root. When you access this script through your web browser, it produces the following output:

```
is 3.14 a double? 1
is 3.14 a string? 1
is 3 an integer? 1
is 3.14 a double? 1
is 1 a boolean? 1
original variable type of 3.14: double
```

Now that you've seen how to change the contents of a variable from one type to another either by using settype() or by casting, consider why this might be useful. It is not a procedure that you will have to use often because PHP automatically casts your variables for you when the context of the script requires a change. However, such an automatic cast is temporary, and you might want to make a variable persistently hold a particular data type, which is why PHP gives you the ability to specifically change types.

For example, the numbers that a user types into an HTML form are made available to your script as the string type. If you try to add two strings together because they contain numbers, PHP helpfully converts these strings into numbers while the addition is taking place. Therefore,

```
"30cm" + "40cm"
```

results in an answer of 70.

NOTE

The generic term *number* is used here to mean integers and floats. If the user input were in float form, and the strings added together were "3.14cm" and "4.12cm", the answer provided would be 7.26.

During the casting of a string into an integer or float, PHP ignores any nonnumeric characters. The string are truncated, and any characters from the location of the first nonnumeric character onward are ignored. So, whereas `"30cm"` is transformed into `"30"`, the string `"6ft2in"` becomes just 6 because the rest of the string evaluates to 0.

You might want to clean up the user input yourself and use it in a particular way in your script. Imagine that the user has been asked to submit a number. We can simulate this by declaring a variable and assigning the user's input to it:

```
$test = "30cm";
```

As you can see, the user has added units to his number—instead of entering 30, the user has entered 30cm. You can make sure that the user input is clean by casting it as an integer:

```
$newtest = (integer) $test;
echo "Your imaginary box has a width of $newtest centimeters.";
```

The resulting output is as follows:

```
Your imaginary box has a width of 30 centimeters.
```

Had the user input not been cast, and the value of the original variable, `$test`, been used in place of `$newtest` when the statement about the width of a box was printed, the result would have been this:

```
Your imaginary box has a width of 30cm centimeters.
```

This output looks strange; in fact, it looks like parroted user input that has not been cleaned up (which is exactly what it is).

Why Test Type?

Why might it be useful to know the type of a variable? In programming, circumstances often arise when data is passed to you from another source, such as a function. In Chapter 13, you will learn how to create functions in PHP; data is often passed between one or more functions because they can accept information as arguments from the code that calls them. For the function to work with the data it is given, it is a good idea to first verify that the function has been given values of the correct data type. For example, a function expecting data that has a type of resource will not work well when passed a string.

Using Expressions and Operators

With what you have learned so far about PHP, you can assign data to variables, and you can even investigate and change the data type of a variable. A programming language isn't very useful, though, unless you can manipulate the data you have stored. Just like in JavaScript, *operators* in PHP are symbols used to manipulate data stored in variables, to make it possible to use one or more values to produce a new value, to check the validity of data to determine the next step in a condition, and so forth. A value operated on by an operator is referred to as an *operand*.

In this simple example, two operands are combined with an operator to produce a new value:

```
4 + 5
```

The integers 4 and 5 are operands. The addition operator (+) operates on these operands to produce the integer 9. Operators almost always sit between two operands, although you will see a few exceptions later in this chapter.

The combination of operands with an operator to produce a result is called an *expression*. Although operators and their operands form the basis of expressions, an expression need not contain an operator. In fact, an expression in PHP is defined as anything that can be used as a value. This includes integer constants such as 654, variables such as $user, and function calls such as is_int(). The expression (4 + 5), for example, consists of two expressions (4 and 5) and an operator (+). When an expression produces a value, it is often said to *resolve to* that value. That is, when all subexpressions are taken into account, the expression can be treated as if it were a code for the value itself. In this case, the expression 4 + 5 resolves to 9.

> **NOTE**
> _____
>
> An *expression* is any combination of functions, values, and operators that resolves to a value. As a rule of thumb, if you can use it as if it were a value, it is an expression.
> _____

Now that you have the principles out of the way, it's time to take a tour of the operators commonly used in PHP programming. These will look quite similar to those used in JavaScript, as you saw in Chapter 7, "JavaScript Fundamentals: Variables, Strings, and Arrays."

The Assignment Operator

You have seen the assignment operator in use each time a variable was declared in an example; the assignment operator consists of the single character =. The assignment operator takes the value of the right-side operand and assigns it to the left-side operand:

```
$name = "Jimbo";
```

The variable $name now contains the string "Jimbo". This construct is also an expression. Although it might seem at first glance that the assignment operator simply changes the variable $name without producing a value, a statement that uses the assignment operator always resolves to a copy of the value of the right operand. Therefore,

```
echo $name = "Jimbo";
```

prints the string "Jimbo" to the browser while it also assigns the value "Jimbo" to the $name variable.

Arithmetic Operators

The *arithmetic operators* do exactly what you would expect—they perform arithmetic operations. Table 12.2 lists these operators along with examples of their usage and results.

TABLE 12.2 Arithmetic Operators

Operator	Name	Example	Sample Result
+	Addition	10+3	13
-	Subtraction	10-3	7
/	Division	10/3	3.3333333333333
*	Multiplication	10*3	30
%	Modulus	10%3	1

The addition operator adds the right-side operand to the left-side operand. The subtraction operator subtracts the right-side operand from the left-side operand. The division operator divides the left-side operand by the right-side operand. The multiplication operator multiplies the left-side operand by the right-side operand. The modulus operator returns the remainder of the left-side operand divided by the right-side operand.

The Concatenation Operator

The concatenation operator is represented by a single period (.) in PHP; in JavaScript you have seen this type of operator, except it is a + symbol. Treating both operands as strings, this operator appends the right-side operand to the left-side operand. Therefore,

```
"hello" . " world"
```

returns

```
"hello world"
```

Note that the resulting space between the words occurs because there is a leading space in the second operand (" world" rather than "world"). The concatenation operator literally smashes together two strings without adding any padding. So, if you try to concatenate two strings without leading or trailing spaces, such as

```
"hello" . "world"
```

you will get this as your result:

```
"helloworld"
```

Regardless of the data types of the operands used with the concatenation operator, they are treated as strings, and the result is always of the string type. You will encounter concatenation frequently throughout this book when the results of an expression of some kind must be combined with a string, as in the following:

```
$cm = 212;
echo "the width is " . ($cm/100) . " meters";
```

Combined Assignment Operators

Although there is only one true assignment operator, PHP provides a number of combination operators that transform the left-side operand and return a result while also modifying the original value of the variable. As a rule, operators use operands but do not change their original values. But combined assignment operators break this rule. A combined assignment operator consists of a standard operator symbol followed by an equal sign. Combination assignment operators save you the trouble of using two operators in two different steps within your script. For example, if you have a variable with a value of 4 and you want to increase this value by 4 more, you might do this:

```
$x = 4;
$x = $x + 4; // $x now equals 8
```

However, you can also use a combination assignment operator (+=) to add and return the new value, as shown here:

```
$x = 4;
$x += 4; // $x now equals 8
```

Each arithmetic operator, as well as the concatenation operator, also has a corresponding combination assignment operator. Table 12.3 lists these new operators and shows an example of their usage.

TABLE 12.3 Some Combined Assignment Operators

Operator	Example	Equivalent To
+=	$x += 5	$x = $x + 5
-=	$x -= 5	$x = $x - 5
/=	$x /= 5	$x = $x / 5
*=	$x *= 5	$x = $x * 5
%=	$x %= 5	$x = $x % 5
.=	$x .= " test"	$x = $x . " test"

Each of the examples in Table 12.3 transforms the value of $x using the value of the right-side operand. Subsequent uses of $x will refer to the new value. Here's an example:

```
$x = 4;
$x += 4; // $x now equals 8
$x += 4; // $x now equals 12
$x -= 3; // $x now equals 9
```

These operators are used throughout the scripts in the book. You will frequently see the combined concatenation assignment operator when you begin to create dynamic text. Looping through a script and adding content to a string, such as dynamically building the HTML markup to represent a table, is a prime example of the use of a combined assignment operator.

Automatically Incrementing and Decrementing an Integer Variable

When coding in PHP, you will often find it necessary to increment or decrement a variable that is an integer type. You usually need to do this when you are counting the iterations of a loop. You have already learned two ways of doing this. You can increment the value of $x using the addition operator, like so:

```
$x = $x + 1; // $x is incremented by 1
```

Or you can use a combined assignment operator, like this:

```
$x += 1; // $x is incremented by 1
```

In both cases, the new value is assigned to $x. Because expressions of this kind are common, PHP provides some special operators that allow you to add or subtract the integer constant 1 from an integer variable, assigning the result to the variable itself. These are known as the *post-increment* and *post-decrement* operators. The post-increment operator consists of two plus symbols appended to a variable name:

```
$x++; // $x is incremented by 1
```

This expression increments the value represented by the variable $x by 1. Using two minus symbols in the same way decrements the variable:

```
$x--; // $x is decremented by 1
```

If you use the post-increment or post-decrement operators in conjunction with a conditional operator, the operand is modified only after the first operation has finished:

```
$x = 3;
$y = $x++ + 3;
```

In this instance, $y first becomes 6 (the result of 3 + 3) and then $x is incremented.

In some circumstances, you might want to increment or decrement a variable in a test expression before the test is carried out. PHP provides the pre-increment and pre-decrement operators for this purpose. These operators behave in the same way as the post-increment and post-decrement operators, but they are written with the plus or minus symbols preceding the variable:

```
++$x; // $x is incremented by 1
--$x; // $x is decremented by 1
```

If these operators are used as part of a test expression, incrementing occurs before the test is carried out. For example, in the next fragment, $x is incremented before it is tested against 4:

```
$x = 3;
++$x < 4; // false
```

The test expression returns `false` because 4 is not smaller than 4.

Comparison Operators

Comparison operators perform comparative tests using their operands and return the Boolean value `true` if the test is successful or `false` if the test fails. This type of expression is useful when using control structures in your scripts, such as `if` and `while` statements. This book covers `if` and `while` statements in Chapter 13.

For example, to test whether the value contained in $x is smaller than 5, you can use the less-than operator as part of your expression:

```
$x < 5
```

If $x contains the value 3, this expression has the value `true`. If $x contains 7, the expression resolves to `false`.

Table 12.4 lists the comparison operators.

TABLE 12.4 Comparison Operators

Operator	Name	Returns True If...	Example ($x Is 4)	Result
==	Equivalence	Left is equivalent to right.	$x == 5	false
!=	Nonequivalence	Left is not equivalent to right.	$x != 5	true
===	Identical	Left is equivalent to right, and they are the same type.	$x === 4	true

Operator	Name	Returns True If...	Example ($x Is 4)	Result
!==	Nonequivalence	Left is equivalent to right, but they are not the same type.	`$x !== "4"`	`false`
>	Greater than	Left is greater than right.	`$x > 4`	`false`
>=	Greater than or equal to	Left is greater than or equal to right.	`$x >= 4`	`true`
<	Less than	Left is less than right.	`$x < 4`	`false`
<=	Less than or equal to	Left is less than or equal to right.	`$x <= 4`	`true`

These operators are most commonly used with integers or doubles, although the equivalence operator is also used to compare strings. Be very sure to understand the difference between the == and = operators. The == operator tests equivalence, whereas the = operator assigns value. Also, remember that === tests equivalence with regard to both value and type.

Creating Complex Test Expressions with the Logical Operators

Logical operators test combinations of Boolean values. For example, the or operator, which is indicated by two pipe characters (||) or simply the word or, returns the Boolean value true if either the left or the right operand is true:

```
true || false
```

This expression returns true.

The and operator, which is indicated by two ampersand characters (&&) or simply the word and, returns the Boolean value true only if both the left and right operands are true:

```
true && false
```

This expression returns the Boolean value false. It's unlikely that you will use a logical operator to test Boolean constants because it makes more sense to test two or more expressions that resolve to a Boolean. For example,

```
($x > 2) && ($x < 15)
```

returns the Boolean value true if $x contains a value that is greater than 2 and less than 15. Parentheses are used when comparing expressions to make the code easier to read and to indicate the precedence of expression evaluation. Table 12.5 lists the logical operators.

TABLE 12.5 Logical Operators

Operator	Name	Returns True If...	Example	Result
`||`	Or	Left or right is true.	`true || false`	`true`
`or`	Or	Left or right is true.	`true or false`	`true`
`xor`	Xor	Left or right is true, but not both.	`true xor true`	`false`
`&&`	And	Left and right are true.	`true && false`	`false`
`and`	And	Left and right are true.	`true and false`	`false`
`!`	Not	The single operand is not true.	`! true`	`false`

You might wonder why are there two versions of both the `or` and the `and` operators, and that's a good question. The answer lies in operator precedence, which we examine next.

Operator Precedence

When you use an operator within an expression, the PHP engine usually reads your expression from left to right. For complex expressions that use more than one operator, though, the PHP engine could be led astray without some guidance. First, consider a simple case:

```
4 + 5
```

There's no room for confusion here; PHP simply adds 4 to 5. But what about the following fragment, with two operators:

```
4 + 5 * 2
```

This presents a problem. Should PHP find the sum of 4 and 5, and then multiply it by 2, providing the result 18? Or does it mean 4 plus the result of 5 multiplied by 2, resolving to 14? If you were simply to read from left to right, the former would be true. However, PHP attaches different precedence to different operators, and because the multiplication operator has higher precedence than the addition operator, the second solution to the problem is the correct one: 4 plus the result of 5 multiplied by 2.

However, you can override operator precedence by putting parentheses around your expressions. In the following fragment, the addition expression is evaluated before the multiplication expression:

```
(4 + 5) * 2
```

Whatever the precedence of the operators in a complex expression, it is a good idea to use parentheses to make your code clearer and to save you from bugs, such as a situation where you apply sales tax to the wrong subtotal in a shopping cart. The following is a list of the operators covered in this chapter in precedence order (those with the highest precedence listed first):

```
++, --, (cast)
/, *, %
+, -
<, <=, =>, >
==, ===, !=
&&
||
=, +=, -=, /=, *=, %=, .=
and
xor
or
```

As you can see, `or` has a lower precedence than `||`, and `and` has a lower precedence than `&&`, so you can use the lower-precedence logical operators to change the way a complex test expression is read. In the following fragment, the two expressions are equivalent, but the second is much easier to read:

```
$x and $y || $z
$x && ($y || $z)
```

Taking it one step further, the following fragment is easier still:

```
$x and ($y or $z)
```

However, all three examples are equivalent.

NOTE

The order of precedence is the only reason that both `&&` and `and` are available in PHP. The same is true of `||` and `or`. In most circumstances, the use of parentheses makes for clearer code and fewer bugs than code that takes advantage of the difference in precedence of these operators. This book tends to use the more common `||` and `&&` operators, and relies on parenthetical statements to set specific operator precedence.

Constants

Variables offer a flexible way of storing data because you can change their values and the type of data they store at any time during the execution of your scripts. However, if you want to work with a value that must remain unchanged throughout your script's execution, you can define and use a *constant*. You must use PHP's built-in `define()` function to create a constant, which subsequently cannot be changed unless you specifically `define()` it again. To use the `define()` function, place the name of the constant and the value you want to give it within parentheses and separated by a comma:

```
define("YOUR_CONSTANT_NAME", 42);
```

The value you want to set can be a number, a string, or a Boolean. By convention, the name of the constant should be in capital letters. Constants are accessed with the constant name only; no dollar symbol is required. Listing 12.4 shows you how to define and access a constant.

LISTING 12.4 Defining and Accessing a Constant

```
1: <?php
2: define("THE_YEAR", "2017");
3: echo "It is the year " . THE_YEAR;
4: ?>
```

TIP

Constants can be used anywhere in your scripts, including in functions stored in external files.

Notice that in line 3 the concatenation operator is used to append the value held by the constant to the string `"It is the year "` because PHP does not distinguish between a constant and a string within quotation marks.

Put these few lines into a text file called `constant.php` and place this file in your web server document root. When you access this script through your web browser, it produces the following output:

```
It is the year 2017
```

The `define()` function can also accept a third Boolean argument that determines whether the constant name should be case sensitive. By default, constant names are case sensitive. However, by passing `true` to the `define()` function, you can change this behavior. So, if you were to set up our `THE_YEAR` constant as

```
define("THE_YEAR", "2017", true);
```

you could access its value without worrying about case:

```
echo the_year;
echo ThE_YeAr;
echo THE_YEAR;
```

The preceding three expressions are equivalent, and all result in an output of 2017. This feature can make scripts a little friendlier for other programmers who work with our code because they will not need to consider case when accessing a constant we have already defined. However, given the fact that other constants *are* case sensitive, this might make for more, rather than less, confusion as programmers forget which constants to treat in which way. Unless you have a compelling reason to do otherwise, the safest course is to keep your constants case sensitive and define them using uppercase characters, which is an easy-to-remember (not to mention standard) convention.

Predefined Constants

PHP automatically provides some built-in constants for you. For example, the constant __FILE__ returns the name of the file that the PHP engine is currently reading. The constant __LINE__ returns the current line number of the file. These are but two examples of what are called "magic constants," because they are not statically predefined and instead change depending on the context in which they are used. For a complete list, see http://www.php.net/manual/en/language.constants.predefined.php.

You can also find out which version of PHP is interpreting the script with the PHP_VERSION constant. This constant can be useful if you need version information included in script output when sending a bug report. The PHP_VERSION constant *is* a predefined constant (and a reserved word). For a complete list of reserved constants, see http://www.php.net/manual/en/reserved.constants.php.

Understanding Arrays

Scalar variables of the types you've seen so far in this chapter can store only one value at a time—for example, the $color variable can hold only a value of red or blue, and so forth, but it cannot be used to hold a list of colors in the rainbow. But arrays are special types of variables that enable you to store as many values as you want, including all seven of those rainbow colors.

Arrays are indexed, which means that each entry is made up of a *key* and a *value*. The key is the index position, beginning with 0 and increasing incrementally by 1 with each new element in the array. The value is whatever value you associate with that position—a string, an integer, or whatever you want. Think of an array as a filing cabinet and each key/value pair as a file folder. The key is the label written on the top of the folder, and the value is what is inside. You'll see this type of structure in action as you create arrays in the next section.

Creating Arrays

You can create an array using either the `array()` function or the array operator `[]`. The `array()` function is usually used when you want to create a new array and populate it with more than one element, all in one fell swoop. The array operator is often used when you want to create a new array with just one element at the outset, or when you want to add to an existing array element.

The following code snippet shows how to create an array called `$rainbow` using the `array()` function, containing all its various colors:

```
$rainbow = array("red", "orange", "yellow", "green", "blue", "indigo", "violet");
```

The following snippet shows the same array being created incrementally using the array operator:

```
$rainbow[] = "red";
$rainbow[] = "orange";
$rainbow[] = "yellow";
$rainbow[] = "green";
$rainbow[] = "blue";
$rainbow[] = "indigo";
$rainbow[] = "violet";
```

Both snippets create a seven-element array called `$rainbow`, with values starting at index position 0 and ending at index position 6. If you want to be literal about it, you can specify the index positions, such as in this code:

```
$rainbow[0] = "red";
$rainbow[1] = "orange";
$rainbow[2] = "yellow";
$rainbow[3] = "green";
$rainbow[4] = "blue";
$rainbow[5] = "indigo";
$rainbow[6] = "violet";
```

However, PHP handles this numbering for you when positions are not specified, and that eliminates the possibility that you might misnumber your elements when order is important, as in this example:

```
$rainbow[0] = "red";
$rainbow[1] = "orange";
$rainbow[2] = "yellow";
$rainbow[5] = "green";
$rainbow[6] = "blue";
$rainbow[7] = "indigo";
$rainbow[8] = "violet";
```

Regardless of whether you initially create your array using the `array()` function or the array operator, you can still add to it using the array operator. In the first line of the following snippet, six elements are added to the array, and one more element is added to the end of the array in the second line:

```
$rainbow = array("red", "orange", "yellow", "green", "blue", "indigo");
$rainbow[] = "violet";
```

The examples used in this section are of numerically indexed arrays, arguably the most common type you'll see. In the next two sections, you learn about two other types of arrays: associative and multidimensional.

Creating Associative Arrays

Whereas numerically indexed arrays use an index position as the key—0, 1, 2, and so forth—associative arrays use actual named keys. The following example demonstrates this by creating an array called `$character` with four elements:

```
$character = array(
            "name" => "Bob",
            "occupation" => "superhero",
            "age" => 30,
            "special power" => "x-ray vision"
            );
```

The four keys in the `$character` array are name, occupation, age, and special power. The associated values are Bob, superhero, 30, and x-ray vision, respectively. You can reference specific elements of an associative array using the specific key, such as in this example:

```
echo $character['occupation'];
```

Here is the output of this snippet:

```
superhero
```

As with numerically indexed arrays, you can use the array operator to add to an associative array:

```
$character['supername'] = "Mega X-Ray Guy";
```

This example adds a key called supername with a value of Mega X-Ray Guy.

The only difference between an associative array and a numerically indexed array is the key name. In a numerically indexed array, the key name is a number. In an associative array, the key name is a meaningful word.

Creating Multidimensional Arrays

The first two types of arrays hold strings and integers, whereas this third type holds other arrays. If each set of key/value pairs constitutes a dimension, a multidimensional array holds more than one series of these key/value pairs. For example, Listing 12.5 defines a multidimensional array called $characters, each element of which contains an associative array. This might sound confusing, but it's really only an array that contains another array.

LISTING 12.5 Defining a Multidimensional Array

```
 1:  <?php
 2:  $characters = array(
 3:                array(
 4:                   "name" => "Bob",
 5:                   "occupation" => "superhero",
 6:                   "age" => 30,
 7:                   "special power" => "x-ray vision"
 8:                   ),
 9:                array(
10:                   "name" => "Sally",
11:                   "occupation" => "superhero",
12:                   "age" => 24,
13:                   "special power" => "superhuman strength"
14:                   ),
15:                array(
16:                   "name" => "Jane",
17:                   "occupation" => "arch villain",
18:                   "age" => 45,
19:                   "special power" => "nanotechnology"
20:                   )
21:                   );
22:  ?>
```

In line 2, the $characters array is initialized using the array() function. Lines 3–8 represent the first element, lines 9–14 represent the second element, and lines 15–20 represent the third element. These elements can be referenced as $characters[0], $characters[1], and $characters[2].

Each element consists of an associative array, itself containing four elements: name, occupation, age, and special_power.

However, suppose you attempt to print the master elements, like so:

echo $characters[1];

In this case, the output will be

```
Array
```

because the master element indeed holds an array as its content. To really get to the content you want (that is, the specific information found within the inner array element), you need to access the master element index position plus the associative name of the value you want to view.

Take a look at this example:

```
echo $characters[1]['occupation'];
```

It prints this:

```
superhero
```

If you add the following lines to the end of the code in Listing 12.5, it prints the information stored in each element, with an added line displayed in the browser for good measure:

```
foreach ($characters as $c) {
        while (list($k, $v) = each ($c)) {
                echo "$k ... $v <br>";
        }
        echo "<hr>";
}
```

The foreach loop is concerned with the master array element, $characters. It loops through this array and assigns the temporary name $c to the element contained within each position. Next, the code begins a while loop. This loop uses two functions to extract the contents of the inner array. First, the list() function names placeholder variables, $k and $v, which will be populated with the keys and values gathered from the each() function. The each() function looks at each element of the $c array and extracts the information accordingly.

The echo statement simply prints each key and value ($k and $v) extracted from the $c array using the each() function and adds a line break for display purposes. Figure 12.1 shows the result of this file, called mdarray.php.

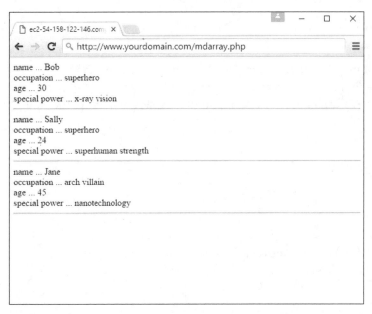

FIGURE 12.1
Looping through a multidimensional array.

Some Array-Related Constructs and Functions

More than 70 array-related functions are built in to PHP, which you can read about in detail at http://php.net/manual/en/ref.array.php. Some of the more common (and useful) functions are described briefly in this section:

- ▶ **count() and sizeof()**—Each of these functions counts the number of elements in an array; sizeof() is an alias of count(). Given the array

  ```
  $colors = array("blue", "black", "red", "green");
  ```

  both count($colors); and sizeof($colors); return a value of 4.

- ▶ **each() and list()**—These functions (well, list() is a language construct that *looks* like a function) usually appear together, in the context of stepping through an array and returning its keys and values. You saw an example of this previously, where we stepped through the $c array and printed its contents.

- ▶ **foreach()**—This control structure (which looks like a function) is used to step through an array, assigning the value of an element to a given variable, as you saw in the previous section.

▶ **reset()**—This function rewinds the pointer to the beginning of an array, as in this example:

```
reset($character);
```

This function proves useful when you are performing multiple manipulations on an array, such as sorting, extracting values, and so forth.

▶ **array_push()**—This function adds one or more elements to the end of an existing array, as in this example:

```
array_push($existingArray, "element 1", "element 2", "element 3");
```

▶ **array_pop()**—This function removes (and returns) the last element of an existing array, as in this example:

```
$last_element = array_pop($existingArray);
```

▶ **array_unshift()**—This function adds one or more elements to the beginning of an existing array, as in this example:

```
array_unshift($existingArray, "element 1", "element 2", "element 3");
```

▶ **array_shift()**—This function removes (and returns) the first element of an existing array, as in this example, where the value of the element in the first position of $existingArray is assigned to the variable $first_element:

```
$first_element = array_shift($existingArray);
```

▶ **array_merge()**—This function combines two or more existing arrays, as in this example:

```
$newArray = array_merge($array1, $array2);
```

▶ **array_keys()**—This function returns an array containing all the key names within a given array, as in this example:

```
$keysArray = array_keys($existingArray);
```

▶ **array_values()**—This function returns an array containing all the values within a given array, as in this example:

```
$valuesArray = array_values($existingArray);
```

▶ **shuffle()**—This function randomizes the elements of a given array. The syntax of this function is simply as follows:

```
shuffle($existingArray);
```

This brief rundown of array-related functions only scratches the surface of using arrays. However, arrays and array-related functions are used in the code examples throughout this book, so you will get your fill soon enough. If you don't, there's always the array section of the PHP Manual at http://php.net/manual/en/ref.array.php that discusses all array-related functions in great detail, including more than 10 different methods just for sorting your arrays.

Summary

This chapter covered some of the basic features of the PHP language. You learned about variables and how to assign values to them using the assignment operator. You also learned a bit about the scope of variables and built-in superglobals. This chapter also covered operators, and you learned how to combine some of the most common of these into expressions. You learned how to define and access constants, which will one day play a meaningful role in any application you build.

This chapter also introduced you to the concepts of arrays, including how they are created and referenced. The three array types are the numerically indexed array, associative array, and multidimensional array. In addition, you saw examples of some of the numerous array-related functions already built in to PHP. You can use these functions to manipulate and modify existing arrays, sometimes even creating entirely new ones.

Now that you have mastered some of the fundamentals of PHP, the next chapter really puts you in the driver's seat. You learn how to make scripts that can make decisions and repeat tasks, with help from variables, expressions, and operators.

Q&A

Q. Why is it useful to know the type of data that a variable holds?

A. Often the data type of a variable constrains what you can do with it. For example, you cannot perform array-related functions on simple strings. Similarly, you might want to make sure that a variable contains an integer or a float before using it in a mathematical calculation, even though PHP will often help you by changing data types for you in this situation.

Q. Should I obey any conventions when naming variables?

A. Your goal should always be to make your code easy to read and understand. A variable such as `$ab123245` tells you nothing about its role in your script and invites typos. Keep your variable names short and descriptive.

A variable named `$f` is unlikely to mean much to you when you return to your code after a month or so. A variable named `$filename`, however, should make more sense.

Q. Should I learn the operator precedence table?

A. There is no reason you shouldn't, but I would save the effort for more useful tasks. By using parentheses in your expressions, you can make your code easy to read while defining your own order of precedence.

Q. How many dimensions can multidimensional arrays have?

A. You can create as many dimensions in your multidimensional array as you can manage, but remember the more dimensions you have, the more you have to manage. If you have data with more than a few dimensions, it might be wise to ask yourself whether that data should be stored differently, such as in a database, and accessed that way.

Workshop

The Workshop is designed to help you review what you've learned and begin putting your knowledge into practice.

Quiz

1. Which of the following variable names are not valid?

```
$a_value_submitted_by_a_user
$666666xyz
$xyz666666
$_____counter_____
$the first
$file-name
```

2. What does the following code fragment output?

```
$num = 33;
(boolean) $num;
echo $num;
```

3. What does the following statement output?

```
echo gettype("4");
```

4. What is the output from the following code fragment?

```
$test_val = 5.5466;
settype($test_val, "integer");
echo $test_val;
```

5. What construct can you use to define an array?

Answers

1. The variable name $666666xyz is not valid because it does not begin with a letter or an underscore character. The variable name $the first is not valid because it contains a space. $file-name is also invalid because it contains a nonalphanumeric character (-).

2. The fragment prints the integer 33. The cast to Boolean produces a converted copy of the value stored in $num. It does not alter the value actually stored there.

3. The statement outputs the string "string".

4. The code outputs the value 5. When a float is converted to an integer, any information beyond the decimal point is lost.

5. array()

Exercises

▶ Assign values to two variables. Use comparison operators to test whether the first value is

   ▶ The same as the second
   ▶ Less than the second
   ▶ Greater than the second
   ▶ Less than or equal to the second

   Print the result of each test to the browser.

   Change the values assigned to your test variables and run the script again.

▶ Create a multidimensional array of movies organized by genre. This should take the form of an associative array with genres as keys, such as Science Fiction, Action, Adventure, and so forth. Each of the array's elements should be an array containing movie names, such as Alien, Terminator 3, Star Wars, and so on. After creating your arrays, loop through them, printing the name of each genre and its associated movies.

CHAPTER 13

PHP Fundamentals: Functions, Objects, and Flow Control

What You'll Learn in This Chapter:

▶ How to define and call functions from within your scripts

▶ How to pass values to functions and receive values in return

▶ How to access global variables from within a function

▶ How to give a function a "memory"

▶ How to pass data to functions by reference

▶ How to create and manipulate objects and the data they contain

▶ How to use the `if` statement to control the execution of code

▶ How to use the `switch` statement to control the execution of code

▶ How to repeat the execution of code using a `while` statement

▶ How to use `for` statements to make tidy loops

▶ How to break out of loops

▶ How to use PHP start and end tags within control structures

It's no coincidence that this chapter has a nearly identical title and structure as Chapter 8, "JavaScript Fundamentals: Functions, Objects, and Flow Control," because the concepts shared between JavaScript and PHP are quite similar. This chapter goes a little deeper into the topics because your backend scripts are likely to handle more intensive programming than your JavaScript (at least early on in your career).

But just like in JavaScript, you'll soon see that functions remain at the heart of a well-organized script and make your code easy to read and reuse. No large project would be manageable without them because the problem of repetitive code would bog down the development process. Throughout this chapter, you investigate functions and learn some of the ways functions can save you from repetitive work. You'll also learn the very basics of object-oriented programming, in which the structure of an application is designed around objects and their relationships and interactions.

Finally, in this chapter you begin to move away from the linear PHP scripts of previous chapters and move toward loops and conditional checks just like you did with JavaScript in earlier chapters.

Calling Functions

You can think of a function as an input/output machine. This machine takes the raw materials you feed it (input) and works with them to produce a product (output). A function accepts values, processes them, and then performs an action (printing to the browser, for example) or returns a new value, or both.

If you needed to bake a single cake, you would probably do it yourself, in your own kitchen with your standard oven. But if you needed to bake thousands of cakes, you would probably build or acquire a special cake-baking machine, built for baking cakes in massive quantities. Similarly, when deciding whether to create a function for reuse, the most important factor to consider is the extent to which it can save you from writing repetitive code.

A *function* is a self-contained block of code that can be called by your scripts. When called, the function's code is executed and performs a particular task. You can pass values to a function, which then uses the values appropriately—storing them, transforming them, displaying them, or whatever the function is told to do. When finished, a function can also pass a value back to the original code that called it into action.

Functions come in two flavors: those built in to the language and those you define yourself. PHP has hundreds of built-in functions. Look at the following snippet for an example of a function in use:

```
$text = strtoupper("Hello World!");
```

This example calls the `strtoupper()` function, passing it the string `"Hello World!"`. The function then goes about its business of changing the contents of the string to uppercase letters; the result is stored in the `$text` variable.

A function call consists of the function name (`strtoupper` in this case) followed by parentheses. If you want to pass information to the function, you place it between these parentheses. A piece of information passed to a function in this way is called an *argument*. Some functions require that more than one argument be passed to them, separated by commas:

```
some_function($an_argument, $another_argument);
```

`strtoupper()` is typical for a function in that it returns a value. Most functions return some information back after they've completed their task; they usually at least tell whether their mission was successful. `strtoupper()` returns a string value, so its usage requires the presence of a variable to accept the new string, such as the following:

```
$new_string = strtoupper("Hello World!");
```

You may now use $new_string in your code, such as to print it to the screen:

```
echo $new_string;
```

This code results in the following text on the screen:

HELLO WORLD!

NOTE

The `print()` and `echo()` functions, which you may see throughout the examples in this book, are not actually functions—they're language constructs designed to output strings to the browser. However, you will find them in the PHP function list, at http://www.php.net/print and http://www. php.net/echo, respectively. These constructs are similar in functionality and can be used interchangeably. Whichever one you use is a matter of taste.

The `abs()` function, for example, requires a signed numeric value and returns the absolute value of that number. Let's try it out in Listing 13.1.

LISTING 13.1　Calling the Built-In `abs()` Function

```php
<?php
$num = -321;
$newnum = abs($num);
echo $newnum;
//prints "321"
?>
```

This example assigns the value -321 to the variable $num. It then passes that variable to the abs() function, which makes the necessary calculation and returns a new value. The code assigns this to the variable $newnum and displays the result.

Put these lines into a text file called abs.php and place this file in your web server document root. When you access this script through your web browser, it produces the following:

321

In fact, Listing 13.1 could have dispensed with temporary variables altogether, passing the number straight to the abs() function and directly printing the result:

echo abs(-321);

This example uses the temporary variables $num and $newnum, though, to make each step of the process as clear as possible. Sometimes you can make your code more readable by breaking it up into a greater number of simple expressions.

You can call user-defined functions in exactly the same way that we have been calling built-in functions.

Defining a Function

You can define your own functions using the `function` statement:

```
function some_function($argument1, $argument2)
{
    //function code here
}
```

The name of the function follows the `function` statement and precedes a set of parentheses. If your function requires parameters, you must place comma-separated names within the parentheses. These parameters are filled by the values passed to your function as arguments. Even if your function doesn't require parameters, you must nevertheless supply the parentheses.

NOTE

The naming rules for functions are similar to the naming rules for variables: Names cannot include spaces, and they must begin with a letter or an underscore. As with variables, your function names should be meaningful and consistent in style. The capitalization of function names is one such stylistic touch you can add to your code; using mixed case in names, such as `myFunction()` or `handleSomeDifficultTask()`, makes your code much easier to read. You may hear this naming convention referred to as *camelCase*.

Listing 13.2 declares and calls a function.

LISTING 13.2   Declaring and Calling a Function

```php
<?php
function bighello()
{
    echo "<h1>HELLO!</h1>";
}
bighello();
?>
```

The script in Listing 13.2 simply outputs the string `"HELLO!"` wrapped in an HTML `h1` element.

Listing 13.2 declares a function, `bighello()`, that requires no arguments. Because of this, the parentheses are left empty. Although `bighello()` is a working function, it is not terribly useful. Listing 13.3 creates a function that requires an argument and actually does something with it.

LISTING 13.3   Declaring a Function That Requires an Argument

```
1: <?php
2: function printBR($txt)
3: {
4:       echo $txt."<br>";
5: }
6: printBR("This is a line.");
7: printBR("This is a new line.");
8: printBR("This is yet another line.");
9: ?>
```

NOTE

Unlike variable names, function names are not case sensitive. In Listing 13.3, the `printBR()` function could have been called as `printbr()`, `PRINTBR()`, or any combination thereof, with success.

Put these lines into a text file called `printbr.php` and place this file in your web server document root. When you access this script through your web browser, it should look like Figure 13.1.

FIGURE 13.1
A function that prints a string with an appended `<br>` tag.

In line 2, the `printBR()` function expects a string, so the variable name `$txt` is placed between the parentheses when the function is declared. Whatever is passed to `printBR()` is stored in this `$txt` variable. Within the body of the function, line 3 prints the `$txt` variable, appending a `<br>` element to it.

When you want to print a line to the browser, such as in line 6, 7, or 8, you can call `printBR()` instead of the built-in `print()`, saving you the bother of typing the `<br>` element.

Returning Values from User-Defined Functions

The previous example output an amended string to the browser within the `printBR()` function. Sometimes, however, you will want a function to provide a value that you can work with yourself. If your function has transformed a string that you have provided, you might want to get the amended string back so that you can pass it to other functions. A function can return a value using the `return` statement in conjunction with a value. The `return` statement stops the execution of the function and sends the value back to the calling code.

Listing 13.4 creates a function that returns the sum of two numbers.

LISTING 13.4   A Function That Returns a Value

```
1: <?php
2: function addNums($firstnum, $secondnum)
3: {
4:      $result = $firstnum + $secondnum;
5:      return $result;
6: }
7: echo addNums(3,5);
8: //will print "8"
9: ?>
```

Put these lines into a text file called `addnums.php` and place this file in your web server document root. When you access this script through your web browser, it produces the following:

8

Notice in line 2 that `addNums()` should be called with two numeric arguments (line 7 shows those to be 3 and 5 in this case). These values are stored in the variables `$firstnum` and `$secondnum`. Predictably, `addNums()` adds the numbers contained in these variables and stores the result in a variable called `$result`.

The `return` statement can return a value or nothing at all. How you arrive at a value passed by `return` can vary. The value can be hard-coded:

```
return 4;
```

It can be the result of an expression:

```
return $a/$b;
```

It can be the value returned by yet another function call:

```
return another_function($an_argument);
```

Understanding Variable Scope

A variable declared within a function remains local to that function. In other words, it is not available outside the function or within other functions. In larger projects, this can save you from accidentally overwriting the contents of a variable when you declare two variables with the same name in separate functions.

Listing 13.5 creates a variable within a function and then attempts to print it outside the function.

LISTING 13.5   Variable Scope: A Variable Declared Within a Function Is Unavailable Outside the Function

```php
<?php
function test()
{
    $testvariable = "this is a test variable";
}
echo "test variable: ".$testvariable."<br>";
?>
```

Put these lines into a text file called `scopetest.php` and place this file in your web server document root. When you access this script through your web browser, it should look like Figure 13.2.

FIGURE 13.2
Output of `scopetest.php`.

NOTE

The exact output you see depends on your PHP error settings. That is, it might or might not produce a "notice," as shown in Figure 13.2, but it will show the lack of an additional string after `"test variable"`.

The value of the variable $testvariable is not printed because no such variable exists outside the test() function. Remember that the attempt in line 6 to access a nonexistent variable produces a notice such as the one displayed only if your PHP settings are set to display all errors, notices, and warnings. If your error settings are not strictly set, only the string "test variable:" is shown.

Similarly, a variable declared outside a function is not automatically available within it.

Accessing Variables with the global Statement

From within one function, you cannot (by default) access a variable defined in another function or elsewhere in the script. Within a function, if you attempt to use a variable with the same name, you will only set or access a local variable. Let's put this to the test in Listing 13.6.

LISTING 13.6   Variables Defined Outside Functions Are Inaccessible from Within a Function by Default

```
1: <?php
2: $life = 42;
3: function meaningOfLife()
4: {
5:     echo "The meaning of life is ".$life";
6: }
7: meaningOfLife();
8: ?>
```

Put these lines into a text file called scopetest2.php and place this file in your web server document root. When you access this script through your web browser, it should look like Figure 13.3.

FIGURE 13.3
Attempting to reference a variable from outside the scope of a function.

As you might expect, the meaningOfLife() function does not have access to the $life variable in line 2; $life is empty when the function attempts to print it. On the whole, this is a good thing because it saves you from potential clashes between identically named variables, and a function can always demand an argument if it needs information about the outside world. Occasionally, you might want to access an important variable from within a function without passing it in as an argument. This is where the global statement comes into play. Listing 13.7 uses global to restore order to the universe.

LISTING 13.7 Accessing Global Variables with the global Statement

```
1: <?php
2: $life=42;
3: function meaningOfLife()
4: {
5:      global $life;
6:      echo "The meaning of life is ".$life";
7: }
8: meaningOfLife();
9: ?>
```

Put these lines into a text file called scopetest3.php and place this file in your web server document root. When you access this script through your web browser, it should look like Figure 13.4.

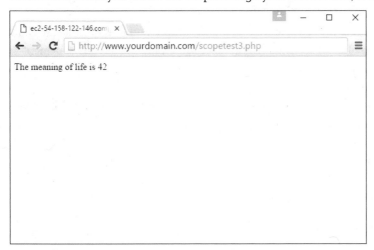

FIGURE 13.4
Successfully accessing a global variable from within a function using the global statement.

When you place the global statement in front of the $life variable when it is declared in the meaningOfLife() function (line 5), it refers to the $life variable declared outside the function (line 2).

You need to use the `global` statement within every function that needs to access a particular named global variable. Be careful, though: If you manipulate the contents of the variable within the function, the value of the variable changes for the script as a whole.

You can declare more than one variable at a time with the `global` statement by simply separating each of the variables you want to access with commas:

```
global $var1, $var2, $var3;
```

CAUTION

Usually, a parameter is a copy of whatever value is passed by the calling code; changing it in a function has no effect beyond the function block. Changing a global variable within a function, however, changes the original and not a copy. Use the `global` statement carefully.

Saving State Between Function Calls with the `static` Statement

Local variables within functions have a short but happy life—they come into being when the function is called and die when execution is finished, as they should. Occasionally, however, you might want to give a function a rudimentary memory.

Assume that you want a function to keep track of the number of times it has been called so that numbered headings can be created by a script. You could, of course, use the `global` statement to do this, as shown in Listing 13.8.

LISTING 13.8   Using the `global` Statement to Remember the Value of a Variable Between Function Calls

---

```
1:   <?php
2:   $num_of_calls = 0;
3:   function numberedHeading($txt)
4:   {
5:       global $num_of_calls;
6:       $num_of_calls++;
7:       echo "<h1>".$num_of_calls." ".$txt."</h1>";
8:   }
9:   numberedHeading("Widgets");
10:  echo "<p>We build a fine range of widgets.</p>";
11:  numberedHeading("Doodads");
12:  echo "<p>Finest in the world.</p>";
13:  ?>
```

Put these lines into a text file called numberedheading.php and place this file in your web server document root. When you access this script through your web browser, it should look like Figure 13.5.

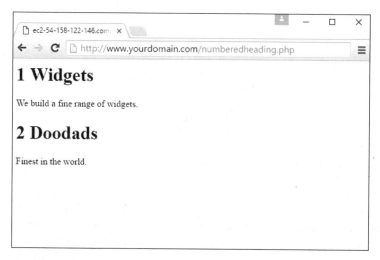

FIGURE 13.5
Using the `global` statement to keep track of the number of times a function has been called.

This does the job. Listing 13.8 declares a variable, $num_of_calls, in line 2, outside the function numberedHeading(). Line 5 makes this variable available to the function by using the `global` statement.

Every time numberedHeading() is called, the value of $num_of_calls is incremented (line 6). You can then print out the heading, complete with the properly incremented heading number.

This is not the most elegant solution, however. Functions that use the `global` statement cannot be read as standalone blocks of code. In reading or reusing them, we need to look out for the global variables that they manipulate.

This is where the `static` statement can be useful. If you declare a variable within a function in conjunction with the `static` statement, the variable remains local to the function, and the function "remembers" the value of the variable from execution to execution. Listing 13.9 adapts the code from Listing 13.8 to use the `static` statement.

LISTING 13.9   Using the `static` Statement to Remember the Value of a Variable Between Function Calls

```php
1:  <?php
2:  function numberedHeading($txt)
3:  {
4:      static $num_of_calls = 0;
5:      $num_of_calls++;
6:      echo "<h1>".$num_of_calls." ". $txt."</h1>";
7:  }
8:  numberedHeading("Widgets");
9:  echo "<p>We build a fine range of widgets.</p>";
10: numberedHeading("Doodads");
11: echo "<p>Finest in the world.</p>";
12: ?>
```

The numberedHeading() function has become entirely self-contained. When the $num_of_calls variable is declared on line 4, an initial value is assigned to it. This assignment is made when the function is first called on line 8. This initial assignment is ignored when the function is called a second time on line 10. Instead, the code remembers the previous value of $num_of_calls. You can now paste the numberedHeading() function into other scripts without worrying about global variables. Although the output of Listing 13.9 is the same as that of Listing 13.8, the code is a bit more elegant.

More About Arguments

You've already seen how to pass arguments to functions, but there's plenty more to cover. This section covers a technique for giving your arguments default values and explores a method of passing variables by reference rather than by value. This means that the function is given an alias of the original value rather than a copy of it.

Setting Default Values for Arguments

PHP provides a nifty feature to help build flexible functions. Until now, you've heard that some functions require one or more arguments. By making some arguments optional, you can render your functions a little less autocratic.

Listing 13.10 creates a useful little function that wraps a string in an HTML span element. To give the user of the function the chance to change the font-size style, you can demand a $fontsize argument in addition to the string (line 2).

LISTING 13.10   A Function Requiring Two Arguments

```
1:  <?php
2:  function fontWrap($txt, $fontsize)
3:  {
4:     echo "<span style=\"font-size:".$fontsize."\">".$txt."</span>";
5:  }
6:  fontWrap("really big text<br/>","24pt");
7:  fontWrap("some body text<br/>","16pt");
8:  fontWrap("smaller body text<br/>","12pt");
9:  fontWrap("even smaller body text<br/>","10pt");
10: ?>
```

Put these lines into a text file called `fontwrap.php` and place this file in your web server document root. When you access this script through your web browser, it should look like Figure 13.6.

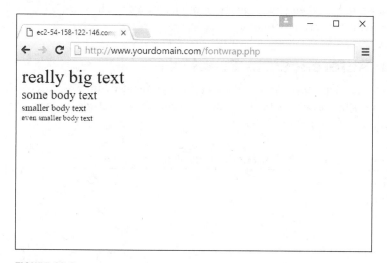

FIGURE 13.6
A function that formats and outputs strings.

By assigning a value to an argument variable within the function definition's parentheses, you can make the $fontsize argument optional. If the function call doesn't define an argument for this parameter, the value you have assigned to the argument is used instead. Listing 13.11 uses this technique to make the $fontsize argument optional.

LISTING 13.11 A Function with an Optional Argument

```
1:  <?php
2:  function fontWrap($txt, $fontsize = "12pt")
3:  {
4:      echo "<span style=\"font-size:".$fontsize."\">".$txt."</span>";
5:  }
6:  fontWrap("really big text<br>","24pt");
7:  fontWrap("some body text<br>");
8:  fontWrap("smaller body text<br>");
9:  fontWrap("even smaller body text<br>");
10: ?>
```

When the `fontWrap()` function is called with a second argument, as in line 6, this value is used to set the font-size attribute of the span element. When this argument is omitted, as in lines 7, 8, and 9, the default value of `"12pt"` is used instead. You can create as many optional arguments as you want, but when you've given an argument a default value, all subsequent arguments should also be given defaults.

Passing Variable References to Functions

When you pass arguments to functions, they are stored as copies in parameter variables. Any changes made to these variables in the body of the function are local to that function and are not reflected beyond it, as illustrated in Listing 13.12.

LISTING 13.12 Passing an Argument to a Function by Value

```
1:  <?php
2:  function addFive($num)
3:  {
4:      $num += 5;
5:  }
6:  $orignum = 10;
7:  addFive($orignum);
8:  echo $orignum;
9:  ?>
```

Put these lines into a text file called `addfive.php` and place this file in your web server document root. When you access this script through your web browser, it produces the following:

10

The `addFive()` function accepts a single numeric value and adds 5 to it, but it returns nothing. A value is assigned to a variable $orignum in line 6 and then this variable is passed to `addFive()` in line 7. A copy of the contents of $orignum is stored in the variable $num.

Although $num is incremented by 5, this has no effect on the value of $orignum. When $orignum is printed, you find that its value is still 10. By default, variables passed to functions are passed by value. In other words, local copies of the values of the variables are made.

You can change this behavior by creating a reference to your original variable. You can think of a reference as a signpost that points to a variable. In working with the reference, you are manipulating the value to which it points.

Listing 13.13 shows this technique in action. When you pass an argument to a function by reference, as in line 7, the contents of the variable you pass ($orignum) are accessed by the argument variable and manipulated within the function, rather than just a copy of the variable's value (10). Any changes made to an argument in these cases change the value of the original variable. You can pass an argument by reference by adding an ampersand to the argument name in the function definition, as shown in line 2.

LISTING 13.13   Using a Function Definition to Pass an Argument to a
Function by Reference

```
1: <?php
2: function addFive(&$num)
3: {
4:       $num += 5;
5: }
6: $orignum = 10;
7: addFive($orignum);
8: echo $orignum;
9: ?>
```

Put these lines into a text file called addfive2.php and place this file in your web server document root. When you access this script through your web browser, it produces the following:

15

Testing for the Existence of a Function

You do not always know whether a function exists before you try to invoke it. Different builds of the PHP engine might include different functionality, and if you are writing a script that may be run on multiple servers, you might want to verify that key features are available. For instance, you might want to write code that uses MySQL if MySQL-related functions are available but simply log data to a text file otherwise.

You can use function_exists() to check for the availability of a function. function_exists() requires a string representing a function name. It returns true if the function can be located, and false otherwise.

Listing 13.14 shows `function_exists()` in action and illustrates some of the other topics we have covered in this chapter.

LISTING 13.14   Testing for a Function's Existence

```
1:   <?php
2:   function tagWrap($tag, $txt, $func = "")
3:   {
4:       if ((!empty($txt)) && (function_exists($func))) {
5:           $txt = $func($txt);
6:           return "<".$tag.">".$txt."</".$tag."><br>";
7:       } else {
8:           return "<strong>".$txt."</strong><br>";
9:       }
10:  }
10:
12:  function underline($txt)
13:  {
14:      return "<span style=\"text-decoration:underline;\">".$txt."</span>";
15:  }
16:  echo tagWrap('strong', 'make me bold');
17:  echo tagWrap('em', 'underline and italicize me', "underline");
18:  echo tagWrap('em', 'make me italic and quote me',
19:  create_function('$txt', 'return "&quot;$txt&quot;";'));
20:  ?>
```

Listing 13.14 defines two functions: `tagWrap()` (line 2) and `underline()` (line 12). The `tagWrap()` function accepts three strings: a tag, the text to format, and an optional function name. It returns a formatted string. The `underline()` function requires a single argument—the text to be formatted—and returns the text wrapped in `<span>` tags with appropriate style attributes.

When you first call `tagWrap()` on line 16, you pass it the string `"string"` and the string `"make me bold"`. Because you haven't passed a value for the function argument, the default value (an empty string) is used. Line 4 checks whether the `$func` variable contains characters, and, if it is not empty, `function_exists()` is called to check for a function by that name. Of course, in this case, the `$func` variable is empty, so the `$txt` variable is wrapped in `<strong>` tags in the `else` clause on lines 7 and 8 and the result is returned.

The code calls `tagWrap()` on line 17 with the string `'em'`, some text, and a third argument: `"underline"`. Then `function_exists()` finds a function called `underline()` (line 12), so it calls this function and passes the `$txt` argument variable to it before any further formatting is done. The result is an italicized, underlined string.

Finally, on line 18, the code calls `tagWrap()`, which wraps text in quotation entities. It is quicker to simply add the entities to the text to be transformed ourselves, but this example serves to illustrate the point that `function_exists()` works as well on anonymous functions as it does on strings representing function names.

Put these lines into a text file called `exists.php` and place this file in your web server document root. When you access this script through your web browser, it should look like Figure 13.7.

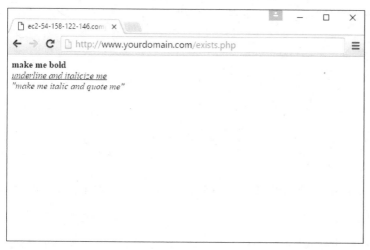

FIGURE 13.7
Output of `exists.php`.

Creating an Object

Having spent a lot of time with functions that often end up manipulating scalar variables, let's move on and spend some quality time with objects. Objects are inherently abstract. An object is a sort of theoretical box of things—variables, functions, and so forth—that exists in a templated structure called a *class*. Although it's easy to visualize a scalar variable, such as `$color`, with a value of `red`, or an array called `$character` with three or four different elements inside it, some people have a difficult time visualizing objects.

For now, try to think of an object as a little box with inputs and outputs on either side of it. The input mechanisms are *methods*, and methods have properties. Throughout this section, we look at how classes, methods, and properties work together to produce various outputs.

As mentioned previously, an object exists as a data structure, and a definition of that structure called a *class*. In each class, you define a set of characteristics. For example, suppose you have created an `automobile` class. In the `automobile` class, you might have `color`, `make`, and `model` characteristics. Each `automobile` object uses all the characteristics, but each object initializes the characteristics to different values, such as `blue`, `Jeep`, and `Renegade`, or `red`, `Porsche`, and `Boxster`.

Using objects creates the potential for highly reusable code. Because classes are so tightly structured but self-contained and independent of one another, you can reuse them from one application to another. For example, suppose that you write a text-formatting class for one project and decide you can use that class in another project. Because a class is just a set of characteristics, you can pick up the code and use it in the second project, reaching into it with methods specific to the second application but using the inner workings of the existing code to achieve new results.

Creating an object is simple; you just declare it to be in existence:

```
class myClass {
     //code will go here
}
```

Now that you have a class, you can create a new instance of an object:

```
$object1 = new myClass();
```

In Listing 13.15, you have proof that your object exists, even though there's nothing in it—it's just been named.

LISTING 13.15   **Proof That Your Object Exists**

```
 1:  <?php
 2:  class myClass {
 3:       //code will go here
 4:  }
 5:  $object1 = new myClass();
 6:  echo "\$object1 is an ".gettype($object1).".<br>";
 7:
 8:  if (is_object($object1)) {
 9:       echo "Really! I swear \$object1 is an object!";
10: }
11: ?>
```

If you save this code as `proofofclass.php`, place it in your document root, and access it with your web browser, you will see the following on your screen:

```
$object1 is an object.
Really! I swear $object1 is an object!
```

This is not a particularly useful class because it does absolutely nothing, but it is valid and shows you how the class template works in lines 2–5. Lines 8–10 use the `is_object()` function to test whether something is an object; in this case, the *something* is `$object1`. Because the test of `is_object()` evaluates to `true`, the string within the `if` statement is printed to the screen.

Next, you learn about using object properties and methods within the class template.

Properties of Objects

The variables declared inside an object are called *properties*. It is standard practice to declare your variables at the top of the class. These properties can be values, arrays, or even other objects. The following snippet uses simple scalar variables inside the class, prefaced with the `public` keyword:

```
class myCar {
    public $color = "silver";
    public $make = "Mazda";
    public $model = "Protege5";
}
```

NOTE

If you use the keyword `public`, `protected`, or `private` before the variable name, you can indicate if the class member (the variable) can be accessed everywhere (public), within the class itself or a parent class or an inherited class (protected), or only by the class itself (private).

Now when you create a `myCar` object, it will always have those three properties. Listing 13.16 shows you how to access properties after they have been declared and values have been assigned to them.

LISTING 13.16 Showing Object Properties

```
1:  <?php
2:  class myCar {
3:      public $color = "blue";
4:      public $make = "Jeep";
5:      public $model = "Renegade";
6:  }
7:  $car = new myCar();
8:  echo "I drive a: " . $car->color . " ".$car->make . " " . $car->model;
9:  ?>
```

If you save this code as `objproperties.php`, place it in your document root, and access it with your web browser, you will see the following on your screen:

```
I drive a: blue Jeep Renegade
```

Because the odds are low that you drive a blue Jeep Renegade, you'll want to change the properties of the `myCar` object. Listing 13.17 shows you how to do just that.

LISTING 13.17   Changing Object Properties

```
1:  <?php
2:  class myCar {
3:      public $color = "blue";
4:      public $make = "Jeep";
5:      public $model = "Renegade";
6:  }
7:  $car = new myCar();
8:  $car->color = "red";
9:  $car->make = "Porsche";
10: $car->model = "Boxster";
11: echo "I drive a: " . $car->color . " " . $car->make . " ". $car->model;
12: ?>
```

If you save this code as `objproperties2.php`, place it in your document root, and access it with your web browser, you will see the following on your screen:

```
I drive a: red Porsche Boxster
```

NOTE

In this instance, even if the `$color`, `$make`, and `$model` properties had no initial values when declared, lines 8–10 would assign a value to them. As long as the properties are declared, you can use them later (initial values or not).

The purpose of Listing 13.17 is to show that as long as you have a well-defined class with properties, you can still easily change the values of the properties to fit your needs.

Object Methods

Methods add functionality to your objects. No longer will your objects just sit there, holding on to their properties for dear life—they'll actually do something! Listing 13.18 shows just that.

LISTING 13.18   A Class with a Method

```
<?php
class myClass {
    public function sayHello() {
        echo "HELLO!";
    }
}
$object1 = new myClass();
$object1->sayHello();
?>
```

Although it is not the most thrilling example of action, if you save this code as `helloclass. php`, place it in your document root, and access it with your web browser, you will see the following on your screen:

```
HELLO!
```

A method looks and acts like a normal function but is defined within the framework of a class. The `->` operator is used to call the object method in the context of your script. Had there been any variables stored in the object, the method would have been capable of accessing them for its own purposes, as illustrated in Listing 13.19.

LISTING 13.19 Accessing Class Properties Within a Method

```php
1:  <?php
2:  class myClass {
3:     public $name = "Jimbo";
4:     public function sayHello() {
5:          echo "HELLO! My name is " . $this->name;
6:     }
7:  }
8:  $object1 = new myClass();
9:  $object1->sayHello();
10: ?>
```

If you save this code as `helloclass2.php`, place it in your document root, and access it with your web browser, you will see the following on your screen:

```
HELLO! My name is Jimbo
```

The special variable `$this` is used to refer to the currently instantiated object as you see on line 5. Any time an object refers to itself, you must use the `$this` variable. Using the `$this` variable in conjunction with the `->` operator enables you to access any property or method in a class, within the class itself.

One final tidbit regarding the basics of working with an object's properties is how to change a property from within a method. Previously, a property's value changed outside the method in which it was contained. Listing 13.20 shows how to make the change from inside a method.

LISTING 13.20 Changing the Value of a Property from Within a Method

```php
1: <?php
2: class myClass {
3:    public $name = "Jimbo";
4:    public function setName($n) {
5:         $this->name = $n;
6:    }
```

```
7:     public function sayHello() {
8:          echo "HELLO! My name is ".$this->name;
9:     }
10: }
11: $object1 = new myClass();
12: $object1->setName("Julie");
13: $object1->sayHello();
14: ?>
```

If you save this code as `helloclass3.php`, place it in your document root, and access it with your web browser, you will see the following on your screen:

`HELLO! My name is Julie`

Why? Because in lines 4–6, a new function called `setName()` was created. When it is called in line 12, it changes the value of `$name` to `Julie`. Therefore, when the `sayHello()` function is called in line 13 and it looks for `$this->name`, it uses `Julie`, which is the new value that was just set by the `setName()` function. In other words, an object can modify its own property—in this case, the `$name` variable.

Constructors

A *constructor* is a function that lives within a class and, given the same name as the class, is automatically called when a new instance of the class is created using `new classname`. Using constructors enables you to provide arguments to your class, which will then be processed immediately when the class is called. You will see constructors in action in the next section.

Object Inheritance

Having learned the absolute basics of objects, properties, and methods, you can start to look at object inheritance. Inheritance with regard to classes is just what it sounds like: One class inherits functionality from its parent class. Listing 13.21 shows an example.

LISTING 13.21   A Class Inheriting from Its Parent

```
1:   <?php
2:   class myClass {
3:       public $name = "Benson";
4:       public function myClass($n) {
5:            $this->name = $n;
6:       }
7:       public function sayHello() {
8:            echo "HELLO! My name is ".$this->name;
9:       }
```

```
10: }
11: class childClass extends myClass {
12: //code goes here
13: }
14: $object1 = new childClass("Baby Benson");
15: $object1->sayHello();
16: ?>
```

If you save this code as `inheritance.php`, place it in your document root, and access it with your web browser, you will see the following on your screen:

```
HELLO! My name is Baby Benson
```

Lines 4–6 make up a constructor. Notice that the name of this function is the same as the class in which it is contained: `myClass`. Lines 11–13 define a second class, `childClass`, that contains no code. That's fine because, in this example, the class exists only to demonstrate inheritance from the parent class. The inheritance occurs through the `extends` clause shown in line 11. The second class inherits the elements of the first class because this clause is used.

Listing 13.22 shows you one last example of how a child class can override the methods of the parent class.

LISTING 13.22   The Method of a Child Class Overriding That of Its Parent

```
1:   <?php
2:   class myClass {
3:       public $name = "Benson";
4:       public function myClass($n) {
5:           $this->name = $n;
6:       }
7:       public function sayHello() {
8:           echo "HELLO! My name is ".$this->name;
9:       }
10: }
11: class childClass extends myClass {
12:     public function sayHello() {
13:         echo "I will not tell you my name.";
14:     }
15: }
16: $object1 = new childClass("Baby Benson");
17: $object1->sayHello();
18: ?>
```

The only changes in this code from Listing 13.21 are the new lines 12–14. In these lines, a function is created called `sayHello()` that, instead of printing HELLO! My name is…, prints the message I will not tell you my name. Because the `sayHello()` function now exists in childClass, and childClass is the class called in line 16, its version of sayHello() is the one used.

If you save this code as inheritance2.php, place it in your document root, and access it with your web browser, you will see the following on your screen:

```
I will not tell you my name
```

Like most elements of object-oriented programming, inheritance is useful when attempting to make your code flexible. Suppose that you create a text-formatting class that organizes and stores data, formats it in HTML, and outputs the result to a browser—your own personal master-piece. Now suppose that you have a client who wants to use that concept, but instead of format-ting the content into HTML and sending it to a browser, he wants to format it as plain text and save it to a text file. No problem; you just add a few methods and properties, and away you go. Finally, the client comes back and says that he really wants the data to be formatted and sent as an email—and then, what the heck, why not create XML-formatted files as well?

Although you might want to pull your hair out in frustration, you're really not in a bad situa-tion. If you separate the compilation and storage classes from the formatting classes—one for each of the various delivery methods (HTML, text, email, XML)—you essentially have a parent-child relationship. Consider the parent class the one that holds the compilation and storage methods. The formatting classes are the children: They inherit the information from the parent and output the result based on their own functionality. Everybody wins.

Switching Flow

Your PHP scripts are going to be full of functions, objects, and logic that control input and out-put. It is common for scripts to evaluate conditions and change their behavior accordingly. These decisions make your PHP scripts dynamic—that is, able to change output according to circum-stances. Like most programming languages, including JavaScript, as you saw in previous chap-ters, PHP enables you to control flow with an if statement.

The if Statement

The if statement is a way of controlling the execution of a statement that follows it (that is, a single statement or a block of code inside braces). The if statement evaluates an expression found between parentheses. If this expression results in a true value, the statement is executed. Otherwise, the statement is skipped entirely. This functionality enables scripts to make decisions based on any number of factors:

```
if (expression) {
    // code to execute if the expression evaluates to true
}
```

Listing 13.23 executes a block of code only if a variable contains the string "happy".

LISTING 13.23   An if Statement

```
1: <?php
2: $mood = "happy";
3: if ($mood == "happy") {
4:     echo "Hooray! I'm in a good mood!";
5: }
6: ?>
```

In line 2, the value "happy" is assigned to the variable $mood. In line 3, the comparison operator == compares the value of the variable $mood with the string "happy". If they match, the expression evaluates to true, and the subsequent code is executed until the closing bracket is found (in this case, in line 5).

Put these lines into a text file called testif.php and place this file in your web server document root. When you access this script through your web browser, it produces the following output:

```
Hooray! I'm in a good mood!
```

If you change the assigned value of $mood to "sad" or any other string besides "happy" and then run the script again, the expression in the if statement evaluates to false, and the code block is skipped. The script remains silent, which leads to the else clause.

Using the else Clause with the if Statement

When working with an if statement, you might want to define an alternative block of code that should be executed if the expression you are testing evaluates to false. You can do this by adding else to the if statement followed by a further block of code:

```
if (expression) {
    // code to execute if the expression evaluates to true
} else {
    // code to execute in all other cases
}
```

Listing 13.24 amends the example in Listing 13.23 so that a default block of code is executed if the value of $mood is not equivalent to "happy".

LISTING 13.24   An if Statement That Uses else

```
1: <?php
2: $mood = "sad";
3: if ($mood == "happy") {
4:     echo "Hooray! I'm in a good mood!";
5: } else {
```

```
6:     echo "I'm in a $mood mood.";
7: }
8: ?>
```

Put these lines into a text file called `testifelse.php` and place this file in your web server document root. When you access this script through your web browser, it produces the following output:

```
I'm in a sad mood.
```

Notice in line 2 that the value of $mood is the string `"sad"`, which obviously is not equal to `"happy"`, so the expression in the `if` statement in line 3 evaluates to `false`. This results in the first block of code (line 4) being skipped. However, the block of code after `else` *is* executed, and the alternate message is printed: `I'm in a sad mood`. The string `"sad"` is the value assigned to the variable $mood.

Using an `else` clause in conjunction with an `if` statement allows scripts to make decisions about code execution. However, your options are limited to an either-or branch: either the code block following the `if` statement or the code block following the `else` statement. You'll now learn about additional options for the evaluation of multiple expressions, one after another.

Using the `elseif` Clause with the `if` Statement

You can use an `if...elseif...else` clause to test multiple expressions (the `if...else` portion) before offering a default block of code (the `elseif` portion):

```
if (expression) {
    // code to execute if the expression evaluates to true
} elseif (another expression) {
    // code to execute if the previous expression failed
    // and this one evaluates to true
} else {
    // code to execute in all other cases
}
```

If the initial `if` expression does not evaluate to `true`, the first block of code is ignored. The `elseif` clause presents another expression for evaluation. If it evaluates to `true`, its corresponding block of code is executed. Otherwise, the block of code associated with the `else` clause is executed. You can include as many `elseif` clauses as you want; if you don't need a default action, you can omit the `else` clause.

NOTE

The `elseif` clause can also be written as two words (`else if`). The syntax you use is a matter of taste, but coding standards employed by PEAR (the PHP Extension and Application Repository) and PECL (the PHP Extension Community Library) use `elseif`.

Listing 13.25 adds an `elseif` clause to the previous example.

LISTING 13.25   An `if` Statement That Uses `else` and `elseif`

```
 1:  <?php
 2:  $mood = "sad";
 3:  if ($mood == "happy") {
 4:      echo "Hooray! I'm in a good mood!";
 5:  } elseif ($mood == "sad") {
 6:      echo "Awww. Don't be down!";
 7:  } else {
 8:      echo "I'm neither happy nor sad, but $mood.";
 9:  }
10: ?>
```

Once again, the $mood variable has a value of "sad", as shown in line 2. This value is not equal to "happy", so the code in line 4 is ignored. The `elseif` clause in line 5 tests for equivalence between the value of $mood and the value "sad", which in this case evaluates to `true`. The code in line 6 is therefore executed. In lines 7 through 9, a default behavior is provided, which would be invoked if the previous test conditions were all `false`. In that case, we would simply print a message including the actual value of the $mood variable.

Put these lines into a text file called `testifelseif.php` and place this file in your web server document root. When you access this script through your web browser, it produces the following output:

```
Awww. Don't be down!
```

Change the value of $mood to "iffy" and run the script. It produces the following output:

```
I'm neither happy nor sad, but iffy.
```

The `switch` Statement

The `switch` statement is an alternative way of changing flow, based on the evaluation of an expression. Using the `if` statement in conjunction with `elseif`, you can evaluate multiple expressions, as you've just seen. However, a `switch` statement evaluates only one expression in a list of expressions, selecting the correct one based on a specific bit of matching code. Whereas the result of an expression evaluated as part of an `if` statement is interpreted as either `true` or `false`, the expression portion of a `switch` statement is subsequently tested against any number of values, in hopes of finding a match:

```
switch (expression) {
     case result1:
          // execute this if expression results in result1
          break;
```

```
     case result2:
         // execute this if expression results in result2
         break;
     default:
         // execute this if no break statement
         // has been encountered hitherto
}
```

The expression used in a switch statement is often just a variable, such as $mood. Within the switch statement, you find a number of case statements. Each of these cases tests a value against the value of the switch expression. If the case value is equivalent to the expression value, the code within the case statement is executed. The break statement ends the execution of the switch statement altogether.

If the break statement is omitted, the next case statement is executed, regardless of whether a previous match has been found. If the optional default statement is reached without a previous matching value having been found, its code is executed.

CAUTION

It is important to include a break statement at the end of any code that will be executed as part of a case statement. Without a break statement, the program flow continues to the next case statement and ultimately to the default statement. In most cases, this results in unexpected behavior, likely incorrect!

Listing 13.26 re-creates the functionality of the if statement example using the switch statement.

LISTING 13.26   A switch Statement

```
1:  <?php
2:  $mood = "sad";
3:  switch ($mood) {
4:      case "happy":
5:          echo "Hooray! I'm in a good mood!";
6:          break;
7:      case "sad":
8:          echo "Awww. Don't be down!";
9:          break;
10:     default:
11:         echo "I'm neither happy nor sad, but $mood.";
12:         break;
13: }
14: ?>
```

Once again, in line 2 the $mood variable is initialized with a value of "sad". The switch statement in line 3 uses this variable as its expression. The first case statement in line 4 tests for equivalence between "happy" and the value of $mood. There is no match in this case, so script execution moves on to the second case statement in line 7. The string "sad" is equivalent to the value of $mood, so this block of code is executed. The break statement in line 9 ends the process. Lines 10 through 12 provide the default action, should neither of the previous cases evaluate as true.

Put these lines into a text file called testswitch.php and place this file in your web server document root. When you access this script through your web browser, it produces the following output:

```
Awww. Don't be down!
```

Change the value of $mood to "happy" and run the script. It produces the following output:

```
Hooray! I'm in a good mood!
```

To emphasize the caution about the importance of the break statement, try running this script without the second break statement. Be sure to change the value of $mood back to "sad" and then run the script. Your output will be as follows:

```
Awww. Don't be down! I'm neither happy nor sad, but sad.
```

This is definitely not the desired output, so be sure to include break statements where appropriate.

Using the ?: Operator

The ?: or *ternary* operator is similar to the if statement, except that it returns a value derived from one of two expressions separated by a colon. This construct provides you with three parts of the whole—hence the name *ternary*. The expression used to generate the returned value depends on the result of a test expression:

```
(expression) ? returned_if_expression_is_true : returned_if_expression_is_false;
```

If the test expression evaluates to true, the result of the second expression is returned; otherwise, the value of the third expression is returned. Listing 13.27 uses the ternary operator to set the value of a variable according to the value of $mood.

LISTING 13.27   Using the ? Operator

```
1: <?php
2: $mood = "sad";
3: $text = ($mood == "happy") ? "I am in a good mood!" : "I am in a $mood mood.";
4: echo "$text";
5: ?>
```

In line 2, $mood is set to "sad". In line 3, $mood is tested for equivalence to the string "happy". Because this test returns false, the result of the third of the three expressions is returned.

Put these lines into a text file called testtern.php and place this file in your web server document root. When you access this script through your web browser, it produces the following output:

```
I am in a sad mood.
```

The ternary operator can be difficult to read, but it's useful if you are dealing with only two alternatives and want to write compact code.

Implementing Loops

So far, you've looked at decisions that a script can make about what code to execute. Scripts can also decide how many times to execute a block of code. Loop statements are specifically designed to enable you to perform repetitive tasks because they continue to operate until a specified condition is achieved or until you explicitly choose to exit the loop. Again, these structures will look familiar to you based on previous chapters that included discussions of loops in JavaScript.

The while Statement

The while statement looks similar in structure to a basic if statement, but it has the ability to loop:

```
while (expression) {
      // do something
}
```

Unlike an if statement, a while statement executes for as long as the expression evaluates to true, over and over again if need be. Each execution of a code block within a loop is called an *iteration*. Within the block, you usually change something that affects the while statement's expression; otherwise, your loop continues indefinitely. For example, you might use a variable to count the number of iterations and act accordingly. Listing 13.28 creates a while loop that calculates and prints multiples of 2 up to 24.

LISTING 13.28   A while Statement

```
1: <?php
2: $counter = 1;
3: while ($counter <= 12) {
4:     echo $counter . " times 2 is " . ($counter * 2) . "<br>";
5:     $counter++;
6: }
7: ?>
```

This example initializes the variable $counter in line 2 with a value of 1. The while statement in line 3 tests the $counter variable so that as long as the value of $counter is less than or equal to 12, the loop continues to run. Within the while statement's code block, the value of $counter is multiplied by 2, and the result is printed to the browser. In line 5, the value of $counter is incremented by 1. This step is extremely important because if you did not increment the value of the $counter variable, the while expression would never resolve to false and the loop would never end.

Put these lines into a text file called testwhile.php and place this file in your web server document root. When you access this script through your web browser, it produces the following output:

```
1 times 2 is 2
2 times 2 is 4
3 times 2 is 6
4 times 2 is 8
5 times 2 is 10
6 times 2 is 12
7 times 2 is 14
8 times 2 is 16
9 times 2 is 18
10 times 2 is 20
11 times 2 is 22
12 times 2 is 24
```

The do...while **Statement**

A do...while statement looks a little like a while statement turned on its head. The essential difference between the two is that the code block is executed *before* the truth test and not after it:

```
do  {
    // code to be executed
} while (expression);
```

CAUTION

The test expression of a do...while statement should always end with a semicolon.

This type of statement is useful when you want the code block to be executed at least once, even if the while expression evaluates to false. Listing 13.29 creates a do...while statement. The code block is executed a minimum of one time.

LISTING 13.29 . The do...while **Statement**

```
1: <?php
2: $num = 1;
3: do {
4:     echo "The number is: " . $num . "<br>";
5:     $num++;
6: } while (($num > 200) && ($num < 400));
7: ?>
```

The do...while statement tests whether the variable $num contains a value that is greater than 200 and less than 400. Line 2 initializes $num to 1, so this expression returns false. Nonetheless, the code block is executed at least one time before the expression is evaluated, so the statement prints a single line to the browser.

Put these lines into a text file called testdowhile.php and place this file in your web server document root. When you access this script through your web browser, it produces the following output:

```
The number is: 1
```

If you change the value of $num in line 2 to 300 and then run the script, the loop displays

```
The number is: 300
```

and continues to print similar lines, with increasing numbers, through

```
The number is: 399
```

The for **Statement**

Anything you want to do with a for statement can also be done with a while statement, but a for statement is often a more convenient method of achieving the same effect. In Listing 13.28, you saw how a variable was initialized outside the while statement and then tested within its expression and incremented within the code block. With a for statement, you can achieve this same series of events, but in a single line of code. This allows for more compact code and makes it less likely that you might forget to increment a counter variable, thereby creating an infinite loop:

```
for (initialization expression; test expression; modification expression) {
    // code to be executed
}
```

NOTE

Infinite loops are, as the name suggests, loops that run without bounds. If your loop is running infinitely, your script is running for an infinite amount of time. This behavior is very stressful on your web server and may render the web site unusable.

The expressions within the parentheses of the for statement are separated by semicolons. Usually, the first expression initializes a counter variable, the second expression is the test condition for the loop, and the third expression increments the counter. Listing 13.30 shows a for statement that re-creates the example in Listing 13.28, which multiplies 12 numbers by 2.

LISTING 13.30   Using the for **Statement**

```
1: <?php
2: for ($counter = 1; $counter <= 12; $counter++) {
3:     echo $counter . " times 2 is " . ($counter * 2) . "<br>";
4: }
5: ?>
```

Put these lines into a text file called testfor.php and place this file in your web server document root. When you access this script through your web browser, it produces the following output:

```
1 times 2 is 2
2 times 2 is 4
3 times 2 is 6
4 times 2 is 8
5 times 2 is 10
6 times 2 is 12
7 times 2 is 14
8 times 2 is 16
9 times 2 is 18
10 times 2 is 20
11 times 2 is 22
12 times 2 is 24
```

The results of Listings 13.28 and 13.30 are the same, but the for statement makes the code in Listing 13.30 more compact. Because the $counter variable is initialized and incremented at the beginning of the statement, the logic of the loop is clear at a glance. That is, as shown in line 2, the first expression initializes the $counter variable and assigns a value of 1, the test expression verifies that $counter contains a value that is less than or equal to 12, and the final expression increments the $counter variable. Each of these items is found in the single line of code.

When the sequence of script execution reaches the for loop, the $counter variable is initialized and the test expression is evaluated. If the expression evaluates to true, the code block is executed. The $counter variable is then incremented and the test expression is evaluated again. This process continues until the test expression evaluates to false.

Breaking Out of Loops with the break **Statement**

Both while and for statements incorporate a built-in test expression with which you can end a loop. However, the break statement enables you to break out of a loop based on the results of additional tests. This can provide a safeguard against error. Listing 13.31 creates a simple `for` statement that divides a large number by a variable that is incremented, printing the result to the screen.

LISTING 13.31 A `for` Loop That Divides 4000 by 10 Incremental Numbers

```
1: <?php
2: for ($counter = 1; $counter <= 10; $counter++) {
3:     $temp = 4000 / $counter;
4:     echo "4000 divided by " . $counter . " is..." . $temp . "<br>";
5: }
6: ?>
```

In line 2, this example initializes the variable `$counter` and assigns a value of 1. The test expression in the `for` statement verifies that the value of `$counter` is less than or equal to 10. Within the code block, 4000 is divided by `$counter`, printing the result to the browser.

Put these lines into a text file called `testfor2.php` and place this file in your web server document root. When you access this script through your web browser, it produces the following output:

```
4000 divided by 1 is... 4000
4000 divided by 2 is... 2000
4000 divided by 3 is... 1333.33333333
4000 divided by 4 is... 1000
4000 divided by 5 is... 800
4000 divided by 6 is... 666.666666667
4000 divided by 7 is... 571.428571429
4000 divided by 8 is... 500
4000 divided by 9 is... 444.444444444
4000 divided by 10 is... 400
```

This seems straightforward enough. But what if the value you place in `$counter` comes from user input? The value could be a negative number or even a string. Let's take the first instance, where the user input value is a negative number. Changing the initial value of `$counter` from 1 to -4 causes 4000 to be divided by 0 when the code block is executed for the fifth time. It is generally not a good idea for your code to divide by 0 because such an operation results in an answer of "undefined." Listing 13.32 guards against this occurrence by breaking out of the loop if the value of the `$counter` variable equals 0.

LISTING 13.32 Using the `break` Statement

```
1: <?php
2: $counter = -4;
3: for (; $counter <= 10; $counter++) {
4:     if ($counter == 0) {
5:         break;
```

```
6:      } else {
7:          $temp = 4000/$counter;
8:          echo "4000 divided by " . $counter . " is... " . $temp . "<br>";
9:      }
10: }
11 ?>
```

NOTE

Dividing a number by 0 does not cause a fatal error in PHP. Instead, PHP generates a warning and execution continues.

Listing 13.32 uses an `if` statement, shown in line 4, to test the value of `$counter` before attempting mathematical operations using this value. If the value of `$counter` is equal to `0`, the `break` statement immediately halts execution of the code block, and program flow continues after the `for` statement (line 11).

Put these lines into a text file called `testfor3.php` and place this file in your web server document root. When you access this script through your web browser, it produces the following output:

```
4000 divided by -4 is... -1000
4000 divided by -3 is... -1333.33333333
4000 divided by -2 is... -2000
4000 divided by -1 is... -4000
```

Notice that the `$counter` variable was initialized in line 2, outside the `for` statement's parentheses. This method was used to simulate a situation in which the value of `$counter` is set from outside the script.

TIP

You can omit any of the expressions from a `for` statement, but you must remember to retain the separation semicolons.

Skipping an Iteration with the `continue` Statement

The `continue` statement ends execution of the current iteration but doesn't cause the loop as a whole to end. Instead, the next iteration begins immediately. Using the `break` statement as in Listing 13.32 is a little drastic. With the `continue` statement in Listing 13.33, you can avoid a divide-by-zero error without ending the loop completely.

LISTING 13.33 Using the `continue` Statement

```php
1:   <?php
2:   $counter = -4;
3:   for (; $counter <= 10; $counter++) {
4:       if ($counter == 0) {
5:           continue;
6:       }
7:       $temp = 4000 / $counter;
8:       echo "4000 divided by " . $counter . " is... " . $temp . "<br>";
9:   }
10:  ?>
```

Line 5 swaps the `break` statement for a `continue` statement. If the value of the `$counter` variable is equivalent to 0, the iteration is skipped, and the next one starts immediately.

Put these lines into a text file called `testcontinue.php` and place this file in your web server document root. When you access this script through your web browser, it produces the following output:

```
4000 divided by -4 is... -1000
4000 divided by -3 is... -1333.33333333
4000 divided by -2 is... -2000
4000 divided by -1 is... -4000
4000 divided by 1 is... 4000
4000 divided by 2 is... 2000
4000 divided by 3 is... 1333.33333333
4000 divided by 4 is... 1000
4000 divided by 5 is... 800
4000 divided by 6 is... 666.666666667
4000 divided by 7 is... 571.428571429
4000 divided by 8 is... 500
4000 divided by 9 is... 444.44444444444
4000 divided by 10 is... 400
```

CAUTION

Using the `break` and `continue` statements can make code more difficult to read because they often add layers of complexity to the logic of the loop statements that contain them. Use these statements with care, or comment your code to show other programmers (or yourself) exactly what you're trying to achieve with these statements.

Nesting Loops

Loops can contain other loop statements, as long as the logic is valid and the loops are tidy. The combination of such statements proves particularly useful when you're working with dynamically created HTML tables. Listing 13.34 uses two `for` statements to print a multiplication table to the browser.

LISTING 13.34 Nesting Two `for` Loops

```
1:   <?php
2:   echo "<table style=\"border: 1px solid #000;\"> \n";
3:   for ($y = 1; $y <= 12; $y++) {
4:       echo "<tr> \n";
5:       for ($x = 1; $x <= 12; $x++) {
6:           echo "<td style=\"border: 1px solid #000; width: 25px;
7:                   text-align:center;\">";
8:           echo ($x * $y);
9:           echo "</td> \n";
10:      }
11:      echo "</tr> \n";
12:  }
13:  echo "</table>";
14:  ?>
```

Before you examine the `for` loops, take a closer look at line 2 in Listing 13.34:

```
echo "<table style=\"border: 1px solid black;\"> \n";
```

Notice that Listing 13.34 uses the backslash character (\) before each of the quotation marks within the string containing the style information for the table. These backslashes also appear in lines 6 and 7, in the style information for the table data cell. This is necessary because it tells the PHP engine that we want to use the quotation mark character, rather than have PHP interpret it as the beginning or end of a string. If you did not "escape" the quotation marks with the backslash character, the statement would not make sense to the engine; it would read it as a string followed by a number followed by another string. Such a construct would generate an error. This line also uses \n to represent a newline character, which makes the source easier to read when it is rendered by the browser, which is useful especially for looking at HTML for tables.

The outer `for` statement (line 3) initializes a variable called `$y`, assigning to it a starting value of 1. This `for` statement defines an expression that intends to verify that the value of `$y` is less than or equal to 12, and then defines the increment that will be used. In each iteration, the code block prints a `tr` (table row) HTML element (line 4) and begins another `for` statement (line 5). This inner loop initializes a variable called `$x` and defines expressions along the same lines as for the outer loop. For each iteration, the inner loop prints a `td` (table cell) element to the browser (lines 6 and 7) as well as the result of `$x` multiplied by `$y` (line 8). Line 9 closes the table cell. After the inner loop has finished, execution falls back through to the outer loop, where the table row closes on line 11, ready for the process to begin again. When the outer loop has finished, the result is a neatly formatted multiplication table. Listing 13.34 wraps things up by closing the table on line 13.

Put these lines into a text file called `testnestfor.php` and place this file in your web server document root. When you access this script through your web browser, it should look like Figure 13.8.

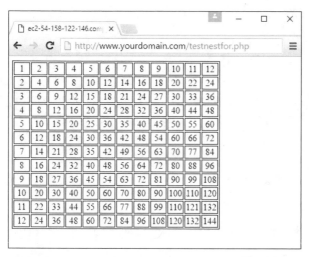

FIGURE 13.8
Output of `testnestfor.php`.

Summary

You saw a lot of code examples and hopefully learned a lot in this chapter. This chapter taught you about functions and how to create and use them. You learned how to define and pass arguments to a function, how to use the `global` and `static` statements, how to pass references to functions, and how to create default values for function arguments. You also learned to test for the existence of functions.

You learned the basics of working with object-oriented code. You learned to create classes and instantiate objects from them, and you learned how to create and access the properties and methods of a class, how to build new classes, and how to inherit features from parent classes.

As if all that wasn't enough, you also learned about control structures and the ways in which they can help to make your scripts flexible and dynamic. Most of these structures reappear regularly throughout the rest of the book and are very similar in both JavaScript and PHP. You should now know enough of the basics to write both front-end and back-end scripts of your own that make decisions and perform repetitive tasks.

Q&A

Q. Can I include a function call within a double- or single-quoted string, as I can with a variable?

A. No. Just like in JavaScript, you must call functions outside quotation marks. However, you can break the string apart and place the function call between the parts of the string, using the concatenation operator to tie them together, as follows:

```
$newstring = "I purchased" . numPurchase($somenum) . " items.";
```

Q. What happens if I call a function that does not exist, or if I declare a function with a name already in use?

A. Calling a function that does not exist or declaring a function with the same name as another existing function causes the script to stop execution. Whether an error message displays in the browser depends on the error settings in your `php.ini` file.

Q. Must a control structure's test expression result in a Boolean value?

A. Ultimately, yes. But in the context of a test expression, `0`, an undefined variable, or an empty string is converted to `false`. All other values evaluate to `true`.

Q. Must I always surround a code block in a control statement with brackets?

A. If the code you want executed as part of a control structure consists of only a single line, you can omit the brackets. However, the habit of always using opening and closing brackets, regardless of structure length, is a good one.

Workshop

The Workshop is designed to help you review what you've learned and begin putting your knowledge into practice.

Quiz

1. True or false? If a function doesn't require an argument, you can omit the parentheses in the function call.

2. How do you return a value from a function?

3. How can you declare a class called `emptyClass` that has no methods or properties?

4. If a variable is declared `private`, where can it be used?

5. How do you use an `if` statement to print the string `"Youth message"` to the browser if an integer variable, `$age`, is between `18` and `35`, and if `$age` contains any other value, the string `"Generic message"` is printed to the browser?

Answers

1. The statement is false. You must always include the parentheses in your function calls, whether or not you are passing arguments to the function.

2. You must use the `return` keyword.

3. Use the `class` keyword, like so:

```
class emptyClass {
}
```

4. Variables declared `private` can only be used in the class itself.

5.

```
$age = 22;
if (($age >= 18) && ($age <= 35)) {
    echo "Youth message";
} else {
    echo "Generic message";
}
```

Exercises

▶ Create a function that accepts four string variables, returns a string that contains an HTML table element, and encloses each of the variables in its own cell.

▶ Create a class called `baseCalc()` that stores two numbers as properties. Next, create a method called `calculate()` that prints the numbers to the browser.

▶ Now create classes called `addCalc()`, `subCalc()`, `mulCalc()`, and `divCalc()` that inherit functionality from `baseCalc()` but override the `calculate()` method, and then print the appropriate totals to the browser.

Working with Cookies and User Sessions

What You'll Learn in This Chapter:

▶ How to store and retrieve cookie information

▶ What session variables are and how they work

▶ How to start or resume a session

▶ How to store variables in a session

▶ How to destroy a session

▶ How to unset session variables

▶ What the differences are between a browser's local and session storage

In an online world controlled by HTTP—the Hypertext Transfer Protocol, or the way data is communicated on the Web—cookies and sessions are a means of storing and transferring small bits of information specific to you to help that communication along. For example, for the duration of the time you spend browsing an online shopping site, a bit of text stored in your web browser identifies your actions—such as adding an item to a shopping cart—as belonging to you.

Both JavaScript and PHP contain built-in language features for managing and keeping track of user information, including both simple cookies and all-encompassing user sessions.

Introducing Cookies

You can use cookies within your JavaScript or PHP scripts to store small bits of information about a user. A *cookie* is a small amount of data stored by the user's browser in compliance with a request from a server or script. Each cookie consists of a name, value, and expiration date, as well as host and path information. Web browsers can handle up to 30 cookies for a single website, as long as the total amount of data stored is not more than 4KB.

After a cookie is set, only the originating host can read the data, ensuring that the user's privacy is respected. Furthermore, users can configure their browsers to notify them upon receipt of all cookies, or even to refuse all cookie requests. For this reason, cookies should be used in moderation and should not be relied on as an essential element of an environment design without first warning users.

The Anatomy of a Cookie

Both JavaScript and PHP scripts can send cookies, and the underlying structure of the information that is sent through HTTP's headers that might look something like this:

```
HTTP/1.1 200 OK
Date: Sat, 15 Jul 2017 10:50:58 GMT
Server: Apache/2.4.18 (Ubuntu) PHP/7.1.6
X-Powered-By: PHP/7.1.6
Set-Cookie: vegetable=artichoke; path=/; domain=.yourdomain.com
Connection: close
Content-Type: text/html
```

This example is specific to a cookie being sent via PHP, but the types of information sent are the same. In this example, the `Set-Cookie` header contains a name/value pair, a path, and a domain. If set, an `expiration` field provides the date at which the browser should "forget" the value of the cookie. If no expiration date is set, as in this example, the cookie expires when the user's session expires—that is, when he closes his browser.

The `path` and `domain` fields work together: The `path` is a directory found on the `domain`, below which the cookie should be sent back to the server. If the path is a slash (/), which is common, that means the cookie can be read by any files below the document root. If the path is /products/, the cookie can be read only by files within the /products/ directory of the specific website.

The `domain` field represents the Internet domain from which cookie-based communication is allowed. For example, if your domain is www.yourdomain.com and you use www.yourdomain.com as the domain value for the cookie, the cookie will be valid only when the user browses the www.yourdomain.com website. This could pose a problem if you send the user to some domain like www2.yourdomain.com or billing.yourdomain.com within the course of his browsing experience, because the original cookie will no longer work. Therefore, it is common simply to begin the value of the domain slot in cookie definitions with a dot, leaving off the host (for example, .yourdomain.com). In this manner, the cookie is valid for all hosts on the "yourdomain.com" domain.

Accessing Cookies

If your web browser is configured to store cookies, it keeps the cookie-based information until the expiration date. If the browser is pointed at any page that matches the path and domain of the cookie, it resends the cookie to the server. The browser's headers might look something like this:

```
GET / HTTP/1.1
Connection: Keep-Alive
Mozilla/5.0 (Windows NT 10.0; WOW64) AppleWebKit/537.36 (KHTML, like Gecko)
Chrome/51.0.2704.106 Safari/537.36
Host: www.yourdomain.com
```

```
Accept: text/html,application/xhtml+xml,application/xml;q=0.9,image/webp,*/*;q=0
Accept-Encoding: gzip, deflate, sdch
Accept-Language: en-US
Cookie: vegetable=artichoke
```

A PHP script then has access to the cookie in the environment variable `HTTP_COOKIE` or as part of the `$_COOKIE` superglobal variable, which you may access three different ways:

```
echo $_SERVER['HTTP_COOKIE']; // will print "vegetable=artichoke"
echo getenv('HTTP_COOKIE');   // will print "vegetable=artichoke"
echo $_COOKIE['vegetable'];   // will print "artichoke"
```

You can access the cookie in JavaScript via `document.cookie`, which returns all the cookies associated with the current document loaded in the web browser. Suppose you were to put a piece of JavaScript in your code like the following:

```
console(document.cookie);
```

In this case, it would print the contents of the cookies (*vegetable=artichoke* in this instance) in the console of the browser, which is typically accessible in the browser's Developer Tools (check the Help menu for your browser of choice).

Setting a Cookie

In this section, you'll learn how to set cookies in PHP as well as in JavaScript. Cookies set by either language are completely accessible by the other (as well as languages not mentioned here) because these bits of information are ultimately stored in your web browser and appended to any server-side or client-side requests that are made. In other words, it doesn't matter how cookies get there; once they're there, they can be read.

You can set a cookie in a PHP script in two ways. First, you can use the `header()` function to set the `Set-Cookie` header. The `header()` function requires a string that is then included in the header section of the server response. Because headers are sent automatically for you, `header()` must be called before any output at all is sent to the browser:

```
header("Set-Cookie: vegetable=artichoke; expires=Sat, 15-Jul-2017 13:00:00 GMT;
path=/; domain=.yourdomain.com");
```

Although not difficult, this method of setting a cookie requires you to build a function to construct the header string. Although formatting the date as in this example and URL-encoding the name/value pair are not particularly arduous tasks, they are repetitive ones. Fortunately, PHP provides a function that does all these things already: `setcookie()`.

The `setcookie()` function does what its name suggests—it outputs a `Set-Cookie` header. For this reason, just as before, it should be called before any other content is sent to the browser.

The function accepts the cookie's name, value, expiration date (in UNIX epoch format), path, domain, and integer (which should be set to 1 if the cookie is to be sent only over a secure connection). All arguments to this function are optional apart from the first (cookie name) parameter.

Listing 14.1 uses `setcookie()` to set a cookie.

LISTING 14.1   Setting and Printing a Cookie Value

```
1: <?php
2: setcookie("vegetable", "artichoke", time()+3600, "/", ".yourdomain.com", 0);
3:
4: if (isset($_COOKIE['vegetable'])) {
5:   echo "<p>Hello again! You have chosen:  ".$_COOKIE['vegetable'].".</p>";
6: } else {
7:   echo "<p>Hello, you. This may be your first visit.</p>";
8: }
9: ?>
```

Even though the listing sets the cookie (line 2) when the script is run for the first time, the `$_COOKIE['vegetable']` variable is not created at this point. Because a cookie is read-only when the browser sends it to the server, you cannot read it until the user revisits a page within this domain.

The cookie name is set to `"vegetable"` on line 2, and the cookie value to `"artichoke"`. The `time()` function gets the current timestamp and adds `3600` to it (3,600 seconds in an hour). This total represents the expiration date. The code defines a path of `"/"`, which means that a cookie should be sent for any page within this server environment. The domain argument is set to `".yourdomain.com"` (you should make the change relevant to your own domain or leave it blank if you are working on `localhost`), which means that a cookie will be sent to any server in that group. Finally, the code passes `0` to `setcookie()`, signaling that cookies can be sent in an unsecure environment. If the value were `1`, the cookie would only be valid in a secure (HTTPS) environment.

Passing `setcookie()` an empty string (`""`) for the string arguments or `0` for integer fields causes these arguments to be skipped.

NOTE
When you're using a dynamically created expiration time in a cookie, as in Listing 14.1, note that the expiration time is created by adding a certain number of seconds to the current system time of the machine running Apache and PHP. If this system clock is not accurate, the machine may send the cookie at an expiration time that has already passed.

You can view your cookies in most modern web browsers using the Developer Tools baked into those browsers. Figure 14.1 shows the cookie information stored for Listing 14.1. The cookie name, content, and expiration date appear as expected; the domain name will differ when you run this script on your own domain.

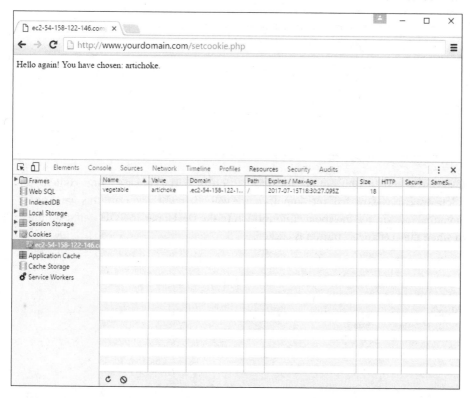

FIGURE 14.1
Viewing a cookie stored by PHP in a web browser.

For more information on using cookies, and the setcookie() function in particular, see the PHP Manual entry at http://www.php.net/setcookie.

To set the same cookie with JavaScript, you must be explicit with the header information, as in the first example in this section:

```
document.cookie = "vegetable=artichoke; expires=Sat, 15 Jul 2017 13:00:00 GMT;
path=/; domain=.yourdomain.com";
```

Listing 14.2 shows setting a cookie in JavaScript and providing a button to check the value of that cookie.

LISTING 14.2   Setting and Checking a Cookie with JavaScript

```
1: <!DOCTYPE html>
2: <html lang="en">
3:   <head>
4:     <title>Setting a Cookie</title>
5:       <script type="text/javascript">
6:       document.cookie = "vegetable=artichoke; expires=Sat, 15 Jul 2017 13:00:00 GMT;
7:                          path=/; domain=.yourdomain.com";
8:     </script>
9:   </head>
10: <body>
11:    <h1>Got a Cookie?</h1>
12:    <button onclick="alert(document.cookie);">Let's See!</button>
13: </body>
14: </html>
```

Figure 14.2 shows the cookie information stored for Listing 14.2. The cookie's name, content, and expiration date appear as expected; the domain name will differ when you run this script on your own domain. You can see the cookie information in the Developer Tools as well as in the alert shown when the "Let's See!" button is clicked.

FIGURE 14.2
Viewing a stored cookie in a web browser by JavaScript.

Deleting a Cookie

In PHP, to delete a cookie, you just have to call `setcookie()` with the name argument only, which effectively resets all stored values:

```
setcookie("vegetable");
```

To be absolutely sure your cookie is no longer valid or storing any values at all, you could also set the cookie with a date that you are sure has already expired—a date in the past:

```
setcookie("vegetable", "", time()-60, "/", ".yourdomain.com", 0);
```

When deleting a cookie in this manner, make sure you pass `setcookie()` the same path, domain, and secure parameters as you did when originally setting the cookie.

Similarly, in JavaScript you delete a cookie with reset values, like so:

```
document.cookie = "vegetable=; expires=Thu, 01 Jan 1970 00:00:00 GMT";
```

In this case, the cookie expiration is set to a specific date in the past, meaning it is expired and thus will never be set.

Overview of Server-Side Sessions

Server-side sessions provide a unique identifier to a user, which can then be used to store and acquire information linked to that ID. When a visitor accesses a PHP session-enabled page, either a new identifier is allocated or the user is reassociated with one that was already established in a previous visit. Any variables that have been associated with the session become available to your code through PHP's `$_SESSION` superglobal.

Session state is usually stored in a temporary file, although you can implement database storage or other server-side storage methods using a function called `session_set_save_handler()`. The use of `session_set_save_handler()` and a discussion about other advanced session functionality are beyond the scope of this book, but you can find more information in the PHP Manual section for sessions for all items not discussed here (http://php.net/manual/en/book.session.php).

To work with a PHP session, you need to explicitly start or resume that session *unless* you have changed your `php.ini` configuration file. By default, sessions do not start automatically. If you want to start a session this way, you must find the following line in your `php.ini` file and change the value from 0 to 1 (and restart the web server):

```
session.auto_start = 0
```

By changing the value of `session.auto_start` to 1, you ensure that a session initiates for every PHP document loaded by the web server. If you don't change this setting, you need to call the `session_start()` function in each script.

After a session is started, you instantly have access to the user's session ID via the `session_id()` function. The `session_id()` function enables you to either set or retrieve a session ID. Listing 14.2 starts a session and prints the session ID to the browser.

LISTING 14.3   **Starting or Resuming a Session**

```
1: <?php
2: session_start();
3: echo "<p>Your session ID is ".session_id().".</p>";
4: ?>
```

When this script (let's call it `session_checkid.php`) is run for the first time from a browser, a session ID is generated by the `session_start()` function call on line 2. If the script is later reloaded or revisited, the same session ID is allocated to the user. This action assumes that the user has cookies enabled, as a cookie is created in the user's browser that holds this information for reference.

For example, when I run this script the first time, the output is as follows:

```
Your session ID is 59f8a4cd676c96986ce293726d66b070.
```

When I reload the page, the output is still

```
Your session ID is 59f8a4cd676c96986ce293726d66b070.
```

because I have cookies enabled and the session ID still exists.

Because `start_session()` sets a cookie when initiating a session for the first time, it is imperative that you call this function before you output anything else at all to the browser. If you do not follow this rule, your session will not be set, and you will likely see warnings on your page.

Sessions remain current as long as the web browser is active. When the user restarts the browser, the cookie is no longer stored. You can change this behavior by altering the `session.cookie_lifetime` setting in your php.ini file. The default value is 0, but you can set an expiry period in seconds.

Working with Session Variables

Accessing a unique session identifier in each of your PHP documents is only the start of session functionality. When a session is started, you can store any number of variables in the `$_SESSION` superglobal and then access them on any session-enabled page.

Listing 14.4 adds two variables into the $_SESSION superglobal: product1 and product2 (lines 3 and 4).

LISTING 14.4 Storing Variables in a Session

```
1: <?php
2: session_start();
3: $_SESSION['product1'] = "Sonic Screwdriver";
4: $_SESSION['product2'] = "HAL 2000";
5: echo "The products have been registered.";
6: ?>
```

The magic in Listing 14.4 will not become apparent until the user moves to a new page. Listing 14.5 creates a separate PHP script that accesses the variables stored in the $_SESSION superglobal.

LISTING 14.5 Accessing Stored Session Variables

```
1: <?php
2: session_start();
3: ?>
4: <!DOCTYPE html>
5: <html lang="en">
6:   <head>
7:     <title>Your Products</title>
8:   </head>
9:   <body>
10:   <h1>Your Products</h1>
11:   <p>Your chosen products are:</p>
12:   <ul>
13:     <li><?php echo $_SESSION['product1']; ?></li>
14:     <li><?php echo $_SESSION['product2']; ?></li>
15:   </ul>
16:   </body>
17: </html>
```

Figure 14.3 shows the output from Listing 14.5. As you can see, you have access to the $_SESSION['product1'] and $_SESSION['product2'] variables in an entirely new page. You can also see the reference to the PHPSESSID cookie in the browser's Developer Tools.

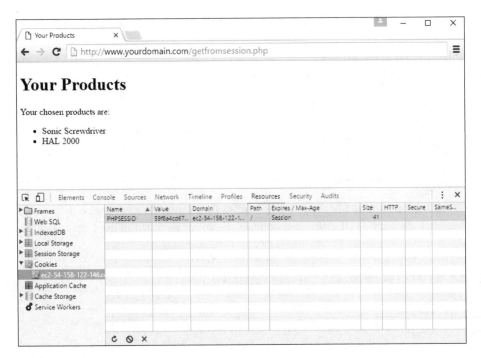

FIGURE 14.3
Accessing stored session variables.

Behind the scenes, PHP writes information to a temporary file on the web server. You can find
out where this file is being written on your system by using the `session_save_path()` function. This function optionally accepts a path to a directory and then writes all session files to
it. If you pass it no arguments, it returns a string representing the current directory to which it
saves session files. On my system, the following prints `/tmp`:

```
echo session_save_path();
```

A glance at my `/tmp` directory reveals a number of files with names like the following:

```
sess_59f8a4cd676c96986ce293726d66b070
sess_76cae8ac1231b11afa2c69935c11dd95
sess_bb50771a769c605ab77424d59c784ea0
```

Opening the file that matches the session ID I was allocated when I first ran Listing 14.5, I can
see how the registered variables have been stored:

```
product1|s:17:"Sonic Screwdriver";product2|s:8:"HAL 2000";
```

When a value is placed in the `$_SESSION` superglobal, PHP writes the variable name and value
to a file. This information can be read and the variables resurrected later—as you have already

seen. After you add a variable to the $_SESSION superglobal, you can still change its value at any time during the execution of your script, but the altered value is not reflected in the global setting until you reassign the variable to the $_SESSION superglobal.

The example in Listing 14.4 demonstrates the process of manually adding variables to the $_SESSION superglobal. This example is not very flexible, however. Ideally, you should be able to register a varying number of values. You might want to let users pick products from a list, for example. In this case, you can use the serialize() function to store an array in your session.

Listing 14.6 creates a form that allows a user to choose multiple products. You use the session variables to create a rudimentary shopping cart.

LISTING 14.6 Adding an Array Variable to a Session Variable

```
 1: <?php
 2: session_start();
 3: ?>
 4: <!DOCTYPE html>
 5: <html lang="en">
 6: <head>
 7: <title>Storing an array with a session</title>
 8: </head>
 9: <body>
10: <h1>Product Choice Page</h1>
11: <?php
12: if (isset($_POST['form_products'])) {
13:     if (!empty($_SESSION['products'])) {
14:         $products = array_unique(
15:         array_merge(unserialize($_SESSION['products']),
16:         $_POST['form_products']));
17:         $_SESSION['products'] = serialize($products);
18:     } else {
19:         $_SESSION['products'] = serialize($_POST['form_products']);
20:     }
21:     echo "<p>Your products have been registered!</p>";
22: }
23: ?>
24: <form method="post" action="<?php echo $_SERVER['PHP_SELF']; ?>">
25: <p><label for="form_products">Select some products:</label><br>
26: <select id="form_products" name="form_products[]" multiple="multiple" size="3">
27: <option value="Sonic Screwdriver">Sonic Screwdriver</option>
28: <option value="Hal 2000">Hal 2000</option>
29: <option value="Tardis">Tardis</option>
30: <option value="ORAC">ORAC</option>
31: <option value="Transporter bracelet">Transporter bracelet</option>
32: </select></p>
33: <button type="submit" name="submit" value="choose">Submit Form</button>
```

```
34: </form>
35: <p><a href="session1.php">go to content page</a></p>
36: </body>
37: </html>
```

The listing starts or resumes a session by calling `session_start()` on line 2. This call gives access to any previously set session variables. An HTML form begins on line 24 and, on line 26, creates a `SELECT` element named `form_products[]`, which contains `OPTION` elements for a number of products.

NOTE

Remember that HTML form elements that allow multiple selections, such as check boxes and multiple select lists, should have square brackets appended to the value of their `NAME` attributes. This makes the user's choices available to PHP in an array.

The block of PHP code beginning on line 11 tests for the presence of the `$_POST['form_products']` array (line 12). If the variable is present, you can assume that the form has been submitted and information has already been stored in the `$_SESSION` superglobal.

Line 12 tests for an array called `$_SESSION['products']`. If the array exists, it was populated on a previous visit to this script, so the code merges it with the `$_POST['form_products']` array, extracts the unique elements, and assigns the result back to the `$products` array (lines 14–16). Then the `$products` array is added to the `$_SESSION` superglobal on line 17.

Line 35 contains a link to another script, which will demonstrate access to the products the user has chosen. This new script is created in Listing 14.7, but in the meantime you can save the code in Listing 14.6 as `arraysession.php`.

Moving on to Listing 14.7, you see how to access the items stored in the session created in `arraysession.php`.

LISTING 14.7 Accessing Session Variables

```
 1: <?php
 2: session_start();
 3: ?>
 4: <!DOCTYPE html>
 5: <html lang="en">
 6: <head>
 7: <title>Accessing Session Variables</title>
 8: </head>
 9: <body>
10: <h1>Content Page</h1>
11: <?php
```

```
12: if (isset($_SESSION['products'])) {
13:     echo "<strong>Your cart:</strong><ol>";
14:     foreach (unserialize($_SESSION['products']) as $p) {
15:         echo "<li>".$p."</li>";
16:     }
17:     echo "</ol>";
18: }
19: ?>
20: <p><a href="arraysession.php">return to product choice page</a></p>
21: </body>
22: </html>
```

Once again, `session_start()` resumes the session on line 2. Line 12 tests for the presence of the `$_SESSION['products']` variable. If it exists, the variable is unserialized and looped through on lines 14–16, printing each of the user's chosen items to the browser. Figure 14.4 shows an example of the output.

FIGURE 14.4
Accessing an array of session variables.

For a real shopping cart program, you are likely to keep product details in a database and validate that user input rather than blindly store and present it, but Listings 14.6 and 14.7 demonstrate the ease with which you can use PHP session functions to access array variables set in other pages.

Destroying Sessions and Unsetting Session Variables

You can use the PHP function `session_destroy()` to end a session, which will erase all session variables managed on the server side. The `session_destroy()` function requires no arguments. You should have an established session for this function to work as expected. The following code fragment resumes a session in PHP and then abruptly destroys it:

```
session_start();
session_destroy();
```

When you move on to other pages that work with a PHP session, the session you have destroyed will not be available to them, forcing the initiation of new sessions. Any previously registered variables will be lost.

The `session_destroy()` function does not instantly destroy registered variables, however. They remain accessible to the script in which `session_destroy()` is called (until it is reloaded). The following code fragment resumes or initiates a session and registers a variable called `test`, which is set to 5. Destroying the session does not destroy the registered variable:

```
session_start();
$_SESSION['test'] = 5;
session_destroy();
echo $_SESSION['test']; // prints 5
```

To remove all registered variables from a session, you have to unset the variable:

```
session_start();
$_SESSION['test'] = 5;
session_destroy();
unset($_SESSION['test']);
echo $_SESSION['test']; // prints nothing (or a notice about an undefined index)
```

Using Sessions in an Environment with Registered Users

The examples you've seen so far have gotten your feet wet with PHP sessions, but perhaps additional explanation is warranted for using sessions "in the wild," so to speak. The following two sections outline some examples of common session usage. In later chapters of this book, you'll use sessions to some extent in the sample applications you build.

Working with Registered Users

Suppose that you've created an online community, or a portal, or some other type of application that users can "join." The process usually involves a registration form, where the user creates a username and password and completes an identification profile. From that point forward, each time a registered user logs in to the system, you can grab the user's identification information and store it in the user's session.

The items you decide to store in the user's session should be those items you can imagine using quite a bit—and that would be inefficient to continually extract from the database. For example, suppose that you have created a portal in which users are assigned a certain level, such as administrator, registered user, anonymous guest, and so forth. Within your display modules, you would always want to check to verify that the user accessing the module has the proper permissions to do so. Thus, "user level" is an example of a value stored in the user's session, so that the authentication script used in the display of the requested module only has to check a session variable—there is no need to connect to, select, and query the database (except to validate that data further down the chain).

Working with User Preferences

If you are feeling adventurous in the design phase of a user-based application, you might build a system in which registered users can set specific preferences that affect the way they view your site. For example, you might allow your users to select from a predetermined color scheme, font type and size, and so forth. Or, you might allow users to turn "off" (or "on") the visibility of certain content groupings.

You can store each of those functional elements in a session. When the user logs in, the application loads all relevant values into the user's session and reacts accordingly for each subsequently requested page. Should the user decide to change her preferences, she could do so while logged in—you could even prepopulate a "preferences" form based on the items stored in the session instead of going back to the database to retrieve them. If the user changes any preferences while she is logged in, simply replace the value stored in the $_SESSION superglobal with the new selection—no need to force the user to log out and then log back in again.

Understanding Local and Session Storage in the Browser

The two scenarios just described can also be performed entirely within the browser itself, using mechanisms in HTML5 called *local* and *session storage*. Both local and session storage can be used to enhance a user's experience with a website by reducing the latency inherent in continually requesting data from the web server.

Local and session storage in the browser do the same thing; the difference is the duration of time they perform their jobs. Local storage allows you to persist data in the user's browser until he explicitly deletes it. This is great for long-term storage of preferences, but really bad when the computer is shared with others since the data will persist even after the browser is closed or the computer is shut down. On the other hand, items in session storage persist only as long as the tab, window, or browser is opened.

To place items in local or session storage, you can use JavaScript to access the HTML5 Web Storage API, like so:

```
localStorage.setitem("loggedIn", true);
sessionStorage.setitem("displayName", "Jane");
```

To access these values later, you can use JavaScript again:

```
var loggedIn = localStorage.getItem("loggedIn");
var displayName = sessionStorage.getItem("displayName");
```

You can learn more about the HTML5 Web Storage API at https://developer.mozilla.org/en-US/docs/Web/API/Web_Storage_API/.

Summary

In this chapter, you looked at different ways of saving state in the stateless protocol of HTTP, including setting a cookie and starting a session. All methods of saving state use some manner of cookies or information in the HTTP headers, sometimes combined with the use of files or databases.

You learned that a cookie alone is not intrinsically reliable and cannot store much information. However, it can persist over a long period. Approaches that write information to a file or database involve some cost to speed and might become a problem on a popular site; this is a matter to explore with your systems administrators.

About sessions themselves, you learned how to initiate or resume a session with `session_start()`. When in a session, you learned how to add variables to the `$_SESSION` superglobal, check that they exist, unset them if you want, and destroy the entire session.

Q&A

Q. **What will happen to my application if users disable cookies?**

A. Simply put, if your application relies heavily on cookies and users have cookies disabled, your application won't work. However, you can do your part to warn users that cookies are coming by announcing your intention to use cookies, and also by checking that cookies are enabled before doing anything "important" with your application. The idea being, of course, that even if users ignore your note that cookies must be turned on in order to use your application, specifically disallowing users to perform an action if your cookie test fails will get their attention!

Q. Should I be aware of any pitfalls with session functions?

A. The session functions are generally reliable. However, remember that cookies cannot be read across multiple domains. So, if your project uses more than one domain name on the same server (perhaps as part of an ecommerce environment), you might need to consider disabling cookies for sessions by setting the

```
session.use_cookies
```

directive to `0` in the `php.ini` file.

Workshop

The Workshop is designed to help you review what you've learned and begin putting your knowledge into practice.

Quiz

1. Which function would you use to start or resume a session within a PHP script?

2. Which PHP function can return the current session's ID?

3. If you want to store user preferences for a long period of time on the client side, would you use local storage or session storage?

Answers

1. You can start a session by using the `session_start()` function within your PHP script.

2. You can access the session's ID by using the `session_id()` function in your PHP script.

3. You would use local storage, but be careful if your use case includes using shared devices.

Exercises

▶ Create a script that uses session functions to track which pages in your environment the user has visited.

▶ Create a new script that lists for the user all the pages she has visited within your environment, and when.

CHAPTER 15

Working with Web-Based Forms

Web forms enable you to receive feedback, orders, or other information from the users who visit your web pages. If you've ever used a search engine such as Google or Bing, you're familiar with HTML forms—those single-field entry forms with one button that, when clicked, gives you all the information you are looking for and then some. Product order forms are also a standard use of forms; if you've ordered anything from Amazon.com or purchased something from an eBay seller, you've used forms.

In this chapter, you'll learn how to create your own forms, including both the front-end display and the back-end processing.

How HTML Forms Work

An HTML form is part of a web page that includes areas where users can enter information to be sent back to you, to another email address that you specify, to a database that you manage, or to another system altogether, such as a third-party management system for your company's lead-generation forms, such as Salesforce.com.

Before you learn the HTML elements that are used to make your own forms, you should at least conceptually understand how the information from those forms makes its way back to you. The actual behind-the-scenes (the *server-side* or *back-end*) process requires knowledge of at least one programming language—or at least the ability to follow specific instructions when using someone else's server-side script to handle the form input.

Forms include a button the user can click to submit the forms; that button can be an image that you create yourself or a standard HTML form button that is created when a form `<input>` element is created and given a `type` value of `submit`. When someone clicks a form-submission button, all the information typed in the form is sent to a URL that you specify in the `action` attribute of the `<form>` element. That URL should point to a specific script that will process your form, sending the form contents via email or performing another step in an interactive process (such as requesting results from a search engine or placing items in an online shopping cart).

When you start thinking about doing more with form content than simply emailing results to yourself, you need additional technical knowledge. For example, if you want to create an online store that accepts credit cards and processes transactions, there are some well-established practices for doing so, all geared toward ensuring the security of your customers' data. That is not an operation you'll want to enter into lightly.

Creating a Form

Every form must begin with an opening `<form>` tag, which can be located anywhere in the body of the HTML document. The `<form>` tag typically has three attributes, `name`, `method`, and `action`, as shown here:

```
<form name="my_form" method="post" action="myprocessingscript.php">
```

The most common `method` is `post`, which sends the form entry results to the back-end script as a document. You could also use `method="get"`, which submits the results as part of the URL query string instead. The `action` attribute specifies the address for sending the form data. You have two options here:

▸ You can type the location of a form-processing program or script on a web server, and the form data will then be sent to that program. This is by far the most common scenario.

▸ You can type `mailto:` followed by your email address, and the form data will be sent directly to you whenever someone fills out the form. However, this approach is completely dependent on the user's computer being properly configured with an email client. People accessing your site from a public computer without an email client will be left out in the cold. Here's an example:

```
<form name="my_form" method="post" action="mailto:me@mysite.com">
```

The form created in Listing 15.1 and shown in Figure 15.1 includes just about every type of user input component you can currently use in HTML forms in modern browsers. Refer to this figure and listing as you read the following explanations of each type of input element.

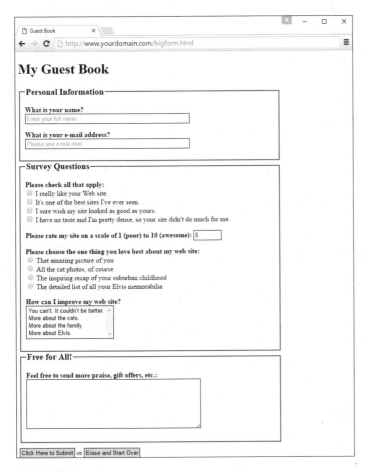

FIGURE 15.1
The code in Listing 15.1 uses many common HTML form elements.

LISTING 15.1   A Form with Various User-Input Components

```
<!DOCTYPE html>

<html lang="en">
  <head>
    <title>Guest Book</title>

    <style type="text/css">
```

```css
      fieldset {
         width: 75%;
         border: 2px solid #ff0000;
      }

      legend {
         font-weight: bold;
         font-size: 125%;
      }

      label.question  {
         width: 225px;
         float: left;
         text-align: left;
         font-weight: bold;
      }

      span.question  {
         font-weight: bold;
      }

      input, textarea, select {
         border: 1px solid #000;
         padding: 3px;
      }

      #buttons {
          margin-top: 12px;
      }

   </style>
 </head>
<body>
   <h1>My Guest Book</h1>
   <form name="gbForm" method="post" action="URL_to_script">

   <fieldset>
      <legend>Personal Information</legend>

      <p><label class="question" for="the_name">
            What is your name?</label>
      <input type="text" id="the_name" name="the_name"
            placeholder="Enter your full name."
            size="50" required autofocus></p>

      <p><label class="question" for="the_email">What is your e-mail
            address?</label>
```

```
    <input type="email" id="the_email" name="the_email"
          placeholder="Please use a real one!"
          size="50" required></p>
</fieldset>

<fieldset>
    <legend>Survey Questions</legend>

    <p><span class="question">Please check all that apply:</span><br>
    <input type="checkbox" id="like_it" name="some_statements[]"
          value="I really like your Web site.">
    <label for="like_it">I really like your Web site.</label><br>
    <input type="checkbox" id="the_best" name="some_statements[]"
          value="It's one of the best sites I've ever seen">
    <label for="the_best">It's one of the  best sites I've ever
          seen.</label><br>
    <input type="checkbox" id="jealous" name="some_statements[]"
          value="I sure wish my site looked as good as yours.">
    <label for="jealous">I sure wish my site looked as good as
          yours.</label><br>
    <input type="checkbox" id="no_taste" name="some_statements[]"
          value="I have no taste and I'm pretty dense, so your site
          didn't do much for me.">
    <label for="no_taste">I have no taste and I'm pretty dense, so
          your site didn't do much for me.</label></p>

    <p><label for="choose_scale"><span class="question">Please rate my
             site on a scale of 1 (poor) to 10 (awesome):</span></label>
    <input type="number" id="choose_scale" name="choose_scale"
           min="0" max="10" step="1" value="5"></p>

    <p><span class="question">Please choose the one thing you love
          Best about my web site:</span><br>
    <input type="radio" id="the_picture" name="best_thing"
          value="me">
    <label for="the_picture">That amazing picture of you</label><br>
    <input type="radio" id="the_cats" name="best_thing"
          value="cats">
    <label for="the_cats">All the cat photos, of course</label><br>
    <input type="radio" id="the_story" name="best_thing"
          value="childhood story">
    <label for="the_story">The inspiring recap of your suburban
          childhood</label><br>
    <input type="radio" id="the_treasures" name="best_thing"
          value="Elvis treasures">
    <label for="the_treasures">The detailed list of all your Elvis
          memorabilia</label></p>
```

```
       <p><label for="how_improve"><span class="question">How can I
           improve my web site?</span></label><br>
       <select id="how_improve" name="how_improve" size="4" multiple>
           <option value="You can't. It couldn't be better.">You
           can't. It couldn't be better.</option>
           <option value="More about the cats.">More about the cats.
           </option>
           <option value="More about the family.">More about the
           family.</option>
           <option value="More about Elvis.">More about Elvis.
           </option>
       </select></p>
   </fieldset>

   <fieldset>
       <legend>Free for All!</legend>
       <p><label for="message"><span class="question">Feel free to send
           more praise, gift offers, etc.:</span></label>
       <textarea id="message" name="message" rows="7" cols="55">
       </textarea></p>
   </fieldset>

   <div id="buttons">
     <input type="submit" value="Click Here to Submit"> or
     <input type="reset" value="Erase and Start Over">
   </div>

   </form>
 </body>
</html>
```

The code in Listing 15.1 uses a `<form>` element that contains quite a few `<input>` tags. Each `<input>` tag corresponds to a specific user input component, such as a check box or radio button. The input, select, and text area elements contain borders in the style sheet, so it is easy to see the outline of the elements in the form. Keep in mind that you can apply all sorts of CSS to those elements.

The next few sections dig into the `<input>` tag and other form-related tags in detail.

Accepting Text Input

To ask the user for a specific piece of information within a form, use the `<input>` tag. Although the tag does not explicitly need to appear between the `<form>` and `</form>` tags, it is good practice and makes your code easier to follow. You can place `<input>` elements anywhere on the page in relation to text, images, and other HTML tags. For example, to ask for someone's name, you could type the following text followed immediately by an `<input>` field:

```
<p><label class="question" for="the_name">What is your name?</label>
<input type="text" id="the_name" name="the_name"
       placeholder="Enter your full name."
       size="50" required autofocus></p>
```

The `type` attribute indicates what type of form element to display—a simple, one-line text entry box, in this case. (Each element type is discussed individually in this chapter.) In this example, note the use of the `placeholder`, `required`, and `autofocus` attributes. You'll learn about the `required` attribute later in this chapter; the `autofocus` attribute automatically focuses the user's cursor in this text field as soon as the browser renders the form. A form can have only one `autofocus` field. The `placeholder` attribute enables you to define some text that appears in the text box but disappears when you begin to type. Using this attribute, you can give the user a bit more guidance in completing your form.

TIP

If you want the user to enter text without the text being displayed on the screen, you can use `<input type="password">` instead of `<input type="text">`. Asterisks (***) are then displayed in place of the text the user types. The `size`, `maxlength`, and `name` attributes work exactly the same for `type="password"` as they do for `type="text"`. Keep in mind that this technique of hiding a password provides only visual protection; no encryption or other protection is associated with the password being transmitted.

The `size` attribute indicates approximately how many characters wide the text input box should be. If you are using a proportionally spaced font, the width of the input will vary depending on what the user enters. If the input is too long to fit in the box, most web browsers automatically scroll the text to the left.

The `maxlength` attribute determines the number of characters the user is allowed to type into the text box. If a user tries to type beyond the specified length, the extra characters won't appear. You can specify a length that is longer, shorter, or the same as the physical size of the text box. The `size` and `maxlength` attributes are used only for those input fields meant for text values, such as `type="text"`, `type="email"`, `type="URL"`, and `type="tel"`, but not check boxes and radio buttons since those have fixed sizes.

Naming Each Piece of Form Data

No matter what type an input element is, you must give a name to the data it gathers. You can use any name you like for each input item, as long as each one on the form is different (except in the case of radio buttons and check boxes, discussed later in this chapter). When the form is processed by a back-end script, each data item is identified by name—you'll see this later in the chapter as you process forms using PHP. This name becomes a variable, which is filled with a value. The value is either what the user typed in the form or the value associated with the element the user selected.

For example, if a user enters `Jane Doe` in the text box defined previously, a variable is sent to the form-processing script; the variable is `user_name`, and the value of the variable is `Jane Doe`. Form-processing scripts work with these types of variable names and values.

NOTE

Form-processing scripts are oversimplified here, for the sake of explanation at this point in the chapter. The exact appearance (or name) of the variables made available to your processing script depends on the programming language of that script. But conceptually, it's valid to say that the name of the input element becomes the name of the variable, and the value of the input element becomes that variable's value on the back end.

To use this text field (or others) in JavaScript, remember that the text object uses the `name` attribute; you refer to the value of the field in the previous snippet like this:

```
document.formname.user_name.value
```

Labeling Each Piece of Form Data

Labeling your form data is not the same as using a `name` or `id` attribute to identify the form element for later use. Instead, the `<label></label>` tag pair surrounds text that acts as a sort of caption for a form element. A form element `<label>` provides additional context for the element, which is especially important for screen reader software.

You can see two different examples in Listing 15.1. First, you can see the `<label>` surrounding the first question a user is asked (`What is your name?`). The use of the `for` attribute ties this label to the `<input>` element with the same id (in this case, `the_name`):

```
<p><label class="question" for="the_name">What is your name?</label>
<input type="text" id="the_name" name="the_name"
       placeholder="Enter your full name."
       size="50" required autofocus></p>
```

A screen reader would read to the user "What is your name?" and then also say "text box" to alert the user to complete the text field with the appropriate information. In another example from Listing 15.1, you see the use of `<label>` to surround different options in a check box list (and also a list of radio buttons, later in the listing):

```
<p><span class="question">Please check all that apply:</span><br>
<input type="checkbox" id="like_it" name="some_statements[]"
       value="I really like your Web site.">
<label for="like_it">I really like your Web site.</label><br>
```

```
<input type="checkbox" id="the_best" name="some_statements[]"
       value="It's one of the best sites I've ever seen">
<label for="the_best">It's one of the  best sites I've ever
       seen.</label><br>
<input type="checkbox" id="jealous" name="some_statements[]"
       value="I sure wish my site looked as good as yours.">
<label for="jealous">I sure wish my site looked as good as
       yours.</label><br>
<input type="checkbox" id="no_taste" name="some_statements[]"
       value="I have no taste and I'm pretty dense, so your site
       didn't do much for me.">
<label for="no_taste">I have no taste and I'm pretty dense, so your
       site didn't do much for me.</label></p>
```

In this situation, the screen reader would read the text surrounded by the `<label>` tag, followed by "check box," to alert the user to choose one of the given options. Labels should be used for all form elements and can be styled using CSS in the same manner as other container elements—the styling does not affect the screen reader, but it does help with layout aesthetics and readability.

Grouping Form Elements

In Listing 15.1, you can see the use of the `<fieldset>` and `<legend>` elements three different times, to create three different groups of form fields. The `<fieldset>` element does just that—it surrounds groups of form elements to provide additional context for the user, whether the user is accessing it directly in a web browser or with the aid of screen-reader software. The `<fieldset>` element just defines the grouping; the `<legend>` element contains the text that will display or be read aloud to describe this grouping, such as the following from Listing 15.1:

```
<fieldset>
    <legend>Personal Information</legend>
    <p><label class="question" for="the_name">What is your name?</label>
    <input type="text" id="the_name" name="the_name"
        placeholder="Enter your full name."
        size="50" required autofocus></p>
...
</fieldset>
```

In this situation, when the screen reader reads the `<label>` associated with a form element, as you learned in the preceding section, it also appends the `<legend>` text. In the preceding example, it would be read as "Personal Information. What is your name? Text box." The `<fieldset>` and `<legend>` elements can be styled using CSS, so the visual cue of the grouped elements can easily be made visible in a web browser (as you saw previously in Figure 15.1).

Including Hidden Data in Forms

Want to send certain data items to the server script that processes a form, but don't want the user to see those data items? Use an `<input>` tag with a `type="hidden"` attribute. This attribute has no effect on the display; it just adds any name and value you specify to the form results when they are submitted.

If you are using a form-processing script provided by your web hosting provider, you might be directed to use this attribute to tell a script where to email the form results. For example, including the following code emails the results to me@mysite.com after the form is submitted:

```
<input type="hidden" name="mailto" value="me@mysite.com">
```

You sometimes see scripts using hidden input elements to carry additional data that might be useful when you receive the results of the form submission; some examples of hidden form fields include an email address and a subject for the email. If you are using a script provided by your web hosting provider, consult the documentation provided with that script for additional details about potential required hidden fields.

Exploring Form Input Controls

Various input controls are available for retrieving information from the user. You've already seen one text-entry option; the next few sections introduce you to most of the remaining form-input options you can use to design forms.

Check Boxes

Besides the text field, one of the simplest input types is a *check box*, which appears as a small square. Users can click check boxes to select or deselect one or more items in a group. For example, the check boxes in Listing 15.1 display after text that reads "Please check all that apply," implying that the user could indeed check all that apply.

The HTML for the check boxes in Listing 15.1 shows that the value of the `name` attribute is the same for all of them:

```
<p><span class="question">Please check all that apply:</span><br>
<input type="checkbox" id="like_it" name="some_statements[]"
       value="I really like your Web site.">
<label for="like_it">I really like your Web site.</label><br>
<input type="checkbox" id="the_best" name="some_statements[]"
       value="It's one of the best sites I've ever seen">
<label for="the_best">It's one of the  best sites I've ever
       seen.</label><br>
<input type="checkbox" id="jealous" name="some_statements[]"
       value="I sure wish my site looked as good as yours.">
```

```
<label for="jealous">I sure wish my site looked as good as
      yours.</label><br>
<input type="checkbox" id="no_taste" name="some_statements[]"
      value="I have no taste and I'm pretty dense, so your site
      didn't do much for me.">
<label for="no_taste">I have no taste and I'm pretty dense, so your
      site didn't do much for me.</label></p>
```

The use of the brackets in the name attribute (`[]`) indicates to the back-end processing script that a series of values will be placed into this one variable instead of just one value (well, it might be just one value if the user selects only one check box). If a user selects the first check box, the text string `I really like your Web site.` is placed in the `website_response[]` bucket. If the user selects the third check box, the text string `I sure wish my site looked as good as yours.` also is put into the `website_response[]` bucket. The processing script then works with that variable as an array of data rather just a single entry.

TIP

If you find that the label for an input element is displayed too close to the element, just add a space between the close of the `<input>` tag and the start of the label text, like this:

```
<input type="checkbox" name="mini">
<label>Mini Piano Stool</label>
```

However, you might see groups of check boxes that do use individual names for the variables in the group. For example, the following is another way of writing the check box group:

```
<p><span class="question">Please check all that apply:</span><br>
<input type="checkbox" id="like_it" name="liked_site" value="yes"
      value="I really like your Web site.">
<label for="like_it">I really like your Web site.</label><br>
<input type="checkbox" id="the_best" name="best_site" value="yes"
      value="It's one of the best sites I've ever seen">
<label for="the_best">It's one of the  best sites I've ever
      seen.</label><br>
<input type="checkbox" id="jealous" name="my_site_sucks" value="yes"
      value="I sure wish my site looked as good as yours.">
<label for="jealous">I sure wish my site looked as good as
      yours.</label><br>
<input type="checkbox" id="no_taste" name="am_dense" value="yes"
      value="I have no taste and I'm pretty dense, so your site
      didn't do much for me.">
<label for="no_taste">I have no taste and I'm pretty dense, so your
      site didn't do much for me.</label></p>
```

In this second list of check boxes, the variable name of the first check box is `"liked_site"` and the value (if checked) is `"yes"` when handled by a back-end processing script.

If you want a check box to be checked by default when the web browser renders the form, include the `checked` attribute. For example, the following code creates two check boxes, and the first is checked by default:

```
<input type="checkbox" id="like_it" name="liked_site" value="yes"
       value="I really like your Web site." checked>
<label for="like_it">I really like your Web site.</label><br>
<input type="checkbox" id="the_best" name="best_site" value="yes"
       value="It's one of the best sites I've ever seen">
<label for="the_best">It's one of the  best sites I've ever
       seen.</label><br>
```

The check box labeled `I really like your Web site.` is checked by default in this example. The user must click the check box to uncheck it and thus indicate that he has another opinion of your site. The check box marked `It's one of the best sites I've ever seen.` is unchecked to begin with, so the user must click it to turn it on. Check boxes that are not selected do not appear in the form output.

If you want to handle values from the `checkbox` object in JavaScript, the object has the following four properties:

▶ `name` is the name of the check box as well as the object name.

▶ `value` is the "true" value for the check box—usually on. This value is used by server-side programs to indicate whether the check box was checked. In JavaScript, you should use the `checked` property instead.

▶ `defaultChecked` is the default status of the check box, assigned by the `checked` attribute in HTML.

▶ `checked` is the current value. This is a Boolean value: `true` for checked and `false` for unchecked.

To manipulate the check box or use its value, you use the `checked` property. For example, this statement turns on a check box called `same_address` in a form named `order`:

```
document.order.same.checked = true;
```

The check box has a single method: `click()`. This method simulates a click on the box. It also has a single event, `onClick`, that occurs whenever the check box is clicked. This happens whether the box was turned on or off, so you'll need to examine the `checked` property via JavaScript to see what action really happened.

Radio Buttons

Radio buttons, for which only one choice can be selected at a time, are almost as simple to implement as check boxes. The simplest use of a radio button is for yes/no questions or for voting when only one candidate can be selected.

To create a radio button, use `type="radio"` and give each option its own `<input>` tag. Use the same `name` for all the radio buttons in a group, but don't use the brackets (`[]`) you used with the check box, because you don't have to accommodate multiple answers:

```
<input type="radio" id="vote_yes" name="vote" value="yes" checked>
<label for="vote_yes">Yes</label> <br>
<input type="radio" id="vote_no" name="vote" value="no">
<label for="vote_no">No</label>
```

The `value` can be any name or code you choose. If you include the `checked` attribute, that button is selected by default. No more than one radio button with the same `name` can be checked.

When designing your form and choosing between check boxes and radio buttons, ask yourself whether the question being asked or implied could be answered in only one way. If so, use a radio button.

NOTE

Radio buttons are named for their similarity to the buttons on old push-button radios. Those buttons used a mechanical arrangement so that when you pushed one button in, any other pressed button popped out.

As for scripting, radio buttons are similar to check boxes, except that an entire group of them shares a single name and a single object. You can refer to the following properties of the `radio` object:

- ► `name` is the name common to the radio buttons.
- ► `length` is the number of radio buttons in the group.

To access the individual buttons in JavaScript, you treat the `radio` object as an array. The buttons are indexed, starting with 0. Each individual button has the following properties:

- ► `value` is the value assigned to the button.
- ► `defaultChecked` indicates the value of the `checked` attribute and the default state of the button.
- ► `checked` is the current state.

For example, you can check the first radio button in the `radio1` group on the `form1` form with this statement:

```
document.form1.radio1[0].checked = true;
```

However, if you do this, be sure you set the other values to `false` as needed. This is not done automatically. You can use the `click()` method to do both of these actions in one step.

Like check boxes, radio buttons have a `click()` method and an `onClick` event handler. Each radio button can have a separate statement for this event.

Selection Lists

Both *scrolling lists* and *pull-down pick lists* are created with the `<select>` tag. You use this tag together with the `<option>` tag, as the following example shows (taken from Listing 15.1):

```
<p><label for="how_improve"><span class="question">How can I
    improve my web site?</span></label><br>
<select id="how_improve" name="how_improve" size="4" multiple>
    <option value="You can't. It couldn't be better.">You can't.
        It couldn't be better.</option>
    <option value="More about the cats.">More about the cats.</option>
    <option value="More about the family.">More about the
        family.</option>
    <option value="More about Elvis.">More about Elvis.</option>
</select></p>
```

Unlike the `text` input type that you learned about briefly in a previous section, the `size` attribute here determines how many items show at once on the selection list. If `size="2"` were used in the preceding code, only the first two options would be visible and a scrollbar would appear next to the list so the user could scroll down to see the third and fourth options.

Including the `multiple` attribute enables users to select more than one option at a time; the `selected` attribute makes an option initially selected by default. When the form is submitted, the text specified in the `value` attribute for each option accompanies the selected option.

TIP

If you leave out the `size` attribute or specify `size="1"`, the list creates a simple drop-down pick list. Pick lists don't allow for multiple choices; they are logically equivalent to a group of radio buttons. The following example shows another way to choose `yes` or `no` for a question:

```
<select name="vote">
  <option value="yes">Yes</option>
  <option value="no">No</option>
</select>
```

The object for selection lists is the `select` object. The object itself has the following properties:

▶ `name` is the name of the selection list.

▶ `length` is the number of options in the list.

▶ `options` is the array of options. Each selectable option has an entry in this array.

▶ `selectedIndex` returns the index value of the currently selected item. You can use this to check the value easily. In a multiple-selection list, this indicates the first selected item.

The `options` array has a single property of its own, `length`, which indicates the number of selections. In addition, each item in the `options` array has the following properties:

▶ `index` is the index into the array.

▶ `defaultSelected` indicates the state of the `selected` attribute.

▶ `selected` is the current state of the option. Setting this property to `true` selects the option. The user can select multiple options if the `multiple` attribute is included in the `<select>` tag.

▶ `name` is the value of the `name` attribute. This is used by the server.

▶ `text` is the text that is displayed in the option.

The `select` object has two methods—`blur()` and `focus()`—that perform the same purposes as the corresponding methods for `text` objects. The event handlers are `onBlur`, `onFocus`, and `onChange`, also similar to other objects.

NOTE

You can change selection lists dynamically—for example, choosing a product in one list could control which options are available in another list. You can also add and delete options from the list.

Reading the value of a selected item is a two-step process. You first use the `selectedIndex` property and then use the `value` property to find the value of the selected choice. Here's an example:

```
ind = document.mvform.choice.selectedIndex;
val = document.mvform.choice.options[ind].value;
```

This uses the `ind` variable to store the selected index and then assigns the `val` variable to the value of the selected choice. Things are a bit more complicated with a multiple selection: You have to test each option's `selected` attribute separately.

No HTML tags other than `<option>` and `</option>` should appear between the `<select>` and `</select>` tags, with the exception of the `<optgroup>` tag (not shown in Listing 15.1). The use of `<optgroup>`, as in the following snippet, enables you to create groups of options (that's where the name `optgroup` comes from) with a label that shows up in the list but can't be selected as an "answer" to the form field. For example, the snippet

```
<select name="grades">
    <optgroup label="Good Grades">
        <option value="A">A</option>
        <option value="B">B</option>
    </optgroup>
    <optgroup label="Average Grades">
        <option value="C">C</option>
    </optgroup>
    <optgroup label="Bad Grades">
        <option value="D">D</option>
        <option value="F">F</option>
    </optgroup>
</select>
```

produces a drop-down list that looks like this:

```
Good Grades
    A
    B
Average Grades
    C
Bad Grades
    D
    F
```

In this situation, only A, B, C, D, and F are selectable, but the `<optgroup>` labels are visible.

Text Fields, Text Areas, and Other Input Types

The `<input type="text">` attribute mentioned earlier this chapter allows the user to enter only a single line of text. When you want to allow multiple lines of text in a single input item, use the `<textarea>` and `</textarea>` tags to create a text area instead of just a text field. Any text you include between these two tags is displayed as the default entry in that box. Here's the example from Listing 15.1:

```
<textarea id="message"  name="message" rows="7" cols="55">Your
    message here.</textarea>
```

As you probably guessed, the `rows` and `cols` attributes control the number of rows and columns of text that fit in the input box. The `cols` attribute is a little less exact than `rows` and approximates the number of characters that fit in a row of text. Text area boxes do have a scrollbar, however, so the user can enter more text than what fits in the display area.

The `text` and `textarea` objects also have a few JavaScript methods you can use:

▶ `focus()` sets the focus to the field. This positions the cursor in the field and makes it the current field.

▶ `blur()` is the opposite; it removes the focus from the field.

▶ `select()` selects the text in the field, just as a user can do with the mouse. All the text is selected; there is no way to select part of the text.

You can also use event handlers to detect when the value of a text field changes. The `text` and `textarea` objects support the following event handlers:

▶ The `onFocus` event happens when the text field gains focus.

▶ The `onBlur` event happens when the text field loses focus.

▶ The `onChange` event happens when the user changes the text in the field and then moves out of it.

▶ The `onSelect` event happens when the user selects some or all of the text in the field. Unfortunately, there's no way to tell exactly which part of the text was selected. (If the text is selected with the `select()` method described previously, this event is not triggered.)

If used, these event handlers should be included in the `<input>` tag declaration. For example, the following text field includes an `onChange` event that displays an alert:

```
<input type="text" name="text1" onChange="window.alert('Changed.');">
```

Let's turn back to the basic `<input>` element for a minute, however, because HTML5 provides many more `type` options for input than simply "text," such as built-in date pickers. The downside is that not all browsers fully support many of those options (such as the built-in date picker). Here are a few of the different input types that *are* fully supported but that we haven't discussed in any detail in this lesson:

▶ `type="email"`—This appears as a regular text field, but when form validation is used, the built-in validator checks that it is a well-formed email address. Some mobile devices display relevant keys (the @ sign, for example) by default instead of requiring additional user interactions.

▶ `type="file"`—This input type opens a dialog box to enable you to search for a file on your computer to upload.

▶ `type="number"`—Instead of creating a `<select>` list with `<option>` tags for each number, this type enables you to specify `min` and `max` values, and the step-between numbers, to automatically generate a list on the browser side. You can see this in use in Listing 15.1.

▶ **type="range"**—Much like the number type just covered, this type enables you to specify min and max values and the step-between numbers, but in this case, it appears as a horizontal slider.

▶ **type="search"**—This appears as a regular text field, but with additional controls sometimes used to allow the user to clear the search box using an x or a similar character.

▶ **type="url"**—This input type appears as a regular text field, but when form validation is used, the built-in validator checks that it is a well-formed URL. Some mobile devices display relevant keys (the .com virtual key, for instance) by default instead of requiring additional user interactions.

You can stay up to date with the status of these and other <input> types using the chart at https://developer.mozilla.org/en-US/docs/Web/HTML/Element/input.

Using HTML5 Form Validation

Many features in HTML5 have made web developers very happy people. One of the simplest yet most life-changing feature might be the inclusion of form validation. Before HTML5 form validation existed, we had to create convoluted JavaScript-based form validation, which caused headaches for everyone involved.

But no more! HTML5 validates forms by default, unless you use the novalidate attribute in the <form> element. Of course, if you do not use the required attribute in any form fields themselves, there's nothing to validate. As you learned in a previous section, not only are fields validated for content (any content at all) but they are validated according to the type they are. For example, in Listing 15.1, we have a required field for an email address:

```
<p><label class="question" for="the_email">What is your e-mail
     address?</label>
<input type="email" id="the_email" name="the_email"
     placeholder="Please use a real one!"
     size="50" required></p>
```

In Figures 15.2 and 15.3, you can see that the form automatically validates for the presence of content, but then also slaps you on the wrists when you try to enter a junk string in the field instead of an email address.

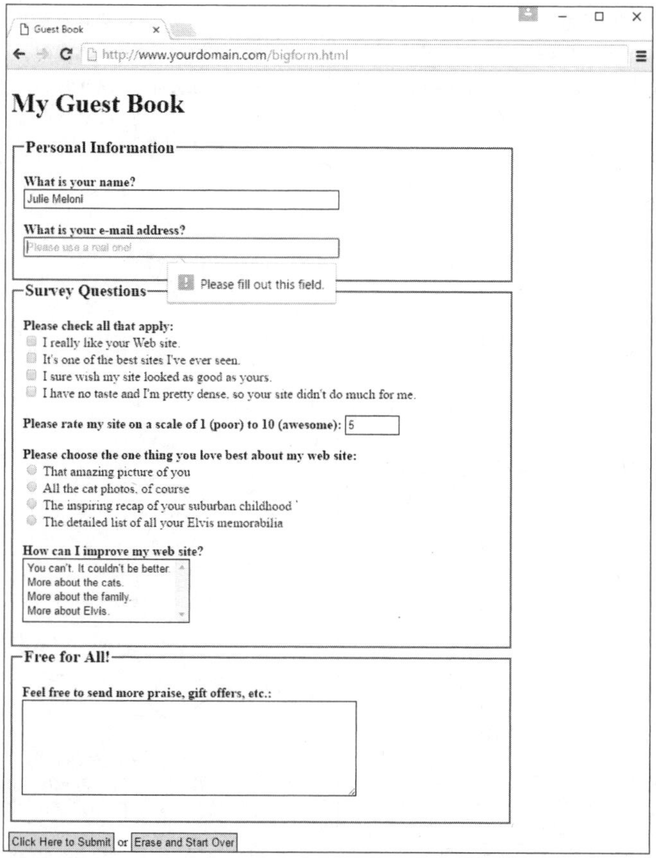

FIGURE 15.2
Attempting to submit a form with no content in a required field causes a validation error.

NOTE

Validation of email addresses begins and ends with the entry simply looking like an email address. This sort of pattern matching is really the only type of "validation" that you can do with email addresses, short of a time-consuming back-end processing script.

You can use the `pattern` attribute of the `<input>` field to specify your own pattern-matching requirements. The `pattern` attribute uses regular expressions, which is a large enough topic to warrant its own book. But consider a little example. If you want to ensure that your `<input>` element contains only numbers and letters (no special characters), you could use the following:

```
<input type="text" id="the_text" name="the_text"
    placeholder="Please enter only letters and numbers!"
    size="50" pattern="[a-z,A-Z,0-9]" required >
```

The pattern here says that if the field contains any letter between a and z, any letter between A and Z (case matters), and any number between 0 and 9, it's valid. To learn more about regular expressions without buying an entire book, take a look at the online tutorial at http://regexone.com/.

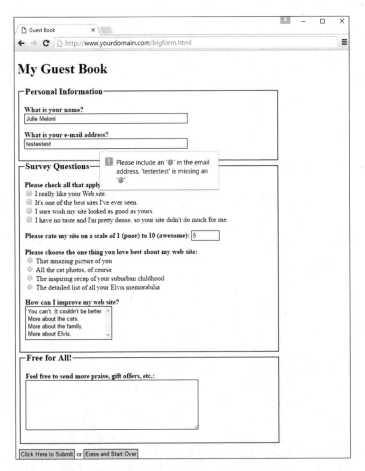

FIGURE 15.3
Attempting to submit a form with badly formed content in a field expecting an email address causes a validation error.

Submitting Form Data

Forms typically include a button that submits the form data to a script on the server or invokes a JavaScript action. For the rest of this chapter, we'll go through some JavaScript actions first and then move into back-end processing using PHP.

So about that button—you can put any label you like on the Submit button with the `value` attribute:

```
<input type="submit" value="Place My Order Now!">
```

Unless you change the style using CSS, a gray button is sized to fit the label you put in the `value` attribute. When the user clicks it, all data items on the form are sent to the email address or script specified in the form's `action` attribute.

You can also include a Reset button that clears all entries on the form so that users can start over if they change their minds or make mistakes. Use the following:

```
<input type="reset" value="Clear This Form and Start Over">
```

If the standard Submit and Reset buttons look a little bland to you, remember that you can style them using CSS. If that's not good enough, you'll be glad to know that there's an easy way to substitute your own graphics for these buttons. To use an image of your choice for a Submit button, use the following:

```
<input type="image" src="button.gif" alt="Order Now!">
```

The `button.gif` image displays on the page, and the form also is submitted when a user clicks the `button.gif` image. You can include any attributes normally used with the `<img>` tag, such as `alt` and `style`.

The form element also includes a generic button type. When using `type="button"` in the `<input>` tag, you get a button that performs no action on its own but can have an action assigned to it using a JavaScript event handler (such as `onclick`).

Using JavaScript for Form Events

The `form` object has two methods: `submit()` and `reset()`. You can use these methods to submit the data or reset the form yourself, without requiring the user to click a button. One reason for this is to submit the form when the user clicks an image or performs another action that would not usually submit the form.

CAUTION

If you use the `submit()` method to send data to a server or via email, most browsers will prompt the user to verify that he or she wants to submit the information. There's no way to do this behind the user's back (nor should you ever do anything with data without the user knowing it).

The `form` object has two events, `Submit` and `Reset`. You can specify a group of JavaScript statements or a function call for these events within the `<form>` tag that defines the form.

If you specify a statement or a function for the `Submit` event, the statement is called before the data is submitted to the server-side script. You can prevent the submission from happening by returning a value of `false` from the `Submit` event handler. If the statement returns `true`, the data will be submitted. In the same fashion, you can prevent a Reset button from working with an `Reset` event handler.

Accessing Form Elements with JavaScript

The most important property of the `form` object is the `elements` array, which contains an object for each of the form elements. You can refer to an element by its own name or by its index in the array. For example, the following two expressions both refer to the first element in the form shown in Listing 15.1:

```
document.gbForm.elements[0]
document.gbForm.name
```

NOTE

Both forms and elements can be referred to by their own names or as indexes in the `forms` and `elements` arrays. For clarity, the examples in this chapter use individual form and element names rather than array references. You'll also find it easier to use names in your own scripts.

If you do refer to forms and elements as arrays, you can use the `length` property to determine the number of objects in the array: `document.forms.length` is the number of forms in a document, and `document.gbForm.elements.length` is the number of elements in the `gbForm` form.

You can also access form elements using the W3C DOM. In this case, you use an `id` attribute on the form element in the HTML document, and use the `document.getElementById()` method to find the object for the form. For example, this statement finds the object for the text field called `name` and stores it in the `name` variable:

```
name = document.getElementById("name");
```

This enables you to quickly access a form element without first finding the `form` object. You can assign an `id` to the `<form>` tag and find the corresponding object if you need to work with the form's properties and methods.

Displaying Data from a Form

As a simple example of interacting with forms purely on the client side, Listing 15.2 shows a form with name, address, and phone number fields, as well as a JavaScript function that displays the data from the form in a pop-up window.

LISTING 15.2 A Form That Displays Data in a Pop-up Window

```
<!DOCTYPE html>

<html lang="en">
  <head>
    <title>Form Display Example</title>
    <script type="text/javascript">
    function display() {
      dispWin = window.open('','NewWin',
      'toolbar=no,status=no,width=300,height=200')

      message = "<ul><li>NAME:" +
      document.form1.name.value;
      message += "<li>ADDRESS:" +
      document.form1.address.value;
      message += "<li>PHONE:" +
      document.form1.phone.value;
      message += "</ul>";
      dispWin.document.write(message);
    }
    </script>
  </head>
  <body>
    <h1>Form Display Example</h1>
      <p>Enter the following information. When you press the Display
      button, the data you entered will be displayed in a pop-up.</p>
      <form name="form1" method="get" action="">
      <p>NAME: <input type="text" name="name" size="50"></p>
      <p>ADDRESS: <input type="text" name="address" size="50"></p>
      <p>PHONE: <input type="text" name="phone" size="50"></p>
      <p><input type="button" value="Display"
                onclick="display();"></p>
      </form>
  </body>
</html>
```

Here is a breakdown of how this simple HTML document and script work:

▶ The <script> section in the document's header defines a function called display() that opens a new window and displays the information from the form.

▶ The <form> tag begins the form. Because this form is handled entirely by JavaScript, the form action and method have no value.

▶ The <input> tags define the form's three fields: yourname, address, and phone. The last <input> tag defines the Display button, which is set to run the display() function.

Figure 15.4 shows this form in action. The Display button has been clicked, and the pop-up window shows the results. Although this is not the most exciting example of client-side form interaction, it clearly shows the basics that form a foundation for later work.

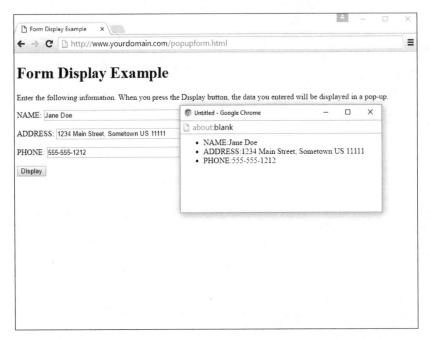

FIGURE 15.4
Displaying data from a form in a pop-up window.

Accessing Form Elements with PHP

To emphasize the process of communicating between a static HTML form and a back-end processing script, let's keep the HTML separate from the PHP code. Listing 15.3 builds a simple HTML form.

LISTING 15.3   A Simple HTML Form

```
1:  <!DOCTYPE html>
2:  <html>
3:    <head>
4:      <title>A simple HTML form</title>
5:    </head>
6:    <body>
7:      <form method="post" action="send_simpleform.php">
8:        <p><label for="user">Name:</label><br>
```

```
 9:        <input type="text" id="user" name="user"></p>
10:        <p><label for="message">Message:</label><br>
11:        <textarea id="message" name="message" rows="5" cols="40"></textarea></p>
12:        <button type="submit" name="submit" value="send">Send Message</button>
13:     </form>
14:   </body>
15: </html>
```

Put these lines into a text file called `simpleform.html` and place that file in your web server document root. This listing defines a form that contains a text field with the name `"user"` on line 9, a text area with the name `"message"` on line 11, and a submit button on line 12. The form element's `action` argument points to a file called `send_simpleform.php` that processes the form information. The method of this form is `post`, so the variables are stored in the `$_POST` superglobal.

Listing 15.4 creates the code that receives user input and displays it within the context of an HTML page.

LISTING 15.4   Reading Input from a Form

```
 1:  <!DOCTYPE html>
 2:  <html>
 3:    <head>
 4:      <title>A simple response</title>
 5:    </head>
 6:    <body>
 7:      <p>Welcome, <strong><?php echo $_POST['user']; ?></strong>!</p>
 8:      <p>Your message is:
 9:      <strong><?php echo $_POST['message']; ?></strong></p>
10:    </body>
11:  </html>
```

Put these lines into a text file called `send_simpleform.php` and place that file in your web server document root.

The script in Listing 15.4 is called when the user submits the form created in Listing 15.3. The code in Listing 15.4 accesses two variables: `$_POST['user']` and `$_POST['message']`. These are references to the variables in the `$_POST` superglobal, which contain the values that the user entered in the `user` text field and the `message` text area. Form processing in PHP really *is* as simple as that.

Enter some information in the form fields and click the Send Message button. You should see your input echoed to the screen. An example is shown in Figure 15.5.

FIGURE 15.5
Form submission complete.

Accessing Form Input with User-Defined Arrays

The previous example showed how to gather information from HTML elements that submit a single value per element name, such as text fields, text areas, and radio buttons. This leaves you with a problem when working with elements such as check boxes because it is possible for the user to choose one or more items. Suppose you name the element with a plain name, like so:

```
<input type="checkbox" id="products" name="products">
```

In this case, the script that receives this data has access to only a single value corresponding to this name ($_POST['products']) and thus only the first check box in the list that the user selected. You can change this behavior by renaming an element of this kind so that its name ends with an empty set of square brackets. You've seen this already in Listing 15.1, as one of the survey questions asked the user to "check all that apply." You could then put the responses in an array called some_statements.

```
<p><span class="question">Please check all that apply:</span><br>
    <input type="checkbox" id="like_it" name="some_statements[]"
    value="I really like your Web site.">
    <label for="like_it">I really like your Web site.</label><br>
    <input type="checkbox" id="the_best" name="some_statements[]"
    value="It's one of the best sites I've ever seen">
    <label for="the_best">It's one of the  best sites I've ever
    seen.</label><br>
    <input type="checkbox" id="jealous" name="some_statements[]"
    value="I sure wish my site looked as good as yours.">
    <label for="jealous">I sure wish my site looked as good as
    yours.</label><br>
    <input type="checkbox" id="no_taste" name="some_statements[]"
    value="I have no taste and I'm pretty dense, so your site
    didn't do much for me.">
    <label for="no_taste">I have no taste and I'm pretty dense, so
    your site didn't do much for me.</label>
</p>
```

In the script that processes the form input, the values of all selected check boxes with the name "`some_statements[]`" are available in an array called `$_POST['some_statements']`. You can cycle through the array, as in the following snippet, which builds a bulleted list of selected items:

```php
<?php
if (!empty($_POST['products'])) {
  echo "<ul>";
  foreach ($_POST['products'] as $value) {
      echo "<li>$value</li>";
  }
  echo "</ul>";
} else {
  echo "None";
}
?>
```

Although the looping technique is particularly useful with check boxes, it can also work with other types of form elements. For example, if you use a SELECT element that allows for multiple selections, you are also enabling a user to choose many values within a single field name.

As long as the name you choose ends with empty square brackets, PHP compiles the user input for this field into an array.

Combining HTML and PHP Code on a Single Page

In some circumstances, you might want to include the form-parsing PHP code on the same page as a hard-coded HTML form. Such a combination can prove useful if you need to present the same form to the user more than once. You would have more flexibility if you were to write the entire page dynamically, of course, but you would miss out on one of the great strengths of PHP, which is that it mingles well with standard HTML. The more standard HTML you can include in your pages, the easier they are for designers and page builders to amend without asking you, the programmer, for help.

For the following examples, imagine that you're creating a site that teaches basic math to preschool children and have been asked to create a script that takes a number from form input and tells the user whether it's larger or smaller than a predefined integer.

Listing 15.5 creates the HTML. For this example, you need only a single text field, but even so, the code listing includes a little PHP.

LISTING 15.5 An HTML Form That Calls Itself

```
1: <!DOCTYPE html>
2: <html>
3:   <head>
4:     <title>An HTML form that calls itself</title>
5:   </head>
```

```
 6:   <body>
 7:     <form action="<?php echo $_SERVER['PHP_SELF']; ?>" method="post">
 8:     <p><label for="guess">Type your guess here:</label><br>
 9:     <input type="text" id="guess" name="guess" ></p>
10:     <button type="submit" name="submit" value="submit">Submit</button>
11:     </form>
12:   </body>
13: </html>
```

The action of this script is $_SERVER['PHP_SELF'], as shown in line 7. This global variable represents the name of the current script. In other words, the action tells the script to reload itself. The script in Listing 15.5 does not produce any output yet, but if you upload the script to your web server, access the page, and view the source of the page, you will notice that the form action now contains the name of the script itself.

In Listing 15.6, you begin to build up the dynamic elements of the script.

LISTING 15.6 A PHP Number-Guessing Script

```
 1:   <?php
 2:   $num_to_guess = 42;
 3:   if (!isset($_POST['guess'])) {
 4:     $message = "Welcome to the guessing machine!";
 5:   } elseif (!is_numeric($_POST['guess'])) { // is not numeric
 6:     $message = "I don't understand that response.";
 7:   } elseif ($_POST['guess'] == $num_to_guess) { // matches!
 8:     $message = "Well done!";
 9:   } elseif ($_POST['guess'] > $num_to_guess) {
10:     $message = $_POST['guess']." is too big! Try a smaller number.";
11:   } elseif ($_POST['guess'] < $num_to_guess) {
12:     $message = $_POST['guess']." is too small! Try a larger number.";
13:   } else  { // some other condition
14:     $message = "I am terribly confused.";
15:   }
16: ?>
```

First, you must define the number that the user guesses, and this is done in line 2 when 42 is assigned to the $num_to_guess variable. Next, you must determine whether the form has been submitted. You can test for submission by looking for the existence of the variable $_POST['guess'], which is available only if the form script has been submitted (with or without a value in the field). If a value for $_POST['guess'] isn't present, you can safely assume that the user arrived at the page without submitting a form. If the value *is* present, you can test the value it contains. The test for the presence of the $_POST['guess'] variable takes place on line 3.

Lines 3 through 15 represent an if...elseif...else control structure. Only one of these conditions will be true at any given time, depending on what (if anything) was submitted from the form. Depending on the condition, a different value is assigned to the $message variable. That variable is then printed to the screen in line 23 in Listing 15.7, which is part of the HTML portion of the script.

LISTING 15.7   A PHP Number-Guessing Script (Continued)

```
17: <!DOCTYPE html>
18: <html lang="en">
19:   <head>
20:     <title>A PHP number guessing script</title>
21:   </head>
22:   <body>
23:     <h1><?php echo $message; ?></h1>
24:     <form action="<?php echo $_SERVER['PHP_SELF']; ?>" method="post">
25:     <p><label for="guess">Type your guess here:</label><br>
26:     <input type="text" is="guess" name="guess"></p>
27:     <button type="submit" name="submit" value="submit">Submit</button>
28:     </form>
29:   </body>
30: </html>
```

Place the PHP and HTML code (all the lines in Listings 15.6 and 15.7) into a text file called numguess.php and put this file in your web server document root. Now access the script with your web browser, and you should see something like Figure 15.6.

FIGURE 15.6
The form created by Listings 15.6 and 15.7.

Make a guess and click the submit button, and you should be directed appropriately to guess again as in Figure 15.7.

You could still make a few more additions, but you can probably see how simple it would be to hand the code to a designer for aesthetic treatment. The designer can do her part without having to disturb the programming in any way—the PHP code is at the top, and the rest is almost entirely HTML.

FIGURE 15.7
Results of guessing incorrectly.

Using Hidden Fields to Save State in Dynamic Forms

The script in Listing 15.6 has no way of knowing how many guesses a user has made, but you can use a hidden field to keep track of this value. A hidden field behaves the same as a text field, except that the user cannot see it unless he views the HTML source of the document that contains it.

Take the original numguess.php script and save a copy as numguess2.php. In the new version, add a line after the initial assignment of the $num_to_guess variable:

```
$num_tries = (isset($_POST['num_tries'])) ? $num_tries + 1 : 1;
```

This line initializes a variable called $num_tries and assigns a value to it. If the form has not yet been submitted (if $_POST['num_tries'] is empty), the value of the $num_tries variable is 1 because you are on your first attempt at guessing the number. If the form has already been sent, the new value is the value of $_POST['num_tries'] plus 1.

The next change comes after the HTML level H1 heading:

```
<p><strong>Guess number:</strong> <?php echo $num_tries; ?></p>
```

This new line simply prints the current value of $num_tries to the screen.

Finally, before the HTML code for the form submission button, add the hidden field. This field saves the incremented value of $num_tries:

```
<input type="hidden" name="num_tries" value="<?php echo $num_tries; ?>">
```

Listing 15.8 shows the new script in its entirety.

LISTING 15.8   Saving State with a Hidden Field

```php
1:  <?php
2:  $num_to_guess = 42;
3:  $num_tries = (isset($_POST['num_tries'])) ? $num_tries + 1 : 1;
4:  if (!isset($_POST['guess'])) {
5:     $message = "Welcome to the guessing machine!";
6:  } elseif (!is_numeric($_POST['guess'])) { // is not numeric
7:     $message = "I don't understand that response.";
8:  } elseif ($_POST['guess'] == $num_to_guess) { // matches!
9:     $message = "Well done!";
10: } elseif ($_POST['guess'] > $num_to_guess) {
11:    $message = $_POST['guess']." is too big! Try a smaller number.";
12: } elseif ($_POST['guess'] < $num_to_guess) {
13:    $message = $_POST['guess']." is too small! Try a larger number.";
14: } else  { // some other condition
15:    $message = "I am terribly confused.";
16: }
17: ?>
18: <!DOCTYPE html>
19: <html lang="en">
20:    <head>
21:       <title>A PHP number guessing script</title>
22:    </head>
23:    <body>
24:       <h1><?php echo $message; ?></h1>
25:       <p><strong>Guess number:</strong> <?php echo $num_tries; ?></p>
26:       <form action="<?php echo $_SERVER['PHP_SELF']; ?>" method="post">
27:          <p><label for="guess">Type your guess here:</label><br>
28:          <input type="text" id="guess" name="guess"></p>
29:          <input type="hidden" name="num_tries" value="<?php echo $num_tries; ?>">
30:          <button type="submit" name="submit" value="submit">Submit</button>
31:       </form>
32:    </body>
33: </html>
```

Save the numguess2.php file and place it in your web server document root. Access the form a few times with your web browser and try to guess the number (pretending you don't already know it). The counter should increment by 1 each time you access the form.

Sending Mail on Form Submission

You've already seen how to take form responses and print the results to the screen, so you're only one step away from sending those responses in an email message. Before learning about sending mail, however, read through the next section to make sure that your system is properly configured.

System Configuration for the `mail()` Function

Before you can use the `mail()` function to send mail, you need to set up a few directives in the `php.ini` file so that the function works properly. Open `php.ini` with a text editor and look for these lines:

```
[mail function]
; For Win32 only.
; http://php.net/smtp
SMTP = localhost
; http://php.net/smtp-port
smtp_port = 25

; For Win32 only.
; http://php.net/sendmail-from
;sendmail_from = me@example.com

; For Unix only.  You may supply arguments as well (default: "sendmail -t -i").
; http://php.net/sendmail-path
;sendmail_path =
```

If you're using Windows as your web server platform, the first two directives apply to you. For the `mail()` function to send mail, it must be able to access a valid outgoing mail server. If you plan to use the outgoing mail server on your machine, the entry in `php.ini` could look like this:

```
SMTP = smtp.yourisp.net
```

The second configuration directive is `sendmail_from`, which is the email address used in the From header of the outgoing email. It can be overwritten in the mail script itself but normally operates as the default value, as in this example:

```
sendmail_from = youraddress@yourdomain.com
```

A good rule of thumb for Windows users is that whatever outgoing mail server you've set up in your email client on that machine, you should also use as the value of SMTP in `php.ini`.

If your web server is running on a Linux/UNIX platform, you use the `sendmail` functionality of that particular machine. In this case, only the last directive applies to you: `sendmail_path`.

The default is sendmail -t -i, but if sendmail is in an odd place or if you need to specify different arguments, feel free to do so, as in the following example, which does not use real values:

```
sendmail_path = /opt/sendmail -odd -arguments
```

After making any changes to php.ini on any platform, you must restart the web server process for the changes to take effect.

Creating the Form

In Listing 15.9, you see the basic HTML for creating a simple feedback form named feedback. html. This form has an action of sendmail.php, which you create in the next section. The fields in feedback.html are simple: Lines 8 and 9 create a name field and label, lines 10 and 11 create the return email address field and label, and lines 12 and 13 contain the text area and label for the user's message.

LISTING 15.9 Creating a Simple Feedback Form

```
1:  <!DOCTYPE html>
2:  <html lang="en">
3:    <head>
4:      <title>E-Mail Form</title>
5:    </head>
6:    <body>
7:      <form action="sendmail.php" method="post">
8:        <p><label for="name">Name:</label><br>
9:        <input type="text" size="25" id="name" name="name"></p>
10:       <p><label for="email">E-Mail Address:</label><br>
11:       <input type="text" size="25" id="email" name="email"></p>
12:       <p><label for="msg">Message:</label><br>
13:       <textarea id="msg" name="msg" cols="30" rows="5"></textarea></p>
14:       <button type="submit" name="submit" value="send">Send Message</button>
15:     </form>
16:   </body>
17: </html>
```

Put all the lines shown in Listing 15.9 into a text file called feedback.html and place this file in your web server document root. Now access the script with your web browser, and you should see something like Figure 15.8.

FIGURE 15.8
The form created in Listing 15.9.

In the next section, you create the script that sends this form to a recipient.

Creating the Script to Send the Mail

This script differs only slightly in concept from the script in Listing 15.4, which simply printed form responses to the screen. In the script shown in Listing 15.10, in addition to printing the responses to the screen, you send them to an email address.

LISTING 15.10   Sending the Simple Feedback Form

```
1:  <?php
2:  //start building the mail string
3:  $msg  = "Name:    ".$_POST['name']."\n";
4:  $msg .= "E-Mail:  ".$_POST['email']."\n";
5:  $msg .= "Message: ".$_POST['message']."\n";
6:
7:  //set up the mail
8:  $recipient = "you@yourdomain.com";
9:  $subject = "Form Submission Results";
10: $mailheaders  = "From: My Web Site <defaultaddress@yourdomain.com> \n";
11: $mailheaders .= "Reply-To: ".$_POST['email'];
12:
13: //send the mail
14: mail($recipient, $subject, $msg, $mailheaders);
15: ?>
16: <!DOCTYPE html>
17: <html>
18:   <head>
19:     <title>Sending mail from the form in Listing 15.9</title>
```

```
20:    </head>
21:    <body>
22:      <p>Thanks, <strong><?php echo $_POST['name']; ?></strong>,
23:      for your message.</p>
24:      <p>Your e-mail address:
25:      <strong><?php echo $_POST['email']; ?></strong></p>
26:      <p>Your message: <br/> <?php echo $_POST['message']; ?> </p>
27:    </body>
28:  </html>
```

The variables printed to the screen in lines 22–26 are $_POST['name'], $_POST['email'], and $_POST['message']—the names of the fields in the form. Their values are saved as part of the $_POST superglobal. That's all well and good for printing the information to the screen, but in this script, you also want to create a string that's sent in email. For this task, you essentially build the email by concatenating strings to form one long message string, using the newline (\n) character to add line breaks where appropriate.

Lines 3 through 5 create the $msg variable, a string containing the values typed by the user in the form fields (and some label text for good measure). This string forms the body of the email. Note the use of the concatenation operator (.=) when adding to the $msg variable in lines 4 and 5.

Lines 8 and 9 are hard-coded variables for the email recipient and the subject of the email message. Replace you@yourdomain.com with your own email address, obviously. If you want to change the subject, feel free to do that too!

Lines 10 and 11 set up some mail headers—namely, the From: and Reply-to: headers. You could put any value in the From: header; this is the information that displays in the From or Sender column of your email application when you receive this mail.

CAUTION

If your outbound mail server is a Windows machine, you should replace the \n newline character with \r\n.

The mail() function uses five parameters: the recipient, the subject, the message, any additional mail headers, and any additional sendmail parameters. In our example, we use only the first four parameters. The order of these parameters is shown in line 14.

Put these lines into a text file called sendmail.php and place that file in your web server document root. Use your web browser and go back to the form, enter some information, and click the submission button. You should see something like Figure 15.9 in your browser.

FIGURE 15.9
Sample results from `sendmail.php`.

If you then check your email, you should have a message waiting for you. It might look something like Figure 15.10.

FIGURE 15.10
Email sent from `sendmail.php`.

NOTE

This example does not include any server-side validation of form elements and just assumes that the user has entered values into the form. In a real-life situation, you would check for the presence and validity of the values entered in the form before doing anything with the mail, perhaps starting with HTML5 form validation as you saw earlier in this chapter.

Summary

This chapter demonstrated how to create HTML forms, which enable your visitors to provide information to you when they are hooked up to a back-end processing script. You learned about all the major form elements, including a little about how the names and value attributes of form elements are interpreted by JavaScript and PHP. Speaking of PHP, you learned how to work with various superglobals and form input. You learned how to pass information from script call to script call using hidden fields. You also learned how to send your form results in email, which is a good milestone to have accomplished.

Table 15.1 summarizes the HTML tags and attributes covered in this chapter.

TABLE 15.1 HTML Tags and Attributes Covered in Chapter 15

Tag/Attribute	Function
`<form>...</form>`	Indicates an input form.

Attributes	Function
`action="scripturl"`	Gives the address of the script to process this form input.
`method="post/get"`	Indicates how the form input will be sent to the server. Normally set to `post` rather than `get`.
`<label>...</label>`	Provides information for the form element to which it is associated.
`<fieldset>...</fieldset>`	Groups a set of related form elements.
`<legend>...</legend>`	Provides a label to a set of related form elements.
`<input>`	Indicates an input element for a form.
`type="controltype"`	Gives the type for this input widget. Some possible values are `checkbox`, `hidden`, `radio`, `reset`, `submit`, `text`, and `image`, among others.
`name="name"`	Gives the unique name of this item, as passed to the script.
`value="value"`	Gives the default value for a text or hidden item. For a check box or radio button, it's the value to be submitted with the form. For reset or submit buttons, it's the label for the button itself.
`src="imageurl"`	Shows the source file for an image.
`checked`	Is used for check boxes and radio buttons. Indicates that this item is checked.
`autofocus`	Puts focus on the element when the form is loaded.
`required`	Indicates that the field should be validated for content, according to type (where appropriate).
`pattern="pattern"`	Indicates that the content of this field should be validated against this regular expression.
`size="width"`	Specifies the width, in characters, of a text input region.
`maxlength="maxlength"`	Specifies the maximum number of characters that can be entered into a text region.

Attributes	Function
`<textarea>`...`</textarea>`	Indicates a multiline text entry form element. Default text can be included.
`name="name"`	Specifies the name to be passed to the script.
`rows="numrows"`	Specifies the number of rows this text area displays.
`cols="numchars"`	Specifies the number of columns (characters) this text area displays.
`autofocus`	Puts focus on the element when the form is loaded.
`required`	Indicates that the field should be validated for content according to type (where appropriate).
`pattern="pattern"`	Indicates that the content of this field should be validated against this regular expression.
`<select>`...`</select>`	Creates a menu or scrolling list of possible items.
`name="name"`	Shows the name that is passed to the script.
`size="numelements"`	Indicates the number of elements to display. If `size` is indicated, the selection becomes a scrolling list. If no `size` is given, the selection is a drop-down pick list.
`multiple`	Allows multiple selections from the list.
`required`	Indicates that the field should be validated for a selection.
`<optgroup>`...`</optgroup>`	Indicates a grouping of `<option>` elements.
`label="label"`	Provides a label for the group.
`<option>`...`</option>`	Indicates a possible item within a `<select>` element.
`selected`	Selects the `<option>` by default in the list when this attribute is included.
`value="value"`	Specifies the value to submit if this `<option>` is selected when the form is submitted.

Q&A

Q. **Is there any way to create a large number of text fields without dealing with different names for all of them?**

A. Yes. If you use the same name for several elements in the form, their objects form an array. For example, if you defined 20 text fields with the name `member`, you could refer to them as `member[0]` through `member[19]`. This also works with other types of form elements.

Q. If HTML5 contains form validation, do I ever have to worry about validation again?

A. Yes, you do. Although HTML5 form validation is awesome, you should still validate the form information that is sent to you on the back end. Back-end processing is outside the scope of the book, but as a rule, you should never trust any user input—always check it before performing an action that uses it (especially when interacting with a database).

Workshop

The Workshop contains quiz questions and activities to help you solidify your understanding of the material covered. Try to answer all questions before looking at the "Answers" section that follows.

Quiz

1. Which of these attributes of a `<form>` tag determines where the data will be sent?

    A. `action`

    B. `method`

    C. `name`

2. Which built-in associative array contains all values submitted as part of a `POST` request?

3. What are the five arguments used by the `mail()` function?

Answers

1. **A.** The `action` attribute determines where the data is sent.

2. The `$_POST` superglobal.

3. The recipient, the subject, the message string, additional headers, and additional parameters.

Exercises

▶ Create a PHP script that processes the big form in Listing 15.1 and sends it to you via email.

▶ Create a calculator script that enables the user to submit two numbers and choose an operation (addition, multiplication, division, or subtraction) to perform on them.

Understanding the Database Design Process

What You'll Learn in This Chapter:

- ▶ Some advantages to good database design
- ▶ Three types of table relationships
- ▶ How to normalize your database
- ▶ How to implement a good database design process

This chapter introduces you to the reasoning behind designing a relational database. Depending on how you decide to focus your technical work in the future—you may want to focus on the front end, the back end, or both—you may never need to work directly in a database or design a *database schema*, or a structure representing a logical view of the database, from the ground up. However, no matter where you focus your work, understanding how data is defined, structured, and stored in a relational database is critical to understanding just what you can do with that data, and how to do it.

After this concept-focused chapter, you jump headlong into learning the basic MySQL commands in preparation for integrating MySQL in your own applications.

The Importance of Good Database Design

A good database design is crucial for a high-performance application, just as an aerodynamic body is important to a race car. If a car does not have smooth lines, it produces drag and goes slower. Without optimized relationships, your database will not perform as efficiently as possible. Thinking about relationships and database efficiency—which includes ease of maintenance, minimizing duplications, and avoiding inconsistencies—is part of *database normalization*, or simply *normalization*.

NOTE

Specifically, *normalization* refers to the process of structuring data to minimize duplication and inconsistencies.

Beyond the issue of performance is the issue of maintenance—your database should be easy to maintain. This includes storing only a limited amount (if any) of repetitive data. If you have a lot of repetitive data and one instance of that data undergoes a change (such as a name change), that change has to be made for all occurrences of the data. To eliminate duplication and enhance your ability to maintain the data, you might create a table of possible values and use a key to refer to the value. That way, if the value changes names, the change occurs only once—in the master table. The reference remains the same throughout other tables.

For example, suppose that you are responsible for maintaining a database of students and the classes in which they are enrolled. If 35 of these students are in the same class (let's call it Advanced Math), this class name would appear 35 times in the table. Now, if the instructor decides to change the name of the class to Mathematics IV, you must change 35 records to reflect the new name of the class. If the database were designed so that class names appeared in one table and just the class ID number was stored with the student record, you would have to change only one record—not 35—to update the name, and you could be sure that the data in your database stays in sync with reality.

The benefits of a well-planned and designed database are numerous, and it stands to reason that the more work you do up front, the less you have to do later. A really bad time for a database redesign is after the public launch of the application using it—although it does happen, and the results are costly.

So, before you even start coding an application, spend a lot of time designing your database. Throughout the rest of this chapter, you learn more about relationships and normalization—two important pieces to the database design puzzle.

Types of Table Relationships

Table relationships come in several forms:

- ▶ One-to-one relationships

- ▶ One-to-many relationships

- ▶ Many-to-many relationships

For example, suppose that you have a table called `employees` that contains each person's Social Security number or other individual identifier, his or her name, and the department in which he or she works. Suppose that you also have a separate table called `departments` containing the list of all available departments, made up of a department ID and a name. In the `employees` table, the Department ID field matches an ID found in the `departments` table. You can see this type of relationship in Figure 16.1. The PK next to the field name indicates the *primary key* for the table, or the key that uniquely defines the records in the table.

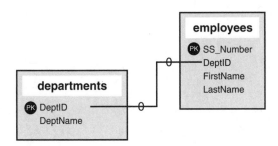

FIGURE 16.1
The `employees` and `departments` tables are related through the DeptID key.

In the following sections, we take a closer look at each of the relationship types.

One-to-One Relationships

In a one-to-one relationship, a key appears only once in a related table. The `employees` and `departments` tables do not have a one-to-one relationship because many employees undoubtedly belong to the same department. A one-to-one relationship exists, for example, if each employee is assigned one computer within the company. Figure 16.2 shows the one-to-one relationship of employees to computers.

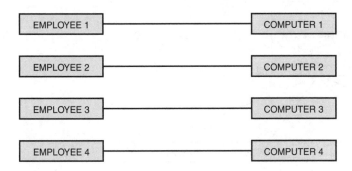

FIGURE 16.2
One computer is assigned to each employee.

The `employees` and `computers` tables in your database would look something like Figure 16.3, which represents a one-to-one relationship.

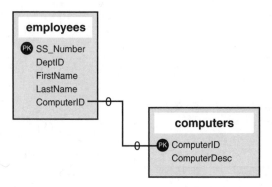

FIGURE 16.3
One-to-one relationship in the data model.

One-to-Many Relationships

In a one-to-many relationship, keys from one table appear multiple times in a related table. The example shown in Figure 16.1, indicating a connection between employees and departments, illustrates a one-to-many relationship. A real-world example is an organizational chart of the department, as shown in Figure 16.4.

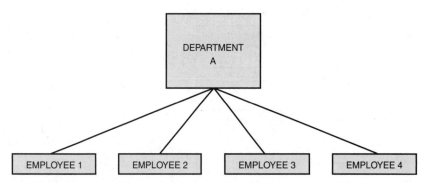

FIGURE 16.4
One department contains many employees.

The one-to-many relationship is the most common type of relationship. Another practical example is the use of a state abbreviation in an address database; each state has a unique identifier (CA for California, PA for Pennsylvania, and so on), and each address in the United States has a state associated with it.

If you have eight friends in California and five in Pennsylvania, you use only two distinct abbreviations in your table. One abbreviation (CA) represents a one-to-eight relationship, and the other (PA) represents a one-to-five relationship.

Many-to-Many Relationships

The many-to-many relationship sometimes causes problems in practical examples of normalized databases—so much so that you may see tables representing many-to-many relationships broken into a series of one-to-many relationships. In a many-to-many relationship, the key value of one table can appear many times in a related table. So far, that just sounds like a one-to-many relationship, but here's the curveball: The opposite is also true, meaning that the primary key from that second table can also appear many times in the first table.

Think of such a relationship this way, using the example of students and classes: A student has an ID and a name. A class has an ID and a name. A student usually takes more than one class at a time, and a class always contains more than one student, as you can see in Figure 16.5.

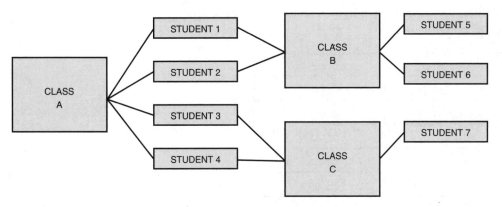

FIGURE 16.5
Students take classes, and classes contain students.

As you can see, this sort of relationship does not present an easy method for relating tables. Your tables could look like Figure 16.6, seemingly unrelated.

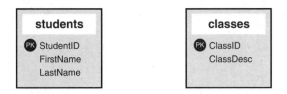

FIGURE 16.6
The `students` table and the `classes` table, unrelated.

To make the theoretical many-to-many relationship a reality, you create an intermediate table, one that sits between the two tables and essentially maps them together. You might build such a table similar to the one in Figure 16.7.

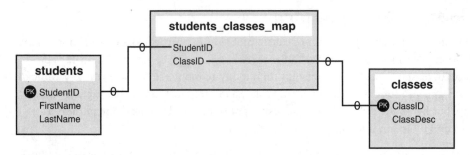

FIGURE 16.7
The students_classes_map table acts as an intermediary.

If you take the information in Figure 16.5 and put it into the intermediate table, you can create something like Figure 16.8.

STUDENTID	CLASSID
STUDENT 1	CLASS A
STUDENT 2	CLASS A
STUDENT 3	CLASS A
STUDENT 4	CLASS A
STUDENT 5	CLASS B
STUDENT 6	CLASS B
STUDENT 7	CLASS C
STUDENT 1	CLASS B
STUDENT 2	CLASS B
STUDENT 3	CLASS C
STUDENT 4	CLASS C

FIGURE 16.8
The students_classes_map table populated with data.

As you can see, many students and many classes happily coexist within the students_classes_map table.

With this introduction to the types of relationships, learning about normalization should be a snap.

Understanding Normalization

Normalization is simply a set of rules that will ultimately make your life easier when you are acting as a database administrator, but also when you are a developer whose responsibility it is to modify data in the database in any way. Normalization is the art of organizing your database in such a way that your tables relate to each other where appropriate and are flexible for future growth.

The sets of rules used in normalization are called *normal forms*. If your database design follows the first set of rules, it is considered in the *first normal form*. If the first three sets of rules of normalization are followed, your database is said to be in the *third normal form*.

Throughout this chapter, you learn about each rule in the first, second, and third normal forms—the most foundational of the nine basic normalizations—and I hope you will follow them as you create your own applications. In the chapter, you use a sample set of tables for a students-and-courses database and take it to the third normal form.

Problems with the Flat Table

Before launching into the first normal form, you have to start with a bunch of data that needs to be normalized. In the case of a database, it's the *flat table*. A flat table is like a spreadsheet—it has many, many columns that define it, and rows of data each have data in, or hold space for, those columns. There are no relationships between multiple tables; all the data you could possibly want is right there in that single flat table. This scenario is inefficient and consumes more physical space on your hard drive than a normalized database.

In your students-and-courses database, assume that you have the following fields in your flat table:

- ▶ `StudentName`—The name of the student.
- ▶ `CourseID1`—The ID of the first course taken by the student.
- ▶ `CourseDescription1`—The description of the first course taken by the student.
- ▶ `CourseInstructor1`—The instructor of the first course taken by the student.
- ▶ `CourseID2`—The ID of the second course taken by the student.
- ▶ `CourseDescription2`—The description of the second course taken by the student.
- ▶ `CourseInstructor2`—The instructor of the second course taken by the student.
- ▶ Repeat `CourseID`, `CourseDescription`, and `CourseInstructor` columns many more times to account for all the classes students can take during their academic career.

With what you've learned so far, you should be able to identify the first problem area: `CourseID`, `CourseDescription`, and `CourseInstructor` columns become repeated groups.

Eliminating redundancy is the first step in normalization, so next you take this flat table to first normal form. If your table remained in its flat format, you could have a lot of unclaimed space and a lot of space being used unnecessarily—not an efficient table design.

First Normal Form

The rules for the first normal form are as follows:

▶ Eliminate repeating information.

▶ Create separate tables for related data.

If you think about the flat table design with many repeated sets of fields for the students-and-courses database, you can identify two distinct topics: students and courses. Taking your students-and-courses database to the first normal form means that you create two tables: one for students and one for courses, as shown in Figure 16.9.

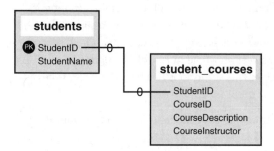

FIGURE 16.9
Breaking the flat table into two tables.

Your two tables now represent a one-to-many relationship of one student to many courses. Students can take as many courses as they want and are not limited to the number of `CourseID`/`CourseDescription`/`CourseInstructor` groupings that existed in the flat table.

The next step is to put the tables into second normal form.

Second Normal Form

The rule for the second normal form is as follows:

▶ No nonkey attributes depend on a portion of the primary key.

In plain English, this means that if fields in your table are not entirely related to a primary key, you have more work to do. In the students-and-courses example, you need to break out the courses into their own table and modify the `students_courses` table.

`CourseID`, `CourseDescription`, and `CourseInstructor` can become a table called `courses` with a primary key of `CourseID`. The `students_courses` table should then just contain two fields: `StudentID` and `CourseID`. You can see this new design in Figure 16.10.

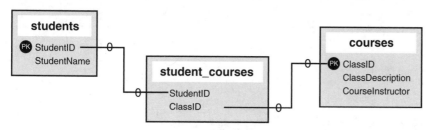

FIGURE 16.10
Taking your tables to second normal form.

This structure should look familiar to you as a many-to-many relationship using an intermediary mapping table. The third normal form is the last form we look at here, and you should find that it is just as simple to understand as the first two.

Third Normal Form

The rule for the third normal form is as follows:

▶ No attributes depend on other nonkey attributes.

This rule simply means that you need to look at your tables and see whether you have more fields that can be broken down further and that are not dependent on a key. Think about removing repeated data and you'll find your answer: instructors. Inevitably, an instructor teaches more than one class. However, `CourseInstructor` is not a key of any sort. So, if you break out this information and create a separate table purely for the sake of efficiency and maintenance (as shown in Figure 16.11), that is the third normal form.

Third normal form is usually adequate for removing redundancy and allowing for flexibility and growth.

The next section gives you some pointers for the thought process involved in database design and where it fits in the overall design process of your application.

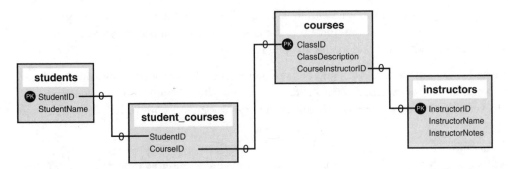

FIGURE 16.11
Taking your tables to third normal form.

Following the Design Process

The greatest problem in application design is a lack of forethought (in anything, really, but in this case we're talking about the database design). As it applies to database-driven applications, the design process must include a thorough evaluation of your database—what it should hold, how data relates to each other, and, most important, whether it is flexible and scalable. The latter point is important because no matter how thorough you think you are being at the beginning, the nature of development is such that you will inevitably have great ideas later as well and you'll need to work those into your flexible design.

The general steps in the design process are as follows:

- ▶ Define the objective.

- ▶ Design the data structures (tables and fields).

- ▶ Discern relationships.

- ▶ Define and implement business rules.

- ▶ Create the application.

Creating the application is the last step, not the first. Many developers take an idea for an application, build it, and then go back and try to make a set of database tables fit into it. This approach is completely backward, inefficient, and will cost a lot of time and money. That is not to say that such an approach doesn't have a place in rapid prototyping or very quick development cycles—it does! I can guarantee that many amazing applications we all use on a regular basis probably started with a poorly structured database. However, at some point, that database schema quickly put together to get an application released as soon as possible will reach its limits; the earlier you focus on the database in your development process, the better, because the database refactoring work will become exponentially more expensive as time goes on and features are added.

So, before you start any application design process, sit down and talk it out. If you cannot describe your application—including the objectives, audience, and target market—you are not ready to build it, let alone model the database.

After you can describe the actions and nuances of your application to other people and it makes sense to them, you can start thinking about the tables you want to create. Start with big flat tables because after you write them down, your newfound normalization skills will take over. You will be able to find your redundancies and visualize your relationships. As you become more experienced, you will be able to minimize the steps in this process, but there's nothing wrong with stepping through them carefully and explicitly.

The next step is to do the normalization. Go from a flat table to the first normal form and so on, up to the third normal form if possible. Use paper, pencils, sticky notes, or whatever helps you to visualize the tables and relationships. There's no shame in data modeling on sticky notes until you are ready to create the tables themselves. Plus, using sticky notes is a lot cheaper than buying software to do it for you; good, full-featured modeling software ranges from hundreds to several thousands of dollars.

After you have a preliminary data model, look at it from the application's point of view. Or look at it from the point of view of the person using the application you are building. This is the point where you define business rules and see whether your data model breaks. An example of a business rule for an online registration application is, "Each user must have one email address, and it must not belong to any other user." If `EmailAddress` is not a unique field in your data model, your model will break based on the business rule.

After your business rules have been applied to your data model, only then can application programming begin with confidence. You can rest assured that your data model is solid and you will not be programming yourself into a brick wall. The latter event is all too common, but easy to avoid.

Summary

Following proper database design is a key way to ensure your application will be efficient, flexible, and easy to manage and maintain. An important aspect of database design is to use relationships between tables instead of throwing all your data into one big flat file. Types of relationships include one-to-one, one-to-many, and many-to-many.

Using relationships to properly organize your data is called normalization. There are many levels of normalization, but the primary levels are the first, second, and third normal forms. Each level has a rule or two that you must follow. Following all the rules helps ensure that your database is well organized and flexible.

To take an idea from inception through to fruition, you should follow a design process. This process essentially says, "Think before you act." Discuss rules, requirements, and objectives, and only then create the final version of your normalized tables.

Q&A

Q. Are there only three normal forms?

A. No, there are more than three normal forms. Additional forms include but are not limited to the Boyce-Codd normal form, fourth normal form, and fifth normal form/Join-Projection normal form. These forms are not often followed in practical application development because the benefits of doing so are outweighed by the cost in man-hours and database efficiency (but it is certainly fine if you implement them). For more information, see http://en.wikipedia.org/wiki/Database_normalization#.

Workshop

The Workshop is designed to help you review what you have learned and begin putting your knowledge into practice.

Quiz

1. Name three types of data relationships.

2. Because many-to-many relationships are difficult to represent in an efficient database design, what should you do?

3. Name a few ways you can create visualizations of data relationships.

Answers

1. One-to-one, one-to-many, and many-to-many.

2. Create a series of one-to-many relationships using intermediary mapping tables.

3. You can use a range of tools, from sticky notes and string (where notes are the tables and string shows the relationships between tables) to software used to draw diagrams, to software programs that interpret your SQL statements and produce visualizations.

Exercises

▶ Explain each of the three normal forms to a person who works with spreadsheets and flat tables.

CHAPTER 17
Learning Basic SQL Commands

What You'll Learn in This Chapter:

▶ The basic MySQL data types

▶ How to use the CREATE TABLE statement to create a table

▶ How to use the INSERT statement to enter records

▶ How to use the SELECT statement to retrieve records

▶ How to use basic functions, the WHERE clause, and the GROUP BY clause in SELECT expressions

▶ How to select from multiple tables, using JOIN or subselects

▶ How to use the UPDATE and REPLACE statement to modify existing records

▶ How to use the DELETE statement to remove records

▶ How to use string functions built in to MySQL

▶ How to use date and time functions built in to MySQL

The preceding chapter explained the basics of the database design process, and this chapter provides a primer on basic SQL syntax, which you use to create and manipulate your MySQL database tables. This is a hands-on chapter, and it assumes that you can issue queries directly to MySQL, either through the MySQL command-line interface or through another management interface such as phpMyAdmin, which is included in the XAMPP installation provided through the Quick Start process in Appendix A, "Installation QuickStart Guide with XAMPP."

Although this might not be the most exciting chapter in the book, it does show you many basic and functional examples of elements you'll use throughout the rest of your work, as you issue these same queries with PHP to create dynamic applications.

Learning the MySQL Data Types

Properly defining the fields in a table is important to the overall optimization of your database. You should use only the type and size of field you really need to use; do not define a field as 10 characters wide if you know you're only going to use two characters—that's eight extra characters the database has to account for, even if they are unused. These field types are also referred to as *data types*, as in the "type of data" you will be storing in those fields.

MySQL uses many different data types, but there are three primary categories to learn: numeric, date and time, and string types. Pay close attention because properly defining the data type is more important than any other part of the table-creation process.

Numeric Data Types

MySQL uses all the standard ANSI SQL numeric data types. So if you're coming to MySQL from a different database system, these definitions will look familiar to you. The following list shows the common numeric data types and their descriptions:

NOTE

The terms *signed* and *unsigned* are used in the list of numeric data types. If you remember your basic algebra, you'll recall that a signed integer can be a positive or negative integer, whereas an unsigned integer is always a nonnegative integer.

- ▶ **INTEGER**, commonly aliased as **INT**—A normal-sized integer that can be signed or unsigned. If it's signed, the allowable range is from −2147483648 to 2147483647. If it's unsigned, the allowable range is from 0 to 4294967295. You can specify a data type width of up to 11 digits.

- ▶ **TINYINT**—A small integer that can be signed or unsigned. If it's signed, the allowable range is from −128 to 127. If it's unsigned, the allowable range is from 0 to 255. You can specify a width of up to four digits.

- ▶ **SMALLINT**—A small integer that can be signed or unsigned. If it's signed, the allowable range is from −32768 to 32767. If it's unsigned, the allowable range is from 0 to 65535. You can specify a width of up to five digits.

- ▶ **MEDIUMINT**—A medium-sized integer that can be signed or unsigned. If it's signed, the allowable range is from −8388608 to 8388607. If it's unsigned, the allowable range is from 0 to 16777215. You can specify a width of up to nine digits.

- ▶ **BIGINT**—A large integer that can be signed or unsigned. If it's signed, the allowable range is from −9223372036854775808 to 9223372036854775807. If it's unsigned, the allowable range is from 0 to 18446744073709551615. You can specify a width of up to 11 digits.

- ▶ **FLOAT(M,D)**—A floating-point number that cannot be unsigned. You can define the display length (M) and the number of decimals (D). This is not required and defaults to 10,2, where 2 is the number of decimals and 10 is the total number of digits (including decimals). Decimal precision can go to 24 places for a FLOAT.

▶ **DOUBLE(M,D)**—A double-precision floating-point number that cannot be unsigned. You can define the display length (M) and the number of decimals (D). This is not required and will default to 16,4, where 4 is the number of decimals. Decimal precision can go to 53 places for a DOUBLE. REAL is a synonym for DOUBLE.

▶ **DECIMAL(M,D)**—An unpacked fixed-point number used to specify exact precision. In unpacked decimals, each decimal corresponds to 1 byte. Defining the display length (M) and the number of decimals (D) is required. NUMERIC is a synonym for DECIMAL.

Of all the MySQL numeric data types, you will likely use some variation of INT most often, but be careful which you choose because you will run into problems if you define your fields to be smaller than you actually need. For example, if you define an ID field as an unsigned TINYINT, you cannot successfully insert that 256th record if ID is a primary key (and thus required).

Date and Time Types

MySQL has several data types available for storing dates and times, and in the past these data types were flexible in their input. In other words, you could enter dates that are not valid, such as February 30 (February has only 28 or 29 days, never 30). Also, you could store dates with missing information. For example, if you know that someone was born sometime in November 1980, you can use 1980-11-00, where 00 would have been for the day, if you knew it. However, in MySQL 5.7 and greater, the ALLOW_INVALID_DATES setting is *not* on by default. For more information please see the MySQL Manual entry at https://dev.mysql.com/doc/refman/5.7/en/sql-mode.html#sqlmode_allow_invalid_dates.

If you are using an older version of MySQL or one with ALLOW_INVALID_DATES turned on, the flexibility of MySQL's date and time types also means that the responsibility for date checking falls on the application developer (that would be you). In these scenarios, MySQL checks only two elements for validity: that the month is between 0 and 12 and that the day is between 0 and 31. MySQL does not automatically verify that the 30th day of the second month (February 30) is a valid date. Therefore, any date validation you want to include in your application should happen in your PHP code before you even attempt to add a record with a bogus date into your database table.

The MySQL date and time data types are as follows:

▶ **DATE**—A date in YYYY-MM-DD format, between 1000-01-01 and 9999-12-31. For example, December 30, 1973 is stored as 1973-12-30.

▶ **DATETIME**—A date and time combination in YYYY-MM-DD HH:MM:SS format, between 1000-01-01 00:00:00 and 9999-12-31 23:59:59. For example, 3:30 in the afternoon on December 30, 1973 is stored as 1973-12-30 15:30:00.

▶ **TIMESTAMP**—A timestamp between midnight, January 1, 1970 and (to be excruciatingly precise) January 19, 2038 at 03:14:07. You can define multiple lengths to the TIMESTAMP field, which directly correlates to what is stored in it. The default length for TIMESTAMP is 14, which stores YYYYMMDDHHMMSS. This looks like the previous DATETIME format, only without the hyphens and colons between numbers; 3:30 in the afternoon on December 30, 1973 is stored as 19731230153000. Other definitions of TIMESTAMP are 12 (YYMMDDHHMMSS), 8 (YYYYMMDD), and 6 (YYMMDD).

▶ **TIME**—Stores time in HH:MM:SS format; this may also include elapsed time, not just clock time. For example, you could store 48:10 for 48 hours and ten minutes.

▶ **YEAR(M)**—Stores a year in two-digit or four-digit format. If the length is specified as 2 (for example, YEAR(2)), YEAR can be 70 to 69 (1970 to 2069). If the length is specified as 4, YEAR can be 1901 to 2155. The default length is 4.

You may end up using DATETIME more often than any other date- or time-related data type, but do understand the differences between it and the others.

String Types

Although numeric and date types are fun, most data you'll store will be in string format. This list describes the common string data types in MySQL:

▶ **CHAR(M)**—A fixed-length string between 1 and 255 characters in length; for example, CHAR(5). The string is right-padded with spaces to the specified length when stored (and stripped when retrieved). Defining a length is not required, but the default is 1.

▶ **VARCHAR(M)**—A variable-length string between 1 and 65,535 characters in length; for example, VARCHAR(192). You must define a length when creating a VARCHAR field.

▶ **BLOB or TEXT**—A field with a maximum length of 65,535 characters. BLOBs are *Binary Large Objects* and are used to store large amounts of binary data, such as images or other types of files. Fields defined as TEXT also hold large amounts of data just like BLOBs; the difference between the two is that sorts and comparisons on stored data are case sensitive on BLOBs and are not case sensitive in TEXT fields. You do not specify a length with BLOB or TEXT.

▶ **TINYBLOB or TINYTEXT**—A BLOB or TEXT column with a maximum length of 255 characters. You do not specify a length with TINYBLOB or TINYTEXT.

▶ **MEDIUMBLOB or MEDIUMTEXT**—A BLOB or TEXT column with a maximum length of 16,777,215 characters. You do not specify a length with MEDIUMBLOB or MEDIUMTEXT.

▶ **LONGBLOB or LONGTEXT**—A BLOB or TEXT column with a maximum length of 4,294,967,295 characters. You do not specify a length with LONGBLOB or LONGTEXT.

▶ **ENUM**—An enumeration, which is a fancy term for *list of allowed values*. When defining an ENUM, you are creating a list of items from which the value must be selected (or it can be NULL). For example, if you want your field to contain A or B or C, you would define your ENUM as ENUM ('A', 'B', 'C'), and only those values (or NULL) could ever populate that field. ENUMs can have 65,535 different values. ENUMs use an index for storing items.

NOTE

The SET type is similar to ENUM in that it is defined as a list. However, the SET type is stored as a full value rather than an index of a value, as with ENUMs, and can only store 64 members.

You will probably use VARCHAR fields more often than other field types, and ENUMs can be quite useful as well.

Learning the Table-Creation Syntax

The table-creation statement requires the following:

▶ Name of the table

▶ Name for each field

▶ Definition for each field

The generic table-creation syntax is

```
CREATE TABLE table_name (column_name column_type);
```

The table name is up to you, of course, but it should be a name that reflects the usage of the table. For example, if you have a table that holds the inventory of a grocery store, you would not name the table s. You would probably name it something like grocery_inventory. Similarly, the field names you select should be as concise as possible and relevant to the function they serve and the data they hold. For example, you might call a field holding the name of an item item_name, not n.

The following table-creation example creates a generic grocery_inventory table with fields for ID, item name, item description, item price, and quantity. Each of the fields is a different type; the ID and quantity fields hold integers, the item name field holds up to 50 characters, the item description field holds up to 65,535 characters of text, and the item price field contains a float:

```
CREATE TABLE grocery_inventory (
  id INT NOT NULL PRIMARY KEY AUTO_INCREMENT,
  item_name VARCHAR (50) NOT NULL,
```

```
    item_desc TEXT,
    item_price FLOAT NOT NULL,
    curr_qty INT NOT NULL
);
```

NOTE

The id field is defined as a *primary key*. You'll learn more about keys in later chapters, in the context of creating specific tables as parts of sample applications, but in brief, a primary key is the unique identifier for a record (or row) in a table. In this field definition, using auto_increment as an attribute of the field tells MySQL to use the next available integer for the id field when the next record is inserted and no value is specified for that field. NOT NULL is used to indicate that the field must contain a value.

The MySQL server responds with Query OK each time a query, regardless of type, is successful. Otherwise, an error message displays, telling you where your query went awry. Depending on the interface to MySQL you are using, you may or may not see this specific response. However, regardless of the interface, it should provide you with some indication of the status of the query.

Using the INSERT Statement

After you have created some tables, you use the SQL statement INSERT for adding new records to these tables. The basic syntax of INSERT is

```
INSERT INTO table_name (column list) VALUES (column values);
```

Within the parenthetical list of values, you must enclose strings within quotation marks. The SQL standard is single quotes, but MySQL enables the usage of either single or double quotes. So, if you are used to working in Oracle, which forces single-quoted strings, there's no need to change your behavior to comply with norms in the world of MySQL. Remember to escape the type of quotation mark used, if it is within the string itself.

NOTE

Integers do not require quotation marks around them.

Here is a classic example of a string where escaping is necessary:

```
O'Connor said "Boo"
```

If you enclose your strings in double quotes, the INSERT statement looks like this:

```
INSERT INTO table_name (column_name) VALUES ("O'Connor said \"Boo\"");
```

If you enclose your strings in single quotes instead, the INSERT statement looks like this:

```
INSERT INTO table_name (column_name) VALUES ('O\'Connor said "Boo"');
```

A Closer Look at INSERT

Besides the table name, the INSERT statement consists of two main parts: the column list and the value list. Only the value list is actually required, but if you omit the column list, you must specifically provide the value for each column in your value list—in the exact order.

Using the grocery_inventory table as an example, you have five fields: id, item_name, item_desc, item_price, and curr_qty. To insert a complete record, you could use either of these statements:

▶ A statement with all columns named:

```
INSERT INTO grocery_inventory
(id, item_name, item_desc, item_price, curr_qty)
VALUES (1, 'Apples', 'Beautiful, ripe apples.', 0.25, 1000);
```

▶ A statement that uses all columns but does not explicitly name them:

```
INSERT INTO grocery_inventory VALUES (2, 'Bunches of Grapes',
'Seedless grapes.', 2.99, 500);
```

Give both of them a try and see what happens. You should get successful response ("Query OK") to both statements.

Now for some more interesting methods of using INSERT. Because id was defined at creation time as an auto-incrementing integer in the grocery_inventory table, you do not have to put it in your value list. However, if there's a value you specifically do *not* want to list (such as id), you then must list the remaining columns in use. For example, the following statement does not list the columns and does not give a value for id:

```
INSERT INTO grocery_inventory VALUES
('Bottled Water (6-pack)', '500ml spring water.', 2.29, 250);
```

The preceding statement produces an error, such as this:

```
ERROR 1136: Column count doesn't match value count at row 1
```

Because you did not list any columns in this statement, MySQL expects all of them to be in the value list; since you did not, the statement results in an error. If your goal was to let MySQL do the work for you by auto-incrementing the id field, you could use either of these statements:

▶ A statement with all columns named except id:

```
INSERT INTO grocery_inventory (item_name, item_desc, item_price, curr_qty)
VALUES ('Bottled Water (6-pack)', '500ml spring water.', 2.29, 250);
```

▶ A statement that uses all columns but does not explicitly name them *and* indicates a NULL entry for id (so one is filled in for you):

```
INSERT INTO grocery_inventory VALUES (NULL, 'Bottled Water (12-pack)',
'500ml spring water.', 4.49, 500);
```

Go ahead and try both so that your grocery_inventory table has four records in total. It makes no different to MySQL which valid statements you use, but as with everything based on your own preferences, be consistent in your application development. Consistent structures are easier for you to debug later because you know what to expect.

Using the SELECT Statement

SELECT is the SQL statement used to retrieve records from your tables. This statement syntax can be totally simple or very complicated, depending on which fields you want to select, whether you want to select from multiple tables, and what conditions you plan to impose on the query. As you become more comfortable interacting with databases, you will learn to enhance your SELECT queries, ultimately making your database do as much work as possible and not over-working your programming language.

The most basic SELECT syntax looks like this:

```
SELECT expressions_and_columns FROM table_name
[WHERE some_condition_is_true]
[ORDER BY some_column [ASC | DESC]]
[LIMIT offset, rows]
```

Look at the first line:

```
SELECT expressions_and_columns FROM table_name
```

One handy expression is the * symbol, which stands for *everything*. So, to select everything (all rows, all columns) from the grocery_inventory table, your SQL query would be

SELECT * FROM grocery_inventory;

Depending on how much data is in the grocery_inventory table, your results will vary, but the results might look something like this:

```
+----+-------------------------+-------------------------+------------+----------+
| id | item_name               | item_desc               | item_price | curr_qty |
+----+-------------------------+-------------------------+------------+----------+
| 1  | Apples                  | Beautiful, ripe apples. | 0.25       | 1000     |
| 2  | Bunches of Grapes       | Seedless grapes.        | 2.99       | 500      |
| 3  | Bottled Water (6-pack)  | 500ml spring water.     | 2.29       | 250      |
| 4  | Bottled Water (12-pack) | 500ml spring water.     | 4.49       | 500      |
+----+-------------------------+-------------------------+------------+----------+
4 rows in set (0.00 sec)
```

NOTE

This output comes from the MySQL command line interface; it creates a lovely, formatted table with the names of the columns along the first row as part of the resultset. If you are using a different interface to MySQL, your results will look different. (Focus on observing the expected data and not the interface differences.)

If you want to select specific columns only—and this is always the recommended option because you should only ask for data you will actually use—replace the * with the names of the columns separated by commas. The following statement selects just the id, item_name, and curr_qty fields from the grocery_inventory table:

```
SELECT id, item_name, curr_qty FROM grocery_inventory;
```

The results are displayed as follows:

```
+----+-------------------------+----------+
| id | item_name               | curr_qty |
+----+-------------------------+----------+
| 1  | Apples                  | 1000     |
| 2  | Bunches of Grapes       | 500      |
| 3  | Bottled Water (6-pack)  | 250      |
| 4  | Bottled Water (12-pack) | 500      |
+----+-------------------------+----------+
4 rows in set (0.00 sec)
```

Ordering SELECT Results

By default, results of SELECT queries are ordered as they were inserted into the table and should not be relied on as a meaningful ordering system. If you want to order results a specific way, such as by date, ID, name, and so on, specify your sorting requirements using the ORDER BY clause. In the following query, the intention is a resultset ordered alphanumerically by item_name:

```
SELECT id, item_name, curr_qty FROM grocery_inventory
ORDER BY item_name;
```

Success! The results are as follows:

```
+----+-------------------------+----------+
| id | item_name               | curr_qty |
+----+-------------------------+----------+
| 1  | Apples                  | 1000     |
| 4  | Bottled Water (12-pack) | 500      |
| 3  | Bottled Water (6-pack)  | 250      |
| 2  | Bunches of Grapes       | 500      |
+----+-------------------------+----------+
4 rows in set (0.03 sec)
```

TIP

When you select results from a table without specifying a sort order, the results may or may not be ordered by their key value. This occurs because MySQL reuses the space taken up by previously deleted rows. In other words, if you add records with ID values of 1 through 5, delete the record with ID number 4, and then add another record (ID number 6), the records might appear in the table in this order: 1, 2, 3, 6, 5.

The default sorting of ORDER BY results is ascending (ASC); strings sort from A to Z, integers start at 0, and dates sort from oldest to newest. You can also specify a descending sort, using DESC:

```
SELECT id, item_name, curr_qty FROM grocery_inventory
ORDER BY item_name DESC;
```

Here are the results:

```
+----+-------------------------+----------+
| id | item_name               | curr_qty |
+----+-------------------------+----------+
| 2  | Bunches of Grapes       | 500      |
| 3  | Bottled Water (6-pack)  | 250      |
| 4  | Bottled Water (12-pack) | 500      |
| 1  | Apples                  | 1000     |
+----+-------------------------+----------+
4 rows in set (0.00 sec)
```

You're not limited to sorting by just one field—you can specify as many fields as you want as long as they are separated by commas. The sorting priority is the order in which you list the fields.

Limiting Your Results

You can use the LIMIT clause to return only a certain number of records from your SELECT query result. Two options apply when using the LIMIT clause: the offset and the number of rows. The *offset* is the starting position, and the *number of rows* should be self-explanatory (and is required).

Suppose that you have more than two or three records in the grocery_inventory table, and you want to select the ID, name, and quantity of the first two, ordered by curr_qty. In other words, you want to select the two items with the least inventory. The following single-parameter limit starts at the 0 position and goes to the second record:

```
SELECT id, item_name, curr_qty FROM grocery_inventory
ORDER BY curr_qty LIMIT 2;
```

Here are the results:

```
+----+-------------------------+----------+
| id | item_name               | curr_qty |
+----+-------------------------+----------+
| 3  | Bottled Water (6-pack)  | 250      |
| 2  | Bunches of Grapes        | 500      |
+----+-------------------------+----------+
2 rows in set (0.00 sec)
```

The LIMIT clause can prove useful in an actual application. For example, you can use the LIMIT clause within a series of SELECT queries to travel through results in steps (first two items, next two items, next two items after that):

▶ `SELECT * FROM grocery_inventory ORDER BY curr_qty LIMIT 0, 2;`

▶ `SELECT * FROM grocery_inventory ORDER BY curr_qty LIMIT 2, 2;`

▶ `SELECT * FROM grocery_inventory ORDER BY curr_qty LIMIT 4, 2;`

If you specify an offset and number of rows in your query, and no results are found, you won't see an error—just an empty resultset. For example, if the grocery_inventory table contains only six records, a query with a LIMIT offset of 6 produces no results.

In web-based applications, when you see lists of data displayed with links such as "previous 10" and "next 10," it's a safe bet that a LIMIT clause is at work.

Using WHERE in Your Queries

You have learned numerous ways to retrieve particular columns from your tables but not specific rows. This is when the WHERE clause comes in to play. From the sample SELECT syntax, you see that WHERE is used to specify a particular condition:

```
SELECT expressions_and_columns FROM table_name
[WHERE some_condition_is_true]
```

An example is to retrieve all the records for items with a quantity of 500:

```
SELECT * FROM grocery_inventory WHERE curr_qty = 500;
```

Here are the results:

```
+----+------------------------+---------------------+------------+----------+
| id | item_name              | item_desc           | item_price | curr_qty |
+----+------------------------+---------------------+------------+----------+
| 2  | Bunches of Grapes       | Seedless grapes.    | 2.99       | 500      |
| 4  | Bottled Water (12-pack) | 500ml spring water. | 4.49       | 500      |
+----+------------------------+---------------------+------------+----------+
2 rows in set (0.00 sec)
```

As shown previously, if you use an integer as part of your WHERE clause, quotation marks are not required. Quotation marks are required around strings, however, and the same rules apply with regard to escaping characters as you learned in the section on INSERT.

Using Operators in WHERE Clauses

You've used the equal sign (=) in your WHERE clauses to determine the truth of a condition—that is, whether one thing is equal to another. You can use many types of operators, with comparison operators and logical operators being the most popular types. Table 17.1 lists the comparison operators and their meanings.

TABLE 17.1   Basic Comparison Operators and Their Meanings

Operator	Meaning
=	Equal to
!=	Not equal to
<=	Less than or equal to
<	Less than
>=	Greater than or equal to
>	Greater than

There's also a handy operator called BETWEEN, which is useful with integer or date comparisons because it searches for results between a minimum and maximum value. Here's an example:

```
SELECT * FROM grocery_inventory WHERE
item_price BETWEEN 1.50 AND 3.00;
```

Here are the results:

```
+----+----------------------+---------------------+------------+----------+
| id | item_name            | item_desc           | item_price | curr_qty |
+----+----------------------+---------------------+------------+----------+
| 2  | Bunches of Grapes    | Seedless grapes.    | 2.99       | 500      |
| 3  | Bottled Water (6-pack)| 500ml spring water. | 2.29       | 250      |
+----+----------------------+---------------------+------------+----------+
2 rows in set (0.00 sec)
```

Other operators include logical operators, which enable you to use multiple comparisons within your WHERE clause. The basic logical operators are AND and OR. When you use AND, all comparisons in the clause must be true to retrieve results, whereas using OR allows a minimum of one comparison to be true. Also, you can use the IN operator to specify a list of items that you want to match.

String Comparison Using LIKE

You were introduced to matching strings within a WHERE clause by using = or !=, but there's another useful operator for the WHERE clause when comparing strings: the LIKE operator. This operator uses two characters as wildcards in pattern matching:

▶ %—Matches multiple characters

▶ _—Matches exactly one character

For example, if you want to find records in the grocery_inventory table where the first name of the item starts with the letter *A*, you would use the following:

```
SELECT * FROM grocery_inventory WHERE item_name LIKE 'A%';
```

Here are the results:

```
+----+-----------+------------------------+------------+----------+
| id | item_name | item_desc              | item_price | curr_qty |
+----+-----------+------------------------+------------+----------+
|  1 | Apples    | Beautiful, ripe apples. |      0.25 |     1000 |
+----+-----------+------------------------+------------+----------+
1 row in set (0.00 sec)
```

NOTE

Unless you're performing a LIKE comparison on a binary string, the comparison is not case sensitive. You can force a case-sensitive comparison using the BINARY keyword.

Selecting from Multiple Tables

You are not limited to selecting only one table at a time. That would certainly make application programming a long and tedious task! When you select from more than one table in one SELECT query, you are really joining the tables together.

Suppose that you have two tables: fruit and color. You can select all rows from each of the two tables by using two separate SELECT statements:

```
SELECT * FROM fruit;
```

This query might result in something like this:

```
+----+-----------+
| id | fruitname |
+----+-----------+
|  1 | apple     |
|  2 | orange    |
|  3 | grape     |
|  4 | banana    |
+----+-----------+
4 rows in set (0.00 sec)
```

SELECT * FROM color;

The second query could result in data like this:

```
+----+-----------+
| id | colorname |
+----+-----------+
|  1 | red       |
|  2 | orange    |
|  3 | purple    |
|  4 | yellow    |
+----+-----------+
4 rows in set (0.00 sec)
```

When you want to select from both tables at once, the syntax of the SELECT statement differs somewhat. First, you must ensure that all the tables you're using in your query appear in the FROM clause of the SELECT statement. Using the fruit and color example, if you simply want to select all columns and rows from both tables, you might think you would use the following SELECT statement:

SELECT * FROM fruit, color;

With this query, you get results like this:

```
+----+-----------+----+-----------+
| id | fruitname | id | colorname |
+----+-----------+----+-----------+
|  1 | apple     |  1 | red       |
|  2 | orange    |  1 | red       |
|  3 | grape     |  1 | red       |
|  4 | banana    |  1 | red       |
|  1 | apple     |  2 | orange    |
|  2 | orange    |  2 | orange    |
|  3 | grape     |  2 | orange    |
|  4 | banana    |  2 | orange    |
|  1 | apple     |  3 | purple    |
|  2 | orange    |  3 | purple    |
```

```
|  3 | grape   |  3 | purple   |
|  4 | banana  |  3 | purple   |
|  1 | apple   |  4 | yellow   |
|  2 | orange  |  4 | yellow   |
|  3 | grape   |  4 | yellow   |
|  4 | banana  |  4 | yellow   |
+----+---------+----+---------+
16 rows in set (0.00 sec)
```

Sixteen rows of repeated information are probably not what you were looking for. What this query did is *literally* join a row in the `color` table to each row in the `fruit` table. Because there are four records in the `fruit` table and four entries in the `color` table, that's 16 records returned to you.

When you select from multiple tables, you must build proper WHERE clauses to ensure that you really get what you want. In the case of the `fruit` and `color` tables, what you really want is to see the `fruitname` and `colorname` records from these two tables where the IDs of each match up. This brings us to the next nuance of the query: how to indicate exactly which field you want when the fields are named the same in both tables.

Simply, you append the table name to the field name, like this:

```
tablename.fieldname
```

So, the query for selecting `fruitname` and `colorname` from both tables where the IDs match would be as follows:

```
SELECT fruitname, colorname FROM fruit, color WHERE fruit.id = color.id;
```

This query produces a better result for you:

```
+-----------+-----------+
| fruitname | colorname |
+-----------+-----------+
| apple     | red       |
| orange    | orange    |
| grape     | purple    |
| banana    | yellow    |
+-----------+-----------+
4 rows in set (0.00 sec)
```

However, if you attempt to select a column that appears in both tables with the same name, you get an ambiguity error:

```
SELECT id, fruitname, colorname FROM fruit, color
WHERE fruit.id = color.id;
```

This query produces the following error:

```
ERROR 1052: Column: 'id' in field list is ambiguous
```

If you want to select the ID from the fruit table, you use this:

```
SELECT fruit.id, fruitname, colorname FROM fruit,
color WHERE fruit.id = color.id;
```

This query produces these results:

```
+------+-----------+-----------+
| id   | fruitname | colorname |
+------+-----------+-----------+
|    1 | apple     | red       |
|    2 | orange    | orange    |
|    3 | grape     | purple    |
|    4 | banana    | yellow    |
+------+-----------+-----------+
4 rows in set (0.00 sec)
```

This was a basic example of joining two tables together for use in a single SELECT query. The JOIN keyword is an actual part of SQL, which enables you to build more complex queries.

Using JOIN

You can use several types of JOINs in MySQL, all of which refer to the order in which the tables are put together and the results are displayed. The type of JOIN used with the fruit and color tables is an INNER JOIN, although it wasn't written explicitly as such. To rewrite the SQL statement using the proper INNER JOIN syntax, you use the following:

```
SELECT fruitname, colorname FROM fruit
INNER JOIN color ON fruit.id = color.id;
```

Your resultset looks like this:

```
+-----------+-----------+
| fruitname | colorname |
+-----------+-----------+
| apple     | red       |
| orange    | orange    |
| grape     | purple    |
| banana    | yellow    |
+-----------+-----------+
4 rows in set (0.00 sec)
```

The ON clause replaces the WHERE clause you've seen before; in this instance, it tells MySQL to join together the rows in the tables where the IDs match each other. When joining tables using ON clauses, you can use any conditions that you would use in a WHERE clause, including all the various logical and arithmetic operators.

Another common type of JOIN is the LEFT JOIN. When you join two tables with LEFT JOIN, all rows from the first table are returned, regardless of whether there are matches in the second table.

Suppose that you have two tables in an address book: one called `master_name`, containing basic records, and one called `email`, containing email records. Any records in the `email` table would be tied to a particular ID of a record in the `master_name` table. For example, look at these two tables (the `master_name` and `email` tables, respectively):

```
+---------+-----------+----------+
| name_id | firstname | lastname |
+---------+-----------+----------+
| 1       | John      | Smith    |
| 2       | Jane      | Smith    |
| 3       | Jimbo     | Jones    |
| 4       | Andy      | Smith    |
| 5       | Chris     | Jones    |
| 6       | Anna      | Bell     |
| 7       | Jimmy     | Carr     |
| 8       | Albert    | Smith    |
| 9       | John      | Doe      |
+---------+-----------+----------+


+---------+-------------------+
| name_id | email             |
+---------+-------------------+
| 2       | jsmith@jsmith.com |
| 6       | annabell@aol.com  |
| 9       | jdoe@yahoo.com    |
+---------+-------------------+
```

Using `LEFT JOIN` on these two tables, you can see that if a value from the `email` table does not exist, an empty value appears in place of an email address:

```
SELECT firstname, lastname, email FROM master_name
LEFT JOIN email ON master_name.name_id = email.name_id;
```

The `LEFT JOIN` query here produces these results:

```
+-----------+----------+-------------------+
| firstname | lastname | email             |
+-----------+----------+-------------------+
| John      | Smith    |                   |
| Jane      | Smith    | jsmith@jsmith.com |
| Jimbo     | Jones    |                   |
| Andy      | Smith    |                   |
| Chris     | Jones    |                   |
| Anna      | Bell     | annabell@aol.com  |
| Jimmy     | Carr     |                   |
| Albert    | Smith    |                   |
| John      | Doe      | jdoe@yahoo.com    |
+-----------+----------+-------------------+
9 rows in set (0.00 sec)
```

A RIGHT JOIN works like LEFT JOIN but with the table order reversed. In other words, when you use a RIGHT JOIN, all rows from the second table are returned, no matter whether matches exist in the first table. However, in the case of the master_name and email tables, there are only three rows in the email table, whereas there are nine rows in the master_name table. This means that only three of the nine rows are returned by this query:

```
SELECT firstname, lastname, email FROM master_name
RIGHT JOIN email ON master_name.name_id = email.name_id;
```

The results are as expected:

```
+-----------+----------+--------------------+
| firstname | lastname | email              |
+-----------+----------+--------------------+
| Jane      | Smith    | jsmith@jsmith.com  |
| Anna      | Bell     | annabell@aol.com   |
| John      | Doe      | jdoe@yahoo.com     |
+-----------+----------+--------------------+
3 rows in set (0.00 sec)
```

Several different types of JOINs are available in MySQL, and you have learned about the most common types. To learn more about JOINs such as CROSS JOIN, STRAIGHT JOIN, and NATURAL JOIN, visit the MySQL Manual at http://dev.mysql.com/doc/refman/5.7/en/join.html. As you continue your learning elsewhere, I highly recommend learning more about and practicing JOINs; they can be one of the most powerful tools in your SQL toolkit.

Using Subqueries

Simply stated, a *subquery* is a SELECT query that appears within another SQL statement. Such queries can prove extremely useful because they often eliminate the need for bulky JOIN clauses, and in the case of application programming, subqueries can eliminate the need for multiple queries within loops.

An example of the basic subquery syntax is shown here:

```
SELECT expressions_and_columns FROM table_name WHERE somecolumn = (SUBQUERY);
```

You can also use subqueries with UPDATE and DELETE statements, as shown here:

```
DELETE FROM table_name WHERE somecolumn = (SUBQUERY);
```

or

```
UPDATE table_name SET somecolumn = 'something' WHERE somecolumn = (SUBQUERY);
```

NOTE

The outer statement of a subquery can be SELECT, INSERT, UPDATE, DELETE, as well as more advanced statements not addressed in this book (e.g. SET and DO).

The subquery must always appear in parentheses—no exceptions!

When you use subqueries, the WHERE portion of the outer statement does not have to use the = comparison operator. In addition to =, you can use any of the basic comparison operators as well as keywords such as IN, which you'll see in a moment.

The following example uses a subquery to obtain records from users in the master_name table who have an email address in the email table:

```
SELECT firstname, lastname FROM master_name
WHERE name_id IN (SELECT name_id FROM email);
```

The results of this query may look something like this:

```
+-----------+----------+
| firstname | lastname |
+-----------+----------+
| Jane      | Smith    |
| Anna      | Bell     |
| John      | Doe      |
+-----------+----------+
3 rows in set (0.00 sec)
```

For a more detailed discussion of subqueries, including limitations, see the "Subqueries" section of the MySQL Manual at http://dev.mysql.com/doc/refman/5.7/en/subqueries.html.

Using the UPDATE Statement to Modify Records

UPDATE is the SQL statement used to modify the contents of one or more columns in an existing record or set of records. The most basic UPDATE syntax looks like this:

```
UPDATE table_name
SET column1='new value',
column2='new value2'
[WHERE some_condition_is_true]
```

The guidelines for updating a record are similar to those used when inserting a record: The data you're entering must be appropriate to the data type of the field, and you must enclose your strings in single or double quotes, escaping where necessary.

For example, assume that you have a table called `fruit` containing an ID, a fruit name, and the status of the fruit (`ripe` or `rotten`):

```
+----+------------+--------+
| id | fruit_name | status |
+----+------------+--------+
|  1 | apple      | ripe   |
|  2 | orange     | rotten |
|  3 | grape      | ripe   |
|  4 | banana     | rotten |
+----+------------+--------+
4 rows in set (0.00 sec)
```

To update the status of the fruit to `ripe`, use

UPDATE fruit SET status = 'ripe';

You receive a response from the database like so:

```
Query OK, 2 rows affected (0.00 sec)
Rows matched: 4  Changed: 2  Warnings: 0
```

Take a close look at the result of the statement. It was successful, as you can tell from the `Query OK` message. Also note that only two rows were affected—if you try to set the value of a column to the value it already is, the update won't occur for that column.

The second line of the response shows that four rows were matched, and only two were changed. If you're wondering what matched, the answer is simple: Because you did not specify a particular condition for matching, the match is `all rows`.

You must be careful and use a condition when updating a table, unless you really intend to change all the columns for all records to the same value. For the sake of argument, assume that the word *grape* is spelled incorrectly in its row in the table, and you want to use UPDATE to correct this mistake:

UPDATE fruit SET fruit_name = 'grape';

This query would have horrible results:

```
Query OK, 4 rows affected (0.00 sec)
Rows matched: 4  Changed: 4  Warnings: 0
```

When you read the result, you *should* be filled with dread: Four of four records were changed, instead of only the one you intended, meaning your `fruit` table now looks like this:

```
+----+------------+--------+
| id | fruit_name | status |
+----+------------+--------+
|  1 | grape      | ripe   |
|  2 | grape      | ripe   |
|  3 | grape      | ripe   |
|  4 | grape      | ripe   |
+----+------------+--------+
4 rows in set (0.00 sec)
```

All your fruit records are now grapes. While you were attempting to correct the spelling of one field, all fields were changed because you failed to specify a condition.

Should you find yourself in an administrative position to dole out UPDATE privileges to your users, think about the responsibility you're giving to someone—one wrong move and your entire table could be grapes. In the preceding example, you could have used the id or fruit_name field in your WHERE clause, as you will see in the following section.

Conditional UPDATEs

Making a conditional UPDATE means that you are using WHERE clauses to match specific records. Using a WHERE clause in an UPDATE statement is just like using a WHERE clause in a SELECT query. All the same comparison and logical operators can be used, such as equal to, greater than, OR, and AND.

Assume that your fruit table has not been completely filled with grapes but instead contains four records, one with a spelling mistake (grappe instead of grape). The UPDATE statement to fix the spelling mistake is as follows:

```
UPDATE fruit SET fruit_name = 'grape' WHERE fruit_name = 'grappe';
```

In this case, only one row was matched and one row was changed, as shown with this result:

```
Query OK, 1 row affected (0.00 sec)
Rows matched: 1  Changed: 1  Warnings: 0
```

Your fruit table should be intact, and all fruit names should be spelled properly:

```
SELECT * FROM fruit;
```

This SELECT query shows the following:

```
+----+------------+--------+
| id | fruit_name | status |
+----+------------+--------+
|  1 | apple      | ripe   |
|  2 | pear       | ripe   |
|  3 | banana     | ripe   |
|  4 | grape      | ripe   |
+----+------------+--------+
4 rows in set (0.00 sec)
```

Using Existing Column Values with UPDATE

Another feature of UPDATE is the capability to use the current value in the record as the base value. For example, go back to the `grocery_inventory` table example, with a table that looks like this:

```
+----+------------------------+--------------------------+------------+----------+
| id | item_name              | item_desc                | item_price | curr_qty |
+----+------------------------+--------------------------+------------+----------+
| 1  | Apples                 | Beautiful, ripe apples.  | 0.25       | 1000     |
| 2  | Bunches of Grapes      | Seedless grapes.         | 2.99       | 500      |
| 3  | Bottled Water (6-pack) | 500ml spring water.      | 2.29       | 250      |
| 4  | Bottled Water (12-pack)| 500ml spring water.      | 4.49       | 500      |
| 5  | Bananas                | Bunches, green.          | 1.99       | 150      |
| 6  | Pears                  | Anjou, nice and sweet.   | 0.5        | 500      |
| 7  | Avocado                | Large Haas variety.      | 0.99       | 750      |
+----+------------------------+--------------------------+------------+----------+
7 rows in set (0.00 sec)
```

When someone purchases a product, such as an apple (id = 1), the inventory table should be updated accordingly. However, you won't know exactly what number to enter in the `curr_qty` column, just that you sold one. In this case, use the current value of the column and subtract 1, like so:

```
UPDATE grocery_inventory SET curr_qty = curr_qty - 1 WHERE id = 1;
```

This query should give you a new value of 999 in the `curr_qty` column, and indeed it does:

```
SELECT * FROM grocery_inventory;
```

The SELECT query shows the new inventory quantity:

```
+----+------------------------+--------------------------+------------+----------+
| id | item_name              | item_desc                | item_price | curr_qty |
+----+------------------------+--------------------------+------------+----------+
| 1  | Apples                 | Beautiful, ripe apples.  | 0.25       | 999      |
| 2  | Bunches of Grapes      | Seedless grapes.         | 2.99       | 500      |
| 3  | Bottled Water (6-pack) | 500ml spring water.      | 2.29       | 250      |
| 4  | Bottled Water (12-pack)| 500ml spring water.      | 4.49       | 500      |
| 5  | Bananas                | Bunches, green.          | 1.99       | 150      |
| 6  | Pears                  | Anjou, nice and sweet.   | 0.5        | 500      |
| 7  | Avocado                | Large Haas variety.      | 0.99       | 750      |
+----+------------------------+--------------------------+------------+----------+
7 rows in set (0.00 sec)
```

Using the REPLACE Statement

Another method for modifying records is to use the REPLACE statement, which is remarkably similar to the INSERT statement:

```
REPLACE INTO table_name (column list) VALUES (column values);
```

The REPLACE statement works like this: If the record you are inserting into the table contains a primary key value that matches a record already in the table, the record in the table is deleted and the new record inserted in its place.

NOTE

The REPLACE command is a MySQL-specific extension to ANSI SQL. This command mimics the action of a DELETE and re-INSERT of a particular record. In other words, you get two commands for the price of one.

Using the grocery_inventory table, the following statement replaces the entry for Apples:

```
REPLACE INTO grocery_inventory VALUES
  (1, 'Granny Smith Apples', 'Sweet!', '0.50', 1000);
```

You should see the following result:

```
Query OK, 2 rows affected (0.00 sec)
```

Notice that the result states 2 rows affected. In this case, because id is a primary key that had a matching value in the grocery_inventory table, the original row was deleted and the new row was inserted: 2 rows affected.

Use a SELECT query to verify that the entry is correct, which it is:

```
+----+-----------------------+------------------------+------------+----------+
| id | item_name             | item_desc              | item_price | curr_qty |
+----+-----------------------+------------------------+------------+----------+
| 1  | Granny Smith Apples   | Sweet!                 | 0.50       | 1000     |
| 2  | Bunches of Grapes     | Seedless grapes.       | 2.99       | 500      |
| 3  | Bottled Water (6-pack)| 500ml spring water.    | 2.29       | 250      |
| 4  | Bottled Water (12-pack)| 500ml spring water.   | 4.49       | 500      |
| 5  | Bananas               | Bunches, green.        | 1.99       | 150      |
| 6  | Pears                 | Anjou, nice and sweet. | 0.5        | 500      |
| 7  | Avocado               | Large Haas variety.    | 0.99       | 750      |
+----+-----------------------+------------------------+------------+----------+
7 rows in set (0.00 sec)
```

If you use a REPLACE statement, and the value of the primary key in the new record does not match a value for a primary key already in the table, the record is simply inserted, and only one row is affected.

Using the DELETE Statement

The basic DELETE syntax is as follows:

```
DELETE FROM table_name
[WHERE some_condition_is_true]
[LIMIT rows]
```

Notice that no column specification is used in the DELETE statement—when you use DELETE, the entire record is removed. You might recall the fiasco earlier in this chapter regarding grapes in the `fruit` table, when updating a table without specifying a condition caused an update of all records. You must be similarly careful when using DELETE.

The statement

```
DELETE FROM fruit;
```

removes all records in the table, assuming the following structure and data in a table called `fruit`:

```
+----+------------+--------+
| id | fruit_name | status |
+----+------------+--------+
|  1 | apple      | ripe   |
|  2 | pear       | rotten |
|  3 | banana     | ripe   |
|  4 | grape      | rotten |
+----+------------+--------+
4 rows in set (0.00 sec)
```

You can always verify the deletion by attempting to SELECT data from the table. If you were to issue the query

```
SELECT * FROM fruit;
```

after removing all the records, you would see that all your fruit is gone:

```
Empty set (0.00 sec)
```

Conditional DELETE

A conditional DELETE statement, just like a conditional SELECT query or UPDATE statement, means you are using WHERE clauses to match specific records. You have the full range of comparison and logical operators available to you, so you can pick and choose which records you want to delete.

A prime example is to remove all records for rotten fruit from the `fruit` table:

```
DELETE FROM fruit WHERE status = 'rotten';
```

Two records were deleted:

```
Query OK, 2 rows affected (0.00 sec)
```

Only `ripe` fruit remains:

```
+----+------------+--------+
| id | fruit_name | status |
+----+------------+--------+
|  1 | apple      | ripe   |
|  3 | banana     | ripe   |
+----+------------+--------+
2 rows in set (0.00 sec)
```

You can also use ORDER BY clauses in your DELETE statements; look at the basic DELETE syntax with the ORDER BY clause added to its structure:

```
DELETE FROM table_name
[WHERE some_condition_is_true]
[ORDER BY some_column [ASC | DESC]]
[LIMIT rows]
```

At first glance, you might wonder, "Why does it matter in what order I delete records?" But the ORDER BY clause isn't for the deletion order, it's for the sorting order of records.

In this example, a table called access_log shows access time and username:

```
+----+---------------------+----------+
| id | date_accessed       | username |
+----+---------------------+----------+
|  1 | 2016-01-06 06:09:13 | johndoe  |
|  2 | 2016-01-06 06:09:22 | janedoe  |
|  3 | 2016-01-06 06:09:39 | jsmith   |
|  4 | 2016-01-06 06:09:44 | mikew    |
+----+---------------------+----------+
4 rows in set (0.00 sec)
```

To remove the oldest record, first use ORDER BY to sort the results appropriately, and then use LIMIT to remove just one record:

```
DELETE FROM access_log ORDER BY date_accessed DESC LIMIT 1;
```

Select all from access_log and verify that only three records exist:

```
SELECT * FROM access_log;
```

The results are as follows:

```
+----+---------------------+----------+
| id | date_accessed       | username |
+----+---------------------+----------+
|  2 | 2016-01-06 06:09:22 | janedoe  |
|  3 | 2016-01-06 06:09:39 | jsmith   |
|  4 | 2016-01-06 06:09:44 | mikew    |
+----+---------------------+----------+
3 rows in set (0.00 sec)
```

Frequently Used String Functions in MySQL

MySQL's built-in string-related functions can be used in several ways within statements and queries. You can use functions in SELECT queries without specifying a table to retrieve a result of the function. Or you can use functions to enhance your SELECT query results by concatenating two fields to form a new string. The following examples are by no means a complete library of MySQL string-related functions, but are some interesting and commonly used functions. For more, see the MySQL Manual at http://dev.mysql.com/doc/refman/5.7/en/string-functions.html.

Length and Concatenation Functions

The group of length and concatenation functions focuses on the length of strings and concatenating strings together. Length-related functions include LENGTH(), OCTET_LENGTH(), CHAR_LENGTH(), and CHARACTER_LENGTH(), which do almost the same thing: count characters in a string.

```
SELECT LENGTH('This is cool!');
```

The result is this:

```
+------------------------+
| LENGTH('This is cool!') |
+------------------------+
|                     13 |
+------------------------+
1 row in set (0.00 sec)
```

The fun begins with the CONCAT() function, which concatenates two or more strings:

```
SELECT CONCAT('My', 'S', 'QL');
```

This query results in the following:

```
+------------------------+
| CONCAT('My', 'S', 'QL') |
+------------------------+
| MySQL                  |
+------------------------+
1 row in set (0.00 sec)
```

Imagine using this function with a table containing names, split into firstname and last-name fields. Instead of using two strings, use two field names to concatenate the firstname and the lastname fields. By concatenating the fields, you reduce the lines of code necessary to achieve the same result in your application:

```
SELECT CONCAT(firstname, lastname) FROM master_name;
```

This query results in the following:

```
+-----------------------------+
| CONCAT(firstname, lastname) |
+-----------------------------+
| JohnSmith                   |
| JaneSmith                   |
| JimboJones                  |
```

```
| AndySmith                 |
| ChrisJones                |
| AnnaBell                  |
| JimmyCarr                 |
| AlbertSmith               |
| JohnDoe                   |
+---------------------------+
9 rows in set (0.00 sec)
```

TIP

If you're using a field name and not a string in a function, do not enclose the field name within quotation marks. If you do, MySQL interprets the string literally. In a CONCAT() example like

```sql
SELECT CONCAT('firstname', 'lastname') FROM master_name;
```

you get the following result:

```
+-------------------------------+
| CONCAT('firstname', 'lastname') |
+-------------------------------+
| firstnamelastname             |
| firstnamelastname             |
| firstnamelastname             |
| firstnamelastname             |
| firstnamelastname             |
| firstnamelastname             |
| firstnamelastname             |
| firstnamelastname             |
| firstnamelastname             |
+-------------------------------+
9 rows in set (0.00 sec)
```

The CONCAT() function would be even more useful if there were some sort of separator between the names, and that's where the next function comes in: CONCAT_WS().

As you might have figured out, CONTACT_WS() stands for *concatenate with separator*. The separator can be anything you choose, but the following example uses whitespace:

```sql
SELECT CONCAT_WS(' ', firstname, lastname) FROM master_name;
```

This query results in the following:

```
+------------------------------------+
| CONCAT_WS(' ', firstname, lastname) |
+------------------------------------+
| John Smith                         |
| Jane Smith                         |
| Jimbo Jones                        |
```

```
| Andy Smith                         |
| Chris Jones                        |
| Anna Bell                          |
| Jimmy Carr                         |
| Albert Smith                       |
| John Doe                           |
+------------------------------------+
9 rows in set (0.00 sec)
```

If you want to shorten the width of your result table, you can use AS to name the custom result field:

```
SELECT CONCAT_WS(' ', firstname, lastname) AS fullname FROM master_name;
```

With this, you get the following results:

```
+--------------+
| fullname     |
+--------------+
| John Smith   |
| Jane Smith   |
| Jimbo Jones  |
| Andy Smith   |
| Chris Jones  |
| Anna Bell    |
| Jimmy Carr   |
| Albert Smith |
| John Doe     |
+--------------+
9 rows in set (0.00 sec)
```

Trimming and Padding Functions

MySQL provides several functions for adding and removing extra characters (including whitespace) from strings. The RTRIM() and LTRIM() functions remove whitespace from either the right or left side of a string:

```
SELECT RTRIM('stringstring   ');
```

This query results in the following, although it is difficult to see the change:

```
+-------------------------+
| RTRIM('stringstring   ') |
+-------------------------+
| stringstring            |
+-------------------------+
1 row in set (0.00 sec)
```

The LTRIM() function results are easier to see:

```
SELECT LTRIM('  stringstring');
```

This query results in the following, with the whitespace clearly stripped:

```
+------------------------+
| LTRIM('  stringstring') |
+------------------------+
| stringstring           |
+------------------------+
1 row in set (0.00 sec)
```

You may have padded strings to trim if the string is coming out of a fixed-width field and either doesn't need to carry along the additional padding or is being inserted into a varchar or other non-fixed-width field. If your strings are padded with a character besides whitespace, use the TRIM() function to name the characters you want to remove. For example, to remove the leading X characters from the string XXXneedleXXX, use

SELECT TRIM(LEADING 'X' FROM 'XXXneedleXXX');

Here is the result of this query:

```
+----------------------------------+
| TRIM(LEADING 'X' FROM 'XXXneedleXXX') |
+----------------------------------+
| needleXXX                        |
+----------------------------------+
1 row in set (0.00 sec)
```

You can use TRAILING to remove the characters from the end of the string:

SELECT TRIM(TRAILING 'X' FROM 'XXXneedleXXX');

The results of this query are as follows:

```
+-----------------------------------+
| TRIM(TRAILING 'X' FROM 'XXXneedleXXX') |
+-----------------------------------+
| XXXneedle                         |
+-----------------------------------+
1 row in set (0.00 sec)
```

If neither LEADING nor TRAILING is indicated, both are assumed:

SELECT TRIM('X' FROM 'XXXneedleXXX');

This query results in this:

```
+----------------------------+
| TRIM('X' FROM 'XXXneedleXXX') |
+----------------------------+
| needle                     |
+----------------------------+
1 row in set (0.00 sec)
```

Just as RTRIM() and LTRIM() remove padding characters, RPAD() and LPAD() add characters to a string. For example, you might want to add specific identification characters to a string that is part of an order number, in a database used for sales. When you use the padding functions, the required elements are the string, the target length, and the padding character. For example, pad the string needle with the X character until the string is 10 characters long using this query:

```
SELECT RPAD('needle', 10, 'X');
```

You will see this result:

```
+-----------------------+
| RPAD('needle', 10, 'X') |
+-----------------------+
| needleXXXX            |
+-----------------------+
1 row in set (0.00 sec)
```

Location and Position Functions

The group of location and position functions is useful for finding parts of strings within other strings. The LOCATE() function returns the position of the first occurrence of a given substring within the target string. For example, you can look for a needle in a haystack:

```
SELECT LOCATE('needle', 'haystackneedlehaystack');
```

You should see this result:

```
+-------------------------------------------+
| LOCATE('needle', 'haystackneedlehaystack') |
+-------------------------------------------+
|                                         9 |
+-------------------------------------------+
1 row in set (0.00 sec)
```

The substring needle begins at position 9 in the target string. If the substring cannot be found in the target string, MySQL returns 0 as a result.

NOTE
_____
Unlike position counting within most programming languages, which start at 0, position counting using MySQL starts at 1.
_____

An extension of the LOCATE() function is to use a third argument for starting position. If you start looking for needle in haystack before position 9, you'll receive a result. Otherwise, because needle starts at position 9, you'll receive a 0 result if you specify a greater starting position.

Substring Functions

If your goal is to extract a substring from a target string, several functions fit the bill. Given a string, starting position, and length, you can use the SUBSTRING() function. This example gets three characters from the string MySQL, starting at position 2:

```
SELECT SUBSTRING("MySQL", 2, 3);
```

The result is as follows:

```
+-------------------------+
| SUBSTRING("MySQL", 2, 3) |
+-------------------------+
| ySQ                     |
+-------------------------+
1 row in set (0.00 sec)
```

If you just want a few characters from the left or right ends of a string, use the LEFT() and RIGHT() functions:

```
SELECT LEFT("MySQL", 2);
```

The result of this query is as follows:

```
+------------------+
| LEFT("MySQL", 2) |
+------------------+
| My               |
+------------------+
1 row in set (0.00 sec)
```

Similarly, using RIGHT(), as in

```
SELECT RIGHT("MySQL", 3);
```

you get the following results:

```
+-------------------+
| RIGHT("MySQL", 3) |
+-------------------+
| SQL               |
+-------------------+
1 row in set (0.00 sec)
```

One common use of substring functions is to extract parts of order numbers to find out who placed the order. In some applications, the system is designed to automatically generate an order number containing a date, customer identification, and other information. If this order number always follows a particular pattern, such as XXXX-YYYYY-ZZ, you can use substring functions to extract the individual parts of the whole. For example, if ZZ always represents the state to which the order was shipped, you can use the RIGHT() function to extract these characters and report the number of orders shipped to a particular state.

String Modification Functions

PHP has numerous functions to modify the appearance of strings, but if you can perform the task as part of the SQL statement, all the better—let the database system do as much work as possible to alleviate the burden further on in the application layer.

The MySQL LCASE() and UCASE() functions transform a string into lowercase and uppercase, respectively. For example, the query

```
SELECT LCASE('MYSQL');
```

produces the following results:

```
+----------------+
| LCASE('MYSQL') |
+----------------+
| mysql          |
+----------------+
1 row in set (0.00 sec)
```

For uppercasing, use the following query:

```
SELECT UCASE('mysql');
```

This query produces the following results:

```
+----------------+
| UCASE('mysql') |
+----------------+
| MYSQL          |
+----------------+
1 row in set (0.00 sec)
```

TIP
_____

A practical use of the LCASE() and UCASE() functions is when you are validating user input against data stored in MySQL—such as in the case of a user login form. If you want the login process to appear not case sensitive, you could attempt to match the uppercase (or lowercase) version of the user input against the uppercase (or lowercase) version of the data stored in the table.

_____

Remember, if you use the functions with field names, don't use quotation marks. For example, you would use the query

```
SELECT UCASE(lastname) FROM master_name;
```

to produce results like this:

```
+-----------------+
| UCASE(lastname) |
+-----------------+
| BELL            |
| CARR            |
| DOE             |
| JONES           |
| JONES           |
| SMITH           |
| SMITH           |
| SMITH           |
| SMITH           |
+-----------------+
9 rows in set (0.00 sec)
```

Another fun string-manipulation function is REPEAT(), which does just what it sounds like—repeats a string for a given number of times:

```
SELECT REPEAT("bowwow", 4);
```

You should see this result:

```
+--------------------------+
| REPEAT("bowwow", 4)      |
+--------------------------+
| bowwowbowwowbowwowbowwow |
+--------------------------+
1 row in set (0.00 sec)
```

The REPLACE() function replaces all occurrences of a given string with another string. For example, the query

```
SELECT REPLACE('bowwowbowwowbowwowbowwow', 'wow', 'WOW');
```

produces the following:

```
+---------------------------------------------------+
| REPLACE('bowwowbowwowbowwowbowwow', 'wow', 'WOW')  |
+---------------------------------------------------+
| bowWOWbowWOWbowWOWbowWOW                           |
+---------------------------------------------------+
1 row in set (0.00 sec)
```

Using Date and Time Functions in MySQL

You can use MySQL's built-in date-related functions in SELECT queries, with or without specifying a table, to retrieve a result of the function. Or you can use the functions with any type of date field such as DATE, DATETIME, TIMESTAMP, and YEAR. Depending on the type of field in use, the results of the date-related functions can be more or less useful, and the following examples are by no means a complete library of MySQL date- and time-related functions. For more functions, see the MySQL Manual at http://dev.mysql.com/doc/refman/5.7/en/date-and-time-functions.html.

Working with Days

The DAYOFWEEK() and WEEKDAY() functions perform the same task but with slightly different results. Both functions find the weekday index of a date, but the difference lies in the starting day and position.

If you use DAYOFWEEK(), the first day of the week is Sunday, at position 1, and the last day of the week is Saturday, at position 7. Here's an example:

```
SELECT DAYOFWEEK('2016-07-04');
```

This query produces the following result:

```
+------------------------+
| DAYOFWEEK('2016-07-04') |
+------------------------+
|                      2 |
+------------------------+
1 row in set (0.00 sec)
```

The result shows that July 4, 2016, was weekday index 2, or Monday. Using the same date with WEEKDAY() gives you a different result with the same meaning:

```
+----------------------+
| WEEKDAY('2016-07-04') |
+----------------------+
|                    0 |
+----------------------+
1 row in set (0.00 sec)
```

The result shows that July 4, 2016, was weekday index 0. Because WEEKDAY() uses Monday as the first day of the week at position 0 and Sunday as the last day at position 6, 0 is accurate: Monday.

The DAYOFMONTH() and DAYOFYEAR() functions are more straightforward, with only one result and a range that starts at 1 and ends at 31 for DAYOFMONTH() and 366 for DAYOFYEAR(). Some examples follow:

```
SELECT DAYOFMONTH('2016-07-04');
```

This query produces the following results:

```
+--------------------------+
| DAYOFMONTH('2016-07-04') |
+--------------------------+
|                        4 |
+--------------------------+
1 row in set (0.00 sec)
```

Now try:

```
SELECT DAYOFYEAR('2016-07-04');
```

This query produces the following results:

```
+-------------------------+
| DAYOFYEAR('2016-07-04') |
+-------------------------+
|                     186 |
+-------------------------+
1 row in set (0.00 sec)
```

It might seem odd to have a function that returns the day of the month on a particular date because the day is right there in the string. But think about using these types of functions in WHERE clauses to perform comparisons on records. If you have a table that holds online orders with a field containing the date the order was placed, you can quickly get a count of the orders placed on any given day of the week, or see how many orders were placed during the first half of the month versus the second half.

The following two queries show how many orders were placed during the first three days of the week (throughout all months) and then the remaining days of the week:

```
SELECT COUNT(id) FROM orders WHERE DAYOFWEEK(date_ordered) < 4;
SELECT COUNT(id) FROM orders WHERE DAYOFWEEK(date_ordered) > 3;
```

Using DAYOFMONTH(), the following examples show the number of orders placed during the first half of any month versus the second half:

```
SELECT COUNT(id) FROM orders WHERE DAYOFMONTH(date_ordered) < 16;
SELECT COUNT(id) FROM orders WHERE DAYOFMONTH(date_ordered) > 15;
```

You can use the DAYNAME() function to add more life to your results because it returns the name of the weekday for any given date:

```
SELECT DAYNAME(date_ordered) FROM orders;
```

This query produces results such as these:

```
+----------------------+
| DAYNAME(date_ordered) |
+----------------------+
| Thursday             |
| Monday               |
| Thursday             |
| Thursday             |
| Wednesday            |
| Thursday             |
| Sunday               |
| Sunday               |
+----------------------+
8 rows in set (0.00 sec)
```

Functions aren't limited to being used in WHERE clauses—you can use them in ORDER BY clauses as well, such as the following:

```
SELECT DAYNAME(date_ordered) FROM orders
ORDER BY DAYOFWEEK(date_ordered);
```

Working with Months and Years

Days of the week are not the only parts of the calendar, and MySQL has functions specifically for months and years as well. Just like the DAYOFWEEK() and DAYNAME() functions, MONTH() and MONTHNAME() return the number of the month in a year and the name of the month for a given date. Here's an example:

```
SELECT MONTH('2016-07-04'), MONTHNAME('2016-07-04');
```

This query produces the following:

```
+---------------------+-------------------------+
| MONTH('2016-07-04') | MONTHNAME('2016-07-04') |
+---------------------+-------------------------+
|                   7 | July                    |
+---------------------+-------------------------+
1 row in set (0.00 sec)
```

Using MONTHNAME() on the orders table shows the proper results but can show a lot of repeated data:

```
+----------------------+
| MONTHNAME(date_ordered) |
+----------------------+
| November             |
| November             |
| November             |
| November             |
```

```
| November                |
| November                |
| November                |
| October                 |
+-------------------------+
8 rows in set (0.00 sec)
```

You can use DISTINCT to get nonrepetitive results:

```
SELECT DISTINCT MONTHNAME(date_ordered) FROM orders;
```

This query produces results like these:

```
+-------------------------+
| MONTHNAME(date_ordered) |
+-------------------------+
| November                |
| October                 |
+-------------------------+
2 rows in set (0.00 sec)
```

For work with years, the YEAR() function returns the year of a given date:

```
SELECT DISTINCT YEAR(date_ordered) FROM orders;
```

This query produces results like the following:

```
+--------------------+
| YEAR(date_ordered) |
+--------------------+
|               2015 |
|               2016 |
+--------------------+
1 row in set (0.00 sec)
```

Working with Weeks

Weeks can be tricky things—there can be 53 weeks in a year if Sunday is the first day of the week and four or more of the days of the same week will be in January. For example, December 30 of 2001 was a Sunday:

```
SELECT DAYNAME('2001-12-30');
```

Here's proof:

```
+-----------------------+
| DAYNAME('2001-12-30') |
+-----------------------+
| Sunday                |
+-----------------------+
1 row in set (0.00 sec)
```

That fact made December 30 of 2001 part of the 53rd week of the year if calculated using the one of the eight different ways to calculate weeks, which you can see using this query:

```
SELECT WEEK('2001-12-30', 4);
```

The week of the year is shown appropriately in the results:

```
+----------------------+
| WEEK('2001-12-30', 4) |
+----------------------+
|                   53 |
+----------------------+
1 row in set (0.00 sec)
```

The 53rd week contained December 30 and 31 and was only 2 days long; the first week of 2002 began with January 1.

If you want your weeks to start on Mondays but still want to find the week of the year, the optional second argument enables you to change the start day. A 1 indicates a week that starts on Monday and four or more days of the same week will be January. In the following examples, a Monday start day makes December 30 part of the 52nd week of 2001, but December 31 is still part of the 53rd week of 2001:

```
SELECT WEEK('2001-12-30',1);
```

This query produces the following results:

```
+----------------------+
| WEEK('2001-12-30',1) |
+----------------------+
|                   52 |
+----------------------+
1 row in set (0.00 sec)
```

While the query

```
SELECT WEEK('2001-12-31',1);
```

produces this result:

```
+----------------------+
| WEEK('2001-12-31',1) |
+----------------------+
|                   53 |
+----------------------+
1 row in set (0.00 sec)
```

The point of this exercise was to show that there are many different date and time manipulation and retrieval functions, with numerous options within each one—always refer to the MySQL Manual if you are unsure or just curious.

Working with Hours, Minutes, and Seconds

If you're using a date that includes the exact time, such as `datetime` or `timestamp`, or even just a `time` field, there are functions to find the hours, minutes, and seconds from that string. Not surprisingly, these functions are called `HOUR()`, `MINUTE()`, and `SECOND()`. `HOUR()` returns the hour in a given time, which is between 0 and 23. The range for `MINUTE()` and `SECOND()` is 0 to 59.

Here is an example:

```
SELECT HOUR('2016-01-09 07:27:49') AS hour,
MINUTE('2016-01-09 07:27:49') AS minute,
SECOND('2016-01-09 07:27:49') AS second;
```

This query produces the following:

```
+------+--------+--------+
| hour | minute | second |
+------+--------+--------+
|    7 |     27 |     49 |
+------+--------+--------+
1 row in set (0.00 sec)
```

That's a lot of queries to get at one time from a `datetime` field. However, you can put the hour and minute together and even use `CONCAT_WS()` to put the colon (`:`) between the results and get a representation of the time, like so:

```
SELECT CONCAT_WS(':',HOUR('2016-01-09 07:27:49'),
MINUTE('2016-01-09 07:27:49')) AS sample_time;
```

This query produces the following:

```
+-------------+
| sample_time |
+-------------+
| 7:27        |
+-------------+
1 row in set (0.00 sec)
```

In the next section, you learn how to use the `DATE_FORMAT()` function to properly format dates and times.

Formatting Dates and Times with MySQL

The DATE_FORMAT() function formats a date, datetime, or timestamp field into a string by using options that tell it exactly how to display the results. The syntax of DATE_FORMAT() is as follows:

```
DATE_FORMAT(date,format)
```

Table 17.2 lists many formatting options for DATE_FORMAT().

TABLE 17.2 DATE_FORMAT() **Format String Options**

Option	Result
%M	Month name (January through December)
%b	Abbreviated month name (Jan through Dec)
%m	Month, padded digits (01 through 12)
%c	Month (1 through 12)
%W	Weekday name (Sunday through Saturday)
%a	Abbreviated weekday name (Sun through Sat)
%D	Day of the month using an English suffix such as 1st, 2nd, 3rd, etc.,
%d	Day of the month, padded digits (00 through 31)
%e	Day of the month (0 through 31)
%j	Day of the year, padded digits (001 through 366)
%Y	Year, four digits
%y	Year, two digits
%X	Four-digit year for the week where Sunday is the first day (used with %V)
%x	Four-digit year for the week where Monday is the first day (used with %v)
%w	Day of the week (0=Sunday...6=Saturday)
%U	Week (0 through 53) where Sunday is the first day of the week
%u	Week (0 through 53) where Monday is the first day of the week
%V	Week (1 through 53) where Sunday is the first day of the week (used with %X)
%v	Week (1 through 53) where Monday is the first day of the week (used with %x)
%H	Hour, padded digits (00 through 23)
%k	Hour (0 through 23)
%h	Hour, padded digits (01 through 12)
%l	Hour (1 through 12)
%i	Minutes, padded digits (00 through 59)

Option	Result
%S	Seconds, padded digits (00 through 59)
%s	Seconds, padded digits (00 through 59)
%r	Time, 12-hour clock (hh:mm:ss [AP]M)
%T	Time, 24-hour clock (hh:mm:ss)
%p	AM or PM

NOTE

Any other characters used in the DATE_FORMAT() option string appear literally.

To display the 07:27 result that we rigged in the previous section, you use the %h and %i options to return the hour and minute from the date with a colon between the two options. Here's an example:

```
SELECT DATE_FORMAT('2016-01-09 07:27:49, '%h:%i') AS sample_time;
```

This query produces the following:

```
+-------------+
| sample_time |
+-------------+
| 07:27       |
+-------------+
1 row in set (0.00 sec)
```

The following are just a few more examples of the DATE_FORMAT() function in use, but this function is best understood by practicing it yourself.

```
SELECT DATE_FORMAT('2016-01-09', '%W, %M %D, %Y') AS sample_time;
```

This query produces the following output:

```
+-----------------------------+
| sample_time                 |
+-----------------------------+
| Saturday, January 9th, 2016 |
+-----------------------------+
1 row in set (0.00 sec)
```

Here's a query to format the time right this second (well, when I wrote this):

```
SELECT DATE_FORMAT(NOW(),'%W the %D of %M, %Y
around %l o\'clock %p') AS sample_time;
```

Here's the output when I ran the query:

```
+----------------------------------------------------------+
| sample_time                                              |
+----------------------------------------------------------+
| Tuesday the 13th of September, 2016 around 1 o'clock PM |
+----------------------------------------------------------+
1 row in set (0.00 sec)1 row in set (0.04 sec)
```

Take some time to play around with date formatting options on your own; there are plenty, and you'll find them easy to follow.

Performing Date Arithmetic with MySQL

MySQL has several functions to help perform date arithmetic, and this is one of the areas where it is typically more efficient to allow MySQL to do the math than your PHP script. The `DATE_ADD()` and `DATE_SUB()` functions return a result given a starting date and an interval. The syntax for both functions is as follows:

```
DATE_ADD(date,INTERVAL value type)
DATE_SUB(date,INTERVAL value type)
```

Table 17.3 shows the possible types and their expected value format.

TABLE 17.3   Values and Types in Date Arithmetic

Value	Type
Number of seconds	SECOND
Number of minutes	MINUTE
Number of hours	HOUR
Number of days	DAY
Number of months	MONTH
Number of years	YEAR
"minutes:seconds"	MINUTE_SECOND
"hours:minutes"	HOUR_MINUTE
"days hours"	DAY_HOUR
"years-months"	YEAR_MONTH
"hours:minutes:seconds"	HOUR_SECOND
"days hours:minutes"	DAY_MINUTE
"days hours:minutes:seconds"	DAY_SECOND

For example, to find the date of the current day plus 21 days, use the following:

```
SELECT DATE_ADD(NOW(), INTERVAL 21 DAY);
```

The query when I ran it produced the following result:

```
+--------------------------------+
| DATE_ADD(NOW(), INTERVAL 21 DAY) |
+--------------------------------+
| 2016-10-04 16:03:41            |
+--------------------------------+
1 row in set (0.02 sec)
```

Using DATE_SUB() produced this result:

```
+--------------------------------+
| DATE_SUB(NOW(), INTERVAL 21 DAY) |
+--------------------------------+
| 2016-08-23 16:03:58            |
+--------------------------------+
1 row in set (0.00 sec)
```

Use the expression DAY, as shown in Table 17.3, despite what might be a natural tendency to use DAYS instead of DAY. Using DAYS results in an error:

```
ERROR 1064: You have an error in your SQL syntax near 'DAYS)' at line 1
```

If you use DATE_ADD() or DATE_SUB() with a date value rather than a datetime value, the result is shown as a date value unless you use expressions related to hours, minutes, and seconds. In that case, your result is a datetime result.

For example, the result of the first query here remains a date field, whereas the second becomes a datetime:

```
SELECT DATE_ADD('2015-12-31', INTERVAL 1 DAY);
```

This query produces the following results:

```
+----------------------------------------+
| DATE_ADD('2015-12-31', INTERVAL 1 DAY) |
+----------------------------------------+
| 2016-01-01                             |
+----------------------------------------+
1 row in set (0.00 sec)
```

While the query

```
SELECT DATE_ADD('2015-12-31', INTERVAL 12 HOUR);
```

produces this result:

```
+-----------------------------------------+
| DATE_ADD('2015-12-31', INTERVAL 12 HOUR) |
+-----------------------------------------+
| 2015-12-31 12:00:00                     |
+-----------------------------------------+
1 row in set (0.00 sec)
```

You can also perform date arithmetic using the + and - operators instead of DATE_ADD() and DATE_SUB() functions, as shown here:

```
SELECT '2015-12-31' + INTERVAL 1 DAY;
```

This query produces the following result:

```
+------------------------------+
| '2015-12-31' + INTERVAL 1 DAY |
+------------------------------+
| 2016-01-01                   |
+------------------------------+
1 row in set (0.00 sec)
```

Special Functions and Conversion Features

The MySQL NOW() function returns a current datetime result and is useful for time-stamping login or access times, as well as for numerous other tasks. MySQL has a few other functions that perform similarly.

The CURDATE() and CURRENT_DATE() functions are synonymous, and each returns the current date in YYYY-MM-DD format:

```
SELECT CURDATE(), CURRENT_DATE();
```

This query produces results like the following:

```
+------------+----------------+
| CURDATE()  | CURRENT_DATE() |
+------------+----------------+
| 2016-09-13 | 2016-09-13     |
+------------+----------------+
1 row in set (0.01 sec)
```

Similarly, the CURTIME() and CURRENT_TIME() functions are synonymous and return the current time in HH:MM:SS format:

```
SELECT CURTIME(), CURRENT_TIME();
```

This query produces results like the following:

```
+-----------+----------------+
| CURTIME() | CURRENT_TIME() |
+-----------+----------------+
| 13:07:23  | 13:07:23       |
+-----------+----------------+
1 row in set (0.00 sec)
```

The NOW(), SYSDATE(), and CURRENT_TIMESTAMP() functions return values in full datetime format (YYYY-MM-DD HH:MM:SS):

SELECT NOW(), SYSDATE(), CURRENT_TIMESTAMP();

This query produces results like the following:

```
+---------------------+---------------------+---------------------+
| NOW()               | SYSDATE()           | CURRENT_TIMESTAMP() |
+---------------------+---------------------+---------------------+
| 2016-09-13 13:07:38 | 2016-09-13 13:07:38 | 2016-09-13 16:07:38 |
+---------------------+---------------------+---------------------+
1 row in set (0.00 sec)
```

The UNIX_TIMESTAMP() function returns the current date in—or converts a given date to—UNIX timestamp format. UNIX timestamp format is in seconds since the epoch, or seconds since midnight, January 1, 1970. Here's an example:

SELECT UNIX_TIMESTAMP();

This query produces results like the following for the time the query was run:

```
+------------------+
| UNIX_TIMESTAMP() |
+------------------+
|       1473782880 |
+------------------+
1 row in set (0.00 sec)
```

This query gets the UNIX timestamp for a specific date:

SELECT UNIX_TIMESTAMP('1973-12-30');

Here is the result of this query:

```
+----------------------------+
| UNIX_TIMESTAMP('1973-12-30') |
+----------------------------+
|                  126057600 |
+----------------------------+
1 row in set (0.00 sec)
```

The FROM_UNIXTIME() function performs a conversion of a UNIX timestamp to a full datetime format when used without any options:

```
SELECT FROM_UNIXTIME('1473782880');
```

The result of this query is as follows:

```
+----------------------------+
| FROM_UNIXTIME('1473782880') |
+----------------------------+
| 2016-09-13 16:08:00.000000  |
+----------------------------+
1 row in set (0.00 sec)
```

You can use the format options from the DATE_FORMAT() functions to display a timestamp in a more appealing manner:

```
SELECT FROM_UNIXTIME(UNIX_TIMESTAMP(), '%D %M %Y at %h:%i:%s');
```

Here is the result of this query at the moment I wrote it:

```
+------------------------------------------------------------+
| FROM_UNIXTIME(UNIX_TIMESTAMP(), '%D %M %Y at %h:%i:%s')     |
+------------------------------------------------------------+
| 13th September 2016 at 04:09:13                            |
+------------------------------------------------------------+
1 row in set (0.00 sec)
```

Summary

In this chapter, you learned the basics of SQL, from table creation to manipulating records. The table-creation statement requires three important pieces of information: the table name, the field name, and the field definitions. Field definitions are important because a well-designed table helps speed along your database. MySQL has three major categories of data types: numeric, date and time, and string.

The INSERT statement, used to add records to a table, names the table and columns you want to populate and then defines the values. When placing values in the INSERT statement, you must enclose strings within single or double quotes. The SELECT SQL query is used to retrieve records from specific tables. The * character enables you to select all fields for all records in a table, but you can also specify particular column names. If the resultset contains too many records for you, the LIMIT clause provides a simple method for extracting slices of results if you indicate a starting position and the number of records to return. To order the results, use the ORDER BY clause to select the columns to sort. Sorts can be performed on integers, dates, and strings, in either ascending or descending order. The default order is ascending. Without specifying an order, results display in the order they appear in the table.

You can pick and choose which records you want to return using WHERE clauses to test for the validity of conditions. Comparison or logical operators are used in WHERE clauses, and sometimes both types are used for compound statements. Selecting records from multiple tables within one statement is as advanced as it gets because JOINs require good planning to produce correct results. Common types of JOINs are INNER JOIN, LEFT JOIN, and RIGHT JOIN, although MySQL supports a few other kinds of JOINs. You also learned that you can use subqueries instead of JOINs when working with multiple tables.

The UPDATE and REPLACE statements modify existing data in your MySQL tables. UPDATE is good for changing values in specific columns and for changing values in multiple records based on specific conditions. REPLACE is a variation of INSERT that deletes and then reinserts a record with a matching primary key. Be careful when using UPDATE or REPLACE to change values in a column because failure to add a condition results in the given column being updated throughout all records in the table.

The DELETE statement removes whole records from tables. This also makes it dangerous, so be sure you give DELETE privileges only to users who can handle the responsibility. You can specify conditions when using DELETE so that records are removed only if a particular expression in a WHERE clause is true. Also, you can delete smaller sets of records in your table using a LIMIT clause. If you have an exceptionally large table, deleting portions is less resource-intensive than deleting each record in a huge table.

You were introduced to MySQL functions that perform actions on strings, dates, and times. If you have strings in MySQL that you want to concatenate or for which you want to count characters, you can use functions such as CONCAT(), CONCAT_WS(), and LENGTH(). To pad or remove padding from strings, use RPAD(), LPAD(), TRIM(), LTRIM(), and RTRIM() to get just the strings you want. You can also find the location of a string within another string, or return a part of a given string using the LOCATE(), SUBSTRING(), LEFT(), and RIGHT() functions. Functions such as LCASE(), UCASE(), REPEAT(), and REPLACE() also return variations of the original strings.

MySQL's built-in date and time functions can definitely take some of the load off your application by internally formatting dates and times and performing the date and time arithmetic. The formatting options used for the DATE_FORMAT() function provide a simple method to produce a custom display string from any sort of date field. The DATE_ADD() and DATE_SUB() functions and their numerous available interval types help you determine dates and times in the past or future. In addition, functions such as DAY(), WEEK(), MONTH(), and YEAR() prove useful for extracting parts of dates for use in WHERE or ORDER BY clauses.

Q&A

Q. What characters can I use to name my tables and fields, and what is the character limit?

A. The maximum length of database, table, and field names is 64 characters. Any character you can use in a directory name or filename, you can use in database and table names, except the slash (/) and period (.) characters. These limitations are in place because MySQL creates directories and files in your file system, which correspond to database and table names. No character limitations (besides length) apply in field names.

Q. Can I use multiple functions in one statement, such as making a concatenated string all uppercase?

A. Sure. Just be mindful of your opening and closing parentheses. This example shows how to uppercase the concatenated first and last names from the master name table:

```
SELECT UCASE(CONCAT_WS(' ', firstname, lastname)) FROM master_name;
```

The result would be something like this:

```
+-------------------------------------------+
| UCASE(CONCAT_WS(' ', firstname, lastname)) |
+-------------------------------------------+
| JOHN SMITH                                |
| JANE SMITH                                |
| JIMBO JONES                               |
| ANDY SMITH                                |
| CHRIS JONES                               |
| ANNA BELL                                 |
| JIMMY CARR                                |
| ALBERT SMITH                              |
| JOHN DOE                                  |
+-------------------------------------------+
9 rows in set (0.00 sec)
```

If you want to uppercase just the last name, use this:

```
SELECT CONCAT_WS(' ', firstname, UCASE(lastname)) FROM master_name;
```

The result would be something like this:

```
+-------------------------------------------+
| CONCAT_WS(' ', firstname, UCASE(lastname)) |
+-------------------------------------------+
| John SMITH                                |
| Jane SMITH                                |
| Jimbo JONES                               |
| Andy SMITH                                |
| Chris JONES                               |
| Anna BELL                                 |
```

```
| Jimmy CARR                                     |
| Albert SMITH                                   |
| John DOE                                       |
+------------------------------------------------+
9 rows in set (0.00 sec)
```

Workshop

The Workshop is designed to help you review what you've learned and begin putting your knowledge into practice.

Quiz

1. The integer 56678685 could be which data type(s)?

2. How would you define a field that could contain only the following strings: `apple`, `pear`, `banana`, `cherry`?

3. What would be the `LIMIT` clauses for selecting the first 25 records of a table? Then the next 25?

4. How do you formulate a string comparison using `LIKE` to match first names of John or Joseph?

5. How do you explicitly refer to a field called `id` in a table called `table1`?

6. Write a SQL query that joins two tables, `orders` and `items_ordered`, each of which has a primary key of `order_id`. From the `orders` table, select the following fields: `order_name` and `order_date`. From the `items_ordered` table, select the `item_description` field.

7. Write a SQL query to find the starting position of the substring `"grape"` in the string `"applepearbananagrape"`.

8. Write a query that selects the last five characters from the string `"applepearbananagrape"`.

Answers

1. `MEDIUMINT`, `INT`, or `BIGINT`

2. `ENUM ('apple', 'pear', 'banana', 'cherry')`

   or

   `SET ('apple', 'pear', 'banana', 'cherry')`

3. `LIMIT 0, 25` and `LIMIT 25, 25`

4. `LIKE 'Jo%'`

5. Use `table1.id` instead of `id` in your query.

6. `SELECT orders.order_name, orders.order_date, items_ordered.item_description FROM orders LEFT JOIN items_ordered ON orders.order_id = items_ordered.id;`

7. `SELECT LOCATE('grape', 'applepearbananagrape');`

8. `SELECT RIGHT("applepearbananagrape", 5);`

Exercises

▶ Take the time to create some sample tables and practice using basic `INSERT` statements and `SELECT` queries.

Interacting with MySQL Using PHP

What You'll Learn in This Chapter:

▶ How to connect to MySQL using PHP

▶ How to insert and select data through PHP scripts

Now that you have learned the basics of PHP and the basics of working with MySQL, you are ready to make the two interact. Think of PHP as a conduit to MySQL: The statements and queries you learned to use in the previous chapter are the same statements and queries that you send to MySQL in this chapter, only this time you send them with PHP. Putting these two pieces together will help form a solid foundation for dynamic applications.

MySQL or MySQLi?

If you are returning to PHP from working with it years earlier, you might have used the `mysql_*` extension and its family of functions.

However, since the release of MySQL 4.1.3 (well over a decade ago), the database system includes functionality necessitating new communications methods in PHP, which are now encompassed in the `mysqli_*` family of functions. A mention of the old extension is still warranted, however, because you are still likely to find code examples all over the Internet that use the `mysql` extension instead of `mysqli`.

All code in this chapter, and throughout the rest of this book, uses the `mysqli` extension for interacting with MySQL using PHP. For more information, see the PHP Manual chapter titled "MySQL Improved Extension," at http://www.php.net/mysqli.

Connecting to MySQL with PHP

To successfully use PHP functions to communicate with MySQL, you must have MySQL running at a location to which your web server can connect (not necessarily the same machine as your web server). You also must have created a user (with a password), and you must know the name of the database to which you want to connect. If you got up and running using Appendix A, "Installation QuickStart Guide with XAMPP," or Appendix B, "Installing and Configuring MySQL," and Appendix D, "Installing and Configuring PHP," you should already have taken care of this. If you are using PHP and MySQL as part of a hosting package at an Internet service provider, make sure you have either been given or have created a username, password, and database name before proceeding with the rest of this chapter.

In all script examples in this chapter, the database name is testDB, the user is testuser, and the password is somepass. Substitute your own information when you use these scripts.

NOTE

All code in this chapter (as well as other chapters moving forward) reflect the procedural use of the mysqli_* family of functions. You can also use these functions in an object-oriented way. For more information on that, visit the PHP Manual at http://www.php.net/mysqli.

If you are coming to PHP from an object-oriented programming language or have an object-oriented mindset, I recommend reviewing the object-oriented functionality in the PHP Manual and substituting it where appropriate—conceptually, these processes are all quite similar.

However, if you are new to programming, or have not yet embraced an object-oriented mindset, there is nothing wrong with learning the procedural style or using it in your daily work. I continue to use procedural programming throughout this book because it has proven to be the best way for new programmers to understand the processes.

Making a Connection

The basic syntax for a connection to MySQL is as follows:

```
$mysqli = mysqli_connect("hostname", "username", "password", "database");
```

The value of $mysqli is the result of the function and is used in later functions for communicating with MySQL.

With sample values inserted, the connection code looks like this:

```
$mysqli = mysqli_connect("localhost", "testuser", "somepass", "testDB");
```

Listing 18.1 is a working example of a connection script. It creates a new connection in line 2 and then tests to see whether an error occurred. If an error occurred, line 5 prints an error message and uses the mysqli_connect_error() function to print the message. If no error occurs, line 8 prints a message that includes host information resulting from calling the mysqli_get_host_info() function.

LISTING 18.1   A Simple Connection Script

```
 1:  <?php
 2:  $mysqli = new mysqli("localhost", "testuser", "somepass", "testDB");
 3:
 4:  if (mysqli_connect_errno()) {
 5:      printf("Connect failed: %s\n", mysqli_connect_error());
 6:      exit();
 7:  } else {
 8:       printf("Host information: %s\n", mysqli_get_host_info($mysqli));
 9:  }
10:  ?>
```

Save this script as `mysqlconnect.php` and place it in the document area of your web server. Access the script with your web browser and you will see something like the following, if the connection was successful:

```
Host information: localhost via TCP/IP
```

You might also see something like this:

```
Host information: localhost via UNIX socket
```

If the connection fails, an error message is printed. Line 5 generates an error via the `mysqli_connect_error()` function. An example is shown here, which is the output that occurs when the password is changed to an incorrect password for this user:

```
Connect failed: Access denied for user 'testuser'@'localhost' (using password: YES)
```

However, if the connection is successful, line 8 prints the output of `mysqli_get_host_info()`, as in the preceding examples.

Although the connection closes when the script finishes its execution, it is a good practice to close the connection explicitly. You can see how to do this in line 9 of Listing 18.2, using the `mysqli_close()` function.

LISTING 18.2   The Modified Simple Connection Script

```
 1:  <?php
 2:  $mysqli = new mysqli("localhost", "testuser", "somepass", "testDB");
 3:
 4:  if (mysqli_connect_errno()) {
 5:      printf("Connect failed: %s\n", mysqli_connect_error());
 6:      exit();
 7:  } else {
 8:      printf("Host information: %s\n", mysqli_get_host_info($mysqli));
 9:      mysqli_close($mysqli);
10:  }
11:  ?>
```

We did not use the `mysqli_close()` function after line 5 because if line 5 is executed, it is because no connection was made in the first place.

That's all there is to basic connectivity to MySQL using PHP. The next section covers the query execution functions, which are much more interesting than simply opening a connection and letting it sit there.

Executing Queries

Half the battle in executing MySQL statements and queries using PHP is knowing how to write the SQL—and you've already learned the basics of this in the previous chapter. The `mysqli_query()` function in PHP is used to send your SQL query to MySQL.

In your script, first make the connection and then execute a statement. The script in Listing 18.3 creates a simple table called `testTable`.

LISTING 18.3   A Script to Create a Table

```
1:   <?php
2:   $mysqli = mysqli_connect("localhost", "testuser", "somepass", "testDB");
3:
4:   if (mysqli_connect_errno()) {
5:        printf("Connect failed: %s\n", mysqli_connect_error());
6:        exit();
7:   } else {
8:        $sql = "CREATE TABLE testTable
9:               (id INT NOT NULL PRIMARY KEY AUTO_INCREMENT,
10:              testField VARCHAR(75))";
11:       $res = mysqli_query($mysqli, $sql);
12:
13:       if ($res === TRUE) {
14:            echo "Table testTable successfully created.";
15:       } else {
16:           printf("Could not create table: %s\n", mysqli_error($mysqli));
17:       }
18:
19:       mysqli_close($mysqli);
20:   }
21:   ?>
```

NOTE

When you issue statements and queries via a script, the semicolon at the end of the SQL statement is not required like it is when accessing MySQL directly via the command-line interface.

In lines 8–10, the text that makes up the SQL statement is assigned to the variable $sql. This is an arbitrary name, and you do not even need to place the content of your SQL query in a separate variable. (It appears as such in the example so that the different parts of this process are clear to you.)

The mysqli_query function returns a value of true or false, and this value is checked in the if...else statement beginning in line 13. If the value of $res is true, a success message is printed to the screen. If you access MySQL through the command-line interface to verify the creation of the testTable table, you will see the following output of DESCRIBE testTable:

```
+-----------+-------------+------+-----+---------+----------------+
| Field     | Type        | Null | Key | Default | Extra          |
+-----------+-------------+------+-----+---------+----------------+
| id        | int(11)     | NO   | PRI | NULL    | auto_increment |
| testField | varchar(75) | YES  |     | NULL    |                |
+-----------+-------------+------+-----+---------+----------------+
```

If this is the case, congratulations! You have successfully created a table in your MySQL database using PHP.

However, if the value of $res is not true and the table was not created, an error message appears, generated by the mysqli_error() function.

Retrieving Error Messages

Take some time to familiarize yourself with the mysqli_error() function; it will become your friend. When used in conjunction with the PHP die() construct, which simply exits the script at the point at which die() appears, the mysqli_error() function returns a helpful error message when you make a mistake.

For example, now that you have created a table called testTable, you cannot execute that script again without an error. Try to execute the script again; when you execute the script, you should see something like the following in your web browser:

```
Could not create table: Table 'testtable' already exists
```

How exciting! Move on to the next section to start inserting data into your table, and soon you'll be retrieving and formatting it via PHP.

Working with MySQL Data

Inserting, updating, deleting, and retrieving data all revolve around the use of the mysqli_query() function to execute the basic SQL statements you learned about in Chapter 17, "Learning Basic SQL Commands." For INSERT, UPDATE, and DELETE statements, no additional scripting is required after the query has been executed because you're not displaying any results (unless you want to). When using SELECT queries, you have a few options for displaying the data retrieved by your query. After an important message about avoiding SQL injection, we start with the basics and insert some data so that you'll have something to retrieve later.

Avoiding SQL Injection

In the table-creation script in Listing 18.3, the data used in the SQL statement was hard-coded into the script. However, in the types of dynamic websites or web-based applications that you are likely to build, you will most often be inserting (INSERT) data into a table or selecting (SELECT) from a table based on user input from a form or other process. If you do not pay attention to this type of user input and do not sanitize it before using it in your queries, you are vulnerable to SQL injection–based security issues.

SQL injection happens when nefarious individuals take the opportunity to type full or partial SQL statements and queries in your form fields, with the assumption that when the script executes these statements and queries, security will be breached and data potentially exposed.

NOTE

A famous XKCD comic strip, informally known as the "Little Bobby Tables" strip, perfectly illustrates the issue of SQL injections. This comic strip is often referenced in discussion forums and other programming-related help sites, with respondents saying "Don't forget Little Bobby Tables!" when providing answers to form input and query-related questions. You can see the comic strip at http://xkcd.com/327/.

Take the following example, which attempts to gather user information from a table called users where the name field matches a value completed in a form; this is much like a web-based login process:

```
$sql = SELECT * FROM users
WHERE name = '".$_POST['username_from_form']."';
```

Imagine the value entered in the username_from_form field is something like this:

```
' or '1'='1
```

This results in a full query, as follows:

```
SELECT * FROM users
WHERE name = ' ' or '1'='1';
```

This query always results in a valid response, because 1 = 1 always returns true.

You probably get the idea, but if not, the PHP Manual has several more examples on the SQL Injection page at http://www.php.net/manual/en/security.database.sql-injection.php. Throughout this book, the code examples limit vulnerability to SQL injection, with one exception: displaying error messages. While you are learning, and operating in a development rather than production environment, I support the printing of error messages to the screen so that you understand what is happening (or not happening). In a production environment, you should suppress error messages, especially when they show the names of database users or tables, to further limit the ability for SQL injection attacks.

TIP

After you have mastered the concepts involved with working with MySQL and PHP in the procedural ways indicated in this chapter, we'll take a look at the PDO (PHP Data Objects) abstraction layer for further hardening of your production applications, as described here: http://www.php.net/manual/en/book.pdo.php.

Inserting Data with PHP

The easiest (and safest) method for inserting data at this stage in the game is to simply hard-code the INSERT statement, as shown in Listing 18.4.

LISTING 18.4   A Script to Insert a Record

```
1:  <?php
2:  $mysqli = mysqli_connect("localhost", "testuser", "somepass", "testDB");
3:
4:  if (mysqli_connect_errno()) {
5:      printf("Connect failed: %s\n", mysqli_connect_error());
6:      exit();
7:  } else {
8:      $sql = "INSERT INTO testTable (testField) VALUES ('some value')";
9:      $res = mysqli_query($mysqli, $sql);
10:
11:     if ($res === TRUE) {
12:         echo "A record has been inserted.";
13:     } else {
14:         printf("Could not insert record: %s\n", mysqli_error($mysqli));
15:     }
16:
17:     mysqli_close($mysqli);
18: }
19: ?>
```

The only changes between this script—for record insertion—and the script in Listing 18.3 for table creation are the SQL query stored in the $sql variable on line 8 and the text modifications on lines 12 and 14. The connection code and the structure for issuing a query remain the same. In fact, most procedural code for accessing MySQL falls into this same type of code template.

Call this script `mysqlinsert.php` and place it on your web server. Running this script results in the addition of a row to the `testTable` table. To enter more records than the one shown in the script, either you can make a long list of hard-coded SQL statements and use `mysqli_query()` multiple times to execute these statements (an atypical use in real-world applications) or you can create a form-based interface to the record-addition script, which we do next.

To create the form for this script, you need only one field, because the `id` field can automatically increment based on the table definition. The action of the form is the name of the record-addition script; let's call it `insert.php`. Your HTML form might look something like Listing 18.5.

LISTING 18.5 An Insert Form

```
<!DOCTYPE html>
<html lang="en">
<head>
<title>Record Insertion Form</title>
</head>
<body>
  <form action="insert.php" method="post">
    <p><label for="testfield">Text to Add:</label><br>
    <input type="text" id="testfield" name="testfield" size="30"></p>
    <button type="submit" name="submit" value="insert">Insert Record</button>
  </form>
</body>
</html>
```

Save this file as `insert_form.html` and put it in the document root of your web server. Next, create the `insert.php` script shown in Listing 18.6. The value entered in the form replaces the hard-coded values in the SQL query with a variable called `$_POST['testfield']` (guarded against SQL injection, of course).

LISTING 18.6 An Insert Script Used with the Form

```
1:  <?php
2:  $mysqli = mysqli_connect("localhost", "testuser", "somepass", "testDB");
3:
4:  if (mysqli_connect_errno()) {
5:      printf("Connect failed: %s\n", mysqli_connect_error());
6:      exit();
7:  } else {
8:      $clean_text = mysqli_real_escape_string($mysqli, $_POST['testfield']);
9:      $sql = "INSERT INTO testTable (testField)
10:             VALUES ('".$clean_text."')";
11:     $res = mysqli_query($mysqli, $sql);
12:
13:     if ($res === TRUE) {
```

```
14:                echo "A record has been inserted.";
15:        } else {
16:            printf("Could not insert record: %s\n", mysqli_error($mysqli));
17:        }
18:
19:        mysqli_close($mysqli);
20:    }
21:    ?>
```

The only changes between this script and the script in Listing 18.4 are in line 8, where the form input is sanitized to avoid SQL injection, and in line 10, where we use the sanitized string $clean_text in place of the hard-coded text string from the previous example. To sanitize the input, we use the mysqli_real_escape_string() function; this function requires that a connection has already been made, and so it is placed in this position within the else portion of the if...else statement.

Save the script as insert.php and put it in the document root of your web server. In your web browser, access the HTML form that you created. It should look something like Figure 18.1.

FIGURE 18.1
The HTML form for adding a record.

Enter a string in the Text to Add field, as shown in Figure 18.2.

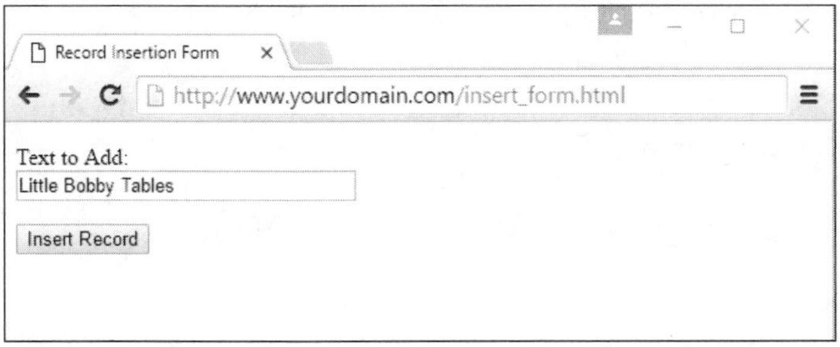

FIGURE 18.2
Text typed in the form field.

Finally, click the Insert Record button to execute the `insert.php` script and insert the record. If successful, you will see results similar to Figure 18.3.

FIGURE 18.3
The record has been successfully added.

To verify the work that has been done with PHP, you can use the MySQL command-line interface to view the records in the table using a SELECT query:

```
SELECT * FROM testTable;
```

The output should be as follows:

```
+----+---------------------+
| id | testField           |
+----+---------------------+
|  1 | some value          |
|  2 | Little Bobby Tables |
+----+---------------------+
2 rows in set (0.00 sec)
```

Next, you learn how to retrieve and format results with PHP, and not just through the MySQL command-line interface as you have previously.

Retrieving Data with PHP

Because you have a few rows in your `testTable` table, you can write a PHP script to retrieve that data. Starting with the basics, we write a script that issues a SELECT query but doesn't overwhelm you with result data. Let's just get the number of rows. To do this, use the `mysqli_num_rows()` function; see line 12 of Listing 18.7.

LISTING 18.7 A Script to Retrieve Data

```php
1:   <?php
2:   $mysqli = mysqli_connect("localhost", "testuser", "somepass", "testDB");
3:
4:   if (mysqli_connect_errno()) {
5:       printf("Connect failed: %s\n", mysqli_connect_error());
6:       exit();
7:   } else {
```

```
8:       $sql = "SELECT * FROM testTable";
9:       $res = mysqli_query($mysqli, $sql);
10:
11:      if ($res) {
12:          $number_of_rows = mysqli_num_rows($res);
13:          printf("Result set has %d rows.\n", $number_of_rows);
14:      } else {
15:          printf("Could not retrieve records: %s\n", mysqli_error($mysqli));
16:      }
17:
18:      mysqli_free_result($res);
19:      mysqli_close($mysqli);
20:  }
21:  ?>
```

Save this script as count.php, place it in your web server document directory, and access it through your web browser. You should see a message like the following. (The actual number will vary depending on how many records you inserted into the table.)

```
Result set has 4 rows.
```

Line 12 uses the mysqli_num_rows() function to retrieve the number of rows in the resultset ($res), and it places the value in a variable called $number_of_rows. Line 13 prints this number to your browser. The number should be equal to the number of records you inserted during testing.

There's a new function in this listing that was not in previous listings. Line 18 shows the use of the mysqli_free_result() function. Using mysqli_free_result() before closing the connection with mysqli_close() ensures that all memory associated with the query and the result is freed for use by other scripts.

Now that you know there are some records in the table (four, according to the output), you can get fancy and fetch the actual contents of those records. You can do this in a few ways, but the easiest method is to retrieve each row from the table as an array.

You use a while statement to go through each record in the resultset, placing the values of each field into a specific variable and then displaying the results onscreen. The syntax of mysqli_fetch_array() is as follows:

```
$newArray = mysqli_fetch_array($result_set);
```

Follow along using the sample script in Listing 18.8.

LISTING 18.8   A Script to Retrieve Data and Display Results

```
1:   <?php
2:   $mysqli = mysqli_connect("localhost", "testuser", "somepass", "testDB");
3:
4:   if (mysqli_connect_errno()) {
```

```
 5:        printf("Connect failed: %s\n", mysqli_connect_error());
 6:        exit();
 7:   } else {
 8:        $sql = "SELECT * FROM testTable";
 9:        $res = mysqli_query($mysqli, $sql);
10:
11:        if ($res) {
12:            while ($newArray = mysqli_fetch_array($res, MYSQLI_ASSOC)) {
13:                $id  = $newArray['id'];
14:                $testField = $newArray['testField'];
15:                echo "The ID is ".$id." and the text is: ".$testField."<br>";
16:            }
17:        } else {
18:            printf("Could not retrieve records: %s\n", mysqli_error($mysqli));
19:        }
20:
21:        mysqli_free_result($res);
22:        mysqli_close($mysqli);
23:   }
24:   ?>
```

Save this script as `select.php`, place it in your web server document directory, and access it through your web browser. You should see a message for each record entered into `testTable`, as shown in Figure 18.4. This message is created in the `while` loop in lines 12 through 15.

FIGURE 18.4
Selecting records from MySQL.

As you can see, you could create an entire database-driven application using just four or five MySQLi functions. This chapter barely scratched the surface of using PHP with MySQL; there are many more MySQLi functions in PHP that you'll learn about in context throughout this book.

Additional MySQL Functions in PHP

More than 100 MySQL-specific functions are available through the MySQLi interface in PHP. Most of these functions are simply alternative methods of retrieving data or are used to gather information about the table structure in question. Throughout this book, especially in the upcoming project-related chapters, you'll gradually be introduced to more of the MySQL-specific functions in PHP. However, for a complete list of functions, with practical examples, visit the MySQLi section of the PHP Manual at http://www.php.net/mysqli.

Summary

Using PHP and MySQL to create dynamic, database-driven websites is a breeze. Just remember that the PHP functions are essentially a gateway to the database server; anything you can enter using the MySQL command-line interface, you can use with the `mysqli_query()` function. You also learned how to avoid SQL injections when receiving user input from a form.

To connect to MySQL with PHP, you need to know your MySQL username, password, and database name. When connected, you can issue standard SQL commands with the `mysqli_query()` function. If you have issued a SELECT command, you can use `mysqli_num_rows()` to count the records returned in the resultset. If you want to display the data found, you can use `mysqli_fetch_array()` to get all the results during a loop and display them onscreen.

Q&A

Q. Is it possible to use both `mysql_*` and `mysqli_*` functions in one application?

A. If PHP was built with both libraries enabled, you can use either set of functions to talk to MySQL. However, be aware that if you use the `mysql_*` set of functions with a version of MySQL later than 4.1.3, you cannot access certain new functionality. In addition, if you are inconsistent with your usage throughout your application, maintenance and upkeep of your application will be time-consuming and produce less-than-optimal results.

Workshop

The Workshop is designed to help you review what you've learned and begin putting your knowledge into practice.

Quiz

1. What is the primary function used to make the connection between PHP and MySQL, and what information is necessary?

2. Which PHP function retrieves the text of a MySQL error message?

3. Which PHP function counts the number of records in a resultset?

Answers

1. The `mysqli_connect()` function creates a connection to MySQL and requires the hostname, username, and password.

2. The `mysqli_error()` function returns a MySQL error message.

3. The `mysqli_num_rows()` function counts the number of records in a resultset. You can also achieve the same goal by counting the number of unique IDs in the table and returning that number as a result, e.g. `SELECT COUNT(id) FROM tablename`.

Exercises

▶ Using an HTML form and PHP script, create a table that contains fields for a person's first and last names. Create another script that adds records to the table.

▶ Once you have records in your table, create a PHP script that retrieves and displays these records in alphabetical order by last name.

Creating a Simple Discussion Forum

What You'll Learn in This Chapter:

▶ How to create tables for a simple discussion forum

▶ How to create input forms for a simple discussion forum

▶ How to display a simple discussion forum

▶ How to add JavaScript to improve a discussion forum

In this chapter, you learn the design process behind a simple discussion forum. This includes developing the database tables and user input forms and displaying the results. When broken into pieces like this, such a task seems simple—and it is! The ultimate goal is to understand the concepts and relationships that go into making something like a discussion forum, not to create the world's most full-functioned system. In fact, you'll see it's quite sparse, but it sure is relational.

Designing the Database Tables

Think of the basic components of a forum: topics and posts. A forum—if properly used by its patrons—should have several topics, and each of those topics will have one or more posts submitted by users. Knowing that, you should realize that the posts are tied to the topics through a key field. This key forms the relationship between the two tables.

Think about the requirements for the topics themselves. You definitely need a field for the title, and subsequently you might want fields to hold the creation time and the identification of the user who created the topic. Similarly, think of the requirements for the posts: You want to store the text of the post, the time of its creation, and the identity of person who created it. Most important, you need that key to tie the post to the topic.

The following two statements, called `forum_topics` and `forum_posts`, create these tables:

```
CREATE TABLE forum_topics (
    topic_id INT NOT NULL PRIMARY KEY AUTO_INCREMENT,
    topic_title VARCHAR (150),
```

```
    topic_create_time DATETIME,
    topic_owner VARCHAR (150)
);
CREATE TABLE forum_posts (
    post_id INT NOT NULL PRIMARY KEY AUTO_INCREMENT,
    topic_id INT NOT NULL,
    post_text TEXT,
    post_create_time DATETIME,
    post_owner VARCHAR (150)
);
```

NOTE
_____

This simple forum example identifies users by their email addresses and does not require any sort of login sequence.

_____

You should now have two empty tables waiting for some input. In the next section, you create the input forms for adding a topic and a post.

Creating an Include File for Common Functions

Previous chapters used an included file of common functions to make your scripts more concise and to help manage information that might change over time, such as a database username and password. The same thing is true in this chapter. Listing 19.1 contains the code shared by the scripts in this chapter.

LISTING 19.1 Common Functions in an Included File
_____

```
1:  <?php
2:  function doDB() {
3:      global $mysqli;
4:
5:      //connect to server and select database; you may need it
6:      $mysqli = mysqli_connect("localhost", "testuser",
7:          "somepass", "testDB");
8:
9:      //if connection fails, stop script execution
10:     if (mysqli_connect_errno()) {
11:         printf("Connect failed: %s\n", mysqli_connect_error());
12:         exit();
13:     }
14: }
15: ?>
```

_____

Lines 2–14 set up the database connection function, doDB. If the connection cannot be made, the script exits when this function is called; otherwise, it makes the value of $mysqli available to other parts of your script.

Save this file as db_include.php and place it on your web server. The other code listings in this chapter include this file within the first few lines of the script.

Creating the Input Forms and Scripts

Before you can add any posts, you must add a topic to the forum. It is common practice in forum creation to add the topic and the first post in that topic at the same time, because from a user's point of view, it doesn't make much sense to add a topic and then go back, select the topic, and add a reply. You want the process to be as smooth as possible. Listing 19.2 shows the form for a new topic creation, which includes a space for the first post in the topic.

LISTING 19.2   Form for Adding a Topic

```
<!DOCTYPE html>
<html lang="en">
<head>
  <title>Add a Topic</title>
</head>
<body>
  <h1>Add a Topic</h1>
  <form method="post" action="do_addtopic.php">

   <p><label for="topic_owner">Your Email Address:</label><br>
   <input type="email" id="topic_owner" name="topic_owner" size="40"
          maxlength="150" required="required"></p>

   <p><label for="topic_title">Topic Title:</label><br>
   <input type="text" id="topic_title" name="topic_title" size="40"
          maxlength="150" required="required"></p>
   <p><label for="post_text">Post Text:</label><br>
   <textarea id="post_text" name="post_text" rows="8"
             cols="40"></textarea></p>

   <button type="submit" name="submit" value="submit">Add Topic</button>

  </form>
</body>
</html>
```

Seems simple enough: The three fields shown in the form, which you can see in Figure 19.1, are all you need to complete both tables; your script and database can fill in the rest. Save Listing

19.2 as something like `addtopic.html` and put it in your web server document root so that you can follow along.

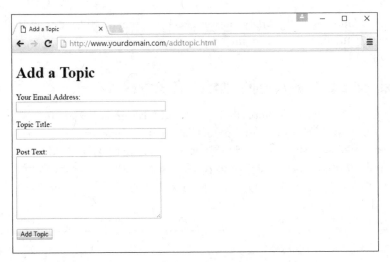

FIGURE 19.1
The topic-creation form.

To create the entry in the `forum_topics` table, you use the values from the `$_POST['topic_title']` and `$_POST['topic_owner']` variables from the input form. The `topic_id` and `topic_create_time` fields will be automatically incremented and added, respectively, via the `now()` MySQL function.

Similarly, in the `forum_posts` table, you use the values of `$_POST['post_text']` and `$_POST['topic_owner']` from the input form, and the `post_id`, `post_create_time`, and the `topic_id` fields will be automatically incremented or otherwise supplied. Because you need a value for the `topic_id` field to be able to complete the entry in the `forum_posts` table, you know that this query must happen after the query to insert the record in the `forum_topics` table. Listing 19.3 creates the script to add these records to the table.

LISTING 19.3   **Script for Adding a Topic**

```
1:  <?php
2:  include 'db_include.php';
3:  doDB();
4:
5:  //check for required fields from the form
6:  if ((!$_POST['topic_owner']) || (!$_POST['topic_title']) ||
7:      (!$_POST['post_text'])) {
8:    header("Location: addtopic.html");
9:    exit;
10: }
```

```
11:
12: //create safe values for input into the database
13: $clean_topic_owner = mysqli_real_escape_string($mysqli,
14:                      $_POST['topic_owner']);
15: $clean_topic_title = mysqli_real_escape_string($mysqli,
16:                      $_POST['topic_title']);
17: $clean_post_text = mysqli_real_escape_string($mysqli,
18:                      $_POST['post_text']);
19:
20: //create and issue the first query
21: $add_topic_sql = "INSERT INTO forum_topics
22:                    (topic_title, topic_create_time, topic_owner)
23:                   VALUES ('".$clean_topic_title ."', now(),
24:                   '".$$clean_topic_owner."')";
25:
26: $add_topic_res = mysqli_query($mysqli, $add_topic_sql)
27:                  or die(mysqli_error($mysqli));
28:
29: //get the id of the last query
30: $topic_id = mysqli_insert_id($mysqli);
31:
32: //create and issue the second query
33: $add_post_sql = "INSERT INTO forum_posts
34:                    (topic_id, post_text, post_create_time, post_owner)
35:                   VALUES ('".$topic_id."', '".$clean_post_text."',
36:                   now(), '".$clean_topic_owner."')";
37:
38: $add_post_res = mysqli_query($mysqli, $add_post_sql)
39:                  or die(mysqli_error($mysqli));
40: //close connection to MySQL
41: mysqli_close($mysqli);
42:
43: //create nice message for user
44: $display_block = "<p>The <strong>".$_POST["topic_title"]."</strong>
45:     topic has been created.</p>";
46: ?>
47: <!DOCTYPE html>
48: <html>
49: <head>
50:   <title>New Topic Added</title>
51: </head>
52: <body>
53:   <h1>New Topic Added</h1>
54:   <?php echo $display_block; ?>
55: </body>
56: </html>
```

Lines 2–3 include the file of user-created functions and call the database connection function. Next, lines 6–10 check for the three required fields needed to complete both tables (the topic owner, a topic title, and some text for the post). If any one of these fields is not present, the user is redirected to the original form. Lines 13–18 create database-safe versions of the contents of those variables.

Lines 21–27 create and insert the first query, which adds the topic to the `forum_topics` table. Note that no value is entered for the `id` field in the table; the automatically incrementing value is added by the system per the original table definition. The MySQL `now()` function is used to timestamp the record with the current time at insertion. The other fields in the record are completed using values from the form.

Line 30 shows the use of a handy function: `mysqli_insert_id()`. This function retrieves the primary key ID of the last record inserted into the database by this script. In this case, `mysqli_insert_id()` gets the `id` value from the `forum_topics` table, which will become the entry for the `topic_id` field in the `forum_posts` table.

Lines 33–39 create and insert the second query, again using a mixture of information known and supplied by the system. The second query adds the text of the user's post to the `forum_posts` table. Lines 44–45 simply create a display string for the user, and the rest of the script rounds out the HTML that is rendered by the browser.

Save this listing as `do_addtopic.php`—the name of the action in the previous script—and place it in the document root of your web server. Complete the form you created from Listing 19.1 and then submit it, and you should see the New Topic Added message. Figures 19.2 and 19.3 show the sequence of events.

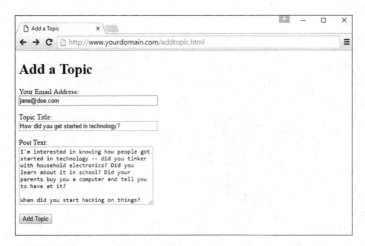

FIGURE 19.2
Adding a topic and first post.

FIGURE 19.3
Successful addition of a topic and first post.

In the next section, you put together two more pieces of the puzzle: displaying the topics and posts and replying to a topic.

Displaying the Topic List

Now that you have a topic and at least one post in your database, you can display this information and let people add new topics or reply to existing ones. In Listing 19.4, you take a step back and create a page that lists all the topics in the forum. This page shows the basic information of each topic and provides the user with a link to add a new topic; you have already created the form and script for that. The code in Listing 19.4 represents an entry page for your forum.

Although Listing 19.4 looks like a lot of code, it's actually many small, simple concepts you've already encountered, starting with the `include()` function and database connection function in lines 2–3.

LISTING 19.4   Topic Listing Script

```
1:  <?php
2:  include 'db_include.php';
3:  doDB();
4:
5:  //gather the topics
6:  $get_topics_sql = "SELECT topic_id, topic_title,
7:                  DATE_FORMAT(topic_create_time,  '%b %e %Y at %r') AS
8:                  fmt_topic_create_time, topic_owner FROM forum_topics
9:                  ORDER BY topic_create_time DESC";
10: $get_topics_res = mysqli_query($mysqli, $get_topics_sql)
11:                  or die(mysqli_error($mysqli));
12:
13: if (mysqli_num_rows($get_topics_res) < 1) {
14:     //there are no topics, so say so
15:     $display_block = "<p><em>No topics exist.</em></p>";
16: } else {
17:     //create the display string
```

```
18:     $display_block <<<END_OF_TEXT
19:     <table>
20:     <tr>
21:     <th>TOPIC TITLE</th>
22:     <th># of POSTS</th>
23:     </tr>
24: END_OF_TEXT;
25:
26:     while ($topic_info = mysqli_fetch_array($get_topics_res)) {
27:         $topic_id = $topic_info['topic_id'];
28:         $topic_title = stripslashes($topic_info['topic_title']);
29:         $topic_create_time = $topic_info['fmt_topic_create_time'];
30:         $topic_owner = stripslashes($topic_info['topic_owner']);
31:
32:         //get number of posts
33:         $get_num_posts_sql = "SELECT COUNT(post_id) AS post_count FROM
34:                     forum_posts WHERE topic_id = '".$topic_id."'";
35:         $get_num_posts_res = mysqli_query($mysqli, $get_num_posts_sql)
36:                     or die(mysqli_error($mysqli));
37:
38:         while ($posts_info = mysqli_fetch_array($get_num_posts_res)) {
39:             $num_posts = $posts_info['post_count'];
40:         }
41:
42:         //add to display
43:         $display_block .= <<<END_OF_TEXT
44:         <tr>
45:         <td><a href="showtopic.php?topic_id=$topic_id">
46:         <strong>$topic_title</strong></a><br/>
47:         Created on $topic_create_time by $topic_owner</td>
48:         <td class="num_posts_col">$num_posts</td>
49:         </tr>
50: END_OF_TEXT;
51:     }
52:     //free results
53:     mysqli_free_result($get_topics_res);
54:     mysqli_free_result($get_num_posts_res);
55:
56:     //close connection to MySQL
57:     mysqli_close($mysqli);
58:
59:     //close up the table
60:     $display_block .= "</table>";
61: }
62: ?>
63: <!DOCTYPE html>
64: <html lang="en">
65: <head>
66:   <title>Topics in My Forum</title>
```

```
67:    <style type="text/css">
68:       table {
69:          border: 1px solid black;
70:          border-collapse: collapse;
71:       }
72:       th {
73:          border: 1px solid black;
74:          padding: 6px;
75:          font-weight: bold;
76:          background: #ccc;
77:       }
78:       td {
79:          border: 1px solid black;
80:          padding: 6px;
81:       }
82:       .num_posts_col { text-align: center; }
83:    </style>
84: </head>
85: <body>
86:    <h1>Topics in My Forum</h1>
87:    <?php echo $display_block; ?>
88:    <p>Would you like to <a href="addtopic.html">add a topic</a>?</p>
89: </body>
90: </html>
```

Lines 6–11 show the first of the database queries, and this particular one selects all the topic information in order by descending date. In other words, these lines gather the data in such a way that the topic that was created most recently will appear at the top of the list. In the query, notice the use of the date_format() function to create a much nicer date display than the raw value stored in the database.

Line 13 checks for the presence of any records returned by the query. If no records are returned, and thus no topics are in the table, you want to tell the user. Line 15 creates this message. At this point, if no topics existed, the script would break out of the if...else construct and be over with; the next action would occur at line 63, which is the start of the static HTML. If the script ended here, the message created in line 15 would be printed in line 87.

If you have topics in your forum_topics table, however, the script continues at line 16. At line 18, a block of text is assigned to the $display_block variable, containing the beginnings of an HTML table. Lines 19–23 set up a table with two columns: one for the title and one for the number of posts. At line 26, you begin to loop through the results of the original query.

The while loop in line 26 says that while there are elements to be extracted from the resultset, extract each row as an array called $topic_info and use the field names as the array element to assign the value to a new variable. So, the first element the script tries to extract is the topic_id field, on line 27. It assigns the value of $topic_info['topic_id'] to the $topic_id variable, meaning that it gets a local value for `$topic_id` from an array called `$topic_info`, containing a field called `topic_id`. Continue doing this for the `$topic_title`, `$topic_create_time`, and `$topic_owner` variables in lines 28–30. The `stripslashes()` function removes any escape characters that may have been input into the table at the time of record insertion.

Lines 33–36 create and issue another query, in the context of the `while` loop, to get the number of posts for that particular topic. In line 43, the script continues the creation of the `$display_block` string, using the concatenation operator (`.=`) to make sure that this string is tacked on to the end of the display string you have built so far. In lines 45–47, you create the HTML table column to display the link to the file that will show the topic (`showtopic.php`) and print the topic owner and creation time.

The second HTML table column, on line 48, shows the number of posts. The script breaks out of the `while` loop on line 51, and on line 60 it adds the last bit to the `$display_block` string to close the table. The remaining lines print the HTML for the page, including the value of the `$display_block` string.

If you save this file as `topiclist.php` and place it in your web server document root, and if you have topics in your database tables, you might see something like Figure 19.4.

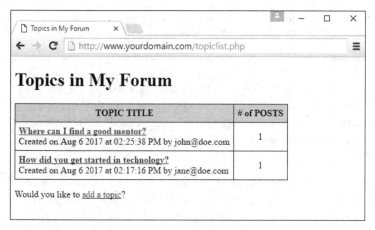

FIGURE 19.4
Topics are available.

Displaying the Posts in a Topic

As you might have guessed, the next item on the task list is to build that `showtopic.php` file to show the topic's postings. Listing 19.5 does just that. In this listing, lines 6–9 check for the existence of a value for `topic_id` in the GET query string. Because you intend to show all the posts within a selected topic, you need to know which topic to use in your query, and this is the manner in which the information is given to you. If a value in `$_GET['topic_id']` does not exist, the user is redirected back to the topic listing page, presumably to try again.

LISTING 19.5 Script to Show Topic Posts

```
1:   <?php
2:   include 'db_include.php';
3:   doDB();
4:
5:   //check for required info from the query string
6:   if (!isset($_GET['topic_id'])) {
7:       header("Location: topiclist.php");
8:       exit;
9:   }
10:
11:  //create safe values for use
12:  $safe_topic_id = mysqli_real_escape_string($mysqli, $_GET['topic_id']);
13:
14:  //verify the topic exists
15:  $verify_topic_sql = "SELECT topic_title FROM forum_topics
16:                      WHERE topic_id = '".$safe_topic_id."'";
17:  $verify_topic_res =  mysqli_query($mysqli, $verify_topic_sql)
18:                      or die(mysqli_error($mysqli));
19:
20:  if (mysqli_num_rows($verify_topic_res) < 1) {
21:     //this topic does not exist
22:     $display_block = "<p><em>You have selected an invalid topic.<br>
23:     Please <a href=\"topiclist.php\">try again</a>.</em></p>";
24:  } else {
25:     //get the topic title
26:     while ($topic_info = mysqli_fetch_array($verify_topic_res)) {
27:         $topic_title = stripslashes($topic_info['topic_title']);
28:     }
29:
30:     //gather the posts
31:     $get_posts_sql = "SELECT post_id, post_text, DATE_FORMAT(post_create_time,
32:                      '%b %e %Y<br>%r') AS fmt_post_create_time, post_owner
33:                       FROM forum_posts
34:                       WHERE topic_id = '".$safe_topic_id."'
35:                       ORDER BY post_create_time ASC";
36:     $get_posts_res = mysqli_query($mysqli, $get_posts_sql)
37:                      or die(mysqli_error($mysqli));
38:
39:      //create the display string
40:      $display_block = <<<END_OF_TEXT
41:      <p>Showing posts for the <strong>$topic_title</strong> topic:</p>
42:      <table>
43:      <tr>
44:      <th>AUTHOR</th>
45:      <th>POST</th>
46:      </tr>
47:  END_OF_TEXT;
```

```
48:
49:        while ($posts_info = mysqli_fetch_array($get_posts_res)) {
50:            $post_id = $posts_info['post_id'];
51:            $post_text = nl2br(stripslashes($posts_info['post_text']));
52:            $post_create_time = $posts_info['fmt_post_create_time'];
53:            $post_owner = stripslashes($posts_info['post_owner']);
54:
55:            //add to display
56:            $display_block .= <<<END_OF_TEXT
57:            <tr>
58:            <td><p>$post_owner</p>
59:            <p>created on:<br>$post_create_time</p></td>
60:            <td><p>$post_text</p>
61:            <p><a href="replytopost.php?post_id=$post_id">
62:            <strong>REPLY TO POST</strong></a></p></td>
63:            </tr>
64:    END_OF_TEXT;
65:        }
66:
67:        //free results
68:        mysqli_free_result($get_posts_res);
69:        mysqli_free_result($verify_topic_res);
70:
71:        //close connection to MySQL
72:        mysqli_close($mysqli);
73:
74:        //close up the table
75:        $display_block .= "</table>";
76:    }
77:    ?>
78:    <!DOCTYPE html>
79:    <html lang="en">
80:    <head>
81:        <title>Posts in Topic</title>
82:        <style type="text/css">
83:            table {
84:                border: 1px solid black;
85:                border-collapse: collapse;
86:            }
87:            th {
88:                border: 1px solid black;
89:                padding: 6px;
90:                font-weight: bold;
91:                background: #ccc;
92:            }
93:            td {
94:                border: 1px solid black;
95:                padding: 6px;
96:                vertical-align: top;
```

```
97:        }
98:        .num_posts_col { text-align: center; }
99:        </style>
100: </head>
101: <body>
102:    <h1>Posts in Topic</h1>
103:    <?php echo $display_block; ?>
104: </body>
105: </html>
```

Lines 15–18 show the first of these queries, and this one is used to validate that the `topic_id` sent in the query string is actually a valid entry by selecting the associated `topic_title` for the topic in question. If the validation fails the test in line 20, a message is created in lines 22–23, and the script breaks out of the `if...else` statement and finishes up by printing HTML. This output looks like Figure 19.5.

FIGURE 19.5
Invalid topic selected.

If, however, the topic is valid, the script extracts the value of `topic_title` in line 27, again using `stripslashes()` to remove any escape characters that may have been automatically added upon insertion. Next, the script creates and issues a query in lines 31–37 to gather all the posts associated with that topic in ascending order by time. In this case, the newest posts are at the bottom of the list. Line 40 starts a block of text, containing the beginnings of an HTML table. Lines 42–46 set up a table with two columns: one for the author of the post and one for the post text itself. The script stops writing the text block momentarily and at line 49 begins to loop through the results of the original query.

The `while` loop in line 49 says that although there are elements to be extracted from the resultset, extract each row as an array called `$posts_info` and use the field names as the array element to assign the value to a new variable. So, the first element the script tries to extract is the `post_id` field on line 50. It assigns the value of `$posts_info['post_id']` to the variable `$post_id`, meaning that it gets a local value for `$post_id` from an array called `$posts_info`, containing a field called `post_id`. Continue doing this for the `$post_text`, `$post_create_time`, and `$post_owner` variables in lines 51–53. The `stripslashes()`

function is again used to remove any escape characters, and the `nl2br()` function is used on the value of `$posts_info[post_text]` to replace all newline characters with line-break characters.

In line 56, the script continues to write to the `$display_block` string, using the concatenation operator (`.=`) to make sure that this string is tacked on to the end of the string you have created so far. Lines 58–59 create the HTML table column to display the author and creation time of the post. The second HTML table row, on lines 60–63, shows the text of the post as well as a link to reply to the post. The script breaks out of the `while` loop on line 65, and on line 75 it adds the last bit to the `$display_block` string to close the table. The remaining lines print the HTML for the page, including the value of the `$display_block` string.

If you save this file as `showtopic.php` and place it in your web server document root, and if you have posts in your database tables, you might see something like Figure 19.6.

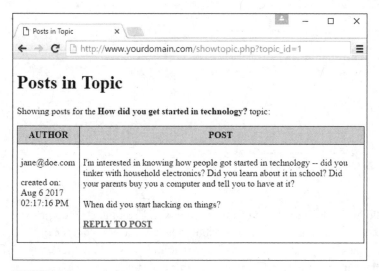

FIGURE 19.6
Posts in a topic.

A one-post topic is boring, so let's finish up this chapter by creating the script to add a post to a topic.

Adding Posts to a Topic

In this final step, you create the `replytopost.php` script, which contains code that looks similar to the script used to add a new topic. Listing 19.6 shows the code for this all-in-one form and script, which begins with the inclusion of the functions file and the initiation of the database connection on lines 2–3. Although the script performs different tasks depending on the status of the form (whether it's being shown or submitted), both conditions require database interaction at some point.

LISTING 19.6   Script to Add Replies to a Topic

```php
1:  <?php
2:  include 'db_include.php';
3:  doDB();
4:
5:  //check to see if we're showing the form or adding the post
6:  if (!$_POST) {
7:      // showing the form; check for required item in query string
8:      if (!isset($_GET['post_id'])) {
9:          header("Location: topiclist.php");
10:         exit;
11: }
12:
13:     //create safe values for use
14:     $safe_post_id = mysqli_real_escape_string($mysqli, $_GET['post_id']);
15:
16:     //still have to verify topic and post
17:     $verify_sql = "SELECT ft.topic_id, ft.topic_title FROM forum_posts
18:                     AS fp LEFT JOIN forum_topics AS ft ON fp.topic_id =
19:                     ft.topic_id WHERE fp.post_id = '".$safe_post_id."'";
20:
21:     $verify_res = mysqli_query($mysqli, $verify_sql)
22:                     or die(mysqli_error($mysqli));
23:
24:     if (mysqli_num_rows($verify_res) < 1) {
25:         //this post or topic does not exist
26:         header("Location: topiclist.php");
27:         exit;
28:     } else {
29:         //get the topic id and title
30:         while($topic_info = mysqli_fetch_array($verify_res)) {
31:             $topic_id = $topic_info['topic_id'];
32:             $topic_title = stripslashes($topic_info['topic_title']);
33:         }
34: ?>
35: <!DOCTYPE html>
36: <html>
37: <head>
38:   <title>Post Your Reply in <?php echo $topic_title; ?></title>
39: </head>
40: <body>
41:   <h1>Post Your Reply in <?php echo $topic_title; ?></h1>
42:   <form method="post" action="<?php echo $_SERVER['PHP_SELF']; ?>">
43:   <p><label for="post_owner">Your Email Address:</label><br>
44:   <input type="email" id="post_owner" name="post_owner" size="40"
45:         maxlength="150" required="required"></p>
46:   <p><label for="post_text">Post Text:</label><br>
47:   <textarea id="post_text" name="post_text" rows="8" cols="40"
48:       required="required"></textarea></p>
```

```
49:   <input type="hidden" name="topic_id" value="<?php echo $topic_id; ?>">
50:   <button type="submit" name="submit" value="submit">Add Post</button>
51:   </form>
52: </body>
53: </html>
54: <?php
55:     }
56:     //free result
57:     mysqli_free_result($verify_res);
58:
59:     //close connection to MySQL
60:     mysqli_close($mysqli);
61:
62: } else if ($_POST) {
63:     //check for required items from form
64:     if ((!$_POST['topic_id']) || (!$_POST['post_text']) ||
65:     (!$_POST['post_owner'])) {
66:         header("Location: topiclist.php");
67:         exit;
68:     }
69:
70:     //create safe values for use
71:     $safe_topic_id = mysqli_real_escape_string($mysqli, $_POST['topic_id']);
72:     $safe_post_text = mysqli_real_escape_string($mysqli, $_POST['post_text']);
73:     $safe_post_owner = mysqli_real_escape_string($mysqli, $_POST['post_owner']);
74:
75:     //add the post
76:     $add_post_sql = "INSERT INTO forum_posts (topic_id,post_text,
77:                       post_create_time,post_owner) VALUES
78:                       ('".$safe_topic_id."', '".$safe_post_text."',
79:                       now(),'".$safe_post_owner."')";
80:     $add_post_res = mysqli_query($mysqli, $add_post_sql)
81:                   or die(mysqli_error($mysqli));
82:
83:     //close connection to MySQL
84:     mysqli_close($mysqli);
85:
86:     //redirect user to topic
87:     header("Location: showtopic.php?topic_id=".$_POST['topic_id']);
88:     exit;
89: }
90: ?>
```

Line 6 checks to see whether the form is being submitted. If $_POST does not have a value, the form has not yet been submitted, and it must be shown. Before showing the form, however, you must check for that one required item; lines 8–11 check for the existence of a value for post_id in the GET query string. If a value in $_GET['post_id'] does not exist, the user is redirected back to the topic listing page.

If you made it past the check for a value in $_GET['post_id'], lines 17–22 create and issue a complicated-looking query that gets the values of the topic_id and topic_title fields from the forum_topics table, based on the only value that you know: a now-database-safe value (thanks to line 14) of $_GET['post_id']. This query both validates the existence of the post and gets information you will need later in the script. Lines 24–27 act on the results of this validity test, again redirecting the user back to the topiclist.php page if the test fails.

If the value of $_GET['post_id'] represents a valid post, you extract the value of topic_id and topic_title in lines 30–33, again using stripslashes() to remove any escape characters. Next, the script prints to the screen the entirety of the form for adding a post, and that's it for this script until the user clicks the form submission button. In the form, you see that the action is $_SERVER['PHP_SELF'] on line 42, indicating that this script will be recalled into action. A hidden field in line 49 holds the information that needs to be passed along to the next iteration of the script.

Moving on to line 62, you can see that this block of code is executed when the script is reloaded and $_POST contains a value. This block checks for the presence of all required fields from the form (lines 64–68) and then, if they are all present, issues the query to add the post to the database (lines 76–81) using safe values created in lines 71–73. After the post is added to the database, the user is redirected to the showtopic.php page (lines 87–88), using the appropriate query string to display the active topic.

Save this file as replytopost.php and place it in your web server document root. If you try it out, you may see something like Figures 19.7 and 19.8.

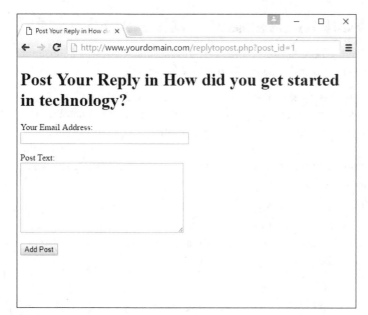

FIGURE 19.7
Preparing to add a post.

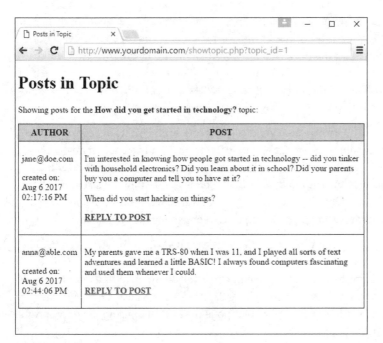

FIGURE 19.8
A post was added to the list.

Modifying the Forum Display with JavaScript

Once you have collected data from a database using PHP, you can manipulate it with JavaScript, because that data has been sent to the browser where JavaScript can get to it.

In the simple forum you created in this chapter, the topic list and posts are displayed automatically in the order defined by the database query, which is by the creation date. But it can be useful to be able to reorder them when you're viewing them in the browser. Although you can reorder them by sending another query to the database and return another page for the browser to render—this time with the information in a different order—it's more responsive for the end user to use JavaScript to reorder them on demand.

In order to sort with JavaScript, you first need to modify the HTML a bit. The new bits of JavaScript will use HTML `tbody` tags to sort the table cells, while leaving the headers at the top. Starting with Listing 19.4, modify lines 18–24 to add JavaScript hooks to make the table sortable, as in Listing 19.7. The modifications have been highlighted in the listing.

LISTING 19.7   Making the Table Sortable

```
18:     $display_block <<<END_OF_TEXT
19:     <table id="myTable">
        <thead>
20:     <tr>
21:     <th><a href="javascript:sortTable(myTable,0,0);">TOPIC
            TITLE</a></th>
22:     <th><a href="javascript:sortTable(myTable,1,0);"># of
            POSTS</a></th>
23:     </tr>
        </thead>
        <tbody>
24: END_OF_TEXT;
```

In addition to adding the `thead` and `tbody` tags, you also need to add an ID to the table, and turn the table head elements into links so that the document can be sorted.

You also need to close the table body, at the bottom of the PHP, by changing line 60 to include the closing `</tbody>` tag.

```
60:     $display_block .= "</tbody>
        </table>";
```

To make this work, you need to add the JavaScript to the HTML on the page. Insert the script in Listing 19.8 before the `</body>` tag (line 89).

LISTING 19.8   JavaScript for Sorting the Table

```
1: <script type="text/javascript">
2:   function sortTable(table, col, reverse) {
3:     var tb = table.tBodies[0];
4:     var tr = Array.prototype.slice.call(tb.rows, 0);
5:     var i;
6:     reverse = -((+reverse) || -1);
7:     tr = tr.sort(function (a, b) {
8:         return reverse // '-1 *' if want opposite order
9:             * (a.cells[col].textContent.trim()
10:                 .localeCompare(b.cells[col].textContent.trim())
11:                 );
12:     });
13:     for(i = 0; i < tr.length; ++i) tb.appendChild(tr[i]);
14:   }
15:   // sortTable(tableNode, columnId, false);
16: </script>
```

This simple script looks at the table identified in the `sortTable()` function call to find the `<tbody>` section (line 3). It puts all the rows in the table body into an array (line 4) and sorts them (line 7). Finally, it appends all the rows on the page in order (line 13). The order of the sort is set by the final parameter. Line 6 changes the direction if the parameter is not zero.

Summary

In this chapter, you saw how forums are hierarchical in nature: Forums contain topics; topics contain posts. You cannot have a topic without a post, and posts do not exist in forums without belonging to a topic. You applied this knowledge to the creation of tables to hold forum topics and posts, and you used PHP scripts to create the input and to display pages for these items. Finally, you added JavaScript to the scripts to enable on-page sorting of the data.

Q&A

Q. What if I want multiple forums? This sequence assumes that only one forum is available.

A. If you want to have multiple forums in your discussion board, create a table called `forums` (or something to that effect) containing fields for an ID, name, and perhaps a forum description. Then, in the `forum_topics` and `forum_posts` tables, add a field called `forum_id` so that those elements lower in the hierarchy are tied to the master forum. Be sure to amend the SQL queries for record insertion to account for the value of the `forum_id`.

Next, instead of starting your display at the topic level, begin it at the forum level. Just as you created a script to display topics, create a script to show the forums. The link to the forum display would contain the `forum_id`, and the page itself would show all the topics within that forum.

Workshop

The Workshop is designed to help you review what you've learned and begin putting your knowledge into practice.

Quiz

1. How is the topic ID value passed to the `showtopic.php` script?

2. What else, besides telling the user that the topic was successfully added, could you do at the end of the `do_addtopic.php` script?

3. Why does the script use the `mysqli_real_escape_string()` function on values from forms?

4. Why is it better to use JavaScript for sorting the displayed data?

Answers

1. Through the `$_GET` superglobal, named as the value of `$_GET['topic_id']`.

2. Just as with the `replytopost.php` script, you could eliminate the message display and simply redirect the user to the topic she just created, showing the new topic and post in all its glory.

3. The `mysqli_real_escape_string()` function guards against SQL injection attacks by preparing "safe" strings for insertion into the database tables.

4. JavaScript allows the data to be sorted more quickly, which makes the page more responsive to the end user. Also, it doesn't require any additional SQL calls so the page loads quickly.

Exercises

▶ You'll notice that none of these pages are really tied together with any sort of navigation. Take these basic framework scripts and apply some navigational flow to them. Make sure that users can always add a topic or return to the topic list from any given page, for example.

▶ Use the information provided in the Q&A section to integrate and display multiple forums into your tidy little discussion board. While you're at it, apply some text styles and colors to jazz up these bare-bones examples.

▶ Modify the JavaScript to create a toggle function on the sorting so that the data sorts both backwards and forwards when clicked. Try adding the sorting functionality to the rest of your data lists as well, to make your forum more functional.

CHAPTER 20
Creating an Online Storefront

What You'll Learn in This Chapter:

▶ How to create relational tables for an online store
▶ How to create scripts to display store categories
▶ How to create scripts to display individual items
▶ How to create JavaScript to enhance the storefront

In this short chapter, you create a generic online storefront. As with the previous project chapter, you learn how to create the relevant database tables as well as the scripts for displaying the information to the user. The examples used in this chapter represent one of many different possibilities to complete these tasks and are meant to provide a foundation of knowledge rather than a definitive method for completing the tasks. You will also get some ideas for how to use JavaScript to make your storefront easier to use and more appealing for your users.

Planning and Creating the Database Tables

Before you tackle the process of creating database tables for an online store, think about the real-life shopping process. When you walk into a store, items are ordered in some fashion: The hardware and the baby clothes aren't mixed together, the electronics and the laundry detergent aren't side by side, and so on. Applying that knowledge to database normalization, already you can see that you need a table to hold categories and a table to hold items. In this simple store, each item belongs to one category.

Next, think about the items themselves. Depending on the type of store you have, your items might or might not have colors, and might or might not have sizes. But all your items will have a name, a description, and a price. Again, thinking in terms of normalization, you can imagine that you might have one general items table and two additional tables that relate to the general items table.

Table 20.1 shows sample table and field names to use for your online storefront. In a minute, you create the actual SQL statements, but first you should look at this information and try to see the relationships. Ask yourself which of the fields should be primary or unique keys.

TABLE 20.1 Storefront Table and Field Names

Table Name	Field Names
store_categories	id, cat_title, cat_desc
store_items	id, cat_id, item_title, item_price, item_desc, item_image
store_item_size	item_id, item_size
store_item_color	item_id, item_color

As you can see in the following SQL statements, the store_categories table has two fields besides the id field: cat_title and cat_desc, for title and description, respectively. The id field is the primary key, and cat_title is a unique field because there's no reason you would have two identical categories:

```
CREATE TABLE store_categories (
    id INT NOT NULL PRIMARY KEY AUTO_INCREMENT,
    cat_title VARCHAR (50) UNIQUE,
    cat_desc TEXT
);
```

Next, we tackle the store_items table, which has five fields besides the id field—none of which are unique keys. The lengths specified in the field definitions are arbitrary; you should use whatever best fits your store.

The cat_id field relates the item to a particular category in the store_categories table. This field is not unique because you will want more than one item in each category. The item_title, item_price, and item_desc (for description) fields are self-explanatory. The item_image field holds a filename (in this case, the file is assumed to be local to your server) that you use to build an HTML <img> tag when it is time to display your item information:

```
CREATE TABLE store_items (
    id INT NOT NULL PRIMARY KEY AUTO_INCREMENT,
    cat_id INT NOT NULL,
    item_title VARCHAR (75),
    item_price FLOAT (8,2),
    item_desc TEXT,
    item_image VARCHAR (50)
);
```

Both the `store_item_size` and `store_item_color` tables contain optional information: If you sell books, they won't have sizes or colors, but if you sell shirts, they will. For each of these tables, the `item_id`, `item_size`, and `item_color` fields are not unique keys because you can associate as many colors and sizes with a particular item as you want:

```
CREATE TABLE store_item_size (
    id INT NOT NULL PRIMARY KEY AUTO_INCREMENT,
    item_id INT NOT NULL,
    item_size VARCHAR (25)
);
CREATE TABLE store_item_color (
    id INT NOT NULL PRIMARY KEY AUTO_INCREMENT,
    item_id INT NOT NULL,
    item_color VARCHAR (25)
);
```

These are all the tables necessary for a basic storefront—that is, for displaying the items you have for sale, which is the limit of what you'll learn in this book.

In Chapter 19, "Creating a Simple Discussion Forum," you learned how to use PHP forms and scripts to add or delete records in your tables. If you apply the same principles to this set of tables, you can easily create an administrative front end to your storefront. We do not go through that process in this book, but feel free to do it on your own. (If you understood what was going on in Chapter 19, you know enough about PHP and MySQL to complete the tasks.)

For now, you can simply issue MySQL queries, via the MySQL monitor or other interface, to add information to your tables. Following are some examples, if you want to follow along with sample data.

Inserting Records into the `store_categories` Table

The following queries create three categories in your `store_categories` table (hats, shirts, and books):

```
INSERT INTO store_categories VALUES
  (1, 'Hats', 'Funky hats in all shapes and sizes!');

INSERT INTO store_categories VALUES (2, 'Shirts', 'From t-shirts to
sweatshirts to polo shirts and beyond.');

INSERT INTO store_categories VALUES (3, 'Books', 'Paperback, hardback,
books for school or play.');
```

In the next section, we add some items to the categories.

Inserting Records into the `store_items` Table

The following queries add three item records to each category. Feel free to add many more.

```
INSERT INTO store_items VALUES (1, 1, 'Baseball Hat', 12.00,
'Fancy, low-profile baseball hat.', 'baseballhat.gif');

INSERT INTO store_items VALUES (2, 1, 'Cowboy Hat', 52.00,
'10 gallon variety', 'cowboyhat.gif');

INSERT INTO store_items VALUES (3, 1, 'Top Hat', 102.00,
'Good for costumes.', 'tophat.gif');

INSERT INTO store_items VALUES (4, 2, 'Short-Sleeved T-Shirt',
12.00, '100% cotton, pre-shrunk.', 'sstshirt.gif');

INSERT INTO store_items VALUES (5, 2, 'Long-Sleeved T-Shirt',
15.00, 'Just like the short-sleeved shirt, with longer sleeves.',
'lstshirt.gif');

INSERT INTO store_items VALUES (6, 2, 'Sweatshirt', 22.00,
'Heavy and warm.', 'sweatshirt.gif');

INSERT INTO store_items VALUES (7, 3, 'Jane\'s Self-Help Book',
12.00, 'Jane gives advice.', 'selfhelpbook.gif');

INSERT INTO store_items VALUES (8, 3, 'Generic Academic Book',
35.00, 'Some required reading for school, will put you to sleep.',
'boringbook.gif');

INSERT INTO store_items VALUES (9, 3, 'Chicago Manual of Style',
9.99, 'Good for copywriters.', 'chicagostyle.gif');
```

NOTE

The preceding queries refer to various graphics which are not included in the code. You can find free-to-use images online or make some placeholder graphics of your own.

Inserting Records into the `store_item_size` Table

The following queries associate sizes with one of the three items in the `shirts` category and a generic "one size fits all" size to each of the hats (assume that they're strange hats). On your own, insert the same set of size associations for the remaining items in the `shirts` category:

```
INSERT INTO store_item_size (item_id, item_size) VALUES (1,'One Size Fits All');
INSERT INTO store_item_size (item_id, item_size) VALUES (2,'One Size Fits All');
INSERT INTO store_item_size (item_id, item_size) VALUES (3,'One Size Fits All');
```

```
INSERT INTO store_item_size (item_id, item_size) VALUES (4,'S');
INSERT INTO store_item_size (item_id, item_size) VALUES (4,'M');
INSERT INTO store_item_size (item_id, item_size) VALUES (4,'L');
INSERT INTO store_item_size (item_id, item_size) VALUES (4,'XL');
```

Inserting Records into the `store_item_color` Table

The following queries associate colors with one of the three items in the `shirts` category. On your own, insert color records for the remaining shirts and hats.

```
INSERT INTO store_item_color (item_id, item_color) VALUES (1,'red');
INSERT INTO store_item_color (item_id, item_color) VALUES (1,'black');
INSERT INTO store_item_color (item_id, item_color) VALUES (1,'blue');
```

Displaying Categories of Items

Believe it or not, the most difficult task in this project is now complete. Compared to thinking up categories and items, creating the scripts used to display the information is easy!

The first script you make is one that lists categories and items. Obviously, you do not want to list all categories and all items at once as soon as the user walks in the door, but you do want to give the user the option of immediately picking a category, seeing its items, and then picking another category. In other words, this script serves two purposes: It shows the categories; then, if a user clicks a category link, it shows the items in that category.

Listing 20.1 shows the full code for `seestore.php`. If you have worked through this book sequentially, you will notice a lot of the same basic construction you saw in previous chapters; these projects are all examples of foundational CRUD—which stands for *create, read, update, delete*—applications. Even so, the code is still explained in detail after the listing.

LISTING 20.1 Script to View Categories

```
1:   <?php
2:   //connect to database
3:   $mysqli = mysqli_connect("localhost", "testuser", "somepass", "testDB");
4:
5:   $display_block = "<h1>My Categories</h1>
6:   <p>Select a category to see its items.</p>";
7:
8:   //show categories first
9:   $get_cats_sql = "SELECT id, cat_title, cat_desc FROM
10:                  store_categories ORDER BY cat_title";
11:  $get_cats_res =  mysqli_query($mysqli, $get_cats_sql)
12:                  or die(mysqli_error($mysqli));
13:
```

```
14: if (mysqli_num_rows($get_cats_res) < 1) {
15:     $display_block = "<p><em>Sorry, no categories to browse.</em></p>";
16: } else {
17:     while ($cats = mysqli_fetch_array($get_cats_res)) {
18:         $cat_id    = $cats['id'];
19:         $cat_title = strtoupper(stripslashes($cats['cat_title']));
20:         $cat_desc  = stripslashes($cats['cat_desc']);
21:
22:         $display_block .= "<p><strong><a href=\"".$_SERVER['PHP_SELF'].
23:         "?cat_id=".$cat_id."\">".$cat_title."</a></strong><br>"
24:         .$cat_desc."</p>";
25:
26:         if (isset($_GET['cat_id']) && ($_GET['cat_id'] == $cat_id)) {
27:             //create safe value for use
28:             $safe_cat_id = mysqli_real_escape_string($mysqli,
29:                 $_GET['cat_id']);
30:
31:             //get items
32:             $get_items_sql = "SELECT id, item_title, item_price
33:                             FROM store_items WHERE
34:                             cat_id = '".$cat_id."' ORDER BY item_title";
35:             $get_items_res = mysqli_query($mysqli, $get_items_sql)
36:                             or die(mysqli_error($mysqli));
37:
38:             if (mysqli_num_rows($get_items_res) < 1) {
39:                 $display_block = "<p><em>Sorry, no items in this
40:                 category.</em></p>";
41:             } else {
42:                 $display_block .= "<ul>";
43:                 while ($items = mysqli_fetch_array($get_items_res)) {
44:                     $item_id    = $items['id'];
45:                     $item_title = stripslashes($items['item_title']);
46:                     $item_price = $items['item_price'];
47:
48:                     $display_block .= "<li><a href=\"showitem.php?item_id=".
49:                     $item_id."\">".$item_title."</a>
50:                     (\$".$item_price.")</li>";
51:                 }
52:
53:                 $display_block .= "</ul>";
54:             }
55:             //free results
56:             mysqli_free_result($get_items_res);
57:         }
58:     }
59: }
60: }
61: //free results
```

```
62: mysqli_free_result($get_cats_res);
63: //close connection to MySQL
64: mysqli_close($mysqli);
65: ?>
66: <!DOCTYPE html>
67: <html lang="en">
68: <head>
69:   <title>My Categories</title>
70: </head>
71: <body>
72:   <?php echo $display_block; ?>
73: </body>
74: </html>
```

Given the length of scripts you saw in Chapter 19, these 74 fully functional lines should be a welcome change. Line 3 opens the database connection because regardless of which action the script is taking—showing categories or showing items in categories—the database is necessary. You can also use an `include` to use to a database connection function, as you did throughout the examples in Chapter 19.

Line 5 starts the `$display_block` string, with some basic page title information added to it. Lines 9–12 create and issue the query to retrieve the category information. Line 14 checks for categories; if none are in the table, a message is stored in the `$display` block variable for display to the user, and that's all this script does. (It jumps to the HTML in line 66 and prints to the screen after freeing up some database results.) However, if categories are found, the script moves on to line 17, which begins a `while` loop to extract the information.

In the `while` loop, lines 18–20 retrieve the ID, title, and description of the category. String operations are performed to ensure that no slashes are in the text and that the category title is in uppercase for display purposes. Lines 22–24 place the category information, including a self-referential page link, in the `$display_block` string. If a user clicks the link displayed by that string, she returns to this same script, except with a category ID passed in the query string. The script checks for this value in line 26.

If a `$_GET['cat_id']` value has been passed to the script (and has been verified as a valid ID) because the user clicked a category link in hopes of seeing listed items, the script builds and issues another query using a safe version of that value (lines 32–36) to retrieve the items in the category. Lines 38–51 check for items and then build an item string as part of `$display_block`. Part of the information in the string is a link to a script called `showitem.php`, which you create in the next section.

After reaching that point, the script has nothing left to do besides free up some resources, and it prints the HTML and value of `$display_block`. Figure 20.1 shows the outcome of the script when accessed directly; only the category information is shown.

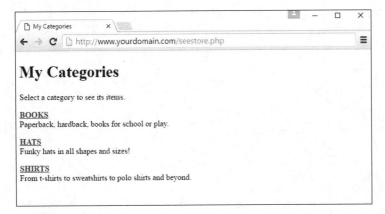

FIGURE 20.1
Categories in the store.

In Figure 20.2, you see what happens when the user clicks the HATS link: The script gathers all the items associated with the category and prints them on the screen. The user can still jump to another category on this same page, and the script will gather the items for that category.

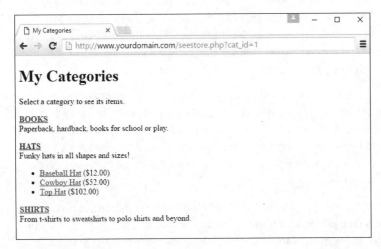

FIGURE 20.2
Items within a category in the store.

The last piece of the puzzle for this chapter is the creation of the item-display page.

Displaying Items

The item-display page that you'll build next shows all of the information for the item that is stored in the database. Listing 20.2 shows the code for `showitem.php`.

LISTING 20.2 Script to View Item Information

```
1:  <?php
2:  //connect to database
3:  $mysqli = mysqli_connect("localhost", "testuser", "somepass", "testDB");
4:
5:  $display_block = "<h1>My Store - Item Detail</h1>";
6:
7:  //create safe values for use
8:  $safe_item_id = mysqli_real_escape_string($mysqli, $_GET['item_id']);
9:
10: //validate item
11: $get_item_sql = "SELECT c.id as cat_id, c.cat_title, si.item_title,
12:                 si.item_price, si.item_desc, si.item_image FROM store_items
13:                 AS si LEFT JOIN store_categories AS c on c.id = si.cat_id
14:                 WHERE si.id = '".$safe_item_id."'";
15: $get_item_res = mysqli_query($mysqli, $get_item_sql)
16:                 or die(mysqli_error($mysqli));
17:
18: if (mysqli_num_rows($get_item_res) < 1) {
19:     //invalid item
20:     $display_block .= "<p><em>Invalid item selection.</em></p>";
21: } else {
22:     //valid item, get info
23:     while ($item_info = mysqli_fetch_array($get_item_res)) {
24:         $cat_id = $item_info['cat_id'];
25:         $cat_title = strtoupper(stripslashes($item_info['cat_title']));
26:         $item_title = stripslashes($item_info['item_title']);
27:         $item_price = $item_info['item_price'];
28:         $item_desc = stripslashes($item_info['item_desc']);
29:         $item_image = $item_info['item_image'];
30:     }
31:
32:     //make breadcrumb trail & display of item
33:     $display_block .= <<<END_OF_TEXT
34:     <p><em>You are viewing:</em><br>
35:     <strong><a href="seestore.php?cat_id=$cat_id">$cat_title</a>
36:         &gt; $item_title</strong></p>
37:     <div style="float: left;"><img src="$item_image" alt="$item_title"></div>
38:     <div style="float: left; padding-left: 12px">
```

```
39:     <p><strong>Description:</strong><br>$item_desc</p>
40:     <p><strong>Price:</strong> \$$item_price</p>
41: END_OF_TEXT;
42:     //free result
43:     mysqli_free_result($get_item_res);
44:
45:     //get colors
46:     $get_colors_sql = "SELECT item_color FROM store_item_color WHERE
47:                       item_id = '".$safe_item_id."' ORDER BY item_color";
48:     $get_colors_res = mysqli_query($mysqli, $get_colors_sql)
49:                       or die(mysqli_error($mysqli));
50:
51:     if (mysqli_num_rows($get_colors_res) > 0) {
52:         $display_block .= "<p><strong>Available Colors:</strong><br>";
53:         while ($colors = mysqli_fetch_array($get_colors_res)) {
54:             item_color = $colors['item_color'];
55:             $display_block .= $item_color."<br>";
56:         }
57:     }
58:     //free result
59:     mysqli_free_result($get_colors_res);
60:
61:     //get sizes
62:     $get_sizes_sql = "SELECT item_size FROM store_item_size WHERE
63:                       item_id = ".$safe_item_id." ORDER BY item_size";
64:     $get_sizes_res = mysqli_query($mysqli, $get_sizes_sql)
65:                       or die(mysqli_error($mysqli));
66:
67:     if (mysqli_num_rows($get_sizes_res) > 0) {
68:         $display_block .= "<p><strong>Available Sizes:</strong><br>";
69:         while ($sizes = mysqli_fetch_array($get_sizes_res)) {
70:             $item_size = $sizes['item_size'];
71:             $display_block .= $item_size."<br>";
72:         }
73:     }
74:     //free result
75:     mysqli_free_result($get_sizes_res);
76:
77:     $display_block .= "</div>";
78: }
79: //close connection to MySQL
80: mysqli_close($mysqli);
81: ?>
```

```
82: <!DOCTYPE html>
83: <html lang="en">
84: <head>
85:   <title>My Store</title>
86: </head>
87: <body>
88:   <?php echo $display_block; ?>
89: </body>
90: </html>
```

Line 3 makes the database connection, because information in the database forms all the content of this page. Line 5 starts the `$display_block` string, with some basic page title information.

Lines 11–13 create and issue the query to retrieve the category and item information, using the safe value created in line 8. This particular query is a table join. Instead of selecting the item information from one table and then issuing a second query to find the name of the category, this query simply joins the table on the category ID to find the category name.

Line 15 checks for a result; if there is no matching item in the table, a message is printed to the user—and that's all this script does. However, if item information is found, the script moves on and gathers the information in lines 23–30.

In lines 34–36, you first create what's known as a *breadcrumb trail*. This is simply a navigational device used to get back to the top-level item in the architecture. In other words, you're going to print a link so the user can get back to the category. The category ID, retrieved from the master query in this script, is appended to the link in the breadcrumb trail.

In lines 37–40, you continue to add to the `$display_block`, setting up a display of information about the item. You use the values gathered in lines 23–30 to create an image link, print the description, and print the price. What's missing are the colors and sizes, so lines 46–57 select and print any colors associated with this item, and lines 62–73 gather the sizes associated with the item.

Lines 77–78 wrap up the `$display_block` string and the master if…else statement. Because the script has nothing left to do after closing the connection to MySQL, it prints the HTML (lines 82–90), including the value of `$display_block`. Figure 20.3 shows the outcome of the script when the baseball hat is selected from the hats category. Of course, your display will differ from mine because you won't have the same images I used, but you get the idea.

FIGURE 20.3
The baseball hat item page.

That's all there is to creating a simple item display that pulls information out of a database.

Using JavaScript with an Online Storefront

One of the biggest challenges to online stores is convincing customers to stay on the site long enough to purchase something. Every time a customer has to take an action, they have an opportunity to abandon the purchase. To prevent this, many online stores show as much information as possible without requiring any action on the part of the customer beyond clicking the Buy button.

In the simple store catalog interface you've created in this chapter, there are several steps before a customer can purchase an item: the customer must choose a category, then choose the item, then alternately a size and color, and then click to purchase or add to a shopping cart (the latter are outside of the scope of this chapter). By removing just one of those steps, you can reduce the abandonment rate and increase sales. And an easy way to do that is to redesign the category lists with a slideshow of the items displayed directly rather than after a click. Figure 20.4 shows how the store might change if you changed the display to a JavaScript slideshow, also referred to as a carousel.

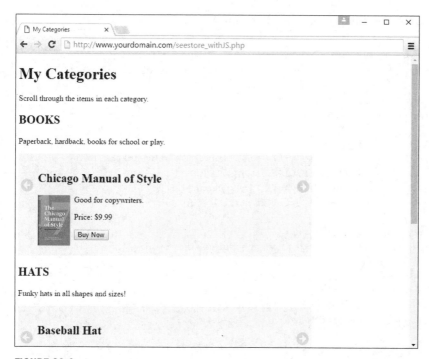

FIGURE 20.4
The store using carousels for the categories.

Although you can create your own carousel from scratch using JavaScript, there are many free and open source options that are much easier to use. For this example, I installed Kevin Batdorf's Liquid Slider, found at https://github.com/KevinBatdorf/liquidslider. This slider has the advantage of being responsive and can include heading tabs as well as slider arrows to make the carousel more usable.

To use this slider library, you must download the library files and place them on your web server, then reference them in your script. Typically when you use third-party libraries they will include documentation for getting started, and this particular slideshow library is no different—at https://github.com/KevinBatdorf/liquidslider you will find download, installation, and sample use instructions.

After downloading the library and putting it in a directory called liquidslider in my web server document root, I then modified the seestore.php script to display the items directly on the category page in a slideshow format. Listing 20.3 shows this new script.

LISTING 20.3   Store Modified to Use a Slideshow

```
1:  <?php
2:  //connect to database
3:  $mysqli = mysqli_connect("localhost", "testuser", "somepass", "testDB");
4:
5:  $display_block = "<h1>My Categories</h1>
6:  <p>Scroll through the items in each category.</p>";
7:
8:  //show categories first
9:  $get_cats_sql = "SELECT id, cat_title, cat_desc FROM store_categories
10:               ORDER BY cat_title";
11: $get_cats_res = mysqli_query($mysqli, $get_cats_sql)
12:               or die(mysqli_error($mysqli));
13:
14: if (mysqli_num_rows($get_cats_res) < 1) {
15:    $display_block = "<p><em>Sorry, no categories to browse.</em></p>";
16: } else {
17:    while ($cats = mysqli_fetch_array($get_cats_res)) {
18:         $cat_id  = $cats['id'];
19:         $cat_title = strtoupper(stripslashes($cats['cat_title']));
20:         $cat_desc = stripslashes($cats['cat_desc']);
21:
22:         $display_block .= "<h2>".$cat_title."</h2>\n<p>".$cat_desc."</p>";
23:
24:         //get items
25:         $get_items_sql = "SELECT id, item_title, item_price, item_desc,
26:            item_image FROM store_items WHERE cat_id = '".$cat_id."'
27:            ORDER BY item_title";
28:         $get_items_res = mysqli_query($mysqli, $get_items_sql)
29:                        or die(mysqli_error($mysqli));
30:
31:         if (mysqli_num_rows($get_items_res) < 1) {
32:            $display_block = "<p><em>Sorry, no items in this category.</em></p>";
33:         } else {
34:            $display_block .= "<section class=\"liquid-slider\"
35:                             id=\"main-slider-".$cat_id."\">";
36:
37:            while ($items = mysqli_fetch_array($get_items_res)) {
38:                $item_id  = $items['id'];
39:                $item_title = stripslashes($items['item_title']);
40:                $item_price = $items['item_price'];
41:                $item_img = $items['item_image'];
42:                $item_desc = $items['item_desc'];
43:
44:                $display_block .= <<<END_OF_TEXT
```

```
45:   <div>
46:   <h2 class="title">$item_title</h2>
47:   <p>
48:   <img src="$item_img" alt="$item_title" style=" float: left;
49:            margin-right:0.5rem;">
50:   $item_desc
51:   </p>
52:   <p>Price: \$$item_price</p>
53:   <p><a href="seestore.php?cat_id=$cat_id"><button id="">Buy Now</button></a></p>
54:   </div>
55:   END_OF_TEXT;
56:            }
57:
58:            $display_block .= <<<END_OF_TEXT
59: </section>
60: <script type="text/javascript">
61: $(function(){
62:   $('#main-slider-$cat_id').liquidSlider({
63:     dynamicTabs: false,
64:     hoverArrows: false
65:   });
66: });
67: </script>
68: END_OF_TEXT;
69:
70:     }
71:     //free results
72:     mysqli_free_result($get_items_res);
73:   }
74: }
75:
76: //free results
77: mysqli_free_result($get_cats_res);
78:
79: //close connection to MySQL
80: mysqli_close($mysqli);
81: ?>
82: <!DOCTYPE html>
83: <html lang="en">
84: <head>
85:   <title>My Categories</title>
86:   <link rel="stylesheet" href="liquidslider/css/liquid-slider.css">
87:   <script src="https://cdnjs.cloudflare.com/ajax/libs/jquery/3.2.1/jquery.min.
      js"></script>
```

```
88:    <script src="https://cdnjs.cloudflare.com/ajax/libs/jquery-easing/1.4.1/
       jquery.easing.min.js"></script>
89:    <script src="https://cdnjs.cloudflare.com/ajax/libs/jquery.touchswipe/1.6.18/
       jquery.touchSwipe.min.js"></script>
90:    <script src="liquidslider/js/jquery.liquid-slider.min.js"></script>
91: </head>
92: <body>
93:    <?php echo $display_block; ?>
94: </body>
95: </html>
```

As you look through the code in Listing 20.3, you will see a number of changes from Listing 20.1. On line 6, the introductory text changed to indicate that you can browse the items in each category by scrolling through them. After each category is displayed with a title and description in line 22, you go right to the SQL statement to get all the items in the category, since no click and backend request is necessary to "open" the category as there was before.

In lines 34–35, a new HTML element is placed; this element will hold the slider contents that will be built up next by fetching the item results and displaying them in a `<div>` created in lines 44–55. This `<div>` now includes all item information so that the user can see it while scrolling on the single page you've displayed. In lines 58–68, the slider script is initialized and ready for action when the user clicks on one of the arrows that will be displayed on the page.

After the PHP code is finished out in line 81, there are a few changes to the HTML in lines 86–90. In these lines, you link to the slider's CSS file, as well as to a few other script libraries that are necessary for the functionality to be complete.

Summary

In this chapter, you applied your basic PHP and MySQL knowledge to the creation of a storefront display. You learned how to create the database table and scripts for viewing categories, item lists, and single items. You also saw how integrating a third-party JavaScript library to adjust how the page displays and interacts with customers can make the whole application more usable and appealing.

Q&A

Q. In the item detail record, you use single filenames in the `item_image` field. What if I want to link to items on a different server?

A. You can enter a URL in the `item_image` field, as long as you define the field to hold a long string such as a URL.

Q. Why can't I just build my entire storefront in JavaScript? Wouldn't that be better?

A. It is possible to create an entire online shopping cart experience using only HTML and JavaScript, but that store could be hacked pretty easily since customers could change the prices on the front end (among other nefarious actions). It's better to use JavaScript for interactivity and enhancement and keep the storefront features in the PHP and the database.

Workshop

The Workshop is designed to help you review what you've learned and begin putting your knowledge into practice.

Quiz

1. Which PHP function was used to uppercase the category title strings?

2. Why don't the `store_item_size` and `store_item_color` tables contain any unique keys?

3. Why do you continue to use `mysqli_real_escape_string()` on values that will be used in database queries?

Answers

1. `strtoupper()`

2. Presumably, you will have items with more than one color and more than one size. Also, items may have the same colors or sizes, so the `item_color` and `item_size` fields must not be primary or unique either.

3. You should use `mysqli_real_escape_string()` to ensure values from the user that will be used in database queries are safe to use, no matter if you've created one script, 10 scripts, or 100.

Exercises

▶ Create three more categories, with an item or two in each, by issuing queries of your own in MySQL.

▶ Create some images (or use Creative Commons licensed images) for each of the items in your store and then put them in an `images` directory on your server. Doing so necessitates one change to the `showitem.php` script (or to the `seestore_withJS.php` script if you used the JavaScript carousel): adding the `image` directory to the file path of the generated `<img>` tag.

## CHAPTER 21

Creating a Simple Calendar

What You'll Learn in This Chapter:

▶ How to build a simple calendar script in both PHP and JavaScript

▶ How to view and add events in your calendar

This chapter pulls together the skills you've learned so far regarding the PHP language and building small CRUD applications—those that create, retrieve, update, and delete data. In this chapter, you continue your learning in the context of creating a small calendar application.

Building a Simple Display Calendar

You'll build upon language constructs and functionality you've learned throughout this book to build a calendar that displays the dates for any month between 1990 and 2020. Those are randomly selected years and have no significance—you can make your calendar go from 1980 to 2025 if you want, or any other range of dates that makes sense to you. The user can select both month and year with pull-down menus, and the dates for the selected month will be organized according to the days of the week.

In this script, we work with two variables—one for month and one for year—that are supplied by user input. These pieces of information are used to build a timestamp based on the first day of the selected month. If user input is invalid or absent, the default value is the first day of the current month.

Checking User Input

When the user accesses the calendar application for the first time, no information will have been submitted. Therefore, we must ensure that the script can handle the fact that the variables for month and year might not be defined. We could use the `isset()` function for this because it returns `false` if the variable passed to it has not been defined. However, let's use the `checkdate()` function instead, which not only will see whether the variable exists but will also do something meaningful with it—namely, validate that it is a date. Listing 21.1 shows the fragment of code that checks for month and year variables coming from a form and then builds a timestamp based on them.

LISTING 21.1   Checking User Input for the Calendar Script

```
 1: <?php
 2: if ((!isset($_POST['month'])) || (!isset($_POST['year']))) {
 3:     $nowArray = getdate();
 4:     $month = $nowArray['mon'];
 5:     $year = $nowArray['year'];
 6: } else {
 7:     $month = $_POST['month'];
 8:     $year = $_POST['year'];
 9: }
10: $start = mktime (12, 0, 0, $month, 1, $year);
11: $firstDayArray = getdate($start);
12: ?>
```

Listing 21.1 is a fragment of a larger script, so it does not produce any output itself. But it's an important fragment to understand, which is why it sits all alone here, ready for an explanation.

In the if statement on line 2, we test whether the month and year have been provided by a form. If the month and year have not been defined, the mktime() function used later in the fragment will not be able to make a valid date from undefined month and year arguments.

If the values are present, we use getdate() on line 3 to create an associative array based on the current time. We then set values for $month and $year ourselves, using the array's mon and year elements (lines 4 and 5). If the variables have been set from the form, we put the data into $month and $year variables so as not to touch the values in the original $_POST superglobal.

Once we are sure we have valid data in $month and $year, we can use mktime() to create a timestamp for the first day of the month (line 10). We will need information about this timestamp later on, so on line 11, we create a variable called $firstDayArray that stores an associative array returned by getdate() and based on this timestamp.

Building the HTML Form

We now need to create an interface by which users can ask to see data for a month and year. For this, we use SELECT elements. Although we could hard-code these in HTML, we must also ensure that the pull-downs default to the currently chosen month, so we will dynamically create these pull-downs, adding a SELECT attribute to the OPTION element where appropriate. The form is generated in Listing 21.2.

LISTING 21.2   Building the HTML Form for the Calendar Script

```php
1: <?php
2: if (((!isset($_POST['month'])) || (!isset($_POST['year'])))) {
3:     $nowArray = getdate();
4:     $month = $nowArray['mon'];
5:     $year = $nowArray['year'];
6: } else {
7:     $month = $_POST['month'];
8:     $year = $_POST['year'];
9: }
10: $start = mktime (12, 0, 0, $month, 1, $year);
11: $firstDayArray = getdate($start);
12: ?>
13: <!DOCTYPE html>
14: <html lang="en">
15: <head>
16:   <title><?php echo "Calendar:".$firstDayArray['month']."
17:     ".$firstDayArray['year']; ?></title>
18: </head>
19: <body>
20: <h1>Select a Month/Year Combination</h1>
21:   <form method="post" action="<?php echo $_SERVER['PHP_SELF']; ?>">
22:     <select name="month">
23:     <?php
24:     $months = Array("January", "February", "March", "April", "May",
25:     "June", "July", "August", "September", "October", "November", "December");
26:     for ($x=1; $x <= count($months); $x++) {
27:         echo"<option value=\"$x\"";
28:         if ($x == $month) {
29:             echo " selected";
30:         }
31:         echo ">".$months[$x-1]."</option>";
32:     }
33:     ?>
34:     </select>
35:     <select name="year">
36:     <?php
37:     for ($x=1990; $x<=2020; $x++) {
38:         echo "<option";
39:         if ($x == $year) {
40:             echo " selected";
41:         }
42:         echo ">$x</option>";
43:     }
44:     ?>
45:     </select>
46:     <button type="submit" name="submit" value="submit">Go!</button>
47:   </form>
48: </body>
49: </html>
```

Having created the $start timestamp and the $firstDayArray date array in lines 2–11, let's begin to write the HTML for the page. Notice that we use $firstDayArray to add the month and year to the TITLE element on lines 16 and 17.

Line 20 is the beginning of our form. To create the SELECT element for the month pull-down, we drop back into PHP mode on line 22 to write the individual OPTION tags. First, for display purposes, we create in lines 23 and 24 an array called $months that contains the names of the 12 months. We then loop through this array, creating an OPTION tag for each name (lines 25–31).

This is an overcomplicated way of writing a simple SELECT element were it not for the fact that we are testing $x (the counter variable in the for statement) against the $month variable on line 27. If $x and $month are equivalent, we add the string SELECTED to the OPTION tag, ensuring that the correct month will be selected automatically when the page loads. We use a similar technique to write the year pull-down on lines 36–42. Finally, back in HTML mode, we create a submit button on line 45.

We now have a form that can send the month and year parameters to itself and will default either to the current month and year or the month and year previously chosen. If you save this listing as dateselector.php, place it in your web server document root, and access it with your web browser, you should see something like Figure 21.1. (Your month and year might differ.)

FIGURE 21.1
The calendar form.

Creating the Calendar Table

We now need to create a table and populate it with dates for the chosen month. We do this in Listing 21.3, which represents the complete calendar display script.

Although line 2 is new, lines 3–64 should be familiar from your work with Listing 21.2, with some style sheet entries added in lines 19–35. That addition in line 2 simply defines a constant variable (in this case, ADAY—for "a day") with a value of 86400. This value represents the number of seconds in a day, which the script uses later.

LISTING 21.3   The Complete Calendar Display Script

```
1: <?php
2: define("ADAY", (60*60*24));
3: if ((!isset($_POST['month'])) || (!isset($_POST['year']))) {
4:     $nowArray = getdate();
5:     $month = $nowArray['mon'];
6:     $year = $nowArray['year'];
7: } else {
8:     $month = $_POST['month'];
9:     $year = $_POST['year'];
10: }
11: $start = mktime (12, 0, 0, $month, 1, $year);
12: $firstDayArray = getdate($start);
13: ?>
14: <!DOCTYPE html>
15: <html>
16: <head>
17:    <title><?php echo "Calendar: ".$firstDayArray['month']."
18:    ".$firstDayArray['year'']; ?></title>
19:    <style type="text/css">
20:    table {
21:        border: 1px solid black;
22:        border-collapse: collapse;
23:    }
24:    th {
25:        border: 1px solid black;
26:        padding: 6px;
27:        font-weight: bold;
28:        background: #ccc;
29:    }
30:    td {
31:        border: 1px solid black;
32:        padding: 6px;
33:        vertical-align: top;
34:        width: 100px;
35:    }
36:    </style>
37: </head>
38: <body>
39:    <h1>Select a Month/Year Combination</h1>
40:    <form method="post" action="<?php echo $_SERVER['PHP_SELF']; ?>">
41:    <select name="month">
42:    <?php
43:    $months = Array("January", "February", "March", "April", "May",
44:    "June", "July", "August", "September", "October", "November", "December");
45:    for ($x=1; $x <= count($months); $x++) {
46:        echo"<option value=\"$x\"";
```

```
47:        if ($x == $month) {
48:            echo " selected";
49:        }
50:        echo ">".$months[$x-1]."</option>";
51:    }
52:    ?>
53:    </select>
54:    <select name="year">
55:    <?php
56:    for ($x=1980; $x<=2010; $x++) {
57:        echo "<option";
58:        if ($x == $year) {
59:            echo " selected";
60:        }
61:        echo ">$x</option>";
62:    }
63:    ?>
64:    </select>
65:    <button type="submit" name="submit" value="submit">Go!</button>
66:    </form>
67:    <br>
68:    <?php
69:    $days = Array("Sun", "Mon", "Tue", "Wed", "Thu", "Fri", "Sat");
70:    echo "<table><tr>\n";
71:    foreach ($days as $day) {
72:        echo "<td>".$day.</td>\n";
73:    }
74:    for ($count=0; $count < (6*7); $count++) {
75:        $dayArray = getdate($start);
76:        if (($count % 7) == 0) {
77:            if ($dayArray['mon'] != $month) {
78:                break;
79:            } else {
80:                echo "</tr><tr>\n";
81:            }
82:        }
83:        if ($count < $firstDayArray['wday'] || $dayArray['mon'] != $month) {
84:            echo "<td> </td>\n";
85:        } else {
86:            echo "<td>".$dayArray['mday']."</td>\n";
87:            $start += ADAY;
88:        }
89:    }
90:    echo "</tr></table>";
91:    ?>
92: </body>
93: </html>
```

We pick up the entirely new code at line 66 of Listing 21.3. Because the table will be indexed by days of the week, we loop through an array of day names in lines 71–73, printing each in its own table cell (on line 72). All the real magic of the script happens in the final `for` statement beginning on line 74.

In line 74, we initialize a variable called `$count` and ensure that the loop will end after 42 iterations. This is to make sure that we will have enough cells to populate with date information, taking into consideration that a four-week month might actually have partial weeks at the beginning and the end, thus the need for six 7-day weeks (rows).

Within this `for` loop, we transform the `$start` variable into a date array with `getdate()`, assigning the result to `$dayArray` (line 75). Although `$start` is the first day of the month during the loop's initial execution, we will increment this timestamp by the value of `ADAY` (24 hours) for every iteration (see line 85).

On line 76, we test the `$count` variable against the number 7, using the modulus operator. The block of code belonging to this `if` statement will therefore be run only when `$count` is either zero or a multiple of seven. This is our way of knowing whether we should end the loop altogether or start a new row, where rows represent weeks.

After we have established that we are in the first iteration or at the end of a row, we can go on to perform another test on line 77. If the `mon` (month number) element of the `$dayArray` is no longer equivalent to the `$month` variable, we are finished. Remember that `$dayArray` contains information about the `$start` timestamp, which is the current place in the month that we are displaying. When `$start` goes beyond the current month, `$dayArray["mon"]` will hold a different figure than the `$month` number provided by user input. Our modulus test demonstrated that we are at the end of a row, and the fact that we are in a new month means that we can leave the loop altogether. Assuming, however, that we are still in the month that we are displaying, we end the row and start a new one on line 80.

In the next `if` statement, on line 83, we determine whether to write date information to a cell. Not every month begins on a Sunday, so it's likely that our rows will contain an empty cell or two. Similarly, few months will finish at the end of one of our rows, so it's also likely that we will have a few empty cells before we close the table.

We have stored information about the first day of the `$firstDayArray`; in particular, we can access the number of the day of the week in `$firstDayArray['wday']`. If the value of `$count` is smaller than this number, we know that we haven't yet reached the correct cell for writing. By the same token, if the value of the `$month` variable is no longer equal to `$dayArray['mon']`, we know that we have reached the end of the month (but not the end of the row, as we determined in our earlier modulus test). In either case, we write an empty `cell` to the browser on line 84.

In the final `else` clause on line 85, we can do the fun stuff. We have already determined that we are within the month that we want to list, and that the current day column matches the day number stored in `$firstDayArray['wday']`. Now we must use the `$dayArray` associative array that we established early in the loop to write the day of the month and some blank space into a cell.

Finally, on line 86, we need to increment the `$start` variable, which contains our date stamp. We just add the number of seconds in a day to it (we defined this value in line 2), and we're ready to begin the loop again with a new value in `$start` to be tested. If you save this listing as `showcalendar.php`, place it in your web server document root, and access it with your web browser, you should see something like Figure 21.2 (your month and year might differ).

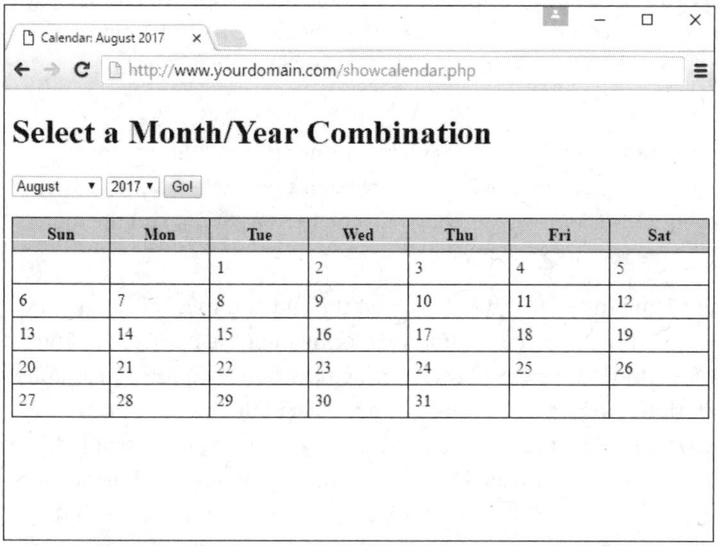

FIGURE 21.2
The calendar form in action.

Adding Events to the Calendar

Displaying the calendar is great, but with just a few extra lines of code, you can make it interactive—that is, you can add and view events on a given day. To begin, let's create a simple database table that holds event information. For purposes of simplicity, these events will occur on only a single day and only their start date and time will be shown. Although you can make the event entries as complex as you want, this example is here just to show the basic process involved.

The `calendar_events` table will include fields for the start date and time, the event title, and an event short description:

```
CREATE TABLE calendar_events (
    id INT NOT NULL PRIMARY KEY AUTO_INCREMENT,
    event_title VARCHAR (25),
```

```
    event_shortdesc VARCHAR (255),
    event_start DATETIME
);
```

We can use the code in Listing 21.3 as our base (the script called `showcalendar.php`). In this new script, we add a link to a pop-up window as part of the calendar display. Each date is a link; the pop-up window calls another script that displays the full text of an event as well as provides the capability to add an event. To begin, add the following JavaScript code at the bottom of the HTML document, before the closing `</body>` tag (after line 90 of the original script in Listing 21.3):

```
<script type="text/javascript">
function eventWindow(url) {
    event_popupWin = window.open(url, 'event', 'resizable=yes, scrollbars=yes,
            toolbar=no,width=400,height=400');
    event_popupWin.opener = self;
}
</script>
```

This JavaScript function defines a 400 × 400 window that will call a URL we provide. We placed the JavaScript at the bottom of the document to give the rest of the page time to load. We use this JavaScript function to replace what was line 85 of the original script in Listing 21.3; we now wrap the date display in this link to the JavaScript-based pop-up window, which calls a script named `event.php`. The new code is as follows:

```
echo "<td><a href=\"javascript:eventWindow('event.php?m=".$month.
"&amp;d=".$dayArray['mday']."&amp;y=$year');\">".$dayArray['mday']."</a>
<br>".$event_title."</td>\n";
```

Not only do we call the `event.php` file, but we also have to send along with it the date information for the particular link that is clicked. This is done via the query string, and you can see we're sending along three variables—what will become `$_GET['m']` for the month, `$_GET['d']` for the day, and `$_GET['y']` for the year.

Only one change remains for this particular script before we tackle the `event.php` script—adding an indicator to this particular view, if events do indeed exist. The query that checks for existing events on a given day appears at the onset of the `else` statement that was originally found at line 85. An entirely new `else` statement is shown; you can see that the database connection is made, a query is issued, and, if results are found, text is printed within the table cell for that day:

```
} else {
    $event_title = "";
    $mysqli = mysqli_connect("localhost", "testuser", "somepass", "testDB");
    $chkEvent_sql = "SELECT event_title FROM calendar_events WHERE
                month(event_start) = '".$month."' AND
                dayofmonth(event_start) = '".$dayArray['mday']."'
```

```
                    AND year(event_start) = '".$year."' ORDER BY event_start";
        $chkEvent_res = mysqli_query($mysqli, $chkEvent_sql)
                    or die(mysqli_error($mysqli));

        if (mysqli_num_rows($chkEvent_res) > 0) {
            while ($ev = mysqli_fetch_array($chkEvent_res)) {
                $event_title = stripslashes($ev['event_title']);
            }
        } else {
            $event_title = "";
        }

        echo "<td><a href=\"javascript:eventWindow('event.php?m=".$month.
        "&amp;d=".$dayArray['mday']."&amp;y=$year');\">".
        $dayArray['mday']."</a><br>".$event_title."</td>\n";

        unset($event_title);

        $start += ADAY;
    }
}
```

In Listing 21.4, you can see the entirely new script, which we'll call `showcalendar_` `withevent.php`.

LISTING 21.4 Calendar Display Script with Entry-Related Modifications

```
 1: <?php
 2: define("ADAY", (60*60*24));
 3: if ((!isset($_POST['month'])) || (!isset($_POST['year']))) {
 4:     $nowArray = getdate();
 5:     $month = $nowArray['mon'];
 6:     $year = $nowArray['year'];
 7: } else {
 8:     $month = $_POST['month'];
 9:     $year = $_POST['year'];
10: }
11:
12: $start = mktime (12, 0, 0, $month, 1, $year);
13: $firstDayArray = getdate($start);
14: ?>
15: <!DOCTYPE html>
16: <html lang="en">
17: <head>
18:   <title><?php echo "Calendar: ".$firstDayArray['month']."
19:    ".$firstDayArray['year'']; ?></title>
20:   <style type="text/css">
```

```
21:     table {
22:         border: 1px solid black;
23:         border-collapse: collapse;
24:     }
25:     th {
26:         border: 1px solid black;
27:         padding: 6px;
28:         font-weight: bold;
29:         background: #ccc;
30:     }
31:     td {
32:         border: 1px solid black;
33:         padding: 6px;
34:         vertical-align: top;
35:         width: 100px;
36:     }
37:     </style>
38: </head>
39: <body>
40:     <h1>Select a Month/Year Combination</h1>
41:     <form method="post" action="<?php echo $_SERVER['PHP_SELF']; ?>">
42:         <select name="month">
43:         <?php
44:         $months = Array("January", "February", "March", "April", "May",  "June", "July",
45:         "August", "September", "October", "November", "December");
46:         for ($x=1; $x <= count($months); $x++) {
47:             echo"<option value=\"$x\"";
48:             if ($x == $month) {
49:                 echo " selected";
50:             }
51:             echo ">".$months[$x-1]."</option>";
52:         }
53:         ?>
54:     </select>
55:     <select name="year">
56:     <?php
57:     for ($x=1990; $x<=2020; $x++) {
58:         echo "<option";
59:     if ($x == $year) {
60:         echo " selected";
61:     }
62:     echo ">$x</option>";
63:     }
64:     ?>
65:     </select>
```

```
66:    <button type="submit" name="submit" value="submit">Go!</button>
67:    </form>
68:    <br>
69:    <?php
70:    $days = Array("Sun", "Mon", "Tue", "Wed", "Thu", "Fri", "Sat");
71:    echo "<table><tr>\n";
72:    foreach ($days as $day) {
73:        echo "<th>".$day."</th>\n";
74:    }
75:    for ($count=0; $count < (6*7); $count++) {
76:        $dayArray = getdate($start);
77:        if (($count % 7) == 0) {
78:            if ($dayArray['mon'] != $month) {
79:                break;
80:            } else {
81:                echo "</tr><tr>\n";
82:            }
83:        }
84:        if ($count < $firstDayArray['wday'] || $dayArray['mon'] != $month) {
85:            echo "<td> </td>\n";
86:        } else {
87:            $event_title = "";
88:           $mysqli = mysqli_connect("localhost", "testuser", "somepass", "testDB");
89:            $chkEvent_sql = "SELECT event_title FROM calendar_events WHERE
90:                    month(event_start) = '".$month."' AND
91:                    dayofmonth(event_start) = '".$dayArray['mday']."'
92:                    AND year(event_start) = '".$year."' ORDER BY event_start";
93:            $chkEvent_res = mysqli_query($mysqli, $chkEvent_sql)
94:                    or die(mysqli_error($mysqli));
95:
96:            if (mysqli_num_rows($chkEvent_res) > 0) {
97:                while ($ev = mysqli_fetch_array($chkEvent_res)) {
98:                    $event_title .= stripslashes($ev['event_title'])."<br>";
99:                }
100:           } else {
101:               $event_title = "";
102:           }
103:
104:           echo "<td><a href=\"javascript:eventWindow('event.php?m=".$month.
105:           "&amp;d=".$dayArray['mday']."&amp;y=$year');\">".$dayArray['mday']."</a>
106:           <br>".$event_title."</td>\n";
107:           unset($event_title);
108:           $start += ADAY;
109:        }
110:    }
```

```
111:        echo "</tr></table>";
112:
113:        //close connection to MySQL
114:        mysqli_close($mysqli);
115:        ?>
116:
117:    <script type="text/javascript">
118:    function eventWindow(url) {
119:        event_popupWin = window.open(url, 'event', 'resizable=yes,
120:            scrollbars=yes, toolbar=no,width=400,height=400');
121:        event_popupWin.opener = self;
122:    }
123:    </script>
124:
125: </body>
126: </html>
```

In Figure 21.3, you can see the new calendar, including the representation of the event title on a date that, for illustrative purposes here, I've prepopulated with an event in the calendar_events table.

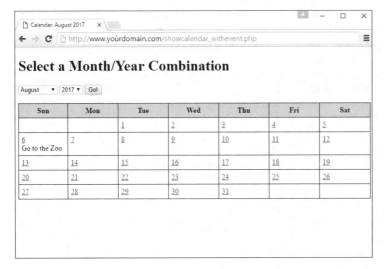

FIGURE 21.3
Showing the calendar with an event.

All that remains is adding the all-in-one event.php script used in the pop-up window to display and also add an event to the calendar (on a particular day). Listing 21.5 contains all the necessary code; the fun part starts at line 8, which connects to the MySQL database. Line 11 checks whether the event entry form has been submitted; if it has, database-safe values are created in lines 14–24, and an INSERT statement is created and issued to add the event to the calendar_events table before continuing (lines 29–34).

LISTING 21.5   Showing Events/Adding Events via a Pop-Up

```
1:   <!DOCTYPE html>
2:   <html>
3:   <head>
4:      <title>Show/Add Events</title>
5:   </head>
6:   <body>
7:      <h1>Show/Add Events</h1>
8:      <?php
9:      $mysqli = mysqli_connect("localhost", "testuser", "somepass", "testDB");
10:
11:     //add any new event
12:     if ($_POST) {
13:
14:         //create database-safe strings
15:         $safe_m = mysqli_real_escape_string($mysqli, $_POST['m']);
16:         $safe_d = mysqli_real_escape_string($mysqli, $_POST['d']);
17:         $safe_y = mysqli_real_escape_string($mysqli, $_POST['y']);
18:         $safe_event_title = mysqli_real_escape_string($mysqli,
19:             $_POST['event_title']);
20:         $safe_event_shortdesc = mysqli_real_escape_string($mysqli,
21:             $_POST['event_shortdesc']);
22:         $safe_event_time_hh = mysqli_real_escape_string($mysqli,
23:             $_POST['event_time_hh']);
24:         $safe_event_time_mm = mysqli_real_escape_string($mysqli,
25:             $_POST['event_time_mm']);
26:
27:         $event_date = $safe_y."-".$safe_m."-".$safe_d."
28:             ".$safe_event_time_hh.":".$safe_event_time_mm.":00";
29:
30:         $insEvent_sql = "INSERT INTO calendar_events (event_title,
31:                 event_shortdesc, event_start) VALUES
32:                 ('".$safe_event_title."', '".$safe_event_shortdesc."',
33:                 '".$event_date."')";
34:         $insEvent_res = mysqli_query($mysqli, $insEvent_sql)
35:             or die(mysqli_error($mysqli));
36:
37:     } else {
38:
39:         //create database-safe strings
40:         $safe_m = mysqli_real_escape_string($mysqli, $_GET['m']);
41:         $safe_d = mysqli_real_escape_string($mysqli, $_GET['d']);
```

```
42:            $safe_y = mysqli_real_escape_string($mysqli, $_GET['y']);
43:        }
44:
45:    //show events for this day
46:    $getEvent_sql = "SELECT event_title, event_shortdesc,
47:                    date_format(event_start, '%l:%i %p') as fmt_date
48:                    FROM calendar_events WHERE month(event_start) =
49:                    '".$safe_m."' AND dayofmonth(event_start) =
50:                    '".$safe_d."' AND year(event_start) =
51:                    '".$safe_y."' ORDER BY event_start";
52:    $getEvent_res = mysqli_query($mysqli, $getEvent_sql)
53:        or die(mysqli_error($mysqli));
54:
55:    if (mysqli_num_rows($getEvent_res) > 0) {
56:        $event_txt = "<ul>";
57:        while ($ev = @mysqli_fetch_array($getEvent_res)) {
58:            $event_title = stripslashes($ev['event_title']);
59:            $event_shortdesc = stripslashes($ev['event_shortdesc']);
60:            $fmt_date = $ev['fmt_date'];
61:            $event_txt .= "<li><strong>".$fmt_date."</strong>:
62:                    ".$event_title."<br>".$event_shortdesc."</li>";
63:        }
64:        $event_txt .= "</ul>";
65:        mysqli_free_result($getEvent_res);
66:    } else {
67:        $event_txt = "";
68:    }
69:    // close connection to MySQL
70:    mysqli_close($mysqli);
71:
72:    if ($event_txt != "") {
73:        echo "<p><strong>Today's Events:</strong></p>
74:        $event_txt
75:        <hr>";
76:    }
77:
78:    // show form for adding an event
79:    echo <<<END_OF_TEXT
80: <form method="post" action="$_SERVER[PHP_SELF]">
81: <p><strong>Would you like to add an event?</strong><br>
82: Complete the form below and press the submit button to
83: add the event and refresh this window.</p>
84:
85: <p><label for="event_title">Event Title:</label><br>
86: <input type="text" id="event_title" name="event_title"
```

```
87:          size="25" maxlength="25"></p>
88:
89:  <p><label for="event_shortdesc">Event Description:</label><br>
90:  <input type="text" id="event_shortdesc" name="event_shortdesc"
91:          size="25" maxlength="255"></p>
92:  <fieldset>
93:  <legend>Event Time (hh:mm):</legend>
94:  <select name="event_time_hh">
95:  END_OF_TEXT;
96:
97:    for ($x=1; $x <= 24; $x++) {
98:        echo "<option value=\"$x\">$x</option>";
99:    }
100:
101:   echo <<<END_OF_TEXT
102: </select> :
103: <select name="event_time_mm">
104: <option value="00">00</option>
105: <option value="15">15</option>
106: <option value="30">30</option>
107: <option value="45">45</option>
108: </select>
109: </fieldset>
110: <input type="hidden" name="m" value="$safe_m">
111: <input type="hidden" name="d" value="$safe_d">
112: <input type="hidden" name="y" value="$safe_y">
113:
114: <button type="submit" name="submit" value="submit">Add Event</button>
115: </form>
116: END_OF_TEXT;
117:    ?>
118: </body>
119: </html>
```

Lines 45–52 create and issue the query and retrieve all records that correspond to events on this given day. The text block used to display entries is created in lines 54–67. However, users also need to see the form for adding an event, and this is built in lines 79–114, effectively the end of the script.

Figure 21.4 shows how a pop-up looks when a link is followed from the calendar and an entry is already present. In this example, we want to add another event on this day, so the form has been completed in preparation for adding the additional event.

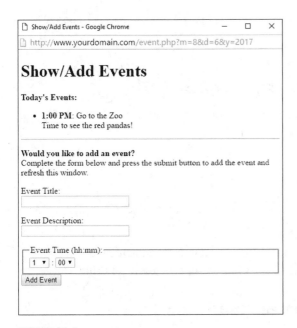

FIGURE 21.4
Showing the day detail, ready to add another event.

In Figure 21.5, a second event has been added to this particular day.

FIGURE 21.5
A second event has been added.

Obviously, this is a simple example, but it shows that it is indeed easy to build a calendar-based application in just a few short scripts.

Creating the Calendar in JavaScript

In order to build the calendar in JavaScript, you do the same things that you do in the PHP:

- ▶ Check the user input.

- ▶ Build an HTML form.

- ▶ Create a calendar table.

- ▶ Add events to the calendar.

You just do them in different ways. For this chapter, you learn how to use jQuery to build your calendar in JavaScript; you learned about jQuery in Chapter 10, "The Basics of Using jQuery."

Creating the HTML for the Calendar

Let's start by creating the basic HTML for the calendar. Since you'll be using jQuery and some unobtrusive JavaScript, you can create a very minimal HTML document. All of the work will be done by the script. You can find this basic HTML in Listing 21.6:

LISTING 21.6 Basic HTML for the JavaScript-based Calendar

```
 1:  <!DOCTYPE html>
 2:  <html lang="en">
 3:  <head>
 4:    <title>My Calendar</title>
 5:    <style type="text/css">
 6:    table {
 7:        border: 1px solid black;
 8:        border-collapse: collapse;
 9:        margin-top: 1rem;
10:    }
11:    th {
12:        border: 1px solid black;
13:        padding: 6px;
14:        font-weight: bold;
15:        background: #ccc;
16:    }
17:    td {
18:        border: 1px solid black;
19:        padding: 6px;
20:        vertical-align: top;
21:        width: 100px;
```

```
22:    }
23:    </style>
24:    <script src="https://code.jquery.com/jquery-3.2.1.min.js"></script>
25: </head>
26: <body>
27:    <h1>Select a Month/Year Combination</h1>
28:    <form id="datePicker"></form>
29:    <div id="myCal"></div>
30:
31:    <script>
32:    // script will go here!
33:    </script>
34: </body>
35: </html>
```

Lines 6–23 are the styles that will be used for the calendar once it's visible. The HTML consists of a header (line 27), a form (line 28), and a <div> container for the calendar (line 29). Lines 31–33 are where the JavaScript will go to build the entire page.

Building the Form to Accept User Input

The first form to place on the page is the date picker, which we'll now build in JavaScript. This JavaScript function, using jQuery at its base, will go in the <script> area lines 31–33) of Listing 21.6 to build that form. Listing 21.7 shows this JavaScript function.

LISTING 21.7   The JavaScript Function for a Date Picker

```
1:  function buildDateForm() {
2:    var months = ["January", "February", "March", "April", "May", "June", "July",
3:    "August", "September", "October", "November", "December"];
4:    $('#datePicker').append('<select id="month"></select>');
5:    for(var i = 0; i < months.length;i++) {
6:      $('#month').append('<option value="'+i+'">'+months[i]+'</option>')
7:    }
8:    $('#datePicker').append('<select id="year"></select>');
9:    for(i = 1990; i < 2021; i++) {
10:      $('#year').append('<option value="'+i+'">'+i+'</option>')
11:    }
12:    $('#datePicker').append('<button id="submit">Go!</button>');
13:
14:    // set date to current month and year
15:    var d = new Date();
16:    var n = d.getMonth();
17:    var y = d.getFullYear();
18:    $('#month option:eq('+n+')').prop('selected', true);
19:    $('#year option[value="'+y+'"]').prop('selected', true);
20: }
```

This script works very much like the PHP-based script from earlier in the chapter worked, except that it builds the HTML elements directly into the DOM. Line 4 of Listing 21.7 looks in the page for the element with the ID `datePicker` and adds a `select` element to select the months. Lines 5–7 walk through the array of months (lines 2–3) and place them as options for the drop-down menu. Lines 8–11 do the same thing for the year drop-down, except they use a `for` loop to populate the years. Line 12 adds a button to the date picker so that the new values can be submitted. Lines 14–20 set the drop-down menus to the current month and year so the calendar is more user friendly.

If we stopped at this point, the page would remain blank because there is nothing to tell the browser to run the script. For this we need to use the jQuery `$().ready` function, which you learned about in Chapter 10. As a reminder, using this function ensures that scripts only run after everything on the page has rendered; if you try to run scripts before the rest of the page has rendered, this can cause problems. For example, if we tried to run the script in Listing 21.6 before the HTML with the `<form id="datePicker"></form>` line had loaded, the script would fail because there would be no element with that ID on the page.

For our calendar, we want to call the `buildDateForm()` function once the DOM is ready, which looks like this:

```
$().ready(function(){
  // build the picker form
  buildDateForm();
});
```

We should add a listener to the function to tell the browser what to do when the form is submitted:

```
  // watch for clicks on the submit button
  $("#submit").click(function() {
    var newMonth = $('#month').val();
    var newYear = $('#year').val();
    var newDate = new Date(newYear, newMonth, 1);
    calendar(newDate);
    return false;
  });
```

This snippet of JavaScript checks for clicks on any element with the ID `#submit`. It then creates a new date with the submitted values and submits them to the calendar script, which redraws the calendar. The `return false;` is important so that the browser doesn't try to submit the form to the server. Let's put these pieces together in the next section.

Creating the Calendar

Once you have the date picker form displaying, you can build the calendar. Like we did with the form, we will add a calendar in a table right inside the empty `div` element in the HTML. The JavaScript functions in a similar way to how the PHP did when building the calendar. Listing 21.7 shows what it looks like.

LISTING 21.7 Building a Calendar with JavaScript

```
 1:  function calendar(date) {
 2:    $( "#myCal" ).empty();
 3:    if (date == null) {
 4:      date = new Date;
 5:    }
 6:    day = date.getDate();
 7:    month = date.getMonth();
 8:    year = date.getFullYear();
 9:    months = new Array('January','February','March','April','May','June',
10:        'July','August','September','October','November','December');
11:    this_month = new Date(year, month, 1);
12:    next_month = new Date(year, month + 1, 1);
13:    days = new Array('Sun', 'Mon', 'Tue', 'Wed', 'Thu', 'Fri', 'Sat');
14:    first_week_day = this_month.getDay(); // day of the week of the first day
15:    days_in_this_month = Math.round((next_month.getTime() - this_month.getTime())
16:        / (1000 * 60 * 60 * 24));
17:
18:    $('#myCal').append('<table id="myCalendar"></table>');
19:    $('#myCalendar').append('<thead><tr></tr></thead>');
20:    for (var i=0; i < days.length; i++) {
21:      $('#myCalendar thead tr').append('<th>'+days[i]+'</th>')
22:    }
23:    $('#myCalendar').append('<tbody></tbody>');
24:    $('tbody').append('<tr>');
25:    for(week_day = 0; week_day < first_week_day; week_day++)  {
26:      $('tbody tr').append('<td id="'+week_day+'"></td>');
27:    }
28:    week_day = first_week_day;
29:
30:    for (day_counter=1; day_counter <= days_in_this_month; day_counter++) {
31:      week_day %= 7;
32:      if (week_day == 0) {
33:        // go to the next line of the calendar
34:        $('tbody').append('</tr><tr>');
35:      }
36:      $('tbody tr:last').append('<td id="day'+day_counter+'">' +
37:        day_counter + '</td>');
38:
39:      week_day++;
40:    }
41:  }
```

The function begins by ensuring the #myCal element is empty (line 2) using the jQuery `empty()` method to remove everything inside the named element. Then we create the date (lines 3–8) using the JavaScript `Date` object. If the `calendar` function is called without any arguments, we use today's date as the starting calendar entry.

Lines 9–16 create the calendar month and days-of-the-week arrays, as well as other variables about the specific calendar month, such as this month, next month, the first day of the month, and the day of the week of the first day. Finally, we use the Math object to determine the days in the month.

Lines 18–27 build the outermost tags of the calendar table. Because jQuery builds the HTML in the DOM, it creates each element separately and then appends it to the parent container. Line 18 adds the <table> element to the <div> element called #myCal and gives it an ID of myCalendar. Line 19 adds the table head and the first row. Lines 20–22 walk through the days-of-the-week array and make them table header cells. Then line 23 adds a tbody section to the table where the main calendar cells will go. Lines 24–27 walk through the empty cells at the beginning of the month before the first day. Then lines 30–39 create each week with a number in each cell indicating the day. To make the calendar display, add the calendar() call to the ready function so that it now looks like this:

```
$().ready(function(){
  // build the picker form
  buildDateForm();
  calendar();

  $("#submit").click(function() {
    var newMonth = $('#month').val();
    var newYear = $('#year').val();
    var newDate = new Date(newYear, newMonth, 1);
    calendar(newDate);
    return false;
  });
});
```

Let's do a little cleanup and place both the buildDateForm() and calendar() functions into their own file, called calendar_functions.js. You can then include it in your HTML file much like you do the jQuery library:

```
<script src="calendar_functions.js"></script>
```

Your HTML file should now look something like Listing 21.8.

LISTING 21.8 Building a Calendar with JavaScript

```
1:    <!DOCTYPE html>
2:    <html lang="en">
3:    <head>
4:      <title>My Calendar</title>
5:      <style type="text/css">
6:      table {
7:        border: 1px solid black;
```

```
 8:          border-collapse: collapse;
 9:          margin-top: 1rem;
10:       }
11:       th {
12:          border: 1px solid black;
13:          padding: 6px;
14:          font-weight: bold;
15:          background: #ccc;
16:       }
17:       td {
18:          border: 1px solid black;
19:          padding: 6px;
20:          vertical-align: top;
21:          width: 100px;
22:       }
23:       </style>
24:       <script src="https://code.jquery.com/jquery-3.2.1.min.js"></script>
25:       <script src="calendar_functions.js"></script>
26:  </head>
27:  <body>
28:       <h1>Select a Month/Year Combination</h1>
29:       <form id="datePicker"></form>
30:       <div id="myCal"></div>
31:
32:       <script type="text/javascript">
33:       $().ready(function(){
34:         // build the picker form
35:         buildDateForm();
36:         calendar();
37:
38:         $("#submit").click(function() {
39:           var newMonth = $('#month').val();
40:           var newYear = $('#year').val();
41:             var newDate = new Date(newYear, newMonth, 1);
42:             calendar(newDate);
43:             return false;
44:         });
45:       });
46:       </script>
47:  </body>
48:  </html>
```

If you load this HTML file in your browser, you should see something like Figure 21.6, which looks strikingly like Figure 21.2 but with the current month's calendar already displayed and none of it being driven by PHP.

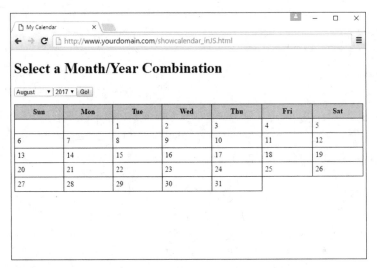

FIGURE 21.6
Showing the calendar created by JavaScript.

Summary

In this chapter, we pulled together the PHP date-related functions you learned about earlier in the book to work within a basic calendar application display. You learned how to test the validity of an input date using `checkdate()`, and you worked through a sample script that applied some of the tools you have learned. You also saw one method for adding and viewing events within your calendar application. You then learned how to build the same type of calendar using JavaScript and jQuery for a better (more efficient) user experience that avoids round-trips back from your web server to compile PHP code to render HTML.

Q&A

Q. Are there any functions for converting between different calendars?

A. Yes. PHP provides an entire suite of functions that cover alternative calendars. You can read about these in the official PHP Manual at http://www.php.net/manual/en/ref.calendar. php. There is also a jQuery plug-in called jQuery Calendars (http://keith-wood.name/calendarsRef.html) that can help you convert between calendars in JavaScript.

Workshop

The Workshop is designed to help you review what you've learned and begin putting your knowledge into practice.

Quiz

1. What PHP function did we use to create a timestamp?

2. What PHP function did we use to create an associative array of date-related information?

3. Why was it important to put the JavaScript function calls within the jQuery `ready` function?

Answers

1. `mktime()`

2. `getdate()`

3. If the function calls were placed outside of the jQuery `ready` function, there would be no guarantee that the required elements had been loaded before attempting to use them.

Exercises

▶ Modify the calendar display script to show an entire year of the calendar—from January through December. After that, display the calendar as a 3 × 4 grid, or four rows of three months on each row.

▶ Modify the JavaScript-based calendar script to combine it with actions based in PHP to add and display events.

CHAPTER 22
Managing Web Applications

What You'll Learn in This Chapter:

▶ Some best practices in web application development
▶ How to write maintainable code
▶ How to get started with version control
▶ The value and use of HTML, CSS, JavaScript, and PHP frameworks

The bulk of this book has led you through the design and creation of basic static and dynamic web content, from text to graphics and multimedia, and with a little JavaScript interactivity and back-end PHP interpretation and database interaction thrown in for good measure. These chapters are the foundation for the next step in your personal and technical development process.

This chapter shows you how to think about developing and managing larger web applications than just the simple prototypes and basic structures you've seen in this book. You'll learn about ways to work with other people on your projects, which includes adding comments and using version control so that you can innovate individually or as part of a team without overwriting work that you might want to have saved. Finally, you'll learn a little bit about application frameworks, which exist so that you and others do not need to reinvent the wheel every time you start a new project—if that were the case, we'd never ship anything!

Understanding Some Best Practices in Web Application Development

If you've learned one thing in this book—and I hope you've learned more than one thing—it's that you can create prototypes and make changes in web-based content and applications *very quickly*. Sometimes you may find yourself in a situation where you're trying to solve a problem and you aren't afforded the luxury of time to systematically approach the solution to your problem—you might end up fiddling around with your style sheets, your HTML, your JavaScript, or your PHP, and only after you've hit on a solution can you go back and say "I totally meant to do that from the beginning." This is normal.

But that doesn't mean you shouldn't *try* to plan your web application development project, or that you shouldn't follow some best practices along the way. You should. However— surprise!—there is no best methodology or project life cycle for web projects, but there are a number of things you should consider. You don't have to follow all of them or in this order if it doesn't suit your project, but be aware of these things and choose the techniques that work for you.

▸ Before you begin, think about what you are trying to build. Think about the goal. Think about who is going to use your web application—that is, your targeted audience. Many technically perfect web projects fail because nobody checked whether users were interested in such an application in the first place.

▸ Try to break down your application into components. What parts or process steps does your application have? How will each of those components work? How will they fit together? Drawing up scenarios, storyboards, and use cases will be useful for figuring out these components and steps.

▸ After you have a list of components, see which of them already exist. This is where frameworks come in, or at least code snippets and libraries that may exist in the open-source community. Determine what code you have to write from scratch and roughly how big that job is, before committing to it. If you do use something from the open source community, be sure you understand what that code is doing—don't use it blindly.

▸ Make decisions about coding standards, directory structures, version control, development environment, and documentation. This step is ignored too often in web projects, and much time is wasted going back and retrofitting code to standards, documenting after the fact, and so on.

▸ Throughout this process, try to separate content and logic in your application. When your team grows beyond just yourself, you are likely to have people who work on content and design, and people who work on logic; you'll want to avoid collisions in your work.

▸ Build a prototype based on all the previous information. Show it to users—design *with* them. Iterate almost incessantly, and test, test, test—but be mindful of a definition of "done" that works for your organization.

We'll look at a few of these in more detail in the following sections.

Separating Logic and Content

For simple projects with a small number of lines of code or scripts, separating content and logic can be more trouble than it's worth. As your projects become bigger, it is essential to find a way to separate logic and content. If you don't do this, your code will become increasingly difficult to maintain. If you or the powers that be decide to apply a new design to your website and a lot of HTML is embedded in your code, changing the design will be a nightmare.

Three basic approaches to separating logic and content follow—some of these should be familiar to you by this point in the book:

▶ Use include files to store different parts of the content. This approach is simplistic, but if your site is mostly static, it can work quite well.

▶ Use a function or class API with a set of member functions to plug dynamic content into static page templates.

▶ Use a templating system. The main advantage of this approach is that if somebody else designs your templates, he or she doesn't have to know anything about PHP code at all. You should be able to use supplied templates with minimum modification. For PHP, a number of template engines are available, such as Smarty (http://www.smarty.net/), Twig (http://twig.sensiolabs.org/), and Plates (http://platesphp.com/).

Prototyping

A *prototype* is a useful tool for working out customer requirements. Usually, it is a simplified, partially working version of an application that can be used in discussions with clients and as the basis of the final system. Often, multiple iterations over a prototype produce the final application. The advantage of this approach is that it lets you work closely with clients or end users to produce a system that they will be pleased with and have some ownership of.

To be able to "knock together" a prototype quickly, you need some particular skills and tools. A component-based approach works well in such situations. If you have access to a set of preexisting components, both in-house and publicly available, you will be able to do this much more quickly. Another useful tool for rapid development of prototypes is templates, which often come from frameworks as discussed later in this chapter.

You will encounter two main problems using a prototyping approach, both easily overcome through communication and planning:

▶ Developers often find it difficult to throw away the code that they have written for one reason or another. Prototypes are often written quickly, and you'll want to throw code away—and ultimately you should. You can avoid this problem by doing a little planning, where you set the expectation with everyone that code will be thrown away at some point. Sometimes it is easier to scrap something and start again than to try to fix a problem.

▶ What you thought would be a quick prototype could end up being an eternal prototype. For example, every time you think you're finished, your client suggests some more improvements or additional functionality or updates to the site. This "feature creep" can stop you from ever signing off on a project. Avoid this by setting expectations and success criteria for your development milestones.

Testing

Reviewing and testing code is another basic point of software engineering that is often overlooked in web development. It's easy enough to try running the system with two or three test cases and then say, "Yup, it works fine." Don't fall into that trap; ensure that you have extensively tested and reviewed several scenarios before making the project production ready.

Adopt a practice of code review within your team. Code review is the process in which another programmer or team of programmers looks at your code and suggests improvements. This type of analysis often suggests

- Errors you have missed

- Test cases you have not considered

- Optimization

- Improvements in security

- Existing components you could use to improve a piece of code

- Functionality defined in the requirements but missing in your work

Finally, find testers for your web applications who represent the end users of the product. The primary difference between web applications and desktop applications is that anyone and everyone will use web applications. You shouldn't make assumptions that users will be familiar with computers. You can't supply them with a thick manual or quick reference card. Instead, you have to make web applications self-documenting and self-evident. You must think about the ways in which users will want to use your application. Usability is absolutely paramount.

Writing Maintainable Code

If you've done any coding before reading this book, you already know how important it is to write code that can be maintained—that is, you or someone else should be able to look at your code later and not be utterly confused by it. The challenge is to make your code as immediately understandable as possible. A time will come when you'll look back on a page that you wrote, and you won't have a clue what you were thinking or why you wrote the code the way you did. Fortunately, there are ways to combat this problem of apparent memory loss.

Many organizations have coding standards for choosing file and variable names, guidelines for commenting code, guidelines for indenting code, and so on. If you are coding on your own or in a small team, you can easily underestimate the importance of coding standards. Don't overlook such standards because your team and project might grow, and it might grow too quickly for you to reasonably document after the fact.

Defining Naming Conventions

The goals of defining naming conventions are twofold:

▶ **To make the code easy to read**—If you define variables and function names sensibly, you should be able to virtually read code as you would an English sentence.

▶ **To make identifier names easy to remember**—If your identifiers are consistently formatted, remembering what you called a particular variable or function will be easier.

As you learned in the early chapters of this book, variable names should describe the data they contain. If you are storing somebody's surname, call it `$surname`. In general, strike a balance between length and readability. For example, storing the name in `$n` makes it easy to type, but the code is difficult to understand. Storing the name in `$surname_of_the_current_user` is more informative, but it's a lot to type (and therefore easier to make a typing error) and doesn't really add that much value.

Decide on capitalization. Variable names are case sensitive in PHP, as you learned earlier in this book. You need to decide whether your variable names will be all lowercase, all uppercase, or a mix—for example, capitalizing the first letter of words. One bad practice some programmers use is to have two variables with the same name but different capitalization just because they can, such as `$name` and `$Name`. I hope it is obvious to you by now why this practice is a terrible idea!

Function names have many of the same considerations as variable names, with a couple of extras. Function names should generally be verb oriented. Consider built-in PHP functions, such as `addslashes()` and `mysqli_connect()`, that describe what they are going to do to or with the parameters they are passed. This naming scheme greatly enhances code readability. Notice that these two functions have a different naming scheme for dealing with multiword function names. PHP's functions are inconsistent in this regard, partly as a result of having been written by a large group of people, but mostly because many function names have been adopted unchanged from various different languages and APIs.

Unlike variable names, function names are *not* case sensitive in PHP. You should probably stick to a particular format anyway when creating your own functions, just to avoid confusion within the code (or your organization).

Additionally, you might want to consider using the module-naming scheme used in many PHP modules—that is, prefixing the name of functions with the module name. For example, all the improved MySQL functions begin with `mysqli_`, and all the IMAP functions begin with `imap_`. If, for example, you have a shopping cart module in your code, you could prefix the function in that module with `cart_`.

In the end, the conventions and standards you use when writing code don't really matter, as long as you apply some consistent guidelines within your codebase and your team.

Documenting Code with Comments

Whenever you develop an HTML page, CSS snippet, JavaScript function, or PHP code, keep in mind that you or someone else will almost certainly need to make changes to it someday. Simple text web pages are usually easy to read and revise, but complex pages with graphics, tables, and other layout tricks can be quite difficult to decipher. The same is true for simple JavaScript or PHP versus longer and more complex code in either language.

Each of the technologies mentioned have a slightly different commenting syntax, and you've seen them all in use throughout this book. Here's a refresher:

▶ To include comments in a style sheet, begin with /* and end with */ (your commented code should be between these characters).

▶ The HTML <!-- and --> comment syntax does not work in style sheets, JavaScript, or PHP, but works like a charm in plain old HTML.

▶ To comment code in JavaScript or PHP, use // before single line comments, and surround multiline comments by /* and */.

To see what I'm talking about, visit just about any page in a web browser and view its source code. Using Internet Explorer, right-click any page and select View Source. Using Chrome or Firefox, right-click any page and select View Page Source. You might see a jumbled bunch of code that is tough to decipher as pure HTML. This might be because content management software systems have generated the markup dynamically, or it might be because its human maintainer has not paid attention to structure, ease of reading, code commenting, and other methods for making the code readable by humans. For the sake of maintaining your own pages, I encourage you to impose a little more order on your HTML markup, style sheet entries, and JavaScript code. And remember: Proper indentation is your (and your future development partner's) friend.

As you have seen in several lessons throughout this book, you can enclose comments to yourself or your coauthors using the HTML beginning and ending comment syntax: <!-- and -->. These comments will not appear on the web page when viewed with a browser but can be read by anyone who examines the HTML code in a text editor or via the web browser's View Source (or View Page Source) function. Here's an example:

```
<!-- This image needs to be updated daily. -->
<img src="headline.jpg" alt="Today's Headline" >
```

As this code reveals, the comment just before the <img> tag provides a clue to how the image is used. Anyone who reads this code knows immediately that this is an image that must be updated every day. Web browsers completely ignore the text in the comment.

Generally, you should consider adding comments to the following items:

▶ **Files**—Whether a complete script or include file, each file should have a comment stating what this file is, what it's for, who wrote it, and when it was updated.

▶ **Functions**—Specify what the function does, what input it expects, and what it returns.

▶ **Classes**—Describe the purpose of the class. Class methods should have the same types and levels of comments as any other functions.

▶ **Any chunks of code within a script or function**—This is especially the case if the code exists as a placeholder or set of pseudocode-style comments.

▶ **Complex code or hacks**—This is especially the case for hacks or things you've have to do in a weird way. Write a comment explaining why you used that approach so that when you or a colleague next looks at the code, you won't be scratching your head and thinking, "What on earth was *that* supposed to do?"

Finally, and perhaps most importantly: comment as you go. You might think you will come back and comment your code when you are finished with a project, but this is likely to be a luxury or rarity in your development life.

Indenting Code for Clarity

I have a confession. Throughout the book, I've been carefully indoctrinating you into an code development style without really letting on. You've no doubt noticed a consistent pattern with respect to the indentation of all the code in the book. For example, in HTML examples, each child tag is indented to the right two spaces from its parent tag. Furthermore, content within a tag that spans more than one line is indented within the tag.

The best way to learn the value of indentation is to see some HTML code without it. You know how the song goes: "You don't know what you've got 'til it's gone." Anyway, here's a very simple table coded without any indentation:

```
<table><tr><td>Cell One</td><td>Cell Two</td></tr>
<tr><td>Cell Three</td><td>Cell Four</td></tr></table>
```

Not only is there no indentation, but there also is no delineation between rows and columns within the table. Now compare this code with the following code, which describes the same table:

```
<table>
  <tr>
    <td>Cell One</td>
    <td>Cell Two</td>
  </tr>
  <tr>
    <td>Cell Three</td>
    <td>Cell Four</td>
  </tr>
</table>
```

This heavily indented code makes it plainly obvious how the rows and columns are divided up via `<tr>` and `<td>` tags.

In JavaScript and PHP, think about the way you lay out your curly braces. Here are two most common schemes followed:

```
if (condition) {
  // do something
}
```

and

```
if (condition)
{
  // do something else
}
```

Which one you use is up to you; just use it consistently. Consistent indentation and other stylistic matters might even be more important than comments when it comes to making your HTML code understandable and maintainable. The main point to take from this section is that it's important to develop a coding style of your own (or your team's own) and then ruthlessly stick to it.

Breaking Up Code

Giant monolithic code is awful. Some people create one huge script that does everything in one giant `switch` statement. Now, I love `switch` statements, and they have their place—especially when first figuring out logic that you want to employ—but it is far better to break up the code into functions and/or classes and put related items into include files wherever possible. You've seen the move from larger scripts to smaller scripts with include files as the book has progressed.

Reasons for breaking up your code into sensible chunks include the following:

▶ It makes your code easier to read and understand, both for yourself later on and for anyone who might join your project later.

▶ It makes your code more reusable and minimizes redundancy. For example, with a single file to set up your database connectivity in PHP, you could reuse it in every script in which you need to connect to your database. If you need to change the way this works, you have to change it in only one place.

▶ It facilitates teamwork. If the code is broken into components, you can then assign responsibility for the individual components to team members. It also means that you can avoid the situation in which one programmer is waiting for another to finish working on `GiantScript.php` so that she can go ahead with her own work.

Implementing Version Control in Your Work

If you've ever used Google Docs, you have encountered a form of version control; when you're using Google Docs, Google automatically saves revisions of your work as you are typing. This is different from simply automatically saving your work (although it does that too) because you can revert to any revision along the way. You might have encountered this concept when using popular blog-authoring software such as WordPress, or even when editing wikis—both of these types of applications also enable users to revise their work without overwriting, and thus deleting for all time, their previous work.

You might be wondering, "Well, what does that have to do with developing HTML, CSS, JavaScript, and PHP? You're just talking about documents." The answer is simple: *everything*. Just as you might want to revert to a previous edition of an article or a letter, you might want to revert to a previous edition of your HTML, CSS, JavaScript, or PHP code. This could be because you followed a good idea to the end, but your markup just proved untenable and you don't want to start over entirely—you just want to back up to a certain point along your revision path. Or, let's say you developed a particularly involved bit of JavaScript and discovered that something in the middle of it just doesn't work with some browsers—you'll want to build on and extend the work you did, not throw it away completely, and knowing what you did in the past will help you in the future.

Version control involves more than just revision history. When you start using version control systems to maintain your code, you will hear terms like these:

► **Commit/check in and check out**—When you put an object into the code repository, you are committing that file; when you check out a file, you are grabbing it from the repository (where all the current and historical versions are stored) and working on it until you are ready to commit or check in the file again.

► **Branch**—The files you have under version control can branch or fork at any point, thus creating two or more development paths. Suppose you want to try some new display layouts or form interactivity, but you don't want an existing site to appear modified in any way. You might have started with one master set of files but then forked this set of files for the new site, continuing to develop them independently. If you continued developing the original set of files, that would be working with the *trunk*.

► **Change/diff**—This is just the term (you can say "change" or "diff") for a modification made under version control. You might also hear *diff* used as a verb, as in "I diffed the files," to refer to the action of comparing two versions of an object (there is an underlying UNIX command called `diff`).

▶ **Fork**—When you find an open-source repository that you want to use as the basis for your own work (or that you want to contribute to), you *fork* the repository to then create a copy of it that you can work on at your own pace. From the forked repository, you can *push* commits to your own version, *fetch* changes from the original repository, and issue *pull requests* to the owner of the original if you would like to contribute your changes to the original repository that you forked.

You will hear many more terms than just these few listed here, but if you can conceptualize the repository, the (local) working copy, and the process of checking in and checking out files, you are well on your way to implementing version control for your digital objects.

Using a Version Control System

Several version control systems are available for use: some free and open source, and some proprietary. Some popular systems are Subversion (http://subversion.apache.org), Mercurial (https://www.mercurial-scm.org/), and Git (http://www.git-scm.com). If you have a web hosting service that enables you to install any of these tools, you could create your own repository and use a GUI or command-line client to connect to it. However, for users who want to get started with a repository but don't necessarily want, need, or understand all the extra installation and maintenance overhead that goes with it, there are plenty of hosted version control systems that can even be used free for personal and open-source projects. These hosted solutions aren't just for individuals—all sorts of companies and organizations both big and small use hosted version control systems such as GitHub (http://www.github.com) and Bitbucket (http://www.bitbucket.org), just to name two. For a few dollars, you can turn your free, public account into a private account, and keep your code to yourself.

For anyone wanting to get started with version control, I highly recommend GitHub for relative ease of use and free, cross-platform tools. The GitHub Help site is a great place to start: See http://help.github.com/. An added benefit of the already-free GitHub account is the capability to use Gist (http://gist.github.com) to share code snippets (or whole pages) with others (those snippets themselves are Git repositories and, thus, are versioned and forkable in their own right). GitHub repositories, including Gist, are also excellent ways to get started with version control of your work.

Understanding the Value and Use of Code Frameworks

A code framework is nothing more than a set of libraries and templates that enable you to rapidly develop feature-rich dynamic sites and web applications without building every piece of the puzzle from scratch. These days, frameworks exist for every popular markup and programming language out there. The use of an application framework allows you to say, "I understand there are many ways to create a login sequence (or shopping cart, or discussion forum, and so on), and instead of starting from scratch, I will implement the [application framework] way of doing things."

Some of these frameworks take the form of an all-encompassing content management system (CMS) such as WordPress (http://www.wordpress.org) or Drupal (http://www.drupal.org), but in the realm of custom web application development you can use frameworks for HTML and CSS, JavaScript, PHP, or any combination thereof. Many of these frameworks are open source and available for download or forking from GitHub repositories.

I recommend three popular HTML, CSS, and JavaScript frameworks:

▶ **Bootstrap**—Developed internally by engineers at Twitter, this framework is open-source software for anyone who wants to use it to get started with modern design elements. Learn more at http://getbootstrap.com/, which includes a simple "Get Started" section that explains what is included and how to use it.

▶ **Foundation**—Another open-source framework, Foundation emphasizes responsive design so that people with all kinds of devices, from desktops to phones, can enjoy and use your website. Learn more at http://foundation.zurb.com/, which includes an extensive "Getting Started" section that details the components of the display templates you can use.

▶ **HTML5 Boilerplate**—One of the leanest frameworks out there, this might be the most useful for beginners because it provides the basics of what you need without overwhelming you with the possibilities. Learn more at http://html5boilerplate.com/ and see the documentation maintained within the GitHub repository.

Many HTML, CSS, and JavaScript front-end frameworks include jQuery, which you learned about in Chapter 10, "The Basics of Using jQuery." I can't emphasize enough how useful these frameworks can be for rapid prototyping, but beware of running the risk of falling into the "cookie cutter" trap, in which your site looks like all the others out there (at least, the ones using the same framework). With a little creativity, and ensuring your prototype doesn't go directly into production, you can easily avoid that trap.

Using JavaScript-Specific Frameworks

There's a big difference between JavaScript libraries—even big ones like jQuery—and JavaScript frameworks: Libraries offer ready-made pieces of code that provide functionality meant to enhance your custom architecture, and frameworks are larger, complicated, and impose an architectural pattern upon your application, such as the *model-view-controller* pattern. In a model-view-controller pattern, or MVC pattern, an application is conceived of as having three interconnected components:

▶ **The model**—Acts as the central component, even though it's listed first in the name. It holds application data, business rules, functions, and other logical elements.

▶ **The view**—Requests information from the model to show to the user.

▶ **The controller**—Sends information to the model for processing through user interactions.

You can think of it this way: In a web-based application, the user interacts with a controller that manipulates the underlying model, which updates the view, which the user then sees in the web browser.

In the traditional web-based application, you will likely have experienced it this way: Both the model and the controller components sit on the back end, away from the browser, and are invoked through form elements or other interactions by the user that say, "Hey, back-end script, go do something with logic and data based on this input I'm giving you, and send the result back to the screen." The screen, in this case, would contain dynamically generated HTML (the view).

In a JavaScript-based MVC application, which most likely has been developed using one of the frameworks you'll learn about in a moment, all three components can sit on the client side—that is to say, a user can interact with data that is stored and manipulated entirely within the front end, never touching a back-end script or database. Or *most* of the three components sit on the front end, and use AJAX requests to invoke a script on the back end, which then sends results back into the view.

If you are building a predominantly read-only website and using a little JavaScript or jQuery for some display features, a framework would be considerable overkill. But if you begin to think about ways to extend that website to include user interactivity, you might consider laying in a framework to handle that work for you.

Following are some major JavaScript frameworks in use today, all of which would be fine starting points for further exploration:

▶ **AngularJS (http://angular.io)**—A very powerful and flexible framework that comes with a steep learning curve. However, it also comes with a very active user community ready to help new developers understand the framework.

▶ **React (https://facebook.github.io/react/)**—Much like AngularJS, React is a powerful, flexible, and efficient component-based JavaScript framework—once you can wrap your brain around it. React has a very active user community and plenty of tutorials.

▶ **Backbone.js (http://backbonejs.org)**—This framework has been around for quite some time (relatively speaking) and has served as the inspiration for many other frameworks. It enables a new developer to get started quickly, but the downside of that, for some, is that your applications will contain a lot of unused templating code.

▶ **Ember (http://emberjs.com)**—Like Backbone.js, Ember enables a new developer to get started quickly. Although it appears "too magical" to some, Ember's strong adherence to common programming idioms can be a benefit to new developers.

There are many more than these few JavaScript frameworks out there at the time of this writing, and I fully expect there will be more in years to come. To stay up to date or to get an overview of the core features of popular JavaScript frameworks and libraries, you can start by bookmarking and revisiting https://github.com/showcases/front-end-javascript-frameworks.

Using PHP-Specific Frameworks

Besides the benefit of reusing a stable codebase for common functionality, using a framework also helps a developer adhere to a consistent software architectural pattern. In the case of PHP frameworks, that pattern is typically the model-view-controller (MVC) pattern—yes, the same type of pattern discussed in the JavaScript section.

The MVC software architecture pattern is ready-made for web-based applications, and in fact many applications (or even just dynamic websites) adhere to some version of this pattern without even trying too hard. Each of the PHP frameworks mentioned explicitly in this section enables you to easily apply an MVC pattern to your software applications. Many other PHP frameworks do as well, and although you might not choose to adhere to the pattern, it is recommended that you do so to enable easier testing, development, deployment, and ongoing maintenance of your applications.

NOTE
_____

For even more examples and explanations of the MVC pattern, see Jeff Atwood's clear and concise blog post "Understanding Model-View-Controller" at http://www.codinghorror.com/blog/2008/05/understanding-model-view-controller.html.
_____

Developers worldwide can choose from more than 20 PHP application frameworks, but the ones I call out here have a (relatively) long history and an active developer community with considerable uptake. In fact, those are three features unrelated to the code itself that you should think about when evaluating a framework for your own purposes: Has it been around a while and is it stable? Are people actively using it? Is the parent company or group of developers actively maintaining it?

Other considerations for selection include the following:

▶ Determining whether the framework is best suited for the type of application you are creating; some frameworks are great for e-commerce, some for content publication, and some for both.

▶ Determining whether the framework provides you with the opportunity to use a software architecture pattern, and if so, whether it is the one you want to use.

▶ Determining whether the framework requires additional PHP modules or server libraries. If it does, but you do not control your server and therefore cannot modify the libraries and modules installed, that framework cannot work for you.

NOTE

You can find a well-maintained list of PHP application frameworks at http://en.wikipedia.org/wiki/Comparison_of_web_application_frameworks#PHP.

The following PHP frameworks are recommended starting points for further exploration:

▶ **Zend Framework (http://framework.zend.com)**—Zend, the company behind the Zend Framework, and its founders have been contributors to the PHP language itself almost since its initial creation. The core PHP engine is often referred to as *the Zend engine*. In other words, if evaluating the Zend Framework according to the criteria I previously mentioned, you would be hard-pressed to find a framework that is more stable, has been around longer, or has more people actively developing the framework and applications with it.

▶ **CakePHP (http://www.cakephp.org)**—At its core, CakePHP is an MVC framework with components for common functionality such as database connections; authentication, authorization, and session management; and consuming and exposing web services—much like the Zend Framework and numerous other frameworks. One of CakePHP's greatest selling points is its ease of use and integration, and it also wins points for having detailed and user-friendly documentation and tutorials.

▶ **Laravel (http://www.laravel.com)**—This framework is a relative newcomer (although it has been around and in use since 2011) but has quickly become one of the most popular, due in part to it having been developed specifically to improve upon earlier popular and feature-rich frameworks such as CodeIgniter (http://www.codeigniter.org).

Regardless of the framework you choose to use—if you even do—remember to take a moment to understand the components of the code you're using and don't just follow the framework blindly.

Summary

This chapter discussed some foundational elements beyond pure code that will help you take the next step in your personal and technical development process. You learned the importance of making your code easy to maintain by adding comments and indentation, and generally following coding standards. Because you likely will soon need code-management tools either for yourself or for yourself and other developers in your group, this chapter introduced you to a few concepts of version control. Version control enables you to innovate without losing your solid, production-quality work and also provides more opportunities for other developers to work within your code base.

Finally, you learned a little bit about HTML, CSS, JavaScript, and PHP frameworks, of which there are many. These frameworks can help you speed up your web development project by giving you templates that already contain modern and validated markup and follow a strong software architecture pattern such as model-view-controller.

Q&A

Q. Won't adding a lot of comments and spaces make my pages load more slowly when someone views them?

A. The size of a little extra text in your pages is negligible when compared to other, chunkier web page resources (such as large images and high-definition multimedia). You'd have to type hundreds of comment words to cause even one extra second of delay in loading a page. Also keep in mind that, with the broadband connections that many people use, text travels extremely fast. Multimedia components slow pages down, so whereas you need to optimize your images as best you can, you can use text comments freely. You can also learn more about the concept of "minifying" your HTML, CSS, and JavaScript at https://developers.google.com/speed/docs/insights/MinifyResources.

Q. Using version control seems like overkill for my tiny personal website. Do I have to use it?

A. Of course not—websites of any type, personal or otherwise, are not required to be under version control or other backup systems. However, most people have experienced some data loss or a website crash, so if you don't use version control, I highly recommend at least performing some sort of automated backup of your files to an external system. By "external system," I mean any external drive, whether a physical drive attached to your computer or a cloud-based backup service such as Dropbox (http://www.dropbox.com).

Workshop

The Workshop contains quiz questions and exercises to help you solidify your understanding of the material covered. Try to answer all questions before looking at the "Answers" section that follows.

Quiz

1. You want to say to future editors of a web page, "Don't change this image of me. It's my only chance at immortality." But you don't want users who view the page to see that message. How can you do this?

2. What are some of the benefits of using an application framework?

3. In the MVC pattern, what does the model do?

Answers

1. Put the following comment immediately before the `<img />` tag:

```
<!-- Don't change this image of me.
     It's my only chance at immortality. -->
```

2. Working with a stable codebase, adhering to a software architecture pattern, and not reinventing the wheel.

3. The model stores and separates data from the controlling and viewing components.

Exercises

▶ Open the HTML, CSS, and JavaScript files that make up your current website, and check them all for comments and code indentation. Are there areas in which the code needs to be explained to anyone who might look at it in the future? If so, add explanatory comments. Is it difficult for you to tell the hierarchy of your code—is it difficult to see headings and sections? If so, indent your code so that the structure matches the hierarchy and thus enables you to jump quickly to the section you need to edit.

▶ Create an account at GitHub and then create a repository for your personal website or other code-based project. From this point forward, keep your repository in sync with your work on your personal computer by committing your changes to the GitHub repository.

▶ Download and install at least one of the frameworks discussed in this chapter. (If you install more than one, delete the old ones first to avoid collisions.) Follow at least one of the tutorials provided by the developers of these frameworks so that you can gain some practical knowledge of using a framework as well as the MVC pattern.

APPENDIX A

Installation QuickStart Guide with XAMPP

What You'll Learn in This Appendix:

▶ How to install Apache, MySQL, and PHP from a third-party installation package on multiple platforms

▶ How to test your installations

In case you want to get started quickly, this appendix steps you through installation from the all-in-one cross-platform installation package XAMPP. Then, the next three appendixes explain how to obtain and install MySQL, Apache, and PHP, respectively, from the Internet so that you can make sure your versions are up to date. In addition, those next three appendixes contain extended explanatory information about each step and other important information relevant to understanding how these technologies work together.

You should familiarize yourself with the extended information for each technology in those next three appendixes. However, if you just want to *get started* working on your local machine, that's fine, too. The screenshots and instructions for XAMPP may refer to MariaDB and not MySQL, but for all intents and purposes here it is the same thing.

Using Third-Party Installation Packages

Third-party installation packages are those bundles of programs that are provided by a company or organization other than the original creator. In this appendix, you learn how to use the XAMPP installation package to install PHP, MySQL, and Apache simultaneously, on whichever operating system you are using (Linux/UNIX, Windows, or Mac).

Besides my own experience as an XAMPP user for several years, I selected it for use in this appendix because of the X in its name: the X indicates it is a cross-platform installation of AMPP—or Apache, MySQL, PHP, and Perl. (Note that Perl is not a topic of this book, so just consider it a bonus.)

Here are two other very good third-party installation packages for Apache, MySQL, and PHP that are specific to operating systems:

- ▶ **WAMP**—Used for installation of Apache, MySQL, and PHP on Windows. See http://www.wampserver.com/ for more information.

- ▶ **MAMP**—Used for installation of Apache, MySQL, and PHP on Mac. See http://www.mamp.info/en for more information.

One potential drawback to using third-party installation packages is that the version of the core technologies that are bundled together will always be a few revision versions behind. This happens because of the work that goes into creating and testing the bundle itself, to ensure that no conflicts exist between the latest versions of the technologies; it also has to go through a quality-assurance process. The upside of this process, however, is that when you install these technologies using a bundled installer, the upgrade process requires nothing more than running the new installer—it takes care of removing and updating all the files for you.

The next three sections describe the basic installation process of XAMPP. You only need to read the section that applies to your operating system. However, be sure to read the "Securing XAMPP" at the end of this chapter; it applies to all operating systems.

Installing XAMPP on Linux/UNIX

The following instructions were tested on Ubuntu Linux 17.04, but they should be the same for other Linux or commercial UNIX distributions. If you encounter unexpected error messages during installation, visit the XAMPP FAQ for Linux users at http://www.apachefriends.org/faq_linux.html.

Download the latest version of XAMPP from http://www.apachefriends.org/download.html. The file will be named similarly to `xampp-linux-x64-VERSION-NUMBER-installer.run` where `VERSION-NUMBER` is based on the bundled PHP release. At the time of this writing, the version is 7.1.6, so the filename is `xampp-linux-x64-7.1.6-0-installer.run`. Later versions will have a different filename, so be sure to adjust the commands accordingly.

Next, make the installer file executable so you can run it:

```
chmod +x xampp-linux-x64-7.1.6-0-installer.run
```

Now you can run the installer. It creates a subdirectory under the `/opt` system directory to install the software to, so you'll need to use `su` or `sudo` to elevate your account privileges to run it:

```
sudo ./xampp-linux-x64-7.1.6-0-installer.run
```

You are presented with a few prompts as part of the XAMPP Setup Wizard. The wizard allows you to specify which components you want to install and set the installation directory. I recommend accepting the default values.

After the installation is complete, you'll find everything under /opt/lamp (or wherever else you specified using the wizard). To start XAMPP (which launches Apache and MySQL), use the following command:

```
sudo /opt/lampp/lampp start
```

You'll see a message such as this:

```
Starting XAMPP for Linux 7.1.6-0...
XAMPP: Starting Apache...ok.
XAMPP: Starting MySQL...ok.
XAMPP: Starting ProFTPD...ok.
```

To test whether the web server is running, open a web browser and enter **http://localhost/dashboard/**. The welcome page for the XAMPP service should display, as shown in Figure A.1.

FIGURE A.1
The XAMPP welcome page.

That's all there is to it; XAMPP has installed Apache, PHP, and MySQL on your machine, and you can read more information about XAMPP through the links at the top of the page when viewing http://localhost/dashboard/.

To stop XAMPP and its services, you can issue the following command at any time from the command line:

```
sudo /opt/lampp/lampp stop
```

Be sure to read "Securing XAMPP" at the end of this appendix for more information about locking down your XAMPP-powered machine (even if it is only for development).

Installing XAMPP on Windows

The following instructions were tested on Windows 10. Windows 2008, 2012, Vista, 7, 8, and 10 are supported, but earlier versions are not. Moreover, only 32-bit builds are available. Because of the nuances in the Windows operating system releases, and because of different security practices and programs that may be installed on Windows machines, if any of the installation steps do not go smoothly, visit the XAMPP FAQ for Windows users at http://www.apachefriends.org/faq_windows.html.

Download the latest version of XAMPP from http://www.apachefriends.org/download.html. The file will be named similarly to `xampp-win32-`*`VERSION-NUMBER`*`-installer.exe`, where *`VERSION-NUMBER`* is based on the bundled PHP release. At the time of this writing, the version is 7.1.6, so the filename is `xampp-win32-7.1.6-0-VC14-installer.exe`. Later versions will have a different filename.

Locate the downloaded file and double-click its icon to launch the wizard-based installer program. Depending on the security of your system, you may see a prompt asking you to confirm whether you want to allow the application to make changes to your system and a warning to avoid installing it in the C:\Program Files (x86) directory. After these prompts, you will see the welcome screen of the installer, as shown in Figure A.2.

FIGURE A.2
The XAMPP installation main screen.

Click the Next button to continue the installation process. You should leave the default installation options as marked and click the Next button to move on past each screen. At this point, the installation process itself happens, as shown in Figure A.3.

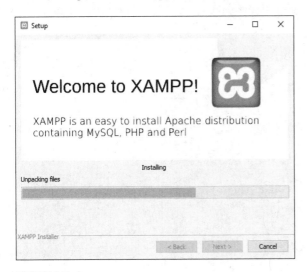

FIGURE A.3
The XAMPP installation continues as the files are extracted.

When the installation process finishes, click the Finish button to complete the installation. Before the XAMPP installation process completely closes, it asks whether you want to start the Control Panel for managing the installed services, as shown in Figure A.4.

FIGURE A.4
The XAMPP installation is complete.

The XAMPP Control Panel, as shown in Figure A.5, provides you with one-click access to starting and stopping the Apache and MySQL server processes running on your machine. If you are running these server processes on your local machine for development purposes only, you might want to turn them on only when you need them; the Control Panel allows quick access to do just that.

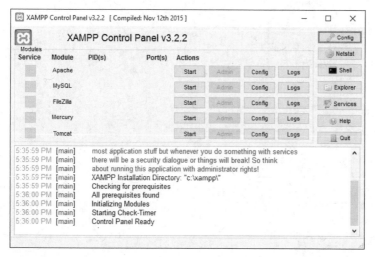

FIGURE A.5
The XAMPP Control Panel.

To test whether the web server is running, open a web browser and enter **http://localhost/dashboard/**. The welcome page for the XAMPP service should display, as shown in Figure A.6.

That's all there is to it; XAMPP has installed Apache, PHP, and MySQL on your machine, and you can read more information about XAMPP through the links at the top of the page when viewing http://localhost/dashboard/.

Be sure to read "Securing XAMPP" at the end of this chapter for more information about locking down your XAMPP-powered machine (even if it is only for development).

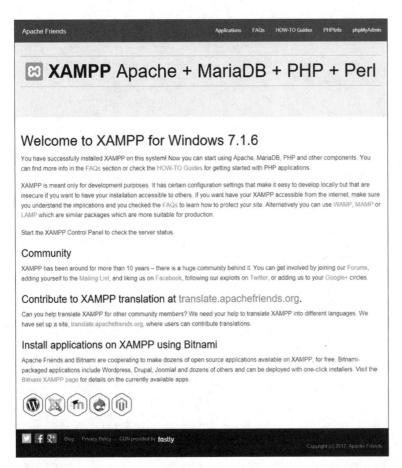

FIGURE A.6
The XAMPP welcome page.

Installing XAMPP on Mac OS X

The following instructions were tested on Mac OS X 10.11 (El Capitan) but they should be the same for other versions. Versions older than 10.6 (Snow Leopard) aren't supported. If you encounter unexpected error messages during installation, visit the XAMPP FAQ for Mac users at http://www.apachefriends.org/faq_osx.html.

Download the latest version of XAMPP from http://www.apachefriends.org/download.html. The file will be named similarly to `xampp-osx-`*VERSION-NUMBER*`-installer.dmg`, where *VERSION-NUMBER* is based on the bundled PHP release. At the time of this writing, the version is 7.1.7, so the filename is `xampp-osx-7.1.7-0-installer.dmg`. Later versions will have a different filename.

Locate the downloaded DMG file and double-click its icon to mount the image. You will see a screen like that shown in Figure A.7.

FIGURE A.7
The XAMPP installation wizard's icon is shown after the DMG image is mounted.

Double-click the installation wizard's icon to launch the wizard-based installer program. Depending on the security of your system, you may see a prompt asking you to confirm whether you want to run the program because it was downloaded from the Internet. You may also need to enter your username and password to give the installer permission to access the Applications directory. After these prompts, you will see the welcome screen of the installer, as shown in Figure A.8.

Click the Next button to continue the installation process. You should leave the default installation options as marked and click the Next button to move on past each screen. At this point, the installation process itself happens, as shown in Figure A.9.

FIGURE A.8
The XAMPP installation wizard's main screen.

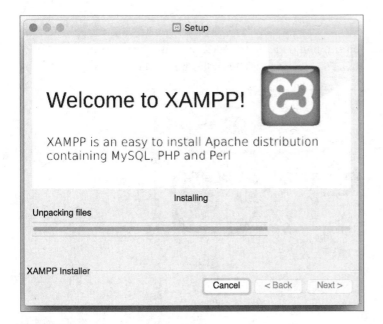

FIGURE A.9
The XAMPP installation continues as the files are extracted.

Before the XAMPP installation process completely closes, it asks whether you want to launch XAMPP, as shown in Figure A.10.

FIGURE A.10
The XAMPP installation is complete.

Once the software is installed, you can find a link to the XAMPP Control Panel in the /Applications/XAMPP folder as manager-osx, as shown in Figure A.11.

FIGURE A.11
Find the link to the XAMPP Control Panel.

Double-click this link to start the XAMPP Control Panel, shown in Figure A.12, through which you can start and stop the Apache and MySQL server processes running on your machine. If you are running these server processes on your local machine for development purposes only, you might want to turn them on only when you need them; the Control Panel allows quick access to do just that.

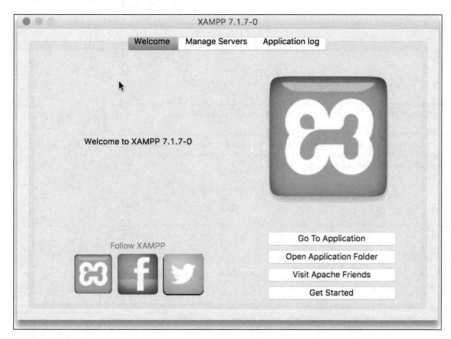

FIGURE A.12
The XAMPP Control Panel.

To test whether the web server is running, open a web browser and enter **http://localhost/dashboard/**. The welcome page for the XAMPP service should display, as shown in Figure A.13.

That's all there is to it; XAMPP has installed Apache, PHP, and MySQL on your machine, and you can read more information about XAMPP through the links at the top of the page when viewing http://localhost/dashboard/.

Be sure to read "Securing XAMPP," next, for more information about locking down your XAMPP-powered machine (even if it is only for development).

FIGURE A.13
The XAMPP welcome page.

Securing XAMPP

The primary purpose of XAMPP is to provide a quick-and-easy installation method for Apache, MySQL, and PHP within a development environment. One of the tradeoffs for this quick-and-easy installation is that some security settings are left incomplete—or, at least, up to the user to determine whether they are important enough to set.

Using the installation right out of the box, the following are some potential security issues:

▶ The MySQL administrator user has no password set. (You can use a blank password.)

▶ Some services are accessible to the network unless you specifically disallow access through your personal firewall.

▶ ProFTPD (an FTP server included in the bundle) uses the password "lampp" for the user "daemon."

However, XAMPP provides a utility for each operating system that you can run to step through the process of securing your XAMPP system, even in a development environment, as follows:

▶ On Linux/UNIX, run the utility by entering the following on the command line:

```
sudo /opt/lampp/lampp security
```

▶ On Windows, open the Security Console by navigating to http://localhost/xampp/index. php in your web browser and selecting Security from the navigation menu on the left side.

▶ On Mac, open a terminal window and enter the following on the command line:

```
sudo /Applications/XAMPP/xamppfiles/xampp security
```

Troubleshooting

If you experience installation problems, first check that you have followed the steps exactly as given in the appendix. Then, check the XAMPP website at http://www.apachefriends.org/ for FAQs specific to this installation package.

If these processes still don't work and you want to try another all-in-one third-party installation package, feel free to try WAMP or MAMP (mentioned at the beginning of this chapter).

You could also try the installations the "long" way, using the extended information found in the next three appendixes. They provide troubleshooting tips and links to additional sites that can help you work through your installation issues.

APPENDIX B
Installing and Configuring MySQL

What You'll Learn in This Appendix:

► How to install MySQL

► Basic security guidelines for running MySQL

► How to work with the MySQL user privilege system

This is the first of three appendixes in which in which you learn how to set up your development environment. We tackle the installation of MySQL first because on some systems compiling PHP requires bits of the MySQL installation to be in place if you're going to use MySQL with PHP.

Current and Future Versions of MySQL

The installation instructions in this appendix refer to MySQL Community Server 5.7.18, the current production version of the software. This version number can be read as "revision number 18 of minor release 7, of the major version 5 of the MySQL server software." Revisions and minor releases do not follow a set release schedule. When enhancements or fixes are added to the code and thoroughly tested, a new version is released with a new revision or minor version number.

By the time you purchase this book, the version number might have changed to 5.7.19 or later. If so, read the documentation at https://dev.mysql.com/doc/refman/5.7/en/installing.html for any installation/configuration process changes. These processes make up the bulk of this appendix.

Although it is unlikely that any installation instructions will change between minor version updates, always check the changelog of software that you install and maintain. If a minor version change does occur while you are reading this book but the changelog notes no installation changes, just make a mental note and substitute the new version number wherever it appears in the installation instructions and accompanying figures.

How to Get MySQL

MySQL AB was the name of the company that developed, maintained, and distributed the MySQL database server; through a series of acquisitions (Sun Microsystems purchased MySQL AB, and Oracle Corporation purchased Sun Microsystems), database giant Oracle now owns MySQL. However, the MySQL Community Edition of the software remains open source, is supported by open-source developers, and is freely available on the MySQL website at http://www.mysql.com. Binary distributions for all platforms, installer packages for Mac OS X, and RPM and DEB packages for Linux platforms are all available.

NOTE

Linux and Mac OS X distributions usually contain some version or another of the open-source MySQL software, although these are usually several revisions or minor versions behind the current release.

The installation instructions in this appendix are based on the official MySQL 5.7.*x* Community Server distribution.

Installing MySQL on Linux/UNIX

Oracle provides up-to-date packages, such as RPMs for Red Hat/CentOS–based distributions and DEBs for Debian/Ubuntu-based distributions, all running on different processor types, such as x86 32- and 64-bit. Although you can download the server and client packages from http://dev.mysql.com/downloads/mysql/5.7.html and install them using `rpm` or `dpkg`, you must have any dependencies already in place. A better option is to register Oracle's MySQL software repositories with your system's online package manager. Then you can use tools like `yum` and `apt-get` to install MySQL, and the dependencies will be installed automatically.

To register the repository for Red Hat/CentOS–based Linux distributions, download the appropriate configuration RPM for your system from http://dev.mysql.com/downloads/repo/yum. The file will be named similarly to `mysqlVERSION-community-release-PLATFORM.noarch.rpm` where `VERSION` is the major and minor number of MySQL and `PLATFORM` denotes the operating system. The file for Red Hat Enterprise Linux 7, for example, is named `mysql57-community-release-el7-11.noarch.rpm`. Be sure to adjust the name accordingly.

Then, install the RPM with the following:

```
sudo rpm -i mysql57-community-release-el7-11.noarch.rpm
```

To register the repository for Debian/Ubuntu-based Linux distributions, download the appropriate configuration DEB from http://dev.mysql.com/downloads/repo/apt. The file will be named similarly to `mysql-apt-config_VERSION_all.deb`, where `VERSION` is the version number of the configuration package. At the time of this writing, the file is named `mysql-apt-config_0.8.6-1_all.deb`.

Then, install the DEB with the following:

```
sudo dpkg -i mysql-apt-config_0.8.6-1_all.deb
```

The configuration interface appears as shown in Figure B.1. The default settings are fine, so use the arrow keys to highlight the Ok option and press Enter.

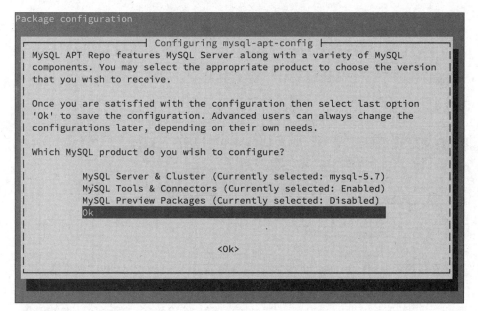

FIGURE B.1
The settings to register the Oracle MySQL repository.

After you install the DEB, you should update the package manager's index files with the following command so it knows to download packages from the new repository. (Note that this isn't necessary on Red Hat systems because yum will automatically refresh its indexes.)

```
sudo apt-get update
```

Now it's time to install MySQL. On Red Hat, this is done with the following command:

```
sudo yum -y install mysql-community-server mysql-community-client
```

On Debian/Ubuntu, use the following:

```
sudo apt-get -y install mysql-community-server mysql-community-client
```

As the installation gets underway, Debian/Ubuntu-based users will be prompted for a password for MySQL's root user, as shown in Figure B.2. Type the desired password, press the Tab key to highlight the <Ok> button at the bottom of the screen, and press Enter.

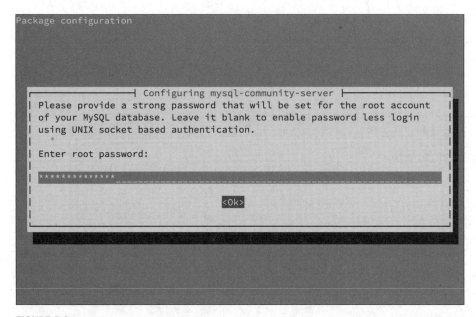

FIGURE B.2
The prompt to set the root account's password.

You're then prompted to enter the password a second time to make sure you didn't make a mistake. Again, type the password, highlight <Ok>, and press Enter.

Red Hat/CentOS–based users will need to perform a few extra setup steps. First, start the MySQL server using the following:

```
sudo systemctl start mysqld
```

When MySQL starts for the first time, a temporary password is generated for the root account. It records the password in its log file, and you can find out what the password is with the following command:

```
sudo grep 'temporary password' /var/log/mysqld.log
```

The output will look something like this:

```
2017-06-26T17:3046.293052Z 1 [Note] A temporary password is generated for root@
localhost:
>XEsegz9q+dn
```

In this case, >XEsegz9q+dn is the root password. To change it, run the mysqladmin command as follows:

```
mysqladmin password -u root -p
```

You will be prompted to enter the temporary password and then to enter and confirm the new password. Type carefully, because the characters won't be displayed on the screen for security purposes.

Now that MySQL is installed and running, skip to the "Basic Security Guidelines" section later in this appendix. If you experienced any issues with your installation, check the "Troubleshooting Your Installation" section.

Installing MySQL on Mac OS X

The MySQL installation process for Mac OS X is fairly straightforward—there is an installation package for Mac OS X. Go to the MySQL downloads page at http://dev.mysql.com/downloads/mysql/5.7.html and select Mac OS X from the drop-down list. The file will be named similarly to `mysql-VERSION-PLATFORM.dmg`, where `VERSION` is the release number of MySQL and `PLATFORM` denotes the version of the Mac OS X operating system. The current file at the time of this writing is named `mysql-5.7.18-macos10.12-x86_64.dmg`. Be sure to adjust the name accordingly.

When you have downloaded the DMG file, double-click the archive. After you open the DMG archive, you will see a package, as shown in Figure B.3.

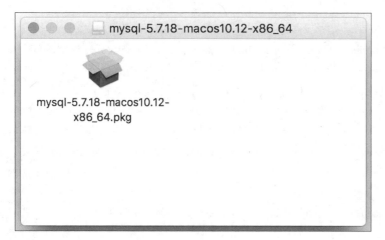

FIGURE B.3
Showing the contents of the MySQL DMG archive.

Double-click the `*.pkg` file in that folder and follow these installation steps to complete the process:

  1. The MySQL installer launches automatically, as shown in Figure B.4. Click Continue to move to the next step.

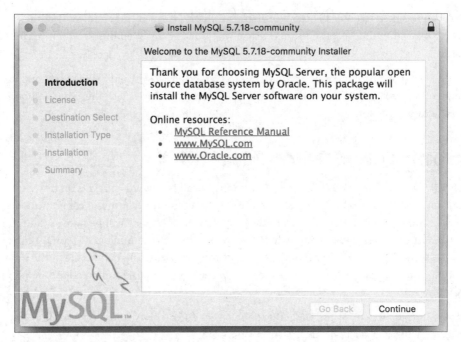

FIGURE B.4
The MySQL Installer for the Mac has started.

2. The next few screens contain general information regarding installation and the MySQL license. Read these screens and click Continue to move through them.

3. The next screen verifies your installation location selection and requires you to click the Install button to continue. At this point, you might be prompted to enter the administrator username and password before the installation process continues.

4. A temporary root password will be generated for the MySQL root account and displayed to you during the installation process, as shown in Figure B.5. Write this password down so you can change it after the installation is complete.

5. MySQL is now installed and you can close the installer and eject the DMG archive.

To change the root account's password, use the mysqladmin utility found in the `/usr/local/mysql-VERSION-PLATFORM/bin` directory, as follows:

```
/usr/local/mysql-5.7.18-macos10.12-x86_64/bin/mysqladmin password -u root -p
```

You will be prompted to enter the temporary password and then to enter and confirm the new password. Type carefully, because the characters won't be displayed on the screen for security purposes.

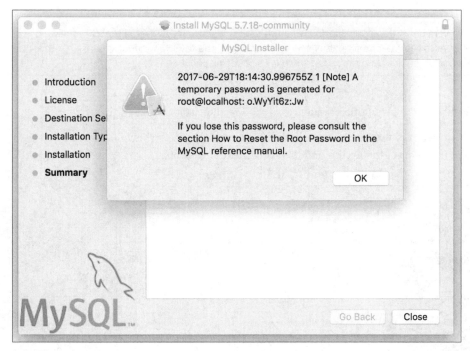

FIGURE B.5
A temporary password is generated for the root account.

Now that MySQL is installed and running, skip to the "Basic Security Guidelines" section later in this appendix. If you experienced any issues with your installation, check the "Troubleshooting Your Installation" section.

Installing MySQL on Windows

The MySQL installation process on Windows uses an all-in-one installer to walk you through the installation and configuration of a variety of MySQL products on your Windows Server 2003, Windows Vista, Windows 7, Windows 8, or Windows 10 machine. The following steps detail the installation of MySQL 5.7.18 on Windows 10; however, the installation sequence follows the same steps regardless of your Windows environment.

Go to the MySQL downloads page at http://dev.mysql.com/downloads/mysql/5.7.html and select the Windows option from the drop-down menu. Then, download the Windows MSI Installer file. Although the installer is 32-bit, it is capable of installing 32- or 64-bit software. When this file has been downloaded, double-click it to begin the installation process.

NOTE

A ZIP Archive version is also available for Windows users. If you want to install the ZIP Archive version, be sure to read the descriptions and instructions in the MySQL Manual at http://dev.mysql.com/doc/refman/5.7/en/windows-choosing-package.html.

Jumping right into the installation sequence, just follow these steps:

1. The first screen of the wizard displays the license agreement, as shown in Figure B.6. Accept the terms of the license and then click Next to continue.

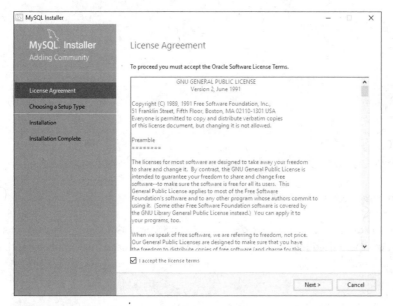

FIGURE B.6
The first step of the MySQL Setup Wizard for Windows.

2. After agreeing to the terms and conditions, you are asked to choose a setup type (see Figure B.7). The Custom option allows you to pick and choose the elements of MySQL to install, whereas the Full option installs all the components of MySQL, which range from documentation to benchmarking suites to integration libraries. Select Custom as the installation method and click Next to continue.

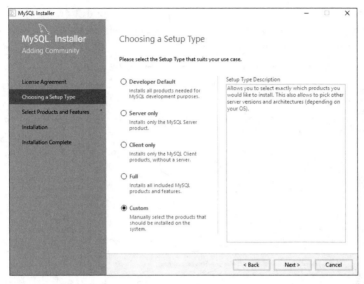

FIGURE B.7
Select an installation type.

3. Navigate the list of products to select the MySQL server version suitable for your system as well as the desired version of MySQL Shell, as shown in Figure B.8. For each selection, click the right arrow between the windows to move the selection to the To Be Installed list. Then click Next to continue.

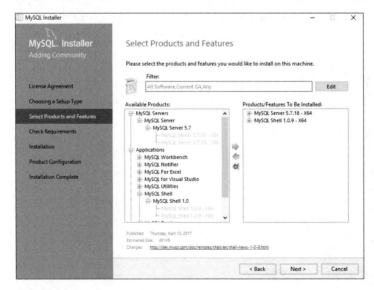

FIGURE B.8
Select the MySQL Server and MySQL Shell.

4. The installer will check to make sure the necessary dependencies are installed on your system, as shown in Figure B.9. If any are missing, the installer will try to download and install them automatically. Click the Execute button to continue.

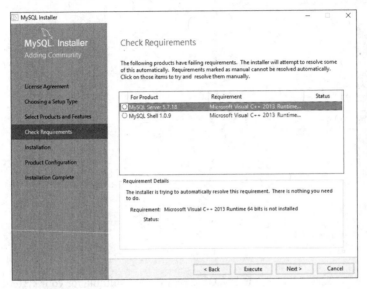

FIGURE B.9
The installer will identify and install missing dependencies.

5. After the dependencies are in place, the installer will list the requested applications it will install on your system, as shown in Figure B.10. Click Execute to proceed.

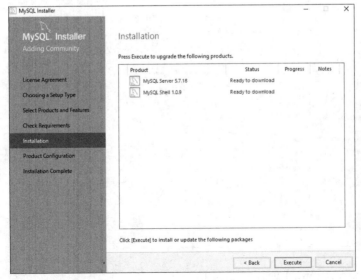

FIGURE B.10
The installer is ready to install the requested software.

6. When the server and shell installation completes, the wizard will guide you through the
   initial configuration and create a custom my.ini file tailored to your particular needs. The
   first of these screens is Type and Networking. Select Standalone MySQL Server, as shown in
   Figure B.11, and click Next.

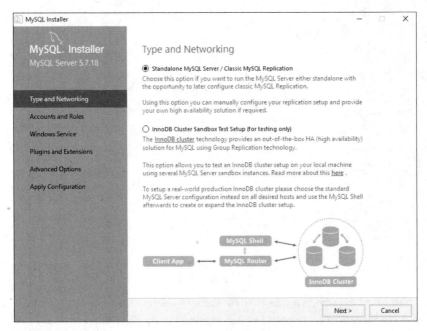

FIGURE B.11
The server will be configured as a standalone MySQL server.

7. Your selection on the next screen, shown in Figure B.12, determines the allotments for
   memory, disk, and processor usage. If you are using MySQL on your personal machine
   for testing purposes, select the Developer Machine option. If MySQL is running on
   a machine with other server software and can take up more system resources than
   if you were running it on your personal machine, select the Server Machine option.
   Select the Dedicated MySQL Server Machine option if MySQL is the primary service
   running on the machine and can take up the bulk of the system resources. Then click
   Next to continue.

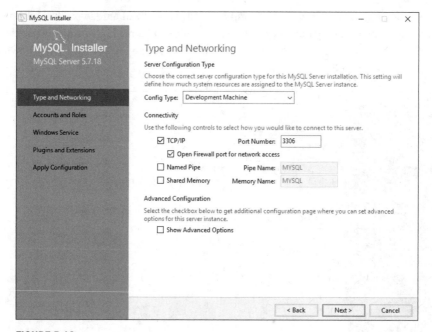

FIGURE B.12
The default config type and port settings.

8. You are then asked to provide a password for the root account. It is important to have a secure password for the root account because it is used to manage the server. You can also create any number of user accounts. Although adding additional accounts is optional (and they can easily be created later), it is convenient to create at least one other account for your own use at this time, as shown in Figure B.13.

FIGURE B.13
A non-root user is created.

9. The default values for the remainder of the wizard's prompts are appropriate, so you're free to click Next, as necessary, until you reach the end of the process. As shown in Figure B.14, the wizard applies the configuration settings, and you may click Finish to close out the process.

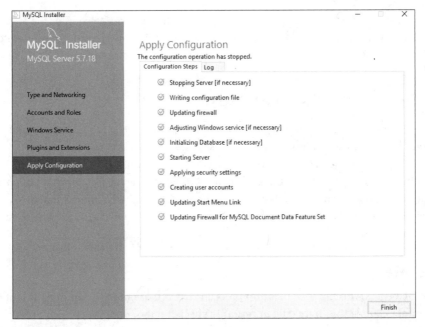

FIGURE B.14
The wizard applies the configuration settings.

Now that MySQL has been started, skip to the "Basic Security Guidelines" section later in this appendix. If you experienced any issues with your installation, check the "Troubleshooting Your Installation" section.

Troubleshooting Your Installation

If you have any problems during the installation of MySQL, the first place you should look is the "Problems and Common Errors" section in the MySQL Manual, which is located at http://dev.mysql.com/doc/refman/5.7/en/problems.html.

The following are just a few of the common installation problems:

▶ On Linux/UNIX and Mac OS X, incorrect permissions do not allow you to start the MySQL daemon. If this is the case, be sure that you have changed owners and groups to match those indicated in the installation instructions.

▶ If you see the message `Access denied` when connecting to MySQL, be sure that you are using the correct username and password.

▶ If you see the message `Can't connect to server`, make sure that the MySQL daemon is running.

If you still have trouble after reading the "Problems and Common Errors" section in the MySQL Manual, sending an email to the MySQL mailing list (see http://lists.mysql.com/ for more information) will likely produce results. You can also purchase support contracts from MySQL AB.

Basic Security Guidelines

Regardless of whether you are running MySQL on Windows, Linux/UNIX, or Mac OS X, and no matter whether you administer your own server or use a system provided to you by your Internet service provider, you must understand basic security guidelines. If you are accessing MySQL through your Internet service provider, there are several aspects of server security that you, as a non-root user, should not be able to modify or circumvent. Unfortunately, many Internet service providers pay no mind to security guidelines, leaving their clients exposed—and for the most part, unaware of the risk.

Starting MySQL

Securing MySQL begins with the server startup procedure. If you are not the administrator of the server, you cannot change this, but you can certainly check it out and report vulnerabilities to your Internet service provider.

If your MySQL installation is on Linux/UNIX or Mac OS X, your primary concern should be the owner of the MySQL daemon—it should not be root. Running the daemon as a non-root user such as `mysql` or `database` limits the ability of malicious individuals to gain access to the server and overwrite files.

TIP

You can verify the owner of the process using the `ps` (process status) command on your Linux/UNIX or Mac OS X system.

If you see that MySQL is running as root on your system, immediately contact your Internet service provider and complain. If you are the server administrator, you should start the MySQL process as a non-root user or specify the preferred username in the startup command line:

```
# mysqld --user=non_root_user_name
```

For example, if you want to run MySQL as user `mysql`, use this command:

```
# mysqld --user=mysql
```

However, the recommended method for starting MySQL is through the `mysqld_safe` startup script in the `bin` directory of your MySQL installation:

```
# bin/mysqld_safe --user=mysql &
```

Securing Your MySQL Connection

You can connect to the MySQL monitor (command-line interface) or other MySQL applications in several different ways, each of which has its own security risks. If your MySQL installation is on your own workstation, you have less to worry about than users who have to use a network connection to reach their server.

If MySQL is installed on your workstation, your biggest security concern is leaving your workstation unattended with your MySQL monitor or MySQL GUI administration tool up and running. In this type of situation, anyone can walk over and delete data, insert bogus data, or shut down the server. Use a screensaver or lock-screen mechanism with a password if you must leave your workstation unattended in a public area.

If MySQL is installed on a server outside your network, the security of the connection should be of some concern. As with any transmission of data over the Internet, data can be intercepted. If the transmission is unencrypted, the person who intercepted the data can piece it together and use the information. Suppose that the unencrypted transmission is your MySQL login information; a rogue individual now has access to your database, masquerading as you.

One way to prevent this from happening is to connect to MySQL through a secure connection such as Secure Shell (SSH), through which all transmissions to and from the remote machine are encrypted. Similarly, if you use a web-based administration interface, such as the highly recommended phpMyAdmin (see http://www.phpmyadmin.net/ for more information, and note that phpMyAdmin is installed as part of the XAMPP-based QuickStart installation in Appendix A, "Installation QuickStart Guide with XAMPP") or another tool used by your Internet service provider, access that tool over a secure connection.

In the next section, you learn about the MySQL privilege system, which helps secure your database even further.

Introducing the MySQL Privilege System

MySQL maintains its own set of user accounts and privilege system separate from the operating system. Moreover, the MySQL privilege system is always on. The first time you try to connect, and for each subsequent action you perform, MySQL checks the following three things:

▶ Where you are accessing the database from (your host)

▶ Who you say you are (your username and password)

▶ What you're allowed to do (your command privileges)

All this information is stored in the database called `mysql`, which is automatically created when MySQL is installed. There are several privilege-related tables in the `mysql` database, such as the following:

- **columns_priv**—Defines user privileges for specific fields within a table

- **db**—Defines the permissions for all databases on the server

- **host**—Defines the acceptable hosts that can connect to a specific database

- **procs_priv**—Defines user privileges for stored routines

- **tables_priv**—Defines user privileges for specific tables within a database

- **user**—Defines the command privileges for a specific user

These tables will become more important to you later as you add a few users to MySQL. For now, just remember that these tables exist and must have relevant data in them for users to complete actions.

Understanding the Two-Step Authentication Process

As you've learned, MySQL checks three things during the authentication process. The actions associated with these three things are performed in two steps:

1. MySQL looks at the host you are connecting from and the username and password pair you are using. If your host is allowed to connect, your password is correct for your username, and the username matches one assigned to the host, then MySQL moves to the second step.

2. For whichever SQL command you are attempting to use, MySQL verifies that your user has permissions to perform that action for that database, table, and field.

If step 1 fails, you see an error about it and you cannot continue on to step 2. For example, suppose that you are connecting to MySQL with a username of `joe` and a password of `abc123`, and you want to access a database called `myDB`. You will receive an error message if any of those connection variables is incorrect for any of the following reasons:

- Your password is incorrect.

- Username `joe` doesn't exist.

- User `joe` can't connect from `localhost`.

- User `joe` can connect from `localhost` but cannot use the `myDB` database.

You may see an error like the following:

```
# mysql -h localhost -u joe -pabc123 test
Error 1045: Access denied for user: 'joe@localhost' (Using password: YES)
```

If user `joe` with a password of `abc123` is allowed to connect from `localhost` to the `myDB` database, MySQL checks the actions that `joe` can perform in step 2 of the process. For our purposes, suppose that `joe` is allowed to select data but is not allowed to insert data. The sequence of events and errors would look like the following:

```
# mysql -h localhost -u joe -pabc123 test
Reading table information for completion of table and column names
You can turn off this feature to get a quicker startup with -A

Welcome to the MySQL monitor.  Commands end with ; or \g.
Your MySQL connection id is 12 to server version: 5.7.18-log
Type 'help;' or '\h' for help. Type '\c' to clear the buffer.

mysql> SELECT * FROM test_table;
+----+------------+
| id | test_field |
+----+------------+
|  1 | blah       |
|  2 | blah blah  |
+----+------------+
2 rows in set (0.0 sec)

mysql> INSERT INTO test_table VALUES ('', 'my text');
Error 1044: Access denied for user: 'joe@localhost' (Using password: YES)
```

Action-based permissions are common in applications with several levels of administration. For example, if you have created an application containing personal financial data, you might grant only `SELECT` privileges to entry-level staff members, but `INSERT` and `DELETE` privileges to executive-level staff with security clearances.

In most cases, when you are accessing MySQL through an Internet service provider, you have only one user and one database available to you. By default, that user has access to all tables in that database and is allowed to perform all commands. In this case, the responsibility is yours as the developer to create a secure application through your programming.

However, if you are the administrator of your own server, or if your Internet service provider allows you to add as many databases and users as you want and to modify the access privileges of your users, you can do so as described in the following subsections.

Adding Users to MySQL

Administering your server through a third-party application might afford you a simple method for adding users by using a wizard-like process or a graphical interface. However, adding users through the MySQL shell is not difficult, especially if you understand the security checkpoints used by MySQL, which you just learned.

To add a new user account, connect to MySQL as the root user and use the `ADD USER` command. The syntax is shown here:

```
ADD USER 'username'@'hostname' IDENTIFIED BY 'password';
```

If, for instance, you want to create a user called `john` with a password of `99hjc!5`, and you want this user to be able to connect from any host, use this command:

```
ADD USER 'john'@'%' IDENTIFIED BY '99hjc!5';
```

Note the use of wildcard `%`. In this example, `%` replaces a list of all hosts in the known world—a very long list indeed.

Here's another example of adding a user with the `ADD USER` command, this time to add a user called `jane` with a password of `45sdg11`. This new user can connect only from a specific host:

```
ADD USER 'jane'@'janescomputer.company.com' IDENTIFIED BY '45sdg11';
```

If you know that `janescomputer.company.com` has an IP address of `63.124.45.2`, you can substitute that address in the hostname portion of the command, as follows:

```
ADD USER 'jane'@63.124.45.2' IDENTIFIED BY '45sdg11';
```

One note about adding users: Always use a password and make sure that the password is a good one!

After you create a user, you use the `GRANT` command to assign that user privileges. The simple syntax of the `GRANT` command is shown here:

```
GRANT privileges ON databasename.tablename TO 'username'@'host';
```

For example, to grant all privileges to `john` on the `myCompany` database, use this command:

```
GRANT ALL ON myCompany.* TO 'john'@'%';
```

Note the use of the wildcard `*` this time, which represents all tables. The `*` can also be used to indicate all databases, like so:

```
GRANT ALL ON *.* TO 'john'@'%';
```

Here's another example, giving `jane` permissions to issue `SELECT`, `INSERT`, `UPDATE`, and `DELETE` commands on all tables in the `myCompany` database:

```
GRANT SELECT, INSERT, UPDATE, DELETE ON myCompany.* TO 'jane'@'janescomputer.
company.com';
```

The following are some of the common privileges you can grant users. For a complete list, see the `GRANT` entry in the MySQL Manual at http://dev.mysql.com/doc/refman/5.7/en/grant.html.

▶ **ALL**—Gives the user all common privileges.

▶ **ALTER**—User can alter (modify) tables, columns, and indexes.

▶ **CREATE**—User can create databases and tables.

▶ **DELETE**—User can delete records from tables.

▶ **DROP**—User can drop (delete) tables and databases.

▶ **INDEX**—User can add or delete indexes.

▶ **INSERT**—User can add records to tables.

▶ **PROCESS**—User can view and stop system processes; only trusted users should be able to do this.

▶ **REFERENCES**—User can create foreign keys.

▶ **RELOAD**—User can issue FLUSH statements; only trusted users should be able to do this.

▶ **SELECT**—User can select records from tables.

▶ **SHOW DATABASES**—User can retrieve a list of databases managed by MySQL.

▶ **UPDATE**—User can update (modify) records in tables

After you add users and grant them privileges, you can issue the FLUSH PRIVILEGES command in the MySQL monitor to reload the privilege tables to have them take effect.

Removing User Privileges

Removing privileges is as simple as adding them; instead of the GRANT command, you use REVOKE. The REVOKE command syntax is as follows:

```
REVOKE privileges ON databasename.tablename FROM 'username'@'host';
```

To revoke the ability for user john to INSERT items in the myCompany database, you issue this REVOKE statement:

```
REVOKE INSERT ON myCompany.* FROM 'john'@'%';
```

Again, for the server to be aware of your changes, issue the FLUSH PRIVILEGES command in the MySQL monitor.

APPENDIX C
Installing and Configuring Apache

What You'll Learn in This Appendix:

▶ How to install the Apache server

▶ How to make configuration changes to Apache

▶ Where Apache log and configuration files are stored

In this appendix, you install the Apache web server and familiarize yourself with its main components, including log and configuration files.

Before installing Apache, make sure you are not currently running a web server (for instance, a previous version of Apache or Microsoft Internet Information Services) on your machine. You might want to uninstall or otherwise disable existing servers. You can run several web servers, but they must run in different address and port combinations.

Current Versions of Apache

The Apache HTTP server website at http://httpd.apache.org shows announcements for releases of the Apache 2.2.*x* and Apache 2.4.*x* versions. The Apache Software Foundation maintains both versions, but the features in Apache 2.4.*x* include the latest and greatest; it is the version used here. However, if you choose to install (or already have installed either in a local or external development environment) Apache 2.2.*x*, all the PHP and MySQL code in this book will still work as described. In fact, you will find a number of hosting providers still using Apache 2.0.*x*—not even Apache 2.2.*x*, let alone the newest Apache 2.4.x branch. The installation instructions in this appendix refer to Apache HTTP server version 2.4.26, except where noted, which is the best available version of the software at the time of this writing.

The Apache Software Foundation uses minor and revision numbers for updates containing security enhancements or bug fixes. Neither minor nor revision releases follow a set release schedule. When enhancements or fixes are added to the code and thoroughly tested, the Apache Software Foundation releases a new version.

By the time you purchase this book, the version number might have changed to 2.4.27 or later. If so, read the list of changes, which is linked from the download area at http://httpd.apache. org/download.cgi, for any installation/configuration process changes. These processes make up the bulk of this appendix.

Although it is unlikely that any installation instructions will change between version updates, always check the changelog of software that you install and maintain. If a minor or revision change does occur while you are reading this book but the changelog notes no installation changes, just make a mental note and substitute the new version number wherever it appears in the installation instructions and accompanying figures.

Choosing the Appropriate Installation Method

You have several options when it comes to getting a basic Apache installation in place. Apache is open source, meaning that you can have access to the full source code of the software, which in turn enables you to build your own custom server. In addition, prebuilt Apache binary distributions are available for most modern UNIX platforms. Finally, Apache comes already bundled with a variety of Linux distributions, and you can even purchase commercial versions with support packages from vendors. The examples here teach you how to build Apache from source if you are using Linux/UNIX, and how to use the installer if you plan to run Apache on a Windows system.

Building from Source

Building from source gives you the greatest flexibility because it enables you to build a custom server, remove modules you do not need, and extend the server with third-party modules. Building Apache from source code enables you to easily upgrade to the latest versions and quickly apply security patches, whereas updated versions from vendors can take days or weeks to appear. The process of building Apache from source is not especially difficult for simple installations, but can grow in complexity when third-party modules and libraries are involved.

Installing a Binary

Linux/UNIX binary installations are available from vendors, or you can download them from the Apache Software Foundation website. Binary installations provide a convenient way to install Apache for users with limited system administration knowledge or with no special configuration needs. Third-party commercial vendors provide prepackaged Apache installations together with an application server, additional modules, support, and so on. The Apache Software Foundation provides an installer for Windows systems—a platform where a compiler is less commonly available than in Linux/UNIX systems.

Installing Apache on Linux/UNIX

This section explains how to install a fresh build of Apache 2.4.26 on Linux/UNIX. The general steps necessary to successfully install Apache from source are as follows:

1. Download and uncompress the software distribution file.

2. Run the configuration script.

3. Compile the code and install it.

The following sections describe these steps in detail.

Downloading the Apache Source Code

The official Apache download site is located at http://httpd.apache.org/download.cgi. You can find several versions of the Apache source code packaged with different compression methods. The distribution files are first packed with the `tar` utility and then compressed with either the `gzip` tool or the `bzip2` utility. Download the `*.tar.gz` version if you have the `gunzip` utility installed on your system. This utility comes installed by default in open-source operating systems such as FreeBSD and Linux. Download the `*.tar.bz2` file if `gunzip` is not present on your system (it isn't included in the default installation of many commercial UNIX operating systems).

The file you want to download will be named something similar to `httpd-VERSION.tar.gz`, where `VERSION` is the most recent release of Apache. For example, Apache version 2.4.26 is distributed as a file named `httpd-2.4.26.tar.gz`.

Uncompressing the Source Code

If you downloaded the tarball compressed with `gzip` (it will have a `tar.gz` suffix), you can uncompress it using the `gunzip` utility (part of the `gzip` distribution).

NOTE
_____
Tarball is a commonly used nickname for software packed using the `tar` utility.
_____

You can uncompress and unpack the software by typing the following command:

```
gunzip < httpd-2.4.26.tar.gz | tar xvf -
```

Uncompressing the tarball creates a structure of directories, with the top-level directory named `httpd-VERSION`. Change your current directory to this top-level directory to prepare for configuring the software.

Preparing to Build Apache

You can specify which features the resulting binary will have by using the `configure` script in the top-level distribution directory. By default, Apache is compiled with a set of standard modules compiled statically and is installed in the `/usr/local/apache2` directory. If you are happy with these settings, you can issue the following command to configure Apache:

```
./configure
```

However, in preparation for the PHP installation in Appendix D, "Installing and Configuring PHP," you need to make sure that mod_so is compiled into Apache. This module, named for the UNIX shared object (`*.so`) format, enables the use of dynamic modules such as PHP with Apache. To configure Apache to install itself in a specific location (in this case, `/usr/local/apache2/`) and to enable the use of mod_so, issue the following command:

```
./configure --prefix=/usr/local/apache2 --enable-so
```

The purpose of the `configure` script is to figure out everything related to finding libraries, compile-time options, platform-specific differences, and so on, and to create a set of special files called *makefiles*. Makefiles contain instructions to perform different tasks, called *targets*, such as building Apache. The `make` utility reads these files and carries out the targets' tasks. If everything goes well, after executing `configure`, you will see a set of messages related to the different checks just performed and will return to the prompt:

```
...
configure ok
creating test/Makefile
config.status: creating docs/conf/httpd.conf
...
config.status: executing default commands
$
```

If the `configure` script fails, warnings appear, alerting you to track down additional software that must be installed, such as compilers and libraries. After you install any missing software, you can try the `configure` command again, after deleting the `config.log` and `config.status` files from the top-level directory.

CAUTION

If the configuration process ends with a warning that you do not have APR installed, go to http://apr.apache.org/ and download both the APR and APR-util packages, and unpack them in the `srclib` subdirectory of your `httpd-VERSION` source directory. Once they are installed, rerun the `configure` command.

Similarly, if the configuration process ends with a warning that you do not have PCRE installed, go to http://www.pcre.org and download the files and install PCRE on your system according to the instructions found at the website. Once PCRE is installed, rerun the `configure` command.

Both of these requirements are changes in the requirements for the Apache 2.4.x installation process, different from the Apache 2.2.x process.

Building and Installing Apache

The make utility reads the information stored in the makefiles and builds the server and modules. Type **make** at the command line to build Apache. You will see several messages indicating the progress of the compilation, and you will end up back at the prompt.

```
make
```

After compilation is finished, you can install Apache by typing **make install** at the prompt. Because make will attempt to install Apache under a system directory (/usr/local), you may need to elevate your account privileges using sudo or su for this step.

```
sudo make install
```

The makefiles then install files and directories and return you to the prompt:

```
...
Installing header files
Installing build system files
Installing man pages and online manual
...
make[1]: Leaving directory '/usr/local/bin/httpd-2.4.26'
$
```

The Apache distribution files should now be in the /usr/local/apache2 directory, as specified by the --prefix switch in the configure command. To test that the httpd binary built correctly, type the following at the prompt:

/usr/local/apache2/bin/httpd -v

You should see the following output (your version and build date will be different):

```
Server version: Apache/2.4.26 (Unix)
Server built:   June 26 2017 19:56:22
```

Unless you want to learn how to install Apache on Mac OS X or Windows, skip ahead to the "Apache Configuration File Structure" section to learn about the Apache configuration file.

Installing Apache on Mac OS X

Lucky you, Apache is already installed on Mac OS X. By default, the Apache server binary is located at /usr/sbin/httpd. Configuration files such as httpd.conf, the master configuration file for Apache, are in /etc/httpd. Because Apache is ready to go and fully prepared to use PHP, skip ahead to the "Apache Configuration File Structure" section to learn more about the Apache configuration file and how to use it.

NOTE

If you want to use an all-in-one package installer for Mac OS X, you can do so as shown with XAMPP in Appendix A, "Installation QuickStart Guide with XAMPP," or you can install the MAMP package from http://www.mamp.info.

Installing Apache on Windows

Apache 2.4 runs on most Windows platforms and offers increased performance and stability over earlier versions for Windows. You can build Apache from source, but because not many Windows users have compilers, this section deals with installing precompiled binaries.

The Apache Software Foundation does not provide compiled binary releases for Windows. However, there are many reputable third-party sites that compile and maintain releases for the benefit of Windows users who want to run a version of the Apache server. One such site is Apache Lounge at http://www.apachelounge.com.

Different sites may package Apache differently. Apache Lounge provides ZIP archives you can download and extract, so the installation process is really nothing more than moving the contents of the archive to the appropriate directory.

When you're ready to begin, go to http://apachelounge.com/download/, look for the download link appropriate for your system, and download the ZIP archive. The file you want to download will be named something similar to `httpd-VERSION-NN-VC-.zip`, where `VERSION` is the most recent release of Apache, `NN` indicates 32- or 64-bit binaries, and `VC` is the version of the Visual C compiler library the software was compiled against. For example, Apache version 2.4.26 for 64-bit systems using VC 15 is distributed as a file named `httpd-2.4.26-Win64-VC15.zip`.

Once the download is complete, right-click the archive and select Extract All... from the context menu, as shown in Figure C.1.

A dialog box will prompt you to specify the extraction destination. For now, leave the default path and click Extract. The archive will be extracted to a new folder in the current directory named similarly to the archive.

After Windows has extracted the contents of the ZIP archive, enter into the new directory. You'll see an `Apache24` folder and some other accompanying distribution files, as shown in Figure C.2.

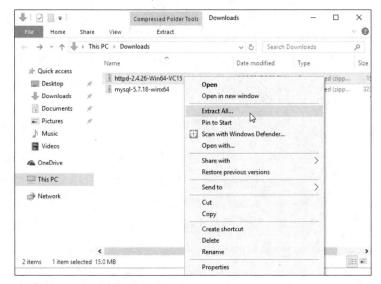

FIGURE C.1
Extracting the downloaded Apache archive.

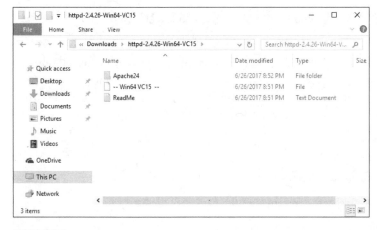

FIGURE C.2
The extracted contents.

Right-click the Apache24 folder and select Cut from the context menu. Then, type c:\ in File Explorer's address bar and press Enter to navigate to the root directory of the C drive. Right-click in any of the white area in the window and select Paste from the context menu to move it to that directory (see Figure C.3).

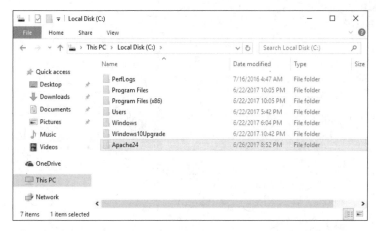

FIGURE C.3
The Apache24 folder after it has been moved to the root of the C drive.

In the next section, you learn about the Apache configuration file and eventually start up your new server.

Apache Configuration File Structure

Apache keeps all its configuration information in text files. The main file is `httpd.conf`. This file contains directives and containers that enable you to customize your Apache installation. *Directives* configure specific settings of Apache, such as authorization, performance, and network parameters. *Containers* specify the context to which those settings refer. For example, authorization configuration can refer to the server as a whole, to a directory, or to a single file.

Directives

The following rules apply for Apache directive syntax:

- ▶ The directive arguments follow the directive name.

- ▶ The directive arguments are separated by spaces.

- ▶ The number and type of arguments vary from directive to directive; some have no arguments.

- ▶ A directive occupies a single line, but you can continue it on a different line by ending the previous line with a backslash character (\).

The Apache server documentation offers a quick reference for directives at http://httpd.apache.org/docs/2.4/mod/quickreference.html. You'll soon learn about some of the basic directives, but you should supplement your knowledge using the online documentation.

The Apache documentation for directives typically follows this model:

- **Description**—This entry provides a brief description of the directive.

- **Syntax**—This entry explains the format of the directive options. Compulsory parameters appear in italics; optional parameters appear in italics and brackets.

- **Default**—If the directive has a default value, it appears here.

- **Context**—This entry details the containers or sections in which the directive can appear. The next section explains containers. The possible values are `server config`, `virtual host`, `directory`, and `.htaccess`.

- **Override**—Apache directives belong to different categories. The Override field specifies which directive categories can appear in `.htaccess` per-directory configuration files.

- **Status**—This entry indicates whether the directive is built in Apache (`core`), belongs to one of the bundled modules (`base` or `extension`, depending on whether they are compiled by default), is part of a multiprocessing module (`MPM`), or is bundled with Apache but not ready for use in a production server (`experimental`).

- **Module**—This entry indicates the module to which the directive belongs.

- **Compatibility**—This entry contains information about which versions of Apache support the directive.

Further explanation of a directive follows these entries in the documentation, and a reference to related directives or documentation might appear at the end.

Containers

Directive containers, also called *sections*, limit the scope for which directives apply. If directives are not inside a container, they belong to the default server scope (`server config`) and apply to the server as a whole.

The following are the default Apache directive containers:

- **`<VirtualHost>`**—A `VirtualHost` directive specifies a virtual server. Apache enables you to host different websites with a single Apache installation. Directives inside this container apply to a particular website. This directive accepts a domain name or IP address and an optional port as arguments.

- **`<Directory>`, `<DirectoryMatch>`**—These containers allow directives to apply to a certain directory or group of directories in the file system. `Directory` containers take a directory or directory pattern argument. Enclosed directives apply to the specified directories and their subdirectories. The `DirectoryMatch` container allows regular expression patterns to be specified as an argument. For example, the following allows a match of all second-level subdirectories of the www directory that are made up of four numbers, such as a directory named after a year and month (0217 for February 2017):

```
<DirectoryMatch "^/www/.*/[0-9]{4}">
```

▶ **<Location>, <LocationMatch>**—These containers allow directives to apply to certain requested URLs or URL patterns. They are similar to their Directory counterparts. LocationMatch takes a regular expression as an argument. For example, the following matches directories containing either "/my/data" or "/your/data":

```
<LocationMatch "/(my|your)/data">
```

▶ **<Files>, <FilesMatch>**—Similar to the Directory and Location containers, Files sections allow directives to apply to certain files or file patterns.

Containers surround directives, as shown in Listing C.1.

LISTING C.1   Container Directives Example

```
<Directory "/some/directory">
    SomeDirective1
    SomeDirective2
</Directory>
<Location "/downloads/*.html">
    SomeDirective3
</Location>
<Files "\.(gif|jpg)">
    SomeDirective4
</Files>
```

Directives *SomeDirective1* and *SomeDirective2* apply to the directory /some/directory and its subdirectories. *SomeDirective3* applies to URLs referring to pages with the .html extension under the /downloads/ URL. *SomeDirective4* applies to all files with a .gif or .jpg extension.

Conditional Evaluation

Apache provides support for conditional containers. Directives enclosed in these containers are processed only if certain conditions are met:

▶ **<IfDefine>**—Directives in this container are processed if a specific command-line switch is passed to the Apache executable. The directive in Listing C.2 is processed only if the -D*MyModule* switch is passed to the Apache binary being executed. You can pass this directly or by modifying the apachectl script, as described in the "Apache-Related Commands" section later in this appendix.

IfDefine containers also allow you to negate the argument. That is, directives inside a <IfDefine !*MyModule*> section—notice the exclamation point before the *MyModule* name—are processed only if no -D*MyModule* parameter is passed as a command-line argument.

▶ <**IfModule**>—Directives in an IfModule section are processed only if the module passed as an argument is present in the web server. For example, Apache ships with a default httpd.conf configuration file that provides support for different MPMs. Only the configuration belonging to the MPM compiled into Apache is processed, as you can see in Listing C.3. The purpose of the example is to illustrate that only one of the directive groups will be evaluated.

LISTING C.2   IfDefine **Example**

```
<IfDefine MyModule>
    LoadModule my_module modules/libmymodule.so
</IfDefine>
```

LISTING C.3   IfModule **Example**

```
<IfModule prefork.c>
    StartServers          5
    MinSpareServers       5
    MaxSpareServers      10
    MaxClients           20
    MaxRequestsPerChild   0
</IfModule>
<IfModule worker.c>
    StartServers          3
    MaxClients            8
    MinSpareThreads       5
    MaxSpareThreads      10
    ThreadsPerChild      25
    MaxRequestsPerChild   0
</IfModule>
```

The ServerRoot **Directive**

The ServerRoot directive takes a single argument: a directory path pointing to the directory where the server lives. All relative path references in other directives are relative to the value of ServerRoot. If you compiled Apache from source on Linux/UNIX, as described earlier in this appendix, the default value of ServerRoot is /usr/local/apache2. The ServerRoot for Mac OS X users defaults to /Library/WebServer. If you used the Apache Lounge binaries on Windows, the ServerRoot is C:\Apache24.

Per-Directory Configuration Files

Apache uses per-directory configuration files to allow directives to exist outside the main configuration file, `httpd.conf`. These special files can be placed anywhere in the file system. Apache processes the content of these files if a document is requested in a directory containing one of these files or any subdirectories under it. The contents of all the applicable per-directory configuration files are merged and processed. For example, if Apache receives a request for the `/usr/local/apache2/htdocs/index.html` file, it looks for per-directory configuration files in the `/`, `/usr`, `/usr/local`, `/usr/local/apache2`, and `/usr/local/apache2/htdocs` directories, in that order.

CAUTION

Enabling per-directory configuration files has a performance penalty. Apache must perform expensive disk operations looking for these files in every request, even if the files do not exist.

Per-directory configuration files are named `.htaccess` by default. This is for historical reasons; they originally protected access to directories containing HTML files.

The `AccessFileName` directive enables you to change the name of the per-directory configuration files from `.htaccess` to something else. It accepts a list of filenames that Apache will use when looking for per-directory configuration files.

To determine whether you can override a directive in the per-directory configuration file, check whether the `Context:` field of the directive syntax definition contains `.htaccess`. Apache directives belong to different groups, as specified in the `Override` field in the directive syntax description. Here are the possible values for the `Override` field:

- ▶ **AuthConfig**—Directives controlling authorization

- ▶ **FileInfo**—Directives controlling document types

- ▶ **Indexes**—Directives controlling directory indexing

- ▶ **Limit**—Directives controlling host access

- ▶ **Options**—Directives controlling specific directory features

You can control which of these directive groups can appear in per-directory configuration files by using the `AllowOverride` directive. `AllowOverride` can also take an `All` or `None` argument. `All` means that directives belonging to all groups can appear in the configuration file. `None` disables per-directory files in a directory and any of its subdirectories. Listing C.4 shows how to disable per-directory configuration files for the server as a whole. This improves performance and is the default Apache configuration.

LISTING C.4   Disabling Per-Directory Configuration Files

```
<Directory />
    AllowOverride none
</Directory>
```

Apache Log Files

Apache includes two log files by default. The `access_log` file is for tracking client requests. The `error_log` file is for recording important events, such as errors or server restarts. These files don't exist until you start Apache the first time. The names of the files are `access.log` and `error.log` on Windows platforms.

The `access_log` File

When a client requests a file from the server, Apache records several parameters associated with the request, including the IP address of the client, the document requested, the HTTP status code, and the current time. Listing C.5 shows an example of `access_log` entries.

LISTING C.5   `access_log` Entries

```
127.0.0.1 - - [26/Jun/2017:20:12:18 -0700] "GET / HTTP/1.1" 200 44
127.0.0.1 - - [26/Jun/2017:20:12:18 -0700] "GET /favicon.ico HTTP/1.1" 404 209
```

The `error_log` File

The `error_log` file includes error messages, startup messages, and any other significant events in the life cycle of the server. This is the first place to look when you have a problem with Apache. Listing C.6 shows an example of `error_log` entries.

LISTING C.6   `error_log` Entries

```
Starting the Apache2.4 service [The Apache2.4 service is running.]
Apache/2.4.26 (Unix) configured -- resuming normal operations
[Mon Jun 26 20:29:34 2017] [notice] Server built: Jun 26 2017 19:56:22
[Mon Jun 26 20:29:34 2017] [notice] Parent: Created child process 3504
[Mon Jun 26 20:29:35 2017] [notice] Child 3504: Child process is running
[Mon Jun 26 20:29:35 2017] [notice] Child 3504: Acquired the start mutex.
```

Additional Files

The `httpd.pid` file contains the process ID of the running Apache server. You can use this number to send signals to Apache manually, as described in the next section. The `scoreboard` file, which is found with Linux/UNIX Apache installations, is used by the process-based MPMs to communicate with their children. In general, you do not need to worry about these files.

Apache-Related Commands

The Apache distribution includes several executables. This section covers only the server binary and related scripts.

Apache Server Binary

The name of the Apache executable is httpd in Linux/UNIX and Mac OS X, and httpd.exe in Windows. It accepts several command-line options, some of which are described in Table C.1. You can get a complete listing of options by typing **/usr/local/apache2/bin/httpd -h** on Linux/UNIX, by typing **/usr/sbin/httpd -h** on Mac OS X, or by typing **httpd.exe -h** from a command prompt on Windows.

TABLE C.1 Some httpd Options

Option	Meaning
-D	Allows you to pass a parameter that can be used for <IfDefine> section processing
-l	Lists compiled-in modules
-v	Shows the version number and server compilation time
-f	Allows you to pass the location of httpd.conf if it differs from the compile-time default

After Apache is running, you can use the kill command on Linux/UNIX and Mac OS X to send signals to the parent Apache process. Signals provide a mechanism to send commands to a process. To send a signal, execute the following command:

kill -*SIGNAL pid*

In this syntax, *pid* is the process ID, and *SIGNAL* is one of the following:

▶ **HUP**—Stop the server.

▶ **USR1 or WINCH**—Graceful restart. Which signal you use depends on the underlying operating system.

▶ **SIGHUP**—Restart.

If you make some changes to the configuration files and you want them to take effect, you must signal Apache that the configuration has changed. You can do this by stopping and starting the server or by sending a restart signal. This tells Apache to reread its configuration.

A normal restart can result in a momentary pause in service. A graceful restart takes a different approach: Each thread or process serving a client continues processing the current request, but when it finishes, it is killed and replaced by a new thread or process with the new configuration. This allows seamless operation of the web server with no downtime.

On Windows, you can signal Apache using the `httpd.exe` executable. Some commands are listed here:

- `httpd.exe -k restart`—Tells Apache to restart

- `httpd.exe -k graceful`—Tells Apache to do a graceful restart

- `httpd.exe -k stop`—Tells Apache to stop

You can access shortcuts to these commands in the Start menu entries that the Apache installer created. If you installed Apache as a service, you can start or stop Apache by using the Windows service interface: In Control Panel, select Administrative Tasks and then click the Services icon.

Apache Control Script

Although it is possible to control Apache on Linux/UNIX using the `httpd` binary, it is recommended that you use the `apachectl` tool. The `apachectl` support program wraps common functionality in an easy-to-use script. To use `apachectl`, type the following:

`/usr/local/apache2/bin/apachectl command`

In this syntax, *command* can be `stop`, `start`, `restart`, or `graceful`. You can also edit the contents of the `apachectl` script to add extra command-line options. Some OS distributions provide you with additional scripts to control Apache; check the documentation included with your distribution.

Starting Apache for the First Time

Before you start Apache, verify that the minimal set of information is present in the Apache configuration file, `httpd.conf`. The following sections describe the basic information needed to configure Apache and to start the server.

Check Your Configuration File

You can edit the Apache `httpd.conf` file with your favorite text editor. In Linux/UNIX and Mac OS X, this probably means `vi` or `emacs`. In Windows, you can use Notepad or WordPad. You must remember to save the configuration file in plain text, which is the only format Apache understands.

You might need to change just two parameters so that you can start Apache for the first time: the name of the server and the address and port to which it is listening. The name of the server is the one Apache will use when it needs to refer to itself (for example, when redirecting requests).

Apache can usually figure out its server name from the IP address of the machine, but not always. If the server does not have a valid DNS (domain name service) entry, you might need to specify one of the IP addresses of the machine. If the server is not connected to a network (you might want to test Apache on a standalone machine), you can use the value `127.0.0.1`, which is the loopback address. The default port value is `80`. You might need to change this value if a server is already running in the machine at port 80 or if you do not have administrator permissions—on Linux/UNIX and Mac OS X systems, only the `root` user can bind to privileged ports (those with port numbers lower than 1024).

You can change both the listening address and the port values with the `Listen` directive. The `Listen` directive takes either a port number or an IP address and a port, separated by a colon. If you specify only the port, Apache listens on that port at all available IP addresses in the machine. If you provide an additional IP address, Apache listens at only that address and port combination. For example, `Listen 80` tells Apache to listen for requests at all IP addresses on port 80. `Listen 10.0.0.1:443` tells Apache to listen at only 10.0.0.1 on port 443.

The `ServerName` directive enables you to define the name the server will report in any self-referencing URLs. The directive accepts a DNS name and an optional port, separated by a colon. Make sure that `ServerName` has a valid value. Otherwise, the server will not function properly; for example, it will issue incorrect redirects.

On Linux/UNIX and Mac OS X platforms, you can use the `User` and `Group` directives to specify which user and group IDs the server will run as. The `nobody` or `www-data` user is a good choice for most platforms. However, there are problems in the HP-UX platform with the `nobody` user ID, so you must create and use a different user ID, such as `www`.

Starting Apache

To start Apache on Linux/UNIX, execute the following command:

```
/usr/local/apache2/bin/apachectl start
```

If Apache listens on a port lower than 1024, you'll need to elevate your account privileges using su or sudo, like so:

```
sudo /usr/local/apache2/bin/apachectl start
```

Mac OS X users can type the following at the prompt:

```
/usr/sbin/httpd
```

To manually start Apache on Windows, click the Start link in the Control Apache Server section, within the Apache HTTP Server 2.4 program group in the Start menu. If you installed Apache as a service, you must start the Apache service instead.

If everything goes well, you can access Apache using a browser. A default installation page displays, such as the one shown in Figure C.4. If you cannot start the web server or an error page appears instead, consult the "Troubleshooting" section that follows. Make sure that you are accessing Apache in one of the ports specified in the `Listen` directive—usually port 80 or 8080.

FIGURE C.4
Apache has been installed.

Troubleshooting

The following subsections describe several common problems that you might encounter the first time you start Apache.

Visual C Libraries Not Installed (Windows)

On Windows, Apache cannot start successfully if the Visual C libraries it was compiled against are not installed. If they are not installed, you will see a message similar to the one shown in Figure C.5.

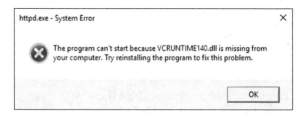

FIGURE C.5
The redistributable Visual C libraries are not installed.

To solve this problem, you need to download and install the missing libraries. For VC14 and VC15, you can use download the library installer from Microsoft at http://go.microsoft.com/fwlink/?LinkId=746571 for 32-bit versions and http://go.microsoft.com/fwlink/?LinkId=746572 for 64-bit versions.

Already an Existing Web Server

If a server is already running on the machine and is listening to the same IP address and port combination, Apache cannot start successfully. You will get an entry in the error log file indicating that Apache cannot bind to the port:

```
[crit] (48)Address already in use: make_sock: could not bind...
[alert] no listening sockets available, shutting down
```

To solve this problem, you need to stop the running server or change the Apache configuration to listen on a different port.

No Permission to Bind to Port

You will get an error if you do not have administrator permissions and you try to bind to a privileged port (between 0 and 1024):

```
[crit] (13)Permission denied: make_sock: could not bind to address 10.0.0.2:80
[alert] no listening sockets available, shutting down
```

To solve this problem, you must either log on as the administrator before starting Apache, elevate your account privileges using su or sudo when invoking the command, or change the port number. 8080 is a commonly used non-privileged port.

Access Denied

You might not be able to start Apache if you do not have permission to read the configuration files or to write to the log files. You will get an error similar to the following:

```
(13)Permission denied: httpd: could not open error log file
```

This problem can arise if the user who built and installed Apache is different from the user trying to run it.

Wrong Group Settings

You can configure Apache to run under a certain username and group. Apache has default values for the running server username and group. Sometimes the default value is not valid and you will get an error containing setgid: unable to set group id.

To solve this problem on Linux/UNIX and Mac OS X, you must change the value of the Group directive in the configuration file to a valid value. Check the /etc/groups file for existing groups.

APPENDIX D
Installing and Configuring PHP

What You'll Learn in This Appendix:

▶ How to install PHP

▶ How to test your PHP installation

▶ How to find help when things go wrong

In this appendix, you acquire, install, and configure PHP and make some basic changes to your Apache installation.

Current and Future Versions of PHP

The installation instructions in this appendix refer to PHP version 7.1.6, which is the current version of the software.

The PHP Group uses revisions and minor releases for updates containing security enhancements or bug fixes. These releases do not follow a set release schedule; when enhancements or fixes are added to the code and are thoroughly tested, the PHP Group releases a new version with a new revision number.

It is possible that by the time you purchase this book the minor version number will have changed to 7.1.7, or beyond. If that is the case, you should read the list of changes at http://php.net/ChangeLog-7.php for any installation/configuration process changes. These processes make up the bulk of this appendix.

Although it is unlikely that any installation instructions will change between minor version updates, always check the changelog of software that you install and maintain. If a revision does occur while you are reading this book but the changelog notes no installation changes, just make a mental note and substitute the new version number wherever it appears in the installation instructions and accompanying figures.

Building PHP on Linux/UNIX with Apache

This section examines one way of installing PHP with Apache on Linux/UNIX. The process is more or less the same for any UNIX-like operating system. Although you might be able to find prebuilt versions of PHP for your system, compiling PHP from source gives you greater control over the features built in to your binary.

To download the PHP distribution files, go to the home of PHP, http://www.php.net/, and follow the link to the Downloads section. Grab the latest version of the source code—for this example, we are using 7.1.6. Your distribution will be named something similar to `php-VERSION.tar.gz`, where `VERSION` is the most recent release number. This archive will be a compressed tar file, so you need to unpack it:

```
gunzip < php-7.1.6.tar.gz | tar xvf -
```

Uncompressing the archive creates a structure of directories, with the top-level directory named `php-VERSION`. Change your current directory to this top-level directory to prepare for configuring the software.

In your distribution directory, you will find a script called `configure`. This script accepts additional information that is provided when the `configure` script is run from the command line. These command-line arguments control the features that PHP supports. This example includes the basic options you need to install PHP with Apache and MySQL support. We discuss some of the available `configure` options later in the appendix and throughout the book as they become relevant.

```
./configure  --prefix=/usr/local/php \
--with-mysqli=/usr/local/mysql/bin/mysql_config \
--with-apxs2=/usr/local/apache2/bin/apxs
```

CAUTION

If you have installed MySQL or Apache in a different location than the paths indicated in the configuration shown here, ensure that you substitute the appropriate directory paths in the command.

If you have installed MySQL via the Oracle repositories as described in Appendix B, "Installing and Configuring MySQL," you will also need to install the `mysql-community-dev` package to make `mysql_config` available.

After the `configure` script has run, you are returned to the prompt. Here's an example:

```
...
creating libtool
appending configuration tag "CXX" to libtool
```

Generating files
```
configure: creating ./config.status
creating main/internal_functions.c
creating main/internal_functions_cli.c
+-------------------------------------------------------------------+
| License:                                                          |
| This software is subject to the PHP License, available in this    |
| distribution in the file LICENSE.  By continuing this installation |
| process, you are bound by the terms of this license agreement.    |
| If you do not agree with the terms of this license, you must abort |
| the installation process at this point.                           |
+-------------------------------------------------------------------+

Thank you for using PHP.

config.status: creating php7.spec
config.status: creating main/build-defs.h
config.status: creating scripts/phpize
config.status: creating scripts/man1/phpize.1
config.status: creating scripts/php-config
config.status: creating scripts/man1/php-config.1
config.status: creating sapi/cli/php.1
config.status: creating sapi/cgi/php-cgi.1
config.status: creating ext/phar/phar.1
config.status: creating ext/phar/phar.phar.1
config.status: creating main/php_config.h
config.status: executing default commands
$
```

CAUTION

If the `configure` script fails and returns the error
```
xml2-config not found. Please check your libxml2 installation.
```

then you can install it using your system's package manager. Users of Debian/Ubuntu-based systems should run the command `sudo apt-get install libxml2-dev`, and Red Hat/CentOS users should run `sudo yum install libxml2-devel`.

From the prompt, issue the `make` command:

make

The command will then compile the PHP source code and return you to your prompt:

```
...
Generating phar.php
Generating phar.phar
```

```
invertedregexiterator.inc
clicommand.inc
pharcommand.inc
directorytreeiterator.inc
directorygraphiterator.inc
phar.inc

Build complete.
Don't forget to run 'make test'.
$
```

Then issue the `make install` command. For this, depending on the target installation location you specified via the `configure` script, you may need to elevate your account's privileges using sudo or su:

sudo make install

The command installs the newly compiled binaries to the appropriate directories.

You need to ensure that two very important files are copied to their correct locations. First, issue the following command to copy the development version of `php.ini` to its default location (you learn more about `php.ini` later in this appendix):

sudo cp php.ini-development /usr/local/php/lib/php.ini

Next, copy the PHP shared object file to its proper place in the Apache installation directory, if it has not already been placed there by the installation process; it usually will be, as you can see in the `make install` output:

sudo cp libs/libphp7.so /usr/local/apache2/modules/

You should now be able to configure and run Apache, but let's cover some additional configuration options before heading on to the "Integrating PHP with Apache on Linux/UNIX" section.

Additional Linux/UNIX Configuration Options

In the previous section, when we ran the PHP `configure` script, we included some command-line arguments that determined some features that the PHP engine will include. The `configure` script itself gives you a list of available options, including the ones we used. From the PHP distribution directory, type the following:

./configure --help

This command produces a long list, so you might want to add it to a file and read it at your leisure:

./configure --help > configoptions.txt

If you discover additional functionality you want to add to PHP after you install it, simply run the configuration and build process again. Doing so creates a new version of `libphp7.so` and places it in the Apache directory structure. All you have to do is restart Apache to load the new file.

Integrating PHP with Apache on Linux/UNIX

To ensure that PHP and Apache get along with one another, you need to check for—and potentially add—a few items to the `httpd.conf` configuration file. First, look for a line like the following:

```
LoadModule php7_module          modules/libphp7.so
```

If this line is not present or only appears with a pound sign (#) at the beginning of the line, you must add the line or remove the #. This line tells Apache to use the PHP shared object file created by the PHP build process (`libphp7.so`).

Next, look for this section:

```
#
# AddType allows you to add to or override the MIME configuration
# file mime.types for specific file types.
#
```

Add the following line to that section:

```
AddType application/x-httpd-php .php
```

This statement ensures that the PHP engine will parse files that end with the `.php` extension. Your selection of filenames might differ; you might want to parse all files ending with `*.html` as PHP, for example.

Save this file and then restart Apache. When you look in your `error_log`, you should see something like the following line:

```
[Fri Jun 30 18:03:47 2017] [notice] Apache/2.4.26 (Unix) PHP/7.1.6 configured
```

PHP is now part of the Apache web server. If you want to learn how to install PHP on a Mac OS X or Windows platform, keep reading. Otherwise, you can skip ahead to the "Testing Your Installation" section.

Installing PHP on Mac OS X

There are a few different options for installing PHP with Apache on Mac OS X, including building from source, as described in the previous section. Some users may find the simplest method is to install PHP from a precompiled binary package, such as one from MacPorts (at http://www.macports.org/), or as part of the all-in-one installation packages from XAMPP (as shown in Appendix A, "Installation QuickStart Guide with XAMPP") or MAMP (at http://www.mamp.info). However, if you are comfortable with the command line, I recommend following the instructions in the previous section, "Building PHP on Linux/UNIX with Apache."

Installing PHP on Windows

Installing PHP on Windows requires nothing more than downloading the distribution archive and extracting its contents to the appropriate directory. To download the PHP distribution files, go to http://windows.php.net/download and grab the latest version of the thread-safe ZIP package—for this example, we are using 7.1.6. Your distribution will be named something similar to php-*VERSION*.zip, where *VERSION* is the most recent release number.

Right-click the archive and select Extract All... from the context menu, as shown in Figure D.1.

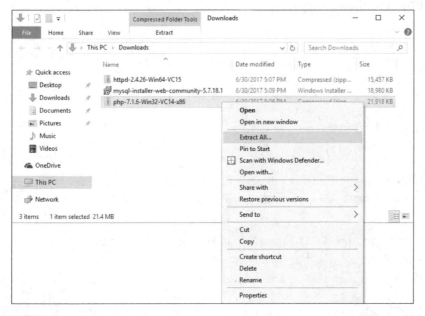

FIGURE D.1
Extracting the downloaded PHP archive.

A dialog box will prompt you to specify the extraction destination. Change the path to `C:\php` and click Extract, as shown in Figure D.2. The archive will be extracted to a new folder named php in the root directory of the C drive.

Next, go to the `C:\php\` directory and copy the `php.ini-development` file to `php.ini`.

Now, to get a basic version of PHP working with Apache, you need to make a few minor modifications to the Apache configuration file.

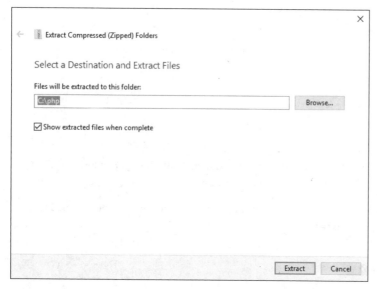

FIGURE D.2
Specifying the destination for the extracted files.

NOTE

On some Windows systems, you might need to set an explicit environment variable in order for PHP to run correctly; setting it will not cause any harm, so even if you are unsure if it is necessary, there's no reason not to. For information on adding the PHP directory to the PATH environment variable, see the entry in the PHP FAQ at http://www.php.net/manual/en/faq.installation.php#faq.installation.addtopath.

Integrating PHP with Apache on Windows

To ensure that PHP and Apache get along with one another, you need to add a few items to the httpd.conf configuration file. First, find a section that looks like this:

```
# Example:
# LoadModule foo_module modules/mod_foo.so
#
LoadModule access_module modules/mod_access.so
...
#LoadModule vhost_alias_module modules/mod_vhost_alias.so
```

At the end of this section, add the following:

```
LoadModule php7_module C:/php/php7apache2_4.dll
```

In addition, add the following to ensure Apache knows where php.ini resides:

```
PHPIniDir "C:/php/"
```

Next, look for this section:

```
#
# AddType allows you to add to or override the MIME configuration
# file mime.types for specific file types.
#
```

Add the following line:

```
AddType application/x-httpd-php .php
```

This statement ensures that the PHP engine will parse files that end with the `.php` extension. Your selection of filenames might differ; for example, you might want to parse all `*.html` files as PHP files.

Save the `httpd.conf` file and then restart Apache. The server should start without warning; PHP is now part of the Apache web server.

`php.ini` **Basics**

After you have compiled or installed PHP, you can still change its behavior with the `php.ini` file. On Linux/UNIX systems, the default location for this file is `/usr/local/php/lib` or the `lib` subdirectory of the PHP installation location you used at configuration time. On a Windows system, this file should be in the `PHP` directory or another directory as specified by the value of `PHPIniDir` in the Apache `httpd.conf` file.

Directives in the `php.ini` file come in two forms: values and flags. *Value directives* take the form of a directive name and a value separated by an equal sign. Possible values vary from directive to directive. *Flag directives* take the form of a directive name and a positive or negative term separated by an equal sign. Positive terms include 1, `On`, `Yes`, and `True`. Negative terms include 0, `Off`, `No`, and `False`. Whitespace is ignored.

NOTE
On Windows systems, it is important to explicitly provide the value for the `extension_dir` directive. If you installed PHP in `C:\php`, then the value of `extension_dir` should be `"C:\php\ext"`.

You can change your `php.ini` settings at any time, but after you do, you need to restart the server for the changes to take effect. At some point, take time to read through the `php.ini` file on your own to see the types of things you can configure.

Testing Your Installation

The simplest way to test your PHP installation is to create a small test script that uses the `phpinfo()` function. This function produces a long list of configuration information. Open a text editor and type the following line:

```
<?php phpinfo(); ?>
```

Save this file as `phpinfo.php` and place it in the document root of your web server—the `htdocs` subdirectory of your Apache installation or the `/Library/WebServer/Documents` directory on Mac OS X. Access this file using your web browser, and you should see something like what is shown in Figure D.3.

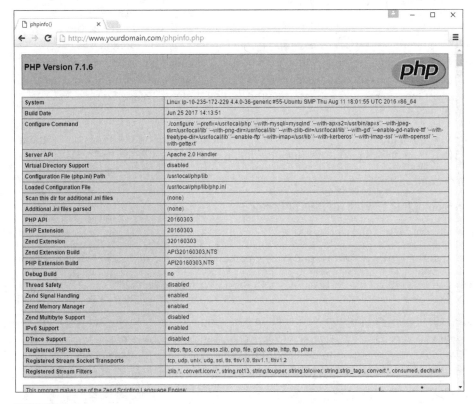

FIGURE D.3
The results of `phpinfo()`.

The exact output of `phpinfo()` depends on your operating system, PHP version, and configuration options.

Getting Installation Help

Help is always at hand on the Internet, particularly for problems concerning open-source software. Wait a moment before you click the Send button, however. No matter how intractable your installation, configuration, or programming problem might seem, chances are you are not alone. Someone has probably already answered your question.

When you hit a brick wall, your first recourse should be to the official PHP site at http://www.php.net/ (particularly the annotated manual at http://www.php.net/manual/).

If you still cannot find your answer, don't forget that the PHP site is searchable. The advice you are seeking may be lurking in a press release or an FAQ file. You can also search the mailing list archives at http://www.php.net/search.php. These archives represent a huge information resource, with contributions from many of the great minds in the PHP community. Spend some time trying out a few keyword combinations.

If you are still convinced that your problem has not been addressed, you might well be doing the PHP community a service by exposing it. You can join the PHP mailing lists at http://www.php.net/mailing-lists.php. Although these lists often have high volume, you can learn a lot from them. If you are serious about PHP scripting, you should certainly subscribe to at least a digest list. After you've subscribed to the list that matches your concerns, consider posting your problem.

When you post a question, it is a good idea to include as much information as possible (without writing a novel). The following items are often pertinent:

- ▶ Your operating system

- ▶ The version of PHP you are running or installing

- ▶ The configuration options you chose

- ▶ Any output from the `configure` and `make` commands that preceded an installation failure

- ▶ A reasonably complete example of the code that is causing problems

Why all these cautions about posting a question to a mailing list? First, developing research skills will stand you in good stead. A good researcher can generally solve a problem quickly and efficiently. Posting a naive question to a technical list often results in a wait rewarded only by a message or two referring you to the archives where you should have begun your search for answers in the first place.

Second, remember that a mailing list is not analogous to a technical support call center. No one is paid to answer your questions. Despite this, you have access to an impressive pool of talent and knowledge, including that of some of the creators of PHP itself. A good question and its answer will be archived to help other coders. Asking a question that has already been answered several times just adds more noise.

Having said this, don't be afraid to post a problem to the list. PHP developers are a civilized and helpful breed, and by bringing a problem to the attention of the community, you might be helping others to solve the same problem.

Index

Symbols

S